Theories of Child Development

Theories of
Child Development

ALFRED L. BALDWIN

DEPARTMENT OF PSYCHOLOGY
NEW YORK UNIVERSITY

JOHN WILEY & SONS, INC., NEW YORK • LONDON • SYDNEY

248 73522

Copyright © 1967 by John Wiley & Sons, Inc.

All Rights Reserved
This book or any part thereof
must not be reproduced in any form
without the written permission of the publisher.

10

Library of Congress Catalog Card Number: 66-26733
Printed in the United States of America

ISBN 0 471 04580 2

In gratitude for his constant encouragement of the author,
and also in recognition of his role of friend, adviser,
and critic to a generation of psychologists,
this book is gratefully dedicated to the memory of

GORDON S. IERARDI

Preface

I WAS led to write a survey of current theories of child behavior and child development in part because developmental psychology is currently a very active discipline. The number of publications in the field has increased greatly over the last ten years, and research is advancing on several fronts. In a situation like this, it is easy for students to become so involved in local research problems that they lose sight of the broader perspective of the field. Theoretical ideas about child psychology come from a variety of sources, and it has been my impression that students at a particular university often see child psychology and child development from parochial perspective. It is the intent of this book to provide in one volume a discussion of some of the diverse major theoretical positions.

This broad perspective of theory in child development seems particularly appropriate because, after examination of the different theoretical viewpoints, I have concluded that they are not so much contradictory as unrelated. While there is a certain amount of theoretical integration of some of the different points of view, a great deal more is possible. Furthermore, the current spectrum of theory of child development contains many suggestions for profitable research, no matter what the particular theoretical predilections of the investigator may be.

I have written this book with the belief that an exploration in depth of a relatively few psychological theories is preferable to a briefer review of a large number of theories. Thus, I have not attempted to cover all of the theories that have some relevance for psychological research. Specifically, a number of important earlier theories have been completely neglected in order that more space may be devoted to current ones.

The book is divided into a number of sections, each devoted to a detailed review of one theoretical position. In no case is this sufficient for an exhaustive review, but it does provide an opportunity to discuss the position in some detail and to review some of the major research on which the theory is based; it also provides me with an opportunity to put the theory into some kind of perspective. Therefore, each theory is introduced by a statement of its philosophical and methodological background and the effect of this background on the development of the theory itself. In addition, the final part of each section is devoted to a critique of the theory.

It is one of my basic assumptions in this book that none of the current theories of child development approaches the degree of rigor and clarity that an adequate theory must achieve. The critique of each theory has, therefore, not concentrated on its methodological shortcomings or on its lack of operational rigor. Rather, the major concepts of each theory have been reviewed in an attempt to assess their possible fruitfulness for the future development of the field.

This book has been in preparation for six or seven years. During this time many people have actively encouraged me in my attempt to produce this kind of a text. I am especially indebted to Gordon S. Ierardi, psychology editor of John Wiley and Sons. He encouraged me from the moment that the book was a gleam in my eye and actively supported my writing over the whole period. I regret very much that Mr. Ierardi's death prevented him from seeing the final outcome. It is therefore with a real feeling of gratitude that I have dedicated the book to Mr. Ierardi's memory.

In addition, I am very grateful to those colleagues who were kind enough to review the different sections of the book. It was my intention to be assured that each section was factually accurate, and so each section was submitted to a reader who would be able to assess its accuracy. These readers all responded with great care and, as a result of their efforts, the book is unquestionably better than it would have been otherwise. At the same time, it is important to acknowledge that the criticisms were not always accepted and that the inadequacies in the final volume are entirely my responsibility. The author expresses his gratitude to: Urie Bronfenbrenner, John Flavell, Bernard Kaplan, Harold W. Stevenson, and Silvan Tompkins.

I also wish to acknowledge the more informal and intangible contributions of my immediate colleagues, especially my wife and collaborator, Dr. Clara P. Baldwin. Her comments and advice on various parts of the book have been very helpful, as well as her sympathetic acceptance of the trials and tribulations that inevitably fall upon the immediate family of an author.

Quotations from various sources are specifically acknowledged in the bibliography, but I wish to thank the following publishers for their permission to quote copyrighted material: Addison-Wesley Publishing Co., Inc., Basic Books, Inc., Harper & Row, Holt, Rinehart & Winston, Inc., International Universities Press, Inc., Liveright Publishing Corp., W. W. Norton & Company, Inc., Stanford University Press, John Wiley & Sons, Inc.

ALFRED L. BALDWIN

New York University
October 1966

Contents

Fritz Heider and Naïve Psychology

CHAPTER 1. Common sense and its role in psychological theory 5

CHAPTER 2. General issues of behavior theory 38

Kurt Lewin and Field Theory

CHAPTER 3. The child psychology of Kurt Lewin 85

CHAPTER 4. Evaluation and critique of field theory 138

The Theory of Jean Piaget

CHAPTER 5. Piaget's fundamental concepts and strategy of research 171

CHAPTER 6. Piaget's description of development during infancy 190

CHAPTER 7. Development of conceptual thought— preoperational stage 221

CHAPTER 8. The periods of concrete and formal operations 249

CHAPTER 9. Piaget's theory of the developmental process 289

Sigmund Freud and the Psychoanalytic Theory of Development

CHAPTER 10. Freudian theory—fundamental strategy and
           concepts   305
CHAPTER 11. Freudian theory of psychodynamics   324
CHAPTER 12. Freudian theory—development of personality   349
CHAPTER 13. Critique of psychoanalytic theory   374

Stimulus-Response Theories

CHAPTER 14. The basic elements of the S-R strategy   391
CHAPTER 15. Social-learning theory of child development   437
CHAPTER 16. Critique of social-learning theory   474

Heinz Werner—The Organismic Developmental Point of View

CHAPTER 17. Heinz Werner's theory of child development   495

Talcott Parsons and Robert F. Bales—The Sociological Viewpoint

CHAPTER 18. The family as a social system   539

Conclusion

CHAPTER 19. Toward an integrated theory of child
           development   579

Bibliography and Author Index   601

Subject Index   609

Theories of Child Development

FRITZ HEIDER

Fritz Heider

and Naïve Psychology

ONE

Common sense and its role
in psychological theory

IT IS PERHAPS NO SERIOUS EXAGGERATION to say that a turning point in
the development of civilization came when man began to invent theories to explain nature. It is not necessary to have theories to live, nor
even to learn skills that improve one's way of life. Theory building is a
luxury, but a luxury that can revolutionize civilization.

In the first few years of a child's life he indulges in no theory building; he modifies his behavior on the basis of the consequences of his
acts. But, according to Jean Piaget, the young child is oriented toward
success. Acts that succeed are preserved; those that fail disappear. It is
only around the age of two or three that the child begins to search for
truth, instead of merely trying to find an act that succeeds. At this
point he begins to try to understand his environment and not merely
to exploit it.

In the history of civilization, such a change in viewpoint led to theory building, because a theory is an attempt to describe how nature
works, and need not be concerned with the conquest of nature for
one's own benefit. This is not to say that the exploitation of nature is
antithetical to its explanation. On the contrary, pure science has led to
the most astounding harnessing of natural forces. There is, however, a
certain detached selfless attitude necessary for involvement in searching for truth regardless of where it leads. This attitude of intellectual
curiosity is a keystone of modern science and a hallmark of scholarship. The outcomes of all such dispassionate inquiries might perhaps
be called theories.

The first attempts to understand the world do not, however, result in the birth of full-grown theories, or even in correct ones. The first real theories are preceded by much vaguer and less formalized descriptions of nature, and it is almost inevitable that the earliest attempts at understanding the world focus on the wrong problems and ask the wrong questions, and that early explanations are often mystical and supernatural.

Common Sense as the Basis of Theory Building

There is, however, a ground from which an understanding of natural phenomena grows. Science grows imperceptibly from the answers that ordinary laymen find for the questions occurring to them. In each science we can find a naïve or common-sense theory that seems to be implicit in what people do to manage their environment. For example, when a boy wants to throw a baseball as far as he can, he does not try to keep the trajectory of the ball nearly parallel to the ground. Instead he aims up in the air, not straight up, but about 45 degress. His behavior implies some sort of intuition about the trajectory of an object; it also implies some appreciation of the fact that the problem of maximum range is to keep the ball in the air long enough to use all the forward momentum, while giving it maximum forward thrust. The accurate solution of the problem involves the calculus.

Presumably, from this common-sense knowledge of nature the early scientific problems and hypotheses emerge. Conant reports, for example, that before the time of Galileo, technicians already knew how to build an ordinary water pump that sucked water up a pipe (1948). They knew that such a pump could not lift water more than 32 feet, and this knowledge posed a scientific problem. One interesting wrong hypothesis to explain the limit of 32 feet suggested that the stream of water broke under its own weight as would a wire if one tried to lift too long a strand of it by one end. Another common-sense belief about this phenomenon still plagues the student. It seems more obvious that the vacuum sucks in air or water than that the outside air pressure pushes either in. "Nature abhors a vacuum" was an elegant way of putting this notion. Such a belief made it difficult to understand why one could not suck water in a vacuum.

Common-sense theory is both a useful aid to scientific theory building and a source of misleading hypotheses that may hamper development for a long time. We shall see, therefore, that within psychology there are marked differences of opinion about the usefulness of common sense as a guide to psychological theory; some people prefer to build a theory that makes no use of common-sense notions, and others prefer to use common-sense theory as a guide. There is a real sense, however, in which common-sense or naïve theory is the prototheory for all science.

Certainly, it is true that people can act wisely in human relations without having any academic knowledge of psychology—really without knowing why at all. We can intuitively realize that it is tactful to ask, "would you mind," or to begin, "if I may make a suggestion," but no established theory encompasses this common sense. When we teach interpersonal skills in education, counseling, or group work, we depend on supervised field experience rather than verbal instruction. Part of the mistrust of theory as impractical or idealistic rests upon the reality that current theory does not offer much help to people who must deal with other people in face-to-face situations. At any rate, we are not far beyond common sense in psychology, so that the tactful leader does many effective things for which there is no adequate theory. In this respect, psychology is in a position similar to that of physics before the time of Galileo.

Common sense may have any of three roles in the strategy of science. It may contain glimmerings, or more than glimmerings, of the truth, but be dimly perceived, poorly stated, and unsystematic. On the other hand, common sense may contain pure mythology like many of the primitive theories of illness. The two may be mixed in varying proportions.

A third possibility is inherent in the nature of social science. What is called common-sense psychology may actually be cultural convention in the field of human relations. Thus, a person who injures another person may accept punishment for doing so with the feeling that the expiation somehow relieves him of his guilt and makes the injured party feel satisfied. This seems to be the consequence of expiation in many cases. The question is, how does it operate? We might make a basic psychological hypothesis that an injured person feels hostility toward the person who injures him, and that his hostility is satisfied by the punishment. We might say that the important psychological principle is that the aggressor must communicate that he is sorry, and that he does communicate this fact by his acceptance of punishment. In other words, expiation may be merely a language for communicating repentance, and so, in another culture, the same communication might take another form. Certainly, common-sense psychology does contain many elements of cultural convention, and part of being socially tactful is being able to communicate the right sentiment in the right language. Thus, common-sense theory in psychology, even if it is completely arbitrary insofar as genuine psychological mechanisms are concerned, is as important as language for purposes of analysis. Nobody would argue that addition of *ed* to a verb is any better than any other suffix for expressing the past tense. Nevertheless, the speaker of English had better use *ed* to express the past tense because that is how it is understood by other people.

Whatever the proper role of common sense in behavioral science, common sense influences the scientist. Even for the scientist who deliberately tries to disavow all common-sense presuppositions, common sense is a source of tacit assumptions which he must uproot. One thesis of this book is that many scientific theories of psychology can be understood as denials of one or another common-sense assumption. Psychoanalysis, for example, denies the assumption that all thinking is conscious. But we shall find that other common-sense assumptions have been taken over tacitly by psychoanalytic theory, even some that create difficulties for the full acceptance of the theory of unconsicoùs thinking.

Thus, the first chapter of this book is devoted to a systematic description of common-sense beliefs about human behavior, or *naïve psychology,* as it is called by Heider, who is mainly responsible for its systematic formulation. In the next chapter, we shall return to the particular problem of theory building, to show how naïve psychology contains the roots of many of the theories of child development to be discussed later in the book, as well as the roots of the persistent problems that have engaged philosophers for several thousand years, and psychologists since their science first emerged.

NAÏVE PSYCHOLOGY

A little boy caught red-handed thumping his little brother's head justifies himself by saying, "Jimmy started it." A mother whose child is doing poorly in school tells her friend that "Danny is bright enough; he's not dull; he's just not interested in school work." Jerry, after being set upon and bullied by some bigger boys, turns to his companion and says, "Why did you just stand there? Why didn't you help me? I thought you were my friend!"

Each of these remarks reflects certain tacit assumptions about human behavior. The person who initiates a conflict is more to be reprimanded than his unwilling victim who is finally forced to retaliate. Success in school, like success in every other task, requires a certain ability and also a motivation. One consequence of friendship is to become angry with the person who harms a friend, and to want to protect a friend from danger. Naïve psychology is this system of tacit assumptions that are reflected in everyday human action, which children must learn as they grow up.

How can one discover the assumptions of naïve psychology? The task of dissecting a naïve theory of behavior is much like the linguist's task in writing the grammar of a strange primitive language. He obtains samples of the speech actually used and tries to formulate some of the rules. As soon as he thinks he has discovered a grammatical rule, he uses it to construct sentences and finds out whether his "grammatically" constructed sentences make sense or not. The rules of the grammar are discovered by studying the way that people actually use words.

Naïve psychology must be investigated in the same way. It is based on what people actually do, particularly how they interpret and respond to other people's actions. The principles underlying these responses can be discovered from the regularities of interpersonal relations and can be checked by seeing if behavior based on those rules seems reasonable. Fritz Heider has devoted a lifetime to formulating the important principles of naïve, or common-sense psychology, and has described them in his book, *The Psychology of Interpersonal Relations* (1958). Heider's book forms one basis for this chapter.

The Distinction between Personal and Impersonal Action

Heider points out that in everyday life we discriminate between impersonal acts, like avalanches, windstorms, or runaway automobiles, and those that are manifestations of personal intention. We respond differently to the two. We do not try to escape impersonal events by such stratagems as hiding to avoid discovery; neither do we try to placate, bribe, or deceive impersonal causes. We do not feel hostile or grateful toward impersonal causes. An impersonal event is accepted as the result of natural forces and as subject to the laws of physical science.

Personal events, on the other hand, are intentional, voluntary, and goal-directed. When an out-of-control automobile comes hurtling toward a person, it is an impersonal event, and all that he needs to do in order to avoid being hit is to get out of the way. The path of the automobile is not responsive to the objects in front of it. However, if a murderer deliberately tries to run down a person with a car, his victim cannot avoid destruction merely by stepping out of the path, because the driver will turn the car to keep it directed toward him. The behavior of the guided car is directed toward certain results and may take any of several pathways to achieve it. This "equifinality"—namely, that different means all have the same final result—is the hallmark of personal events involving goal-directed intentional action.

Naïve theory in psychology is concerned with the nature of personal causation. There is a naïve physics concerned with impersonal events which describes people's conceptions of space and time, velocity and number, volume and density, and other such topics. The naïve theory of psychology, on the other hand, is concerned with people's conceptions of intention, perception, emotion, and feeling.

Although personal events are intentional and goal-directed, some of their results are unintended, and thus have some characteristics of the results of impersonal action. A personal act is generally the result of an intention to produce some more-or-less complex result. In addition to this intended result, there are always consequences that were not foreseen and not part of the intention. Some of these consequences may, in fact, be completely accidental, that is, the actor cannot foresee them. Other unintended consequences of action may be incidental rather than accidental. They are more-or-less clearly recognized by the actor, but are not part of his intention. If he must adapt his behavior to accomplish the intention, the failure to achieve incidental consequences does not influence him. For example, in trying to kill the mosquitoes on his property, the owner may spray with DDT and accidentally kill the bees that produce honey. The DDT is chosen because it kills mosquitoes, and if it were not effective in achieving this end, it would not have been selected. It happens that the same spray kills bees, but its effect on bees unfortunately did not influence the owner's behavior one way or the other. In short, intention is as blind to its accidental consequences and as unconcerned about its incidental consequences as the impersonal event.

Can and Try

Since personal events are intentional and goal-directed, they require a motivation. A person does not accomplish his intention without trying to bring it about. Thus, that the individual try is one condition which must be fulfilled before a personal act can be successful. *Trying* indicates that the result is actually intended and that the behavior is directed toward it. A second condition to be fulfilled concerns ability or power. The ability to produce a result is ordinarily described by the word *can*. Both the motivational factor and the ability are necessary: If a person is able to cause some effect and tries to cause it, then he will cause it.

Once this distinction is described by Heider, it is, of course, perfectly obvious. Evidence that this view of human behavior is held by people in everyday life can be observed in many situations. If, for example, we wish to influence a powerful person, we try to persuade him or motivate him to want to do the things we want done. If he is not powerful, we may not spend much effort in trying to change his motivation. Rather, we ignore his wishes, since he cannot do much anyway.

The distinction between *can* and *try* is also implicit in many social judgments. A teacher reacts differently to the student who "isn't trying" and to one who "can't do the work." Psychological examiners testing for abilities feel strongly that they must motivate the child to try as hard as he can, so that the test can measure the child's ability.

THE RELATION BETWEEN THE ABILITY, THE DIFFICULTY, AND CAN. In everyday psychological thinking, the term *ability* is not left undefined. A number of the word's implications constitute the naïve theory of ability. Whether a person can cause some event or not is attributed to two factors: (1) a characteristic of the person himself (ability) and (2) a characteristic of the task (its difficulty). These two concepts are related, because a person *can* perform an act if the difficulty of it is not greater than his ability. Some failures are attributed to the difficulty of the task. If a person fails to break the world's record in an athletic event, for example, it is seen as a result of the extreme difficulty of the task. If a person fails to do something that is easy, the failure is ordinarily attributed to the weakness of the person.

Although the concepts of ability and difficulty seem perfectly natural from a common-sense standpoint, they introduce complications of definition and scientific investigation. Whereas the individual's success in performance is an observable fact, the factors of individual ability and task difficulty are neither easy to define empirically nor to measure. From one point of view, they seem unnecessary concepts.

Heider speculates on the values and functions of these concepts. They are examples of a broad class of variables called *dispositional variables*. A dispositional variable describes a property of an object which is rather permanent and which is manifested in a variety of circumstances, but which is attributed to the object even when not manifested. Scientific explanations frequently employ dispositional variables. The fragility of an egg, for example, is a dispositional property. This property is reflected in many ways, such as when the egg breaks after a short fall or after being hit by an object or squeezed in the hands. The egg is "fragile," however, even when it is not being broken, that is, when it is not manifesting its fragility.

There are good functional reasons for attributing dispositional properties to people in everyday life. It is important in interpersonal relations to know what to expect from another person. If we are to rely on him to succeed in a task he accepts, we need to know whether he is likely to succeed; that is, how much *ability* he possesses. Furthermore, his ability is not necessarily revealed by his momentary behavior. Information about it can be obtained from our past experiences with him, but the process is not a simple counting of successes. We come to a high assessment of a person's ability by observing that he has succeeded at tasks at which other people have failed, and failed only at tasks at which other people have also failed. Another person who has failed many tasks, including those which many others have performed successfully, is judged to have low ability. Thus, by a distillation of past experiences, we determine which people are able and which tasks are difficult, and thus build up expectations about who will succeed on what task. All of this complicated factoring of the data on success and failure into the two variables, *personal ability* and *task difficulty,* is carried out more-or-less intuitively in ordinary, everyday, interpersonal relations.

Naïve psychological theory contains more than a general concept of ability: in everyday life we also have some realization that there are different kinds of abilities. We expect a calculus problem to be easy for a mathematics professor and a 14-foot pole vault to be easy for an athlete, but do not necessarily expect the reverse. Thus, in making our assessments of other people's abilities, we tacitly limit our review of the evidence to tasks that seem relevant. To some degree, we perform an armchair factor analysis and distinguish such abilities as athletic ability, intellectual ability, business acumen, and others. At the level of naïve psychology, however, these factors have only a vague meaning and there does not seem to be a clear prescribed organization of abilities into definite factors.

Naïve Theory of Motivation

The naïve theory of ability is not uncomplicated, but the common-sense theory of goal-directed behavior is even more elaborate. The naïve theory of motivated action includes tacit assumptions about knowledge and the process of knowing, and about desire and enjoyment and the conditions necessary for each, as well as theories about the actual execution of intended actions.

Perception, Cognition, and Consciousness

Motivated intentional behavior is assumed in naïve psychology to require an organism who "knows what he is doing." It is not necessary to make such an assumption; there are many mechanical devices that show guided behavior. In everyday life, however, we do assume that personal actions are performed by knowing organisms whose behavior is guided by information from the environment.

How is this assumption of cognition evident in everyday life? Hiding is one example. Hiding from another person is a sensible strategy only if one believes the other person's actions are controlled by information from his environment obtained through vision. Even at young ages, children seem to have acquired this assumption. They try to hide from their pursuers and to remain inconspicuous when jobs are being handed out or the teacher is getting ready to call on someone. On the other hand, children who want to attract attention know a variety of means for accomplishing their purpose.

Knowing what one is doing is an essential element in being given credit or in being held responsible for one's acts. In one experiment by Baldwin and Baldwin (1965) the subject is read two short stories in which one child benefits another—in this case a larger boy knocks a ball down from a high box so that a little boy can get it to play with. In one story the larger boy performs this act accidentally, not even knowing the little boy wants the ball; in the other story he performs the same act in response to the little boy's request for help. Even four-year-olds generally see the second act as kinder than the first. In justifying their answers, many children say that the first boy did not know what he was doing.

Thus, naïve psychology assumes that cognition plays an essential part in the causation of human behavior. The first link in the causal chain leading to behavior is to receive and process information from the environment. This processing of information is assumed to lead to a conscious perception of the external world, and to a cognitive representation of the individual's environment.

PERCEIVING. In naïve psychology, perception is conceived as direct passive registration or awareness of the external world. Although scientific psychology has shown that perception is a complicated reconstruction of a picture of the external world from disjointed and unarticulated sensory information, in naïve psychology this complexity is unrecognized. In everyday life we assume that an event occurring before our eyes is more-or-less photographically perceived. Because of this confidence in perception, eyewitness reports of a crime have an importance quite out of proportion to their accuracy.

Naïve psychology does not assume, however, that perception is complete. Objects can be too small or too well-hidden to be perceptible. For good perception, the visual medium must be clear; darkness, fog, a blindfold, or bad eyes may interfere with the chain that mediates vision. If these minimal conditions are met, however, we assume that people perceive whatever is in front of them. If an acquaintance looks straight at someone but does not greet him, the latter feels snubbed; he tacitly assumes that the acquaintance did perceive him and deliberately refused to greet him. If, on the other hand, the friend is blind, or if the night is dark and foggy, then he admits the possibility that he could not be recognized.

COGNITION. According to common-sense psychology, the individual's knowledge of his environment includes more than what he directly perceives. We may know that the drugstore is around the corner without being able to perceive it right now. We may infer the presence of objects because of indirect evidence. By talking toward backstage, an actor can create a convincing illusion of a person in the next room. The murderer can create a convincing alibi by playing a tape recording of a conversation in his room while he is actually out murdering his rich uncle.

Regardless of how the information is obtained, the person as conceptualized in naïve psychology knows his environment in an organized way, integrating information from different sources about the same object. His knowledge, or cognitive representation, includes the past, the future, the observed, the known, and the inferred. It includes knowledge of the properties of objects and relationships among them. Furthermore, this knowledge is assumed to be conscious, or to be readily available to consciousness. To know something is to be conscious of it, as far as naïve theory is concerned. Naïve theory contains little or no provision for unconscious ideas, perceptions, motives, or feelings. In everyday life, we assume that other people, as well as ourselves, are consciously aware of what goes on around them.

Naïve theory assumes, furthermore, that people can report on what they know—if they can talk. They may choose to tell a lie or refuse to talk, but they can tell what they know if they will. The translation of knowledge into words can also go in the reverse direction. People can acquire knowledge by being told. Language is one medium for obtaining information that may become part of one's knowledge.

In everyday life, children as well as adults do distinguish between immediately conscious thoughts that seem to be mental events occurring right now, and stored knowledge that is available but not active. We are never at any one time thinking about all the knowledge we possess, but we can voluntarily think about it on demand. In summary, we can say that naïve theory is a thoroughgoing cognitive theory in which conscious awareness is an essential link in the actual causation of behavior.

These statements are expressed didactically and somewhat overstate the naïveté of the man on the street. The ordinary person does have some conception of slips of the tongue, or momentary forgetfulness of facts that he knows well, and does realize that people can sometimes be blind to what is right in front of their eyes. It is not people's lack of awareness of these facts that keeps such concepts out of our formulation of naïve theory. Rather, such events do not fit into the ordinary person's general conception of human behavior. They are errors in the functioning of people, and are therefore not integrated into a coherent set of beliefs. They are like dreams about which everybody knows, but which have no place in naïve theory.

Naïve theory is primarily a theory of rational behavior which assumes that people perceive accurately, use information logically to form reasonable judgments, experience appropriate emotions and motives, and generally adopt sound strategies for obtaining their objectives. It is not exclusively a theory of rational behavior, because feelings such as revenge, envy, and jealousy, rational or not, are understandable within it. On the other hand, some behavior that people do know about is inexplicable in naïve theory because it is not integrated into a broad set of beliefs.

Naïve theory can thus be viewed as an organization of concepts that encompasses most of the behavior in everyday life, but, like most theories, it fails to account for some behavior. Since behavior that fails to fit the theory is not frequent, it is tolerated as exceptional and does not force a basic revision. Naïve theory is also somewhat like a cultural norm which states what ought to be done, rather than reports what is done. Behavior which departs from it is viewed as deviant and is subjected to cultural pressure to conform. Thus, the apparent rarity of such deviant behavior may signify that people hide it or rationalize it to fit the culturally understandable psychological processes, or are actually coerced into feeling and behaving in the way that is culturally expected of them. In any case, naïve theory does not encompass all behavior, or even all the behavior that the man in the street is aware of, but it does describe the behavior that seems sensible and understandable in everyday life.

Effort and intention. In the chain of concepts used to explain motivated behavior, the first link is the cognition of the environment and of one's own actions. Given this first step, what is the naïve conceptualization of the actual motivation itself? One feature of motivated behavior is *trying*. In common-sense psychology, trying has two aspects. There is a qualitative factor, namely, what is the person trying to do? This describes his *intention*. We also speak of how hard he is trying. This factor may be called *effort*.

Effort is related in naïve theory, on the one hand, to the strength of the motivation, and on the other hand, to the probability of success. The more a person wants something, the harder he tries; and, the harder he tries, the more likely he is to succeed, especially if the difference between his ability and the difficulty is not very great. In other words, effort can actually increase a person's power to some extent.

What a person tries to do is his *intention*. Trying is taken as an unequivocal sign of intention in naïve theory. If an individual tries to do something, he may produce other results than those he tries to, but he never tries to do something he does not intend to do.

Trying indicates intention, but as Heider uses the term, it does not necessarily indicate *wanting*. The person may not *want* to achieve the result he is trying to achieve. Heider defines *want* as wanting something for itself. A person may therefore perform an action he does not want to do, perhaps as a necessary step to achieve something he does want, or because somebody he is very fond of wants him to do it or because he believes he ought to do it. Although the word *want* is not used in everyday life in such a restricted way, the distinction between wanting something for itself and doing it for an ulterior motive certainly reflects a common-sense notion.

In all, Heider describes five possible sources of intention: (1) a want, (2) an ulterior reason, (3) a sentiment, (4) a compulsion, and (5) an obligation. Any of these factors may induce the person to try to achieve a particular goal. Of the five possible bases of intention, wanting is perhaps more completely analyzed than any of the others. Heider proposes the following conceptualization of the naïve theory of desire: *Desire* is a feeling that occurs when one does not have something one *likes*. Both conditions are necessary; one must like something to desire it, and one must not have it. When a person desires something and then obtains it, the desire disappears and is replaced by another feeling called *enjoyment*. These two feelings are related, one is elicited by not having what one likes, the other by having what one likes.

This concept is implicit in many aspects of interpersonal relations. If we see a person try to get something and succeed, we assume that he is pleased and enjoys it. If we find he does not enjoy it, we may explain his lack of enjoyment by deciding that he was acting out of duty, necessity, or some other reason. If a person protests he is doing something only because he should—for example, when the salesman explains to his wife that he had to take the out-of-town buyer to a strip-tease nightclub, and then shows pleasure, we suspect that he desired it all the time. If a person says he desires something, we assume that if we can help him get it, he will be pleased. If we know that a person expressed enjoyment when he last had some object, we assume that he likes it and that it would be a suitable present to give him.

To summarize, *like* describes a dispositional property of the person, while *desire* and *enjoyment* describe two feeling states that depend upon liking, and also upon the presence or absence of the liked object. Some other feelings are incorporated into the same system. *Hope,* for example, is a feeling that accompanies the desire for something and the expectation that it will be attained. *Despair* is sometimes used to describe the intense desire for something accompanied by a conviction that it will not be achieved.

Although Heider does not elaborate on the corresponding concepts that accompany *dislike,* the relations seem generally complementary. The presence of a disliked object causes displeasure just as the presence of a liked object causes pleasure. The complement of desire might be called aversion. It is found to accompany displeasure and disappears when the disliked object is no longer present. Aversion, like desire, is a want and contributes to trying, but the wanted change is to become separated from the object rather than united to it.

In everyday language there is some confusion concerning whether the escape from a disliked event brings about the same pleasure that accompanies the accomplishment of a liked event. In one sense, it does; it is a pleasure to be rid of troubles, but is not the enjoyment of positively liked events something more than merely the absence of unpleasantness? We shall see that this same confusion plagues scientific theories of behavior in controversies over drive reduction (see p. 411).

Heider summarized the naïve theory of motivation in the diagram shown in Figure 1-1.

DISTANCE. The discussion of separation as a condition for desire illustrates how the concept of distance is involved in everyday thinking. It is not logically necessary to conceive of "not enjoying a wanted experience" as "being separated from a goal," but the spatial analogy appears frequently in naïve psychology.

Another illustration of how distance is psychologically important is the enjoyment that comes from physical proximity to liked objects, people, etc., even when there is no further interaction involved. Just being near his mother can quiet an anxious child. A quite different effect of distance in the arousal of feelings occurs in what Heider calls *almost* situations. To almost attain a goal is particularly frustrating and teasing. Bare escape of a disaster elicits a particularly intense feel-

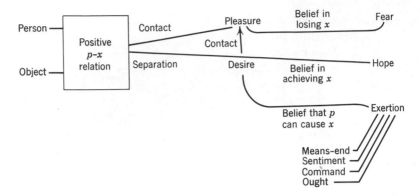

Figure 1-1. Desire and pleasure in the naïve psychology of motivation.

ing of relief. A psychological *near-miss* or a *close escape* need not have any real basis in the actual probability of the event. If, for example, the person next to you receives the first prize in a lottery, or if your number is just one lower than the lucky number, this closeness makes it psychologically a near-miss, even though it was not a near-miss in any realistic way.

These considerations have led Heider to believe that a spatial representation is tacitly involved in much naïve psychology. He feels that desire can be coordinated to "being distant from a liked object," and that "trying to cause a desired event" can be equated with "trying to reduce the distance." As we shall see, Lewin tried to formalize this geometry. In a later chapter we shall look closely at the problems involved in such an attempt (see p. 157 ff.).

LIKES AND DISLIKES. One of the conditions for desire is that we like the object we desire. Like is a dispositional concept involved in the analysis of *want,* somewhat analogous to the ability concept in the analysis of success. Liking is a dispositional property because it is relatively enduring, and a knowledge of a person's likes permits us to anticipate what sorts of things he will be motivated to achieve. Perhaps it is because enduring likes permit predictability in social interaction that fickleness of preference is a source of irritation and puzzlement.

Just as the person's ability interacts with the difficulty of the task to permit prediction of success, there is also an environmental aspect to liking and disliking. Some desires are attributed to the desirability of certain objects, while others are viewed as a more personal and idiosyncratic manifestation of individual likes or tastes. If an object is highly desirable, the person need have no special taste for it to enjoy it. It is viewed as natural for children to like candy, but the liking of spinach is due to the child's special taste. A dislike for candy is also to be accounted for by a particular distaste for it.

The assumption of some commonly accepted standards of desirability greatly eases social interaction. We assume that a person will like a box of candy, and thus it is an acceptable, if uninspired, gift that communicates good wishes. To send a dead rat, on the other hand, is a clear act of unfriendliness. It might just happen that the recipient is allergic to candy, and has a particular fetish for dead rats, but this does not modify the meaning attributed to the gifts, unless it is quite clear that the giver is well aware of the recipient's special tastes. The assumption of a general factor of desirability essentially simplifies the prediction of a person's likes and dislikes.

In summary, wanting or desiring is conceived in naïve theory as a result of two factors: first, a liking for the object, and second, separation from it. Separation from the object and changes in the amount of separation play important roles in the momentary feelings that situations arouse. Liking describes a more enduring characteristic of the person which permits his desires and pleasure to be anticipated. However, liking itself is in part culturally standardized. Some objects are viewed as desirable. They can be used to convey one's feelings about a person even without any special knowledge of his special tastes. Liking also contains idiosyncratic elements that may or may not agree with the cultural norm.

Sentiment

In the naïve theory of action, sentiment is one of the roots of behavior. We do things because people we like want us to, or because we think the actions will please them. In attempts to influence other people, one strategy is to make them like us, and if a firm friendship does exist, we may exert leverage by an appeal to sentiment: "Even if you won't do it yourself, do it for me."

In some ways sentiments resemble likes and dislikes. In everyday language we use the word "like" both for liking money and for liking a new acquaintance, but there are important differences between the two uses. Feelings about objects are relatively undifferentiated; they include likes and dislikes, and perhaps fears. But sentiments toward people are much more varied; they include hate, contempt, admiration, and sympathy. Sentiment toward objects is related to desire and enjoyment in relatively simple ways, but the statement that one person likes another is much more complicated to describe, despite its being quite understandable in everyday life. We know what to expect of a person who likes another, but it is not easy to express these expectations in a few clear principles.

The positive sentiment, "liking a person," seems to have the following manifestations:

1.   It implies a desire to benefit the person. In fact, it implies more. It is as if the other person replaced the self in situations normally eliciting desire, enjoyment, hope, and fear. If my son does not have something he likes, my sentiment toward him creates in me the desire to obtain it for him, and I enjoy it when he has obtained something he likes. What makes him unhappy, makes me unhappy for him. When he is in danger, I am afraid.

2.   The sentiment of liking also makes certain kinds of relationships with the other person pleasant and unpleasant. We tend to enjoy contact with the people we like and to desire that contact in their absence. The exact kind of contact varies with the variety of positive sentiment. The contact that lovers desire is not the same as the contact desired by intellectual colleagues, but the word *contact* covers both.

3.   The sentiment of liking also facilitates similarity. One wants to agree with a friend's opinions and to have similar tastes and values. Thus, mutual friendship within a group of people tends to produce conformity among them. Similarity can also be a cause of friendship; similarity of tastes and opinions, even similarity in background or physique, all contribute to the development of friendship.

4.   A positive sentiment toward a person is also reflected in a generally favorable opinion of him. A friend is generally seen as good, kind, wise, trustworthy, etc.—the fact of friendship casts a halo about the entire person.

Of these four manifestations of liking, the most salient and peculiarly human feature is the desire to benefit the other person, and the arousal of a whole set of tender altruistic motivations toward him. It is this desire to benefit that lies behind the potency of such sentiments in causing behavior. Naïve theory assumes a genuine desire to make one's friends happy and a genuine distress at their misfortunes.

THE BALANCE PRINCIPAL AMONG SENTIMENTS. The effect of these four manifestations of a sentiment, particularly the tendency toward similarity, is to make certain sets of sentiments compatible with each other and other sets relatively incompatible. For example, to like a man but dislike his wife results in a certain strain. Sentiments toward other people are most compatible when there is a homogeneity to them.

Heider calls a sentiment of liking a "plus" relation, and he also calls the relationship of *belonging* or *union* a "plus" relation. If someone owns an object, then it belongs to him; if he performs some action, that action belongs to him even more intimately; if he is a member of the same organization, same family, same nationality, or same race as someone else, there is, to some degree, a relationship of belonging.

According to Heider's balance principle as applied to three objects, the relation is balanced if there is a plus relation between each object and every other one. Thus, if one likes a man and admires a book he has written, the situation is balanced: There is a plus relation between the two men, between the admirer and the book, and, since the man wrote the book, there is a belongingness or a plus relation between him and the book. To like all the members of a family similarly produces a balanced situation.

Another kind of balance is achieved if there are two negative relationships out of the three. Thus, if one likes a person and shares with him a dislike of a third person, the shared dislike creates a balance. There is a minus relation between the third person and each of the pair. On the other hand, a single negative relation among the three produces imbalance. If *A* likes *B*, and *B* likes *C*, but *A* dislikes *C*, the situation is more unbalanced than if two of them mutually dislike the third, or if one of them dislikes both of the others.

If one learns that a friend has done something one considers quite wrong, this creates an imbalance. Heider has pointed out how the imbalance can be resolved in any of three ways. One can decide that the thing the friend did was not really wrong, that one does not like him any more, or that the friend did not really do it. Any of these three decisions brings the situation into balance again.

DISLIKE. The negative sentiment of dislike is, generally speaking, the opposite of like. It is expressed by a desire to harm the other person rather than to benefit him, and by a desire to be distant rather than close. Various complexities and dilemmas arise in the expression of negative sentiment which are less apparent when liking is involved. For one thing, harming a person and withdrawing from him are often incompatible with each other, whereas benefiting and approaching are frequently mutually supporting actions.

A second complication arises because of the relation of fear to dislike. Fear implies a belief that the other person is hostile, and that he has power and can carry out his hostile intention. This belief frequently accompanies one's own hatred of the other person and presents one with the uncomfortable conflict between the desires for fight and flight.

No comparable dilemma arises on the positive side. The result of benefiting another person, as we shall see later, tends to be that he becomes friendly, and this response on his part facilitates the expression of a positive sentiment. Mutual friendliness is a balanced situation in which the expressions of one person's friendliness facilitate the expressions of the other person's. Negative sentiments, on the contrary, do not fit each other quite as well. Mutual avoidance of each other results in a stable, reasonable, and harmonious situation in which two enemies never see each other and both are satisfied as a result. But attack on each other is seldom satisfactory to both parties. Thus, the problem of harming, yet staying out of harm's way, arises in negative sentiments and creates problems that do not exist in a mutual friendship.

In everyday human relations we intuitively recognize a variety of negative sentiments, including hatred and readiness to attack, hatred but cautiousness about direct attack, and fearfulness. Ordinary language is not specific in making these distinctions, and we can all become lost in the complexity of subtle sentiments. However, an appreciation of the varieties of sentiments and their different associated behaviors is quite general among laymen as well as among psychologists.

Requests and Commands

Returning to Figure 1-1 which outlines the various sources from which intentional action may stem, we have seen how personal desires and sentiments toward other people may lead to intentional behavior. A third possible reason for a voluntary action is that another person requests or commands it. The distinction between obeying an order and acquiescing to a request to do what a friend wants is not always clear. In order to put the problem in perspective, Heider discusses the various strategies presented in naïve psychology for inducing another person to do something.

INDUCTION OF BEHAVIOR. If one person wants another person to perform some action, he may try to make the other person want to perform it by persuading him that it is enjoyable. In other words, he tries to create a wish to perform the action by attaching the action to the other person's motivational system. If he succeeds in creating this desire, he is not making direct use of the other person's sentiment toward him, although his persuasion may be more readily accepted if the two are friends.

A second method for inducing another person to do something is to ask him. The motivation for acceding to a request is the desire to do what another person wants or needs. If the two people are friends, the positive sentiment provides a strong basis for acquiescence, but friendship is not necessary for acquiescence to a request. Almost anyone will tell a stranger what time it is, or will direct him if he is lost, and some people will go to great lengths to benefit other people, whether they are particular friends or not. As we shall see later, the desire to benefit another person is aroused—according to naïve theory—by his needing help. Thus, people may sacrifice their own plans to help victims of an accident, even though the victims are complete strangers, but they would not be so helpful if the need were trivial. Beggars are highly adept at capitalizing on the sympathy of strangers by telling an unfortunate story, appearing to be crippled, etc.

A third means of inducing another person to perform some action is to command him to do it. Commands operate through power, rather than through sentiment or sympathy. If the person who issues the order possesses naked power, he is able to punish disobedience so severely that people obey. Although commands can be enforced through strength alone, they are more effective if the person giving the command is either personally respected or has an acknowledged right to give orders, such as an army officer has. These two bases for commanding obedience are often found in the same person, but a subtle difference exists between them. Respect for a person seems to imply that his commands can be trusted to be wise ones, even if the person receiving the command does not understand the reason for the action. Authority, however, gives a person's commands an obligatory character. We "ought" to obey the commands of a person who has the "right" to give orders.

Just as obedience to a command depends partly on the sentiments or attitudes toward the person giving it, it may also depend upon the characteristics of the person receiving it. Like the generalized kindness that describes a readily aroused desire to benefit others, there is a generalized dispositional characteristic of submissiveness which consists of a susceptibility to commands, no matter who may give them.

CAN AND MAY. One feature of a command is that it works upon the person's volition, not his ability. No matter how forceful or effective the command is, it does not physically force the person to do what is commanded. The bars and locks of a safe deposit vault prevent stealing, but not by means of a command. Even when a command rests on naked power, it rests on the strength of the commander to control the consequences of obedience or disobedience, and so influences the person through his voluntary obeying.

Although obedience is a voluntary act, the force of a command can be so great that the obeyer is relieved of responsibility for the action. Ordinarily, the presence of an intention behind an action makes one responsible for it and for its intended consequences. In fact, the responsibility may extend to some of the unintended consequences—as in culpable negligence. If a beggar asks a man for money and receives it, he is certainly not guilty of robbery. If he points a gun at his victim and asks, then he is guilty of robbery. In the first case, the man voluntarily gives away money and is responsible for his action; in the second case, the giving itself is intentional, but is done under such a powerful threat that the act is viewed as acquiescence to force rather than a voluntary giving of money. The general principle is that if an action is induced by a threat of severe punishment, responsibility tends to shift from the actor to the inducer, whereas induction through promise of reward does not relieve the actor of responsibility. To bribe a bank teller to open a safe is a crime, but it does not lessen the crime of the bank teller who accepts the bribe. To threaten a bank teller with death at gunpoint if he does not open the safe is interpreted as forcing him to open the safe; in such a circumstance the teller bears no responsibility for the crime: It rests entirely on the man with the gun.

Ought Forces

Ethical and moral issues have already appeared in our discussion of naïve theory, but the nature of moral influence has not been directly considered. However, what Heider calls *ought forces* are another source of intentional action. One may perform an act merely because one feels he ought to do so, even though the act itself may be unpleasant.

Heider shows that an obligation and a command are similar, except that no clear agent issues the command implied in an obligation. First, both operate through intentional action, that is, they prevent behavior not by making it physically impossible but by forbidding it. Secondly, both obligations and commands are enforceable by reward and punishment. The rewards of virtue and the punishment of sins stem from the conscience, but are nevertheless powerful. Third, both obedience and conformity to obligation involve a respect for authority. The sense of conscience is based upon one's convictions about what is right, and is much weakened whenever one begins to doubt the validity of the moral principles upon which the obligation depends. Conscience is not, however, based entirely upon validity. People can feel guilty over actions that they are convinced are not wrong. Sexual relations in marriage may arouse guilt feelings even though they are completely acceptable. Conscience has a certain force of its own, and this fact is recognized in naïve psychology. Psychoanalytic theory, of course, emphasizes the importance of this force in human feeling.

Because of the similarity between command and obligation, Heider conceives of obligations as the commands of some respected and powerful authority. What is this authority? For some people it may be God, but it is not necessarily so personalized. People who have vague beliefs about God, or are even atheistic, may still have a strong sense of obligation. Heider, therefore, uses the term "the objective order" to describe the fact that moral principles are felt to be objectively right. The phrase "it just isn't done" expresses this same feeling of prohibition but without any clear agent doing the prohibiting.

If one carries this analogy farther, then "values" are "those things that the authority likes." The commands of an authority are seen as expressing his sentiments, and if one knows the sentiments of the authority, one may well anticipate commands by bringing about the things that the authority likes, even without being told to do so. In moral behavior, one seldom feels that a particular act is being commanded or prohibited in isolation. Instead, one has a set of values or principles that describe what is right and wrong. Moral behavior thus consists in bringing about what is right and avoiding what is wrong.

In everyday life, children and adults alike believe their values are universal and objectively right. Values are not just a matter of tastes; they are right, not only for oneself, but also for everybody. That the values of different cultures are not the same does not change the fact that the person feels values as objective facts. There is an essential difference—from the person's own point of view—between a taste for olives and a sense of justice.

The absoluteness and universality of values is, of course, only a subjective impression: in fact, there are wide differences among cultures about what is considered right and wrong. These cultural variations produce serious difficulties in international relations, because each culture tends to view the deviant values of the others as error or sin. The resulting dilemma is a poignant one: Intolerance of other cultures' values leads to conflict and dogmatism, but tolerance of deviant values makes them matters of taste so that all values lose some of their reality and conviction.

VIOLATION AND OUGHTS. In the view of naïve psychology, the violation of a moral requirement or an ought force brings three consequences.

1. The violator deserves punishment. In the special case where the violation has harmed some person, that person is in a special position of demanding punishment, but generally speaking, the punishment

need not be inflicted by the victim of the crime. The criminal deserves to be punished merely because he committed a wrong.

2.   The violation of a moral law is followed by guilt feelings on the part of the person himself. Logically, one might feel that committing a crime was a sign of a defective or absent conscience, but in everyday life we recognize that the pangs of guilt can punish acts that conscience did not prevent. Criminals are therefore expected to be appropriately conscience-stricken and the criminal who does not show any signs of repentance may be treated with special severity. Sins in our society are punished even if the criminal is conscience-stricken, but his pangs of guilt give his crime the appearance of a weakness of will, not a deliberate cold-blooded violation of moral law unhampered by any moral feeling. It is the calm unperturbed criminal confessing with no sign of guilt that he killed his five-year-old daughter because she kept pestering him who seems beyond the pale of human decency and who arouses public demands for severe punishment.

3.   Guilt is expiated by punishment. By being punished the guilty person's conscience is appeased so that he can live with himself again. Punishment is also supposed to appease the rest of society, so that the violator can be reinstated in his former place in it. "He has paid his debt" and in some way the balance which he upset by committing the crime is restored. This feeling that a certain punishment is appropriate and expiates the crime exists among criminals as well as the outside world. Farber (1945) has shown that up to a certain point in serving out their sentences, criminals may feel that they are getting what they deserve. At some point they feel, however, that they have paid enough. Now the balance begins to turn in the other direction and society is wronging them.

In summary, the naïve theory of action is concerned with the various concepts that are thought to underlie voluntary action. We have described several sources of intention: personal wants, ulterior reasons, the promptings of sentimental attachment, the inclination to accede to requests, obedience to commands, and moral obligations. Each of these sources of intentional behavior involves certain dispositional characteristics of the person, his tastes, his sentiments, his values, and his general personality traits like kindness or submissiveness. In naïve psychology, some of these variables are attributed to the objective reality, and others are considered to be personal and subject to individual differences. Intentional behavior is viewed as stemming from the person himself, as being active rather than passive in its nature. However, naïve psychology also conceptualizes the events that impinge on the person and arouse feelings and reactions. These will be discussed in the next section.

ENVIRONMENTAL EFFECTS. One of the important distinctions in naïve psychology is between stimuli that merely present a person with something to perceive and perhaps respond to, and stimuli that forcefully impinge on the person causing effects over which he has no control. The person perceives the stimulus simply because it is present and is thus provided with the opportunity for voluntary intentional action. However, naïve psychology recognizes that some events press themselves on the person, or impose on him in a sense. They may make him suffer, as does an injury, or they may make him happy, as does an unexpected gift; they may demand something of him or they may forbid him to do something. Such events are, of course, perceived by the person, but are also "undergone" or "suffered," and Heider uses the term "suffer" in this general sense. These events have sometimes been labeled "press" (Murray, 1938).

Environmental impositions are perceived and attributed to causal factors, perhaps to an impersonal source, perhaps to another person. An injury, for example, is seen as having a cause; in some cases the cause is another person, perceived as inflicting the injury intentionally or accidentally. If it is intentional, it may be attributed to hostility, to sadism, to revenge, or to some other motivation.

When these impositions occur, they are expected to arouse certain feelings and certain types of responsive behavior. The loss of a loved one is expected to produce sorrow; exposure in a *faux pas* brings shame or embarrassment; the good fortune of another person may elicit envy. Naïve psychology thus contains explanations of one's response to an environmental event which make the response seem natural or expected. An unexpected response, such as guilt over winning first prize or scorn of a popular hero, appears peculiar and requires some explanation to justify it.

Two general principles are detectable in people's expectations of the response to impositions: a tendency to reciprocate and a tendency to resist. It is natural to expect that an injury will arouse the desire for revenge, and that a kindness will tend to elicit kindness in return, and special feeling of poetic justice is aroused if an act is perfectly reciprocated. Thus, saving a life is reciprocated in an especially appropriate way if he whose life is saved later saves the life of his rescuer. Of all these reciprocations, the most obvious is the tendency to take revenge for injury and to return a benefit, however.

All impositions tend to evoke some resistance. Thus, it is quite understandable that people may resent being helped if they are capable of helping themselves and that even benefits may be resented because of the obligation they impose. One of the most tactful ways to benefit somebody is to provide him with an opportunity to obtain what he desires. This leaves him free to operate on his own wishes and is less of an imposition than if the benefit is bestowed so that there is no way of avoiding it.

Along with these reactions to impositions, certain feelings are felt to be natural. Thus, injury angers the injured party, a benefit produces gratitude, and domination generates a stubborn, resistant feeling. Other sorts of press also have their typical emotional response. Loss elicits sorrow or mourning; misfortune in others elicits sympathy; exposure of one's defect produces shame.

Thus far we have been primarily describing the responses to personal press, that is, press attributed to other people. Impositions or press from the impersonal world are primarily classified as good or bad fortune. Heider points to a balance principle in the consideration of good and bad fortune. There is a common belief that fortune balances out. Some people may undergo a series of lucky experiences with an increasing feeling that they are going to pay for them with corresponding bad luck. Certainly, a piece of misfortune does not arouse nearly as much sympathy from others if the person has just had some good luck as when it is piled on top of other misfortunes.

Naïve Theory of Personality

Since in this book we are primarily concerned with theories of child development, it is appropriate to look back over naïve theory for what it has to say about the development of personality. First, it distinguishes between a theory of personality and a theory of action. Some of its concepts describe *events,* like feelings, wishes, desires, and behavioral acts, and other concepts describe *dispositional properties* of either the person or the environment. An object may be attractive, another person may be pitiful, or a situation may be difficult: these are dispositional properties of the environment. Naïve theory also describes the dispositional properties of people's likes and preferences, envy, etc.

In naïve theory, however, there is a tendency to find the cause of a psychological event in either the environment or the person, but not in both. Thus, naïve psychology seems to regard personality as relevant only when the behavior is unexpected or difficult to predict. No personality concept is needed to explain that a person desires an attractive object, or that he succeeds in an easy task; personality is involved, however, when a person does not desire an attractive object, or when he succeeds in a difficult task. It is as if there were a standard set of responses that are natural to human beings and for which no personality concepts are necessary; however, when behavior deviates from the expected, personality explains the deviation. There are some areas where cultural norms are less prescribed, like envy or pleasure at others' good fortune. In these areas personality concepts are involved, no matter what the behavior is. Personality dispositions, then, are used to describe individual differences among people, but to the degree that a certain feeling or reaction is universal, it is explained by the environment, not by a personality trait.

Personality traits in naïve theory are systematically related to the kinds of psychological events which occur. Thus, there are traits that describe abilities, which are correlated with success and failure; there are also traits related to desires, which are essentially statements of preference and likes among goal objects; there are personality traits that describe one's desire to benefit or harm other people, the sentiments or attitudes; and there are personality traits that describe one's reaction to press, such as being revengeful or hot-tempered. Within each of these personality dispositions, naïve theory does not provide much organization. There is some recognition that certain traits are related to others and may have a common factor, but traits are largely tied to a restricted psychological event. Personality as a whole is, in naïve psychology, more a catalog than an organization of interrelated traits.

It is not entirely true, however, that in naïve theory personality traits are not organized. There is, for example, a general tendency to consider ability a single variable, so that people who are capable and competent in one area are generally given respect in all areas; thus, movie stars can recommend which brand of soap to use, and admirals are listened to respectfully when they talk about the public schools.

In the area of motivation there is a similar general trait, goodness or badness. People who are good are expected to be unselfish, to pay their debts promptly, to be unenvious, and to resist the temptation to steal, lie, and commit adultery. Bad people behave in the opposite way.

The organization of descriptive adjectives into clusters has been extensively investigated by Osgood and his colleagues in their studies of the "semantic differential" (Osgood, Suci, & Tannenbaum, 1957). Various objects, people, and concepts can be rated on a list of bipolar adjectives, such as *fast–slow,* and in this way the connotative meaning of the word can be charted. Many studies have shown that three general factors are involved in the connotative meanings of words: *good–bad, strong–weak,* and *active–passive.* These general traits are recognized in everyday life to be fallible, but they still exert considerable influence on our expectations. It is difficult for an exconvict or a cripple to get a job because one is viewed as bad and the other as weak.

Naïve Theory of Development and Change

Heider's primary concern is with the naïve theory of social behavior and interpersonal relations. Because our interest is in child and developmental psychology, we shall attempt to expand Heider's description of naïve psychology to include common-sense notions about the psychological characteristics of children and the processes of learning and development.

In everyday life we not only interpret the behavior of other people and adjust to it, but may also attempt to change their personalities or to educate them. The educational aim is, of course, most common in the school and family where the responsibility for child rearing primarily rests. Parents, in particular, are expected to inculcate in children the proper values of interpersonal behavior—in short, to inculcate the naïve psychology that we have just been describing. By observing how people proceed to educate a child, we can discern their tacit assumptions about children and learning.

SIMILARITIES BETWEEN CHILDREN AND ADULTS IN NAÏVE THEORY. The naïve theory of children's behavior seems to be a mixture of two assumptions: that in certain fundamental aspects human behavior is innate and appears without training, and that in other important respects children are not like adults because they are uninformed and untaught.

Some characteristics are attributed to children as if little or no specific learning is required. In general, the aspects of human behavior that seem natural and self-evident are those attributed to children at an early age. They are not necessarily attributed to children at birth, however. For many adults the newborn child seems so random in his behavior, so unfocused in his vision, and so preoccupied with eating and sleeping that he is hardly seen as human in the sense of being responsive and purposive. Ordinarily, at about the age of three or four months the child begins to respond and focus his attention. Mothers often say at this age that he is beginning to act like a real person.

As soon as the child begins to take on certain important human characteristics, it is natural for adults to attribute to him many subtleties of intention, perception, and feeling. These are essentially the same as those they would attribute to an older child or an adult. At the same time, adults do not unselectively assume that the child is adultlike in all respects. Those features that depend on mechanisms of response like purposiveness, perception, emotional feeling, and certain self-evident logical principles are viewed as natural for the child, while those features of adult behavior that depend on knowledge and training are assumed to be acquired through experience.

One natural function is perception. Since perception is believed in naïve psychology to be a more-or-less direct registration of the environment, it is assumed that as soon as children can see clearly, they perceive shapes and colors and sizes as an adult does, even though they may not have the language to describe them. Thus, even young babies are "shown" presents and other objects with the expectation that they see them even if they do not know what they are.

One evidence of this naïve assumption in the innateness of perception is the common belief that if a congenitally blind person recovers his vision, he will immediately see that triangles and squares are different in shape, and that colors are different from each other. Experiments on the congenitally blind (Senden, 1932) have shown this expectation to be quite wrong. It actually requires a long time for the newly sighted person to learn to discriminate one shape from another. Nevertheless, the naïve expectation is that shapes will look different even if one has never seen them before.

Children are also expected to know intuitively some of the so-called self-evident axioms of physics and logic. For example, when a father performs a magic trick for his two-year-old child—say, making a coin disappear by sleight-of-hand—he expects the child to be surprised. The basis for his expectation is that the child should know that something cannot disappear without going somewhere. Therefore, if it apparently disappears into thin air, the child should be surprised at the phenomenon. Our common-sense intuition also suggests that the child does not need to learn that a statement cannot be true and false at the same time, or that an object cannot be in two places at once, or that the same object cannot be both a dog and a cat. As it turns out, these self-evident axioms of logic and physics are not self-evident at all to the three-year-old child (see Chapter 7).

Certain kinds of instrumental action are also seen as natural in naïve theory. The fact that a child goes toward the object he wants does not require any explanations. We may point to the child's ball or doll in an attempt to help him get it. Such an action tacitly assumes that following a pointer is a primitive ability and that knowing the whereabouts of an object is sufficient to allow the child to go after it.

Finally, some emotional reactions are naïvely viewed as innate. Crying is interpreted as meaning distress even in the newborn child; a forceful loud bellow is assumed to mean anger; when the baby is in a stranger's arms and begins to cry, he is assumed to want his mother and is expected to become happy when handed back to his mother; a baby's smile is assumed to mean that he likes the person he smiles at. Examples like this could be multiplied indefinitely. Naïve theory assumes that the basic structure of behavior, intention, effort, pleasure, pain, etc., appears spontaneously and without training.

CHILDREN LACK KNOWLEDGE. Although children are assumed to perceive like an adult and to intuit certain physical laws, they are also assumed not to know many things that give meaning to experience. They are, of course, ignorant of language, and thus adults can talk about their private affairs freely in front of a young child with no concern that he will understand. Children must be taught the difference between right and wrong, and they cannot be expected to have any moral sense without such training. They are assumed to be sexually innocent, so there is no real taboo on undressing in front of a young child. Parents have sexual intercourse in the presence of infants and young children on the assumption that they do not know what is happening. Children must learn almost all actual behavioral skills. They must learn to sit up, stand up, walk, and talk. They have no habits when they are born, and must acquire them. To summarize, in naïve psychology information, meanings, values, habits, and skills are seen as acquired.

How Do Children Learn?

The principles of learning that seem to be implicit in child-rearing practices reflect the importance of cognition in naïve psychology. Since almost all behavior is assumed to be intentional and guided by the knowledge of what act will have what result, it is reasonable in naïve psychology to view most learning as the acquisition of knowledge. Thus, a readily understood mechanism of learning is that by the results of his action a person discovers what behavior is effective and what is not. When the same situation arises again, he is guided by the knowledge acquired from past experience. When a serious consequence has followed from an action, it is assumed to be especially effective in learning because it is impressed so strongly on the memory. "He won't forget that again!" The child is apparently thought to remember or to forget the information that should guide his action, and thus to behave wisely or unwisely. Thus, naïve psychology conceives of a law of effect in which rewards and punishments are important factors in learning, but, unlike the usual formulation of the law of effect in psychology, the rewards and punishments are pictured as operating through teaching the child the consequences of actions.

Because learning is cognitive, it is possible, according to naïve theory, to substitute instruction for learning through experience. Thus, we can tell children what to do and how to do it, and instill wise and proper behavior without the actual necessity of rewarding and punishing them. It is a common belief among naïve educators, however, that verbal instruction is not nearly as effective as actual reward or punishment. Thus, socializing agents do not limit their instruction to verbal teaching, but actively arrange rewards and punishments for good and bad behavior, respectively.

Repetition and its consequences in naive psychology. Although the naïve theory of reward and punishment emphasizes the cognitive effects of the two, we believe in everyday life that repetition has important effects in learning certain kinds of actions. For example, memory is strongly influenced by repetition: The drill of multiplication tables in traditional education is based upon the principle of repetition. But memory is not acquired cognitively; memory affects behavior through cognition, though remembering itself is not an act that fits the naïve theory of action. The memory of past experience that guides one into proper behavior often simply pops into one's head and is not intentionally remembered in the same way that a memorized poem is recalled voluntarily.

Naïve theory also includes the concept of habit. Habits are pictured as actions which were first performed voluntarily, but which, through repetition, come to occur automatically without thinking. There are good habits and bad, and the naïve theory of education includes ways of forming good habits and breaking bad ones. The method is to try hard on every occasion to perform the proper behavior, especially if one is trying to replace a bad habit with a good one. The good habit may be practiced repeatedly, but it is important never to forget to perform it. There is certainly a naïve belief that one failure to resist a bad habit undoes more learning than is achieve by one success in performing the good habit. Bad habits range all the way from typing *the* as *hte,* to not hanging up one's jacket when coming into the house, to being alcoholic. In naïve theory all of these must be remedied in much the same way, through will power and effort. However, some habits like alcoholism are recognized as being more difficult to break because of the actual pleasure involved in the addiction which must be resisted by will power, in addition to expending the effort involved in remembering to perform the right action. Thus, repetition is a essential factor in memorization and habit formation.

Naïve theory also recognizes the role of repetition in learning motor skills. The individual first tries to perform the motor act voluntarily and someone may instruct him in how to do it. Once he gets it right, he should practice it over and over again, until it becomes automatized or habitual. There also seems to be a belief in naïve psychology that there is value in just trying over and over again to perform the action; a gradual improvement takes place which is not really accompanied by cognitive knowledge of exactly what one is doing. It is important, of course, to practice the correct action rather than the incorrect one, but improvement comes through practice even without intellectual knowledge.

There is a fourth area of naïve psychology where repetition is an important factor, namely, habituation. Habituation involves a change of feelings about a situation. We become accustomed to new food and even learn to like it, whereas at first it was not at all pleasant. Some people learn not to get mad at being bossed around if they have to live under a dictatorial authority for a long time. We can become acclimated to high altitude, cold weather, braces on the teeth, or bifocal glasses merely by living with them for a period of time. A certain amount of effort may be required, but in everyday life we believe that most of the change is due to the passage of time.

The naïve theory of learning, it appears, makes repetition an important factor in changing certain psychological reactions, namely, memory, automatized habits, motor skills, and feelings. All of these reactions involve factors that seem to go beyond cognition and intention; none of them fit exactly into naïve theory of action, because they do not seem to be entirely under voluntary control. Memories pop into and out of consciousness without effort; habits can apparently operate without our thinking about them or even being aware of their operation; feelings are, at best, only partly controllable; and a motor skill, although under voluntary control as a whole, is composed of molecular actions that somehow occur in the proper sequence and organization without our knowing much about how this happens. It thus seems fruitful to distinguish between the naïve theory of voluntary behavior and the much vaguer naïve theory of other reactions. The concepts underlying voluntary action are much better explicated, depend much more on cognition, and act in the service of conscious motives. The less voluntary reactions are not so well understood; they can be modified, but not in so predictable a way, by repetition and practice.

THE DEVELOPMENT OF SENTIMENTS. Besides beliefs about learning, there is also common sense about the growth and development of sentiments, including personal tastes of all sorts. As a matter of fact, naïve theory contains two apparently contradictory explanations for the development of sentiments and tastes, one based upon habituation and continued contact, the other based upon reaction to deprivation.

Habituation is frequently used as an explanation for tastes and sentiments. People like the kind of music, scenery, food, climate, and traditions to which they have become accustomed; social attitudes of children are thought to reflect the prevalent attitudes in their homes; putting people together in groups is believed to facilitate their becoming friends; living in a foreign country is felt to be one way to develop an appreciation for that country's culture and tastes. Curiously enough, though, the opposite result is also understandable to one's common sense. The child who grows up on a farm may never want to see a farm again; adults may hate oatmeal because they had it for breakfast every morning as a child. It is not completely inexplicable if the son of a businessman hates business or if the children of a conservative grow up to be radicals. It seems understandable if a child particularly cherishes financial security because of a poverty-stricken childhood, or if an uneducated parent insists upon his child's going to college.

In terms of the naïve theory of action, desire is stimulated by the absence of things one likes. The effect of living for a long time in a state of ungratified desire may, therefore, accentuate the liking for the desired object, perhaps until the desire becomes insatiable. On the other hand, the result may be that the person grows accustomed to what he does not have, so that he loses an active desire for the unattainable. Thus, opposite results are equally explainable.

There is no reason why both mechanisms cannot operate, but it is important to know what conditions determine which. Within common sense, there are some indications of the conditions that distinguish between accentuation or habituation. When habituation is the aim, the child is encouraged, rather than forced, and is made to suffer only a small amount of imposition while the rest of the situation is made as pleasant as possible. If some important food or necessary imposition can be introduced in this way, common sense says that it will be likely to become gradually accepted. On the other hand, if it is introduced suddenly, violently, and forcibly, and if it becomes a source of contention, common sense leads us to expect a permanent dislike rather than habituation.

NAÏVE THEORY OF MATURATION. Finally, the naïve theory of child development contains some tacit assumptions about the limitations of learning. In every culture there are concrete beliefs about what the child can be expected to do and to learn at every age, and it is generally felt that children cannot learn any skill or habit earlier than the time assigned for it.

Whiting and Child (1953), basing their conclusions on their observation of many cultures, describe socialization as a "period of indulgence" followed by a "period of socialization." The infant exhibits many types of behavior which must change before the child becomes an adult, but in no culture is he expected to change them all at once. The process of socialization may be begun gradually or suddenly, gently or violently, by one means or another. In most cultures there is a period of transition during which the child is being socialized, but the socialization is not expected to be completed. This does not mean that the child is treated leniently, but that the socializing agents are not condemned if the child does not behave in an adult manner. After a while, however, the child is expected to behave like an adult in this particular respect. In the naïve theory of all cultures, therefore, there is a theory of maturation. The child must be taught the skills and controls that govern the behavior of adults, but his ability to acquire the knowledge and controls is acknowledged to have an inherent limitation. Maturity comes gradually with age and is assumed to be reached by the time the child has become adult.

Summary

In this chapter, Heider's presentation of naïve theory has been closely followed, except for some extensions of it to include the special problems of child development. We have seen that the naïve everyday view of human behavior is in one way far from naïve. It implicitly contains a complex set of assumptions and laws that govern much of our understanding of other people. It has been Heider's great contribution to make these assumptions explicit. Briefly they are that:

Nearly all human behavior is cognitively directed, that is, directed toward the attainment of goals which must be cognized before they can become operative. This cognition is seen in naïve theory as a natural process depending merely upon the exposure of the person to the external world. We see what is in front of us, and nearly everyone sees the same thing when he is exposed to the same external situation.

Differences in the behavior of different people depend upon differences in motivation, which in turn depend upon differences in dispositional characterstics. In interpersonal relationships, much effort goes into analysis of the dispositional characteristics or personality of other people.

As well as being motivated by appropriate goal objects, people also respond to external press or imposition, which may arouse hostility, gratitude, fear, disgust, etc. These feelings and their accompanying behavioral consequences are reasonably predictable, according to naïve theory.

Two other classes of psychological mechanisms, according to common-sense theory, are sentiments and feelings of moral obligation or "ought."

Despite the widespread predominance of cognitively controlled mechanisms in our everyday view of human nature, some more automatic or involuntary mechanisms are also recognized. These are particularly important in the naïve theory of child behavior. The effect of repetition on behavior is assumed to be effective in: (1) learning motor skills, (2) learning habits, (3) acquiring associations, and (4) habituation.

Children, according to naïve theory, are primarily ignorant adults. Their behavior is not governed by laws markedly different from those governing adults; they simply lack much of the knowledge necessary for sensible action. Thus, the socialization and education of children is seen as a process of giving them knowledge, either through experience or verbal instruction. At the same time, there is some recognition that children, even if informed, cannot be held responsible for their actions because they are not adequately controlled by their knowledge of right and wrong and of consequences. This responsibility seems to be seen as a result of the maturation that comes automatically with age.

TWO   General issues of behavior theory

UPON SITTING BACK to take a detached look at naïve psychology, one
may be amazed that common sense is so sophisticated and systematic,
and may feel like the man who discovered that he had been speaking
prose all his life. The systematization is largely Heider's doing, just as
the systematic formulation of a grammar is the work of a linguist, but
it could not have been done if the essential discriminations had not
been present. Without detracting from Heider's achievement, we can
be gratified that everyday naïve notions are so impressive.

It is important to realize, however, that naïve psychology is not a
stated theory but a body of beliefs about human behavior. Only the
systematic description of naïve psychology gives it the look of a theory.
Common-sense beliefs are the ground out of which theories of human
behavior may grow, but they are equally the ground in which literary
criticism, the historian's understanding of social processes, and the the-
ologian's ideas of the relation of God to man are rooted. Many different species of flora grow in the soil of common-sense psychology.

It is easy for psychologists to believe that a scientific psychological
theory provides the only solid basis for an understanding of man and
his behavior. Although this volume is concerned only with attempts to
devise a scientific theory of human behavior and development, we
must recognize that psychologists are not the only people trying to understand human beings and their behavior. The construction of a psychological theory depends on certain assumptions about the nature of
man, but it depends also upon the nature of the explanation. It is possible to make other assumptions and to define the task of explaining

human behavior in a different manner. Before examining the problems that naïve psychology poses for the psychologist constructing a scientific theory, let us review some other approaches to the problem to discover, if possible, what is common to all approaches and what is distinctive about the psychological approach based on the model of theories in natural science.

The Search for Truth Takes Many Forms

What is common to all scholarly attempts to understand man is devotion to the search for truth. As we pointed out earlier, it is not necessary to understand nature to adapt successfully to it. The search for truth may take many forms, but all require a certain detachment and a willingness to accept the results wherever they may lead. The searcher for truth constantly discovers how wrong, how blind, and how thoughtless he has been. It requires a certain humility and a genuine self-confidence to spend one's life uncovering one's past errors and yet to continue to believe in the accessibility of the truth.

In this age of science, we may easily believe that the scientific method is the only method used in the search for truth. Nothing could be more wrong. The search for truth has taken many forms in the history of civilization, and still assumes many guises in modern life. Thomas Aquinas presented a theory of psychology one thousand years ago based largely on what he felt had been revealed to him. The true prayer of the religious man contains the essence of the search for truth, namely, the struggle of fallible man hampered by his prejudices and personal wishes to understand what God is trying to reveal.

The effort to rid oneself of presuppositions and to subdue one's wish for a particular outcome must constantly accompany the search for truth. This effort is particularly obvious in many attempts of ancient philosophers to find some self-evident axioms which could serve as the foundations for the construction of a theory; for example, Euclid thought he had self-evident axioms in such fundamental geometrical assumptions as "one and only one straight line may be drawn through any two points." Early writings in psychology were also very concerned with discovering axioms from which principles of human behavior may be derived. Descartes proposed his dictum, "I think, therefore I am" as one such assumption, and Spinoza based his philosophy upon a number of axioms, such as: (1) everything which is, is either in itself or in another, (2) that which cannot be conceived through another, must be conceived through itself, or (3) the knowledge of an effect depends upon and involves the knowledge of the cause, (4) a true idea must agree with that of which it is the idea.

One important distinction between revealed truth and self-evident truth is that the latter is recognized as obviously true once it is discovered, although, like the solution to a good detective story, it may be difficult to discover. There is no reason, on the other hand, that a revelation should appear obvious to anyone but the one to whom it is revealed. The rest of us must accept it second hand on faith. Thus, not all philosophers have assumed that the truth would be obvious once it was seen; some have even assumed that the ordinary human being cannot trust his judgment at all in the search for truth, and must instead accept the truth on the authority of those few people who have been smart enough to discover it or to whom it has been revealed. In medieval medicine, the writings of Aristotle and Galen were taken as authoritative, and when Renaissance scientists showed by actual anatomical dissection that these authorities were inaccurate, some scientists considered the evidence irrelevant to the truth. Although such a reliance on authority is now considered antithetical to the scientific attitude, we must realize that the subjection of one's beliefs to the review of authority requires a sort of discipline not unlike that required to let one's favorite hypothesis be disproved by facts. Furthermore, the search for authoritative backing for one's belief is a genuine variety of scholarship that should not be deprecated.

Basic Methodological Principles of Natural Science

Modern science has been built in opposition to these procedures for discovering the truth, and its tenets are partly to be understood in the light of the opinions against which it fought so vigorously in its early days. Thus, modern science adopts the position that no axiom may be accepted as self-evident, but instead may be viewed in either of two ways. In mathematics, it is merely a statement from which other statements are rigorously deduced, and its truth or self-evidence is quite irrelevant; this view was achieved only after a long struggle, however. Euclid's famous parallel axiom that "through a point not on a line, one and only one line may be drawn parallel to the line," was first denied by the Italian geometer Saccheri, solely as a means of proving that to deny it led to contradictions with other, more obviously self-evident, axioms. Instead, Saccheri proved a whole series of theorems of non-Euclidean geometry. It later became clear that complete and self-consistent geometries could be constructed with some other parallel axiom besides Euclid's. One of these, Riemannian, describes the geometry of a spherical surface. Mathematics, therefore, is concerned with constructing rigorous logical systems of self-consistent theorems, without being concerned with the empirical truth of these systems.

Empirical science is also concerned that its system of theorems be logically coherent and self-consistent; a scientific statement may be condemned as illogical if it does not follow from the assumptions of the theory.

A basic assumption may also be viewed as a statement whose falsity may be established by showing that it logically leads to a false empirical statement. If it does lead to false predictions, its self-evidence cannot save it; if it does not lead to false testable statements, its lack of self-evident truth is quite irrelevant. Many basic assumptions of science are far from self-evident; for example, it is quite contradictory to common sense to assume that a body in motion will continue in motion forever if not affected by some force. Thus, modern science has denied the importance of self-evidence of its basic assumptions.

Insistence upon empirical evidence for confirmation of hypotheses combined with rejection of authority as a criterion of truth has produced a second vital feature of natural science. Evidence must be public evidence; the experiments upon which a theory is based must be described so that other people can perform them, and if others follow the instructions and get different results, the evidence is suspect.

This requirement of repeatability has two important consequences. First, it puts a premium upon clear, simple, easily interpreted observations. It takes no skill to verify a pointer reading; therefore, if evidence can be stated as a pointer reading it is readily tested. If, however, the evidence required for verification is an aesthetic judgment, it is more difficult for another person to verify it. Second, the criterion of repeatability puts a premium on scientific laws whose operation can be produced at will. Thus, natural science searches for general laws that can be repeatedly demonstrated, and deals with unique events like the origin of the solar system as something to be explained by laws rather than as evidence for laws.

To summarize, logical coherence, public repeatability, and empirical validity are the hallmarks of theory in natural science.

Is a Natural Science of Human Behavior Possible?

The procedural rules of natural science have been very helpful, and the progress made in the natural sciences during the last two hundred years has been so phenomenal that it seems to many people that all scholarship must use natural science as an ideal. In other fields, however, these procedural rules are not easy to apply. History, for example, cannot be repeated and the truth of an hypothesis about the causes of the French Revolution must be investigated in a quite different way from an hypothesis about the inheritance of blue eyes in cats. Nevertheless, although criteria for the establishment of historical facts are different from those for science, they are very severe, and responsible scholarship is just as demanding in history as in physics.

History is a particularly good example of a discipline that is by its very nature concerned with the concrete sequence of events and their relation to one another. It is this concern for the unique, concrete, and unrepeatable event such as the assassination of Caesar that may make many of the methods of natural science inappropriate to it, although many of those methods are valuable tools in historical research.

Psychology presents many of the same problems as history if it is primarily concerned with the concrete facts of individual life histories. The biographer's search for an understanding of his subject and the psychiatrist's evaluation of a case history both involve judgments about the causes and effects of unique unrepeatable events. In this sense, the principles of natural science are not readily applied.

Psychology may in a still different way present problems for the natural scientist if one assumes that the primary data are the subjective phenomena of consciousness. By definition, a "perception" cannot be made publicly verifiable in the same sense as the velocity of a falling object. (See p. 57 for a fuller discussion.)

There are thus good bases for claiming that the rules and procedures of natural science are inappropriate for psychology; and there are psychologists who make this claim. Most psychologists and other behavioral scientists assume, however, that a natural science of human behavior is possible and that theory building in behavioral science should conform to the rules of other natural sciences. Psychology does not, by that decision, become freed from all the difficulties of understanding the individual case or of subjectivity, but it does become committed to solving these problems in the framework of natural science.

In this book we shall discuss only theories of child development which try to describe and explain human behavior in the same sense that theories in chemistry and biology account for the data in those fields. At the same time we must admit that there are other ways of viewing human behavior and that there is no proof that the point of view of natural science is the most appropriate.

Even if we adopt the procedures and criteria of natural science, we must admit that human behavior does pose special problems for the development of a science. For example, it is the only field where the widespread publication of a theory—like Freudian theory—may actually change the behavior of the organisms with which the theory is concerned. In psychology, theory building itself is an activity that the theories should explain. This kind of a logical regression seems to

cause trouble wherever it occurs. The special role of subjective phenomena in psychology also causes difficulties. For these and other
reasons, theories of human behavior and development have not been
well designed.

In any science there is untidiness preceding the development of
good theories, and we cannot expect that early ones will be neat, crys-
tal clear models. Every science must achieve its wise definitions and its
rigorous deductions through a long struggle. Each has asked many
nonsense questions and has toyed with many poorly defined concepts,
before clarifying the issues and tackling the problem efficiently.

Psychology is now in this stage of frustration. Psychologists are not
in a position to choose among a variety of rival theories each of which
is well-developed, but are rather fumbling in the dark, trying to decide
the most likely direction in which to search for an adequate formulation of human behavior. Despite the fact that psychologists are not at a
stage at which they can design well-defined theories, they must operate
within the framework of scientific theories. Our next step, therefore, is
to explore the characteristics of a scientific theory.

NATURE OF SCIENTIFIC THEORY

Theory as an Explanation

A theory is intended to provide an explanation for some class of
events. Thus, in physics, the pressure of the gas within a box is believed
to be explained by the hypothesis that the gas is composed of millions
of free molecules each moving in random manner. Some of these molecules are constantly hitting the sides of the container; this bombard-
ment by millions of molecules every second produces an almost
constant pressure. This is one example of a theory that has been successful because it explains the pressure of the gas. If the molecules are
assumed to move more rapidly as the gas is heated, then the increase of
the pressure with temperature becomes understandable. Other phenomena also fit into the same theory. This might be taken as an example of a kind of theory that it would be satisfying to have in psychology: It explains an unknown phenomenon in terms of concepts already familiar.

On closer examination the word "explanation" gives us some trouble, however. It is not easy to determine the essential elements in an
explanation and when a statement is a description rather than an
explanation. For example, are the tables predicting the times of high
tide each day for a year ahead explanatory or descriptive? Perhaps

most people would feel that these tide tables are based upon an explanatory theory, but they may feel that the equally accurate predictions of sunrise and sunset are merely descriptions of the movements of the earth around the sun. A second difficult question concerns the difference between the origin of a phenomenon and its mechanism of operation. Does an accurate picture of the way the lungs work constitute an explanation of the lungs, or is it necessary to show how the human species developed this particular organ? Some people might feel that neither of these is an explanation, and the explanation of the lungs is to be found in its functional significance in providing oxygen to the tissues of the body.

In natural science it is the present custom to avoid these questions about the exact meaning of explanation because it seems fruitless to dispute over such issues. A theory consists of a set of statements, some of which can be logically derived from others in the system. If these derived statements predict under what conditions various events will occur and if these predictions are verified, then the theory is validated. Thus, the tide tables and the predictions of sunrise and sunset are certainly accurate statements derived from general formulas. They meet the criteria of a valid theory, and whether they explain or describe need not be answered.

The fact that such terms as "explanation" are avoided in the formal definition of a theory does not mean that the issue does not arise in more informal evaluations of theories. A set of statements may fit the definition of a theory perfectly, and be quite trivial and uninteresting. By contrast, theories that make surprising new predictions, that encompass many fields, or that involve only a few basic assumptions and nevertheless predict many events accurately—all tend to excite more interest and admiration than narrow superficial theories. Such properties as breadth or depth or uniqueness or elegance are not, however, part of the minimal standards for a theory.

Minimal Standards for a Theory

THEORIES MAKE PREDICTIONS. The idea that theories provide explanations for data is difficult to formalize. The current tendency is to concentrate upon the capabilities of theories to predict accurately and not to worry about whether the basis for the prediction is an accurate description or an explanation.

It is important, however, to consider carefully the kind of predictions that a scientific theory makes. Science is surrounded with an aura of magic and mystery perhaps inherited from the times when science and magic were almost indistinguishable. Soothsayers in ancient days also made predictions, and laymen are inclined to think of the predictions of science in much the same terms. Actually, science makes few predictions in the sense of foretelling the future. When Roman generals consulted the augurs they were interested in who would win the battle tomorrow morning—they wanted to know in advance what particular events were going to occur. When astronomy predicts eclipses of the sun it is making that same kind of a prediction. However, most scientific predictions are not of this type; instead, they are predictions about what will happen if certain specific conditions are met. For example, from the theory that the gene for color blindness is on the Y chromosome in human beings and that the Y chromosome is the chromosome which determines the male sex of a child, one can predict that there are many more color-blind men than color-blind women. This "prediction" does not foretell the future in the same way the astronomer foretells eclipses, because the statement that "color-blind men are much more common than color-blind women" can be verified over and over again; it was presumably just as true a thousand years ago as it is today. The so-called "prediction" is really just an accurate empirical statement, but it is a statement that follows logically from theories in the field of genetics.

It is better, therefore, not to think of scientific predictions as foretelling the future, but as empirical statements whose accuracy may be checked. Sometimes those statements will assert that a specific event will occur at a paricular time, but more frequently the prediction will not have any precise time label. Ordinarily, the statement will be capable of being tested any time and repeatedly. In fact, repeatability is a particularly valuable test of the theory because it means that it can be checked by other people besides the person who formulated the theory.

To summarize, a scientific prediction is an *if-then* statement. It states that *if* certain conditions are brought about, *then* a certain observable event will occur: Any time the specified conditions are met, the same event will occur, and so most predictions can be checked repeatedly by anybody who wishes to do so. It is this repeatability that gives the theory the public verifiability so central to the concept of an empirical science.

Is there any sense, then, in which the ordinary scientific prediction foretells the future? There are two ways in which a prediction that actually foretells the future is preferred over other kinds, although neither of these is strictly necessary for a scientific theory.

First, a theory is generally more readily accepted if it predicts what is not already known to be true than if it merely predicts already known facts. A good theory must, of course, make no errors in predicting known facts, but if, in addition, it suggests a new experiment which has never before been done and predicts an unexpected result that proves valid, it has scored a triumph.

Although there is no requirement that a theory must predict unexpected events, there is a good reason why such predictions are especially valued. The scientist who constructs a theory has many choices and much freedom to build any kind of theory he wants to fit the facts, and so if he is ingenious he might construct several theories that would predict them.

One interesting example of pseudo-science illustrates this point. In the 1860's John Taylor and Charles P. Smyth advanced the theory that the great pyramid in Egypt was not constructed by idolatrous ancient Egyptians but was a divinely inspired construction, built by ancestors of the Jews and embodying in its measurements much modern scientific knowledge and a cryptographic chronicle of the past and future history of the world (Smyth, 1867). For example, the ratio of the vertical height of the pyramid to the breadth of the base is equal to $\pi/2$. Number π was unknown to the Egyptians at the time the pyramid was built. Taylor and Smyth also found that the base line of the pyramid, when divided by 366 (almost the number of days in a year), was "a length approaching nearly one ten-millionth of the earth's semiaxis of rotation." The measuring unit, however, had to be the "pyramid inch" equal to .999 British inches. The Great Pyramid Theory also correlates the turns and varying heights of the tunnels in the pyramid to various historical events that occurred long after the pyramid was built, although not after the theory was devised.

This bizarre theory illustrates that theories can be built to fit many sets of facts. In fact, many theories can be fit to the same facts. If, however, the theory can predict facts that are unknown when the theory is constructed, it gains much more stature.

There is a second sense in which a theory that predicts the future is preferred to one that does not. If the conditions that form the "if" part of the prediction precede the predicted event in time, then the theory may specify the necessary causes of that event. One of the assumptions of modern natural science is that causes must precede and immediate causes must immediately precede their effects; a cause cannot work backward in time. (We shall discuss this assumption later in connection with psychological theories, but for the moment we must take it as an assumption.) Thus, if we predict that a person with pneumonia will show on a tissue culture test that his sputum contains pneumococcus, we are making a perfectly good scientific prediction; if the prediction is validated, the validation helps to support the theory that pneumococcus is a necessary condition for pneumonia. Notice, how-ever, that the finding itself is just as compatible with the theory that the pneumococcus is the result of the disease as that it is its cause. Now, if an hypothesis could be advanced and validated that a person who did not have pneumonia would soon display symptoms of the disease whenever a test revealed the presence of pneumococcus in his body, such a finding would be incompatible with the hypothesis that the pneumococcus was the result of the disease, and it would also sug-gest methods for controlling and predicting pneumonia before it de-veloped. (Incidentally, neither of these hypotheses is actually valid. There are kinds of pneumonia that do not depend on pneumococcus, and people often have the bacteria present in their bodies without contracting the disease. The actual evidence supporting the hypothesis that pneumococcus is a causal agent of pneumonia would be lengthy and out of place in this discussion.)

There are then two advantages to scientific predictions that foretell the future. Such predictions ensure that the theory was not constructed to fit the predicted event, and they suggest causal agents and facilitate the development of control over the predicted event. Such predictions are not, however, a necessity for a scientific theory. As long as the the-ory logically leads to the prediction the validation provides some sup-port for the theory, whereas the failure to predict invalidates it.

One other aspect of a theoretical prediction is also important: It is not the scientist but the theory that must make the prediction. A sci-entist can make an amazing prediction, but if he cannot show how he derived his prediction from his theory, the theory is not strengthened. Perhaps the scientist was lucky, or perhaps he intuitively understood relationships that he could not put down explicitly. In either case his theory is not strengthened. Only if the prediction derives from the the-ory is the theory confirmed by an accurate prediction.

PUBLIC VERIFIABILITY OF A SCIENTIFIC THEORY. Repeatability has been stressed because it permits a theory to be verified by people other than the theorist himself. The requirement that a scientific theory be pub-licly verifiable is extremely important in modern science, and its con-sequences should be examined carefully.

The actual physical repeatability of a prediction is not the most sig-nificant aspect of public verifiability; much more important is the clarity of the language of the theory and the prediction, which makes it possible for anybody to follow the derivation of the prediction from the assumptions of the theory, to set up the conditions necessary for observing the predicted event, and to recognize the predicted event when it happens. Clarity of language is not just a matter of literary style. If the deduction of the prediction from the general theory is to be repeatable, the rules of deduction must be quite explicit. For example, if a theory deduces from the fact that the child is frustrated the fact that he is irritable, the theory must contain the statements necessary to make that deduction logical. It cannot leave the deduction to psychological common sense. Thus, a scientific theory is frequently much more detailed and explicit than a more casual explanation. Students beginning the study of geometry frequently feel that the proofs go to tremendous lengths to arrive at an obvious result because they do not realize the importance of making the proof airtight.

Let us take as an example of this, a rather casual proof that two triangles are congruent (exactly alike) if two angles and the included side for one is equal to two angles and the included side of the other (see Figure 2-1). After a little thought this seems obvious. We can put the lower side of B over the lower side of A, and then the unknown sides of B must lie along the sides of A, because the angles are equal. The two sides of A must then meet at the point C that is the same place as the third corner of A. This proof is essentially valid, but to make it rigorous several additional steps are necessary. For example, is it true that if two lines the same length are superimposed, their end points will correspond? Some such assumption must be put into the theory. If two lines are superimposed on two other lines and the second two cross each other, will the first two necessarily cross each other at the same point? This is necessary for the proof and requires some assumption that two straight lines cannot intersect in more than one point. By the time all the necessary gaps are filled in, we have built up a rather complicated set of geometrical assumptions and theorems, yet all this is necessary for a logically rigorous proof. The naïve proof depended on a certain ability to visualize triangles, to extend lines in imagination, and to

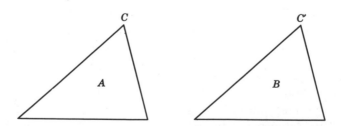

Figure 2-1. An intuitive proof of the congruence of two triangles.

recognize intuitively what would happen if this were done. The rigorous proof does not depend on a figure at all. It can be reduced to substituting one phrase for another in a sequence of sentences until the last sentence says what was to be proven. It is more publicly verifiable, although most young geometry students are convinced that it is more difficult than common sense.

Not only must the logical derivation of the prediction from the theory by publicly verifiable; the accuracy of the prediction itself must also withstand public test. In a way, the latter is more difficult because it involves several steps. First, the terms in the prediction must have a clear meaning. For example, suppose that some prediction from a psychological theory stated that if a person were intentionally hurt by another person he would become angry at the person who injured him. Before this prediction can be tested, we must be able to determine when a person is intentionally hurt by another, and when he is angry at another. Unless different investigators would agree on the circumstances in which the condition was met and those in which it was not, they might not be testing the same hypothesis at all. Similarly, unless there were some definition of anger so that the observer could tell when someone was angry or not in this experiment, the conclusions might well be different for different investigators. Thus, it is necessary for the terms in a scientific prediction to be so clearly defined that any other investigator would apply the term to the same situations as the original investigator. Such a definition of a term is called *empirical* or, alternatively, *operational*. The reason for those designations is clear: An empirical definition of "angry" says what signs indicate that a person is angry; an operational definition of "angry" tells how the investigator determines whether a person is angry. Both terms imply the same thing.

Not only must the terms be empirically defined, but the observational situation or the experiment must be described in sufficient detail so that it can be reproduced by another investigator who wishes to test the prediction. All of these requirements of a scientific prediction have been developed to ensure that a theory is accepted or rejected because of empirical evidence, not because some famous scientist says that it is true or because it seems that it ought to be true. This reliance upon evidence has been achieved only through many struggles in the history of science; hence, it is not surprising that it is considered vital for the acceptance of a scientific theory.

FALSIFIABILITY OF A SCIENTIFIC THEORY. One important further requirement of a scientific theory is that it must be testable or falsifiable.

This does not mean that the theory must be proved false, but only that it is possible to prove it so. The most common way that a theory fails to be falsifiable is that the empirical prediction proves to be a restatement of the definitions in different words. Suppose, for example, the prediction is made that a hungry man will choose food rather than money. This sounds like a straightforward prediction, but suppose that "hungry" were defined as a condition in which a person puts a higher value on food than on any other goal object. Since the term *value* has been introduced it must be empirically defined. Suppose the method for determining that object A has a higher value than object B is to present the person with the alternatives of having A or B and assigning the higher value to the one he selects. By now we have built a neat little logical circle, so that anybody who prefers money to food is by definition not hungry. The theory is not falsifiable because no matter how the person behaves, he cannot go against the theory. This example seems ludicrous because it is so obvious, but in complicated theories it is very easy to set up definitions that make some of the most desired predictions of the theory nonfalsifiable.

An hypothesis may also fail to be falsifiable because the theory is not specific enough to provide a good test. Suppose, for example, than an hypothesis stated that if a person were hungry enough he would prefer food to any amount of money. This hypothesis might be true, but it is not testable unless we can specify more exactly how hungry the person must be. Otherwise, the theory cannot be proved false. If the person does not prefer food to money, it may well be that he is not hungry enough.

These, then, are the important requirements for a scientific theory: First, it must make empirical predictions which can determine its validity by their accuracy. Second, the predictions must be publicly verifiable, which implies that the logical derivation is explicit and rigorous, that the terms in the predictions are empirically defined, and that the conditions are clearly specified. Finally, the theory must be falsifiable—that is, it must be possible to conceive of results which would disprove it, although, of course, the scientist hopes that such results will not actually be produced.

How public must the public verifiability be? The various requirements set up for a scientific theory to ensure that it deals with evidence in a publicly verifiable way are generally quite reasonable, but careful scrutiny reveals that there are still some sources of difficulty. These are a few of the most relevant for behavioral science.

One problem concerns just who is included in the "public" that should be able to test a scientific theory. Obviously, a theory does not need to be put in terms such that anyone could test it; A certain amount of intelligence and competence is expected. In a science where mathematics is important, the so-called operations for testing a theory may include integral calculus, theory of complex variables, and matrix operations. This restricts the public that can actually follow the derivations and proofs to a small proportion of the total population. Essentially, it limits it to professionally trained scientists, although in principle many people could acquire this training and would then be able to perform the operations. Similarly, the actual experimental operations for testing a theory may require special skills and special experience. It is not uncommon for a competent biochemist to require several months to repeat an experiment that has been "fully described" in a scientific journal.

Within the field of personality study, just who should be able to verify a psychological hypothesis? Suppose that the hypothesis required a trained psychoanalyst to test it. For example, suppose an hypothesis predicted a causal factor in the repression of homosexual wishes. It might happen that a trained psychoanalyst would verify such a finding from analysis of dreams and free associations, but that a nonpsychoanalyst would not consider the terms clearly enough defined to permit such a test. He would challenge the analyst to explain how he could tell from a dream whether there were repressed homosexual wishes or not. If a layman raised such objections about a derivation involving tensor analysis in physics, the physicist would tell him that he must acquire the necessary training before he is competent to test the theory, but is the psychoanalyst entitled to make the same response? The danger, of course, of restricting too closely the people who are competent to test the theory is that proof of the theory eventually rests upon acceptance of authority rather than upon acceptance of evidence. All sorts of knowledge based upon revelations from God could then be defended as "publicly verifiable," provided that the public was restricted to the proper people.

There is no straightforward foolproof way out of this dilemma. In general, however, the policy to be followed is clear. The simpler and more easily reproducible the logical derivation and the experimental testing of a theory, the better, because the ease of reproduction helps to ensure that the conclusions are based upon evidence. On the other hand, evidence that requires a very special kind of training or skill should not be discredited just because it is not commonly reproduci-

ble. The hope is that theories supported by such restricted evidence
can become testable in more unrestricted ways and thus more widely
accepted or rejected.

Formal Statement of a Theory

Having described most of the features of a scientific theory we can
now put them together in a more formal way. We follow the terminology of Braithwaite (1955). First, a theory can be described as a set of
statements, although some theories are presented in the form of pictures or models. If we think of the usual set of axioms, theorems, and
proofs as a theory we can see what this set of statements is like. It includes all the sentences in the definitions, assumptions, proofs, and
theorems of geometry, which can be arranged in a sort of order because
some follow logically from others in the set. Thus, the theorem, *one
and only one circle can be drawn through any three points on a plane
but not on a straight line,* can be logically deduced from various other
statements in geometry: some postulates, axioms, and previous theorems. However, some of the statements are not deduced from any
other set of statements in the system. Such statements are either
assumptions or *definitions.* Sometimes there is some choice about what
will be called assumptions and what will be derived from them, but
that uncertainty creates no real problem.

On the other hand, there are some statements in a scientific theory
that are derived from other sentences in the system, but from which
nothing further derives. In a scientific theory these are empirical statements of the form, "at a certain time, in a certain place, a certain
event will occur." They correspond to the raw data of the observation
or experiment which would confirm the theory. In a personality theory
such an empirical statement might be that "Ralph Marshal, when
shown card III in the Rorschach test, will give a response employing
the colored parts of the blots."

In a theory, the specific hypotheses the investigator is testing appear
just above such strictly empirical statements. For example, the hypothesis that *"impulsive people tend to give color responses on the Rorschach"* constitutes such a statement. Before it can be translated into a
strictly empirical statement, the actual experimental sample must be
substituted for the term "impulsive people" as a particular group of
such people and the term "color response" must be further specified. In
general, however, the lowest-level empirical statements are generally
specific examples of second-level hypotheses. The second-level hypotheses are usually considered to be predictions from the theory
under test. Between the top-level assumptions and the low-level em-

pirical hypotheses may be a more or less complicated structure of statements all derived eventually from the basic assumptions, and all leading logically to the lower-level testable propositions.

The statements in a theory are divided into two classes by another criterion: Some are contingent statements, which have some testable empirical consequences and which may, therefore, be disproved if the results do not confirm the empirical predictions. Contingent statements include assumptions, middle-level hypotheses, and empirical hypotheses.

On the other side are various types of noncontingent statements. These statements are not subject to disproof because they are merely statements of certain conventional practices. Some are definitions which must be accepted by anyone who wishes to use the theory. If a theory defines a criminal as a person who does not blush easily, we may feel that it is an unfortunate use of the word, but as long as that meaning is consistently used in the theory and criminal is not defined in some other inconsistent way, there is no disproving the definition.

Another kind of statement that is not subject to proof is one that describes the way one statement may be derived from another. Thus, if the theory involves solution of equations, then, strictly speaking, the laws of algebra are a part of the theory as rules of operation.

On the contingent side of the theory, therefore, there are statements of various degrees of generality, from assumptions to empirical statements. On the noncontingent side of the theory there are definitions and rules of operation, which make it possible to derive the lower-level hypotheses from the higher-level ones and thus to enter intimately into the workings of the theory, but which are not subject to disproof.

Now, what happens when an empirical statement proves true or false? The essential point is that the particular result of the observation or the experiment is only one case of the empirical hypothesis and that no single positive result can prove the hypothesis true. The hypothesis that all men are mortal cannot be proved by showing that one man died. It can, however, be disproved by finding just one man who lived forever. The result of a test of an hypothesis may therefore only disprove it or fail to disprove it and so leave it tenable. This is why in actual tests of hypotheses the scientist often sets up a "null" hypothesis that states the condition that he hopes is not true and then tests that. It can be disproved. Thus, if a scientist has an hypothesis that boys and girls are treated differently by their parents, he may well test the hypothesis that they are not treated differently. If he can disprove this with a sufficient level of confidence, the alternative hypothesis receives support.

Because empirical tests can never prove hypotheses, it is important for a theory to be falsifiable. The hypothesis discussed earlier that a person will prefer food to any amount of money if he is hungry enough is an empirical statement, not merely a restated definition, and so it would receive support whenever a hungry person chose food upon being offered the alternative of a great deal of money. It could not be specifically disproved, however, and only a disproof has a marked effect upon theory.

Every failure to disprove a hypothesis does lend it some sort of support, and after repeated failures to disprove an hypothesis, the scientist may come to have a great deal of confidence in it, just as we have considerable confidence that the sun will rise tomorrow morning. Strictly speaking, though, he can never be satisfied that the hypothesis has been proven true. Various attempts have been made to estimate how much an empirical test supports an hypothesis if the test does not disprove it, but these attempts have not been very successful.

The scientist is thus left without any clear guide for determining when his experiment is successful. Sometimes he will mistrust the results and repeat the experiment to confirm it, and sometimes he will test some other implication of his theory to see if it will hold up under empirical test; or, he may go on to use the hypothesis in applied science as if it were true. How much evidence he requires may well depend upon the consequences of error. He will require more proof that a new vaccine against poliomyelitis can never cause the disease than he will that a new dandelion spray cannot injure the lawn, more proof about a new vaccine if the disease is rare than if it is threatening a disastrous epidemic, and more if the disease is fatal than if it is only a minor illness like a cold. Despite the lack of clear rules, the scientist does use the results both of his successful and unsuccessful predictions.

The implication of an unsuccessful prediction is not clearly prescribed, either. When an empirical test fails, it is clear that something is wrong somewhere in the assumptions and hypotheses from which the test was derived, but the failure seldom precisely locates the error in the theory. Suppose, for example, the structure of the theory is as shown in Figure 2-2: If J is the empirical test, then its disproof clearly disproves H from which it is derived. Either E or F or both must be in error, but there is no way to tell which. At the top level, A, C, and D all enter into the derivation of H and J, so there must be an error there somewhere. It is clear that B cannot be the cause of the difficulty in H, but that is the only assumption clearly not involved. Even this

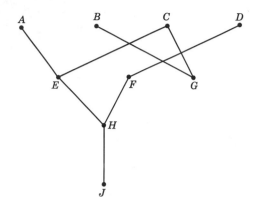

Figure 2-2. Logical structure of
an hypothetical theory.

does not exhaust the possibilities, however. There are many definitions of terms involved in this derivation of *J* which cannot be tested, but that does not mean that a change in a definition might not cure the difficulty. Suppose, for example, hypothesis *H* involved the term *aggression,* and in this experiment aggression was measured by a projective test involving the telling of stories about pictures. If this were the definition of aggression, it could not be tested directly, but one might still find that a change in scoring the test eliminated the cases that made the prediction come out wrong.

It is clear that the precise effects of confirmation and disconfirmation of a theory cannot be spelled out. How to modify a theory that makes a wrong prediction or how to extend it after a successful prediction are both matters involving a great deal of judgment. This judgment constitutes part of the art of scientific research, but has not yet been reduced to clear rules and procedures.

In summary, the minimal requirements for a scientific theory are that its assumptions and rules of derivation be clear and explicit, and that its terms be empirically defined. In addition, its theorems and definitions must be constructed so that it is falsifiable. Besides the minimal requirements, a theory that makes new predictions that are then verified is particularly valuable. Theories whose derivations permit causal control over important phenomena are more useful than those that do not. Theories that are elegant and encompass many empirical phenomena, deriving them from a relatively simple set of assumptions, are also desirable. However, none of these criteria is necessary for a theory. None of the theories of development completely meets the minimal requirements for a theory, although some of them are elegant theories about restricted sets of phenomena. Scientists proceed to construct an adequate theory by trying to maintain the parts of their model that seem to predict well and by discarding and modifying the parts that cause trouble. As we have seen, even with clearly stated, operationally defined theories, the proper interpretations of a confirmation are not yet reducible to rules. It is a part of the art of theory building.

Therefore, although we can readily point to defects when examining the theories presented in this book, including naïve theory, it is more difficult to estimate what portions of these prototheories are likely to become incorporated in an eventually satisfactory theory or to lead to a fruitful line of empirical research. This is the task we have set, and only one thing is clear: Any theory must be evaluated against the criteria for the scientific theory which all scientific psychologists are striving to develop.

THE EVALUATION OF NAÏVE THEORY

With this background, we return to an examination of commonsense psychology, with particular emphasis upon some of the knotty problems it raises for scientific psychology. These problems can largely be encompassed under three headings: subjective experience, teleology, and free will.

The Problem of Private Experience

One requirement of a scientific theory is that it be testable. It must lead to statements which are expressed in empirical terms and which can be publicly verified. Therefore, the terms in which these statements are couched must be operationally or empirically defined so that any scientist who wishes to test a statement will be able to do so.

Naïve theory contains many terms like *intend, want, like, pleasure, try,* and *ought.* Many scientific psychologists contend that such terms have no empirical definition and therefore no place in a scientific theory of human behavior. It is this view that we want to examine thoroughly.

Because of its complexity, the issue will require a careful examination. On the one hand, the requirement that terms be empirically defined may be so interpreted that it is unnecessarily restrictive; such terms as *goal* or *intention* have sometimes been condemned without sufficient examination. On the other hand, it may be that such terms really are undefinable in empirical language: That a concept has been condemned on unjust grounds does not mean that it is free of sin.

EMPIRICAL DEFINITION OF TRY. In naïve theory, *try* and *can* describe the two necessary conditions for action. If a person can do something and tries to do it, he will succeed in doing it. The converse does not hold, however, because people may bring about results which they do not try to bring about. If a person does not produce some result, it may not be because he has not tried, but because he could not do it, or because both conditions were lacking.

If we are going to use *intention* as a term in scientific psychology, we need to be able to determine a person's intentions from his behavior and its effects. Sometimes the term intention has been condemned because the same action may be intended or unintended, and the same intention may lead at times to one action and at times to another. Such condemnation is clearly unjustified. There are many well-established scientific terms which have different symptoms under different conditions. A temperature of 0°C is defined in terms of the freezing of water, but water does not always freeze at 0°C. Only if the water is pure, the pressure is standard, and the nuclei of crystallization are present will water actually freeze at 0°C. So, the mere fact that an intention is not unequivocally related to a particular action or its effect is not a sufficient basis for condemning it as unscientific.

Sometimes the term intention is condemned because it is not identifiable under all conditions. If a person walks along the street meeting the variety of conditions which a street provides, should we as scientists be able to recognize from a complete record of his behavior what his intentions are? It would undoubtedly be useful to have such a diagnostic procedure, and for some practical problems such a diagnosis might be necessary, but an intention need not be manifest under all possible conditions for it to be a satisfactory scientific term, and its basic definition certainly need not be applicable under all conditions. The fragility of a china cup is a well-defined property: Presumably a cup is fragile even when it is sitting on a table, yet the basic definition of fragility is couched in terms of how easily it is broken. There are, of course, ways to measure the fragility of a cup without breaking it, and such diagnostic methods are very useful, but they are not necessary for the scientific use of the concept of fragility.

It may be that intention can be defined only in some very special, well-controlled experimental situation. Perhaps the situation must be arranged so that the intended result is not difficult to attain, so that no other results of the action can ensue, and so that there is no possibility for some other intention to be operative. The fact that the intention could be tested only under very special conditions would not mean that it was an unsuitable term for a scientific theory. On the other hand, the term must be defined in terms of some situation; merely to admit that it may be defined only in very special situations does not relieve us of saying exactly what those conditions are. If we feel that the intention to open a door is manifested unequivocally only when the arm movement has no other effect than to open a door, we must describe just how we will arrange the situation so that such a one-to-one relation between an action and its effect can occur. We cannot merely describe the situation in theoretical terms if it is to be used as an empirical definition.

The question is, therefore, what sort of empirical definition for *trying* is provided in naïve theory? Certainly it is not any highly specialized experimental definition, but instead a number of suggestions about the diagnosis of a person's intentions. In everyday life, we frequently make judgments about the intentions of other people. There does not appear to be any single defining symptom, but rather a combination of evidence of various kinds which leads to judgment. The more evidence, the more confident we are in the judgment, but in many circumstances no judgment is possible.

What are some of these lines of evidence?

1.   If a person performs a series of actions, each of which might reasonably cause a result X, we tend to believe that the person is trying to cause X. Thus, if we see a person try one key after another in a door, we believe he is trying to open it.

2.   If a person shows increasing signs of annoyance and anger as each action fails to produce X, we have further evidence that he is trying to cause X.

3.   If he performs a series of actions, each of which is a necessary step in a chain of events that will cause X, we are certain he seeks to cause X. Thus, if he first opens an outer door, then asks for the key to the inner door, searches the attic for a box of old keys, and then brings the box down to the inner door, and tries the keys one at a time, we are quite convinced that he wants to open the door.

4.   We are more confident that the immediate result of the action is intended than a more remote result. We are sure that the person wants to unlock the door; we are not as confident about why he wants to unlock the door or what he intends to do once the door is open.

5.   We take into account any statement by the person that "I want X."

Such a verbal statement is not necessarily sufficient nor is it necessary, and its value as evidence depends on possible reasons for making a mistake or telling an untruth.

6. We tend to attribute to another person an intention which we would have if we were in his position.

This list by no means exhausts the cues to the perception of intentions, but it presents a clear picture of their variety, and also illustrates that some of the bases for perceiving intentions are reasonably sound, whereas others are probably unsound. The question now is whether such a set of cues constitutes an adequate empirical definition of the term intention.

Admittedly, such a collation of evidence is frequently used in science to establish belief in a theory, and it is not unscientific to piece together evidence from a variety of sources to confirm or deny an hypothesis. Although such procedure does not always lead to complete belief, it may, under some circumstances, result in firmly established hypotheses. In everyday life, such a convergence of evidence is used in courtroom trials and a jury may feel that it establishes the guilt of the defendant "beyond a reasonable doubt." The diagnosis of disease depends in many instances upon just such a procedure.

In fact, such procedures are sometimes used in other sciences for defining concepts. For example, in the many studies of identical twins, their identification is based upon the convergence of many different bits of evidence: Similarities of blood type, fingerprints, and hair whorls, are all combined. Certain dissimilarities rule out the possibility that the twins are identical, others only reduce it. Evidence from the birth of the pair is added. A common amnion is excellent, but not conclusive, evidence that twins are identical. For practical purposes, the definition of identical twins is based upon just such a combining of evidence for and against, and is reached with a recognition of its fallibility. Some pairs of children just cannot be classified as identical or not.

There is an important difference, however, between *definition* and *identification*. Gradually, in the history of biology, the term *identical twins* has been replaced by the term *homozygous twins*. Homozygous twins are twins that develop from a single fertilized egg. All the evidence from blood types, fingerprints, common amnion, etc., is based upon a theory about the consequences of two individuals developing from a single fertilized egg. The validity of fingerprints as evidence for homozygosity can properly be debated. If anyone questions, however, whether two individuals who developed from the same fertilized egg are really homozygous, he clearly does not understand what homozygous means. *Homozygous* is *defined* as developing from a single egg cell.

In actual biological research on twins, the basic empirical definition of homozygosity is almost never used; probably, it has never even been observed in humans. For research purposes, it is replaced by some probabilistic diagnostic procedure, based upon observable symptoms. But "developing from a single egg cell" remains the definiton of homozygosity and is related by an elaborate theoretical structure to the actual symptoms employed for research purposes.

Now what is the situation with regard to the definition of *intention*? The symptoms listed earlier are not intended to constitute a definition of intention in naïve theory, but are merely symptoms of intention; any one or any group of them might be considered fallible.

What, then, is the definition of an intention? In naïve theory the definition is private. The person knows his own intention but may hide it so successfully that nobody else can discover it. Further, he may pretend so successfully to an intention he does not have that other people will be fooled. The actual definition, however, is his own private knowledge, because in naïve theory the idea that a person does not know his own intention is unthinkable. In Freudian theory, however, we shall see that this private knowledge of intention is considered fallible and that the ultimate defining properties of intentions are purely conceptual.

This ultimate definition of intention as the private knowledge of the person himself constitutes a genuine impasse in the evaluation of naïve theory, making it unacceptable as a scientific theory according to the criteria described earlier. The whole development of natural science has been a struggle to make its basic definitions public, so that its theories can be tested by other scientists and need not rest upon some special private information of an individual person who claims to know the truth over and above the evidence.

Although defining intention as the private knowledge of the individual weakens the scientific basis of the concept, the absence of a basic definition need not hamper research greatly, at least for a while. Most research on perception has taken the individual's report of what he perceives as the defining criterion. If he says that one line looks longer than another, his report is taken to describe his perception; many important advances have been made on this basis. Using various criteria for determining intention or purpose, researchers have similarly carried out important work on goal-directed behavior, with only a hazy notion of fundamental definition.

In the long run, however, the lack of a basic empirical definition is a serious flaw. The various criteria for determining an intention are not entirely consistent with one another, but without some basic definition there is no way to establish their fallibility. Defining intention by referring to private experience alone leads to serious problems when we begin to study young children and lower animals. Do we attribute a private consciousness to all organisms, or do we deny intention to organisms to which we deny private experience? If we let ourselves become involved in these problems, how can we possibly find any reasonable basis for resolving them? The problem posed by naïve theory's acceptance of private experience is a real one, not merely an academic problem of interest to hair-splitting philosophers.

Optional Resolutions to the Problem of Private Experience

If we admit that the problem of private experience is a serious one, what are the optional resolutions? There are three basic courses which various theorists have taken, and since the same three arise in connection with other theoretical issues raised by naïve theory, we shall spend some time describing each of them.

S-R BEHAVIORISM. One approach is to scrap all the concepts of naïve theory as misleading, and to search for a basically new approach to the problem of predicting human behavior. The basic strategy here is to completely divorce the concepts of human behavior as experienced by the behaving organism from the concepts of human behavior described by an outside observer. If we forget that we ourselves are examples of the organism we are studying, we can look at human behavior from the outside, just as we look at the activities of stars, chemical reactions, or electrical currents. Our task as scientists is to try to build a theory that will predict how people behave in various circumstances.

We shall do this best, radical behaviorists argue, if we drop all the preconceptions of naïve theory which were developed by people looking at their own experience and other people's behavior, and go back to actual behavior. We can see that when a person is subjected to certain kinds of situations, he behaves in certain ways. Our job is to describe such behavior, to establish descriptive laws relating the two, and to build a theory that will account for the behavior.

This strategy we call S-R behaviorism. It represents one basic approach to the problems of human behavior and one basic method for solving those problems. Within this approach there are many different opinions and a multitude of different concrete theories of behavior, but a detectable similarity in basic technique. All such theorists accept the necessity for publicly verifiable operational definitions of concepts;

this implies that the definitions must be stated in terms of action or behavior rather than subjective experiences. A second similarity among all such theorists is the belief that the concepts of naïve theory are misleading and should be discarded. Thus, the terms stimulus and response tend to be the elemental concepts of this strategy.

COGNITIVE BEHAVIORISM. A second basic strategy adopted by some psychological theorists resembles the first in its acceptance of the fundamental tenets of behaviorism. This second strategy assumes that the basic definitions of the science of human behavior must be empirical, operational, and couched in terms of behavior. However, this type of behaviorist does not throw away all the concepts of naïve psychology to start out from a wholly fresh beginning; instead, he tries to rework and rewrite such concepts of naïve psychology as purpose, feeling, or cognition. If properly rewritten, these can be rigorously defined in behavioral terms. We shall call this strategy *cognitive behaviorism,* reflecting the fact that many people adopting this strategy accept the concept of "cognition" from common-sense psychology.

The argument for such a strategy runs as follows: Naïve theory contains many difficulties stemming from its assumption that people's consciousness provides the basic definitions for concepts. However, naïve theory did not develop primarily to allow people to understand themselves, but rather to allow them to understand one another, and so common-sense notions contain many hypotheses about the behavioral consequences of purposes, feelings, and sentiments. Therefore, the concepts of naïve theory are likely to be definable in behavioral terms. It is unwise not to take advantage of all the wisdom about human behavior that is implied in naïve theory, and so we should begin with those concepts and try to build on them, although we may need to redefine them, to limit their scope, and perhaps even to change them completely.

Within the general cognitive-behaviorist viewpoint there is again great room for difference. Some theorists take the theoretical difficulties of naïve concepts very seriously, and others are inclined to pass them off as only minor problems. Some theorists are quite resistant to any change in theory that violates common sense, and others expect than an adequate theory will probably look quite different from naïve theory. Despite the differences, such psychologists do show a certain unity of spirit, a respect for the wisdom of naïve psychology, and a feeling that its concepts have some resemblance to reality. They also accept the basic tenets of natural science and the necessity for publicly verifiable scientific hypotheses.

NONBEHAVIORISM. A third strategy is also adopted in modern psychology. Psychologists following this path maintain their convictions about the inherent nature of man, regardless of the tenets of natural science. They insist that human beings do have a consciousness which is an essential feature of human nature, and that if the rules of natural science do not permit such a concept, it is because these rules were not developed to explain human nature. Such theorists argue that we should not permit arbitrary rules of science to govern us in psychology. Psychology is different from physical science precisely because its subject matter is personal. This fact may cause problems, but these cannot be resolved by denying the fundamental subjectivity of psychological phenomena.

Psychology and the other social sciences that deal primarily with man and society must develop their own criteria for the adequacy of scientific theories because the rules for natural science are just not suitable. Let us then develop methods that are natural for psychology; we are interested in how people behave, but also in how they feel and think. Let us continue to develop our considerable wisdom about human nature by using the same procedures that have been tried for hundreds of years. This attitude will be labeled *non-behaviorism*.

As we shall see, these three strategies arise in connection with a variety of theoretical issues and provide useful ways of relating more specific theoretical positions to one another, but they should not be viewed as three clear-cut theories. Several words of caution are in order.

1. Not every scientist takes only one of these courses. Although there is some tendency for scientists to cluster about each of the three, there are all varieties of intermediate positions and all degrees of rigidity about adhering to only one strategy.
2. Within any strategic approach there is room for enormous theoretical differences. The clearest conflicts are likely to develop within one strategy because of the common agreement on terminology and criteria.
3. These positions generally do not differ on matters of fact or specific prediction. Much fruitless effort has been spent in trying to devise clear-cut empirical tests of one or the other position, but if one is shown to be best it will be on the basis of the general fruitfulness of the approach rather than on the basis of any crucial experiment. All are strategies, not theories, faiths, not empirical hypotheses.
4. For some psychologists, these basic strategic considerations are extremely important. Some S-R behaviorists are convinced that the

term *purpose* cannot be used without being mystical, and some cognitive behaviorists believe that any explanation couched in S-R terms is necessarily superficial and wooden, while other psychologists view these differences with little emotional involvement. Since they do represent basic strategies for theory building, they may be very important indeed, just as basic strategic decisions are very important for conducting a war, but it is important to recognize that findings made under one strategy remain findings for people following a different strategy. There is no reason why the different strategies cannot stimulate as well as disagree with one another.

Actually, there is no rational basis for choosing among the strategies at present or for knowing how each may best contribute to an understanding of human behavior. Probably the worst mistake one could make would be to outlaw any of the strategies upon the basis of the prejudgment that it is valueless. Fortunately, since scientists are individualists, there is no real danger that any of the strategies will be completely abandoned.

The Problem of Cognitive and Teleological Mechanisms

A second problem in naïve theory arises from the failure to describe mechanisms for achieving cognition and intentional action. Under this theory, the existence of a cognitive picture of the environment and the fact that muscles carry out intentions are assumed, but neither phenomenon is seen as posing any particular explanatory problem. Naïve theory assumes that all direct perception is an automatic and accurate registration of the objects in the environment. Although the possibility of error is recognized, its possible sources are viewed as defects in the person or unclearness in the medium. No fundamental problem of accurate perception is recognized.

Perceptual research has shown, however, that visual perception is a complicated process; it is not merely "taking a picture" through the eye. Many queer shapes can look like everyday objects if viewed from a particular point of view, and innumerable different physical objects can all produce exactly the same image on the retina of the eye, owing partly to the fact that we are really quite insensitive to differences in depth. Thus, objects can be seriously distorted in the depth dimension without our noticing it. How, then, does it happen that the retinal image results in only one perception most of the time and that the perception is so frequently accurate? Our perception shows the third dimension even though that dimension has been largely removed in the retinal image. It is as though we heard a symphony concert through a filter that cut out all differences in pitch, so that each note came through with the same pitch as every other note, but instead of hearing just a pitchless series of notes, we perceived the original symphony in all its clarity. Of course, there is nothing magic about visual perception; the cues to depth do exist and are used to create a three-dimensional perception. The process of rebuilding a coherent perception out of the cues available in the retinal image is, however, as complex as the process of inferring from the cues provided in the detective story that the presumably paralyzed grandmother committed the murder.

Once the problem involved in achieving a correct perception is recognized, any theory that provides no explanation for it appears either to have a tremendous gap or to be frankly mystical. Suppose that some theory assumed—without any explanation of the mechanism—that we were aware of what other people are thinking. Knowing the difficulty involved, we would believe that the theory invoked a mystical clairvoyance. To those who are aware of the difficulties in accounting for accurate perception, a theory that avoids the whole issue by assuming that perception is direct, or one that starts the explanation of behavior with what is perceived, seems unsatisfactory.

A similar problem arises in naïve theory at the point where intentions are translated into actions. In naïve theory there seems to be no problem in going directly toward a goal object once the person knows where the goal is and how to get there. In this theory the motor mechanism by which the correct muscles are contracted at the correct times to move the individual directly and efficiently toward a desired object is completely ignored; the naïve theory seems to assume even complicated indirect paths are taken automatically. The child remembers that he had left his baseball behind the garage, so he goes and gets it. The whole series of complex adjustments involved in "going to get it" is ignored.

The carrying out of simple intentions does pose a number of psychological problems that have not yet been solved by scientific psychology, however. It is therefore not difficult to see how the naïve psychological view is incomplete. Saying that you know where you want to go does not sufficiently explain the process you use to get there. If just knowing the ball was behind the garage were sufficient, the boy could obtain it with his eyes shut. Actually, of course, the boy at every moment is responding to immediate visual stimuli that do not emanate from the final goal of the action. If the boy finds something in his path, he does not blindly stumble into it as a person might who is completely fixed on the goal. He steps over or around the obstacle but still does not lose his direction toward the baseball. Psychology cannot yet describe the mechanisms underlying all of these simple goal-directed actions, but it is quite clear than a purely cognitive knowledge of the goal itself is insufficient.

Whenever a theory explains an event solely in terms of its final result or its functional value without describing the mechanism by which that result is obtained, the theory is called *teleological*. Thus, naïve psychology is teleological because it explains the individual's action by citing its purpose. As far as naïve psychology is concerned, the intention is translated directly into action and the action itself is apparently governed and guided by the end result.

Teleological explanations have often been proposed in other sciences to explain adaptive processes. If the evolution of gills into lungs is explained by the fact that land animals need to breathe air, such an explanation is teleological. Similarly in physiology, bile has the function of digesting fats, and absence of bile causes illness, but to explain bile production in terms of its usefulness of digestion is teleological.

Whenever these teleological explanations have arisen in physics or biology, they have been eventually superseded by causal explanations which describe the mechanism bringing about the end result, without ignoring the fact that biological processes do have functional value.

No one doubts the importance of respiratory processes for maintaining life in the organism. Biologists describe the mechanism by which oxygen is taken from the air, transported to the tissues, and used, but none of the scientific principles used to explain the process involves the fact that respiration is necessary for life. The blood would take up oxygen and the heart would pump blood into the arteries, if the proper causal conditions existed, even though there were no tissue to use the oxygen at the other end.

In other examples, the mechanism and its functional value are even more intimately related. In some species of sea animal, for example, the tentacles wave more-or-less randomly until they come into contact with food. Then they stop. Since the tentacles contain the mouth, this cessation of activity facilitates the organism's feeding. The mechanism, however, depends on the fact that some substance in the food inhibits the movement of the tentacles and if this substance were supplied in some other fashion, the tentacles would stop their motion even though the organism might be starving. The operation of the causal mechanism does not depend on its functional value.

Animal and human behavior is frequently adapted to the environment so that the behavior helps maintain the organism. Much human behavior is guided toward functionally valuable end results, even though the environment offers unusual and unexpected obstacles. This is goal-directed behavior and it is a phenomenon important for psychologists to understand. The behavior must be explained, however, by a causal mechanism that does not depend on the functional value of the behavior in reaching a goal. It is the absence of any such causal mechanism in naïve psychology that makes it teleological.

Purely teleological laws are not permitted in natural science because in natural science it is assumed that all causes are efficient ones, and that no cause of an event can occur after the event itself. Furthermore, all causes must be transmitted to the objects they affect. A cause in one place cannot produce an effect in another without some mechanism connecting the two; the beginning of a chain of causes can be far distant from the effect, but there must be an unbroken sequence of events linking the beginning of the chain to the end. Similarly, causes in the past must be connected to the events they cause in the present; since time goes in just one direction, there cannot be a causal chain from a future cause to a present effect. Thus, teleological explanations are inadmissible in natural science.

Despite the inacceptability of teleological causation in natural science, there is no strictly logical reason for excluding such a law. As we described earlier, a scientific theory consists of a body of statements in which the lower-level ones, including the empirical observations, are derived from the upper level ones like assumptions and postulates. There is no reason that the logical deduction cannot go from later events to earlier ones rather than from earlier ones to later ones. If there is only one hallway leading to a room and no other room on that hall, then it is equally logical to deduce from a person's going down the hall that he will reach the room or to deduce from his being in the room that he must have gone down the hall. Logical deductions frequently do go both directions; we try to predict the future consequence of a present situation or we try to reconstruct the events leading up to a particular end result.

Thus, a teleological theory could be written that would meet all the logical requirements of theory building; that is, it could be coherent, logical, and testable. The assumption that the causal chain of events goes in only one direction is a specific assumption of natural science, a particular constraint upon the word *cause*.

Even though causal laws are not logically necessary for a theory, it is not just a whim of natural scientists to require that causes precede effects. We can easily concede that one of the functions of science is to predict future events and eventually to control them. It is then clear that we must base predictions upon facts that already have occurred because a teleological theory would not allow such prediction and control. Psychologists who believe that psychology is one of the natural sciences accept this principle of causation and deny teleological explanations in their scientific theories.

Naïve psychology, however, does not provide any causal mechanism to account for the process of perception or for the execution of intentions.

What can psychologists do about this unfortunate gap in naïve theory? As with the problem of private experience, there are three solutions. For radical behaviorists, teleology is another reason to scrap naïve theory and to start theory building on a sounder basis which does not involve such mystical ideas as goals, intentions, and cognitive pictures of the external world. They argue that we can assume that stimuli elicit behavior, an assumption which permits a causal law; we do not need to assume that there is any cognitive representation of the external world, and indeed, had better not assume it because of the danger of mysticism. Neither should we adopt the concept of intention or goal, because that would involve teleology; instead, psychology should begin with stimuli and end with motor actions, and try to build a theory to connect the two. Such a course has clear implications for the way that behavior can be described. To say that a boy catches a ball or insults his enemy is to describe behavior in terms of its effect upon the environment, but a behavioral theory should stop with the description of the act itself and not include its subsequent effects upon the environment. The boy does not, behaviorally speaking, catch the ball: He holds out his hand in a cupped position. The fact that such an act has the function of catching the ball is just as irrelevant to the mechanism of behavior as the fact that the heart's pumping blood has the function of supplying oxygen to the tissues.

It would not be inconsistent with radical behaviorism to study the effect of stimuli from the ball upon the position of the boy's hand—the stimuli may very well direct the hand to a particular position. Neither would it be inconsistent to study the effect of catching or not catching the ball on previous occasions upon the way the boy responds to the stimuli from the ball. Once the ball is caught, it is a stimulus and can influence future behavior, but the later consequences of the boy's action cannot be relevant to the causal explanation of the action itself.

Cognitive behaviorism would not deny the force of these arguments, but would maintain that no such radical denial of all the concepts of naïve psychology is necessary. The only thing required is that a mechanism of perception and intentional behavior be provided in the theory to make it acceptable on scientific grounds. Even if perception is not a direct reproduction of the external world, it can be conceived as a representation that is somehow constructed on the basis of information provided by stimuli from the external world, although it may well be less accurate than is assumed in naïve theory. Even if it is accurate, it still requires an explanation. The concept of cognition plays an important role in naïve theory, however, the cognitive behaviorists argue that we would do well to try to refine the theory rather than to discard it. Furthermore, it might be argued that the evidence indicates that perceptual representations are quite accurate on the whole, and so it may be useful for research on some problems to assume that cognition is an accurate reproduction of the external world and go from there. We need not put off the investigation of other psychological problems until the problem of perception is solved, provided we are perfectly clear that the mechanism of perception must be described before any theory has a sound foundation.

Similar arguments are used to justify the desire of cognitive behaviorists to retain the concept of intention or goal. The mechanism by which intentions are carried out is important, but the intentions are important, too. Since in so many types of situations intentions are carried out effectively, we may take the end result of the behavior as one sort of evidence for the intention, if we recognize that it is a fallible symptom. Many important psychological problems are involved in understanding how intentions are formed, and these can be effectively studied without having a complete theory of the mechanism of goal-directed action.

One further line of argument advanced by the cognitive behaviorists is that perception and intention pose with special clarity the problem of the adaptiveness of behavior. The concern of radical behaviorists to avoid teleology may lead them to ignore the adaptiveness of behavior and to deny that adaptiveness is an important empirical fact which a theory must take into account. Although general outlines for a mechanism to explain guided behavior have been available since the end of World War II, and have been used repeatedly in the design of automated machines in industry and in guided missiles, there has been remarkably little psychological research to work out the details of even the simplest sort of guided human behavior. One reason for this may be a reluctance to admit the existence of guided behavior among those psychologists best equipped to investigate its mechanism.

The third strategy, nonbehaviorism, can obviously be applied to the study of perception, too. Goal-directed rational behavior is one of the hallmarks of human beings. If purposes and intentions do not fit the conception of a proper natural science, then psychology should not try to fit into the prescriptions of natural science. Purposiveness is to be accepted, whether there is a mechanism for it or not.

Thus, the three strategies reappear when the problems of accurate perception and teleology are examined. They will arise once more when the problem of free will is considered.

The Problem of Free Will

The problem of free will is raised in naïve psychology by the distinction between "can" and "try." The actions a person cannot perform or cannot keep himself from performing are obviously determined. The person has no choice about whether he breaks into a bank vault with his bare hands, or about whether he hits the ground if he falls out of an airplane. On the other hand, the statement that a person tries or does not try to do something suggests that he could have done something else if he had so chosen. Power enables one to be free to decide what to do, weakness leaves one helpless and unable to exercise any choice.

This suggestion of free will is certainly accepted as valid in naïve psychology, at least in the specific sense that a person could have chosen to do something else. The concept of freedom of action is also valued highly by the ordinary man. Being predicted seems to many people the same as being coerced. The desire for liberty that makes us resist imposition and dictation also makes us resist any theory that says human behavior is predetermined and predestined; thus, for example, there is a general rejoicing when social scientists fail to predict an election accurately, because we do not like our election behavior to be predictable. Similarly, we in the United States are tolerant of all sorts of efforts to convince us to buy one sort of toothpaste rather than another. We do not resent having advertisers lie to us or use all sorts of extravagant claims to convince us that one brand of cigarette is less dangerous than another. Yet, when subliminal advertising was reported to be effective, it aroused immediate apprehension and anger. So-called subliminal advertising is flashed upon the movie or television screen for very short periods—too short to be recognized. The claim is that such exposure unconsciously influences us to buy what is advertised, and we believe that such advertising violates our freedom of action, while to claim falsely that a toothpaste prevents decay does not appear to do so.

Curiously enough, the acceptance of free will in naïve theory does not imply that people do not have reasons for what they do. On the contrary, naïve theory suggests that behavior is nearly always directed toward achieving some goal, yet such behavior is considered voluntary, in the sense that the individual could have done something else had he wanted. Even when a person is forced to perform some action because of so potent a threat that he is not considered responsible for his behavior (for example, at the point of a gun) he is judged to have operated through motives and to have chosen to do what he did.

This assumption violates the scientific principle of determinism. Determinism assumes that the results of a situation are always completely predictable from a complete knowledge of the circumstances, so that when the circumstances are duplicated the results will be too. A science that tries to build a theory to predict human behavior must assume that the behavior can be predicted, although such a science might admit unpredictability in restricted areas or in certain respects.

The problem of free will in human behavior is even further confused by the fact that most physicists now believe that the behavior of individual subatomic particles is not predictable. This indeterminism in physics has led some psychologists to assume that there is a respectable scientific precedent for asserting that human beings have free will. Free will in psychology is quite different, however, from indeterminism in physics. In physics, indeterminism means that the behavior of individual particles is random and unpredictable, so that, for example, we cannot predict just which radium atom will disintegrate although we can predict the number that will disintegrate in any reasonable time interval. This is not true in the naïve conception of free will, however. We would like to have freedom of action, yet have our free action be sensible, logical, and based upon sound reasons. We do not naïvely conceive of freedom as the capacity to behave randomly, but rather as the capacity to behave rationally; therefore, indeterminism in physics does not resemble free will in the usual sense. It may be that there is an indeterminism in human behavior in exactly the sense that there is in physics, but if so, it will not bolster one's belief in the freedom of man's will, but will rather further demonstrate its powerlessness and subservience to the laws of probability.

Free will is, therefore, a genuine issue in the science of human behavior, and the various ways of meeting the problem take on the now-familiar pattern. For the radical behaviorist, free will is merely one further example of the futility of trying to salvage the concepts of naïve psychology. If one adopts the radical behaviorist position, one may easily assume determinism or some sort of indeterminism in the sense of probability laws, should the data eventually justify it.

The cognitive behaviorist must also be prepared to accept a deterministic position, but he will perhaps inquire into the function of free will in naïve theory. He can argue, for example, that there is an important distinction between those actions that are voluntary because they operate through one's motives, goals, and intentions, and those actions that do not depend upon motivation for their operation, even though both are in principle predictable. If voluntary action means doing what one wants to do, whereas involuntary action means doing something whether one wants to or not, there may be good psychological meaning to the distinction even if voluntary action is not assumed to be unpredictable or undetermined. The cognitive behaviorist would try to see what psychological insights are contained in the concepts of responsibility and ought, and whether those insights might be preserved without denying an essentially deterministic position.

At first it seems that the whole structure of criminal law is nonsense unless one admits the validity of the concept of responsibility for one's behavior. How can one be responsible for behavior if it was determined? But, on further thought it is possible to recognize the functional value of the concept. If the function of laws and punishments is to deter criminal behavior, then only behavior that can be so deterred should be dealt with by means of law and punishments. If laws deter some sorts of behavior but not others, the distinction between the two is quite sensible, even if, in an ultimate sense, neither sort is less determined than the other.

Such arguments make it more reasonable than it at first appears to examine the concepts of naïve theory, even those that imply freedom of choice, for their possible contributions to a scientific theory of human behavior.

The third course, that of the non-behaviorists, is to accept genuine free will as characteristic of human behavior. There is no proof for determinism; it is, in a sense, forced upon natural science by the task it has chosen for itself, namely, prediction. Therefore, one can make a different assumption and adopt a different attitude toward one's subject matter. Human behavior can be understood even if it cannot be predicted, and in fact, one can easily argue that if one's purpose as a scientist is to influence human behavior, the possibility of modifying future events is nonsensical if one assumes that those future events have already been determined. Under this strategy, the search for truth takes on a different complexion from our picture of scientific research, but that is no incontrovertible argument against it.

The Problem of Incomplete Specification

The issues arising from naïve theory which have claimed our attention thus far are the perennial philosophical problems that have drawn attention for two thousand years, and so it is not surprising to find them inherent in naïve theory and in everyday concepts of human behavior. However, naïve theory raises other problems and other difficulties than these traditional philosophical issues. Let us now consider these.

In many ways, naïve psychology seems better adapted to providing an understanding of human behavior *after* it occurs than to predicting the behavior ahead of time. The relation of *like* to *desire* and of both to *try,* can be used to illustrate the point. It seems reasonable for desire to occur only when we do not have something that we like. The theory here seems to specify a necessary condition for desiring, but is far from specifying the sufficient conditions. We do not actively desire every object that we like but do not have. At this moment the reader is not enjoying many things he likes, such as a movie, a visit with a friend, a good meal, a trip to the mountains, or a game of tennis. To predict ahead of time just what a person will desire in a situation, we need to know much more about the laws of motivation than those contained in naïve theory. Other conditions besides the mere absence of something liked are required to predict just which desire will be aroused and which will not.

Much the same argument can be made in regard to other dispositional variables. One does not feel actively obligated to strive for the achievement of everything that one considers "good," and so other conditions are necessary to predict just which good one will actively try to achieve and which good one will not.

It may be that the lack of complete specification of the causes of behavior in naïve theory is related to the assumption of free will. Of all the possible things that a person might reasonably try to obtain at any moment, it is by no means easy to determine exactly which one he will choose. Common sense recognizes some of the factors that may make one goal chosen above others, such as the amount of liking or the opportunity which the situation may provide to reach various goals. In many circumstances, however, it seems as if the person just happens to choose one goal rather than another. In naïve theory this can be seen as the exercise of free choice, but if we strive for a more deterministic theory we must search for more of the factors that single out one particular goal at one particular time.

The Problem of Single-Factor Explanations

The final difficulty in naïve theory to be discussed in this chapter is the tendency to attribute causality to only one of the various factors that play a role in a situation. Sometimes one of the factors is changing and thus actually precipitates the behavior; in naïve theory this factor is made causal, and the importance of the other circumstances in the situation is ignored. In other cases in which one of the factors is unusual, naïve psychology may often overemphasize that one.

Heider describes, for example, how enjoyment of a situation is sometimes attributed to the desirability of the objects and sometimes to the characteristic of the person. For example, if a person likes a kind of food that is generally liked (especially if the observer himself likes it) the food is seen as desirable and the fact that a person likes it is attributed to its desirable properties. However, if a person likes a kind of food that is generally thought to be distasteful, then the liking is attributed to the particular characterstics of the person, and the properties of the food are not considered relevant in accounting for his liking it.

In each case, the attribution goes in one direction or the other and neglects the other factor. Actually, the tastes of the person and the desirability of the food are both relevant. If the food is generally liked, the person's tastes are similar to those of other people; nevertheless, those tastes are crucial for understanding his liking the food. The particular properties of the food that make it liked are also important. In the other case, the person may have unique tastes, but that does not mean that his likes and dislikes are unrelated to the properties of the food. In order to account for his liking, we must consider both the properties of the food and his own food preferences. The enjoyment of the food results from the two, not from either one by itself.

This tendency in naïve psychology is frequently met in naïve thinking in other fields, and is one source of error that the scientist must avoid. For example, disease is generally attributed to the germ that is said to be the causal agent, but medicine now knows that people are frequently exposed to a disease without contracting it. Various other conditions, sometimes called the *predisposing causes,* must be met before the person actually sickens, although the germ is the *precipitating cause* of the disease. Awareness of both is required to understand the disease itself, but naïve psychology frequently ignores the predisposing causes and concentrates upon the precipitating cause, just as in everyday life a person is inclined to pick out a causal factor that stands out in his mind and to ignore all the contributing factors. We can see other examples of this same error in the attribution of responsibility for an action in naïve theory. Under most conditions a person who performs an act is responsible for it, but under some circumstances he may be put under such pressure to do it that the responsibility is shifted to the person who exerted the pressure. A soldier who tells secrets to the enemy is a traitor, but if he does so under sufficient torture he is absolved of responsibility. Actually, there are at least two factors involved in determining whether he tells: the amount of pressure and his resistance to telling. Some people refuse to talk under any pressure, and others will talk under mild pressure. It is an error to shift the attribution of responsibility suddenly from the person to the situation at some point when the pressure passes a threshold.

In many ways this feature of naïve theory is its most insidious error and creeps most easily into attempts to develop a better, more scientific theory of human behavior. In our experiments we are constantly changing one factor in a situation and holding others constant. If we find that while A is changed and B is held constant the behavior changes, then we are justified in attributing the change of behavior to the change in factor A. But it is very easy, though quite unjustified, to make the further statement that the behavior is the result of factor A. We know that A influences behavior under some conditions, but we have no evidence that B is not even more influential, or that various combinations of A and B might not have quite different consequences.

Summary of Naïve Theory

Thus far, we have examined the naïve theory of human behavior to evaluate its significance and possible contribution to the science of psychology. We have found that although the theory is much more sophisticated and complex than we would expect "common sense" to be, it nevertheless contains many features that create serious difficulties for the scientific study of human behavior. These difficulties are of three sorts.

The first type of difficulty lies in the fact that naïve theory depends ultimately on private experience for its definitions, and accepts teleological causation and free will. Each of these three points of view violates important, generally accepted criteria for natural science. We have seen that a scientist may take any one of three points of view about these difficulties: He may feel that they completely invalidate naïve theory and point to the wisdom of building a new science of human behavior from entirely different premises, and may feel that any attempt to salvage hypotheses from naïve theory is likely to lead to mishap; this point of view we have called radical behaviorism. A second tack agrees on the necessity for a behavioristic approach and for the recognition that the subjectivity, teleology, and free will of naïve theory must be changed if a scientific psychology is to be formulated. Holders of this second position maintain, however, that much of this modification can be done within the general structure of naïve theory, and that, despite its difficulties, naïve theory contains much of genuine scientific value. We have called this position cognitive behaviorism because of its attempt to retain the basic notions of cognition and purposiveness in naïve theory. A third position can be called mentalistic or nonbehavioristic because it disavows the principles and criteria of natural science on the grounds that they are not suitable for the study of human affairs. Holders of such a view feel free to accept teleology, free will, and the validity of private experience as basic data for the understanding of human nature.

Each of these three approaches has been adopted by one or another psychological theorist, and as specific theories are presented in the remainder of this book we shall see how each of them modifies naïve theory more or less radically. We shall also see how each frequently accepts aspects of naïve theory tacitly, sometimes without full appreciation of their implications.

In addition to the three perennial problems of psychology—dependence on private experience for definition, and acceptance of teleological causes and free will—we have pointed to two other difficulties in naïve theory, more in the nature of weaknesses rather than fundamental philosophical flaws; nevertheless, they creep insidiously into attempts at more careful, rigorous formulations of psychological theory. One of these is the incomplete specification of the conditions for behavior. Naïve theory can frequently explain what happened after the action is complete, by pointing to some of the necessary conditions that led to it; in order to predict behavior, however, the causal factors must be more thoroughly specified. In addition, naïve theory often does not attempt to specify the details of the mechanism by which behavior occurs. Secondly, in naïve theory one of the contributing factors to behavior is selected out and made "the" cause of the action. All of this search for the single cause leads to the neglect of contributory causes and frequently poses problems that are both insoluble and quite unnecessary.

Neither of this last pair of defects in naïve theory would require any major modification of the theory, because in many cases the theory contains terms for describing more than one contributing cause to an action; it is only in its tacit assumption that events have single causes that the theory creates unnecessary difficulties for itself.

STRATEGIES FOR THE DEVELOPMENT OF A SCIENCE

We have now examined naïve psychology in some detail, pointing to the problems it poses for the construction of a scientific theory, and to some of the controversial alternatives adopted by psychologists in re-

sponse to these problems: to discard it, to use it as the basis for a behavioristic theory, or to accept its truth even if it requires the acceptance of different standards for theory construction. These reactions to naïve psychology are reflected in the variety of strategies
adopted by psychologists in their efforts to attain a theory of human
behavior. Psychologists expect that attaining a theory of human behavior will be a slow process and that a good theory will be attained
only by the gradual replacement of poor theories by better ones that
lead to empirically verified predictions. There are, however, two
different strategies concerning the sequence of theories which, it is
hoped, leads to an adequate one.

One strategy is to make each theory in the sequence rigorous and
operationally defined. Early theories will be wrong in many respects,
of course, but if a theory is clear, logical, and well-defined, its errors
can be more easily located than if it is vague and untestable. The
many supporters of this strategy argue strongly that progress is fastest
and most efficient if every proposed theory, regardless of how primitive, is a model of clarity and rigor. These people usually adopt the S-
R behavioristic approach that naïve psychology is inherently vague
and diffuse, and that even if it contains valuable elements these must
be transplanted into a clear rigorous theory that permits the errors to
be identified and removed. The result of this strategy is that the early
theories are generally restricted in scope. Such theories may, for example, be limited to rote learning of nonsense syllables presented under
certain standard conditions (Hull et al, 1940). Many of the mathematical models of learning (Estes, 1950) or discrimination are similarly
tailored to predict data within a narrow range of situations. The strategy is to expand the range of data to which the theory can apply until
it finally encompasses the entire range of human behavior.

To other psychologists this strategy seems to result in a concentration of scientific effort on trivial problems. Such theories seem more
like mathematical games than attempts to understand human behavior. Consequently these psychologists employ a different strategy.
They prefer to begin with broad theories that deal with the significant
problems of psychology, even if they do so loosely and intuitively,
assuming that the theory can gradually be refined in the light of findings. Supporters of this strategy argue that the first approach actually
succeeds in rigor only by avoiding the very problems that must be
faced in order to develop a rigorous theory of human behavior. They
point to the fact that when this S-R behavioristic approach has been
applied to significant human problems it becomes as unoperational
and as vague as other theories that stem from the cognitive behavior-

istic strategy. The truth of this assertion will be examined in the discussion of social-learning theory (see Chapters 15 and 16).

It is not our purpose to decide the matter here, although it is perhaps appropriate to indicate that the question is genuinely debatable. The fact that adequate theories must be testable and rigorous does not imply that their initial steps should have these same properties. Neither does the fact that adequate theories must encompass all human behavior mean that early theories must attempt the same scope. At the present stage of knowledge it is healthy to argue over which strategy is preferable, without condemning either as demonstrably wrong.

The third strategy is to avoid theory building entirely and to concentrate on establishing facts. In its extremest form such a strategy is based on the assumption that the facts will eventually lead so obviously and clearly to a set of rules for predicting behavior that no complex task of theory building is required. At the other extreme some people maintain that any fact that does not stem from a theory is useless, and that facts have meaning only in terms of the theories from which they derive.

Here again the issue is genuinely debatable, but either extreme position seems to create unnecessary trouble in actual research. Disavowal of all theory building often opens the door to tacit, unexamined assumptions that are, in fact, theoretical guides to research. The insistence upon a theory to guide every study means that every empirical investigation must have an hypothesis. It is as if one should not investigate sex differences in intelligence without having an hypothesis about which sex is smarter or that there is no difference between the two sexes. The insistence on hypotheses frequently means that the investigator pulls them out of the blue rather than derives them from a theory. Such hypotheses comply only *pro forma* to the requirement for theory-guided research. Recently, therefore, there has been an increasing tolerance for purely fact-finding investigations, even though only a small minority of psychologists maintains the position that science should completely avoid theory building.

SUMMARY

This chapter has been devoted to an analysis of various problems of theory building. Although common sense is the ground in which theories grow, it is also the ground for other views of human nature. Scientific theories are not the only ways in which man's understanding of human nature is expressed; literary critics and biographies, historians and social philosophers, theologians and philosophers of ethics all are searching for the truth, and all their activities are rooted in naïve psychology just as scientific theories are.

Scientific theories represent the result of centuries of development of the natural sciences and emphasize certain basic assumptions about the nature of evidence: that it should be publicly verifiable, and testable, and have clear logical derivations and clear empirical definitions. These are the minimum requirements for a scientific theory, but even given them, the actual work of testing theories, modifying them in the light of new evidence, and constructing more satisfactory ones is not routine. Good theory building requires decisions based upon intuition, good judgment, and sometimes pure luck.

Naïve psychology has been examined in this chapter for its strength and weaknesses as the basis for theory building. There are serious problems inherent in naïve psychology, namely, the subjectivity of evidence, the reconciliation of teleological and causal principles, the problem of free will, and a general faulty tendency to fasten upon single-factor explanations. Different psychologists have responded differently to these problems. Some, S-R behaviorists as we have called them, prefer to discard naïve psychology and to construct theories on the basis of a completely external view of human behavior. Others, cognitive behaviorists, accept the need for behavioral definitions but have tried to construct theories that refine naïve psychology without losing the wisdom and sophistication they believe is inherent in it. Still another viewpoint discards the canons of natural science as inappropriate for the understanding of human behavior.

The specific theories of human behavior and development that will be examined in later chapters represent the first two strategies, and a detailed study of them will disclose the liabilities and assets of each.

(Photographed by Dr. Robert R. Holt)

KURT LEWIN

Kurt Lewin
and Field Theory

THREE

The child psychology of Kurt Lewin

IN 1932 A NEW FIGURE arrived on American shores. Reports had it that he was a child psychologist, but he was certainly a new variety of the species. Instead of charting the ages at which children first utter a complete sentence or pick up a block between thumb and forefinger, he took movies of them having trouble sitting down on a rock because they could not sit down and see what they were sitting on at the same time. His theories were equally strange. He conceived of children being pulled around by forces and attracted to places with positive valences. In place of saying "the child chose the toy he liked best" he put down such formulae as $f_{pg_1} > f_{pg_2}$. He intrigued psychologists by proposing that a queer sort of mathematics, topology, was the proper language for psychological theory.

This psychologist was Kurt Lewin, and we begin our survey of scientific theories of psychology with his, because it is an example of the attempt to build a scientific theory upon the concepts and hypotheses of naïve theory, trying first to make them more explicit, more rigorous, and more refined, and then to progress to major modifications and revisions.

There are many examples of such theories in social science; in fact, some of these are actually simplifications of naïve theory. For example, some behavioral scientists try to describe all behavior as goal directed (Tolman, 1932); their theories try to simplify naïve theory to the point of describing all emotional reactions as anger, all guidance of behavior by ethical principles, and all sentimental factors in behavior as different varieties of goal-directed action. Other investigations include concepts like values, beliefs, or attitudes in their theories.

Several possible theories present themselves as good examples of this strategy. Tolman's purposive behaviorism (1932) is one example, and Carl Rogers's client-centered psychotherapy (1959) is another. There are three reasons, however, for selecting Lewin's field theory for a detailed discussion. First, Lewin had a deep interest in the problems of child and developmental psychology, and we are here describing developmental theories. Second, Lewin was articulate about many general theoretical issues: If he adapted a revision of naïve theory it was not because he was reluctant to break away from common sense. Third, his theory has led to ramifications almost unthought of in common-sense psychology. It can serve to show how the strategy of beginning with naïve theory need not restrict the development of theory building to common-sense notions.

Kurt Lewin was born in Mogilno, Germany in 1890 and received his doctorate from the University of Berlin just before World War I. After his military service, Lewin returned to Berlin and began the development of his theories in the 1920's. With Hitler's rise to power, Lewin emigrated to the United States and spent the rest of his life in this country, settling first at Cornell for a short time, then at Iowa State University, and finally at MIT.

More than most theorists', his life was a progression from one substantive field to another. In his early career he was primarily interested in the experimental study of motivation and its conceptualization. Though child behavior attracted his attention because of its openness, purely practical considerations probably dictated that in the United States he and his students study children primarily. However, little in his writings about child behavior is not equally applicable to any sort of human behavior. Even if Lewin's earlier theory had not been limited to child psychology it was a theory of individual psychology: and so it represented a real shift in 1941 when his interests turned to social psychology and the study of group processes. His interest has been perpetuated in the Research Center for Group Dynamics, which he founded.

Lewin differed from most other psychological theorists in still another way. He resisted formalizing his theory into a definite "Lewinian" theory because he was convinced that premature formalization of a theory makes it rigid and inflexible. Thus, he would first introduce some concept in a casual, common-sense way, and would gradually decide through further experiment what was the best way to give the concept some formal definition. Even then, he was more interested in whether a concept "made sense" and served him well, than in its purely logical implications.

Thus, it is more accurate to speak of the Lewinian approach to problems than of the Lewinian theory of behavior. The truth of this statement is best illustrated by considering the fate of the Lewinian "school." He collected a number of enthusiastic students and colleagues at every stage of his career. Some of them are now clinical psychologists, others are in child psychology, others in the study of small groups, and others in industrial psychology. It would be difficult to find even three or four substantive concepts upon which all these Lewinians would have a common point of view, yet there is a common trait perceptible in the group wherever they meet—as they do periodically: their approach to a problem and their strategy of attack.

BASIC CONCEPTS

Despite the rather scattered nature of Lewin's theory of human behavior, some specific concepts are essential to it. We shall begin with a survey of these concepts (Lewin, 1935, 1936, 1946, 1951).

Life Space

Wishing to analyze some of the problems of psychological conflict, Lewin represented one sort of conflict as in Figure 3-1. In this conflict a person has two mutually exclusive goals; he cannot attain one of them without abandoning the other. In Figure 3-1 the small circle labeled P is the person; he is shown in the middle of three regions. The regions to the right and the left of him are marked G_1 and G_2, to indicate that they are two goal regions; the $+$ signs, called positive valences, in each of the regions indicate they are goals. The arrows represent forces pulling the person toward each of the two goal regions; the mutual exclusivity of the regions is represented by the lack

Figure 3-1. The Lewinian representation of an approach-approach conflict.

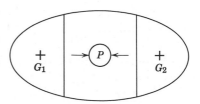

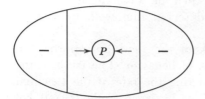

Figure 3-2. Lewinian representation of a conflict between two unpleasant alternatives.

of overlap and by the fact that if P takes the path to one of them he must move away from the other.

This representation contrasts with a second type of conflict, in which Lewin saw the person compelled to choose between two negative or unpleasant alternatives (see Figure 3-2). We shall discuss the particular problem of conflict presently, but these two examples introduce the Lewinian way of looking at problems and some of the best-known Lewinian concepts.

The total area within the oval in the diagrams is called the *life space*. Lewin defined the life space as the sum of *all the facts that determine the person's behavior at a given time.* Lewin conceived his task of analyzing and explaining any behavior as the job of describing the life space at that moment in verbal, pictorial, or symbolic terms.

The term *life space* suggests that it includes all the facts of a person's life. This is not true, however; indeed, as Lewin conceived it, the life space is surprisingly limited. In the first place, Lewin meant it to include only those facts that are relevant to the behavior in question. The person in conflict between going to a movie and a baseball game has memories of his mother, hopes for the future, and anxieties about the fate of the world, but they are not represented in the life space unless they influence his behavior at the moment.

HISTORICAL, VERSUS SYSTEMATIC, CAUSATION. Furthermore, the life space contains only facts that are directly relevant to the behavior. By this Lewin meant that past events were never directly represented in the life space but only indirectly as they were reflected in current influences. For example, the young man trying to decide between the movie and the ball game may enjoy baseball partially because he grew up in a town with Little League baseball, because his father once played first base for the Giants, or because he played baseball in college. These facts are not irrelevant to the young man's conflict, but their influence is represented and summarized in the strength of the plus valence of the *watching a baseball game* region.

Lewin distinguished between historical and systematic causation, contending that systematic causes contemporary with the behavior were sufficient to explain the behavior. To take an example in a different field, it is the strength of the fish line at the moment of the fish's tug that determines whether the line breaks or not; its strength may have been affected by the line having been left out in bad weather, by it having rubbed against underwater logs on past fishing trips, and by countless other events, but the result of these past events is reflected in the present strength of the line which determines whether or not the fish severs it. Thus Lewin included only contemporary facts in the life space because all past events operate only through their representatives in the present.

Lewin also theorized that many present facts are no more directly relevant to behavior than past ones and so decided these are not to be represented in the life space. For example, the whole institution of professional baseball, the farm system, the contracts of the players, etc., are contemporary facts but are only indirectly relevant to the young man's choice. Lewin said such facts are nonpsychological and lie outside the life space, but are represented in the life space by the existence of the region *"watching baseball."* Thus, the life space does not include just any fact having some bearing on the behavior but only those facts in the present situation that directly influence the behavior.

ARISTOTELIAN AND NON-ARISTOTELIAN EXPLANATION. Another term in Lewin's definition of *life space* which contains considerable hidden meaning is the word *fact*. Lewin said that the life space contains the sum of *facts* that determine a person's behavior; he insisted that the causes of behavior had to be concrete facts. This statement has two sides: On the one hand it excludes some explanations of behavior that have been accepted by other theorists, but on the other hand it classes things like forces as facts which other people might feel do not have that status.

Lewin intended to exclude those explanations of behavior which attribute behavior to one of the person's characteristics, which in turn merely asserts that he shows such behavior. Lewin argued that one of the marks of primitive periods in science was the explanation of a phenomenon merely by pointing out that it belonged to a certain class of events that exhibited the phenomenon. If, for example, one of the defining characteristics of the robin is that the species has a red breast, it is no explanation to say that the bird has a red breast because it is a robin. To explain that a wolf killed a chicken because of his "killing instinct" or that a person's quarrel with another stems from his aggressiveness are further examples of what Lewin called *Aristotelian explanations.*

This does not mean that such classifications are not useful in science. The term aggressiveness indicates that a person is easily aroused to hostility. But when such a person is actually involved in a fight, his aggressiveness is not a satisfying explanation of his fighting. More satisfying explanations lie in statements that submission to domination has a high negative valence for this person or that making other people suffer has a positive valence for him. For Lewin the explanation lies in the dynamics of the immediate situation.

Whether one accepts Lewin's arguments may well depend upon the meaning given to the word causation. There are less restrictive ways in which to use the term *cause,* but Lewin pointed to certain distinctions between some kind of causal statements and others. These distinctions are quite important and will be treated more fully in the critical discussion of Lewinian theory (see p. 144).

If Lewin excluded some concepts because they were not concrete, he included others like *force* and *valence* and *tension* that his critics might not agree were concrete. In this he was following the lead of physical science. Physics has made great progress by postulating factors such as forces and using them as links in the causal chain of various physical events. A magnetic field, for example, exerts a force upon a steel needle suspended in the field; *field, force,* and *needle* are all treated in this sentence as equally concrete facts. Lewin adopted the same strategy in psychology and argued strongly that such concepts were important steps in attaining more adequate theories of human behavior. No matter whether his particular terms are eventually accepted as the most fruitful ones, his insistence upon introducing such hypothetical concepts seems to have been increasingly accepted in recent attempts at theory building. Many terms in modern psychological theories are hypothetical facts or events that describe the mechanism leading from the directly observable cause of behavior to the behavior itself.

The totality of facts that constitute the life space are divided by Lewin into two large classes, those that describe the *person* and those that describe the *environment.* Let us examine each of these in turn.

The Psychological Environment

In the representations of psychological conflict shown in Figures 3-1 and 3-2, nearly everything is part of the psychological environment. The person in these figures is indicated only by the point *P,* and *P*'s function is to provide a reference that locates the individual in the environment. We shall see later that the person can also be represented in considerable detail.

In a general way the psychological environment is a representation of the physical environment in which the person lives. It is different in one important way from the physical environment, however: It pictures how the external environment impinges on the person or determines his behavior. For example, many aspects of the physical environment may have no psychological effect on the person because he does not know about them. The fact that there is a buried treasure directly under my feet may have not the slightest influence on my behavior if I have no idea that it is there. If, on the other hand, I am convinced that a colleague is hostile to me, my behavior may be much influenced by that belief, whether he actually is hostile or not.

Obviously, any theory of behavior must recognize that behavior is influenced by events in the external world; it is equally obvious that there is some selectivity in what is effective. One way to handle this problem is to hypothesize a psychological environment that is a picture of the real outside environment but not a complete nor an entirely accurate one.

PSYCHOLOGICAL VERSUS PHENOMENAL ENVIRONMENT. For some psychologists the psychological environment is defined as the environment that the person perceives or believes to exist. The term *phenomenal* environment is sometimes used to indicate this meaning. Such a phenomenal environment is part of the private experience of the individual. We saw in the discussion of naïve theory how the definition of a psychological concept in terms of private experience meets serious objections, yet to many psychologists it has seemed necessary to define the psychological environment as the phenomenal environment.

Lewin carefully avoided defining the psychological environment as a phenomenal world of which the person is conscious. Instead, he defined it in terms of its effect on behavior. By definition, all parts of the psychological environment influence the person's behavior, and therefore the psychological environment is a description of the external situation as it affects behavior. It is not necessary to raise any questions about private experience or consciousness. For example, magnetic fields have no effect upon a block of wood. Therefore the effective environment of the block of wood does not contain magnetic fields. Such a concept does not assume that the wood perceives or is conscious of its environment.

By this definition of the psychological environment, Lewin tried to reap the advantages of the concept, in order to describe the world as it exists for the person but at the same time to maintain a strict behaviorism in the definition of the concept. We shall see later how successful this device is.

In some ways Lewin was more radical than similar theorists because he did not explicitly include the physical environment in his representation; the psychological environment does not, for Lewin, have any specified relation to the physical environment. In a sense the theory suggests that the individual could function if there were no external world. If something is represented in the psychological environment it affects behavior; if it is not represented, it does not affect behavior; if it does not affect behavior, then it is irrelevant to a psychological explanation of the behavior. The theory does not distinguish between the accurate and inaccurate features of the psychological environment as a picture of reality. Lewin recognized, of course, that the physical objects were represented psychologically by some perceptual process, and he admitted it was important to understand how perception operates, how objects are perceived the way they are, and how they may thus acquire psychological significance for the person; however, Lewin essentially ignored this perceptual process in theory building and left it to be investigated by psychologists who are especially concerned with the problem of perception.

DEFINITION OF BEHAVIOR. Because Lewin rooted his theory so firmly in the psychological environment, he had to logically define behavior itself in a peculiar way. Behavior for the Lewinian theory is not physical activity, but merely a change in the psychological environment. Thus, if a person thinks through a problem and sees how to reach a goal where he could not before, this activity has changed the psychological environment; the environment will at that point have different effects upon his behavior than it did before. This change in the environment is one kind of behavior.

Probably the commonest way that the psychological environment changes is through actual physical activity. The person is separated from his goal; he acts and reaches the goal. As long as his position and activity are accurately reflected in his psychological environment, his psychological environment will change as a result of his physical activity. Thus such a change fits the Lewinian definition of behavior. But strictly speaking, behavior in the Lewinian sense consists of the change in the psychological environment not in the physical. A person might suffer the delusion that he had reached the goal; in this case his psychological environment would have changed, and, in the Lewinian sense of the word, he would have behaved.

Actually, such a definition is quite reasonable; as psychologists we are as interested in the causes of the delusion as in the physical motion. It makes a difference, of course, whether the person is deluded or not in his belief, just as it makes a difference in all other cases whether the psychological environment is an accurate representation of the physical environment. Nevertheless, all changes in the psychological environment are phenomena to be explained by psychological theory and can well be called behavior.

This broadened definition of behavior also permits us to include other sorts of important psychological activity in it. A change of loyalty from one country to another may not be marked by any clear physical activity, but it certainly is a kind of psychological behavior in which we should be interested. To give up an aspiration after a long struggle to attain it is a sort of behavior. Similarly, to lose hope or to acquire new hope, to change one's opinion of another person, or to become angry with another person are all examples of behavior in this broad sense of the word.

NATURE OF PSYCHOLOGICAL LAWS IN LEWINIAN THEORY. The psychological laws described in Lewinian theory clearly do not relate overt behavioral responses to physical stimuli; rather, they predict how a psychological structure spontaneously changes under the pressure of its own internal dynamics. In this, they are somewhat like the laws of the pendulum in physics. Given the field of forces on a pendulum, we can predict that if we release the pendulum at the top of the swing, it will go through a predictable series of motions and finally reach some stable position. A psychological environment in which the person is not in the goal region is like a pendulum at the top of its swing. The environment will tend to change in a predictable way until the person is in the goal region, provided there are no barriers in the way. This change in the structure of the psychological environment is what Lewinian laws predict. Whether this change in psychological structure is accompanied by certain overt physical actions or not is of interest to psychology, but it is not encompassed by the Lewinian laws.

The reader may believe that such laws are so detached from behavior that they are not testable; he may even believe that they are not good first steps toward building a theory of behavior. Many psychologists would agree with him. Even Lewin would have admitted that his theory was not complete and that it would eventually have to be tied to physical stimuli and to overt behavior, but he would also have argued that such purely psychological laws were not incompatible with a completely sound theory. Most important of all, this strategy permitted him to experiment with many psychological problems that had proved recalcitrant to experimental investigation.

As we shall see, Lewinian research is not at all divorced from the world. In actuality, psychological concepts are closely tied to physical situations and to overt behavior. Lewin and his followers are greatly concerned with the proper design of an experimental situation; situations must have definite predictable psychological effects if they are employed in Lewinian research. When Barker, Dembo, and Lewin (1941) wanted to study frustration, they went to great lengths to assure themselves that the experimental situation was actually frustrating in a psychological sense. Lewinians may put themselves in the experiment, interview the subjects carefully, obtain a variety of questionnaire responses, or employ other behavioral measures to check upon the adequacy of the experimental manipulation.

However, Lewin did not formalize this process, or establish objective criteria to guide the experimenter in determining whether the desired psychological situation actually was achieved. Instead, Lewinians are guided by their psychological judgment and their common sense, and so tacitly depend a great deal upon naïve theory.

If such a dependence on intuition seems unscientific, we should say that no psychological theory is detailed enough to completely specify the experimental conditions. The design of experimental situations depends a great deal upon the "art" of experimentation, and the difference between a successful and unsuccessful experiment frequently depends upon the good intuition of the experimenter. We may debate whether or not Lewinian experiments depend on these intuitive considerations more than those of other theories. In any case, the difference between Lewinian experiments and more rigorous ones is only a matter of degree.

GEOMETRICAL REPRESENTATION. A unique feature of the psychological environment in Lewinian theory is its formal description in geometrical language. Many features of naïve theory suggest the possible usefulness of a geometrical picture. For example, friends are described as "close" and estrangement is described as having become more "distant." We speak in problem solving of "getting close to a solution" and "being on the right track." Many psychologists label aversive responses "withdrawal."

In Lewinian theory, however, a geometrical representation should not be merely metaphorical. It ought to be a genuine mathematical model of human behavior in which action is described as a movement in geometrical space. Many actions are actually locomotions in physical space, but other behavior, such as passing examinations, becoming a doctor, marrying the boss's daughter, or writing a book, even though they involve physical movement, cannot be directly represented as physical locomotions. The geometrical representation of such behavior is based on the behavior's being goal-directed. The behavior is a means for attaining some goal; it is viewed as a locomotion in the direction of the goal within some defined space.

When it comes to representing this abstract geometry in detail, it is apparent that many of the concepts in Euclidian geometry which describe ordinary physical space are difficult to apply. For example, we can conceive of a movement toward a goal or away from it. Lewin, however, considered certain activities irrelevant to attaining a goal; these activities take the individual no closer to or farther from the goal and therefore seem to have no sensible geometrical meaning.

An abstract kind of geometry called *topology,* Lewin discovered, was mathematically precise, yet seemed to have many of the properties required for the geometry of human action. In topology, the only properties described are those that would not change if the space were stretched or distorted. For this reason it is sometimes called a rubber-sheet geometry. Distances and angles and shapes are not preserved in distorted space. If three points, *A, B,* and *C,* on a straight line were drawn on a sheet of rubber with *B* between *A* and *C,* and the rubber was then stretched, we could easily change the distance between *A* and *B* and *A* and *C.* We could distort the rubber so that the line was no longer straight. But, no matter how we stretched the rubber (provided we did not tear it) we could not put *C* between *A* and *B* on the line connecting them. If two regions sharing a common boundary were marked out on the rubber sheet, no stretching could separate those regions, although we might make the boundary much shorter or longer than it was. Thus properties like neighboringness and betweenness are said to be topological, because they do not change by stretching or other kinds of deformation of the space.

Topology seemed to fit the description of human behavior in many ways. If a person must carry through a sequence of three activities to get from the starting point to a goal, we can represent them as three regions between the starting region and the goal region, although in our primitive state of knowledge we would be unable to say that one region was bigger than the other. This sequence is a topological property of the structure.

The number of regions between the start and the end could be counted; this is a topological "distance." If there were two different pathways from the starting point to the end and it were impossible to shift from one path to the other after the starting point, the structure would look like that shown in Figure 3-3. All the properties described in the previous sentence are topological.

STRUCTURE OF THE ENVIRONMENT. In Lewinian theory, therefore, the psychological environment is described in geometrical terms. In the first place, the environment is composed of regions, which, for different purposes, may correspond to varied psychological events.

Sometimes "region" refers to an activity of the individual; a series of regions arranged in linear order then concerns a sequence of activities. Two regions are neighboring if the individual can shift from the one activity to the other without engaging in any intervening step.

Sometimes the region corresponds to events that happen to the individual. There might, for example, be a region corresponding to "being insulted" or "being praised." There might be one corresponding to "danger." Again, the neighboringness of two regions depends on whether the conditions can shift from one to another without any intervening step.

Sometimes regions have been used to represent group membership. Thus, the process of being discharged from the army and becoming a civilian can be thought of as a movement from one region to another, perhaps through several intermediate regions; or, a shift in one's loyalty from one country to another might be represented as a locomotion from one region to another.

Simplest of all, regions sometimes correspond to physical areas. Thus, in many experimental situations where a particular structure of regions is to be studied, the simplest representation may be actual compartments that are connected to one another in specified ways.

In all these cases the person is said to be "in the region" when he is performing the activity, or suffering the experience, that is, in general, whenever he meets the criteria that define the region.

Whenever the individual goes from one region to another without

Figure 3-3. Topological structure of two alternative paths to goal.

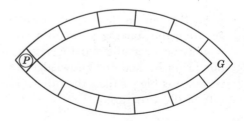

passing through a third, then the two regions, as we have noted, are neighboring. On the other hand, there may be a barrier that prevents a person from moving from one region to a neighboring one. Sometimes it is convenient to represent a barrier as a blockage which prevents movements from one region to its neighbor, but sometimes it is more convenient to represent a barrier as being the lack of any connection between one region and another (see Figure 3-4). Both representations indicate that locomotion is not possible.

When there is a series of such steps from one region to its neighbor, as from *A* to *B*, *B* to *C*, *C* to *D*, and *D* to *E*, we say there is a "path" from *A* to *E*. *A* and *E* need not be neighboring, but there are intermediate regions that permit the individual to shift from the activity described by *A* to the activity described by *E*. When an individual changes his activity in such a way that he is successively in regions *A*, *B*, *C*, *D*, and *E*, we describe him as *moving* or *locomoting* along the path from *A* to *E*.

The arrangement of the regions therefore describes the possible locomotions of the individual. Two regions may be far apart so that there is no way to move from one to the other without going through several intervening regions; by contrast, an arrangement of regions may be quite compact so that every region neighbors every other one, as in Figure 3-5. This arrangement of the regions in the psychological environment is called the "cognitive structure."

Dynamics of the Environment

In the cognitive structure the person is located in some region (see Figure 3-5) and he may or may not be moving. The purpose of dynamic laws in Lewinian theory is to predict when a person will locomote and, if so, from what region through what to what. If we can find laws of such generality that they apply to any set of regions, these same laws will make a number of specific predictions about the behavior in

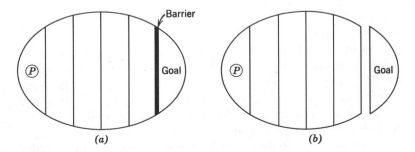

Figure 3-4. Two representations of a barrier.

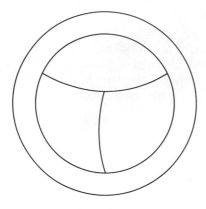

Figure 3-5. A compact arrangement
of regions.

concrete situations and exemplify a particular cognitive structure. If
such laws can be found, then the theory is very powerful because it
relates many different behaviors to a single set of general principles.

PSYCHOLOGICAL FORCES. Lewin proceeded as follows: He postulated
the existence of psychological forces in the environment. The movement of the person from one region to another was to be explained in
terms of a *force* on the person in the first region in the direction of the
second region. Any force must have: (1) a point of application, (2) a
strength, and (3) a direction. To postulate such forces was in itself no
advance. One had to know under what conditions there would be
forces and in what direction they would operate.

The mere postulation of forces suggests interesting problems, however. For example, there might be no movement because there were no
forces on the person or because equal and opposite forces canceled
each other out, or because an impassable barrier prevented the person
from leaving the region. These distinctions seemed to offer some promise for the study of conflicts.

A second suggestion which arises from the notion of psychological
forces is that two forces in different but not opposite directions might
push the person along the "resultant" of the two, just as in physics a
vertical and horizontal force may combine to produce a force at a 45°
angle. Psychological examples of such resultants are not easy to find;
perhaps they do not even exist. These suggestions illustrate, however,
how a purely theoretical concept may indicate further research and
lead the scientist to phenomena that he would not have discovered before the theory was formulated. If the theory is a good one, its suggestions will turn out to describe empirical events; if they do not, the theory will require some kind of modification.

When Lewin introduced the concept of force, he found that he needed to elaborate his geometry somewhat. Nothing in topology corresponds to the concept of direction from one region to another, yet forces must have directions and the force must be in the direction of the goal region. To show conflict, a theory must clearly specify what is meant by two forces in opposite direction. As it turns out, the concept of direction from one region to another is troublesome and once more raises the persistent problem of teleology.

To illustrate this problem, suppose we had a cognitive structure like the one shown in Figure 3-6. Suppose the person were in region *A* and his goal in region *E*. We would like to say that there was a force acting on him in region *A* going in the direction of region *E*. Clearly, he could not go directly from *A* to *E*, and so if the theory were to predict what the person did, it would have to predict how he gets from *A* to *E*. Obviously, the person will first move to *B*, then from *B* to *C*, then to *D*, and finally to *E*. As the force in *A* impels him in the direction of *E*, it first produces a locomotion from *A* to *B*. Lewin therefore defined the direction from *A* toward *E* as the direction of the first step in the path from *A* to *E*; in other words, the force is directed toward *E*, but its immediate effect on the person is to make him move from *A* to *B*.

This seems straightforward enough and corresponds to the way forces are used in physics. For example, gravitation is a field of force whose center is the center of the earth but it produces a movement on a body that is quite local and predictable. There is no predictable difference in the momentary movement of a rock whether it is operating under gravity oriented toward the center of the earth, or under the influence of a magnet that produces a force of the same size in the same direction. Direction is therefore locally defined, and there is

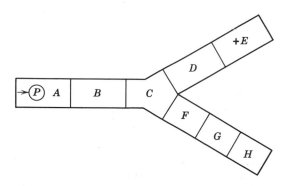

Figure 3-6. The forces moving *P* to goal.

nothing about the local force on an object to indicate what distant point in space may be the center of that force field. By defining direction locally, physics avoids teleology. The center of the earth may be the end of a falling body if nothing stops it, but there is nothing about the force on the body at any moment which indicates that end point. The local force is indistinguishable from any other force in the same local direction, regardless of what its end point might be.

Can psychologists be content with such a formulation? Consulting Figure 3-6, we see that the existence of E as a goal sets up a force on the person in A impelling him in the direction of B. Once he is in B, it moves him in the direction of C, and then D, and finally E. Is he going in the same direction all the time as he follows the path from A to E? In naïve thinking, we would say yes. Psychologically the person is going in the same direction as long as he stays on the path to the goal, yet in Figure 3-6 we can easily see the predicament to which such an assumption leads. Suppose the person's goal were H, not E. While he was at A or at B, he would make the same locomotion as he would with E as his goal: The initial step in the two pathways is the same. But at C the two pathways diverge, so that the pathway toward E is in a different direction from the pathway toward H. Obviously, if in going from A to E or from A to H the person does not change direction, and CD is a different direction from CF, then the step AB cannot be the same direction for the person going toward E as for the person going toward H.

In common-sense psychology, each step of the pathway to a goal is governed by the goal, that is, the end point of the path; at the same time, we recognize that the pathways to two goals may start out in the same direction, as Figure 3-6 shows. We must resolve this problem if we are to have a rigorous theory. In his solution Lewin actually compromised and spoke of A to E and A to H as being "partly equal" in direction (Lewin, 1938) without being more specific about how directions change as the person moves along the pathway.

In a sense, this is a minor point, yet it illustrates an important problem of building a rigorous theory out of naïve theory. We must be ready to violate common-sense ideas when they lead to contradictions. Here it is apparent that the common-sense term *direction* has two meanings which are not always compatible with each other. A rigorous theory must avoid such terms.

How the problem of direction is to be resolved is not clear. In terms of actual locomotion, if the action of going from A to B toward E is, in fact, identical with going from A to B toward H, the direction at point A from A to E is the same as from A to H. If the action of going from A to B is different depending on the goal, then probably B is not common to the two paths. When two paths with a common first segment separate, the direction to the goal presumably changes for one or both paths. Unfortunately, there are no criteria for deciding whether *AB* is the same direction as *BC*. It would perhaps be best if directions were defined only for single steps of a path and two directions compared only if they had a common initial point. Whether the individual were headed toward *E* or *H* could be ascertained at *A,* and the valence of the region would indicate the direction, but the distinction would not be reflected in the locomotion.

To complete the basic picture of the structure and dynamics of the environment, an additional concept is required: *valence.* In the discussion of direction, forces were tacitly assumed to be oriented to goals, but Lewin tried to further formalize the statement of a goal. In the first place he did not assume that every force on the person was a force impelling him to one of his goals. Lewin distinguished between *own forces, induced forces,* and *impersonal forces.* Own forces do correspond to goals, but induced forces need not. Some of the interesting problems Lewin investigated had to do with conflicts between own forces and induced forces, as well as the methods by which forces might be induced.

VALENCE FORCES. An own force is a force toward the individual's goal; a goal is represented in the environment as a region that has a *positive valence.* In a sense, a valence is psychologically more fundamental than a force. The force on a person depends not only on his goal, but also in what region he happens to be. A valence, however, represents a *force field* that is manifested in a particular force on a particular person. Suppose we have a cognitive structure such as the one shown in Figure 3-7 (*a*); further, suppose we did not know what regions, if any, had a positive valence. We could diagnose which re-

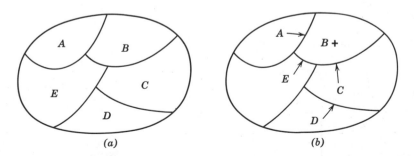

Figure 3-7. A positive force field.

gions of that structure were positive in the following manner: If we put the person in region A and find that he locomotes to region B, we are justified in indicating a force in A toward B. If we put the person in region B and he stays there, we say there is no force in region B. We may put him in region C and find there is a force toward B, in D and find there is a force toward C, or in region E and find there is a force toward B. With this information we can fill in the blank structure, as shown in Figure 3-7b. From that structure we can see that there is a field of forces oriented toward B: All roads lead to B and stop there. A field of forces with this kind of pointing toward some single region is what is implied when we say that region B has a *positive valence*. Knowing that B has a positive valence, we can predict what the force upon the person will be, no matter where in the field he is located.

Now, suppose we have a field like the one in Figure 3-8, in which all the forces seem to point away from region B, but in which there is no region toward which they point consistently. This state of affairs signifies that region B has a *negative valence*. There is a force away from B at every point in the field.

Lewin's procedure defines a goal as a region with a positive valence It also describes another sort of region for which there is no single term in ordinary language, but which is like an unpleasant or dangerous region. In Lewinian terminology this region has a negative valence. Of course, in a real situation there may be several regions in the life space that have positive or negative valences.

With these concepts the dynamics of the environment can be summarized. Corresponding to each positively or negatively valent region, there is a force field. Thus, if a person is located in any region of the environment, he will be affected by a force operating in the direction

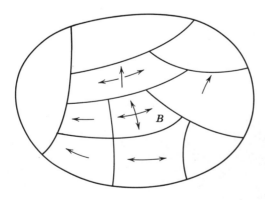

Figure 3-8. A negative force field.

of a region with positive valence and away from one with negative valence. If there are many different regions with valences, there may be various forces upon the person. Some of these may be in the same direction and reinforce one another, and some may be in different directions and conflict with one another. Consequently there will be movement in the direction containing the greatest forces, but the presence of the opposing forces may be evident in other aspects of the individual's behavior, such as his hesitation in deciding where to go.

CONFLICT. Having this set of terms for describing dynamics, we can turn to the Lewinian analysis of conflict. To make this analysis, Lewin further assumed that *the strength of the force toward or away from a valent region increased with decreasing distance.* He held that the force toward a region of positive valence gradually increased the closer the person was to the region. Correspondingly the forces away from a negative region were stronger the closer the person was to the negative region, but here Lewin assumed that the decrease was much more rapid. Figure 3-9 shows a graph of Lewin's conception of the forces.

Lewin could draw several conclusions and make several predictions from this assumption. Suppose the person were in a conflict between two positive regions; he would be at the point where the forces in the two different directions exactly balanced. If he made a tentative decision and began to move in the direction of one of the two regions, the force toward the one he approached would increase and the force to-

Figure 3-9. Graph of strength of a negative valence.

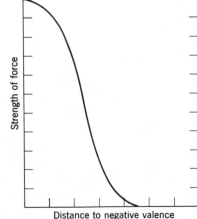

Strength of force

Distance to negative valence

ward the one he was leaving would decrease. The conflict would become more and more unequal and therefore he would tend to keep on moving in the direction he started out. In other words, the equilibrium between two positive regions is unstable. Thus, Lewin predicted that the person would not take long to come to a decision and that once he made it he would not be inclined to change it or to vacillate.

Consider, on the other hand, the conflict between two negative valences. The forces are balanced as before, but as the person moves toward one of the two regions, the repelling force increases, so that it becomes increasingly difficult to carry out the decision; therefore he will tend to move back toward the point of equilibrium. The same will be true if he starts out in the opposite direction. In other words, a person in this sort of conflict tends to go in one direction, then back, then in the other direction, then back, and to vacillate back and forth around the equilibrium. This led Lewin to predict that longer periods of decision and more vacillation would be involved in conflicts between two negative regions than would be involved in conflict between two positive regions. This prediction has been confirmed. Barker (1942) contrasted the behavior of children choosing between two pleasant alternatives, pineapple juice and orange juice, with the behavior of children forced to choose vinegar or salt water. He found that the second choice was much more difficult and involved much more hesitation.

Furthermore, Lewin predicted that the presence of the two negative valences in a field actually made the equilibrium region negative. If there were any region available which permitted the person to take neither alternative, this region would be preferred. Thus, we would expect that people in conflict over two unpleasant alternatives would be strongly motivated to escape from the decision situation altogether.

In some experiments with this sort of conflict, subjects excuse themselves to go to the bathroom, remember appointments they must keep, or frankly devise some ruse to cease being an experimental subject. Lewin called this kind of behavior "leaving the field." The terminology is unfortunate because it suggests that the person leaves the entire psychological environment, which is impossible. The behavior itself is quite understandable though, and the subject is leaving the field established by the experimenter.

In a third type of conflict, a region simultaneously has a positive and negative valence, so that there is a force toward and a force away from a particular region. In this situation, the strength of the forces toward and away are balanced at only one particular point. Further away, the approach forces are greater than the avoidance ones; closer,

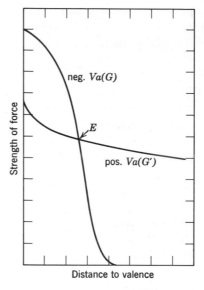

Figure 3-10. Forces in an approach-avoidance conflict.

the reverse is true (see Figure 3-10). Lewin predicted that the person in such a case would tend to stay at the equilibrium point, neither getting closer nor further away. This same prediction may be made on the basis of an S-R theory (see Chapter 14). Miller and Brown, having extensively investigated conflict in terms of their theoretical system, have confirmed this prediction.

Another sort of conflict arises in a situation where a barrier blocks a person from reaching a goal. When goal-directed behavior is blocked, it is usually called "frustration" rather than conflict. The term conflict is reserved for the situation where the person is simultaneously impelled to carry out two incompatible actions.

However, Lewin hypothesized that a barrier that originally merely blocked the goal-directed behavior gradually acquired a genuine negative valence of its own; this valence might actively drive the person away from the barrier. We have all experienced this barrier effect when we have tried in vain to solve a problem, until finally we were impelled to give up in order to escape the frustration. The state of frustration itself becomes so unpleasant that we give up the goal rather than continue to feel frustrated.

One of the effects of conflict is to produce restless movements. We are all familiar with how difficult it is to sit still when we must wait for some important event, such as when a husband waits for the delivery of his child. People who pace the floor while puzzling over a problem

also show restless movements. These movements may occur where a
physical barrier prevents access to a goal. Now, however, the restlessness is constrained because people are not going to move away from
the goal in their restlessness: there is a force preventing that direction
of movement. The physical barrier prevents the person from approaching the goal. The restless movements then tend to occur perpendicular
to the force toward the goal. Thus, in the situation diagrammed in
Figure 3-11 for example, where a child is kept out of a goal region by a
circular barrier, his restless movements result in a continuous circling
of the region. In one film of a child in such a situation, he finally circles the region at a dead run.

DETOUR. Two of the phenomena that convinced Lewin of the reality
of psychological forces were their pressure in actual physical situations
and their obvious orientation to the physical directions involved.
Thus, the observer cannot help but be impressed by the feeling that
the child in the foregoing example is just as securely tied to the goal
object as if he were on the end of a rope and that the circling is as
physically determined as the circular path of a satellite.

Another striking example of the physical coerciveness of psychological forces may be seen in *detour problems.* Woodcock (1941) reported
how a group of nursery school children eager to get through a door
that opened toward them jammed against it so vigorously that it could
not be opened. The children were in some sense irresistibly pulled to-

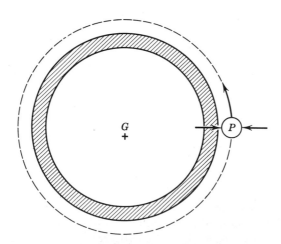

Figure 3-11. Direction of restless movements.

ward the door and held it shut, just as a rock on a manhole cover prevents its being opened.

If a chicken is put into a detour situation such as the one shown in Figure 3-12, and if attractive food is placed just in front of it yet behind the transparent fence, the chicken will be captured, because it cannot go away from the food to discover the roundabout path. A dog, on the other hand, can discover the detour unless he is very hungry. If the motivation is too strong, he is tied to the food by his sight of it as if by a string (Kohler, 1926).

Lewinian theory is intuitively convincing in these situations. The forces toward the goal are plain to be seen. Furthermore, Lewinian theory here goes beyond naïve theory. The "irrational" nature of a force toward a goal which prevents the person from reaching it is something not encompassed by naïve theory. Lewin did not discover

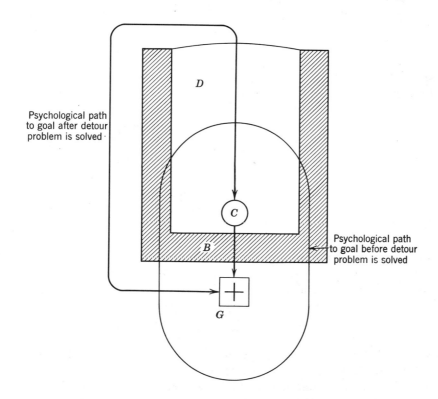

Figure 3-12. A detour problem. B = transparent U-shaped fence; C = chicken; G = goal object.

detour problems and their difficulty, but his theory is at its best in explaining them.

How does the theory account for the behavior of people who readily take the detour and are not puzzled by it? In the psychological environment of these people, the direction of the force is no longer in the physical direction of the goal but rather in the direction of the first step in its path; this psychological direction to the goal is different from the one for those who cannot solve the detour problem.

These Lewinian analyses of conflict and detour situations illustrate some of the strengths and difficulties of the Lewinian approach. They admirably fit a common-sense analysis of the problem, but clearly go beyond common sense. Naïve theory lacks some of the essential concepts that make the Lewinian analysis possible; yet, once the analysis has been made, the results are readily integrated into our naïve understanding of the problem. It is for this reason that Lewinian analyses of practical psychological problems have often helped greatly in clarifying our understanding.

For example, Lewin's analysis of educational problems has been most helpful. Many psychologists have found that "drawing the life space" helps a person to understand a puzzling behavior pattern, puts his intuitive knowledge on a more systematic basis, and suggests implications that were not previously obvious.

On the other hand, these analyses are far from providing a complete deductive theory of the behavior in question. They are full of common-sense assumptions that seem reasonable, but which are difficult to state in a rigorous fashion. For example, it makes sense that the physically straight pathway to the goal will frequently determine the cognitive structure of the situation, so that the person will get physically close to the goal object even if a barrier prevents it from being attainable. However, this assumption is not an explicit part of Lewinian theory and is not even easily stated in Lewinian terminology; the assumption describes how the physical environment relates to the psychological environment, and Lewinian theory is concerned with the relation of psychological environment to changes in its structure.

Lewin recognized clearly enough that the theory did not contain enough assumptions to permit a rigorous deduction of the behavior of a person in a detour situation. He could readily have added some assumption such as, "in the psychological environment of a naïve subject, the pathway from one region to another will correspond to the physically straight line between the two regions." This assumption would permit the rigorous derivation of some of the intuitive predictions he made about the behavior of an organism in a detour situation, but it would have several disadvantages. First, it would hold only for the cognitive structure of physical situations. It would not be applicable to the cognitive structure of an algebra problem, for example. Furthermore, it would not describe some of the real detour situations in which children find themselves. For example, children who are eager to get through a door to whatever is on the other side sometimes press fruitlessly against it when all they need to do is to step back and pull the door toward them because it opens in that direction. Stepping back from the goal seems to require "detour" behavior, but here the goal is not visible. The children know what is on the other side of the closed door, and that knowledge gives direction to the force pushing them toward the goal object.

Lewin would have argued that the explicit statement of such an assumption would be an example of premature formalization. It would reduce the theory to a "miniature" theory of the behavior of naïve organisms in certain sorts of physical situations, and although it would be a more elegant theory of that specific behavior, it might restrict the potential usefulness of the basic concepts in broader situations.

For example, one useful extension of the concept of detour would be to apply it to more abstract problem-solving situations. Children have great difficulty with problems such as the following:

If a person drives the first ten miles of a trip at a speed of 30 miles per hour, how fast must he drive the last ten miles of the trip to achieve an average speed of 60 miles per hour for the whole trip?

The child first facing this problem is tempted to say "90 m.p.h.," because the average of 30 and 90 is 60. This is wrong. Actually the man cannot possibly achieve an average of 60 miles per hour, no matter how fast he drives the last ten miles. In order to average 60 miles per hour he must make the 20 miles in 20 minutes, yet he has already used up his twenty minutes on the first ten miles.

When the junior high school student jumps to the conclusion that he can average the two speeds, his behavior resembles that of the younger child who tries to follow a straight path to a goal even though a barrier obstructs his way. If we could define "detours" in sufficiently general terms, we might find that many examples of problem solving are equivalent to "discovering a detour." Much of the research on physical detour problems could then be transferred to the general field of problem solving and thus might lead to some new and interesting implications.

PREMATURE FORMALIZATION. Lewin felt that the potential usefulness of many of his concepts would be hampered if he formalized them prematurely. It was his practice to use new concepts intuitively for a long time and to add them to the formal structure of his theory only after sufficient experience convinced him that they were defined so that, in addition to "handling" the data already at hand, they would permit valuable extensions of the theory.

A good example of premature formalization is to be seen in level of aspiration. Lewin introduced the notion of a "level of aspiration" as the goal that the person engaged in a task sets for himself. Though such a definition is subjective, Lewin and a student nevertheless designed a situation to measure the level of aspiration (Hoppe, 1930). The subject was asked to say in advance what score would satisfy him in the next trial in one test situation. In another situation, the subjects were allowed to select how difficult a task they wished to attempt.

For Lewin it was important to determine whether the subject's announced goal was in fact the subject's level of aspiration. Was it the level of performance that would satisfy him? The announced goal might not be the level of aspiration; it might be a wild hope that was not realistic, or it might be a pessimistic level of expectation that would not be satisfying even if achieved. The announced goal was an indication, but an imperfect one, of the level of aspiration.

The "level of aspiration" experiments appealed to other investigators, and in the early 1940's there was a flurry of them, summarized by Lewin, Dembo, Festinger, and Sears (1944). In these experiments it was typical for the announced goal to be taken as the operational definition of level of aspiration, rather than as a fallible indicator of it. These studies established relationships between the announced level of aspiration and many other factors. For example, a success on one trial tends to raise the announced level of aspiration for the next trial (Jucknat, 1937). If the subject is given information about the level of performance of various classes of subjects—young children, experts, etc.—his own announced level of aspiration changes.

Although these findings are interesting, from the Lewinian point of view, they confuse factors influencing level of aspiration with those influencing the "announcement" of a level of aspiration. Simple laws of level of aspiration are thus not likely to be found because the concept was made operational prematurely, in the Lewinian approach.

This view about the formalization of concepts is obviously a judgment about broad research strategy and not an opinion about the nature of scientific theory *per se*. It is certainly debatable. Many, perhaps most, current psychological theorists would disagree with it. It is not a readily testable position. At the present time it cannot be demonstrated to be either a sound or an unsound strategy. In Lewin's case it was a considered judgment, not a result of ignorance or of nonchalance about operational definitions or empirical verification of theories. He felt that setting up good operational definitions might be a poor strategy of scientific investigation.

Structure and Dynamics of the Person

Thus far we have discussed only the psychological environment and the concepts used to describe it systematically. A second important component of the life space is the *person*.

NEEDS. The concepts in Lewinian theory that describe the dynamics of the person came earlier in Lewin's career than the topological concepts which formed the basis for describing the environment. In the 1920's Lewin was much concerned with the problem of motivation and tried to conceptualize many of its aspects as a "need system in a state of hunger." The hunger for food was the model for the concept as it is for so many theories of motivation, but Lewin introduced an innovation. Most theories concerned with needs and need reduction focus upon so-called primary needs which are presumed to have some innate biological basis; Lewin also adopted the hunger model, but he applied it to such needs as the intention to mail a letter, or to complete an unfinished task. He admitted that there must be relationships between these "quasi-need systems" and the basic biological needs, but he restricted his own research to the study of quasi-needs almost exclusively. Thus, for example, when a person accepts the task of mailing a letter and forms the intention to do so, he puts a quasi-need system into a state of hunger.

When a need system is in a state of hunger, several consequences follow. Most obviously, needs are correlated to forces in the psychological environment. Thus, one possible effect of a need system in hunger—or, as Lewin later came to call it, in a state of tension—is that some region in the environment acquires a positive valence. Consequently, there is a force on the person in the direction of that region. Directed action to satisfy the need is thus one possible consequence of a need system being in tension.

This is by no means a complete picture, however. A person who intends to mail a letter does not always head toward the nearest mailbox. He may go about his regular business until he encounters a mailbox, at which time the mailbox acquires a positive valence. A need in hunger does not therefore always imply that there is a corresponding force in the environment. Unfortunately, Lewin was not very clear about how the need in tension sometimes created a positive valence and sometimes remained latent until the appropriate goal became available.

Another part of the mechanism is that a need in a state of tension tends to make the person think about the situation that would satisfy the need. Lewin stated this hypothesis explicitly. The so-called *"Zeigarnik effect"* is the tendency for a person to remember more about a task that was interrupted after he began it than about a task that he was allowed to finish. The primary research on this phenomenon was carried out by Zeigarnik (1927). She gave each subject a number of little tasks, such as stringing beads, filling in squares of a checkerboard, or putting together a small jigsaw puzzle. The subject was allowed to complete some of these tasks, and was interrupted before he had finished others. After the entire list had been presented to the subject, he was asked to recall all the tasks in which he had been engaged. Zeigarnik found that more of the incompleted ones were remembered than the completed ones.

This finding has been confirmed several times, but nevertheless it is a complex phenomenon not easily obtained. For example, not every unfinished task is psychologically incomplete. If there is no clear end in sight, as in assembly line work, stopping does not leave as strong a tension to complete it as if there were a clear end to the task. Furthermore, it is easy to interrupt tasks so that the subject feels that he has failed them, whereas he can feel that he succeeds on the complete ones. In this case other motivational factors are involved, and some subjects remember more successes than failures.

The hypothesis that people tend to think about the situations that are connected with unsatisfied needs is a common one. Freud hypothesized that the hallucination of need satisfaction was the root of all cognitive activity (see Chapter 10). This hypothesis is the explicit basis for many projective techniques. Such a hypothesis can, for example, certainly help to account for a person's tendency to remember his intentions, even if the actual carrying out of them is postponed for a period of time after their formation. When a man reaches the office, he remembers to mail the letter his wife gave him; the child remembers to meet his friends for a football game after school is dismissed. The mechanism may be that thoughts related to intention come readily to mind and are easily stimulated by reminders.

Still another line of experimentation followed directly from the thinking underlying the Zeigarnik experiment. If a person is interrupted in a task, the tension of the unsatisfied need should also be reflected in a tendency to resume the interrupted task. Ovsiankina (1928) carried out this experiment. Subjects were set at a task and then interrupted before it was complete. Later, the subjects had an opportunity to resume the interrupted task but under conditions where it was clear that they were no longer required to do so by the instructions of the experiment. Most subjects did resume filling in a checkerboard or completed some other equally trivial task just because they had started and then been interrupted. In fact, Ovsiankina tried to prohibit some subjects from resuming the task, but even then, some of them would surreptitiously complete it.

The concept of a need in a state of tension also led Lewin and his students to other interesting experiments. If a need can be in a state of hunger, can it also be too well satisfied as is physical hunger after a too-lavish Thanksgiving dinner? Can any quasi-need become satiated? Thus, Karsten (1928) created a quasi-need by asking a subject in an experiment to draw a simple figure like a moon face. She then kept the subject drawing moon faces until he was more than ready to stop; eventually the subject refused to go on. Examination of the moon faces he drew showed typical phenomena. One was that the subject attempted to vary the faces; some were drawn in great detail, others were just scrawled; some were drawn fast, and some slow. The characteristic seemed to be the attempt to stave off boredom by introducing all sorts of variations into the otherwise repetitive task. The concept of a need system in tension thus led to a variety of experimental studies that have proved fruitful.

Lewin was also greatly interested in the relationships between need systems, and it was this line of research that resulted in the formulation of the Lewinian view of the person.

THE RELATION BETWEEN NEEDS. One real problem arises in describing in rigorous terms just what regions acquire a positive valence because some need is in a state of hunger. To satisfy the intention to mail a letter, any one of many mailboxes would obviously suffice. However, the intention might also be fulfilled by giving the letter to someone else to mail. Or, if one happened to see the person to whom the letter was addressed, it might be given directly to him without being mailed at all. Seldom is there one and only one region of the environment that could become positively valent because a need was in a state of hunger.

Problems also arise at another level. When a task is interrupted as in the Ovsiankina experiment (1928), the person tends to seize every opportunity to complete the interrupted task. But even if that opportunity does not arise, the valence of other tasks can be changed by the interruption of that particular one. Suppose the incompleted task were a jigsaw puzzle. A different jigsaw puzzle might become more attractive if the original task had not been completed. If so, this new task is said to have acquired a *substitute valence*. Suppose, instead, that this so-called substitute task is performed and completed. Will the person still try to complete the original unfinished task? If the substitute task has the effect of reducing the tendency to complete the original incomplete task, then it is said to have *substitute value*.

This area of problems was originally investigated by Lissner (1933) and subsequently by other students of Lewin (Adler, 1939). They found that some tasks have substitute valence, and some have substitute value but that, in general, the range of tasks with substitute value is much smaller than those having substitute valence.

Lewin tried to conceptualize these relationships in terms of the neighboring quality of regions in the person. He conceived of the person as composed of regions that corresponded to various need systems. That one of these need systems was in a state of hunger was described by saying that the corresponding region in the person was in a state of tension. This tension tended to spread to other regions. Whether it spread to a neighboring region depended upon the strength of the boundary between the two; if it did spread it would affect neighboring regions before distant ones.

If one need system (A) is in tension, and the tension spreads to a neighboring region (B), that system is also in tension. Tension in the neighboring region (B) is shown by the activities appropriate to that need system acquiring a positive valence. This valence is a substitute valence, in the sense that it is derived from the spread of tension from A to B. If the substitute task were performed, the tension in the neighboring system (B) would be reduced. If communication between the two systems was so good that the reduction of tension in B drained off the tension from the original region (A), then the task would have substitute value as well as substitute valence.

Not only can attractiveness of a task spread from one task to another, but Kounin (1941) and others have shown that the boredom from satiation can also spread. In these experiments a subject is given one drawing to perform, say a simple picture of a cat (see Figure 3-13). He continues with that drawing until he is satiated. He is then given a different task, drawing a bug (see Figure 3-13). When he is satiated on bugs, he is asked to draw turtles, and, finally, to draw rabbits. As one might suspect, he does not take as long to become satiated with bug figures as with cat figures, nor as long as he would have taken on bugs

Figure 3-13. Figures used in satiation experiment.

if he had started out drawing them. The time to satiate on each successive figure decreases. Lewin conceptualized this as a spreading of tension from one region to another, and called it "co-satiation."

This is the general thought model underlying Lewin's conceptualization of the substitution of one motivation for another. It is an attractive model, but much research would be required to transform it into a satisfactory theory and to test its fruitfulness. For example, if neighboring were important, one would hope that if one task had substitute value for another, the second would have substitute value for the first. This hypothesis has not been tested. If a test failed, the boundaries between two regions would have to be given the property of transmitting tension in only one direction. One would also hope that activities that were neighboring as measured by substitute valence would also be neighboring when measured by co-satiation. This hypothesis has not been tested either.

Instead of building a solid body of evidence for these fundamental conceptions, however, Lewin and his students moved in a somewhat different direction: They described the structure of systems of regions. The effort began with Lewin's attempt to describe in topological terms how adults differed from children.

Differentiation

One of the concepts that has frequently been used to describe development is that of *differentiation*. Perhaps the most important source of the notion is Coghill's work on the development of salamanders (1929), in which he first described a general mass action in response to stimulation, which he found to be replaced at a later developmental period by segmental differentiated responses. The concept of differentiation has never been entirely clear, however, and we shall see in the later discussion of Werner and also of Parsons, a serious attempt to define the concept (see Chapters 17 and 18).

Lewin adopted the hypothesis that children became more differentiated as they developed; but for him, the concept had a specific conceptual meaning somewhat similar to Coghill's. Differentiation is defined in Lewinian theory as an increase in the number of regions in the person (Barker, Dembo & Lewin, 1941). If a system of regions is changed by the division of one region into two or more, the process is described as *differentiation*. Lewinian theory implies that if the differentiation occurred in the psychological environment, it would mean that what was formerly one activity was now two. If, for example, writing the word cat, came to be seen as writing the letter *c*, followed by *a*, followed by *t*, then we could speak of differentiation. Or, if one's undivided loyalty to one's country became a more discriminating approval of some of its policies but a disapproval of others, we might label such a change differentiation.

We have seen that the regions in the person are separated by boundaries that resist the spread of tension. If, therefore, a boundary separates two regions that were previously undivided it means that two needs, previously indistinguishable, have become sufficiently independent that one can be in tension without the other necessarily being so.

Lewin described two processes in the development of the person: 1) differentiation, or an increase in the number of regions, and 2) a *rigidification* or an increase in the strength of the boundaries between regions. He hypothesized that both processes went on simultaneously.

These concepts were investigated by Kounin (1941) who specifically hypothesized that rigidity increased with chronological age, while differentiation increased with mental age. Therefore, we would hypothesize that feebleminded adults and normal children of the same mental age have similar degrees of differentiation, but different degrees of rigidity. Kounin tested some of the logical implications of this hypothesis. For example, he predicted that feebleminded subjects would show less co-satiation than normal subjects of the same mental age, because if the boundaries of the regions were more rigid there would be less spread of tension from the region of drawing cats to the region of drawing turtles. His prediction was confirmed; the feebleminded subjects drew turtles nearly as long as they did cats, while the normal subjects drew turtles a much shorter time than they did cats (see Figure 3-14).

In the monograph *Frustration and Regression* (1941), coauthored by Barker, Dembo, and Lewin, we find the most serious attempt to formulate that Lewinian theory of development. The task they set themselves was to describe the main differences between behavior at different age levels and to show how these differences might be encompassed by the concept of differentiation. As Lewin saw it, the prelimi-

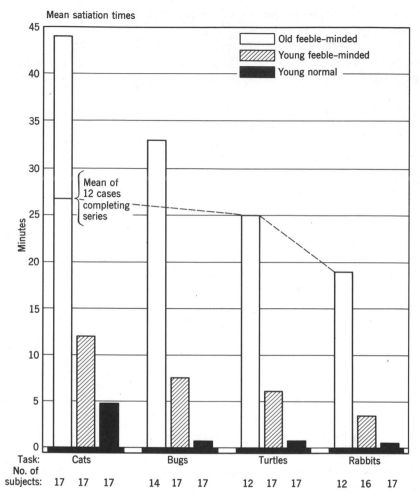

Figure 3-14. Velocity of satiation and co-satiation with individuals of different chronological age and the same mental age. (From *Experimental Studies of Rigidity as a Function of Age and Feeblemindedness*, by J. S. Kounia. Unpublished Ph.D. dissertation, U. of Iowa, 1939.)

nary description of the difference between age levels poses the problem. He distinguished the following aspects of development:

1. As the child grows older he exhibits a greater *variety* of behavior. Some activities drop out, but on the whole he shows more and more

varieties of behavior, emotional expressions, needs and interests, knowledge, and social relations.

2. Despite the increased repertoire, a child's behavior becomes more organized as he grows up, that is, it becomes increasingly guided by a governing purpose, a main theme, or a leading idea.

(a) In this organization, behavior is divided into large units composed of subparts. Thus, the functioning unit of behavior becomes more complex. In play, for example, the unit of action might be "building a tower." This necessitates many steps, where at an earlier age "putting one block on another" might be the unit.
(b) The organization tends to become hierarchical. Each level provides guidance to the level below and is guided by the level above. Thus, if a boss decided not to accept the recommendation of a subordinate, the guiding idea of his discussion with the subordinate might be (1) to reject the recommendation but (2) not to hurt the subordinate's pride more than necessary. This leads to a tactical decision to emphasize the reasons for rejection which the subordinate could not have known about, which in turn dictates an utterance that "gives reasons." This leads to the selection of a sentence of the form, "There is no way you could have known———, it is necessary———." This form in turn dictates the parts of speech employed, etc.
(c) Besides being hierarchical, the organization may be complicated by the need to carry on an activity through interruptions, to carry on two activities simultaneously, or to devise a strategy that fits two different purposes, as in the example just given.
All these sorts of organization increase with age, but as Barker, Dembo, and Lewin indicated, not every adult act is so highly organized. It is the maximum level of organization of the behavioral unit that increases with age.

3. The psychological environment of the child expands both in the area covered and in the time span. The life space of the young child does not contain many regions that are only remotely connected to the one he occupies, nor does the young child's psychological environment contain hopes and expectations for the distant future or regrets and satisfactions connected with long past events. Therefore, not only does the life space itself increase in size, but the portion of it that is accessible to the child also increases. Thus Lewin said: (1) The life space of the child is smaller than that of the adult, and (2) the space of free movement increases as the child grows up.
Notice in these statements that there is no necessary relation be-

tween the regions of the life space and the physical activities that correspond to them. The psychological environment is large if it contains long pathways involving many regions. The far ends of these pathways need not correspond to physically distant regions or to activities that would be difficult to perform.

4.   The growth of child involves changes in the dependence of his activities on one another. These changes are probably the most difficult for any theory to account for, or even describe systematically. On the one hand, the young child has difficulty in performing activities independently of one another. For example, if the infant's head is turned, he tends to take up the "fencing position" involving extension of one arm and retraction of the other (Gesell, 1928). The young child's behavior is governed more by impulse and feelings, whereas the adult, despite the existence of impulses and feelings, does not act them out so readily. Thus, there is some increase in the independence of one action from others as the child grows up. This is the type of change referred to frequently as differentiation.

On the other hand, the activities of the adult are much more interdependent in the sense that they are organized into complex, purposive patterns. This aspect of development is often called increased integration. It thus seems that the actions of the adult are both more and less interdependent than those of the child.

Lewin attempted to solve this problem by distinguishing between *simple interdependence* and *organizational interdependence*. Simple interdependence is reflected in the readiness with which tension in one region of the person spreads to other regions. Thus, both the differentiation of the person and the increasing rigidity of the boundaries between regions are consistent with the decrease of simple dependence between regions.

Organizational dependence, on the other hand, does not decrease with age. On the contrary, the hierarchical organization of the life space tends to increase with age. This increased organization can be described to some degree by the complexity of means-end relationships in the psychological environment; Lewin never did devise any satisfactory method for describing the hierarchical relation of regions in the person, however, and he described no mechanism like the spread of tension to account for the way one need system might control subordinate needs, establish subgoals, etc. He did believe that the distinction between simple and organizational dependence was a step in the right direction.

We can see in a concrete example how the two kinds of dependence are in opposition to each other. A boy with a number of lawn cutting jobs decides to build a small wagon to carry his equipment. He draws up his plans, and at some point in the process needs to find suitable wheels for the wagon, and so he starts out looking for them. The search for wheels is a subgoal—in Lewinian terms, a region on the path to building the wagon that has acquired a valence of its own. The boy's behavior is now directed toward that region as a goal.

Corresponding to the behavior of searching for wheels is a region in the person that is in a state of tension; the region corresponding to building the wagon is also under tension. These two regions are *not* neighboring in the system of regions that constitute the person. Tension in the one region creates tension in the other, but not by spreading across the boundary. The tension in the second region is due instead to the means-end relationship between the two activities in the psychological environment.

Suppose that the boy cannot readily find wheels for his wagon. We might expect from the work on substitute valences that he would be attracted to all sorts of similar objects, such as roller-skate wheels and old tire casings. In this case, though, the range of wheels that attracts his attention and arouses his motivation is strictly limited to the group of those that meet the functional demands of a wagon. If the tension did spread to such neighboring regions as the search for tire casings, it would hamper the boy's functioning in getting the wagon built. In a younger child such a shift might actually occur. He might find a set of skate wheels and shift to making a sidewalk coaster, or might make a collection of all sorts of wheels to add to the clutter in the family basement.

Tension maintenance in a region even after its functional utility is gone is a similar phenomenon; for example, the child might set himself the task of searching the junk pile for wheels and might keep collecting wheels even after he found the ones he wanted. For effective action, the tension in the regions corresponding to subgoals should not spread—or at least not beyond the substitutes that are functionally equivalent in reaching the goal.

5.   A fifth change during development is an increase in *realism*. To explain this notion, we must specify that one of the dimensions of the psychological environment is its level of reality. Parts of the environment may be more unreal than others; for example, hopes and fears or wishes. People may well distinguish between "how things are" and "how I wish they were." One's wishes are not without effect on behavior, and therefore they are part of the life space. On the other hand, they do not influence behavior in the same way that beliefs do, and so must be distinguished. For example, if children are put into a

make-believe mood, they will accept pieces of cardboard as a substitute for candy, but they are much less likely to do so in a serious situation (Sliosberg 1934). Evidence of this sort led to the postulation of degree of reality as one dimension of the life space. The term *realism* means the development of this distinction between levels of reality. Where realism is high, the boundaries between regions are relatively rigid; goals are not reached merely by wishing or imagining but only by behavior that conforms to some rules. It probably represents the child's acquiring the concept of an objective world external to himself.

Realism is not defined, however, in terms of external reality. It is not defined as behavior that is more accurate, more appropriate, or more governed by facts outside the individual. Although it is probably true that the rigidity of the barriers at the high levels of reality is due to the genuine intractability of physical obstacles, such an assumption is not necessary. Realistic behavior is identifiable by its psychological properties and behavior could conceivably be "realistic" yet completely deluded as far as external reality is concerned.

Realistic behavior does increase with age, however, and thus it is one aspect of development that Lewin felt had to be explained by a scientific theory.

Structure of Dynamic Wholes

The features of development that Lewin described are partly empirical generalizations, but they are expressed in the language of his theory. Lewin did not think that they constituted a theory of development, but rather a description of the problems that such a theory had to encompass. He clearly believed that these developmental levels were best conceived in terms of general properties of the life space considered as a dynamic whole. He thought that they depended on the global properties, such as unity, of a system of regions.

In *Frustration and Regression* Lewin therefore turned to a general theoretical analysis of the structural properties of dynamic wholes. This analysis obviously referred to the properties of the person, but it was an exercise in highly abstract conceptualization.

We, too, must begin our exploration of these concepts with a discussion at a very abstract level. Suppose that Figure 3-15 represents any dynamic whole, any system composed of regions. Suppose further that some state might exist in any of these regions, and that the state could spread to neighboring regions as we have described. Finally, assume for the present that all of the boundaries between the regions have the same strength.

One question we might ask is whether all of the regions in the sys-

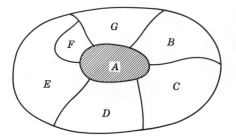

Figure 3-15. A central region.

tem are equally important. If by importance we mean the extent to which changes in one region will affect the states of all the others, then it is clear that the influence of one region on another depends upon the length of the pathway connecting the two. Neighboring regions will influence one another more than those separated by two or three other regions—in general, the fewer the regions separating two regions, the more dependent they will be on each other. In Figure 3-15 region *A* is neighboring to all the others. If there is a state of tension in *A,* it will spread to all the other regions in the system as soon as it is great enough to cross the boundary of *A.* Suppose, on the other hand, that there were a tension in region *C;* it would not affect the tension level of region *F* until the tension had first spread to *A* and *B,* and then further to *F.* Lewin therefore argued that in one sense region *A* was in a special position of being able to influence all the other regions more quickly than any of the others could, but in the reverse sense it is the most susceptible to influence. No matter what other region is under tension, *A* is influenced as soon as any other region. *A*'s position is said to be *central* because of this property.

This centrality is formally defined in the following way: The distance between any two regions is defined as the smallest number of regions that must be crossed to go from one to the other. This is the same definition of distance that was used in describing the environment. Further, the *centrality* of any region *P* in a system of regions is defined as the longest distance from *P* to any other region of the system. If the most distant region were two regions away, that distance would determine the centrality of *P.*

Centrality is greatest when distance is minimal. Of course, the most central region is the one whose centrality is greatest, that is, whose distance to the most distant region is minimal.

It is important to distinguish between central and inner regions. Inner regions are those that are a long distance from the outside boundary

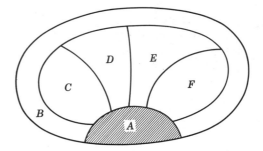

Figure 3-16. A central region
that is also an outer region.

of the whole system. Central regions are those that are close to all the
other regions in the system. We can think of situations where a region
on the outside boundary would be the most central, even though some
other region were further in. For example, Region A in Figure 3-16 is
an "outer" region yet a "central" region.

Once we have the concept of dependence as a function of distance
between two regions, we can define a property of the whole system,
namely, its *diameter*. The diameter of a system is the maximum distance between any two regions in the system. If this maximum distance
is 2, then any influence on any region has only to cross two boundaries
before all regions are affected (Figure 3-15). In Figure 3-17, on the other
hand, which has the same number of regions, a tension in region A must
cross three boundaries to reach region F. Thus, the diameter of the system in Figure 3-17 is greater than the diameter of the system in
Figure 3-15. It is apparent that the unity of a system does not solely
depend on its differentiation (the number of regions); in general,

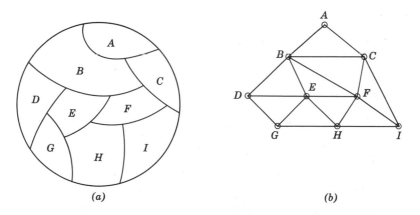

(a) (b)

Figure 3-17. A system with a diameter of 3.

however, an increase in differentiation tends to increase the diameter of a system of regions.

The diameter of a system is closely related to an important dynamic property of its unity. If unity means the readiness with which all regions of a system are influenced by a disturbance in any part of the system, then, other things being equal, the greater the diameter the less the unity.

One further theoretical derivation of these concepts concerns the variety of patterns of tension which can exist in a system of regions. We can readily see that this variety depends on the number of regions, the differentiation. If a whole is all one region, it must be homogeneous. If it is composed of two regions, one region can be in tension and the other not—provided the boundary is strong enough. If there are three regions, various other patterns may exist. It is also clear that the weaker the boundaries between the regions, the more the whole system tends to be homogeneous—and the smaller the variety of patterns of tensions that it can support.

How much does this theory of dynamic wholes contribute to the explanation of developmental levels? The basic assumption is that development involves an increase in the number of regions (differentiation) and an increase in the strength of boundaries. From the theory it would seem likely that such an hypothesis might predict an increase in the variety of behavior patterns and a decrease in simple dependence. The concept of differentiation as Lewin used it would not lead, however, to predictions about the scope of the life space or the increase in organizational dependence, or to an increase in realism.

Lewin recognized the importance of building a theory of organizational dependence upon a different basis but hardly made more than the first few exploratory efforts toward such a theory. He felt that one possible line for theory building was to describe organizational dependence in terms of the power of one region over another. He had begun to use this concept in social psychology before his death and it has been greatly developed in this area since then, but so far no one has attempted to use it to describe the influence of one region on another within the person.

DEVELOPMENT OF LEWINIAN THEORY IN SOCIAL PSYCHOLOGY

After the beginning of World War II, Lewin became more and more interested in social psychology; and this interest has remained alive at the Research Center for Group Dynamics which he founded. Since this book is primarily concerned with child development the developments of Lewinian theory in social psychology will not be fully reported, although many of the ideas could be studied developmentally.

Only one portion of the social psychological theorizing will be reported, the development of a *graph theoretical* description of systems of regions. The mathematical concept of graph will be referred to later, so it is important to see its relation to Lewinian theory.

Although these descriptions of the properties of dynamic wholes were developed in connection with the problem of describing the development of the individual person, their usefulness in explaining the phenomena of development is still not established. These same concepts have proven to be useful in describing some of the total properties of social groups, however. If, for example, each person in a group were represented by a region and his communication with other members of the group were indicated by neighborliness, then information can spread through the group just as Lewin conceived of tension spreading through the person.

Application of Topology to Communication Patterns in Groups

Bavelas (1950) has been mainly responsible for the application of these concepts to the communication patterns of groups. For example, he and his colleagues have compared the four groups whose communication patterns are shown in Figure 3-18. These diagrams do not look like the drawings used heretofore, but Figure 3-17 will make the translation clear. The two methods of presentation are completely compatible. The traditional representation shown in *a* is mathematically the same as the representation shown in *b*. The second form of representation replaces regions by points and adjacency of regions by lines connecting the points. This representation is called a *graph* representation. A *graph* is a mathematical concept defined as a set of points and a set of lines connecting some or all the points with one another. There is a well-developed branch of mathematics called *graph theory,* part of the more general field of topology which consists of various theorems about graphs; the concepts of centrality and peripherality, inner and outer, and diameter, all appear in this branch of mathematics, although sometimes under other labels. Lewin was apparently unacquainted with these developments in graph theory when he described the properties of dynamic wholes in 1941. Hereafter in this presentation we shall use the graph representation of systems of regions.

Returning to the representation of communication patterns in

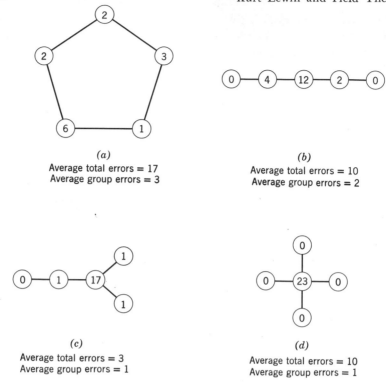

(a)
Average total errors = 17
Average group errors = 3

(b)
Average total errors = 10
Average group errors = 2

(c)
Average total errors = 3
Average group errors = 1

(d)
Average total errors = 10
Average group errors = 1

Figure 3-18. Graphical representation of a system of regions. Errors and lead-ership attribution in different communication patterns. Average total errors is the average number of switches thrown wrong per problem, and average group errors is the average number of groups whose final solution contains an error. (From Harold A. Leavitt, Ph.D. dissertation M.I.T., 1949, as reported in Bavelas, 1950.)

groups, we see in Figure 3-18 four patterns within a five-person group. Each of these groups of people was given a problem to solve, and each member of the group was given a card upon which appeared five sym-bols taken from a collection of six. Each group member had a set of five symbols different from any other member of the group, but one of the six symbols was common to all five cards. The group's task was to discover which symbol was the one all had in common, and to com-municate this information to everybody in the group. Each member of the group had a set of six electrical switches in front of him and when he thought he knew which symbol was common to all five members of the group, he pressed the switch representing that symbol. The problem was solved correctly when all members of the group had turned on the correct switch. If any of the members had the wrong switch thrown when the group was finished with a problem this was counted a group error.

Below each pattern in Figure 3-18 is shown the average number of errors made by groups in fifteen tests using these problems. More interesting than the number of errors is the appearance of recognized leaders at some particular point in the pattern. Each person in every group was asked whether his group had a leader and if so, who. All groups were composed of strangers whose communication was limited to that shown in the pattern, and so the assignment of leadership status emerged solely through the solution of the problems. The number in each of the circles in the pattern indicates the number of times in the entire experiment that the person in the spot was nominated as a leader by someone in the group. It seems clear that the centrality of the position in the communication pattern is strongly related to the emergence of leadership in this particular sort of experiment. There is also evidence that people in peripheral positions liked their jobs less than those in central positions and were less satisfied with the job done by the group.

Applications of Graph Theory to Attitudes

We have seen an interesting development in a theoretical concept. The topological representation was first conceived to describe the psychological environment; it was then adapted to the description of certain aspects of the person. The concepts developed were then found applicable for the description of communication patterns within small groups. But the development did not stop there. For example, Harary (1953) and Cartwright and Harary (1956) have considered the problem of graphs in which the lines may have either positive or negative valences or signs. They are interested in this type of mathematics because of its possible uses in representing the like or dislike of members of a group for one another. From the theory of signed graphs they have been able to describe in a mathematical way the principles of balance enunciated by Heider (see p. 20) and have generalized these principles to balance in sets of more than three elements.

Heider described the relations among three social objects: two people, and a third object that might or might not be a person. For the present let us consider it to be a group of three people, p, o, and r. If p likes o, p likes r, and o likes r, the situation is in balance. If p likes o and both dislike r, the situation is also in balance. Two friends share a common dislike. If, however, p likes o, p dislikes r, but o likes r, then for p, the situation is unbalanced or strained.

These can be represented as three signed graphs (see Figure 3-19). Heider used the same representation without realizing that it had such a fancy name. He described the general principle in terms of the number of pluses and minuses: One plus or three pluses among the three people was balanced, but two pluses was unbalanced (see p. 000).

Let us see what happens to this notion in a more mathematical treatment. One of the concepts in graph theory is a cycle. A cycle is a connected pathway from one point through some other points and back to the starting place. Thus, in each representation in Figure 3-19, there is only one cycle (or two, if the same path in reverse order is counted). In the balanced situation the cycle contains an even number of minus signs; in the unbalanced situation it contains an odd number of minus signs.

In generalizing this notion, Cartwright and Harary defined a balanced graph as one in which every possible cycle among the points contains an even number of minus signs. Let us apply this to a graph having four points where every point is directly connected to every other point. Such a graph is called *complete* (see Figure 3-20a). There are seven different cycles in such a graph: $ABCA$, $ABDA$, $ADCA$, $ABDCA$, $ABCDA$, $ADBCA$, and $BCDB$.

Now suppose the plus and minus signs are arranged as in Figure 3-20b. We can list the seven cycles in a table and count the number of minus signs in each. By the definition, the group is balanced. Notice that it could be described as two pairs of friends AB and CD who dislike each other. Each person likes his friend and dislikes both members of the other pair.

In Figure 3-20c only some of the cycles are balanced. Such a group is unbalanced according to our definition. Notice also that there is no way to divide the group into two cliques so that all minus signs are between the two and all plus signs within each clique.

This last point is important because it can be proved that if a graph

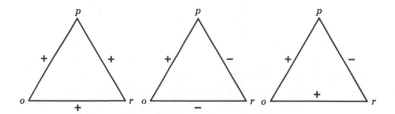

Figure 3-19. Balance and imbalance in a 3-element signed graph.

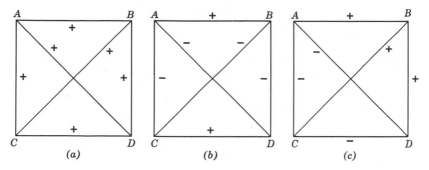

Figure 3-20. Balance and imbalance in a 4-element signed graph.

is balanced, it can be divided into two sections or subgraphs such that every line within each is positive and every line connecting the two is negative. If this theorem is expressed in social psychological terms, it means that any group is balanced if it is divided into two cliques such that everybody likes everybody else within his clique and dislikes everybody in the other clique. In 3-20a the second clique is missing and everybody likes everybody else. In 3-20b the two cliques are *AB* and *CD*. What keeps 3-20c from being balanced is that the friendships are mixed up. Everybody likes *B,* but dislikes everyone else.

These conceptualizations represent some of the most recent developments in the use of topology to represent psychological situations. The developments have not been used in the study of children, although they readily can be. It is also interesting to note that these developments in the field of signed graphs do not have obvious implications in the representation of either the psychological environment or the person.

Number of minus signs in each

	Fig. 3-20a	Fig. 3-20b	Fig. 3-20c
ABCA	0	2	1
ABDA	0	2	1
ADCA	0	2	3
ABDCA	0	2	2
ABCDA	0	2	2
ADBCA	0	2	2
BCDB	0	2	1

Figure 3-21. Number of minus signs in each cycle of Figure 3-20.

PSYCHOLOGICAL ECOLOGY

We have seen that the psychological environment as it is described in Lewinian theory is not intended to picture the physical environment. Behavior is defined in terms of the change in the psychological environment, and may or may not occur through actual overt behavior in the external environment.

Lewin conducted experiments and used a variety of behavioral indicators to describe the content of the life space. He also set up experimental situations that were in the external world as far as the subject was concerned, and expected these situations to have predictable effects upon the psychological environment of the subject. He did not, however, make any of these operational definitions a formal part of the theory; instead, they were devised on an intuitive basis for the conduct of a particular experiment.

At the same time, Lewin was quite clear that the external world had important effects upon the life space. He spoke of these external events as belonging to the "alien hull" of the life space. The death of a child's mother is obviously an important event for the child. It is most difficult to see how in Lewin's theory the death is to be represented in the psychological environment, however. The experience is certainly unpleasant to the child, but it can hardly be pictured as a region with a negative valence. If the child denied the event, we might picture that behavior as withdrawal from an unpleasant region. But how should we describe mourning? Mourning itself could be thought of as a region that the child entered and eventually left, but how could the relation of mourning to the death of the mother be presented?

Lewin and his followers have never satisfactorily solved this problem, but curiously enough they have been more active than any other group in trying to describe the environment of the individual in psychologically relevant terms.

One factor that has led Lewinians to analyze the individual's environment is their conviction that the causes of behavior can be found in the present situation. Thus, they are led to analyze a conflict situation, a cheating situation, a choice of easy or difficult goals. More than any other important theoretician, Lewin attempted to assess the full psychological impact of the experimental situation, rather than to consider it merely the carrier of the specific variable he was investigating. For example, the experiments on the resumption of interrupted tasks were primarily designed to show the persistence of tension in a region if the goal were not reached; when the experiments were performed, however, Lewin and his students looked at the experimental situation as a whole and found, naturally enough, that interruption was not the sole determinant of resumption of an activity. For example, the structure of the task, either having a definite goal or being an endless sequence of actions, made a big difference in whether or not it was resumed. So Lewin asked, "What is the situation—psychologically speaking—at the moment of resumption?" This question, "What is the situation?" is one of the characteristic marks of Lewinian experimentation.

If one asks this question, "What is the situation—psychologically speaking?" not about a particular experimental situation but about the person's total environment, one is approaching the field of psychological ecology. Lewin was concerned with the question, but two of his followers, Barker and Wright (1951, 1955), have carried out the most extensive studies in the field.

In the general field of biology, ecology is an important subject. It deals with the total environment of the organism and describes that environment in terms that are relevant for the organism. For example, the adequacy of the food supply is an ecological fact. Obviously, species tend to survive where there are sufficient food supplies, and some species migrate to richer environments or move around until they find an adequate one. The existence and density of natural enemies is another ecological fact. Here we can illustrate the interdependence of ecological facts. The threat posed by a natural enemy is a function not only of the numbers of that enemy, but also of the numbers of the species itself. Natural enemies may keep the population of deer down to where there is enough winter feed for it and thus may actually improve the probability that the species will survive in the region. Or to take another example, the coexistence of other food supply for the enemy may make real differences. There might not, for example, be enough deer in a region to provide an adequate food supply for wolves, but if there are plenty of rabbits, then the wolves would survive by eating rabbits and so pose a more serious threat to the deer population.

This sort of analysis of the environment of human individuals is most important, although it is not, of course, primarily oriented toward questions of survival. In psychological ecology we still ask elementary questions comparable to "How many rabbits does a fox kill in a winter?" Barker and Wright were interested in questions such as the following: How many of a child's interpersonal contacts with adults are friendly? How many are dominated by adults? How many are frustrating to the child's own goals? Questions might also be directed to many other topics, such as length of contact. In some homes, there is almost never a parent-child conversation that deals with one topic for longer than a minute or two, yet such children are expected to engage in sustained attention and participation for perhaps ten minutes when they enter school.

In behavioral science we need many facts about the environments of individuals, but one of the problems is to discover how to organize our descriptions of environment. In the work of Lewin and his students we find several suggestions about this problem.

In his work on the modification of food habits during World War II, Lewin (1945) found that the homemaker played a role of gate-keeper in feeding her family. By and large, people eat whatever is put on the table; the absence of new varieties of food does not stem primarily from the refusal of people to eat them if they are served, but rather from the fact that they are not served. In the description of the environment, therefore, one phenomenon is a selective gatekeeper or filter, which determines what sorts of situations the individual is confronted with. It is obvious that the parent is a gatekeeper of the child's environment. He provides some kinds of experiences, allows others, and refuses admission to some. This suggests the obvious fact that the parent is crucial in the child's environment, but it further suggests a whole program of research in which the parent's values, or anxieties, or personal moods are correlated with large sectors of the child's environment.

A second description of the environment of the children in a group emerged from the study of autocratic and democratic atmospheres (White & Lippitt, 1960). In this experiment groups of school-age children were studied under three types of leadership: autocratic, democratic, and laissez-faire. The leaders in each of the three types of leadership roles were carefully instructed in the principles of how to behave. Figure 3-22 shows the three sets of instructions.

Observers were present in each of the club meetings and recorded the behavior of the leader and all the members. The behavior of the leaders differed markedly in the three types of leadership, not only in the ways determined by the instructions, but in other ways as well. For example, the autocratic leader interrupted activity more than the democratic leader.

Group atmosphere is an ecological variable characteristic not of a particular situation, but of a whole environment. Whenever there was a task to be done, the autocratic leader behaved in a characteristic fashion although the details of his behavior varied from one situation to another. This sort of an atmosphere variable could be used to describe prevailing characteristics of the environment and might be de-

Laissez-faire	Authoritarian	Democratic
1. Complete freedom for group or individual decision without any leader participation.	All determination of policy by the leader.	All policies a matter of group discussion and decision, encouraged and assisted by leader.
2. Various materials supplied by leader, who made it clear that he would supply information when asked. He took no other part in work discussions.	Techniques and activity steps dictated by the authority, one at a time, so that future steps were always uncertain to a large degree.	Activity perspective gained during first discussion period. General steps to group goal sketched, and where technical advice was needed the leader suggested two or three alternative procedures from which choice could be made.
3. Complete nonparticipation by the leader.	The leader usually dictated the particular work task and work companions of each member.	The members were free to work with whomever they chose and the division of tasks was left to the group.
4. Very infrequent comments on member activities unless questioned, and no attempt to participate or interfere in the course of events.	The denominator was "personal" in his praise and criticism of the work of each member, but remained aloof from active participation except when demonstrating. He was friendly or impersonal rather than hostile.	The leader was "objective" or "fact-minded" in his praise and criticism and tried to be a regular group member in spirit without doing too much of the work.

Figure 3-22. Criteria for Diagnosing a Laissez faire, an authoritarian, and a Democratic Atmosphere. (Ronald Lippitt and Ralph K. White, "The Social Climate of Children's Groups," in R. G. Barker, J. Kounin and H. F. Wright (eds.), *Child Behavior and Development*, McGraw-Hill, New York, 1943.)

fined by the regular occurrence of symptomatic behaviors in key situations.

Still another environmental variable appeared in the study of Barker, Dembo, and Lewin on frustration and regression (1941). In that experiment children were allowed to play in a pleasant room full of toys, and were then removed to another room with less inviting toys. The nice room was still visible to them through a chickenwire fence separating the two areas. Needless to say, the children were frustrated by being shut off from the more attractive toys, and most of them spent a good deal of time trying to get into the nice room. They asked the experimenter, tried the door, etc.

Not all of the time was spent, however, in trying to reach the pleasant toys. The children also played with the available toys. The investigators distinguished two sorts of play with the toys. One was called secondary play and was marked by the child's looking at the forbidden region or otherwise paying attention to it even while he played with the available toys. As Lewin described it, the children were in an overlapping situation, behaving in two different environments at the same time.

As would be expected, their half-hearted play was not very constructive or imaginative. Some of the children also showed a period of primary play, during which they gave no behavioral signs that they were concerned about the frustrating situation, and seemed absorbed in playing with the available toys. The observers judged that they did not manifest frustration as part of their psychological environment at that time, yet even during these periods the children were less constructive and imaginative than they had been during the control session before the pleasant toys were first revealed to them. How was this effect of the situation to be described? It apparently did not affect behavior in terms of producing any goal-directed activity or even any evidence of awareness of the frustration. Nevertheless, constructiveness was reduced.

Here we have experimental evidence for an important hypothesis: frustrations in the child's background may have consequences for his behavior even if he is unaware of the frustration. Barker, Dembo, and Lewin called this a *background of frustration*. This was not represented in the life space as a particular region, but as a sort of shadow falling on the whole life space and producing general effects. As a theoretical explanation this leaves much to be desired, but nevertheless the general concept is important. If we are to describe the child's environment, we must describe such background properties of the environment as may affect behavior without producing any signs of direct behavioral response.

Barker and Wright's Description of the Psychological Environment

By far the most ambitious attempt to describe the psychological environments of children has been carried out by Barker and Wright.

They have devised several sorts of techniques and have introduced some new concepts.

One of their tools is a behavior record. They have recorded in great detail a child's behavior and experiences over an entire day. One of their objectives in doing this was to sample behavior at all hours from first arising until retiring. Such a record can and does serve as a tool for describing the child. Barker and Wright, however, wanted to use it primarily to describe the environment as it impinged upon the child.

The running behavior record is first divided into *episodes,* viewed by Barker and Wright as the units of description. An episode is a behavior sequence during which the child has the same immediate goal. If uninterrupted, it ends when the child reaches the goal, but it may be broken off by some other influence which establishes a different goal, as when a mother calls her child to lunch in the middle of his changing a bicycle tire.

These episodes are then described in terms of a number of categories. For example, an episode may be classified according to the number and kind of associates the child had during the episode. It may also be described as self-initiated or as externally initiated (like being called to lunch). It may be described as gratifying or frustrating, according to whether the child reached his goal or was prevented from attaining it. It may be classified according to whether the associates of the child bossed him, flattered him, asked his advice, hurt him, etc.

Assuming that a representative sample of episodes has been observed, one may then make such statements as: John's goal-directed behavior was blocked in 15% of the episodes, reached in 65%, and shifted of John's own accord in 20%. These statements are data describing John's psychological environment. For Henry the comparable figures may be 25% blocked, 50% attained, and 25% shifted. These data raise useful questions, such as, it Henry's environment more frustrating or is Henry less effective in meeting difficulties? The resolution of such questions demands further information, but the *psychological environment* of Henry contains more blocking of his goal-directed activities than does John's.

These studies produce data which are important for building a science of human behavior; often the facts do not bear out our presuppositions. For example, Barker and Wright found that the environment of a boy with a congenital heart defect contained less blocking of goals than one of a roughly comparable normal child.

Another type of description of the environment is based upon an analysis of the people and objects involved in the various episodes of the child's behavior record. It might well be that the portrait of its first principal that hangs in the entrance hall of the child's school never enters into the child's behavior record; as far as we can tell, it has no influence upon his behavior and therefore does not exist as an object in his life space. On the other hand, flat rocks that skip well when thrown over the surface of a pond may be an important set of behavior objects for the child, but may be of no significance to an adult. Thus, from a behavior record we can map the objects that influence the child's activity and measure the prominence of such objects in the sense of the times they enter into episodes of behavior.

A third concept used by Barker and Wright to describe the child's environment is *behavior setting*. A behavior setting is some situation or set of situations which prescribes to some degree the behavior of any person who finds himself in that setting. A setting may be a geographically segregated region like a street crossing with a traffic light, or may be a temporally separate situation like Christmas. Often it involves both spatial and temporal aspects like the church on Sunday morning, which requires different behavior than any place else on Sunday, and also demands different behavior than other times in the week.

For Barker and Wright behavior settings have several distinct properties. First, they are perceptually segregated from one another; they are times and places that people see as distinct. Second, they are regions in the Lewinian sense that one may enter and leave. Third, associated with each setting are certain constraints on behavior which operate on each person who enters the setting. People do not yell, discuss business, drink cocktails, or kiss passionately at a funeral service. Not every setting has such rigid restraints as a funeral service, but every setting has some restrictions on some behavior and provides special opportunities for other sorts of behavior. A grocery store, for example, provides an opportunity to buy dill pickles which does not occur in most other settings in a community.

These criteria are clear, but in actual practice many problems arise in arriving at a list of the behavior settings in a community. For example, is every street corner with a traffic light a separate setting or are they all parts of the same one? How about two grocery stores? Is a drug store the same setting for a man who comes to buy medicine, a couple who come for a coke date, and a ten-year-old who comes to read comic books? Should the prescription counter and the soda fountain be different settings? Suppose they were in neighboring stores; would that make them different? Can we say that an infant who conforms to none of the restraints and takes advantage of none of the opportunities really "enters" a setting? Is it part of his environment?

These are very knotty problems, and have probably not yet been well solved. Barker and Wright have described a set of criteria for measuring the independence of two settings, however. One many choose how finely or how grossly one wishes to define settings. Two settings are more dependent to the extent that:

1. the same people enter both settings.
2. the same power figures or leaders are active in both settings.
3. both settings use the same space.
4. both settings occur at the same time or close together in time.
5. the same objects and equipment are used in both settings.
6. the same action units span the two settings.
7. the same behavior mechanisms occur in both settings.

Barker and Wright devised rating scales for each of these criteria and thus could estimate the degree of dependence between two settings. On their particular scales a value of 21 was taken as the criterion that two settings were independent. Thus, they speak of the K 21 level of independence. To illustrate concretely, it turned out that the academic programs of the first and second grade were considered two settings because the K values for the pair was 21. The music programs of the first and second grades were more dependent, perhaps because the same music teacher functioned in both, and so these programs did not reach the K 21 criterion of independence.

Once the settings are described, Barker and Wright want to record the extent to which various people participate in the setting—or "penetrate" it, in their language. There are six levels of penetration: (1) onlooker; (2) audience or invited guest; (3) member of the group; (4) active functionary; (5) joint leader; and (6) single leader. Such a measure of participation permits the authors to describe the average penetration of settings of different age levels of children, etc., in communities of different sizes. They can also use the penetration to distinguish between accessible and inaccessible settings.

It is not possible to review all the variables recorded in Barker and Wright's description of the small midwestern town they chose as a psychological environment. The examples we have cited illustrate the methods and strategies employed and give some picture of the kind of description to which Barker and Wright aspire. It is not clear yet how these concepts fit with many sociological concepts such as custom, role, status, etc., that resemble them. Neither is it to be expected that these variables will be Barker and Wright's last word on the description of the environment. Nevertheless, their research indicates a new sort of investigation for social psychology and represents one of the fruits of Lewin's interest in psychological ecology.

FOUR

Evaluation and critique
of field theory

FIELD THEORY IS BEWILDERING and perplexing because of its curious tendency to be both exceedingly formal and very loose at the same time. Lewin's explicit statements about the structure of a theory, his recognition of the role of operational definitions in a theory, his use of symbolic formulas, his employment of topology, and his mathematical creativity have all led to the expectation that field theory would be constructed in accordance with the general description of scientific theory discussed in Chapter 2.

However, Lewinian theory is not like that. It is loose; as a formal theory it contains almost no operational definitions, and even the conceptual structure is not rigorous. It is probably fair to say that Lewin was more interested in using his theory to obtain an increased understanding of human behavior than in using it to develop a sound theoretical explanation of human behavior. He viewed a theory as an instrument rather than as an object of affection, but at the same time held a deep conviction that science had to progress through theory building. The purpose of this chapter is to appraise the advantages and disadvantages of this attitude of mind about theories and theory construction.

Lack of Operational Definitions

The commonest criticism of field theory is its lack of operational definitions. It is apparent that the theory lacks coordinating definitions which tie the concepts to the observable situation or to observable behavior; in actual experiments these links are supplied through intuition and common sense. This characteristic of field theory appears not only in experiments conducted by Lewin himself, but also in the many experiments carried on by his colleagues and students since his death.

It is easy to view this lack of operational definitions as a fatal defect of the theory and to dismiss the theory on that basis. One must recognize, however, that neither Lewin nor his followers have been unaware of this weakness of the theory. If it is a fatal defect it is an error of judgment, not an oversight or a lack of appreciation of the role of operational definitions.

We must ask how fruitful it is to invest years in building up a formal system of concepts related by definitions and laws, expecting that the system will fit into a complete theory once the coordinating definitions have been properly designed? It is a little like prefabricating the middle section of a bridge before one knows how to attach it to solid ground at either end, because one expects that it will fit into place *in toto* once the problem of how to build the abutments and approaches has been solved.

The analogy is prejudicial to the fact. Although the fruitfulness of the strategy is certainly debatable, it is not obviously nonsense. To adopt such a strategy requires a deep faith that a good theory of human behavior can be constructed using such concepts as psychological environment, goals, need systems, and tension. This is exactly the faith that Lewin had; furthermore, he felt that first approximations to operational definitions were available even though they could not be spelled out in any final form.

Thus, Lewin defined the psychological environment as the sum of the factors that influenced behavior. He did not define it in terms of consciousness or the phenomenal world. Yet, Lewin must have believed (tacitly if not explicitly) that when a subject reported that he was frustrated by a problem, he was describing his psychological environment with some degree of accuracy. If this report was accompanied by other behavior, such as trying one possible solution after another and expressing more and more angry words, then a number of behavioral signs of frustration seemed to have converged on the interpretation that he was frustrated. Although no two subjects may have shown exactly the same symptoms of frustration, each showed a pattern of verbal and expressive behavior that was convincing to the experimenters. Lewin did not believe that he could formalize this diagnostic process as an operational procedure by which frustration could always be identified, but he was reasonably confident that it was being identified accurately in the particular case. He based his interpretation of the subject's report and behavior on common sense, or as we would say now, on an acceptance of naïve theory as a first approximation to the truth.

Lewin's approach fits together into a reasonable and defensible strategy. The theory is a restatement and refinement of naïve theory; in those areas still unexplored by careful investigation, naïve theory is generally accepted as a first approximation. To return to the bridge building analogy, assume that the construction of the whole bridge were being guided by a threadlike structure that crossed the stream but could not carry much weight. First one portion and then another of this gossamer bridge would be duplicated in steel but would also be changed and modified when it was made of more solid material. The middle part would be done first because the structure would seem clearer there, but it would be designed to fit as well as possible the vague preexisting structure that links the middle portion to the two banks of the stream.

The fruitfulness of this strategy rests primarily on the essential soundness of naïve theory: If it is a good guide to theory building, then the Lewinian strategy is reasonable; if naïve theory is inherently defective, Lewinian strategy is less likely to be the wise choice.

Even if one accepts the basic strategy, one still might quarrel with the sequence in which Lewin formulated his concepts. Perhaps the analysis of perception is the best place to begin, or perhaps Lewin should have spent his life studying individual motivation. These points of view may, of course, be true, but they rest upon personal taste and judgment. One may consider these choices within the freedom of the theory builder to tackle the problems in which he is interested and to which he thinks he can best contribute.

Contamination of Formal Theory by Common Sense

Besides lacking formal definitions which are coordinated to observable facts, the theory proposed by Lewin is not rigorously and tightly constructed even in its formalized portion. Lewin always experimented with concepts for a long time before incorporating them in a formal theory, and thus many notions in his writings have never been formalized. Furthermore, the formal theory itself leads to insoluble difficulties.

For example, the concept of "barrier" is well-established, and can be described as the impassable boundary between two neighboring regions. On the other hand, one definition of neighboring is the possibility of moving from one region to the other without intervening steps.

By this definition, a barrier makes the two regions unconnected, and Lewin at times described a barrier in these terms. However, when the difficulty in solving a problem was ignorance about what to do, Lewin tended to describe a barrier as a lack of connection between the region where the person was and the goal region. And, if the difficulty was an inability to do what was necessary to reach the goal, he tended to describe it as a barrier.

This is a good example of how common sense contaminates formal theory. It makes sense to distinguish between "not knowing what to do" and "knowing what to do but not being able to do it," because the two difficulties lead to different sorts of behavior, and probably represent psychologically different types of frustration. But Lewin's formal theory does not permit this distinction. In our concept of physical space, it is quite possible for two regions to be separated by only a small distance, despite the fact that a person would have to use a long detour to go from one to the other or might not have a path available to do so at all. This possibility depends upon a concept of distance that is independent of actual paths. The concept of barrier requires two different sorts of relations between regions, so that it is possible for them to be neighboring by one criterion and distant or even unconnected by another. The formal theory could be enlarged to encompass such a concept, but Lewin and his followers have not done so. Instead, they use barrier in its common-sense context with its unexplicated implications, alongside the formally refined notions of topological distance.

There are other similar examples to be found in Lewinian writings. The concept of "partly equal" directions discussed earlier is one (see p. 100). In most such examples, the problem can be traced to the difficulty in identifying the common-sense implications of the terms employed and the failure either to deal with them in a formal way or to renounce them clearly. These difficulties are not surprising. One of the hazards of reformulating and redefining everyday concepts is that they carry unintended connotations or actual denotations into formal theories and so cause logical difficulties. One argument used by those who would build a new theory from the bottom up is that these unintended confusions can be better avoided if we do not attempt to rework and refurbish naïve theory.

Lack of Systematic Construction

In addition to these specific difficulties in Lewinian theory, one is inclined to believe that the theory has been constructed in an unsystematic way. There seems something almost capricious in the way that concepts appear here and there rather disconnected from one another.

For example, the neighboring character of two regions in the person is investigated through experiments on substitute value and substitute valence, and on cosatiation. All three phenomena are steps in the direction of establishing operational definitions for the neighboring nature of regions, yet the relations among the three have not been carefully investigated to see whether they agree with one another in the study of structure.

A similar problem appears in the way in which the term *region* is coordinated with other terms in different parts of the theory. A region is sometimes coordinated with an activity, sometimes with a state, and sometimes with an event that happens to the person, yet in all these cases it is a part of the psychological environment. One is led to conceive of the environment as a continuous connected space surrounding the person. Apparently, however, the psychological environment cannot consist of a set of connected regions; instead, it must be viewed as a combination of qualitatively distinct sets of regions whose relation to one another is uninvestigated.

All these features of Lewinian theory contribute to the impression that it is discoordinated and loose. Upon first reading it appears to be a coherent theory, and the words in which it is couched convey that impression. However, closer investigation suggests that it is better characterized as a "style of investigation." Field theorists share a common approach to problems and much of the same terminology, but they have not exerted much effort to build a coherent total theory of a mechanism that governs human behavior. The contributions of field theory are piecemeal, although not necessarily less valuable for that reason. This feature also seems to stem from its naïve approach: Lewinian investigators often use some common-sense term as the starting point for research, without being too concerned about how the concepts will eventually fit others in the theory. They seem to have a faith that if individual problems are carefully investigated and analyzed, the working hypotheses will eventually fit together.

This opportunistic strategy is perfectly defensible, and if it were explicitly espoused, there would be no problem. It seems to cause difficulty only because field theory appears to be aiming for a single general theory and to claim at times that it is well on its way. Once the strategy of field theory is explicit, however, it is seen to be perfectly reasonable, though possibly more modest than at first appears.

Lack of Dispositional Variables

Field theory is primarily concerned with the immediate causal chain that results in action; the concepts of force and valence all are parts of the event sequence that leads to action. The theory is much less concerned with the dispositional variables that underlie behavior. Tension is one such variable, in so far as it is used to explain the maintenance of a motivating state from the time an intention is formed until it has been carried out. Some region in the person stays in tension after a task is interrupted and predisposes the person to think about the task and finish it when an opportunity arises. Although Lewinians hypothesize this, they do not hypothesize the way the mechanism works. For tension to be assigned dispositional properties, there must be some fuller description of the mechanism by which tension causes a valence in a region of the environment. The intention to mail a letter (conceptualized as tension in a region of the person) need not result in a positive valence nor in an actual force until the opportunity to mail the letter arises. The theory does not describe how this selection occurs.

More fundamental dispositional characteristics of the individual are embodied in the description of the cognitive structure of the environment, and of the structure of regions in the person. The environmental cognitive structure describes the individual's knowledge of his environment, but Lewinian theory contains no description of the way this knowledge is stored or the way in which the stored knowledge interacts with information from the situation to produce a particular cognitive structure.

The structure of the person embodies a number of dispositional features. The number of regions and the rigidity of boundaries are described as the "degree of differentiation"—and this is a dispositional variable that describes the maturity of the individual. The particular arrangement of regions in the person describes the activities which are substitutes, and the general pattern of simple dependence of activities. Whether this pattern is sufficiently constant to characterize important aspects of the individual's personality remains to be empirically established.

There are other possible dispositional variables such as anxiousness, generosity, tolerance of ambiguity, musical ability, or antisemitism that seem quite difficult to describe in the language of field theory. The manifestations of these traits can be described in Lewinian theory, but the traits themselves cannot. This is in contrast to most personality theories, which describe the trait but not its manifestation in behavior. In general, then, Lewinian theory is weak in its treatment of dispositional variables and in its handling of the problem of how latent potentialities of the individual are brought into overt behavior.

CONCRETE CAUSAL EXPLANATIONS

Lewin said, in the *Principles of Topological Psychology,* that "only what is concrete can have effects." He therefore limited the content of the life space to *facts*—observed or hypothetical—because facts are concrete. Another way of stating this position is to define a theory of behavior as a hypothetical sequence of events leading from the situation to the behavior. This insistence upon couching theory in terms of concrete facts and events is not unique with Lewin, but it does distinguish his theoretical point of view. It also has consequences for his theory and lies behind some of the central features of field theory.

In this section, therefore, the distinction between a *concrete causal explanation* and other sorts of theories will first be illustrated in the field of physics and then be translated into behavioral science. Certain features of Lewin's theory will be traced back to his convictions about concrete causal explanations.

Lewin (1951) used the graphic representation of the gas laws in physics as an example of what he did *not* mean by a field theoretical explanation. Let us look at this example to gain insight into the general distinction between concrete explanations and other kinds.

Suppose there is a *volume* of gas at a certain *temperature* and *pressure.* We learn in elementary physics that these properties are related by a set of laws called the *general gas law.* If the gas is closed up in a container so that its volume cannot change and is then heated, the pressure will increase. That is, pressure increases with temperature if the volume is held constant. If, on the other hand, the volume of gas is allowed to change in order to keep the pressure constant, the volume increases as the temperature increases. One way these laws can be represented is in the graph shown in Figure 4-1. The graph shows a number of curves, each of which relates pressure to volume. If pressure on a body of gas is high, it is compressed and its volume is small. As the pressure decreases, the gas expands to larger and larger volume. The exact curve that is followed depends upon the temperature. If the temperature is high, then curve t_4 describes how pressure and volume relate. If the temperature is lower, the t_1 curve predicts the pressure from the volume.

In this case pressure, temperature, and volume are represented geometrically. The curves of Figure 4-1 describe a set of laws that accurately predict the way that any of these three properties will change if the other two change. Do these gas laws then constitute a theory of the behavior of gases?

Lewin did not deny the extreme usefulness of the gas laws, but he

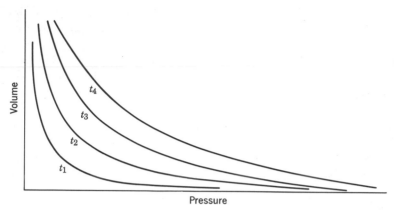

Figure 4-1. Graph showing relation of volume, pressure, and temperature.

did contend that they did not provide a theoretical explanation of the sort he valued. If not, what sort of theory did he want?

There is a concrete explanatory theory of the behavior of gases, the *molecular theory* of gases. According to this theory in its simplest form, a gas is composed of molecules in rapid motion. It is something like a jar full of bees all flying constantly at full speed. These molecules continuously collide with one another and with the walls of the container, and since there are billions of molecules in the container, many of them are hitting the sides of the container at the same instant, each exerting a small amount of force against the walls. The sum of these tiny forces constitutes the pressure that the gas exerts on the container. Since these molecules are distributed at random and are moving in random fashion, the number of them hitting any particular area of the wall is approximately equal to the number hitting any other area, and consequently the pressure is equal in all directions.

If the volume is suddenly decreased, the same number of molecules remain, but they are confined within a smaller area. They must be more crowded, and more of them must be colliding with the wall and one another at any instant. Thus, the pressure on the wall of the container will increase.

What happens if the temperature is changed? According to the theory, an increase in temperature increases the speed of each molecule. Thus, there are the same number of bees but they are flying faster. This will increase the number of collisions and the pressure on the wall of the container.

This molecular theory is an example of a concrete explanation of the behavior of gases, as distinct from the general gas laws. The two are completely compatible, but are quite different kinds of theories. In the geometry of Figure 4-1, the dimensions are pressure, temperature, and volume. In the space description in molecular theory, the dimensions are height, width, and depth. The molecules are concrete objects—essentially little balls as far as this oversimplified form of the theory is concerned. They are moving around in ordinary space, colliding, bouncing off walls, etc. The theory is a picture of what is actually happening in the container. It conjures up an image, whereas the geometric representation in Figure 4-1 is a purely mathematical formulation. Some people would consider the difference between the two as a distinction between description and explanation. The general gas laws *describe* how each property changes under the influence of other properties and permits accurate predictions. The molecular theory *explains* the gas laws.

Lewin wanted a concrete explanation of human behavior which was something like the molecular theory of gases. We shall see shortly how this connection makes real differences in his theory and research. But first let us pause to recognize that the distinction between such descriptions and concrete explanations is highly controversial.

The Argument against Concrete Models in Science

There are many scientists and philosophers of science who would deny that the molecular theory of gases represents any advance over the general gas laws. They contend that it accounts for no more, and predicts no better; they claim that it merely adds untested and useless surplus assumptions to the stark precision of the mathematical statements of the laws.

Furthermore, these people maintain that the scientist's desire for concrete pictures of the causal chain leading up to the events he tries to explain can generate serious trouble. The most striking example of this is in atomic physics where for years physicists tried to draw a picture of the atom that fitted their data. None of these physical models was satisfactory. However, once they were satisfied with purely mathematical expressions that predicted the observations, many of the previous problems disappeared. When scientists tried to conceive of an electron as a particle in the usual sense of the word, they faced the problem of explaining situations where it could be demonstrated that the particle went simultaneously through two slits in a plate. Modern physicists now feel they cannot attempt a picture of subatomic phenomena, and that mathematical equations are the only representations available.

Just because the search for concrete explanations is fruitless or even worse in physics does not mean that it is misleading in other fields. One can argue that the search for concrete causal mechanisms, even when it has led to postulation of such concepts as a "force of gravitation," has oftener than not been a stimulus to progress. "Chemical bonds" began as hypothetical constructs to permit a concrete causal explanation of chemical reactions, and the "gene" in the science of genetics was originally a hypothetical construct used to explain certain phenomena of inheritance, yet both concepts have been of great value in their fields.

We must not decide too hastily whether the search for concrete explanations in psychology is the broad highway of delusion or the narrow path to a better theory. Let us examine the problem more closely. MacCorquodale and Meehl (1948) draw a distinction between intervening variable and hypothetical construct. They believe the difference between the two is the *surplus meaning* of the hypothetical construct. By a *hypothetical construct,* they mean a scientific fiction such as force, gene, or bond that is invented to provide a possible concrete causal explanation of behavior. By an *intervening variable* they mean a concept whose only function is to reduce the data to a form in which their lawfulness is more readily expressed. Intervening variables have no surplus meaning. Like P, V, and T in the gas laws, they are variables that enter into laws that predict behavior. As MacCorquodale and Meehl point out, it is not necessary to draw on the surplus meaning of the hypothetical construct to arrive at a prediction.

This argument cannot be refuted as far as testing a theory is concerned. Once a theory is developed, its adequacy is determined by its predictions, and two theories making the same predictions are equivalent. But the argument is not necessarily valid if theory building is involved. The surplus meaning in a concrete causal hypothesis is frequently the part of the hypothesis that suggests the next experiment, because it has implications beyond the body of data it was devised to explain. On the other hand, the same surplus meaning may blind the scientist to other hypotheses that fit the data but not the tacit assumptions carried in the surplus meaning.

It is this fact that justifies the term surplus meaning. For example, there is a method for measuring the strength of motives called the obstruction box method. In this method, an animal is placed in a box on one side of an electric grid and some goal-like food is placed on the other side. The experimenter can vary the charge on the grid until it is strong enough to make the animal refuse to cross it.

A theory builder might use the construct *force* to explain such behavior and say that its strength toward the goal list pitted against the force away from the grid. If the second force is equal to or greater than the first, the animal refuses to cross the grid. If this is the sole function of force in the theory, it could be replaced by an intervening variable, *response strength*. The term force has properties like direction that are unused in explaining the behavior in the obstruction box. The direction is therefore part of the surplus meaning of forces; it adds nothing to the prediction and is dispensable. On the other hand, the fact that force has direction might suggest a further experiment that involves the direction of the response.

Some Examples of Concrete Theory in Psychology

Laying aside for the moment the question of whether it is wise to demand a concrete explanation, let us see what the consequences of such a position might be for psychological research.

One example of the two different approaches to a problem can be found in the study of children's abilities. Factor analysis of test scores approaches the problem by looking at the similarities and differences among scores on various tests. If two tests are found to be highly correlated so that children who do well on one test tend to do well on the other, this is evidence that the two tests are to some degree measuring the same ability. A set of five tests might have so much in common that a properly constructed pair of tests could convey as much information as the entire five, so that instead of five scores for each person, two scores do the job. These two scores are then called factor scores and are said to measure two primary abilities.

If there are good tests for each of these primary abilities it is possible to predict fairly accurately the score an individual will earn on any of a whole battery of other measures of performance that involve these primary abilities in varying degrees. Primary abilities identified for children include the following (Thurstone & Thurstone, 1946):

1. Verbal ability
2. Number ability
3. Perceptual speed
4. Rote memory
5. Inductive reasoning
6. Deductive reasoining
7. Word fluency
8. Ability to visualize objects in space

A child's failure in arithmetic might be predictable from his low number ability, low deductive reasoning ability, and poor rote memory. The question is, do these low abilities explain his poor performance in arithmetic?

Before attempting to explain, we must assert that the value of such primary mental abilities and their tests is no in question; for both practical and theoretical viewpoints they are useful. There is, however, considerable controversy about whether these primary abilities explain the child's performance on an arithmetic test. The search for primary abilities does not involve the description of any causal mechanism by which an ability influences performance. A child with high word-fluency is able to think of a long series of words that begin with the letter *s*, but if we ask by what sequence of events do the various words come to mind, the primary ability provides no answer.

It is important to note, however, that the facts about the primary ability do provide data which the theorist must take into account. If, for example, he wants to explain the child's high productivity of words beginning with *s* primarily in terms of the size of the child's vocabulary, the lack of high correlation between rote memory and word fluency will create difficulty.

A different analysis of arithmetic performance seems to lead toward a causal explanation. If long division is analyzed into a sequence of actions—division, multiplication, subtraction, etc.—then the final answer is seen as the result of a causal chain of events. The role of an error in multiplication is clear. This analysis is quite different from an analysis into primary mental abilites and seems to be more causal.

Lewin would certainly have preferred to analyze the performance of children on a long division problem in terms of the steps they needed to take, and how those steps had to be organized. One of the characteristic methods of the theorist searching for a concrete explanation is to take a certain behavior and to ask what series of events led to its occurrence. This causal chain of events might be partly observable, but some of the links in the chain might be hypothetical constructs. Once achieved, the concrete explanation provides a description of the process leading to the behavior. Lewin was demanding such theory when he wrote that, "only what is concrete can have effects."

Lewin is not the only theorist who searched for a concrete explanation of behavior in this sense of the term. Most of the theories described in this book are attempts to build a causal chain linking the various antecedents of behavior to the behavior itself, but Lewin was more explicit than most about this feature of his theory. We want to see how this faith in a concrete causal explanation leads to a number of important consequences for Lewinian research, but first we must discuss his meaning of the term "concrete."

The Metaphysical Status of Concepts

If one took the molecular theory of gases as an example of a concrete causal explanation, one might well ask what Lewin was doing with such concepts as *force, valence,* and *tension.* These are certainly not concrete facts like the moving molecules suggested by the molecular theory; they are not even hypothetically concrete facts. One might argue that if Lewin were really interested in a concrete causal explanation of behavior, he should have developed a physiological explanation of behavior because the only material causal chain of events leading from the situation to the behavior is through the sense organ to the brain to the motor nerves and muscles.

It is certainly true that one causal explanation of behavior might be a tracing of the chain of physiological events from the stimulus situation to the response of the organism, and some psychologists desiring concrete explanations have decided that a physiological explanation is the only true explanation of human behavior. Their belief is largely based upon the argument that the only concrete causal connection between the stimulus and the response is physiological. Lewin denied this, and all of the theorists represented in this volume would also deny that a causal explanation of behavior must be physiological.

Lewin directly discussed the nature of concepts such as *force* and *valence* (1951). He argued that the development of a science was largely a matter of changing its definition of what is real. The acceptance in physics of force as real was important to the development of the field. The velocity of a falling body can be predicted from an equation that involves only such terms as the mass of the two bodies, the distance between them, and the acceleration of the moving bodies. The term force can be eliminated mathematically, but not in physics; in the latter, it is given the same reality as mass, speed, and acceleration. In modern physics it is assumed that forces are propagated through space at some finite speed.

Lewin felt, therefore, that the introduction of similar hypothetical constructs in psychology was quite justifiable. He argued that to refuse reality status to psychological concepts such as intention, motivation, group atmosphere, and group goals blocked effective research on these topics. Such research has constantly to fight against the "nothing but" philosophy that says, for example, that group atmosphere is nothing but the actions of the leaders and the members of the group.

The people who argue that group action is nothing but the action of its members or that a symphony is nothing but the sound waves are, of course, trying to avoid mystical factors. This aim is quite important, because their opponents sometimes believe that a group goal is something over and above the behavior of the members. The concept of *mediation* used so much by Heider is important here. The group atmosphere is mediated through the activities of the members of the group just as the symphony is transmitted by means of sound waves. Furthermore, the symphony is entirely mediated through sound waves; there is no other means of mediation, and so, in a sense, the sound waves completely contain the symphony. If the complex sequence of pressure changes on the ear is the same for two different sounds, the sounds are indistinguishable. The sound waves contain all the information that reaches the individual.

This is not quite the same as saying that the symphony is nothing but the sound waves, because it has different effects. To say that the mood of a piece of music is mediated through the sound waves does not deny reality to the mood or discourage research on it, but to say that the mood is *nothing but* the sound waves suggests that the only worthwhile research is on the sound waves. In fact, we can reliably identify and quantitatively study many features of sound without being able to translate them into some property of the sound waves themselves. And, even if the representations of these features in the sound wave were known, they could still be effectively investigated in a direct manner. Similarly, it is quite effective to directly investigate meaning, style, and other features of written language, even though they are mediated through letters in a perfectly known way.

The same argument seems to apply to making psychology physiological. All human behavior is mediated through physiological mechanisms and it is extremely important to discover those mechanisms, but it is also quite defensible to build theories of behavior that are not couched in physiological language. There are dangers, to be sure. Dichotomies such as functional and organic mental disease, for example, suggest that functional disorders are not mediated through organic physiological processes. A genuine belief in such a distinction involves a mystical entity or ghost that arouses horror in the minds of some behavioristic psychologists.

SOME CONSEQUENCES OF LEWIN'S INSISTENCE ON CONCRETE CAUSAL EXPLANATION. One very important consequence of Lewin's belief in the concrete causal explanation of events is his insistence that the behavior of the individual is lawful. If there is a chain of events linked by deterministic relations which lead from the antecedents of behavior to the behavioral act, then the chain occurs in each individual person. That 75% or 95% of the cases behave as the theory predicts is merely a challenge to account for what happened in the other cases. Lewin deplored the tendency to take some statistical basis such as a probability of .01 as a criterion for proof of an hypothesis. If acceptance of such a criterion means that the investigator is satisfied when a large majority of individuals act according to his theory, yet is willing to accept the fact that others do not, then he is truly traitorous to the principle of determinism. We should therefore examine the extent to which Lewin's mistrust of statistical tests was a necessary consequence of the acceptance of a determinism. There are several circumstances under which one might be satisfied if some percentage of the individuals in a sample did not behave as predicted.

One such circumstance might be that the theory has some genuine randomness built into it. In several theories, including one from the Lewinian school, it is assumed that some of the events in the causal chain have a range of random variation. Cartwright and Festinger (1943), for example, were interested in predicting the time required for an individual to make a decision. Their basic prediction depends on the relative strengths of the forces in the direction of the alternatives. The theory states that the more nearly equal the forces, the longer it will take for the individual to reach a decision, yet that even if the forces are indeed equal the individual does make a decision eventually. Cartwright and Festinger assumed that the difference in the forces had to exceed some threshold value before the decision could be made. They also assumed that the strength of each force varied at random to a slight degree. Using these assumptions, the investigators were able to predict (1) the increased time needed to make a decision as the forces approached equality, (2) the subject's inclination to make a decision when the forces were roughly equal, and (3) the unpredictability of the direction of the decision in case of equality of forces and the occasional wrongness of predictions when the forces are only slightly different. Such randomness in the causal mechanism is not explained in their theory. It might be considered a genuine indeterminism, as in some laws of atomic physics, or it might merely be an admission that unknown minor factors might be influencing the strength of the force in an apparently random way.

It is not necessary for randomness to be expressly postulated as part of the causal mechanism, however. Much more frequently the theory specifies only some of the factors involved in the causation of the behavior, but the investigator recognizes that other uncontrolled factors may introduce error into the predictions. Although this degree of ignorance is typical for most studies of human behavior, it is a far from satisfactory state of affairs. If there are so many uncontrolled factors that their total effect is to appear as random variation, we are ignorant indeed.

A third sort of randomness may arise bacause of genuine individual differences among subjects in their susceptibility to the conditions under study. In the investigation of the effect of frustration upon constructiveness, for example, the children varied considerably in their preoccupation with trying to get into the room with the nicer toys (see p. 116). This variable was never predicted. Thus, the degree of effect of the frustration was not predicted, but any child who showed increased constructiveness in the free play following frustration disconfirmed the theory and was singled out for special study.

And so, there are various places in a concrete causal theory where elements of randomness may enter and prevent perfect predictability. On the other hand, such a theory is ordinarily more demanding than the sort of hypothesis so frequently encountered in psychological literature which states that the experimental and control groups are statistically different. Depending on the specificity of the theory, the investigator testing a genuine causal theory can usually maintain that certain results are impossible in any individual; in this sense, every individual is seen as showing lawfully predicted behavior.

SYSTEMATIC CAUSATION. Another implication of Lewin's assumption that a theory should hypothesize a concrete causal mechanism is his well-known distinction between systematic and historical causation (see p. 88). If one believes that the explanation of an event is a chain of causal events leading from antecedent conditions to the phenomenon itself, then this chain must be described up to the point where it dircctly influences the behavior in question. In othcr words, there can be no effect over a distance.

The practical consequence of such a belief upon an investigator is to make him search for the connection linking cause to effect. In many investigations he finds some indications of relationship. For example, there is a great deal of evidence suggesting that institutionalization of young children has detrimental effects on their personality development. Such studies have been valuable by pointing to an important practical problem and posing an interesting problem for the investigator. From the standpoint of theory building, however, these findings raise problems rather than solve them. By what chain of events does institutionalization produce its consequences? If the investigator takes the search for a causal explanation seriously, he will be led to study the causal chain linking institutionalization to child personality. Such investigations have been made, but unfortunately too many investigators have been satisfied merely to show the existence of differences between institutionalized children and children raised in individual homes.

This same belief in the necessity of tracing a causal chain from antecedent to consequence led Lewin to criticize Freudian theory as historical. Lewin did not maintain that past events in the individual's life had no bearing upon his present personality. Rather, he was expressing his conviction that an explanation that did not spell out the connecting links between the past experiences and their present effects was not satisfactory; and, he believed that the Freudian theory of the early 1930's did not specify the causal connection between childhood experience and adult personality. In the chapter on Freudian theory, we shall see to what extent this criticism is valid.

ARISTOTELIAN VERSUS GALILEAN THOUGHT MODELS. The conviction that concrete causal explanations were the proper objects of scientific theorizing also led Lewin to reject what he called Aristotelian thinking in favor of Galilean (see Chapter 3). In so-called Aristotelian theories, a class of individuals is said to have some property in common. For example, a group of individuals may show various sorts of hostile reactions to other people; on the basis of this similarity, these individuals might be categorized as aggressive, in distinction to another class of people who are different from them. If a group is said to have the trait of aggressiveness, it is easy to conclude that its members behave with hostility, fight a lot, attack one another, etc., *because* of their aggressiveness. Lewin rejected such explanations as Aristotelian and criticized many trait theories of personality on these grounds. He argued that the cause of fighting had to be found in the causal chain leading from the antecedent conditions to the fighting, and that to treat aggressiveness as the cause of fighting does not specify how or when the aggressive person fights. Furthermore, it attributes the fighting solely to the individual in the fight and leaves no place for the fighting to be instigated by the situation.

Although Lewin's criticism does not do justice to the trait theories of 1960, there is still real danger in making traits the causes of behavior. Nobody seriously believes that aggressive people are constantly fighting, attacking, criticizing, etc.; we assume that they do not manifest their aggressiveness all the time. It has, however, been common practice to count the instances of hostility and to use that frequency as a measure of aggressiveness. Thus, the child in the nursery school who is in the most fights is labeled the most aggressive in such studies, regardless of whether he was picked on unmercifully and finally fought back in desperation, whether he walked around with a chip on his shoulder and took offense at every remark and insult, or whether he attacked other children without provocation.

Lewin was not attacking a straw man with his criticism of Aristotelian thinking. On the other hand, he was not entirely fair to the trait point of view. Traits need not be defined in ways that ignore the situation. A trait like "irritability" can be defined as sensitivity to certain kinds of situational factors and as the tendency to respond to them with anger and hostility. Even defined in this way, though, irritability does not do more than name a certain class of responses to certain situational factors.

If one is searching for a concrete causal explanation of the hostile behavior, one must find some way of describing the personality structure of the irritable person so that stimuli that are not annoying to other people are annoyances to him, or so that annoyance instigates him to overt hostility whereas other people do not show their feelings. The trait of irritability must be described in conceptual terms that are consistent with a behavior theory, so that the manifestations of the trait may be logically derived. As we shall see presently, one of the serious gaps in Lewinian theory is its nearly total failure to conceptualize such personality variables.

THE NECESSITY FOR DESCRIBING THE TOTAL SITUATION. A final consequence of Lewin's insistence on concrete causal explanations is the preference for the treatment of the experimental data that such a viewpoint entails. The investigator ordinarily designs an experiment to study only one or at most a few variables. In most cases other variables are operating, but in the usual treatment of the experimental results these are handled in either of two ways. If they are considered to be powerful, disturbing variables, they are controlled experimentally. If they are not considered powerful, the sample for the experiment is chosen in random fashion so that these other variables do not bias the results; here the data are treated statistically to establish the significance of the experimental variable.

Lewin's philosophy led him to a much more detailed study of the records of the individuals in his experiment—to an almost clinical analysis of them. For example, in the experiment by Ovsiankina (1928) which studied the effect of interruption of a task upon its resumption, the primary intent was to see if the interruption would leave an unresolved tension to complete the activity. This tension would appear as a tendency for the person to complete the task even if there were no reason to do so or if completion were forbidden by the experimenter, Ovsiankina hypothesized. Once the concrete experiment was set up with specific tasks and specific interruptions, many other variables entered into the situation, however. In a sense, the task of the investigator changed. Instead of studying the relation between interruption and tension to complete the task, the investigator tried to explain why the people who resumed the task did so and why those who did not resume failed to do so. She also tried to explain why some tasks were resumed more frequently than others, and why one particular mode of interruption led to more resumption than others.

The basic hypothesis of the experiment touches on all of these problems, but other issues are also studied. Thus, some tasks seem to have a definite end, and others do not, and those with ends are resumed more reliably than those without them. The interruption can be made to occur in such a way that the subject is led to think that the experimenter expects resumption, or it can occur as if it were external and out of the control of the experimenter—like being called to the telephone. It can be made to occur so that the subject believes he has failed the task by not finishing it, or so that the subject thinks he has completed the essential features of the task but has not carried through all the details. If the investigator adopts the position that every individual's resumption or lack of it must be explained, he is led to a different analysis of the data than if he is satisfied with obtaining a statistically significant percentage of resumption in comparison with a control group.

Whether this determination to account for every case leads to a wise or unwise strategy is debatable. On the positive side, one can argue that it leads to a more detailed and carefully constructed theory. The importance of accessory factors is frequently discovered through the analysis of conflicting results when a second investigator attempts to confirm the findings of a first one. In all scientific research the resolution of conflicting findings has proved a fruitful source of new theoretical formulations. One can argue that the same advantages exist if the individual experimenter seriously attempts to analyze his own contrary cases.

On the negative side one can argue that such a detailed searching of the data is merely saving the theory by explaining away the negative findings through some *ad hoc* reasoning. If any of the cases fails to produce positive results one can find some individual factor that will explain it away. What one must do, according to this position, is to decide before accepting the hypothesis what is being tested and what criteria the results must meet. Then one does the experiment, applies the criteria, and notes the results.

This conflict has no clear resolution, but one of its features should be noted. The first argument is based on the fruitfulness of the strategy in *suggesting new theory*, but the second argument is based on the importance of rigor in *testing old theory*. One can, in principle, test the theory rigorously as advocated in the second argument, and then adopt the first strategy to search for new leads. The danger of over-interpreting data can be avoided if the result of the intensive interpretation of individual cases is to set up a new and more refined experiment to test the validity of the interpretations made in the analysis of the previous data. But this only partially resolves the conflict in strategies. The differences lie deep and perhaps cannot be reconciled. The wise use and wise avoidance of detailed analysis of the data of an experiment are part of the art of scientific research.

The search for concrete causal explanations thus led Lewin to a number of beliefs and research practices which are typical of the field theoretical position. These practices are not logically necessary consequences of a belief in causal explanations, but they fit the pattern of such research and lead to a better understanding of the special features of field theory.

GEOMETRIZATION

One of Lewin's strategies throughout his research and theory building was to employ a geometrical representation of psychological processes. He tried to describe the psychological environment geometrically, and to describe the person through a geometrical model. His students have successfully employed graph theory in describing certain sorts of group problems.

The idea of representing the individual's activities in his psychological environment by a cognitive map or cognitive picture is attractive to many other cognitive theorists. Everyday language contains many suggestions of metaphorical usage of geometrical language, for example, getting close to a decision or getting off the track in problem solving. These considerations lead to a question: Is it possible to represent all behavior as a movement from one point to another in a geometrical space? The purpose of this section is to assess the probable fruitfulness of this course.

In the case of physical locomotion, it is obvious that all actions can be represented as a movement from one point to another in physical space. The same representation can also include most, if not all, of the relevant information that determines which path the individual takes; one path is avoided because it leads to a bad result, another is taken because it leads to the individual's goal, and a third leads to the goal but involves danger along the way. Thus, the cognitive map not only represents the actions of the individual as movements along a path from one point to another, but also contains the relevant information that determines the action.

Advantages of Graph-Map Representation

There are three advantages of a map or graph representation of a problem if it can be made to fit the data.

First it is an efficient representation. Consider the map of railroad lines in a region (shown in Figure 4-2). It represents all possible trips that can be taken on the region's railroads. To duplicate that information by an inventory or listing of all the possible trips would quickly fill up the page, as seen in the partial list given in the legend. Furthermore, the list, once prepared, does not explicitly contain such information as, "there is no way to get from Knox Junction to Petersburg that does not go through Johnson City."

It is important to recognize that such a listing is possible and that it implicitly contains all the information shown in the map. No trip in the list starts at Knox Junction and ends at Petersburg without going through Johnson City. Therefore, it is not that the geometrical representation is required, but merely that it is efficient.

A second advantage of a geometrical representation is that it is part of a mathematical theory which is already organized and worked-out. Many additional problems and lines of investigation are likely to be suggested as soon as the proper representation is obtained.

Third, since we can think intuitively about motions in space we may understand the relations among a series of non-spatial movements if they are represented in the form of a graph. This can be easily illustrated. Suppose we had a two-by-two board with two checkers on it (see Figure 4-3a). Either checker can be moved to an adjacent square that is on the same horizontal or vertical line, but not on a diagonal. If the squares are labeled a, b, c, and d, all the possible positions of the checkers can be represented by pairs of letters, ab, ad, bc, etc. There are six possible positions shown in Figure 4-3b. The lines show the moves that can be made: from position ab one can get to ac or bd in one move, and there is a direct line from ab to ac and bd. The graph representation in Figure 4-3b immediately shows the structure of the moves. The positions ac and bd are in some sense central, because

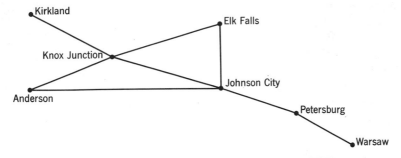

Figure 4-2. Railroad lines in a region. All possible trips that can be taken on the region's railroad.

1. There is direct route from:

    a. Kirkland to Knox Junction   e. Kirkland to Elk Falls

    b. Anderson to Knox Junction   f. Knox Junction to Johnson City

    c. Knox Junction to Elk Falls   g. Johnson City to Petersburg, and

    d. Anderson to Johnson City   h. Petersburg to Warsaw.

2. One can make a trip from:

    a. Kirkland to Elk Falls (via Knox J.)

    b. Kirkland to Johnson City (via Knox J.)

    c.   "   "   "   " (via Elk Falls)

    d.   "   "   "   " (via Knox J. and Elk Falls)

    e.   "   "   "   " (via Elk Falls and Knox J.)

    f.   "   "   "   " (Knox J. and Anderson)

    g. Kirkland to Anderson via Knox Junction,

    h.   "   "   "   " Elk Falls and Knox Junction

    i.   "   " Petersburg via Elk Falls and J. C.

    j.   "   "   "   " Knox J. and J. C.

    k.   "   "   "   " Elk Falls, Knox J., and J. C.

    l.   "   "   "   " Knox J., Elk Falls, and J. C.

    m.   "   "   "   " Knox J., Anderson, and J. C., and

    n.   "   "   "   " Elk Falls, Knox J., Anderson, and J. C.

either leads directly to all of the other four, and one of them must be an intermediary step for any of the other four to be changed into another of the four. Just why the graph representation lays bare the structure of the possibilities better than the rules themselves is not

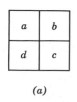

(a)

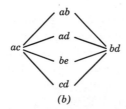

(b)

Figure 4-3. Graph representation of a simple game.

obvious; however, the graph does clearly indicate the structure and help one to understand the situation better.

Requirements for a Graph Representation

It might seem that any set of acts could be represented in the form of a graph. If we list all the possible conditions that can exist as we did in picturing the game in **Figure 4-3a,** we can draw lines between any two conditions that are directly reachable. For example, if we consider that the effect of any action is to change an antecedent situation into a consequent situation, we can represent the first situation by a point, the action by a line, and the consequent situation by a second point.

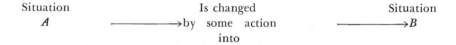

Situation   Is changed   Situation
   A   ——————→by   some   action   ——————→*B*
                                      into

One could thus imagine mapping how every situation could be connected to every other situation into which it might be transformed by some action or series of actions. Such a map would be possible and might be very useful, but in many circumstances might not be as useful as it seems. There are certain inherent assumptions in a linear graph that may or may not fit the demands of a psychological representation. These assumptions are the following:

1. The function of a line in a graph is to connect one point to another. It therefore best fits a psychological system in which actions are to be explained by their antecedents and consequences.
2. Locomotion is the traversing of one line in a graph. Since a person can be in only one spot at a time, all immediate consequences of an action must be represented by only one point. It therefore is difficult to separate the different consequences of a single action on on a graph.
3. Each line in a graph is independent of every other line. This implies, for example, that the path from *A* to *B* is available to any person at *A,* regardless of the path by which they reached *A*.

An examination of each of these assumptions will show how some behaviors are difficult to represent on a graph and others fit it perfectly; for example, instrumental acts fit the geometrical model excellently because they are carried out only because they lead to certain results, and, in the pure case, have no significance of their own. Means that lead from the same situation to the same result are equivalent, except for possible differences in efficiency.

There is much instrumental human behavior. However, several theories, including Lewin's, foster the idea that all behavior is instrumental and determined by its results, and therefore, that any way of efficiently representing means-end activity is useful. A graphic theoretical representation can be valuable in this way. We may ask, however, whether the result of an action is the only feature that should be represented in a theory, or whether there is behavior that is not instrumental, and whether it can be represented geometrically.

One sort of noninstrumental behavior is consummatory. In field theory, consummatory behavior is not viewed as a locomotion at all, but merely as occupation of a region. For many purposes this is a satisfactory representation, although in another sense consummatory behavior changes the situation and should be viewed as moving, not as standing still.

Even more difficult is the distinction between actions unreflected in their results. For example, suppose that, for ethical reasons, a car salesman told only the truth about his product and avoided any false claims. How is this ethical behavior to be represented? To begin with, it is clear that the truth is not a result of an action; we do not go from a nontruth region to a truth region when we tell the truth. We might argue that a lie is a locomotion into nontruth and that Honest John avoids all such paths. But where does such locomotion begin?

For some purposes we could represent "telling the truth" as one region, "telling a lie" as another, and could picture the person as choosing between the two. The two paths may have different consequences like a "guilty conscience" and "sense of virtue," which we could represent, and they also have different consequences like "customer has accurate knowledge" and "customer has misinformation." The problem here would be to show the dilemma of telling the truth and selling the car. The sequence of acts of selling the car involves making contact with the customer, demonstrating the car, offering him a price for his old car, telling him the features of the new car, etc. This sequence can be represented in graph form, but only some of the acts involve truth or falsehood. If a region of "telling the truth" is represented, the salesman goes out of it not only by telling a falsehood but also by doing something else for which truth is meaningless.

The problem in this and other situations is that there are certain tacit assumptions in any graphic representation. One assumption is that the use of the path between two points does not depend upon the path by which the first point is reached. The railroad map indicates that anyone who is at Johnson City can take the path to Knox Junction whether he arrived at Johnson City by way of Petersburg or Elk Falls. From a purely mathematical standpoint, Johnson City is not a town at all, but merely the point to which one can get from Petersburg and from Elk Falls, and from which one can get to Knox City. If, by some peculiar railroad rule, one cannot arrive at Johnson City on the train from Elk Falls and change to the train to Knox City, then in the mathematical representation the train from Elk Falls does not go to Johnson City at all—or else it goes to a different Johnson City from which there is no path to Knox City. It would not be satisfactory, however, to have two Johnson Cities on the railroad map. Johnson City on the map is not just a point on a pathway; it is a city with a name and an operational definition that is independent of its location on the railroad system.

We can give this concrete illustration a more general statement. We can say that when some concrete problem is given a graphic theoretical interpretation, both the points and the lines in the graph must have operational definitions. The points are not merely the ends of lines nor are the lines merely connections between the points. If it happens that any line in the graph exists only if one reaches its end point by one path rather than another, then the particular graphic interpretation of the concrete problem is inappropriate. Such situations often arise. For example, the consequences of a giving b some money may be entirely different, depending on whether the act was preceded by b having given a some money or by a having given b some money previously. An even clearer example is the fact that a injuring b may be quite different if it is in retaliation for a previous injury by b or if it is unprovoked. In still another example, suppose a problem can be solved only by performing act A and act B, but it makes no difference in what order they are performed; in this situation A leads to the goal only if B has already been performed.

The last example is not difficult to represent in graph theory. If act A represents unhooking the chain of the door and act B represents turning the latch, the door can be opened only if both are done. The situation can be represented by a graph similar to the one in Figure 4-4. Notice, however, that the act of unhooking the chain is represented by two different points and that there is nothing in the graphic theoretical representation to indicate that the two points represent the same action.

A similar set of problems arises if one wishes to show graphically that an action may have a number of different consequences. A single line in a graph cannot connect A with more than one other point B. If

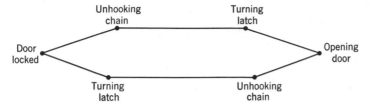

Figure 4-4. Graph representation of two alternative sequences of acts.

John has two tickets to a play, he can either go by himself and throw away the other, or give the other to his roommate. Each act has two consequences: One of them benefits himself and deprives his roommate; the other benefits himself and benefits his roommate. His roommate is likely to be angry if John goes by himself and does not use the other ticket. In this instance, both acts have one consequence in common: they both benefit John. They differ, however, in that one deprives his roommate and the other benefits him. If we tried to represent this situation in the form of a graph it could be done as in Figure 4-5. But notice that there is no indication that the two acts have one consequence in common and differ in one respect.

Another sort of graphical picture, as in Figure 4-6, seems reasonable, but when we use it we must introduce the notion that performing an act may result in following two pathways simultaneously. One assumption in these geometrical pictures is that the person is only at one place at a time. Furthermore, another difficulty arises in the second attempt to picture the situation. The lines to points A, B, C, and D are actions, but the lines beyond the points are consequences that are entailed by reaching the point. Thus, the solid lines and dotted lines mean two different things.

To what does this discussion lead? First, it illustrates some of the ways that a graphic theoretical interpretation of concrete problems

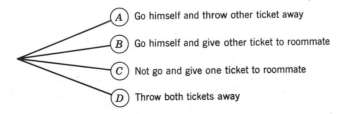

Figure 4-5. Graph representation of a social action.

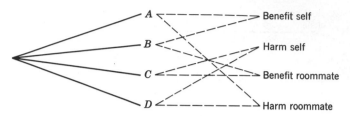

Figure 4-6. An alternative representation to Figure 4-5.

might be made and it shows some of the advantages of such an interpretation. Second, it indicates some of the problems which may arise.
In a map of physical locomotion, such as the railroad map, few such
difficulties are encountered. Each point is a real town and each line is
an actual railroad. When two people reach the same town by different
routes, they arrive at the same physical city and follow distinctively
different railroad tracks. In physical locomotion, the only consequence
of following a path is to get to its end. The problem of multiple consequences of an action does not arise; neither does the situation of a person performing acts to achieve a goal. In other words, a railroad system
in many ways excellently fits the properties of the graph. The movement of messages around a group is almost as perfect a fit. In both
representations, all the possibilities and all the possible actions and
their consequences are neatly and efficiently represented by a graph.

This does not imply that representation of other human behavior by
means of graphs is not useful. It is not necessary to be able to represent
all the psychologically interesting features of a situation on graphs for
them to be useful in representing some features. A graph need not be
considered a mathematical interpretation or a picture, however, in the
sense that a railroad map represents the railroad.

Finally, it is not essential for a theory to be couched in geometrical
terms. The value of a geometrical representation is partly its efficiency,
but it may not always be efficient. A railroad map is efficient, but for
some sorts of cognitive representations verbal description may be better. The following might be a verbal description of some of the relevant factors in a behavioral action:

"If he thinks I hurt him intentionally he will be angry, but if he thinks it was
entirely an accident he will not be angry or punish me. If it were deliberate,
I would know that I had hurt him, but if it were accidental I might know or
might not know that I had hurt him. If I pretend that I don't even realize that
he was hurt, then he will think it was accidental. So that is what I will do."

This reasoning is not difficult to understand and could almost be reduced to a set of theorems. However, it would be difficult indeed to picture this complex of factors and reasons in an efficient graphic theoretical representation that would explain the behavior as effectively as the verbal description does.

In summary, therefore, Lewin's assumption that topology was the appropriate language for describing human behavior seems only partly justified. Topology can indeed be very useful, but if it should restrict field theoretical explanations, the field theoretical positions will find it difficult to deal with certain sorts of problems.

FINAL SUMMARY

Perhaps field theory can best be summarized by trying to identify its recurrent themes and values.

COMMON-SENSE INTUITIVE BASIS. Its common-sense roots in naïve theory are apparent at many points: The concepts themselves are naïvely sensible; the willingness to dispense with formal operational definitions implies a trust in common sense to fill in the gaps; and the search for concrete causal explanations is consistent with a naïve notion of the nature of causality and determinism.

GRADUALISM IN FORMALIZING. Although there is naïvete in field theory, its lack of formal definition is largely intentional and is based upon a real mistrust of formalism in psychology. This seems hard to believe in the light of the proliferation of formulas in many Lewinian writings and the development of new mathematical systems, yet field theory has also resisted rigid definitions, and its proponents have a real tolerance for ambiguity until the appropriate formal conceptualization arrives.

EMPHASIS ON THEORY CONSTRUCTION RATHER THAN THEORY TESTING. It seems possible that the real basis for this resistance to formalization lies in the conviction that the theory should remain open to change and development. This is more than merely being open-minded; it is the building of a theory whose constructs have surplus meaning which lead on to new experiments and new investigation. Such theories are forever incomplete, but also stimulating.

NEGLECT OF OPERATIONAL DEFINITIONS. This same orientation toward theory construction rather than theory testing can also explain the neglect of operational definitions by theorists who know better.

Making a theory operational most clearly limits its freedom to change and grow; it does not necessarily do so, however, and field theory can be quite properly criticized for its lack of empirical definitions. Nevertheless, the preference for a looser, more intuitive coordination of concepts over observable data is understandable.

SEARCH FOR CONCRETE CAUSAL EXPLANATIONS. The previous themes in field theory are quite general, perhaps tacit, assumptions and unformalized values. The search for concrete causal explanations is, however, completely explicit. We have seen how it is consistent with a number of special features of Lewinian theory, namely:

a. The assumption of lawfulness in the individual case.
b. The emphasis given to systematic causation.
c. The denial of trait psychology.
d. The emphasis upon description of the total situation.

GEOMETRIZATION. Geometrization is also an obvious and explicit feature of field theory. The possibility of a graphic theoretical representation of all human behavior has been examined and found to be excellently suited to some problems but inherently unsuited to others. It has so many attractive features when it is suitable that it should not be discarded, but there is a danger that a too-complete dependence on graphic theoretical representations may be stultifying.

In sum, field theory represents a strategy of theory building which is not popular among rigorous, scientific psychologists and contains serious dangers of bias and unsoundness, but which may, in careful hands, have real advantages. As a strategy of research, it has been fruitful and promises to be viable; as a theory, it contains serious weakness but it does not purport to be more than a promissory note that a sound theory along its general lines will eventually be delivered. Only the future can tell.

JEAN PIAGET

The Theory
of Jean Piaget

FIVE

Piaget's fundamental concepts
and strategy of research

PROFESSOR JEAN PIAGET of the University of Geneva is doubtless the
century's most prolific writer and theorist on the development of the
child. Born in 1896, Piaget received his doctorate in biological science
in 1918. Even at that time he was interested in developmental processes, however. Out of his experiences in testing and studying the reasoning process in children he developed his first research on developmental psychology, published in 1921. He was then offered the
position of Director of Studies at the Institut J. J. Rousseau in
Geneva; he has held that position ever since. Piaget also holds the
principal post at the Center of Genetic Epistemology at Geneva. Under his direction, volume after volume of empirical investigations and
theoretical discusson has emeiged, many of them supporting findings
that were not only original, but almost too surprising to be believable.

A flurry of interest in his work appeared in the United States in the
years around 1930; then interest died for some twenty years before re-
viving actively about 1955. At present, there are many research efforts
stimulated by his theoretical ideas or his thought-provoking empirical
discoveries.

In discussing Piaget's theory, we shall first introduce some of the
basic concepts and their background, and then review his formulation
of the development of the child, proceeding from infancy to adolescence. In the final chapter of this section, we shall present a more critical review of his research and theory.

171

BIOLOGICAL FRAMEWORK

Piaget's approach to the problems of psychology reflects his background of biological training. This does not mean that he searches for physiological explanations of human behavior, however. In fact, he seems quite unconcerned in his writings with the possible physiological basis of the psychological mechanisms that he hypothesizes. His biological training reveals itself in a different way.

One of the central interests of biology is the explanation of the adaptiveness and development of biological structures. It is both apparent and amazing to a naturalist how the various species of fauna and flora are so well fitted to meet the environmental demands of their habitats and to exploit the resources of those habitats. Most intriguing of all is the way the adaptive structures often develop from the most unlikely material. For example, the curiously shaped parts of our bodies that we call our ears are quite important in helping us locate the direction from which sound emanates. We know they developed through evolution from one of the gill arches of fish. This ingenious use of a structure having one function for quite another purpose after the original function has become obsolete certainly seems to be intelligent problem solving. A biologist must ask, how can such intelligent adaption occur? A biologist turned psychologist is, by his experience, sensitized to the existence of similar sorts of adaptive mechanisms in human beings.

Biologists are also impressed by the complexly patterned interrelationships among the flora, fauna, and resources of a region. It seems as if there were some sort of pressure for a species to develop to fill every niche in the environment which might support life. A striking example of this tendency is to be found in the comparison of the animal life of Australia and other countries. Australia has a large number of *marsupial* animals, those like opossums and the kangaroos, who give birth to living young in a very immature stage and raise them in external pockets instead of internal uteri. On other continents, most species of marsupials have disappeared, but in Australia there are a large number of them, apparently because the continent was isolated from other large land masses at a relatively early period. At any rate, marsupials have evolved in Australia to resemble externally analogous species in other continents. There are marsupial herding animals of large size that live on grassy plains; tiny marsupials that burrow and feed upon roots like rats and mice; marsupials that resemble squirrels and dwell in trees; wolf-like marsupials that live solely on flesh; and marsupial moles and shrews. Nearly every group of mammals has its counterpart among the marsupials, which must, however, have evolved quite independently.

Such examples suggest that many biological structures are somehow stimulated into evolutionary changes that fit the life of an area to its geography and climate. Within this adaptation there are many balances and counterbalances, regulatory devices, and reactions to regulations. The supply of food roughly matches the supply of consumers; predators keep down the population that would overtax the food supply, etc. Piaget's view of the behavior of a human strongly resembles this picture of a complex, mutually regulatory system in equlibrium.

Piaget transfers two features of biological evolution to his theories of the development of the individual. One is the continuous fitting of old structures into new functions, and the development of new structures to fill old functions under changed circumstances. Development is solidly rooted in what already exists and displays a continuity with the past. At the same time, the structures change to fit new demands. Secondly, these adaptations do not develop in isolation. All of them form a coherent pattern so that the totality of biological life is adapted to its environment. Although each species is adapted to its environment, the particular nature of its adaptation is a function not of its own nature alone, but of the total system. In biology, this sort of dynamic equilibrium of the flora and fauna can be explained without violating the principle of natural science that teleological adaptation must be based upon mechanisms that operate according to causal laws.

Piaget applies this biological viewpoint to his theorizing about human behavior. He tries to identify the structures of each age level and to show how they adapt to environmental demands and to one another, and how they in return modify what the environment demands. For example, when the child walks, he is able to attain goals otherwise unattainable. At the same time, walking puts the child in a position to have goals that he would not have otherwise had. The interrelatedness of the entire pattern is illustrated by the fact that because people walk, our whole social environment is set up to require walking.

Furthermore, walking and other behavior patterns are interrelated. The pattern of holding an object in the hand is modified when the child must hold it while walking, and the walking behavior changes depending upon what the child is carrying—a sack of flour, a fishing pole, or a brimful bowl of soup.

The Schema

With this knowledge of the biological background, it is easier to understand some of Piaget's concepts. The first question is, "What in behavior corresponds to the biological structure that changes and adapts?" For Piaget, the behavioral parallel of structure in biology is the *schema* (Piaget, 1950). The schema may be simple and unitary or it may be a whole system, just as some structures, like the finger, are unitary and others, like the digestive system, are highly differentiated and distributed through the body.

In its simplest form, a schema can be nothing more than a reliable response to a stimulus; in practice, however, it is usually more complicated. The "sucking reflex," for example, is one of the earliest schemas. If it consisted of nothing more than a sucking response to stimulation on the inside of the mouth, this reflex would be a schema. In fact, it is more complicated than that. Even at birth, the response involves turning of the head when the cheek is stimulated, opening the mouth when the lips are touched, sucking when the inside of the mouth is stimulated, swallowing when the liquid reaches the throat. In the early weeks and months after birth, the sucking schema rapidly expands to include searching for the breast when the child is placed against the mother's body, sucking movements performed while the child watches his mother prepare to feed him, and nonnutritive thumb-sucking or sucking and chewing blocks and spoons. Thus, we see that the schema generally includes a variety of acts in many different circumstances, not just a response to a specific stimulus.

A schema is also different in another way from a response to a stimulus; it is *mobile;* in addition, the mobility of schemas increases with age. By mobility of a schema, Piaget means that it can be applied to a variety of objects, even objects never before encountered. Grasping, for example, is a schema that may function with bottles, blocks, beads, cloths, and noses—including both the child's own and other people's. The specific muscular movements involved differ for each object, but the term schema describes the action of grasping in its numerous forms as it occurs in varying circumstances.

Mobility also has a further connotation in Piaget's theory. The mobility of a schema increases when the action becomes instrumental, that is, when it is employed as a means for obtaining some goal, in addition to being an action that functions as an end in itself. The child's behavior is much more adaptable when he can grasp objects, pull them aside, and then release them in order to get at whatever lies behind them than when he can grasp objects only for the intrinsic satisfaction of grasping them.

All of the examples of schemas described thus far have involved overt actions. In Piaget's language, they are *sensorimotor* schemas. Piaget also uses the term to describe cognitive schemas like the number system, the concept of space, or the laws of logic. Piaget can include both cognitive schemas and sensorimotor schemas under the same conceptual label, because he believes that cognitive processes are best conceptualized as actions.

In his description of infancy, Piaget speaks of looking at an object and listening to a sound as actions that form a schema. Perhaps because of the tacit assumptions of naïve psychology, psychologists have sometimes viewed looking and listening as passive receptive processes: The child sees whatever is at the spot where his eyes are pointed. There is growing evidence that this naïve assumption is wrong, however. The schema of looking involves movement of the eyeballs, adaptive movements of the lens of the eye, and paying attention, even though we have no clear idea of what physiological processes this last action involves.

Piaget puts cognitive schemas and sensorimotor schemas into the same class for another reason. He believes that cognitive schemas derive from sensorimotor schemas by a process of internalization. The visual image is, for Piaget, an internalized form of looking. For him, thinking certainly involves internalized use of language, although he does not mean that thinking is nothing but subvocal speech (see p. 415 for further discussion of this problem). Conceptual thinking to him also involves such mental acts as adding, drawing implications, or judging distances. When these internal actions become integrated into a coherent logical system, they are considered logical operations, and the child who employs such systems of operations is said to be in the stage of concrete or formal operations. One of Piaget's important theoretical hypotheses describes the type of interrelationship that must exist among these acts for them to be called *operations* (see p. 186).

Thus, *schema* is a complex concept encompassing both overt motor behavior patterns and internalized thought processes. It includes simple, predictable responses practically at the reflex level, but also complex organizations like a person's understanding of the number system. Piaget argues that every schema has certain unitary properties which justify the assertion that all the actions involved in it are parts of a single schema. A further justification for using the label to describe varying kinds of psychological patterns stems from the belief that one can show developmentally how the primitive schemas of the neonate gradually broaden, merge with one another, differentiate, become internal, become more mobile, and acquire the organization that marks operational systems. Both the unity of the schema at any one time, and the continuity of one schema with a later one, warrant the use of a concept having such widely different meanings.

Adaptation: Assimilation and Accommodation

The schema represents the structure that adapts. *Assimilation* and *accommodation* describe the adaptation process; they are complementary processes (Piaget, 1952). Broadly speaking, assimilation describes the capability of the organism to handle new situations and new problems with its present stock of mechanisms; accommodation describes the process of change through which the organism becomes able to manage situations that are at first too difficult for it. Actually, however, the two processes are more complicated and interrelated than this description would indicate.

Assimilation is a term borrowed from biology. When a person eats food, it is digested and assimilated. The food is changed so that it becomes usable in the physiological functioning of the body; the digestive process does not ordinarily change to fit the demands of the food. If a new kind of food is introduced into the diet, though, the digestive process might actually change slightly to accommodate to it. It is obvious that in the course of evolutionary change, the digestive systems of different animals have accommodated to vastly different diets. Thus, assimilation means that the organism has adapted and can handle the situation presented to it; accommodation means that it must change in order to adapt.

This is an oversimplified picture of the process, however. One way in which the two processes are interrelated is that the organism must to some degree assimilate a new situation before it can accommodate to it. A new food must be edible and not fatally poisonous before accommodation can occur.

Consider a psychological example. The child who is eight months old may be unable to pick up a small object even though he can pick up slightly larger ones. To adapt to the demands of his environment, the child's grasping schema must accommodate to the demands of the tiny object. The gradual acquisition of the ability to pick up tiny objects can be described as an *accommodation* process. Once the ability has been acquired, the grasping schema can *assimilate* such tiny objects.

But this accommodation cannot begin unless the child tries to grasp such tiny objects, and he will not try to pick them up unless in some way they activate the grasping schema. Young infants do not try to pick up everything indiscriminately. At eight months of age, a rug on the floor does not elicit grasping; neither does the surface of the table. The object must in some sense appear to be graspable before the grasping schema is activated. This is the sense in which the grasping schema must assimilate the object to some degree before it can accommodate to the object's particular properties. Whether the grasping schema can assimilate the object sufficiently for the attempt to be made is a problem that would be called motivational in other theories. The child must want and try to grasp an object before he can learn to grasp it. Piaget includes both the motivational and learning aspects in his depiction of the accommodation process.

Let us put this relationship between motivation and ability in more general terms, using Piaget's technical language. The child is confronted by a new situation. How he responds to it depends on what schema is activated, and this is determined by whether the schema assimilates the relevant feature of the situation. If the situation is not completely assimilated by the schema, Piaget considers the experience to constitute a food or *aliment* for the schema. The term *aliment* implies that a situation is assimilated, but that the situation also demands some accommodation from the schema. In other words, it is a challenge. As a result of its interactions with such aliments, the schema gradually accommodates until it reaches an equilibrium with respect to them. At this point, the schema is capable of assimilating the situation completely. In the case of grasping a small pellet, this statement merely means that the child can grasp it effectively. At that point, however, the motivational aspect is also changed. Because the situation is no longer challenging, it does not activate the schema so readily and the child is not attracted by the intrinsic properties of the situation. He does not spend the rest of his life picking up small objects just because he can. The task is no longer motivating, precisely because it is performed so easily and effectively. Thus, the child is attracted to those tasks that are assimilable, but not completely so.

It is easy to see how this process brings about development and why the term aliment is not inappropriate. Those aspects of the situation that are assimilable but not completely assimilated evoke schemas and motivate the use of the schema until the situation has been mastered. Then the schema becomes available as a tool, but the activity is no longer intrinsically attractive. Instead, some novel feature of the situation that has now become assimilable captures the child's behavior and serves as food for his growth until he attains an equilibrium with respect to that problem. In this way, as he grows up, the child gradually becomes equilibrated to a broader and broader range of situations which he achieves through the acquisition of increasingly broad range, organized, and systematic schemas.

These are some of the consequences of Piaget's biological orientation. In biological studies, the problem of adaptation is prominent. In

Piaget's view of behavior, the schema is the element of structure that adapts. The process of adaptation is described by the twin concepts of assimilation and accommodation. These concepts not only show that the behavioral patterns are sometimes adequate to cope with a problem and other times are in need of modification to become effective, but also indicate that the individual is attracted to problems that stretch his adaptation, and that he "feeds" upon such challenges to grow in behavioral effectiveness.

PHILOSOPHICAL BACKGROUND OF PIAGET'S THEORIES

Piaget's developmental theories are influenced by his biological interests, but they are also part of his broader philosophical interests. This interest is concerned with the basis for our human conception of a real external world, the topic which is called *epistemology* in philosophy.

We have already touched upon this problem in our discussion of naïve psychology (see p. 13). In naïve theory, perception is supposed to provide an accurate representation of the external world in some automatic way that hardly needs explanation. As indicated in the critique of the theory (see p. 64), an accurate perception of the external world is really quite an achievement, considering the fact that it must be based solely upon the information entering through the sense organs.

The classical problem of epistemology is whether there is any justifiable basis for assuming that one's picture of the external world is accurate. We receive visual, auditory, and tactual information through separate channels of sensation; we all assume that these sense modalities are three channels to the same external world, not sources of information about three different external worlds. Is there any justification for such an assumption? When we turn away from an object, we no longer receive any sensations from it. Have we any sound evidence that the object does not disappear as soon as our perception of it disappears? Finally, we all assume that there are other individuals like us in the world—despite the fact that we look different to ourselves than others look to us. Not only do we assume these other people exist, but we make the even more daring assumption that they perceive the world the same way as we do, that their sensations of red are the same as our own. What is the justification for such beliefs? These are all problems of epistemology.

Philosophers have considered these problems for centuries. Some of the questions depend on knowledge about the young infant's view of the world. Does the baby see objects as located in a space? Does he have any sense that one experience follows another in time? The two major positions have been either that the child has some inborn predisposition to use space and time as the framework for his perceptions, or that his experiences with objects moving around and causing sensations in various modalities gradually teach him that there is an external world with the properties of space and time, and that his various sensory modalities all communicate information from the same external world. Various viewpoints of these developmental questions have generally had no empirical basis; instead, they have been argued in the absence of valid information.

Piaget set himself the task of investigating the problem empirically, in order to take a position on the problems of epistemology by actual investigation of the child's understanding of space, time, logic, and mathematics. He speaks of this endeavor as *genetic epistemology*. As we shall see, Piaget describes in great detail the development of the assumptions that the external world is stable, independent of the child's perceiving it, and that it is composed of permanent objects moving around in space and possibly changing their properties over time. During childhood, this basic epistemological assumption is conceptualized by the child, who also acquires the basic notions of logic and mathematics, coming to view these also as parts of reality. An important factor in the acquisition of these general notions and their conceptualizations is the fact that the child must adapt to other people and assume that they have much the same type of experience as he has.

THE CONCEPTS OF GROUP AND GROUPING

In his description of the course of development, Piaget places great emphasis upon the child's achievement of certain sets of interrelated intellectual actions which the psychologist says have the properties of a *group* or a *grouping* (Piaget, 1950). To understand what he is trying to say, we must first understand what a *group* is, because Piaget has taken this concept over from mathematics, where the term has a specific meaning. Second, we must see how the concept of *group* is closely related to the notion of equilibrium.

The Concept of Group

In mathematics, a *group* is a set of elements whose relations with one another have certain properties. These elements may be thought of as numbers, points, people, classes of objects, operations, or anything. Piaget usually considers the elements as certain logical or numerical operations, such as the operation of combining two classes of objects into a single class or the operation of adding two numbers.

Not every set of elements forms a *group*. For the set to be a *group* there must be some law of combination of elements. Ordinarily this operation is given the general label "multiplication," but it need not be similar to multiplication in arithmetic. If the elements of the *group* are operations or actions, the law of combination often performs the two actions in succession. For example, "adding 1" and "adding 2" combined together are equivalent to the operation of "adding 3." If we first add 1, then add 2, the result of the two actions is the same as if we had added 3.

Consider another example that will illustrate how nonquantitative elements and operations may be treated. Suppose we let the elements of a set be the permutations in the order of three beads: a red one, a yellow one, and a green one. If the original order of the three were *Y G R* and we rearranged the beads so that the new order were *G R Y,* we could describe the rearrangement in the following notation: *(RGY)* (see Figure 5-1). This notation can be translated into English as follows: The red bead goes to green's position, the green goes to yellow's position, and the yellow goes to where red was. A different permutation, *(RYG)*, means *R* goes to where *Y* was, *Y* goes to *G*'s position, and *G* goes to where *R* was. Notice that this operation can be carried out no matter what the original order of the beads was. Thus, if the original order were *R G Y*, then the same permutation *(RGY)* would rearrange the beads into the order *Y R G*. If a bead is left alone, that fact is represented by putting that letter into parentheses by itself. Thus, *(RG)(Y)* means that *R* goes to where *G* was and *G* goes to where *R* was, but *Y* stays in its same position.

There are six different possible permutations in this set: 1. *(RGY)* 2. *(RYG)* 3. *(RG)(Y)* 4. *(RY)(G)* 5. *(R)(GY)* 6. *(R)(G)(Y)*. Each of these can be written in several different ways. For example, *(GYR)* might appear at first to be different from any of the six, but if it is spelled out, it is identical to *(RGY)*. In each case *R* goes to *G*, *G* goes to *Y,* and *Y* goes to *R*.

The elements in the set are the six rearrangements listed. *The elements in this set are not the three colored beads, but the six possible rearrangements of them.* Now what is the law of combination of these elements? In this example it is the result of performing the two rearrangements in succession. Thus, *(RY)(G)* × *(RGY)* means that we first rearrange the three beads *(RY)(G)* and then perform the second

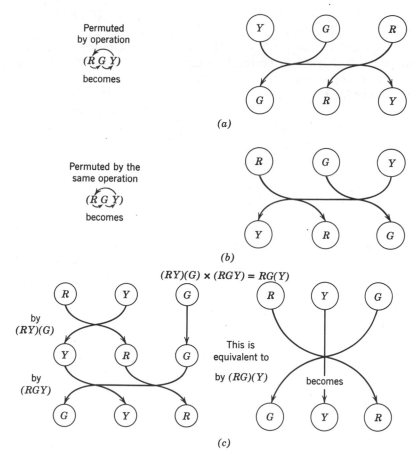

Figure 5-1. Illustrations of permutations and combinations of permutations.

rearrangement (RGY) on the result of the first. Let us illustrate this with a concrete case (see Figure 5-1c). Suppose the original order of the beads were $R\,Y\,G$. Rearranging them by the operation $(RY)\,(G)$ would result in the following order: $Y\,R\,G$. R and Y would change places and G would say where it was. Let us apply the second operation (RGY) to the beads. After the first operation they are $Y\,R\,G$. Now they become $G\,Y\,R$—R is where G was, G is where Y was, and Y is where R was.

As a result of the two operations, $R\,Y\,G$ first becomes $Y\,R\,G$ and then $G\,Y\,R$. Is there an operation that would accomplish the result of these two successive operations in a single step? Yes, $(RG)\,(Y)$ would change $R\,Y\,G$ into $G\,Y\,R$. Therefore, we can say that the two operations, $(RY)(G)$ followed by (RGY), are equivalent to $(RG)(Y)$, or in symbolic form $(RY)(G) \times (RGY) = (RG)(Y)$.

We can think of many other operations besides permutations of the order of beads that might be combined. In the life space of Lewinian theory, for example, we can think of the path from region A to region B being combined with the path from B to C to make the path from A to C. In this case, of course, some paths cannot be combined. One cannot combine the path from A to B with the path from M to N. We can also think of 120-degree, 240-degree, and 360-degree rotations of a wheel as operations that would be the elements of a set.

Thus far we have illustrated the *elements* of a set and some *laws of combination* of those elements. What is necessary for that set of elements with a particular law of combination to form a group? First, the law of combination must be applicable to every pair of elements. It must be possible to combine every element with every other one, and the result of that combination must be one element of the set itself. If this is true, then we say that the set is *"closed under that operation."* To return to the rearrangement of the beads: Unless all six rearrangements were included, the set of elements would not be closed; there would be some combinations of rearrangements that would be equivalent to no single rearrangement in the set. This set of six permutations of the beads is, however, closed. Figure 5-2 is a multiplication table of the operations and shows the result of combining every pair of rearrangements. Each permutation at the left of a row, if followed by the permutation at the top of a column, is equivalent to the permutation at the intersection of that row and column.

	(RGY)	(RYG)	$(RG)(Y)$	$(RY)(G)$	$(R)(GY)$	$(R)(G)(Y)$
(RGY)	(RYG)	$(R)(G)(Y)$	$(R)(GY)$	$(RG)(Y)$	$(RY)(G)$	(RGY)
(RYG)	$(R)(Y)(G)$	(RGY)	$(RY)(G)$	$(R)(YG)$	$(RG)(Y)$	(RYG)
$(RG)(Y)$	$(RY)(G)$	$(R)(GY)$	$(R)(G)(Y)$	(RGY)	(RYG)	$(RG)(Y)$
$(RY)(G)$	$(R)(GY)$	$(RG)(Y)$	(RYG)	$(R)(G)(Y)$	(RGY)	$(RY)(G)$
$(R)(GY)$	$(RG)(Y)$	$(RY)(G)$	(RGY)	(RYG)	$(R)(G)(Y)$	$(R)(GY)$
$(R)(G)(Y)$	(RGY)	(RYG)	$(RG)(Y)$	$(RY)(G)$	$(R)(GY)$	$(R)(G)(Y)$

Figure 5-2. Multiplication table of the six permutations forming a group.

If we consider paths from one region to another as elements, they cannot form a *group* because there is no rule for combining each element with every other element. Only pairs of elements in which the end point of the first corresponds to the beginning point of the second can be combined. The rotations of a wheel, on the other hand, are closed. The set of positive integers is closed when addition is the law of combination, but all positive integers must be included. The sum of any two integers is an integer.

A second requirement for a *group* is that it be *associative*. If three elements are combined, as $1 + 4 + 7$ might be, it makes no difference whether 1 and 4 are first combined and then 7 is added to the result as in $(1 + 4) + 7$, or the result of the second and third is combined to the first as in $1 + (4 + 7)$. Notice that the same law holds for the combination of permutations shown in Figure 5-1. Thus, $(RGY) \times (RG)$ $(Y) \times (R)(GY)$ always equals $(R)(G)(Y)$. It makes no difference whether one first multiplies (RGY) by $(RG)(Y)$ to get $(R)(GY)$ and then the result by $(R)(GY)$, or one first multiplies $(RG)(Y) \times (R)$ (GY) to get (RYG) and then the first term (RGY) by this product.

The third requirement for a *group* is that one of the elements be called the *identity* element because the effect of its combining with any other element is to leave that other element unchanged. As far as addition of numbers is concerned, 0 is the identity element. Zero added to any number leaves it unchanged. In the set of permutations, $(R)(G)(Y)$ is the identity element. It leaves the arrangement just as it was, no matter how it began. The products of $(R)(G)(Y)$ with other permutations are shown in the last column of Figure 5-2.

The fourth and last criterion for a *group* is that every element have an *inverse*. The inverse of an element is that element which, combined with the original, results in the identity element. The inverse of $+5$ in addition must be a number that, added to 5, gives 0 as a result. This is obviously -5. Thus, in order to include the inverses of the positive integers in the set of elements, we must include the negative integers. This means that the positive integers alone do not form a *group;* they are closed and associative, but contain neither an identity element nor inverses. If, however, zero and the negative integers are included, the entire set forms a *group*. The set of permutations does contain the inverse for every element. (RGY) and (RYG) are inverses of each other; $(R)(YG)$ is its own inverse, etc. Each row of Figure 5-2 contains $(R)(G)(Y)$. The two elements whose product is $(R)(G)(Y)$ are inverses.

A set of elements, then, forms a *group,* under some specified law of combination, if:

1. There is a law of combination that applies to every pair of elements in the set, and the result of that combination is, in every case, a member of the set. This is the criterion of *closure*.

2. Any combination of three or more elements is *associative*.

3. There is an *identity* element whose combination with any element leaves it unchanged.

4. Each element has an *inverse* element in the set such that the combination of the element and its inverse is the identity element.

Relation of Group Properties to Equilibrium

By now the reader may well be asking, "so what? This makes an interesting game for those who enjoy that sort of thing, but what has it to do with the problems of human behavior?" In partial answer, we can point out that the concept of equilibrium is closely connected with these properties of groups. If a system is in stable equilibrium, it must be able to counteract disturbances and return to its original state, or if the organism is engaged is goal-directed behavior, it must be able to adjust to external disturbances and find another way of reaching the goal. Thus, the reversibility of changes in the system is essential for equilibrium. In the language of groups, reversibility means that the operation describing the disturbances must have an inverse within the set of possible changes in the system. If all of the changes in a system form a group, then it is possible for the system to remain stable even though disturbances may arise. That such a mathematical group exists does not ensure the maintenance of a stable state, however, because there may be no mechanism by which the system actually responds to a disturbance by engaging in the necessary inverse operations. The existence of such inverse operations is necessary but not sufficient to insure equilibrium.

Piaget speaks of equilibrium in cognitive processes. His thesis is that for the individual to be in cognitive equilibrium with his environment he must have cognitive schemas representing the various kinds of changes or disturbances that may occur in the system, and that the cognitive schemas must also contain the inverses of all these changes. Reversibility within a cognitive schema is thus for Piaget an important characteristic. His notion is that every time a child combines two groups of objects, adds two numbers, or draws a logical implication, an entire schema is activated, that is, the child performs this particular operation against a background of knowledge of the results of all the other operations within the schema and of the inverses of each of them. He does not explicitly or consciously think of them all, but he "knows where he is" within the system and knows how to bring about various other desired results. Such a schema is operational and is marked by reversibility. If all of the operations in the schema form a mathematical group, then such a schema has this reversibility and equilibrium.

Groupings

Is it necessary for the set of operations to form a group before it has this property of reversibility? No. As it turns out, many reversible schemas are composed of operations that do not form a group. Piaget has coined the term "grouping" to describe a set of operations that, though not forming a group, have many of the properties of groups that are most important for the establishment of an equilibrium. Piaget's most detailed example is the schema describing the process of classification and adding of classes.

A typical classification system is that of animals into phylum, class, order, genus, and species. In Figure 5-3 we see an example of a classifi-

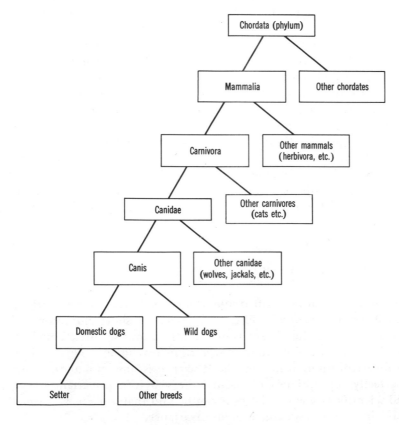

Figure 5-3. Classification of animals.

cation. The group of individual animals called setters can be combined with dogs of other breeds to form the class, domestic dog. These dogs can be combined with various wild dogs to form the genus Canis, etc.

This operation of combining classes to form larger classes can also be reversed by the operation of dividing the members of a large class into subclasses. This system of operations resembles a group in some respects. There is a sort of closure in that any class in the system can be obtained from any other class by a sequence of operations. Sequences of these operations show them to be associative. There is reversibility in that any sequence of legitimate operations can be undone by some other sequence of operations. At the same time, the operations that make up this schema do not form a group, primarily because only certain classes may be legitimately combined. Thus, there is no class representing the combination of domestic dogs and noncarnivorous mammals. One can only combine certain classes. There is also the peculiar fact that the combination of a class with itself results in the same class: $A + A = A$. There is no single identity element in this system; neither in the form of a null class that can be combined with any other class, nor in the form of an identity operation that leaves any class unchanged. Regardless of these deficiencies, from the point of view of the formal characteristics of groups, the system does have a form of closure, completeness, and reversibility that led Piaget to give it the special name *grouping*.

Piaget distinguishes eight types of groupings. These groupings of concrete operations, as he calls them, mark the achievements of the child at about the age of seven when he reaches the stage of concrete operations, and will be described in a later section. At the moment we are interested in the general role of groups and groupings in Piaget's theory.

THE CONCEPT OF INVARIANCE

Still another technical term frequently encountered in the writings of Jean Piaget is *invariance*. The term deserves a short discussion because it is one of the important words in all natural science, though it has not become part of common parlance in psychology. This neglect of the invariance notion in behavioral science is unfortunate, because it is perfectly appropriate and because the search for invariances is a fruitful scientific strategy. Indeed, it can be said that a scientific theory is always, in a sense, a statement of an invariance.

Let us begin with a simple primitive example to illustrate the concept. We shall choose this example so that it also illustrates some of the particular invariances that the child must recognize if he is to understand the physical world. If we can imagine ourselves back in some unknown earlier stage of human culture, we might think of some of the uses to which rocks and stones were put. They were used to pound with; they were sharpened and used to cut with; they were thrown at birds and animals and people as weapons; they were used to hold down light objects when it was windy; some were worn as jewelry; some were heated in a fire and used to heat water in vessels that could not be put directly on a fire.

For several of these purposes the functional property of a rock which determines whether it is useful or not is what we now call its *weight*. For other purposes the weight of a rock is irrelevant, whereas a quite different property such as its shininess or hardness, or the particular way it chips when struck with another stone, is relevant. There is no reason to suppose that originally the particular property of weight was clearly distinguished from its other properties; the concept of weight had to be discovered or invented.

When weight is the relevant property, many different rocks and collections of rocks are equivalent, and many different things can be done with a rock without changing its heaviness. First of all, a rock can be transported from one place to another with no gross change in weight. This is not logically self-evident; it is an empirical fact which might or might not be true. (In fact, it is false if the rock is carried to the moon.) Other properties of rocks are not so easily transportable. The effectiveness of a hot rock for heating water, for example, dissipates as the rock is moved from one place to another. The shininess of a pretty rock disappears if it is carried into a dark cave. The fact that weight remains unchanged or *invariant* when a rock is moved from one place to another is an empirical fact, but it is also in a sense a part of the definition of weight. If it were not true, it is probable that the concept of weight as we know it would not exist as part of our body of knowledge about inanimate objects.

Another important property of weight is closely related. The weight of a collection of rocks does not depend upon their particular arrangement in space; the weight of a collection is equal to the sum of the weights of the individual members. This invariance does not hold for other functional uses of rocks. For example, the usefulness of the particular trapezoidal-shaped stone that forms the keystone of an arch depends very much upon its being placed at the very top of the arch; the stability of an arch would be completely destroyed if the rocks in it were rearranged.

Thus we see that some of the functional and adaptive uses to which rocks are put depend upon the fact that weight is invariant under certain sorts of changes that may drastically alter other characteristics. An understanding of *weight* requires a tacit knowledge of these invariances, and one reason the term was invented and retained in science was to describe what is invariant under these changes.

To carry the story a little further into modern science, the concept of weight was gradually refined and modified because as originally conceived it was not invariant under some important changes. As usually measured, weight changes slightly when an object is taken from sea level to the top of a mountain; we also know, of course, that in a space satellite objects are weightless. These problems were resolved by Sir Isaac Newton when he distinguished between the weight of an object and its mass. The term mass describes the property of an object that is invariant no matter where it may be transported and that also remains unchanged no matter how fast the object may be moving. Mass remains constant, but weight varies with the particular gravitational field in which the object is located. Still more recently, with the Einstein revolution in physics, the mass of an object has been conceived as changing with its velocity, and what is now thought to be invariant is a complicated function describing the energy of the system.

This side excursion into the history of physics illustrates how many scientific concepts are invented and changed to describe those observable properties of nature that remain invariant under various sorts of changes or transformations.

The concept of invariance is now formalized, but it is rooted in the practical everyday uses to which objects are put. Without our realizing it, many of our naïve notions of physics, space, time, and logic can be studied in terms of invariances. For that matter, much of naïve psychology as described in Chapter 1 of this book describes invariances. Thus, dispositional properties such as ability are useful concepts because they describe properties of people that are more or less invariant. Ability is intended to describe the characteristics of a person that do not change as he goes from one situation to another, attacks a difficult problem or an easy one, and sometimes fails and sometimes succeeds. A scientific theory will someday define ability, no doubt, in a way that makes it even more invariant, or else some new concept will be invented to describe the invariant property that underlies the changes in ability from one situation to another.

For an understanding of Piaget's research and theories, we must see two aspects of his interest in invariance. On the one hand, a theory of a child's cognitive development must describe and explain the process by which children come to understand the invariances of properties of objects in their environment. Thus, the child comes to assume that weight does not change if an object is moved from one place to another, or if the object is reshaped as long as nothing is added or taken away. When does this understanding develop? Does it come spontaneously, or is it taught to the child? What conditions foster or retard its development? These are important problems in developmental psychology when the child's understanding of invariance is the phenomenon to be explained.

On the other hand, Piaget is equally interested in discovering the invariances in the child's thought processes themselves. As developmental psychologists, how shall we describe and explain the invariances in the child's functioning that enable him to transfer knowledge from one situation to another, while maintaining a cognitive stability that allows him to meet the pressures of changing situations? Piaget believes that it is the structure of groups and groupings in the child's thought processes which underlies this invariance and makes him cognitively stable and anchored.

The next chapters describing Piaget's conceptualization of the developmental process will illustrate some of the kinds of cognitive stability that are important for effective adaptive behavior.

SUMMARY

This chapter has been concerned with some of the basic concepts in Piaget's theory that are needed to understand the theory itself. We have seen how Piaget's biological background and philosophical interests have gone far toward defining his conception of the problem of developmental psychology. The biological interests have led him to the problem of adaptation and equilibrium, as well as to the conception of adaptation as a double process of assimilation and accommodation. The problem of epistemology or the nature of man's conception of reality has been an important guide to the problems of development which seem significant to him.

Piaget is also very interested in a formal description of the process of thinking. In his search for such a description, he has developed a unique view in terms of the structure of cognitive schemas. If these schemas form groups or groupings that are marked by coherence, closure, and especially reversibility, they have the kind of stability needed for effective adaptation. We have therefore introduced the concepts of group and grouping in this chapter.

SIX

Piaget's description
of development during infancy

PIAGET DIVIDES the child's development into four main periods: infancy, the preoperational period, the period of concrete operations, and the period of formal operations. Following a bird's-eye view of these stages, we shall dwell in this chapter on a detailed consideration of the period of infancy. In the later chapters we will explore each of the other periods, and examine Piaget's theory about the developmental process—how the child moves from one stage to another and what factors in his environment are relevant.

Stage 1: Sensorimotor Period—Birth to Two Years

The sensorimotor period of development corresponds in time to the commonly defined limits of infancy, the first two years of life (Piaget, 1952, 1954, a, b). The important unifying feature of this period, as Piaget sees it, is that the child is acquiring skills and adaptations of a behavioral kind. The schemas of this early period are sensorimotor schemas; they organize sensory information and result in adaptive behavior, but are not accompanied by any cognitive or conceptual representation of the behavior or the external environment. The behavior during infancy is, however, genuinely adaptive and intelligent, and the sensorimotor schemas are the historical roots out of which later conceptual schemas develop.

During infancy, the child becomes able to coordinate information from the various sensory modalities and integrate it as though the different modalities were sources of information about the same objects rather than unrelated ones. Thus, the infant becomes able to look at what he is listening to; his prehension or his walking can be guided by auditory, visual, or tactual cues and the three sorts of cues act as if they were interchangeable. Schemas involving different parts of the body are also integrated. Thus, for example, the infant can hold his hand still so that he can look at an object held in it, and can integrate the two hands so that they function cooperatively.

A second major acquisition of the sensorimotor period is the infant's capacity to operate as if the external world were a permanent place, not one whose existence depended upon his perceiving it. For example, he becomes able to search for objects that have disappeared and to search for them on the basis of information about where they went. He can take a pathway to an object which is different from the pathway the object took, as though he had some notion of a surrounding space that permits taking a variety of paths to the same point. He is also able to return to his own starting point, perhaps by a different route from the one taken.

Finally, he is able to exhibit goal-directed behavior that is governed from its beginning by some intention. He can string together two or three actions, all under the motivation to reach the end point of the sequence. He can even, by the end of infancy, construct new actions never before attempted to reach objectives that are otherwise unattainable. In a sense, he can experiment with new objects, trying out his schemas one after another as if he were searching for the behavioral potentialities of the object. He can spontaneously and deliberately vary his actions.

This is a remarkable achievement for the child by the age of two years—but the child still has serious troubles, because of his lack of conceptual schemas that correspond to these behavioral ones. His behavior is very concrete despite its adaptivity, and this concreteness seriously limits how far ahead the child can plan a sequence of actions. He can actually do more than he "knows" how to do and, like the traditional centipede who does not "know" which leg to move first, his adaptability is seriously hampered.

Stage 2: Preoperational Period—Two to Seven Years

Following the period of infancy there is, according to Piaget, a period of several years during which the child's internal cognitive picture of the external world with its many laws and relationships is gradually growing. It begins in piecemeal fashion; the first conceptual schema is merely an internal copy of a sensorimotor schema. Gradually, however, the conceptual schemas become organized into interrelated systems which Piaget calls *operational*. The term implies that the internal acts which are the elements of the system are related by the laws of groups or groupings. When this happens the child has reached the period of concrete operations.

The preoperational stage is primarily a transitional one, not marked by a stable equilibrium. The end of the sensorimotor stage represents a kind of equilibrium at the behavioral level. The stage of concrete operations represents a new, higher-order equilibrium, and the preoperational stage is the transition between the two. Properly speaking, Piaget should limit himself to only three periods of development, and in some writings he actually does: the sensorimotor stage concluding with the end of infancy, a stage of concrete operations ending with the acquisition of the various groupings to be described in the next section, and a final stage of formal operations. Each of these periods represents for Piaget the achievement of a level of equilibrium and stability that marks it off from other stages.

During the preoperational period, the child is painfully unequilibrated in his conceptual thinking. He falls into obvious self-contradictions; he may at one moment say that *A* is greater than *B*, and a moment later say that *B* is greater than *A,* without quite realizing that the two are incompatible.

Much of the child's everyday behavior is stable and integrated, however, and as long as his language is closely tied to behavioral schemas it too shows many signs of logical thinking. Thus, one of Piaget's children heard the water running in the bathroom one morning and announced, "Daddy is shaving." This seems like a logical deduction based upon the propositions "Daddy always shaves in the morning," and "Daddy runs the water when he shaves." We realize how wrong such a picture of the child's psychological processes must be, when we find that same child cannot look at a set of blue and red squares and circles and say whether "all the blue ones are circles." Yet "all *A* is *B*" is an essential step in every logical deduction.

This period is, therefore, one of the most puzzling to understand. It is so easy to underestimate the child's ability on the basis of his blatant failures at simple logical problems, but it is just as easy to overestimate his ability on the basis of his sensible and logical behavior in free-play situations.

Stage 3: Stage of Concrete Operations—Age Seven to Eleven

At about the age of seven, the child's formal thought processes become much more stable and reasonable. He can, for example, arrange objects in order of size and fit new ones into the series. He can understand that equality of number of two sets of objects depends upon a one-to-one correspondence between the objects in the two groups. He understands that the number of objects in a group is not changed by purely spatial rearrangements. He can understand many of the simpler relationships between classes of objects; for example, he can realize that a class cannot have fewer members than any of its subclasses. He understands what will happen to the sequence of objects if they are rotated. He can distinguish between the distance between two objects and the length of a path between them. In short, he has acquired a rudimentary conception of time, space, number, and logic, those fundamental conceptions in terms of which our understanding of events and objects is ordered.

There are other things, however, that the child cannot yet grasp at this stage of development. Some concepts like volume, which involve the product of quantity and density, are too difficult. The child may be able to perceive relationships between factors when they are presented to him, but he finds it much more difficult to arrange situations ahead of time so that they will reveal the relation between factors. The scientific method which consists of holding control variables constant while varying one experimental variable at a time is still not understood, even intuitively. Piaget describes the child's problem at this stage as one of understanding the relationships among the concrete operational groupings that he has already acquired.

Stage 4: Stage of Formal Operations: Beginning at Age Eleven

The final achievements come in early adolescence. At that point the child can understand the basic principles of causal thinking and scientific experimentation, and can perform experiments and deduce the proper implications—at least in some instances. Although he still has much to learn, as do all scientists, he has the fundamental grasp that underlies logical thought.

SENSORIMOTOR PERIOD (INFANCY)

Piaget describes development during infancy in three books. In the first of these, *The Origins of Intelligence in Children* (Piaget, 1952), he describes the development of adaptive behavior and points to the gradual development of sensorimotor schemas during infancy. In the second, *The Construction of Reality in the Child* (Piaget, 1954a), Piaget devotes himself to the analysis of the child's epistemology: how his behavior reflects various assumptions about the nature of objects, time, space, and causality. In the third, *Play Dreams and Imitation* (Piaget, 1954b), which is only partially devoted to the period of infancy, Piaget describes the development of play and imitation during the sensorimotor period.

These books contain detailed descriptions of six stages within the sensorimotor period, but they also describe in a more general way the sorts of psychological changes that are necessary before the child can achieve the level of adaptive functioning attained at the end of the period.

Accomplishments of This Period

By the end of this period children show considerable insight into their environment. They can use simple tools to obtain objects. They can anticipate the relatively immediate consequences of actions and can recognize the causes of events that occur. They can make use of such external forces as gravity, or they can employ the agency of other people to accomplish the results they want. All of these abilities are limited, but that they exist at all is quite an achievement.

In order to attain these accomplishments certain prerequisites must be met.

THE ACQUISITION OF INTERNALLY CONTROLLED, MOBILE SCHEMAS. The child must acquire a repertoire of schemas that function smoothly through good internal control; it is equally important, however, that these schemas be mobile. Each schema must be internally articulated. The behavior is a sequence of motor acts in which each leads smoothly into the one that follows, like a well-rehearsed routine. This smoothness of functioning is implied by the term internally well-controlled.

Mobility, however, implies that each schema must be adaptable to ranges of situations and objects. The child of two can pick up objects with some precision, grasping each one accurately and delicately in a smooth, unhesitating way. At the same time the prehension is variable and adapted to different circumstances. Small differences in hand and finger position are required to pick up an object from one angle of approach rather than another, and the details of the schema depend upon the particular orientation of the object. But prehension is also applicable to quite different objects that put different requirements on the organism. A marble, a piece of clay, a piece of string, and a burr all require appreciable different actions. Thus, the schema must be generalized and applicable in a variety of circumstances.

Mobility also implies that the schemas must be combinable with one another in different ways. Sometimes schemas fall into a sequence in which the early ones function as a means or as instrumental acts and the last one is a consummatory action, but sometimes schemas must function simultaneously, such as when the child stoops down and reaches for the object he wants. Another sort of union of schemas is demanded when the child tosses a ball: He must move his hand in a certain path and release the ball at a certain point in the trajectory.

THE CONCEPT OF REALITY. In addition to developing a repertoire of schemas, the child must recognize some major characteristics of his environment. During infancy he comes to assume that external objects are relatively permanent and continue to exist even when not directly perceived. The sensory information changes radically whenever the child closes his eyes or turns his head and also when the objects in the environment themselves move or change shape. The child's actions must be responsive to the relevant features of the sensory input and must be uninfluenced by irrelevancies.

Piaget calls the assumption of a permanent identity of objects, the "object concept." When the child looks away, or when an object goes out of sight, the child must be able to return to it, to look for it, and to anticipate its reappearance. The primary data on this feature of development are the child's reaction to the disappearance of objects from his field of perception.

It is not sufficient, however, for the child merely to know that the vanished object is still in existence; he must be able to organize his information about it so that his search for it is appropriate. This means that he must understand that the objects and actions of the world are located in a continuous space and time, which has several characteristics.

In the first place, it must be unitary and not dependent upon the particular channel of information to it. Vision, hearing, and touch must be treated as optional channels of information from the same external world. If the child watches a marble disappear behind a screen, hears it roll to a stop, and then goes after it rather than waiting for it to come out on the other side of the screen he is demonstrating the integration of information from different sources.

Second, the child's space in which objects move must be so organized that he takes advantage of the fact that movements in space form a group. Behaviorally this means that the child can take alternate paths to a point, retrace his steps, rotate an object in different directions, and still know that it is the same "other side" that is revealed.

Third, this space must contain the child's own body. In fact, he must act as though his body were an object in space like any other. Since his sensory information about his own body comes in a far different form from information about other objects, it must be difficult for the child to recognize his own body as an object in space. One interesting strategy for investigating this development is to study the child's imitation. When he can imitate a facial movement, he in some way recognizes from the feel of his own facial movement that it corresponds to the facial movement he sees someone else making. The two-year-old child can do this perfectly well.

RECOGNITION OF CAUSE AND EFFECT. In addition to a repertoire of schemas and a notion of external space, the child must be able to handle problems involving cause and effect. Here again, the task seems enormously difficult when we try to outline it. The causal relation between two events is perceivable only through such cues as their contiguity, their spatial proximity, or the sequence of mediating events. None of these types of evidence is at all infallible. Completely unrelated events can occur close together in time. The child may kick his feet in the air, and by doing so set a swinging rattle into motion; it is not necessarily true, though, that the same action will always cause the same result. If, however, the child does produce the effect several times, he may act as if he thought that the kicking automatically produced the swinging. By the end of infancy the child is more aware of the mediating events and has made considerable progress in recognizing the external factors that are involved in a causal sequence. He can even use external impersonal causes, for example, when he puts a ball at the top of an incline and lets gravity roll it down for him.

It is difficult to describe these behavioral adaptations of the child without making him appear to have an intuitive conceptual knowledge of many abstract principles. It is perfectly clear from the things that he fails to do at the age of two that he has no such knowledge, yet his behavior is in some way delicately and finely adapted to those very principles. Just how this adaptation occurs is still a mystery in most respects, but largely as a result of Piaget's interest in these epistemological issues, the problem is clear.

Theoretical Principles

As Piaget sees it, there is a basic ground plan for all these developments that occurs over and over again. It varies somewhat, of course, from one age to another, but the basic scheme is general enough for it to be fruitful to spell it out before moving on to the concrete details of the specific developments of infancy.

THE CIRCULAR REACTION. One central theoretical concept is the circular reaction. By means of this reaction, the actions involved in the circuit gradually consolidate into a predictable schema. A circular reaction is a response pattern that tends to prolong its own existence because the acts composing it produce the eliciting stimuli; the stimulus elicits the response which produces the stimulus which elicits the response. This type of mechanism is well-known in engineering, where it is labeled "positive feedback."

The sucking behavior of the neonate illustrates the circular reaction. The sucking is elicited by the tactual stimuli on the inner surface of the lips and mouth. As liquid reaches the back of the mouth, swallowing is triggered, which is incompatible with suction. As soon as the swallowing ends, however, the stimuli for sucking are present so that the next cycle is initiated. This is an early form of *circular response*.

Other examples of circular responses are less mechanically complete. The infant with an object lying in the palm of his hand may grasp it tightly because of the grasp reflex. This is a grasping response to a stimulus in the palm. If the pressure is constantly exerted on the object in the palm, the tight grasp will be maintained. The baby may even be lifted up by this mechanism. Without such pressure, the infant may rhythmically or periodically grasp and release the object. In the case of sucking a thumb or some other object that does not give milk, the sucking is repeated rhythmically and repetitively, but one cannot diagram the precise cycle of stimulation. Thus, perhaps some psychological state may serve to maintain the circular reaction. It is as though the response were satisfying or pleasurable so that its ending left the infant wanting to repeat it—and, of course, all the conditions for repetition are present. The circular response is a sort of consummatory or pleasure-giving response pattern.

What is different about Piaget's conception of the circular response is that he views all such schemas (not only those that relieve biological tensions but all others as well) as potentially satisfying. In other words, Piaget conceives of a sort of sensuous satisfaction in the exercise of schemas, especially those that are not yet fully adapted to the circumstances. Furthermore, he conceives these schemas to include looking, listening, etc., as well as motor behavior.

What evidence leads Piaget to adopt such a view of motivation? He mainly cites evidence that these circular patterns of behavior depend upon exercise for their development and existence. Chicks, for example, that are prevented from pecking for long periods lose the ability (Padilla, 1935). Similarly, there is evidence that animals raised without being permitted to see develop serious visual defects (Riesen,

1950). The notion that stimulation and exercise of behavior patterns function as an aliment or food for their development can be defended, although not perhaps for every circular response.

Even if the evidence were clear that a tendency to repeat and exercise infantile behavior patterns was biologically adaptive, it would constitute no proof that there was a motivation to exercise. The obvious fact that infants indulge in long chains of repetitive action certainly suggests, however, that there is some motivational base for such behavior. Furthermore, there is no evidence that contradicts such an assumption; as we shall see in later chapters, this sort of repetitive behavior in infants poses one of the most difficult problems for a "drive reduction" theory of motivation (see p. 411). Regardless of how strongly the position is supported, Piaget's theory maintains that the circular responses, including the elementary reflexes of the neonate, are self-motivating and inherently satisfying.

Piaget's theory goes a little further. It specifies that the repetitive circular exercise of a schema is most strongly motivated when the schema is not completely adapted to the demands of the situation. When the schema assimilates the situation sufficiently to be elicited by it but some accommodation is required before the schema can cope effectively with the situation's demands, then the exercise of the schema is strongly motivated. Such situations constitute the food or aliment for the schema, because they stimulate the improvement of the schema through practice. This particular feature of the schema was described earlier in the section on assimilation and accommodation (see pp. 176 ff.).

Thus, there appear to be different kinds of assimilation and several ways that the schema may accommodate to the demands of the environment. These varieties of assimilation and accommodation are best illustrated in infant development, but they appear over and over again at different stages.

The Four Varieties of Assimilation

1. REPRODUCTIVE ASSIMILATION. This type describes the fact that the schema tends to be repeated over and over again, coming to function stably and smoothly in the process. This sort of repetition occurs even in the earliest reflexes, despite their being relatively well established by the time the child is born. Reproductive assimilation is more important, however, when new schemas are established through the child's accidentally producing some action or result that stimulates assimilation. Through such assimilation these new behavior patterns

become established and mastered. Reproductive assimilation is Piaget's theoretical term for the phenomenon commonly known as learning through exercise.

Piaget gives an example of this process in the following observation made on one of his children at the age of three months five days (written 0; 3 (5)).

Lucienne shakes her bassinet by moving her legs violently (bending and unbending them, etc.) which makes the cloth dolls swing from the hood. Lucienne looks at them, smiling, and recommences at once. These movements are simply the concomitants of joy. When she experiences great pleasure Lucienne externalizes it in a total reaction including leg movements. As she often smiles at her knick-knacks she caused them to swing. But does she keep this up through consciously coordinated circular reaction or is it pleasure constantly springing up again that explains her behavior?

That evening, when Lucienne is quiet, I gently swing her dolls. The morning's reaction starts up again, but both interpretations remain possible.

The next day at 0;3(6), I present the dolls: Lucienne immediately moves, shakes her legs, but this time without smiling. Her interest is intense and sustained and there also seems to be an intentional circular reaction.

At 0;3(8) I again find Lucienne swinging her dolls. An hour later I make them move slightly: Lucienne looks at them, smiles a little, then resumes looking at her hands as she was doing shortly before. A chance movement disturbs the dolls: Lucienne again looks at them and this time shakes herself with regularity. She stares at the dolls, barely smiles and moves her legs vigorously and thoroughly. At each moment she is distracted by her hands which pass again into the visual field: she examines them for a moment and then returns to the dolls. This time there is a definite circular reaction. (*Origins of Intelligence*, pp. 157–58)

In addition to illustrating the gradual stabilization of a circular reaction, these observations also illustrate Piaget's approach to a problem, his devising experiments on the spot, and his use of a variety of behavioral cues to satisfy himself that the behavior pattern was a circular reaction. While a "look of intense interest" is not the most satisfying evidence that one might wish for, it is often all that can be had in naturalistic observations. In any case it is clear that Piaget is being a responsible investigator, even if his evidence is not the most objective in the world.

2. GENERALIZING ASSIMILATION. This kind of assimilation extends the breadth and mobility of schemas. As a circular reaction is established, the child does not always come into contact with precisely the same stimuli. Nevertheless, he frequently encounters objects that serve

to elicit the behavior pattern. They must be assimilated in order to induce the response, but when he makes the response the schema becomes generalized; it responds to a range of stimuli. Through generalizing assimilation, the infant's schemas accommodate to the range of specific stimulus objects that occur in his particular environment.

Because we will discuss generalization of a learned response (see p. 406) later, it is worth noticing that generalizing assimilation is not merely the making of an old response to a stimulus that resembles the one to which the response was learned; this type of assimilation also includes cases where the schema changes slightly in response to different objects. In other words, both accommodation and assimilation are involved in the generalization of a schema to include new objects.

A good example of generalizing assimilation occurs in Lucienne's behavior a few days after the observations already reported.

At 0;3(13) Lucienne looks at her hand with more coordination than usual. In her joy at seeing her hand come and go between her face and the pillow, she shakes herself in front of this hand as when faced by the dolls. Now this reaction of shaking reminds her of the dolls which she looks at immediately after as though she foresaw their movement. She also looks at the bassinet hood which also moves. (*Origins of Intelligence,* p. 158)

3. RECOGNITORY ASSIMILATION. This term is used by Piaget to describe a different sort of behavior. Piaget wants to emphasize that, owing to the reciprocal processes of assimilation and accommodation, schemas gradually become differentiated and enlarged. The schema exists, one might say, in a number of forms, each adapted to particular circumstances. The variants all resemble one another closely because they are all part of a single schema and are adapted to bring about the same result on a variety of objects; yet, they also differ from each other and the differences among them correspond to the respective demands that individual objects put on the schema. Thus, one might say that when one of these variants is elicited the child is recognizing the object. He is discriminating it from other objects that the schema can assimilate, and this is the only sort of recognition of which the young infant is capable.

Piaget also says that the difference in the schemas is the basis of recognition. The properties of the object are not recorded passively and objectively when the infant sets eyes on the object, says Piaget. Instead, a variety of schemas, looking schemas as well as manipulative ones, must be acquired. The various shapes of objects correspond to different visual schemas or at least to different variants of some particular looking schema. The difference between "round" and "square" thus depends upon the fact that the visual inspection and assimilation of round and square objects involve slightly different schemas. This does not imply that the shapes are tracked by eye movements, although that may happen; it does mean, however, that Piaget conceives of perceptual as well as motor processes as being active schemas.

Thus, by the term *recognition* Piaget signifies the fitting of a schema to the demands of the object. But there is another aspect to it, the act of acknowledging the familiarity of the object and the fact that one has "fitted" it, so to speak. Often this fact is acknowledged by the child in a sort of lightly sketched-in replica of the schema itself. Once the schema is well adapted to the object so that it no longer poses problems for mastery, the child ceases to engage in repetitive schematic action toward it; he may, however, express a feeling of "I know you and I have you mastered" in a shadow-like version of the schema itself. For example:

At 0;5(3) Lucienne tries to grasp spools suspended above her by means of elastic bands. She usually uses them in order to suck them, but sometimes she swings them while shaking herself when they are there. She manages to touch but not yet grasp them. Having shaken them fortuitously, she then breaks off to shake herself a moment while looking at them (shakes of the legs and trunk) when she resumes her attempts at grasping.

Why has she broken off in order to shake herself a few seconds? It was not in order to shake the spools because she did not persevere. . . . Everything transpires as though the subject, endowed for the moment with reflection and internal language, had said to himself something like this, "Yes I see the object could be swinging, but it is not what I am looking for. . . ." The short interlude of swinging would thus be equivalent to a sort of motor recognition.

Such an interpretation would remain completely hazardous when confronted by a single fact. But its probability increased along with the following observations. For instance at 0;5(10) Lucienne again relapses into states identical to those vis-à-vis a rattle. So also at 0;6(5) she shakes herself several times in succession, very briefly each time, as soon as she has caught sight of her hand (which comes out of her mouth or by chance enters the visual field). One cannot see what this movement might mean if not that it is the outline of some action suggested by this sight. (*Origins of Intelligence,* p. 186)

4. MUTUAL COORDINATION AND ASSIMILATION OF SCHEMAS. These actually involve nothing basically new or different from what happens in other assimilation except that here two schemas are interacting with each other and assimilating each other. For example, when the child learns to look at his own hand and hold it still enough to see, the looking schema and the manipulative schema are responding and adapting to each other.

Another sort of coordination of schemas occurs among the various schemas that can assimilate a particular object. Several looking and listening schemas as well as some manipulative ones may be simultaneously elicited by some object. This simultaneous activation of several different schemas by a single object helps to build an object concept in which stability and permanence are attributed to the object, while the perception of it may be more transitory.

Both of these sorts of coordination of schemas occur fairly early in the infant's life. By the time he is six months to a year old, his range of schemas has expanded so much that there are many different types of interrelations among them.

DIFFERENTIATION OF SCHEMAS. Schemas expand, become discriminative, and coordinate to one another, but during the course of infancy the schemas mature in a more fundamental way. While the basic principles remain constant, the internal structure of the schemas gradually differentiates. One way this happens is that the schema gradually separates from its object. At first the schema is not distinct, as far as the child is concerned, from the sensory feedback it elicits. Then the schema gradually becomes a channel of information from the external world or the mechanism of action on an external object. The schema becomes exteriorized so that, for example, the looking schema is not just looking for the sake of looking but looking to see the object. It is not so much that the act of looking is any different when it becomes exteriorized, but rather that it fits into a broader system of schemas. Many schemas in the system have one end in the external world and the other in the self, so to speak. Because of their equivalences as channels of information, the child gradually constructs an external world to which his acts extend. Not all schemas, of course, are links to an exterior reality; some coordinate the individual's actions with one another and thus remain part of the self. It is this polarization of self and exterior world that represents such an important development for the child's adaptive functioning.

In another way, also, schemas become more differentiated. The infant becomes capable of intentional actions. For many psychologists, intention is taken to mean that the individual has a cognitive picture of what he wants to do before he actually does it, and probably many intentional actions of older children and adults do have this form, or at least have a conceptual accompaniment. For Piaget, though, intention is distinguished from cognitive representation. Piaget argues that internal cognitive picturing of the environment or of the actions of the self comes only during the preoperational stage, Stage 2, not during the sensorimotor stage. It seems impossible not to describe the problem-solving behavior infants engage in intentionally, however. In fact, Piaget believes that the first signs of intentional behavior appear somewhere between four and six months.

What evidence of intention is there, and how is an intentional action theoretically distinguished from the reflexes or automatic habits that are attainable by the very young infant? In Piaget's view, the essential criterion is the time gap between the need aspect of the schema and the instrumental action that the schema provides. If the need exists prior to the action that satisfies it, the action is intentional. If several schemas are linked in a means-end sequence, it is clear that the need is functional before the final consummatory action. It is possible, however, for intentional behavior to occur even when only one schema is involved. Piaget often comments upon the child's interest in and rapt attention paid to external objects, followed by a carefully executed action. These observations convince Piaget that the action is an intentional one. In the reflex behavior of the neonate, on the other hand, the need to suck and the sucking are indistinguishable. One cannot say that the child wants to suck and then does it. Exercising the schema is satisfying and motivated, but only in the actual doing of it. It may be a little like the episode recorded in the "Lost Chord" in which the beautifully saitsfying sound of the piano chord only emerged in the playing of it. It was unintended but nevertheless satisfying. The hypothetical protagonist in the song then tried for years to recapture that sound, that is, to perform the same act intentionally.

The child of Stage 3 who by accident discovers an interesting spectacle or event repeats what he is doing to prolong or recapture the event. Thus, he seems to want the event in advance of his achieving it. At the same time he does not necessarily have a mental image of what he wants. He feels the yearning, so to speak, and this prolongs his behavior, but he does not have a picture of what he is yearning for.

It is not necessary, however, to describe the infant's phenomenal experience of intending to describe intention in conceptual terms. When the intended action involves only one schema, differentiation between need and the instrumental act is difficult to demonstrate and can only be suggested by such behavioral signs as intense attention before the action is begun. When two schemas are coordinated, however, so that one of them is the instrumental act and the other is the consummatory act, the differentiation of need from behavior becomes clearer.

The Stages of Infant Development

After this long introduction to Piaget's empirical research on the behavior of infants, let us survey briefly his formulation of the development of the child's adaptive resources during the sensorimotor stage.

STAGE 1 (0–1 MO.): THE USE OF REFLEXES. By the term *reflex* psychologists often mean a highly rigid and predictable response to a well-specified stimulus. The knee jerk that results from tapping the tendon just below the knee cap is an example of such a predictable response. Many behavioral responses of the newborn child are innate, but they are not all rigid and predictable like the knee jerk. Piaget provides us with observations to illustrate, for example, both the predictability and variability of the sucking reflex.

Sucking ordinarily occurs when the mouth, lips, or cheeks of the young infant are touched. There is a nuzzling toward the source of stimulation and when the object gets into the mouth it is repeatedly sucked. But this behavior is not invariable. Sucking movements may occur without any apparent stimulus to the mouth region. On the other hand, some infants may not suck even if the nipple is put directly into the mouth. Sometimes the infant may appear quite undiscriminating about what he sucks on; he will suck away on a finger, or a cloth, or just a spot on the skin. At other times he may be quite discriminating and after a tentative suck or two reject all suckable objects except the nipple. Because of this variability, Piaget thinks the neonate's reflexes are much like other schemas because they show assimilation and accommodation, profit from repetition, and provide satisfaction. The only difference between reflexes and other schemas is that reflexes are innate.

It may also be important that the particular reflexes that are the historical roots of later behavioral development are less rigidly organized than the knee jerk or the neonatal startle response. Another factor that may explain which reflexes develop into voluntary motor behavior is that the important ones have a built-in circularity, whereas the knee jerk and some of the others do not. At any rate the early reflex behaviors that Piaget finds important are sucking, grasping, the visual accommodations and eye movements, and those having to do with hearing and phonation.

During Stage 1, these reflexes stabilize, generalize, and become more discriminating, but are limited to the predetermined end result. Thus, the distinction between Stage 1 and Stage 2 is the appearance of the first acquired adaptations.

STAGE 2 (1–4 MO.): THE FIRST ACQUIRED ADAPTATIONS. The first new adaptations are identified by the fact that the child's behavior now brings about, prolongs, and repeats some state of affairs that had not previously occured. In other words, circular responses and schemas are identified by the result they produce. One of the first acquired adaptations is thumb-sucking. This does not mean that the child has never sucked his thumb before—thumb-sucking may even occur prenatally—nor that he has not sucked it for a prolonged time. Up to now, however, he has not possessed a set of behavioral adjustments that enable him effectively to bring his thumb to his mouth and to keep his thumb in his mouth once it is there. By Stage 2, thumb-sucking and nursing represent two different activities, each occurring at its appropriate time and each with its own set of stabilizing adjustments.

Thumb-sucking is therefore called a *primary circular response*. The term implies that the behavioral adaptation is acquired, but it also implies that the actual content of the behavior *is* included among the hereditary mechanisms. Thus, sucking is part of an innate reflex, but systematic thumb-sucking is acquired. In the next stage, in contrast, accidental external events can provoke a repetition of the act that brought them about even though that action occurred quite accidentally and was not part of the innate endowment of the infant. In this way, the child adds to his repertoire of actions. Piaget calls these new behaviors *secondary circular responses*. In principle, the distinction between primary and secondary circular responses is clear, although there are many borderline cases.

Another set of primary circular responses involves vision. The child at birth is capable of looking at a light, providing it is not moving too fast and does not go too far toward the periphery of the retina. The eyes tend to keep the light in the center of the retina. This type of looking seems to be merely fixation.

By the age of one month, Piaget feels something new is added. The infant begins to examine stationary objects, not merely fixate on them. The observer's impression that the child is actively looking probably results from a certain intentness of expression and an alertness in the eye, but it is obviously difficult to define the difference between looking and fixation in clear operational terms.

It is important to realize that Piaget does seriously maintain that looking is a primary circular reaction, different from mere fixation of the eyes. It is a part and parcel of his systematic attempt to describe all perception and cognition as actions and to identify as well as he can the individual acts in the same way that acts are identified in manipulative behavior.

Although it is clear how Piaget intends to treat vision as a set of circular responses and schemas, it is not clear from his discussion just what constitutes the schema. Is each visual form, for example, to be viewed as a separate schema? Or is the schema the acts of visual inspection in the sense of getting visual information? Piaget would probably answer that vision operates analogously to other motor schemas. Grasping behavior is in one sense all one schema, but the details are accommodated to the particular shaped object to be grasped and these are sources of information about different shapes—and each form of the schema constitutes a tactual recognition of the shape.

If the same is true of vision, then "looking" actions must also be accommodated to the specific properties of the visual stimulus so that the differences in the looking behavior permit the discrimination of stimuli. Piaget does not go into detail, but there is some evidence that the infant's looking follows the contours of the stimulus. These movements would then constitute the accommodations of the looking schema to shapes. Recognitory assimilation is especially important in visual behavior since so much recognition depends upon visual identification of the stimulus.

Piaget reports from his observations that one of the earliest signs of recognition is the baby's smile. Later the smile becomes more restricted to interaction with social objects, but Piaget reports early smiles to all sorts of familiar objects, actions, and stimuli. This hypothesis is completely contradictory to the observations reported by Spitz (1946), Kaila (1932), and other investigators, but the field has not been well enough investigated for us to be sure of the facts about the stimuli that elicit smiling in young infants.

During Stage 2, the child's looking behavior, although more than mere fixation of the eyes, is still not object perception. What the child looks at are merely sights or luminous spots. In order for the child to perceive objects, he must develop some idea about objects as detached from himself. During Stage 2, we see some of the preliminary experiences for the later development of an *object* concept. There is, for example, some coordination of looking, hearing, and grasping so that the same stimulus is simultaneously the object of visual, auditory, tactual, and motor actions. This is a necessary step in the acquisition of the idea of an object and a single external world, but it is not sufficient. During Stages 1 and 2, there is no evidence that the child ever searches for an object that has disappeared, although he does encounter, lose contact, and reencounter objects in the course of his activity. These experiences probably constitute the basis for acquiring an object concept. Psychologically, however, there is no indication that the child in Stage 2 recognizes these encounters as anything more than fleeting flashes. The first signs of the object concept come at stage 3.

Finally, we must say something about the development of the infant's prehension, his ability to grasp and obtain objects. Although prehension has its roots in Stage 1 in the grasping of an object pressed into the palm of his hand, even the simplest acts of reaching for an object that he sees do not occur until Stage 3. The discussion of prehension will therefore serve as a transition into the description of the behavior of Stage 3.

The neonate tightly grasps a finger or rod that is pushed into the palm of his hand; in fact, some infants grasp so tightly they can be lifted off the ground by the rod they are grasping. But if an object is merely laid into the palm of the infant he does not grip it constantly. He closes his fist on it, then relaxes, perhaps grasps again, etc. He often loses the object during the rest intervals because he is not ordinarily lying quietly. His arms wave, his feet kick, his body squirms. Gradually, however, his grasp becomes firmer and less precarious.

The next clear advance in prehension is the infant's bringing objects to his mouth to suck. This pattern represents a mutual assimilation of the thumb-sucking schema and grasping. Since the thumb is permanently attached to the hand, it poses no prehension problem for the infant, but soon after the child is able to suck his own thumb or finger, this schema assimilates other objects that happen to be in the hand. Such behavior involves grasping and holding onto objects, and also foreshadows a more general schema of prehension by which objects are retrieved not merely to be sucked but for other reasons as well.

The next problem to be solved in the development of prehension is the coordination of grasping and vision. Eventually, the infant must be able to reach out and grasp an object merely by seeing where it is. At this point, according to Piaget's observations, the abilities of Stage 3 are required. Piaget reports two steps in this development. The first is the ability to reach for an object through visual guidance when the hand and object are in the same field of vision. The child has to see his hand move and correct its path of motion to keep it on the track toward the object. Finally, he is able to bring in his hand from outside the visual field to grasp the object he wants to retrieve. This last step requires coordination of kinesthetic and visual activities. The child must know what it feels like to move his hand to any specific spot in the visual field.

STAGE 3 (4–8 MO.): SECONDARY CIRCULAR REACTIONS—BEGINNING OF INTENTIONAL ADAPTATIONS. Piaget speaks of the behavior in Stage 3 as intentional because it seems there is "desire" in advance of its gratification. This time lag between the need and its satisfaction is Piaget's criterion of intention (see p. 203). In Stage 3, the child also acquires new action patterns that are not merely extensions of previously existing schemas, but that are patterns which happen to produce interesting results. In this stage Piaget also observed the prolongation of accommodation movements to recapture a lost object. Both developments seem to imply that the desire aroused by the loss exists in advance of the action that recaptures the object.

The secondary circular response that headlines this stage of development is illustrated by the following observation made by Piaget.

Laurent from the middle of the third month, revealed global reactions of pleasure, while looking at the toys hanging from the hood of his bassinet, or at the hood itself, etc. He babbles, arches himself, beats the air with his arms, moves his legs, etc. He thus moves the bassinet, and recommences more vigorously. But it is not yet possible to speak of circular reaction: there is no connection felt between the movements of his limbs and the spectacle seen, but only an attitude of joy and of physical exertion. Again at 0;2(17), I observe that when his movements induce those of the toys, he stops to contemplate them, far from grasping that it is he who produces them; when the toys are motionless, he resumes and so on. On the other hand at 0;2(24) I made the following experiment which set in motion a beginning of secondary circular reactions. As Laurent was striking his chest and shaking his hands which were bandaged and held by strings attached to the handle of the bassinet (to prevent him from sucking), I had the idea of using the thing and I attached the strings to the celluloid balls hanging from the hood. Laurent naturally shook the balls by chance and looked at them at once (the rattle made a noise inside them). As the shaking was repeated more and more frequently Laurent arched himself, waved his arms and legs—in short, he revealed increasing pleasure and through this maintained the interesting result. But nothing yet authorizes us to speak of circular reaction; this could be a simple attitude of pleasure and not a conscious connection.

The next day at 0;2(25) I connect his right hand to the celluloid balls but leave the string a little slack in order to necessitate ampler movements of the right hand and thus limit the effect of chance. The left hand is free. At first the arm movements are inadequate and the rattle does not move. Then the movements become more extensive, more regular and the rattle moves periodically while the child's glance is directed at this sight. There seems to be a conscious coordination, but both arms move equally and it is not yet possible to be sure that this is not a mere pleasure reaction. The next day, same reactions.

At 0;2(27) on the other hand, conscious coordination seems definite for the following four reasons: (1) Laurent was surprised and frightened by the first shake of the rattle which was unexpected. On the other hand since the second or third shake, he swings his right arm (connected to the rattle) with regularity, whereas the left remained almost motionless. Now the right could move freely without moving the rattle, the string being loose enough to permit Laurent to suck his thumb for instance, without pulling at the balls. It therefore seems the swinging was intentional. (2) Laurent's eye blinks beforehand, as soon as his hand moves and before the rattle moves as though the child knew he was going to shake it. (3) When Laurent temporarily gives up the game and joins his hands for a moment, the right hand alone resumes the movement while the left stays motionless. (4) The regular shakes that Laurent gives the rattle reveal a certain skill; the movement is regular and the child must stretch his arm backward sufficiently to make the rattle sound. (*Origins of Intelligence,* pp. 160–161)

Notice the differences between this behavior pattern and thumb-sucking. In the first place, the action itself, moving the right arm up and down, is not part of any previous circular response. The infant moves his arm earlier in life than Stage 3, but not as part of a stable pattern. Thumb-sucking, although not a reflex, is a piece segregated from an already existing stable behavior pattern. Thus, by comparison with primary ones, secondary circular responses are more novel in the child's life.

Further, notice that the rewarding event is something external; it is the shaking of the celluloid balls and their rattling. Piaget insists that these balls are not yet perceived as objects, but merely as sights. Nevertheless, the schema of looking and listening to the balls jiggle is more separate from the hand shaking that produces the movement than the arm movement that brings the thumb into the mouth is separate from the sucking movement. Means and ends are gradually differentiating, and subjective action and external results are gradually becoming more distinguishable.

Stage 3 is remarkable for the rapid proliferation of new schemas. Up to this stage, most children have much the same repertory of schemas because these are rooted in the innate behavior patterns of the neonate. But now there is opportunity for tremendous expansion of the child's repertoire and also for great individual differences between children, depending upon what opportunities their environments provide for establishing secondary circular responses.

It is impressive how little conception the child has during this stage of the causal relation between the act and its consequence. Thus, these secondary schemas can generalize almost without limit. Lucienne, for example, learned to shake her legs vigorously to shake dolls that hung from her crib as described in an earlier observation (see p. 199). Leg shaking became for Lucienne one of the things to do to cause events. For example, she executed this same action to make a jack-in-the-box jump out and in all sorts of other unlikely situations.

Stage 3 also marks the beginning of the child's conception of a stable external world in which objects maintain their identity and move around in a continuous space. Such a concept is far from completely acquired at Stage 3, but acquisition does begin.

The basic experiment for Piaget's investigation of the object concept is to observe the child's reaction to a vanished object. If he searches at all, it is one important indication of his apparent belief that objects out of sight are not necessarily out of existence. Furthermore, the nature of his search, if he makes one, indicates a great deal about his understanding of space. To the extent that his reaction when an object disappears is negligible or that he merely repeats the action by which he originally encountered the object, he evidently fails to appreciate that the object has a permanence, and that its location is related to what was happening when it disappeared.

In Stage 3, the child begins to recover disappeared objects, but only under certain special conditions, namely, when he can prolong the accommodative movement that was occurring when the object vanished. For example, when Piaget slowly pulled on an object one of his children was holding, the child at Stage 3 could accommodate to the motion and move his hand accordingly. If the object was suddenly jerked out of his hand, however, he continued to move his hand along the trajectory it was already following. In some instances, this prolongation of the accommodating movement did bring him into contact with the object again. In the same way, a child may recapture an object visually if he is already following it with his eyes when he loses contact with it and if the object stays in its straight-line pathway. At Stage 3, however, there is no searching for the object outside of that path and no retracing to look for it. In fact, it is not clear that the child is actually searching at all; he is merely continuing what he was doing when the object was lost. Nevertheless, this behavior is a step in the right direction and does not occur before Stage 3.

The child also shows some tacit assumption of the permanence of objects in his recognizing and seeking objects that are partially invisible. The following observation illustrates the point.

When I make only part of the bottle disappear and Laurent sees a small fraction of it near my hand, or a cloth, or the table, the manifestations of his desire are more imperious than when he saw the whole bottle. At the very least, they remain identical: Laurent kicks and cries while staring fixedly at the visible portion of the object. Up to 0;7(1) he has not stretched out his arms because he has not been in the habit of holding his bottle, but from that date on, he tries to take it. If I offer it to him half covered by a cloth, he takes possession of what he sees, never doubting for a single second that his bottle is involved. (*Construction of Reality,* p. 30)

These, then, are the main achievements of Stage 3: the development of visual motor prehension; the learning of new schemas that reproduce or prolong an interesting event, even though the schema must be constructed from the beginning out of heretofore random activities; and finally, the prolongation of accommodations that are in process when an object disappears.

STAGE 4 (8–12 MO.): ACQUISITION OF INSTRUMENTAL BEHAVIOR AND ACTIVE SEARCH FOR THE VANISHED OBJECT. From the point of view of problem solving, the big change that comes with Stage 4 is the child's new ability to use familiar schemas in new situations as means to an end. The following sequence of observations illustrates the first appearance of instrumental schemas in Laurent's behavior.

The task is to put aside an obstacle that prevents Laurent from reaching the object he wants. Until 0;7(13) Laurent has never really succeeded in setting aside the obstacle; he has simply attempted to take no notice of it. . . . For instance at 0;6(0) I present Laurent with a matchbox extending my hand laterally to make an obstacle to his prehension. Laurent tries to pass over my hand, or to the side, but he does not attempt to displace it. . . . At 0;7(10) Laurent tries to grasp a new box in front of which I place my hand (at a distance of 10 cm). He set the obstacle aside, but not intentionally; he simply tries to reach the box by sliding next to my hand and when he touches it, tries to take no notice of it. . . . Finally at 0;7(13) Laurent reacts quite differently almost from the beginning of the experiment. I present a box of matches above my hand, but behind it, so that he cannot reach it without setting the obstacle aside. But Laurent, after trying to take no notice of it, suddenly tries to hit my hand as though to remove or lower it; I let him do it to me and he grasps the box.—I recommence to bar his passage, but using as a screen a sufficiently supple cushion to keep the impress of the child's gestures. Laurent tries to reach the box, and, bothered by the obstacle, he at once strikes it, definitely lowering it until the way is clear. (*Origins of Intelligence,* p. 217)

The interesting feature of Laurent's activity is, of course, the use of the separate schema—pushing aside the hand or pounding the cushion—as a preliminary to reaching for the object. It is important, as Piaget makes clear in the observation, that the child not merely push aside the obstacle in the course of reaching for the object, but that he do so as a separate act in advance of reaching, in order to reach for the object.

The use of one schema as a means to an end reflects an ability that can be described in a more general fashion, namely, the ability to execute in an intentional manner old behavior patterns in new situations. The well-practiced pattern at the fourth stage is used as a means to an end, but this stage seems to mark the freeing of a learned behavior mechanism from its instigating situation, an additional step in the separation of the motivational aspect of schemas from the manipulative aspect. As long as schemas must be instigated, they are performed when the child enjoys them, for example, when they are interesting or challenging. But once they become a part of the child's repertoire of voluntary behavioral actions, he can employ them as means to an end or for any other reason, whether they are intrinsically enjoyable or not. Thus, the end result, the consummatory schema, serves to motivate the entire sequence of schemas leading up to it. The means, however, are performed freely in the service of a variety of motives. This freedom is what Piaget means by mobility of schemas.

A further example of this same freedom of schemas can be seen in Piaget's observations of the child's imitation. Stage 4 marks the time that any schema in the child's repertoire can be used in imitation of a model.

According to Piaget, the child can systematically imitate movements earlier than Stage 4, but only when he has observed his own behavior in the same way that he observes the model. Thus, he can imitate his father's closing and opening his hand as soon as he has acquired the schema of opening and closing his own hand, but this early imitation depends upon the fact that he has watched his own hand opening and closing. The model can therefore be considered as directly replacing the feedback stimulation from the child's own behavior. Similarly, he can imitate sounds that are in his repertoire because he has heard himself make the sound.

At Stage 4, the added feature is that the child can begin to imitate actions that are already in his repertoire but that he has never watched himself make—facial grimaces, for example. When behaving this way, the model does not instigate the imitative action directly; the child must recognize what action is being performed and then reproduce it. The imitative action is performed voluntarily. It is not directly instigated. In this sense such imitation also reflects the new mobility of schemas in Stage 4.

Along with the use of a schema as an instrumental act, the child in Stage 4 shows important advances in his object concept. In the observations of Laurent, we saw that the object was quite visible, although separated from the child by a barrier. Visibility of the goal is not essential; the child at this stage can remove the obstacle from an object hidden that much. Thus, when an object is placed underneath a cushion while the child watches he can search for the vanished object and push or pull aside the pillow to recapture it. A curious deficit in the child's understanding of the location of objects is revealed, however, when two pillows are used. The object is put under the red pillow and the child is allowed to retrieve it. Then, while the child watches, it is placed under the red pillow, taken out, shown to the child, and placed under the blue pillow. The question is, where will the child look for it? At Stage 4, he looks under the red pillow.

What does this mean? It actually represents an important failure in the child's understanding. The belief that objects continue to exist when they are invisible also requires some belief that objects are located at some point in space. When objects move they go to the point at the end of the path of movement. Therefore, we look for objects where they were last seen or at the end point of the pathway we think they followed. This strategy for recovering vanished objects is in some ways the exact opposite of what the child discovered in Stage 3, namely, to repeat the action that produced the interesting event. When the child obtains the object from under the red pillow and now looks for it there even though he has seen it put under the blue one, he is repeating the action that found him the object last time rather than looking for it where he last saw it.

If we think of the various problems of everyday life, we realize that we sometimes use the strategy of repeating a previously successful act, but on other occasions we base our action on the tacit assumption that the events we are trying to cope with are organized in some sort of "group" structure. When we turn on a light, we repeat the same action every time we want to produce the light, because a light is not something that goes someplace and is obtained by bringing it back. Whenever events are organized into a continuous process in space or time, repetition of previously successful acts is not necessarily adaptive. The appropriate action depends upon the point in the process at which we are intervening. One application of fertilizer makes a plant grow, but its repetition every hour would kill the plant. Pericles once differentiated between Greeks and barbarians in that a barbarian guards the spot where he was hit last time, whereas a Greek guards the spot where his foe is trying to hit him.

From these examples we see how Piaget has captured a fundamental feature of the child's understanding of objects and space by his investigation of the child's reaction to sequential displacements. In Stage 4, the child is beginning to have a clear idea of the permanence of objects, but he still lacks the essential notion that displacements in space form groups. This achievement comes with Stage 5.

STAGE 5 (12–18 MO.): TERTIARY CIRCULAR REACTIONS AND THE DIS-
COVERY OF NEW MEANS. The central feature of Stage 5 is the child's ability to invent new behavior patterns which he has never before performed. The term "tertiary circular response" describes the kind of
repetitive behavior that engages and fascinates the child of about one
year of age where he repeats an action over and over again, but not in
any stereotyped form nor even with the random variations that ordinarily occur. Rather, now he plays variations on a theme, repeating
the action but also deliberately varying it.

The following observation from Piaget illustrates what is meant by
the tertiary circular response.

One recalls how at 0;10(2) Laurent discovered in "exploring" a case of soap,
the possibility of throwing this object and letting it fall. What interested him
at first was not the objective phenomenon of the fall, that is to say, the object's
trajectory—but the very act of letting go. He therefore limited himself, at the
beginning, merely to reproducing the result observed fortuitously, which still
constitutes a "secondary" reaction, derived it is true, but of typical structure.

On the other hand at 0;10(10) the reaction changes and becomes tertiary.
That day Laurent manipulates a small piece of bread and lets it go continually.
He even breaks off fragments which he lets drop. Now, in contradistinction to
what has happened on the preceding days, he pays no attention to the act of
letting go, whereas he watches with great interest the body in motion; in
particular he looks at it for a long time when it has fallen and picks it up when
he can.

At 0;10(11) Laurent is lying on his back but nevertheless resumes his experiments of the day before. He grasps in succession a celluloid swan, a box,
etc., stretches out his arm and lets them fall. He distinctly varies the position
of the fall. Sometimes he stretches out his arm vertically, sometimes he holds
it obliquely, in front of or behind his eyes, etc. When the object falls in a new
position (for example on his pillow) he lets it fall two or three more times on
the same place, as though to study the spatial relations; then he modifies the
situation. At a certain moment the swan falls near his mouth; now he does
not suck it (even though this object habitually serves this purpose) but drops
it three times more while merely making the gesture of opening his mouth.
(*Origins of Intelligence,* p. 268)

In this observation we see the type of spontaneous new actions in
which the child engages. They do not spring out of nothing but are
really variations upon a theme that is one of the familiar schemas
well-established in the child's repertoire. Nevertheless, the schema expands to include new variants deliberately performed by the child.
These new actions make the schema more adaptive; more importantly,
the ability to create new variations of familiar schemas provides a valuable tool for problem solving.

One of the methods by which all of us solve problems is to stumble on a solution without deciding ahead of time that it was a solution. Many problems do not permit the analysis necessary to plan a wise solution; in others, we may lack the information for a good one. Hence, we try something and see if it works, not an elegant strategy, but in many cases the best we have.

There are two variations on ths strategy. In one, the solution is literally stumbled on. By the purest accident we hit upon an action that works, perhaps when we are trying to do something else. Blotting paper was reportedly invented because someone forgot to put in an ingredient that was necessary for regular paper. The ability to profit from pure accidents is first observed in Stage 3 of the infant's development. At that time he is able to reproduce interesting events that occur accidentally in the course of his activity.

A more sophisticated variation is trial and error. This is employed in many scientific research projects where different variables are systematically manipulated until one of them offers a solution to the problem. By the intentional variation of actions, one increases the likelihood of the occurrence of the happy accident. The ability to vary one's behavior deliberately is therefore an important adaptive tool. We see the first signs of it in Stage 5.

Owing to the tertiary circular response, we find that the infant in Stage 5 can discover solutions to problems by trial and error. In one of his informal experiments Piaget placed the object the child wanted on a pillow. The object itself was out of reach, but the corner of the pillow was within reach. The child in the course of his struggles happened to move the pillow and observed the object move. This occurred by pure accident. As it happened the accidental event did not bring the object close enough for the child to grasp. What happened was that the child began to move the pillow while watching the object, exploring this new tool, so to speak. Soon he had begun to pull the pillow toward himself and thus secured the object. In this episode the basic idea that objects move when their support is moved was hit upon quite accidentally. The movement of the object by means of its support elicited deliberate exploratory actions which made the solution to the problem possible. Thus, the infant capitalized upon an accidental discovery without having actually hit upon a complete solution of his problem.

Another accomplishment of this stage which also depends upon the ability to vary one's actions deliberately is the facility to imitate actions that have never before been performed. Until this time the child has only been able to imitate actions already in his repertoire. Now he can add to the supply.

Another aspect of the tertiary circular response which may not be obvious is its effect on the infant's understanding of space. The observation cited contains many references to the fact that when the child shifted from a secondary to a tertiary circular reaction, his interest moved from the action of letting go to the trajectory of the falling object. After all, the act of releasing an object is no different in one position than in another; the variations appear in the path of the fall, the spot where the object lands, etc. The kind of exploration that the tertiary response permits teaches the child a great deal about the continuous nature of space and the way that variation in acts correlate with variation in results.

One of the achievements of infancy not easily understood is how the child coordinates all his related schemas with one another. Suppose that a hypothetical person had one schema for tossing a ball into a box two feet away, another one for a box four feet away, and a third for a box six feet away. To be effective, ball tossing cannot consist merely in such a set of isolated schemas; the schemas must be coordinated in two ways. First, the gaps must be filled between the three points on the range, and second, there must be a responsiveness to feedback, so that if the ball goes too far the next toss is less forceful. In other words, the actions must be arranged in some sensorimotor representation of a continuous line. We can see how the tertiary circular response provides the sort of exploration that can fill in the gaps between the child's schemas and help to put them in some sort of order so that they can be changed on the basis of feedback.

Stage 5 marks progress also in the development of the object concept. During Stage 4, the child's search for a hidden object included the removal of obstacles to finding it, but by the end of the stage he was still unable to decipher a successive sequence of hidings of the object. If the ball were put under one pillow and then removed and put under a second pillow, the child looked for it under the first pillow. By Stage 5 the child looks for the ball where he last saw it go, but Stage 5 still lacks an important kind of inference about the location of a vanished object, namely, the possibility of invisible movements. Thus in this stage if an object is put into one's hand, which is put behind a pillow, leaving the object there, and the closed hand is then brought out for the child to examine, he will search the hand vigorously; he will not try the hypothesis that the object may have been left behind the pillow while the hand was there, however, because that movement was invisible to him and requires an inference about a possible movement of the object. As we shall see, in Stage 6 the child copes with invisible movements.

Stage 5 is thus an important one. It is the last stage, according to Piaget, that does not involve actual mental representation of the external world, imagery, anticipation, etc.; it represents the peak of the purely sensorimotor adaptations in the infant's development. Of course, the child later develops far more elaborate, refined, and complex sensorimotor schemas than the behaviors of Stage 5, but no new principles are involved.

STAGE 6 (18–24 MOS.): INTERNAL REPRESENTATION OF ACTIONS IN THE EXTERNAL WORLD. Stage 6 marks the beginning of cognitive representation. At this time the child can picture events to himself and to some degree follow them through mentally. Thus, he can discover solutions to problems without overt trial and error and can imitate actions after the model has disappeared—deferred imitation. He can also fill in invisible portions of an object's trajectory and thus anticipate its final location. The ability to represent events internally requires, of course, some intuitive understanding of the nature of objects, the relationships between different paths in space, and some understanding of causality.

In the remainder of this chapter we shall merely quote some observations illustrating these accomplishments. Piaget's theory of the actual process of acquisition of mental representation will come in the next chapter.

First, let us look at the problem-solving behavior of two children, one in Stage 5 (Jacqueline) and one in Stage 6 (Lucienne), both faced with the same task: putting a watch chain into a matchbox with a narrow opening, slightly less than ½ inch by 1 inch. First Jacqueline, Stage 5.

During the first fifteen attempts she goes about it in the following way: First she puts one end of the chain into the box (2 to 4 cm of it), then she grasps the chain about 5 cm. from this end and thus puts a second segment in the box. She then gets ready to do the same with a third segment when the chain, no longer supported by the child's hand, slides out of the box and falls noisily. Jacqueline recommences at once and fourteen times in succession sees the chain come out as soon as it is put in. It is true that around the tenth attempt, Jacqueline has tired of it and was about to give up; but I placed the chain in the box (without the child's seeing how) and then she regained hope by noting that such a result was not impossible.

At the sixteenth attempt, a new phenomenon; Jacqueline having grasped the chain nearer the middle, the chain no longer lengthened as before at the time when the child raises it but takes the form of two entwined cords. Jacqueline then understands the advantage she can take of this new presentation and tries to make the two ends enter the box together.—She no longer lets the chain go after putting one of the ends into the box, as was the case in attempts 1–15, but tries to put all of it in. But, as always occurs when a child of this age manipulates flexible objects, Jacqueline considers the chain as being rigid and lets go of the whole of it when both extremities have been put in the box. The chain then comes out again somewhat, but Jacqueline gently reintroduces the part that hangs.

Attempt 17: Jacqueline distinctly tries to repeat the preceding movement. At first she does not grasp the chain at one end but pulls it together somewhat and grasps the middle part. She again succeeds in putting both ends in together.

Attempt 18: Resumes the initial procedure and fails.

Attempt 19: Rediscovers the procedure of attempts 16 and 17. (*Origins of Intelligence*, pp. 318–319)

In this description we see how Jacqueline makes the major discoveries in her problem solution by accident, but how she then takes advantage of them and deliberately modifies her behavior in small ways to fit the demands of the situation. Now let us look at the behavior of Lucienne, who did not encounter the problem of putting a watch chain into a matchbox until she was sixteen months old (in Stage 6).

At 1;4(0) without even having contemplated this spectacle, Lucienne looks at the box which I bring nearer and return without her having seen the contents. The chain spreads out on the floor and she immediately tries to put it back into the box. She begins by putting one end of the chain into the box and trying to make the rest follow progressively. This procedure which was first tried by Jacqueline, Lucienne finds successful the first time (the end put into the box stays there fortunately) but fails completely at the second and third attempts.

At the fourth attempt, Lucienne starts as before but pauses, and after a short interval, herself places the chain on a flat surface nearby, rolls it up into a ball intentionally, takes the ball between three fingers and puts the whole thing in the box. The fifth attempt begins by a very short resumption of the first procedure. But Lucienne corrects herself at once and returns to the correct method. (*Origins of Intelligence*, pp. 336–337)

The difference between the two solutions is striking, although it is not easy to know just what happened inside Lucienne's head when she solved the problem so brilliantly. It is clear that she did not need to happen onto the correct strategy by an accidental variation of the fruitless attempt to feed the chain into the box link by link. Piaget hypothesizes that Lucienne constructed the solution in her imagination and then was able to carry it out. This ability to form a mental representation of events is the hallmark of Stage 6 and the end of infancy.

Other evidences of this ability to picture events mentally can be found in the child's search for objects that have disappeared and in his understanding of spatial relations. First, it is important to understand why Piaget believes that mental representation is essential for the understanding of spatial relations. The essential insight that the child must acquire is that space is a continuous medium within which all displacements of objects occur. Objects may take various paths to an end point and return to the starting point either by retracing the path or by taking another one.

There are two senses in which this continuity and group structure are not visible. The first is that one object may go behind another. The continuity of the path is therefore not perceptible, and so it must be mentally constructed and given an image. Thus, a child who is mentally unable to represent invisible displacements, has an incomplete grasp of the nature of space—his space is full of holes, so to speak.

A second reason why mental representation is necessary is that the child must put his own body into the same space with other objects. He must in his cognition take an outside view of his own movements. His plan or cognitive picture of his path from the front door to the kitchen cannot merely be a recreation of the series of perceptions he would experience in following the path; it must be like a map in which he sees himself following the path. This ability to picture oneself as from the outside means the mental construction of a picture that one never actually sees. Piaget believes therefore that the child cannot have a genuine intuitive understanding of objects in space without being capable of mentally representing events.

The best evidence that such mental representation occurs at Stage 6 is the child's ability to solve problems that involve invisible displacements of objects. For example:

At 1;6(8) Jacqueline throws a ball under a sofa. But instead of bending down at once and searching for it on the floor she looks at the place, realizes that the ball must have crossed under the sofa and sets out to go behind it. But there is a table at her right and the sofa is backed against a bed on the left; therefore she begins by turning her back on the place where the ball disappeared, goes around the table and finally arrives behind the sofa at the right place. Thus she has closed the circle by an itinerary different from that of the object and has thereby elaborated a group through representation of the invisible displacement of the ball and of the detour to be made in order to find it again. (*Construction of Reality*, p. 205)

It is interesting to note in passing how this kind of detour behavior is viewed similarly and yet differently by Piaget and Lewin. Lewin was primarily concerned with how the child could turn her back on the wanted object and go away from it against the force; but he was not very concerned with just what sort of cognitive reconstruction was required to see the movement away from the goal as the first step in the pathway toward it. Piaget, on the other hand, with his preoccupation with the group structure of displacements views this behavior as interesting because it reflects the child's understanding of an elaboration of the group, and he sees no problem of overcoming forces against turning the other way.

Two other manifestations of Stage 6 are the child's ability to imitate an action after the model is no longer present and his ability to pretend. These abilities are involved so closely with the actual process of forming an image and a conceptual schema that they will be described and discussed in the next chapter.

SUMMARY

We have seen the child progress through the six stages of infancy. At first his behavior is limited to those reflexes with which he is born, although even those are modified and expanded through experience. Then he begins to acquire new schemas that are extensions of these reflex patterns but have new end results. By Stage 3 he can acquire completely new behavior patterns which occur accidentally in the course of random movement and reproduce or prolong an external event. In Stage 4 the child becomes capable of genuinely intentional activities and can put together sets of schemas in a means-end relationship using his schemas much more freely and flexibly, and in a more mobile manner. Stage 5 is marked by the appearance of intentional variation of behavior to produce new behaviors; and finally Stage 6 is characterized by the possibility of mental representation.

SEVEN

Development of conceptual

thought—preoperational stage

WITH THE APPEARANCE of Stage 6 in infancy, the child begins to experience mental pictures of the external world and of his own actions. These schemas are the first signs of a conceptual thinking that will eventually come to fruition in logical thinking. According to Piaget, these schemas are basically different from sensorimotor schemas. What is their difference and how do they influence the overt behavior of the child?

To discover how perceptions and habits differ from conceptual thought, let us examine in some detail Piaget's view of perception and habit. He has a distinctive notion about those processes which must be understood before one can appreciate his view of the accomplishments of conceptual thinking.

NATURE OF PERCEPTION

Within pyschology there are many controversies about the nature of perception. In naïve theory the problem of perception is virtually ignored; it is taken for granted that people perceive the outside world with relative accuracy; in a sense they merely register what is there. As soon as one begins to trace the mechanism, however, it becomes obvious that accurate perception is an amazing phenomenon, in view of the many sources of distortion and the many restrictions on the kind of information that can be transmitted from the sense organ to the brain. The basic fact is that many different arrangements of shapes and objects can all produce exactly the same pattern of stimulation on the sense organs. What the individual reports he perceives is only one of a number of interpretations that would be equally justified on the basis of the momentary sensory information.

This fundamental ambiguity of the sensory information is well illustrated in the demonstrations devised by Ames (1951). Figure 7-1, for example, shows a pair of pictures of what look like two chairs. Both pictures are seen through a peephole in a particular position. Figure 7-2 then shows the two objects from a different perspective. The one "chair" is now seen to be composed of a set of stretched strings. In the momentary stimulation represented in Figure 7-1, the two very different physical objects were perceptually equivalent.

Why are both objects seen as chairs in Figure 7-1 rather than as sets of strings? If there is so much possibility of misinterpretation, why is perception normally as accurate as it is? Various factors contribute to this accuracy. For example, the grotesque object in Figure 7-2 looks like a chair only if one views it from a particular angle and through a small peephole, as in Figure 7-1. If one viewed it with both eyes, "chair" would not be so reasonable an interpretation of the data. Additional sensory information reduces the ambiguity. Still more in-

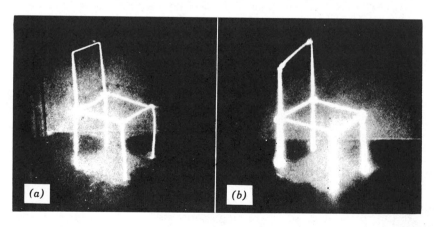

Figure 7-1. Chairs as seen in the Ames demonstration. The person looks through a peephole *a* and sees Figure 7-1*a*. He then looks through peephole *b* and sees Figure 7-1*b*. These photographs were made by placing the camera lens at the peephole. Would you say that the chairs are very much the same size, the same distance away, etc? (Figures 7-1 and 7-2 are taken from Stagner and Karwaski, *Psychology*, copyright, 1952, McGraw-Hill Book Company, Inc. McGraw-Hill Book Company. Used by permission.

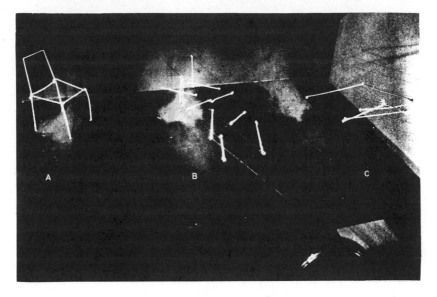

Figure 7-2. The setup of the Ames demonstration. After the person looks through the peepholes, he is invited to look behind the screen and this is what he sees. Do both *a* and *b* now look the same? (*c* is also seen as a chair when viewed through the peephole.) How can string pattern *b* give rise to the perception of a chair? Does this show that the organism contributes something to the nature of what is perceived "out there?"

formation resulting from moving the head would distinguish Figure 7-1*a* from Figure 7-1*b* even more clearly. It might be impossible for an observer who remained motionless to tell which of two lighted lines in a dark room were nearer; with some small head movement, though, he could obtain more information from the relative motion of the two retinal images and so make a judgment.

Past experience plays a role in perception and generally leads to more accurate perception. Both figures in Figure 7-1 look like chairs rather than like scattered rods partly because the chair is a familiar object. In Figure 7-1*b*, this past experience leads to a misperception, but generally familiarity is a reliable indicator of what the object is.

Difference between Perception and Conceptual Judgment (Piaget, 1950)

We can also sometimes arrive at accurate judgments about sizes and shapes by taking other information into account, even if the actual perception is illusory. Thus, Figure 7-3 shows the familiar Müller-Lyer

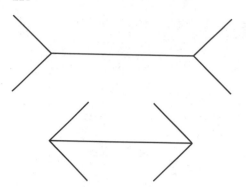

Figure 7-3. Muller-Lyer illusion.

illusion. The lines in the figure do not look the same length, yet if we measured them with a two-inch object and found that in each case the ends of the lines coincided with the ends of the two-inch rule, we would judge they were the same length. This measurement, of course, presumes that a two-inch rule does not change length when it is moved from one place to another in space.

This last example illustrates one way that thought and perception differ. One can know something is one way, yet perceive it differently. In such cases, the knowledge is usually based upon a broader body of information than is the perception, although this broader body of information is somehow not integrable into a perception. The cues available for judgments that do not influence perception are perhaps remote either in time or in space, or perhaps come by way of some other channel of information. Thus, we may take someone's word for something, even if we cannot perceive it directly.

For Piaget, one of the important developments in the child's acquisition of conceptual thought is the gradual appearance of the effects of previous knowledge upon his thinking. One of the most striking experiments on this topic is by Piaget and Taponier (1955–6). They presented two sticks of equal length that were set off as in Figure 7-4(a) to children of various ages. To eight-year-olds, the top line looks longer than the bottom. To five-year-olds, however, there is no illu-

(a)   (b)

Figure 7-4. The sticks used in conservation of length.

sion; the two lines look equal in length. The illusion gradually increases until the age of eight and then gradually decreases with increasing age. To adults the top line looks slightly longer than the bottom, but not as much longer as it does at the age of eight. The illusion is a perceptual one in this situation.

Now suppose that the child of five is shown two sticks, but one is directly above the other as in Figure 7-4b. Under these conditions the sticks appear equal in size and the child of five readily agrees that they are. Now in front of his eyes, the top stick is moved to the right until Figure 7-4a is constructed. The child is asked whether the two sticks are equal. Under this procedure he generally says that the top line is longer. He may say the top is longer or shorter, but he always says the two are not equal. By the age of eight, he is perfectly certain that the two *are* the same length (not that they look the same length but that they are the same length). Piaget considers that the second experiment demands conceptual thinking because it involves the integration of temporally distinct experiences, whereas the first depends upon immediate perception. This experiment neatly shows that the two developments are not the same. Thus, one important difference between the child who functions at the preconceptual level and the child who is capable of conceptual thought is that the latter can integrate two temporally separate experiences into a single judgment, whereas a dependence upon perception markedly limits the ability to perform this sort of integration.

Perceptual Activity

At the same time, however, Piaget believes that perception itself can achieve a limited amount of such temporal integration, and that the ability to do so increases with the child's age. Piaget distinguishes between perception and perceptual activity. Perception is a momentary view of a stimulus, such as might be obtained if the eyes were fixed and the stimulus were exposed for a fraction of a second. Shapes and relations can be seen, moving objects can be seen as moving, but the view is nevertheless a momentary one. This perception is subject to many distorting factors, but the most important one is that the portion of the visual stimulus that is fixated or attended to is enhanced or expanded. One example of this is the so-called "error of the standard" reported by Piaget and Lambercier (1943). They found that when one of two objects was made the standard and another object was compared to it, the former tended to be seen as bigger than it would have been if it had been made a comparison object rather than a standard.

These "still pictures" are, therefore, in Piaget's view, markedly and unpredictably distorted, because the subject may happen to fixate any one of a number of spots. If the visual stimulus is a steady one, however, and the subject examines it in a leisurely way, his eyes wander over it and he fixates first on one place and then on another as his attention is called here and there. Thus, he actually has a number of views of the stimulus field, each centered differently and each distorted in its own way. The subject does not, however, realize that he is getting a multiple viewing of the stimulus; without knowing it, he integrates these different views into a single perception of the stimulus. If he is comparing the size of two figures, for example, he may fixate half the time on one, which, during that time, appears bigger than the other; if he fixates the rest of the time on the other, though, during that time it appears bigger. If the total fixation on each of the two is equal, the result of these diverse perceptions is that the two seem equal. If, however, one is labeled the standard, it tends to be looked at more than the comparison stimulus so that it may be perceived to be the larger of the two. This shift of fixation and attention is one kind of perceptual activity that produces a perception perhaps different from any of the momentary views.

There are other kinds of perceptual activity. If, for example, one is asked to compare the sizes of objects that are quite far apart, one may perceptually transport one of them onto the other to make a comparison. One does not, of course, actually see the two images superimposed, but one nevertheless transports the distance across the intervening space. Or, if the subject is asked whether an arrow out in space is pointing at a target, he may mentally prolong the stick or extend the straight line to see if it hits the target object. Subjects perform many such actions in a perceptual experiment to come to the judgment required of them.

Piaget does not believe that these perceptual actions are integrated logically in the same way that conceptual thought integrates temporally separate events, but they do tend to make perception more veridical and to compensate for some of the distortions present if no such perceptual activity is employed. Furthermore, they increase and become more effective with age. As a result, some illusions that depend upon the distortion of momentary perceptions decline as the child becomes older and compensates for them through perceptual activity. Other illusions, however, depend upon the activity itself and increase with age.

Conceptual Invariance and Perceptual Constancy

Another feature of perception that distinguishes it from thinking is the lack of invariance of perceptual objects. In our conception of the external world, objects remain unchanged unless something specific changes them. In particular, we tacitly assume that such actions as observing an object, moving it from one place to another, or putting another object close to it do not change its size and shape.

In perception, this invariance does not hold true. It is almost a rule in perception that nearby stimuli interact with each other so that the perception of either in isolation is detectably different from the perception of the same object in close proximity to another. A circle surrounded by smaller circles, as in Figure 7-5a, appears larger than the

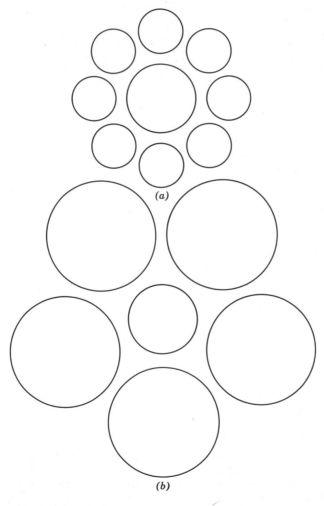

(a)

(b)

Figure 7-5. Size contrast.

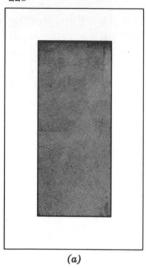 

(a)   (b)

Figure 7-6. Brightness contrast.

same size circle surrounded by larger circles, as in Figure 7-5b. In Figure 7-6 two gray squares appear, one in the middle of a black background, and the other in the middle of a white one. The gray square in the middle of the black background appears lighter. These figures illustrate the principle of contrast. In thinking, however, we do not assume that the size or color of an object changes when it is moved around unless something is done to the object itself to add more color or change its size. One would assume with complete confidence that if a piece of colored paper were stored in a box, it would keep its color all the time it were there and if it were removed in five minutes it would have the same color it had when it entered.

In other ways also, our thinking about the world rests on tacit assumptions. For example, the assumption that the length of a line is equal to the sum of the lengths of its components is logically consistent with the assumption that lengths can be moved from one place to another without change. In perception this principle of additivity does not hold exactly, although it does hold approximately.

We have been emphasizing that perceptions do not entirely fit our conception of the nature of the world, but it is important to recognize that perceptions do show considerable constancy, in view of the much more serious distortions that exist in the retinal image. For example, the same object at different distances does look about the same size, within fairly wide limits of distance, despite the decrease of the retinal image to half its size when the distance of the object doubles.

Parallel Development of Perception and Conception

Thus, on the whole, perception is a fair approximation to the world that we conceive to exist through our thought processes, but it is nevertheless only an approximation. The discrepancies between perception and our intellectual conception of the same situation are large enough for Piaget to insist that conceptual thought is actually different from perception. Even though perception is relatively accurate and its accuracy improves with age, conceptual thinking does not merely correct or build on perception. The child's conception of the world is constructed *de novo* in the course of development.

This basic assumption that conceptual thinking develops independently means that the preschool child's conceptual thinking may be less veridical than his perception. His perceptions and sensorimotor habits may result in more realistic and adapted behavior than his conceptual thinking. Thus, the child of two has no difficulty recognizing familiar objects from any perspective, yet he may totally fail to realize conceptually that the object looks different from different points of view. As we saw in the Piaget and Taponier experiment (see p. 224), the five-year-old's judgment of the equality of the two sticks may be completely thrown off by giving him evidence that logically demonstrates their equality.

The child, in building his conception of the world and its laws, seems to repeat at the conceptual level many of the types of errors that he made during infancy at the sensorimotor level, even though at the time he is making the conceptual errors he can behave adaptively on the basis of his sensorimotor adjustments. This suggests that all of us probably operate on both levels. The sensorimotor adaptations of infancy are not replaced by the later, more conceptual, and cognitive types of adaptations; in fact, the sensorimotor adaptations continue to develop throughout childhood and become more adapted and skillful. But along side of them develops a new way of dealing with problems, an intellectual-conceptual way. Eventually, the conceptual approach becomes more effective and more powerful, but it takes the long period of preschool development for it to catch up and eventually transcend the inherent limitations of the sensorimotor and perceptual mode of adaptation.

Piaget makes no great point of it, but it is entirely likely that even in adult life each approach has its advantages and disadvantages. For standard, repetitive situations, a well-adapted set of sensorimotor habits is probably better suited and more important for effective action than is a clear conceptual understanding. The automatization of habits reflects how conceptually guided behavior may bring about corresponding sensorimotor adaptations that are vital to efficient action. In some areas of life, the artistic and socioemotional, the human race's conceptual understanding may be so poor that too intellectualized an approach may fail where a more perceptual-intuitive approach succeeds.

Regardless of these speculations, Piaget conceives of conceptual thinking as a capacity that gradually develops during the period after infancy. Furthermore, it must grow from the ground up in a different way from the continuing development of the perceptual and sensorimotor adaptations.

THE PREOPERATIONAL PERIOD

Criteria of a Symbolic Schema (Piaget, 1954b)

Piaget believes the roots of the development of conceptual schemas are the mental image and the symbolic schemas involved in the play of the child at the end of infancy. Both phenomena involve an internal schema that pictures an external situation or a sensorimotor schema. The essential feature of all symbolic schemas, as Piaget uses the term, is that the symbol signifies something but is distinguished by the individual himself from its significate. Thus, a word does not function as a sign for the object it represents unless the person using the word realizes what the word means and also realizes that the word is not the same as its meaning. It is this last criterion that excludes perceptions and sensorimotor schemas from the class of symbolic schemas. Sensorimotor schemas contain elements that are internal and that can be viewed as referring to external events, but for the child in the sensorimotor period there is no distinction between the schema and what it represents. Similarly, perception is sometimes considered a mental representation of what is perceived, but as far as the person is concerned he perceives the external event and does not separate his perception from what is perceived. When he describes an event verbally, however, he does distinguish his description from what he is describing. It is this duality of symbolic processes that distinguishes them from nonsymbolic psychological processes.

The Mental Image

For Piaget, a mental image is not an image unless the child distinguishes it from a perception. He must differentiate the image from what it pictures. One indication of such a distinction occurs when the child is able to imitate some action of a model after the model is no longer present. This is called *deferred imitation* and does not occur until Stage 6 of infancy.

Piaget insists that the image is something that the child must construct, just as he originally constructed sensorimotor schemas. It is not an after-effect of perception or an attenuated perception of some kind; it is an independent schema but does not involve external overt activity. Like all mental activity in Piaget's system, the image is an internal act, a schema; it is, in fact, an internalized imitation of an overt sensorimotor action. The child builds up internal imitations of many of his sensorimotor schemas, according to Piaget.

An image is a mental representation of a specific action or event and is just as concrete and specific as the event itself. It is neither a generalization nor a conceptual schema, although there may be visual imagery accompanying more general conceptual schemas. As adults, we may imagine "adding any two numbers." If there is specific visual imagery in this process, the imagery is of some particular two numbers or some concrete event. Along with it, however, there is a conceptual schema in which the two numbers represent all pairs of numbers. It is important to realize that at Stage 6 the child's images have none of this generality. Like a motor schema his image of it may be reproducible over and over, but for him the image does not represent the class of actions described by the schema; it is a specific imitation of a specific action. It may be that the image does not contain all the details of what it represents, particularly the minor accommodations that fit the action to the specific situation. It may be more of a stereotype of the action, and thus perhaps facilitate the child's eventually recognizing that it is really a representation of a class of actions rather than a specific imitation. But, to begin with, an image is not a conceptual, but a concrete, mental representation.

Symbolic Schemas

While one root of conceptual schemas lies in internal imitations, another lies in the process of play. At Stage 6 of infancy, along with deferred imitation the child shows the first evidence of genuine pretending. One action is used by the child to represent another but is still distinguished from it. To pretend to hit someone without distinguishing the pretense from the action is actually to hit the other. The very word *pretend* requires that the pretense represent reality but be distinguished from it. Sometimes young children lose the distinction and suddenly shift from pretending to playing for real or suddenly begin

to believe their own pretense; but, if on occasion the child can genuinely pretend, he must be capable of some degree of symbolic thought.
He must have some mental representation of the action he is pretending to perform which is distinguished from the action that he is really
performing.

But play has other features than pretending. For one thing, it is fun.
The reason this is true, says Piaget, is that play emphasizes assimilation rather than accommodation: Play need not fit the demands of
reality. When one of Piaget's children pretends to go to sleep using a
shawl as a pillow, the child's idea was probably stimulated by the
vague similarity of the edge of the shawl to the edge of a pillow. But
the play makes no demand that the shawl really look like a pillow, and
the child does not need to be convincing in his pretense of going to
sleep; he can stop the game whenever he feels like it. This is the spirit
of play that accompanies assimilatory activity and is in sharp contrast
to the seriousness of the child's attempts to solve problems, to accomplish results, and to fit his behavior to the demands of reality, which
are all part of the process of accommodation.

Despite the fact that imitation is primarily viewed as a process of
accommodation and play as assimilation, the child can often combine
the two. Thus, many kinds of pretend games involve imitating people
or roles, and all complex play certainly depends on mental imagery—
which has its roots in the process of imitation.

In the process of imitation and play, Piaget sees the first appearance
of *symbolic schemas,* internal schemas that permit symbolic behavior.
Behavior is symbolic whenever something in it is used to represent
something else.

Piaget's next point of emphasis is that there are two sorts of symbolic
schemas. One kind is private, idiosyncratic, nonverbal, and more or
less incommunicable. The other is verbal and communicable. It is
adapted to other people and conforms to social rules and customs.

The difference between the two depends on the fact that some
schemas are verbal and use words as symbols. Words are largely arbitrary; they have hardly any inherent resemblance to what they signify,
and their meaning depends on social convention. Furthermore, language is the medium of social communication; whenever it is important for two people to come to an agreement upon their understandings, they must put them into words. Verbal schemas are therefore subject to interpretation, correction, and modification by the verbal
schemas of other people; in short, they become socialized.

Not all mental representations take this verbal form. There is also a
private world of symbolic schemas. These idiosyncratic schemas color

our thinking; they may facilitate or hamper problem solving, and they play an especially important role in both emotional life and interpersonal relations. These nonverbal schemas contain strong elements of concrete imagery, and because of their nonverbal form, they can hardly be communicated to other people in any explicit manner. They appear in our fantasies, our dreams, and our play. Artistic productions frequently represent the artist's attempt to express and communicate his private, feeling-laden, symbolic schemas to other people.

Children's play is one activity where symbolic schemas can be seen clearly and studied. This is true partly because play is often nonverbal, or, if it is verbal, the words used are not communications so much as free expressions. Another reason that play is a good window on the child's symbolic schemas is that it is less accommodated to reality than routine or problem-solving behaviors. Symbolic schemas are also less accommodated to reality than socialized verbal schemas. Quite often they are perfectly accurate, but as they do not need to be adapted to reality. They are freed from a *demand* for accuracy. In symbolic schemas the separation of the person's own feelings from the reality about which he has feelings is less complete than in verbal schemas where subject and predicate are grammatically distinct. Thus, play, dreams, free associations, reveries, and the like offer access to the individual's private symbolic schemas and are widely used for that purpose in psychotherapy and projective testing.

Stages in Children's Play

Piaget has attempted to describe the stages in the development of symbolic schemas as they appear in the play of the preschool child. Exples are presented briefly as follows. All of these are found in the early preschool period, age 2 to 4 approximately, and to some degree the numbering indicates the chronological order of appearance.

TYPE IA: PROJECTION OF SYMBOLIC SCHEMAS ONTO NEW OBJECTS.
At 1;6(30) J said "cry, cry" to her dog and herself imitated the sound of crying. On the following days, she made her bear, a duck, etc. cry. At 1;7(1) she made her hat cry. (*Play, Dreams and Imitation*, p. 121)

TYPE IB: PROJECTION OF IMITATIVE SCHEMAS ONTO NEW OBJECTS.
At 1;7(12) L pretended to be reading a newspaper, pointed with her finger at certain parts of the sheet of paper she was holding, and muttered to herself. At 1;8(2) she pretended to be telephoning, then made her doll telephone (assuming a head voice). On the following days she telephoned with all kinds of things (a leaf, instead of a receiver). (*Play, Dreams and Imitation*, p. 122)

TYPE IIA: SIMPLE IDENTIFICATION OF ONE OBJECT WITH ANOTHER.

At 1;8(30) J stroked her mother's hair, saying, "pussy, pussy." At 1;9(0) she saw a shell and said "cup." After saying it she picked it up and pretended to drink. (pretending to drink had occurred earlier, but here it seems as if the identification of shell and cup instigated the pretense, whereas previously the pretending seemed to appear spontaneously. (*Play, Dreams and Imitation,* p. 124)

TYPE IIB: IDENTIFICATION OF CHILD'S BODY WITH THAT OF OTHER PEOPLE OR THINGS.

In the case of J, the assimilation of the ego to others was achieved directly through games of type IB. At 1;10(30) she pretended to be playing hide and seek with a cousin who had been away for two months. Then she herself became her cousin: "Clive running, Clive jumping, Clive laughing" and she imitated him, strutting up and down (*Play, Dreams and Imitation,* p. 125).

TYPE IIIA: SIMPLE SYMBOLIC COMBINATIONS INVOLVING WHOLE SCHEMAS INSTEAD OF SIMPLE OBJECTS.

At 2;1(9) J put her doll's head through the balcony railings with its face turned towards the street, and began to tell it what she saw. "You see the lake and trees. You see a carriage, a horse," etc. The same day she seated her doll on a sofa and told it what she herself had seen in the garden (*Play, Dreams and Imitation,* p. 127).

TYPE IIIB: COMPENSATORY COMBINATIONS.

At 2;4(8) J, not being allowed to play with the water being used for washing, took an empty cup, went and stood by the forbidden tub and went through the actions, saying "I'm pouring out water." At 2;6(28) she wanted to carry Nonette (the new baby). Her mother told her she could try later on. J folded her arms and said: "Nonette's in there. There are two Nonettes." The same day the game was played again, but became more and more secret. J stopped talking when I went up to her and whispered to Nonette (*Play, Dreams and Imitation,* p. 131).

Another variety of Type IIIB is catharsis:

At 2;9(14) L was afraid of a tractor in a field next to the garden. She then told her doll that "Dolly told me she would like to ride on a machine like that." At 3;0(0) the same thing happens with airplanes (*Play, Dreams and Imitation,* p. 132).

TYPE IIIC: LIQUIDATING COMBINATIONS.

J at 2;1(7) was afraid when sitting on a new chair at the table. In the afternoon she put her dolls in uncomfortable positions and said to them: "It doesn't matter. It will be all right," repeating what had been said to her.

At 2;7(2) she had fallen down and cut her lip. After the usual scene, she consoled herself by projecting it all onto "Cousin Andre" who took the form of a doll: "Oh, it's Cousin Andre. They're washing her because she fell down and hurt her lip. She made a little hole in it. She cried."

At 4;6 I knock J's hands with a rake and made her cry. I said how sorry I was and blamed my clumsiness. At first she didn't believe me, and went on being angry as though I had done it deliberately. Then she suddenly said, half appeased, "You're Jacqueline and I'm daddy. There!" (she hit my fingers) "Now say: 'You've hurt me'" (I said it). "I'm sorry, darling, I didn't do it on purpose. You know how clumsy I am." In short, she merely reversed the parts and repeated my exact words. (*Play, Dreams and Imitation,* p. 133)

TYPE IV: ANTICIPATORY SYMBOLIC CONTRIBUTIONS.

J at 4;6(23) was walking on a steep mountain road; "Mind that loose stone, Marecage" (an imaginary playmate). "One trod on a stone, you know, and didn't take care, and she slipped and hurt herself badly." At 4;6(26) on another rather precipitous path, I pointed out to J the rushing stream at the foot of the mountain and told her to be careful. "Do you know what my little negress friend did? She rolled right to the bottom of the mountain into the lake. She rolled for four nights. She scraped her knee and her leg terribly. She did not even cry. They picked her up afterwards. She was in the lake and she couldn't swim and was nearly drowned. At first they couldn't find her and then they did." (*Play, Dreams and Imitation,* p. 134)

These examples of symbolic play illustrate the complexities of trying to understand just what is going on psychologically. In every example one object or event is represented by another. The representation may be exact as in some of the reenactment of events, or it may be quite different, even the opposite. There is a concreteness about the relationships in these play events which is quite different from that which occurs in more conceptual relationships between two objects. Thus, the cup and shell do not seem to be seen by the child as two objects of the same shape; it is merely that the shell reminds the child of a cup. One also senses that although the symbolization has various functional values, it is not an intentional drawing of comparisons, such as occurs when one makes up a story to illustrate a point; it is merely that the symbolic schema is evoked by the situation.

Verbal Schemas

For several reasons verbal schemas are important in the development of concepts. In the first place, words are our most nearly arbitrary signs. Although some words have an inherent resemblance to what they represent, they are, in the main, quite arbitrary, and there is no inherent reason to prefer "hund" to "dog" or "chien" as the best word for signifying the barking mammal we have for a pet. The definition of the word must, therefore, be acquired from other people, and the meaning of the word must be clear, transmissible, and constant. When one event is symbolic of another as thunder is of anger, the two events have an implicit and inherent connection that does not require a definition to be understandable. Yet, because they have no definitions, symbols are vaguer and hazier in what they signify.

Words also distinguish between external objects and the person's action toward them. Sensorimotor schemas concerning an external object, like a bottle or a ball, are actions that involve the object. In a sense, therefore, the object itself is represented and described by all the schemas that involve it; by being assimilable to schemas of rolling, throwing, grasping, bouncing, looking, etc., the ball is distinguishable from other objects. There is, however, no single sensorimotor schema that represents the object "ball" in the same way that the word "ball" does.

Further, it is especially important that there is no representation of the class of objects called "balls" in the sensorimotor system of schemas. That all balls are assimilable to the same set of schemas reflects the fact that all balls have some common properties. Those properties are the defining characteristics of the class, but the set of sensorimotor schemas would be the same whether only one ball entered and reentered the child's experience with high frequency or many different members of the class balls served him as stimuli.

The need for words to be defined in order to be used helps create the concept of ball as a class, since the definition of the word is the definition of the class. The arbitrariness of words also makes it possible to have words that represent unknown, unperceivable, or even unimaginable concepts.

The thought processes that Piaget describes in his discussion of symbolic schemas are similar to the primary thought process described by Freud (see Chapter 10). In fact, Piaget is deliberately trying to encompass primary-process thinking within his general theoretical framework and is drawing upon Freud's description. The difference between the Freudian and the Piagetian conceptualizations is primarily a matter of emphasis. Freud emphasized the primitiveness of the thinking and its relationship to motives. Piaget recognizes the way that motivational and defensive emotional reactions may shape the symbolic schemas, but he argues that such symbolic thinking is organized even though it is neither verbal nor logical. He also believes that the capacity for symbolic thinking develops after infancy, rather than being a primitive mode of thought found during infancy. Despite the differences, however, there are many similarities between Piaget's and Freud's conceptualizations.

Although words play a tremendously important role in facilitating the development of concepts, conceptual thinking does not automatically occur when the child learns to talk. When he first uses words, the child is not using them as signs or representations for objects and events, but merely as utterances that function as speaking schemas and assimilate various environmental events. Thus, saying "mama" when mother appears need not be psychologically different from hugging her when she holds the child in her lap; shouting "mine" can merely be an instrumental act for keeping an object, just as one would cling tightly to it.

Gradually, however, words become used in a more representative way. At first they are merely accompaniments of action, and perhaps in some way represent the action they accompany. Thus, for example:

At 1;1(0) J used the conventional onomatopoeic sound, "tch, tch" to indicate a train passing her window, and repeated it each time a train passed, probably after the suggestion had first been made to her. But she afterward said "tch, tch" in two quite distinct types of situations. On the one hand she used it indiscriminately for any vehicle she saw out of another window; cars, carriages, even a man walking, at 1;1(4). At about 1;1(6) and on the following days any noise from the street as well as trains produced "tch, tch." But on the other hand, when I played bo-peep, appearing and disappearing without speaking, J at 1;1(4) also said "tch, tch," probably by analogy with the sudden appearance and disappearance of the trains. (*Play, Dreams and Imitation*, p. 216)

In reading this quotation, we find it almost irresistible to think that Jacqueline meant something by her "tch, tch" and to try to decide what it was. It might mean "vehicles," but how could it mean both "vehicles" and "sudden appearances and disappearances"? Its meaning seems to shift unaccountably, but this predicament arises from the assumption that at the time she said "tch, tch," Jacqueline was naming the object that was out there. Even Piaget uses words like "indicate" or "used it for" that suggest naming. But if we think of Jacqueline's utterance as something like a tune one hums as one works, then its inconstancy of meaning and its occurrence in quite different situations become more intuitively understandable. One may hum the tune when part of it or some similar music is heard, in a situation where one has heard it frequently, when a certain mood descends, or in connection with thoughts about a certain person. It is, in a sense, symbolic of all those situations, but it is not a label for them. For the young' child words are not labels either, and we are led into dilemmas if we assume that the 18-month-old child is naming objects in the sense that we do.

Gradually, the child does use words as names, or representations of objects and events, and verbal schemas as descriptions. One clear evidence of this is the appearance of memory and verbal recall of past events. Like deferred imitation the representative behavior implies the existence of an internal representation. Thus, Jacqueline at 1;7(4), while presumably having a nap and not realizing she was overheard, repeated a list of the kinds of food she had had for lunch.

Even when words are used by children as names in a clearly representative way, they need not be concepts in the way that they are for adults. Most nouns, like pencil or book, are for adults not names of unique objects but names of classes of objects. In a sentence a noun is used to refer to a specific object, but the word is clearly understood to be applicable to any of the class of pencils or books. This makes many difficulties for the child of 2 to 4 years of age, even when he can use language fairly well in everyday situations. For example, in Piaget's record of Jacqueline:

At about 2;6, she used the term "the slug" for the slugs we went to see every morning along a certain road. At 2;7(2) she cried: "There it is" on seeing one and when we saw another ten yards further on she said "There is the slug again". I answered, "But isn't it another one?" J went back to see the first one. "Is it the same one?" "Yes," she answered. "Another slug?" "Yes," she answered again. The question obviously had no meaning. (*Play, Dreams and Imitation,* p. 225)

Piaget speaks of these terms as preconcepts. The child does not clearly understand either that members of a class differ from one another, or that they are all alike in their membership in the class.

When the child struggles with the notion that a word is a label for a class of objects or actions, he meets for the first time the necessity for understanding a genuine concept; and, when he does really understand what a noun signifies, he has achieved his first genuinely conceptual thinking. It is conceptual in the sense that a class cannot be pointed to. An aggregate of objects can be pointed to, and children of two who do not understand classes or classification do form aggregates of objects that are alike in some single respect. However, the formation of such aggregates takes place by a different psychological process than conceptual thinking.

Inhelder and Piaget (1964), for example, gave young children no more than two years old, a number of colored shaped mosaics and let them play with them. The subjects in this experiment did not manipulate the pieces at random. They might group together the red ones or the squares; often they formed some sort of geometrical pattern composed of pieces of a single shape. This behavior made it appear that the children were classifying the objects according to shape and picking out all the members of a class to form the geometrical shape, but Piaget denies this interpretation. He describes it as the successive assimilation of square objects by a sensorimotor schema and perhaps also the recognition of homogeneity of the line of objects if they are all the same shape. But they are not grouped into a class on the basis of squareness. Some of the evidence for Piaget's interpretation is the fact that other sorts of building also occur; there may be a chain reaction in which the first shape is matched by the second in shape, but the third matched to the second by color, etc. It is not a defining criterion, but merely a momentary clustering of the two objects because of their similarity.

Piaget says that for a classification of the objects into groups, there must be a mental representation of a set of categories throughout the sorting process; each category has a defining characteristic that determines whether an object is put into that category. Furthermore, each set of objects must be considered as a number of distinct individual objects with a common feature that defines the class. We saw in the example of Jacqueline and the slugs that she did not really have any idea of the difference between one slug appearing over and over again and several different slugs that were all alike. Her bewilderment is perhaps a little like what any of us might feel if we were asked whether the feeling of awe one had in the Cathedral of Notre Dame was the same feeling or a different one from what is experienced two weeks later at Notre Dame, or on another occasion at Chartres.

This puzzlement about the feeling of awe indicates that we do not have a concept of the feeling. We cannot define it, cannot verbally describe it, and can hardly decide whether to ascribe it to ourselves or to the spectacle that inspires it. It is a recognizable feeling that is elicited by appropriate circumstance, but it is not a label for a class of experiences whose individual members have distinctiveness but also certain common features that put them into the same class.

Although there is no reason to suppose that the child's notion of "slug" is like the adult's notion of "awe," it is instructive to discover that the same questions that puzzled Jacqueline puzzle us, and that we cannot justify the existence of a concept of "feeling of awe."

Classification

Having introduced the idea of a class and having shown how Piaget believes that the young child is not necessarily classifying objects when he puts similar ones into a group or names them correctly, we must now shift to a more abstract discussion of classes and classifications. A great deal of Piaget's theory and research about the changes that take place between the ages of two and twelve involves the child's understanding of the nature of classes and the relationships between them. We will try to present a total overall picture of the nature of classifications and their relation to logical thinking, to serve as a background for describing the child's deficits in understanding classification and the course of his development.

A class, as was indicated earlier, is a set of objects or events that has certain characteristics in common. The common characteristics define the class and often some label in the language designates the class. The members of a class need not, of course, be physically clustered; in addition, there need not even be any real members in the class, and the defining characteristics can be of many sorts. Thus, we can think of the class of *red books,* even though the books might be scattered all over every place. We can also think of the class of *red books on the planet Mars* even though it is unlikely that there are any such; such a class is empty but it is clearly defined.

Classes can have a variety of relationships with one another. One class can be included in another, which means that the two classes have the same defining properties, but that the subclass has additional defining characteristics which the class does not have. The class of poodles, for example, is included in the class of dogs; all of the defining properties of dogs apply to poodles, but in addition to being a dog, a poodle must have some additional specific characteristics that distinguish it from other dogs.

Many of the kinds of relationships described in science can be described in terms of the relationships among classes. The relationship of implication is an example. The statement that Fido is a poodle implies that Fido is a dog. This is true because all poodles are dogs; the class "poodle" is completely contained in the class "dog." Another way of stating this fact is to say that there are no members in the class "poodle —but not dog." If, in a scientific experiment, we observe that there are no metals that do not conduct electricity, we conclude that "all metals conduct electricity" and that the statement "this object is metallic" implies the statement "this object conducts electricity."

By the time the child is adolescent, he has mastered the fundamentals of this sort of logical thinking. He draws conclusions from information and designs ways of getting the relevant information for conclusions. This is the end point of the process, however, and there are many understandings that the child must master before he gets there. The first is to understand what a class is; the second is to understand some of the elementary relationships among classes that Piaget calls groupings of concrete operations; the third is to master the more complex relationships among classes that are described in formal logic and that Piaget calls formal operations.

The earliest age level at which the child understands the relation between two classes has been formally investigated and the findings are described in Inhelder and Piaget (1964). The child is shown a number of counters, some blue and some red, some circular and some square. This particular set of counters is constructed so that all the blue ones are circular. The child is asked whether this is true. The youngest children, about three, do not agree. They say in essence that, "No, it is not true that all the blue ones are round, because here is a round one that is red."

Another experiment related to the child's understanding of this relationship of inclusion of one class in another has been described many times (Piaget, 1952). The child is shown a box of wooden beads, some brown and some white. He first agrees that all of the beads are wooden, that some of them are brown, and some are white. Then he is asked whether there are more wooden or brown beads. The young child's answer is usually that there are more brown beads than wooden beads. Why? "Because there are so few white ones." Not until the age of seven, according to Piaget, does the child solve this problem correctly. Before that time, he cannot maintain one cognitive system in which both the brown beads and the white beads are included in the class of wooden beads, and therefore cannot compare the brown beads to the wooden; all he can do is to compare them to the white, a class that is distinct from the brown.

These experiments illustrate the problems that trouble preschool children with the simplest relationships between classes, and illustrate why Piaget believes that children of this age are not capable of conceptual thinking. Conceptual schemas require that there be some sort of a representation of a class of objects, events, or instances and that the member of the class be viewed both as an individual and as a member of the class.

Invariances

Earlier in the chapter in a discussion of the differences between perception and thinking, we saw that one important distinction is that thinking brings evidence from past times to bear upon a problem, whereas perception is limited to data that are more or less immediately available. This feature of thought and conceptual schemas has been called "time binding," although Piaget has not used that word to describe it. The concept is very important, however, for Piaget's theory of the child's thinking in the preoperational period. One of the child's serious problems is that he may not be able to integrate data from past experiences in order to arrive at correct judgments that would otherwise not be possible.

One illustration of such a failure is the experiment described earlier (see p. 225) where the comparison of lengths of two sticks was required. If two sticks are judged equal when adjacent to each other, the preschool child may believe they are unequal after one of them is moved. This is one example of a number of invariance problems that Piaget has investigated, all of which depend upon the use of past experience to make a judgment. One frequently confirmed experiment is on the invariance of quantity. If two identical glasses are filled to equal heights with a liquid, the child readily agrees that the amount of liquid in the two containers is equal. If the liquid in one of them is then poured from its container into another one which is differently shaped—say one much taller and narrower—the child may not believe that the amount of liquid is still the same. The pouring is carried out, of course, right in front of the child's eyes and he may agree that all the liquid was transferred and that none was added, yet none of these facts lead the child to the conviction that the two quantities are equal.

There are several possible explanations for this behavior. The apparently simplest is that the child does not understand what the words "more," "less," and "equal" mean when used with quantities of liquid. The preschool child in the experiment generally believes that the tall narrow container contains more than the short squat one and he points to the differences in the height of the liquid to justify his judgment. It seems as if perhaps he thinks that the words "more" and "higher" are synonymous. We can check on this interpretation. If we show the child containers of different widths in which the height of the liquid is equal and ask him to judge whether either container has more liquid in it, we find that some children who fail the original invariance problem do correctly judge that the wider container contains more than the narrow one. When widths are equal he judges amount in terms of height; when heights are equal he judges amount in terms of width; it is when they both vary that he becomes confused.

The failure on the invariance problem is not primarily a problem of simple vocabulary. On the other hand, it may well be that the child does not mean exactly what adults mean by the words "more" and "less." The adult definiton of quantity does contain the assumption that quantity does not change when the contents are reshaped or rearranged. The invariance is part of the concept of quantity, and the child obviously does not use the words in the same way the adults do, but this merely restates the problem rather than explains the child's behavior.

Piaget hypothesizes that the child in the preoperational stage fails the invariance experiment because of four factors. One factor is his failure to integrate temporally separate events. At the time the question is asked, the child does not use the evidence from the original situation in which the containers are identical. Perhaps he is responding as an adult might do if he were presented with two differently shaped containers each partly full of liquid and asked to judge whether the quantities of liquid were equal. For the adult, this would be a completely different problem from the one where he saw the water poured from one of the original containers into the new one. Yet for the child, the evidence of equality is apparently unusable. Children in the preoperational stage frequently inspect the containers very carefully, as if they believe that the answer to their problem lies in the immediate situation. The older child or the adult, of course, does not care how the liquid looks in the new container. The relevant data are in the original equality and in the pouring.

Piaget also believes that the preoperational child is revealing the lack of reversibility in his schemas when he fails the invariance problem. The child does not realize that the liquid can be poured back into the original container to restore the original equality. When children do solve the invariance problem they may justify their answer by pointing out that the water can be poured back into the original glass.

Reversibility does not, of course, ensure the invariance of quantity. The quantity of water can be increased by adding water, but the original amount can be restored by reversing the process and taking some away. So, when the child uses reversibility to justify his answer that the amounts are equal, he is not giving a valid reason unless he is tacitly assuming that pouring all the liquid does not change the amount.

Another factor required for invariance is therefore the assumption that if nothing is added and nothing taken away, the amount of water remains constant. It seems likely that some children believe this basic assumption, but then they get into conflict when they see that the levels of the liquid in the two glasses are so different. Some children will answer correctly if the containers are covered with sleeves or hidden behind a screen, but will change their minds if the containers are made visible again (Bruner, 1964).

Hence, in order to maintain a stable belief in the invariance of the quantities, the child must also be able to reconcile the assumption of invariance with the appearance of the liquid in the two containers. That is, he must realize how an increase in height and a decrease in width can compensate for each other. Thus the child may justify his correct answer by pointing out that one container is higher but that it is also narrower, and that is how the amounts are equal. This understanding is not sufficient, though. Some children accurately predict and explain how high the liquid is in the new container, but still insist that the quantities are unequal.

Egocentrism in Childhood Thinking

In addition to his difficulties with the concept of class and class relations, and certain troubles in the integration of temporally separate bits of information, the preschool child has trouble understanding the effect of different points of view on the same event. He does have perceptual and sensorimotor schemas that enable him to deal effectively with simple objects, no matter what his perspective of them; on the level of conceptual thought, however, he cannot anticipate how an object will look from another point of view or even realize that it will look any different.

This is well illustrated in an experiment in which the child is shown a model of a landscape with three mountains in a roughly triangular arrangement, each identifiable by specific objects upon it (Piaget, Inhelder, & Szeminska, 1960). With the model in front of him, he is asked to draw or to pick out pictures that represent the way it looks from another perspective. This is different from ordinary perceptual constancy, in which the child is able to represent actual geometrical relations from his view of the landscape and to identify the landscape as the same arrangement, no matter what perspective he is given. In this experiment he must explicitly recognize that different views are different and know what each one is like. It is as if the child were asked to view a round ball at fifteen feet, and then to draw how big it would *look* at five feet, instead of merely making the same size judgment at five and fifteen feet.

Actually, anybody would find it difficult to judge how big an object would appear to be at a different distance. In a purely perceptual situation, we do not distinguish between the properties of the view of the object and the properties of the object itself. We do not generally have cognitive schemas of size constancy.

In problems of changing the perspective of a landscape, however, the cognitive schema contains representations not only of the arrangement of objects in space, but also of their appearance from various perspectives. The schema explicitly draws a distinction between the

representation (namely the view) and what it represents (the arrangement in space). This duality which makes it a representative schema is
difficult for the preschool child to grasp.

One of the important factors growing out of egocentrism is the
necessity of coordinating the diverse views different people have of the
same thing. For example, to anyone riding along in a car at night
when there is a moon in view on one side, the moon appears to follow
the car. We all learn one way or another that this is only an appearance. One conflict that could force some change in belief is the fact that
two people riding opposite directions would each insist the moon was
following him. The acceptance of both opinions would require the
moon to move simultaneously in opposite directions. This is of course,
contradictory to our tacit assumptions about objects. Thus, the con-
frontation between the two perspectives may require the separation
of appearance from reality. The moon is actually stationary but it
seems to each person that it is following him.

The loss of egocentrism occurs, of course, in many other areas than
understanding the apparent movement of the moon. In social interaction of all kinds, one is constantly faced with the necessity of knowing
other people's views of an event and how they differ from one's own.

Intuition and the Intuitive Period

The preoperational period is a long one in which many changes
gradually occur. Piaget divides the preschool period from 2 to 7 years
into two parts, labeling the portion from 4 to 7 the intuitive stage.
During this stage the child acquires a mode of dealing with many of
the problems of integrating different viewpoints and information from
different sources. He can frequently feel his way through a problem
to a correct answer but he still does not have a clear conceptual representation.

We can introduce Piaget's use of the term *intuition* in relation to a
specific problem. One of the experiments Piaget and his students have
performed is concerned with the child's understanding of what happens
to a sequence of objects when the entire set is rotated in space (Piaget,
1946). There are, for example, three beads strung on a wire like a
miniature clothesline. In the middle of this wire is a tube through
which the beads can move but which hides them from view. The beads
are moved into the tube from the left-hand end so that a red one goes
first, followed by a yellow, and then a blue. The child is asked to draw
from memory the order of the beads in the tube just to be sure he is
clear about the original order. He is then asked various questions.
Which one will come out first, if the beads are pushed on out the right-

hand end of the tube? Which will be first if they are pushed back out the left-hand end? Suppose the entire apparatus, platform, wire, tube, etc., is revolved 180°. Now which color will come out which end? Suppose it is revolved 360°, or some other number of turns?

The young child under the age of four is thoroughly confused by this procedure. He may think that the yellow bead in the middle will sometimes come out first because it is its turn. But the older preschool child often can solve the simpler problems of one or two revolutions. Sometimes he will be able to tell which bead will come out first, but unable to tell which one will come out next or last.

Piaget says that the five-year-old's successes are due to his intuitive understanding of the problem. What he does is to perform operations on his mental images of the beads in the tube and see what happens. He takes a mental picture in all its concreteness, then mentally manipulates it to get new information. It is as if his mental picture followed laws that governed the real object, but he could not formulate those laws conceptually and thus see the problem through in a strictly logical fashion to an answer. The probability of this interpretation increases when one discovers the mistakes children make in the intuitive stage. For example, they may solve one, two, and even three revolutions with increasing difficulty, but find it impossible to know what will happen after seven turns. They just cannot revolve a mental image seven times and keep track of all of its parts. Or it may happen that the experimenter turns the tube by holding onto one end; some children may then be able to track in their minds the path of the bead at that end and know where it is located in the tube after rotation. But they may then have lost track of what happened to the other end since they do not have a conceptual schema of the process that enables them to reconstruct the situation. Or if the experimenter is revolving the tube through two 180-degree turns, he may hold onto the tube by one end for one turn, move his hand to the other end, and turn it another half-revolution. Now the poor child is lost; he had tracked it for the first half, but lost the other end, then suddenly his attention is pulled to the other end and he loses track of both ends.

When the child reaches the stage of concrete operations, at about age seven, Piaget reports that he solves the problem in a different fashion. He grasps the principle that one turn reverses the order, a second turn restores it, the middle bead always stays in the middle, and reversing the order puts the bead that was on one end at the other. Thus even without the concept of odd and even numbers, he can solve more than two or three turns because he does not have to keep so many moving beads in mind. With the notion of odd and even number of turns, of course, he can solve any number of turns in a formal way without having to imagine the tube and its beads at all.

Even though the child can transcend the intuitive approach after the age of seven, it still remains a part of his repertoire. We all use this intuitive approach in simple problems involving interpersonal relations; it seems likely that we must frequently operate intuitively because we do not understand the principles of interpersonal behavior that enable us to transcend the intuitive approach. We must frequently imagine ourselves in the position of the other person and try to feel the way he would feel. In this way we can often discover ways to express a criticism or make a suggestion which arouse less antagonism than would a blunter unfeeling approach.

Decentering

The general principle that Piaget believes describes all of the changes of the preschool period which culminate in the period of concrete operations is *decentering*. Perception is centered on the focus of the moment; a certain amount of decentering can occur through the reconciliation and coordination of successive, differently focused perceptions with different distortions owing to centering. The child's earliest symbolic and representative schemas are centered, since they are concrete pictures involving centered perceptions and focused sensorimotor schemas. The preschool child has trouble conceiving of a class because he centers on one member at a time, with only the vaguest idea of the existence of other members. Thus, he neither discriminates among members nor recognizes the similarity that defines the class. In the experiment on brown and white beads in which he needs to compare a subclass with a whole class, he cannot simultaneously represent both the part and the whole. In the invariance problem, he centers first on the present situation, so that information from previous events is not brought into the conceptualization; he then centers upon one or another aspect or phase of the situation, so that information from other phases or the entire configuration is not brought into the conceptualization. Finally, centering prevents the child from taking any point of view other than the one he has at the moment.

Just as perceptual activity with its shift of centering can bring about relatively decentered perception, so mental experiments involving the active moving of mental imagery can bring about an intuitive appreciation of temporal change, or another viewpoint. Such imagery can reflect laws and thus help the child solve problems intuitively, without the child having explicit knowledge about the laws. This imaginal activity helps to decenter thought, but it has its limitations when the required activity becomes too complex. It is only when the schema becomes genuinely conceptual and operational that all of the effects of various kinds of change of perspective and transformations over time are simultaneously represented in the thought process. Then thinking can become truly decentered and truly logical. This occurs around the age of seven, Piaget believes, and marks the period of operational thought. This period will be the subject of the next chapter.

SUMMARY

The preoperational period in the development of the child marks the interval from the earliest beginnings of cognitive representations in the form of concrete imagery and rudimentary symbolic play to the time in which the child's conception of his environment and its operation is coherently organized.

Conceptualization permits a more decentered adaptation to the world than either sensorimotor schemas or perception. It is not that those systems are completely centered; it is that they cannot integrate temporally and spatially distinct information as effectively as can conceptual thinking.

The first step in cognitive representation is the mental image. Out of this beginning a variety of representative schemas gradually develop. Some of these—primarily because they become verbal—become objective, fitted to the cultural norms, and communicable. Others remain symbolic, idiosyncratic, and subjective.

The child's concepts begin as piecemeal acquisitions that are not coherently organized. Thus, he does not behave consistently, particularly when he must integrate temporally separate events. Before the final development of coherent logical structures, there is a more concrete intuitive stage where the child's imagery becomes quite serviceable for picturing and predicting the effect of various changes; but even at best this stage results in only a limited predictability.

EIGHT

The periods of concrete
and formal operations

THE CHILD'S THINKING during the preoperational period is marked
more by his failure to think operationally than by a clear definition of
his thought process. During this period the inconsistencies and lack of
organization in the child's thinking stand out. At times, the preschool
child seems to behave in a perfectly logical fashion, and then, quite
mysteriously, he fails to follow through an apparently simple logical
pattern.

In the periods of concrete and formal operations the child's thinking
appears to be stabilized. It seems as if all the logical implications of
any one belief are also present and available for his thought process.
There are things that he does not understand, true enough, but he no
longer gives the impression that he understands something, only to reveal two sentences later that he does not understand it after all.

According to Piaget, this stable, equilibrated type of thinking results
from the organization of operational thoughts into interrelated systems. This organization makes it possible for the child to behave consistently and logically and to follow through the implications of his
ideas.

Furthermore, says Piaget, this organization of mental actions in operational thinking can be described in terms of mathematical groups
and groupings and, as we shall see a little bit later, also in terms of a
lattice. The concept of grouping has already been introduced (see p.
179), and the description of a mathematical lattice will come later in
this chapter (see p. 282).

Piaget describes nine different groupings which he believes underlie the thinking of children during the period of concrete operations (Piaget, 1950). We shall survey these and then take one of them as a topic for careful study; we will show the various experiments that are necessary to explore fully the implications of such an organization. We shall then move on to the period of formal operations.

LOGICAL VERSUS INFRALOGICAL GROUPINGS

Piaget first distinguishes between what he calls logical groupings involving logical classes and infralogical groupings involving the relationships between the parts and whole of a concrete object or concrete collections of objects. The difference between logical and infralogical groupings is not primarily one of level, although it is true that the child is able to solve some problems at the infralogical level before he is able to solve the same problems logically.

The essential difference between logical and infralogical systems is based upon the notion of a logical class. A class is an abstraction; the class of all trees, books, or dogs does not describe an actual physical collection of trees or dogs or books. Two logical classes may be related in various ways: one may be completely included in the other, they may partially overlap, or they may be mutually exclusive. One can define the class formed by the union of two classes, or by the intersection of two classes. All of these are terms in the field of logic and deal with abstract classes.

There are relationships between the part of an object and the whole, or between one member of a collection of objects and the entire collection, which are analogous to the relation between a member of a class and the class as a whole. Just as classes can be arranged so that the larger one includes all the smaller ones within it, so physical collections can be arranged so that one collection contains all the members of a subcollection. We can also think of a whole object containing parts, which in turn contain still smaller parts. All these relationships of inclusion and the relationships involved in the ordering of size can be applied equally well to logical classes, to physical objects, or to collections of objects.

Even though the abstract descriptions of the relationship of parts to wholes and of the relationship of members to classes are not essentially different, it is important to distinguish the two. As we shall see in some of the experiments on young children, the child may be able to solve problems that he cannot answer in an abstract way once he can perceive the objects in a physical collection. Piaget believes, however, that the child comes to understand the implications of infralogical groupings at approximately the same time that he comes to understand logical groupings. The concepts of logical thinking are not, therefore, built upon the previous understanding of physical collections.

Piaget describes a set of nine groupings that apply equally well to logical classes or to infralogical collections. Further, he perceives a basic similarity between the groupings concerned with classes, particularly the inclusion of one class in another, and the groupings concerned with relationships, such as those of *greater than* or *less than*. Piaget describes four groupings concerned with the logic of classes and a parallel four groupings concerned with the relations. In addition, he recognizes an earlier simpler kind of grouping concerned merely with the relationship of identity or equivalence. This makes nine groupings in all, any one of which may be applied to logical classes and relations, or to parts and wholes in an infralogical set.

In the next section, we shall discuss each of the first eight kinds of organizations or groupings, but shall not attempt to justify, in a strictly rigorous way, the hypothesis that all of these organizations can be described as a grouping in Piaget's sense. The definition of a grouping (see p. 185) includes the criteria that the elements be so organized that there is some kind of transformation, pathway, or relationship that relates every element of the organization to every other one. Furthermore, it is important that these relationships be reversible; that is, the relationship of A to B can be matched or counterposed to an inverse relationship between B and A. It is also important that the organization contain alternate pathways as described by the assumption of associativeness. Piaget himself in *Classes, Numbers, and Relationships* attempts a much more rigorous definition of the concept of grouping, but the understanding of the concept does not require the degree of mathematical rigor that Piaget attempts to employ.

THE NINE BASIC GROUPINGS OF CONCRETE OPERATIONS

Preliminary Grouping of Equalities

If there are a number of classes or sets that are all completely equivalent to one another, the child must understand this fact. This kind of an organization is very simple, in the sense that if A is equal to B and B equal to C then A is equal to C; the child must be able to recognize this, so that he can go from the equality of A and B and the equality of B and C to recognize the equality of A and C. In terms of an organization, a set of elements whose relationship to one another is that of equivalence can be considered an organization of elements in which the child can go from any one to any other one by means of this equivalence relationship. He can also go backwards, in the sense that he must recognize that if A is equal to B then B is equal to A. There is a kind of identity element in this grouping, in the sense that A is equivalent to A. To understand this kind of a grouping the child must merely be able to recognize the equivalence of all of the elements and to reason from any one to any other one by virtue of the relationship: to wit, if A is equal to B and B equal to C, then A is equal to C.

This preliminary grouping of equalities is tacitly involved in all later groupings. It is important to recognize that Piaget does not include in this preliminary grouping elements that are equal to each other only in some particular property. A chair and a table can be the same height, and equality of height, of course, has the transitive relationship of equality. But to abstract one particular property and recognize its equality in two different objects requires more sophistication than to recognize the equivalence of two objects that are exactly alike in all respects. It is this simpler kind of equivalence which Piaget includes in this preliminary grouping.

Grouping: Additive Composition of Classes

This first grouping has been the most thoroughly studied of any of the eight and we have already used it to illustrate the concept of grouping in general (see p. 185). It describes the organization among a set of nested classes where each one is included in the next larger one, which in turn is included in the next larger, until we finally come to the largest class that includes all the members of the set (see Figure 8-1). We can think of each class as consisting of the next smaller one plus another set of elements that are not part of the smaller class. These other elements do not necessarily have any specific common characteristic of their own, but merely represent the residual elements. Thus, Piaget usually describes this kind of a grouping as $A + A' = B$; $B + B' = C$; $C + C' = D$ and so on, until we get to the largest class.

The $A, B,$ and C are the nested classes and A' represents the rest of B that is not in A, with B' representing the rest of C that is not in B, etc. By definition, A and A' have no elements in common: they are distinct classes whose combination includes all the elements of B. This kind of network, which is found in certain biological classifications and in a

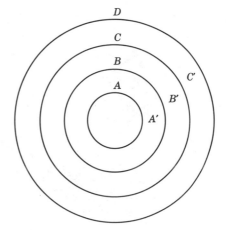

Figure 8-1. A set of nested classes illustrating Grouping I.

variety of other contexts, can be considered an organization that fits the requirements of a grouping. There is a relationship that leads from A to B, namely adding A' to A (see Figure 8-1). There is an inverse relationship that leads from B to A, namely subtracting A'. One can move from any class in this system to any other class by means of these relationships.

A number of elements function as identity elements. On the one hand, $A + A = A$, because the union of any class with itself is equivalent to the class itself. There is also an identity element in the sense of adding zero to a class and thus leaving it unchanged. This organization of elements, although it does form a grouping, does not meet the requirements for a group (see p. 184) for a variety of reasons. One of the most important is that there is no rule by which any element can be combined with any other element. The only elements that can be combined are those that are neighboring, so to speak. A and A' can be combined and A and B can be combined, but there is no rule that defines the meaning of such an element as A plus C'.

This additive grouping of classes is one of the most thoroughly studied in Piaget's research, and in a later section we shall use it to illustrate the experimentation necessary to establish that the child does understand all the implications of this organization of classes.

Grouping II: The Secondary Addition of Classes

Whereas Grouping I covers the relationships of inclusion of one class in the superordinate class that contains it, Grouping II is concerned with the relationships between alternative divisions of the same

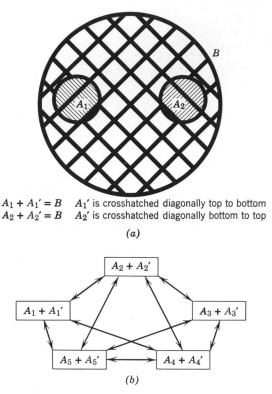

$A_1 + A_1' = B$ A_1' is crosshatched diagonally top to bottom
$A_2 + A_2' = B$ A_2' is crosshatched diagonally bottom to top

(a)

(b)

Figure 8-2. Complete class of mammals—sum of dogs and non-dogs. Grouping of vicariences.

class. Thus, for example, we can divide the class of mammals into dogs and non-dogs. This would be described by Piaget as: A_1 (dogs) plus A_1' (non-dogs) equals B (mammals). We can also divide the class of mammals in some other way—cats and non-cats, for example. There is an equivalence between the sum of the two classes $A_1 + A_1' = B$ and $A_2 + A_2' = B$. Each sum represents the complete class of mammals (see Figure 8-2a). These equivalences, or "*vicariences*" as Piaget calls them, have a logical organization with respect to each other. One can shift from one division of a class to an alternative division and still leave the class as a whole invariant, as illustrated in Figure 8-2b. There are also some implicit relationships between the elements in these two divisions. The class of cats (A_2) is included in the class of non-dogs, A_1'. Similarly, the class of dogs (A_1) is included in the class of non-cats (A_2'). There are more non-dogs than there are cats, because all the cats are non-dogs and there are other animals that are not dogs either. Similarly, there are more non-cats than there are dogs. When the child is able to answer such questions as this and to recognize the equivalence of these alternate ways of subdividing a class into parts, then his logical thinking is governed by the laws of organization of Grouping II.

Grouping III: The Bi-univocal Multiplication of Classes

Piaget describes four groupings that involve classes. The first two involve addition of classes, the second two involve multiplication of classes. Multiplication can be best understood if we think of all the elements in a set as being divided on the basis of two different properties. Thus, for example, they might be separated into the red and non-red ($A + A' =$ total). At the same time they might be separated into the square and non-square ($B + B' =$ total). The relationship between A versus A' and B versus B' is different from the relationship between A_1 versus A_1' and A_2 versus A_2' described in the previous section, because A_1 (dogs) and A_2 (cats) are mutually exclusive, while A and B are not. We can thus multiply $(A + A')(B + B') = AB + AB' + A'B = A'B'$.

In our concrete example, AB corresponds to the class of objects that are red and square, AB' corresponds to the objects that are red and not square, $A'B$ describes the objects that are neither red nor square. Thus, by multiplying a dichotomy, we can divide the total set into four subclasses. $A + A'$ is equal to the total set; $B + B'$ is also equal to the same total.

If we think of these separations of a class of objects (A versus A') (B versus B') as elements, we can see that the separation (A versus A') is connected to the separation (AB versus $A'B$ versus AB' versus $A'B'$) by a relationship of multiplication by (B versus B'). The separation can be multiplied further by (C versus C') to obtain (ABC versus $A'BC$ versus $AB'C$ versus $A'B'C$ versus ABC' versus $A'BC'$ versus $AB'C'$ versus $A'B'C'$). In this way a whole series of separations can be arranged in a

	Red (A)	Non-Red (A')
Square (B)	Red, Square (AB)	Non-red, square ($A'B$)
Non-square (B')	Red, non-square (AB')	Non-red, Non-square ($A'B'$)

Figure 8-3. Grouping III. The bi-univocal multiplication of classes.

sequence. These multiplications are reversible; we can think of removing the classification (B versus B') from the fourfold classification (AB versus AB' versus $A'B$ versus $A'B'$) to return to the original (A versus A') separation. Thus, this whole set of multiplications can be thought of as an organization with consistent relationships among the elements; it therefore forms a grouping in Piaget's sense of the word.

There are various logical relationships among the classes in these different divisions. For example, the class AB is included in the class A and also in the class B (see Figure 8-3). When the child is able to perform these kinds of multiplications—to recognize the four classes that come from dividing objects on two criteria and to recognize the relationship between one division and a finer division—he has mastered Grouping III.

Grouping IV: Co-univocal Multiplication of Classes

The difference between Grouping III and Grouping IV is that in Grouping III the multiplication of red versus non-red by square versus non-square leads to a division containing all four classes: red-square versus red-non-square versus square-non-red versus non-square, non-red. There are a variety of special cases, however, where the multiplication of two attributes does not result in all four classes. For some reason, it is logically impossible for certain classes to have any members. For example, if we multiply the division (dogs versus non-dogs) by (cats versus non-cats) we find there are no animals which are both dog and cat, although there are members in all the other three possible classes. This is the situation in Grouping II.

Grouping IV represents for Piaget a logical completion of the groupings of multiplication. Grouping IV includes cases where each class in one classification corresponds to differing numbers of classes in another. Thus, in one of the matrices Piaget describes, the classification shown on the left in Figure 8-4 is labeled K_1 and has as classes A_1, B_1, and C_1. The classification along the top labeled K_2 has the classes A_2, A_2', and B_2'. When these are multiplied together, only the classes in the triangle on the lower left-hand side of the matrix contain any members. Differing numbers of categories in K_2 correspond to each category in K_1.

This kind of multiplication matrix can be realized concretely if we define the classes in the following way. A_1 is the class of sons of a particular person P, B_1 is the class of grandsons of that person P, and C_1 is the class of great-grandsons of P. This is the K_1 division of the male members of the geneological tree. Another classification of the same male members of the family can be written as follows: A_2 is the class

$$K_2$$

	A_2	A_2'	B_2'
A_1	A_1A_2		
K_1 B_1	B_1A_2	B_1B_2	
C_1	C_1A_2	C_1B_2	C_1C_2

Figure 8-4. Grouping IV. Co-univocal multiplication of classes.

of brothers (everyone is a brother of everyone else) and A_2' is a class of first cousins of people in A_2. What is implied in this notation is that $A_2 + A_2' = B_2$, the class of males who are children of the same grandfather. Class A'_2' consists of those males who are grandchildren of the same person but who are not members of the class A_2 of brothers. Defined formally, A_2' consists of first cousins of the people in A_2. The third class is labeled B_2', second cousins of A_2. They are the remainder of the class C_2 who are not in B_2. The class C_2 consists of great-grandchildren of the same person. Now if these two classifications K_1 and K_2 are multiplied together, we find that all those in A_1, who are sons of the same person, are all brothers. People who are in B_1 may be either brothers (A_2) or first cousins of those brothers (A_2), and people who are all great-grandchildren of P (C_1) may be either members of a group of brothers (A_2) or first cousins (A_2') or second cousins (B_2').

This classification system no doubt appears quite arbitrary and there is no empirical research on children's understanding of this complicated kind of relationship; neither is there evidence that it is a particularly important grouping in the cognitive development of children. As Piaget sees the matter, however, it does represent a logically necessary member of the set of groupings, so he includes it in his list of eight fundamental logical groupings.

Grouping V: Addition of Asymmetrical Relations

Groupings I to IV represent groupings of classes; Groupings V through VIII are all concerned with relationships rather than classes. There is a general one-to-one correspondence between the four groupings of relationships and the four groupings of classes, however. Thus, Grouping V and Grouping I correspond.

In order to understand these groupings, it is necessary to consider briefly some of the different kinds of relationships and the names that have been given to them in the study of logic and mathematics. A relationship is frequently written as A r B, meaning that A has relation to

B. What different kinds of relationships are there? One term used to describe a relationship is whether it is symmetric or asymmetric. The relation of siblings is symmetric, for example. If *A* is a brother or sister of *B*, then *B* is a brother or sister of *A*. In a symmetric relationship, *A* has the same relationship to *B* that *B* does to *A*. This is also illustrated by the relationship of equality. If *A* is equal to *B*, *B* is equal to *A*. The relationship of inequality is also symmetrical. If *A* is not equal to *B*, *B* is not equal to *A*. A special kind of symmetrical relationship is one that is also reflexive. A reflexive relationship is one that holds between the element and itself. Thus, the relationship "equal-to" is reflexive: *A* is equal to *A*. On the other hand, the relationship "unequal," although symmetrical, is not reflexive. It is not true that *A* is unequal to *A*. The relation brother-of is not reflexive: *A* is not a brother of *A*. If we reword it so that the relationship is described as "son of the same father as," then it becomes a reflexive relationship: *A* is the son of the same father as *A*. Another kind of relationship is asymmetrical. If *A* has an asymmetric relationship to *B*, then *B* cannot have this relationship to *A*. The relationship "is greater than" is asymmetric. If *A* is greater than *B* then *B* cannot be greater than *A*. The relationship "son-of" is also asymmetrical. If *A* is the son of *B*, *B* cannot be the son of *A*.

Grouping V describes operations that are performed upon the asymmetrical relationships between two or more individuals, objects, or classes. The analogy between Grouping V and Grouping I stems from the fact that the sizes of the classes in a nested set described in Grouping I form an asymmetrical series in which each member is asymmetrically related to other members of the series. There are fewest members in the smallest class, the second class has more than the first, the third has more than the second, the fourth more than the third, and so on. This example is an asymmetrical relationship between classes, but objects can also be arranged in order of size, in order of weight, or along any other dimension and thus put into an asymmetrical series in which each element is in some respect greater than all the elements below it and less than those above it (see Figure 8-5).

Arranging a series of objects in order of size, or fitting new elements into such a series requires cognitive operations involving these asymmetrical relations. The operations form a grouping in the same sense that the nested sequence of classes in Grouping I forms a grouping. One can move from one element to the next by way of a relationship, and there is an inverse relationship which moves from the second element back to the first; thus, *A* is less than *B* has an inverse relation such that *B* is greater than *A*.

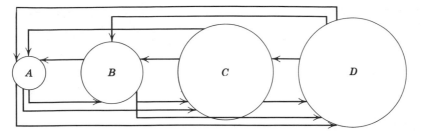

Figure 8-5. Grouping V. Addition of asymmetrical relations. The network of asymmetrical relations in a series. "Less than" relationships are shown below, "greater than" relationships are shown above.

Piaget points to the fact that the inverse in Grouping I and Grouping V are really different. In Grouping I, the inverse consists of a subtraction or a negation. Thus, class B is reduced to the class A by taking away certain of its members leaving only those in A. The relationship within an asymmetrical series is, however, reciprocal. The relationship A is less than B is reciprocal to the relationship B is greater than A. These two different kinds of inverses, "negation" and "reciprocation," will be seen later to be important for some of Piaget's conceptualizations about the thinking of older children in the stage of formal operations. At that time, the child is capable of understanding an organized set of relationships in which both kinds of inverses exist within the same organization. The combination of the two makes it possible to define a special group called the "4-group," which will be described later in this chapter.

Piaget also points to the relation of Groupings I and V for the development of a true number system. The cardinal number 5, for example, is a label for any set containing five members. The fact that 5 is less than 10 is established by the members still left in the larger set after exhaustion of those in the smaller one when a set of five is matched one-to-one with a set of ten. Thus 5 describes a class that is included in 10, as in Grouping I. Numbers are also used ordinally as points on a line where they form an asymmetric series. Thus, both Groupings I and V are involved.

But something else important is involved in moving from an ordered series to a number system of integers, namely, the establishment of a unit. The operation involved in transforming a set of five to a set of six is "adding one unit"; this operation can be repeated over and over again. As long as the classes are merely nested, the operation of going from A to B cannot be compared to the operation of going from B to C.

Once there is a unit operation, though, the classes can be given cardinal numbers. As a result, the numbers form a true group rather than a mere grouping. But it all depends upon Groupings I and V.

Grouping VI: Addition of Symmetrical Relations

The preliminary grouping of equalities is a special case of the grouping of symmetrical relationships, but there are other kinds of symmetrical relationships besides equality that can be related to one another. As an example of Grouping VI, Piaget once again uses the relationships within a genealogical tree. If the relationship A signifies "brother-of," A, "first-cousin-of," and B, "has-the-same-grandfather-as," we can build up a hierarchical set as was illustrated in Grouping IV (see p. 256). These relationships can be combined; thus, if X is the brother of Y and Y is a brother of Z, then X is a brother of Z. Or, if X is a brother of Y and Y is a first cousin of Z, then X is a first cousin of Z. Thus, there are logically necessary relations among these different kinship terms and altogether they constitute an organized system of relationships which Piaget describes as Grouping VI. There has been no research on the importance of this group in the cognitive development of children, but it represents a logical necessity in view of the importance of the asymmetrical relationships described in Grouping V.

Grouping VII: Bi-univocal Multiplication of Relations

This grouping is quite important because it describes the kinds of relationships that can exist when objects are ordered asymmetrically with respect to two attributes at the same time. Thus, Figure 8–6 represents the arrangement of a series of rectangles in terms of width and height. A dimension of asymmetrical relationships extends horizontally: B_1 wider than B_2, B_2 wider than B_3, etc. The rectangles can be arranged so that the widest ones are in the first column, the next widest in the second column, the next widest in the third column, and so on. Notice that the widths do not necessarily decrease evenly from column to column. Furthermore, the rectangles can be arranged in an asymmetrical sequence with respect to height. The elements in the first row are taller than those in the second which, in turn, are taller than those in the third, and so on down to the shortest. When we multiply the two sets of relations together, we get a matrix in which there is decreasing width as one moves from left to right across the table and decreasing heights as one moves from the top down through the table.

The child's understanding of this kind of a table is important in his understanding of the invariance problem, in which he is faced with an amount of liquid which is taller and at the same time narrower. Further-

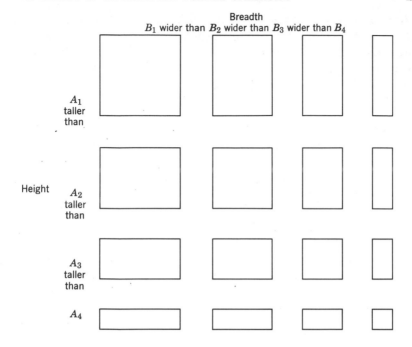

Figure 8-6. Group VII. Bi-univocal multiplication of relations.

more, the two attributes are related to each other so that the amount of liquid remains constant as one moves diagonally across the table from lower right to upper left; that is, a body of liquid that is taller but narrower may have the same amount of liquid as one that is shorter but wider.

When a child puts two sequences in one-to-one correspondence he is also using this set of relationships. In one of Piaget's experiments the child is asked to arrange a series of dolls and then a series of canes in order of size so that the right cane goes with the right doll. This represents the multiplication of two asymmetrical series, but in this case only the diagonal cells in the matrix are occupied. The tallest doll (A_1) has the tallest cane (B_1), the next tallest doll has the next tallest cane, the third tallest doll the third tallest cane, and so on. There is no complete matrix but rather a series of diagonal cells running from the upper left to the lower right. It is Piaget's contention that the child's ability to pair one asymmetrical relation with another to put two series in one-to-one correspondence with each other requires an understanding of the possibility of multiplying an asymmetrical series with another.

In still other research, the child is shown a matrix arranged in this fashion with certain cells missing and is asked to select what goes into a particular cell in terms of where it fits on the horizontal dimension and on the vertical dimension. This tests whether children understand the essentials of this kind of multiplication of asymmetrical relationships.

Grouping VIII: Co-univocal Multiplication of Relations

Grouping VIII, co-univocal multiplication of relations, is to Grouping VII what Grouping IV is to Grouping III. Grouping VIII is concerned with such multiplication of relationships as the asymmetrical series A_1 is the father of A_2, A_1 is the grandfather of A_3, which can be written along one dimension. On the other dimension, B_2 is brother of B_1, B_3 is first cousin of B_1, etc. These kinds of relationships can also be predictably multiplied together; thus, if A is the father of B and B is a brother of C, this implies that A is the father of C. If A is the father of B and B is a first cousin of C then A is an uncle of C. This kind of combination of symmetrical and asymmetrical relationships also forms a logical organization that Piaget describes as Grouping VIII.

THE DEVELOPMENT OF CHILDREN'S CONCEPTS OF CLASSES AND ADDITIVE CLASSIFICATIONS

The nine groupings discussed by Piaget are all abstract, and some of them have never been related by empirical research to actual thinking processes in children. They are part of Piaget's attempt to form a logically consistent system, but many of them are difficult to translate into empirical studies. On the other hand, the exploration of some of the groupings has led to an abundance of empirical research. Of all of the groupings, Grouping I, the additive classification system, has been the most thoroughly investigated. This investigation has been reported in a number of sources, but most recently in a volume by Inhelder and Piaget entitled *The Early Growth of Logic in the Child* (1964). This research program clearly illustrates the variety of implications that follow from a notion of an operational organization that forms a grouping. It also illustrates how the different aspects of the grouping do not necessarily appear simultaneously in the child's development, although, in general, the child seems to acquire the organization within a reasonably short time.

The Sorting Task

How might this grouping of additive classes be investigated empirically? One method that suggests itself is to present the child with a variety of classifiable objects having differing properties, in order to see whether he is able to arrange these objects into a classification. Inhelder and Piaget presented various groups of children with different sets of objects, but the following description of one experiment will serve to illustrate their procedure. In this experiment, the ·child was presented with a variety of objects, some square, some triangular, some rings, some half-rings, some made of wood, and others made of plastic. In addition a variety of colors was represented among sets of objects of the same shape. The child was shown this collection of objects and was asked to "put together the things that are like" or "put them so that they are all the same," or "put them here if they are the same and over there if they are different from this one but the same as each other."

Such a collection of material provides the child with an opportunity to make a number of different kinds of classifications. He can separate objects by shape, ignoring color; he can separate them by color, ignoring shape; he can classify them according to the material of which they are made. Or, if he felt inclined, he could classify them according to two or three different criteria and put together in a single class only those objects that were exactly alike. There is no single correct classification that can be required of the child in order to be sure he understands what a classification system is; even adults who understand the classification problem quite well, might show individual differences in the particular attributes they use to classify the objects. On the other hand, a classification system must meet some criteria for it to be a classification and these criteria determine whether the child can be said to understand the structure of an additive classification system.

Inhelder and Piaget list a number criteria of a classification:

1. When the child has finished classifying the objects, there should be no isolated elements; every element should belong to one or another class within the set. If there is only one object of a particular kind, then it should be put in a class by itself, but should not be left out of the classification system.
2. There should be no isolated classes. For every specific class there should be another class represented by its complement, that is, those objects that do not have those attributes. Thus, if one class is "red," there should be one or more "non-red" classes. It might be that this complement is further subdivided into its own classes. The child might not classify the objects as squares and non-squares, but rather as squares, triangles, rings, and half-rings, but nevertheless, for there to be a classification there should be no partitioning of the set in which there is just one class.
3. Once a classification criterion is established, it should be carried

out consistently. If there is a class of squares, then it should include *all* the squares and it should include *only* squares. Whatever the criterion for a particular class is, it should include all the objects having that attribute and no others.

4. All classes at the same rank should be mutually exclusive; there should be no objects that are classified both *A* and non-*A*.

5. The complementary class in a finite classification system will have its own defining characteristics, although not necessarily a single common attribute. It will not be merely "non-squares," for example; it can also be described as those objects that are triangles, rings, or half-rings.

6. A particular class is included in every higher-ranking class that contains all its elements. Thus, if there is a class of wooden objects, which is further subdivided into squares and triangles, then both squares and triangles should be included in the class of wooden objects. This criterion means that the child should be able to recognize that all of the objects in a subclass are members of the higher ranking class, but that they are only *some* of the objects in the ranking class.

   Finally, there are certain criteria which are necessary before a classification can be called elegant.

7. There ought to be simplicity and a minimal number of classes.

8. The criteria used to distinguish classes of the same rank ought to be similar. For example, if one class of objects is distinguished by being red, objects in other classes of the same rank ought to be characterized by some other color rather than by some different criterion.

9. Finally, for the sake of elegance, if a particular class is subdivided according to one criterion, there is elegant simplicity in using the same criterion to subdivide another class. Thus, if there is a class of square objects which are subdivided into different colors and if there are triangular objects which could also be subdivided by different colors, there is some preference for using colors to subdivide both squares and triangles rather than subdividing the squares by color and the triangles by the material out of which they are made. These ten criteria are required before a child can be said to have really understood the additive system of classification.

When children of various ages are presented with these materials and given simple instructions to put together the things that belong together there is an age progression in the way they approach the task. The youngest children tend to form some kind of graphic collection of objects that generally do not meet any criterion of a classification system. For example, they may make a row of objects in which the first few are all alike; then at some point the color may hold constant, but the shapes change. It is as if each object were put next to its neighbor on the basis of some kind of similarity, but that the particular basis for the similarity shifted from one point to another.

Another feature of *graphic collections,* as these arrangements are called, is that they are arranged in some kind of a geometrical form. In other words, they are not logical classes that are independent of neighboring or being physically together, but are rather mosaics of objects that are put together geometrically. The youngest children tend to have simple kinds of designs that perhaps just form a row. The slightly older children may make more complex designs in which the objects are arranged in squares or in triangles or where the shapes fit together so that they represent a house or form some kind of symmetrical pattern. The important criterion of these graphic collections is that the geometrical arrangement is in some sense an essential part of the way the child arranges the objects, whereas, when the child gets to be seven or eight, the physical location of the different classes of elements becomes irrelevant. Some examples of these graphic collections are seen in Figure 8-7.

Following this stage of graphic collections, there appears a stage of nongraphic collections which is a transition stage between the notion of a collective object, in which the elements are parts, and the notion of a class, in which the elements are members. These nongraphic collections are marked by the continued importance of the geometrical proximity of a collection's elements to the child's ability to think about them though the child does not physically arrange them in patterns when given sorting instructions. The objects are collections in the sense that they are put together, but they are not objects in the sense that they are arranged to have a particular total shape. There are a number of discernible types of nongraphic collections that gradually approach a classification. Thus, the earliest ones include a number of small collections, each based on different criteria, together with an unclassified, heterogeneous residual. For example:

Jud (5;7) makes up six collections: five rectangles, four squares, three letters A, three letters of the same color (M, P, and T), four large circles and one small one. But he leaves a residue of various letters with different colors (Inhelder and Piaget, 1964, p. 53).

Notice, incidentally, that the materials referred to in this protocol vary somewhat from those described earlier. One of the habits of Piaget's

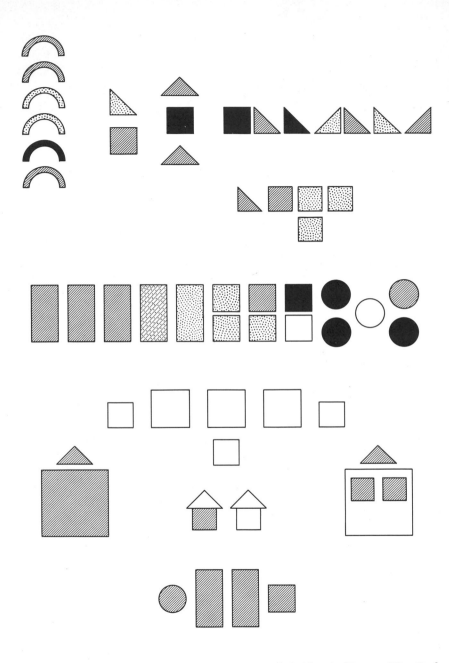

Figure 8-7. Examples of graphic collections. (Inhelder & Piaget, *The Early Growth of Logic*)

investigators is to change materials from one child to another, guided presumably by their own ideas about what is likeliest to bring out the potentialities of the child's thought processes.

At a slightly higher level, there are many small collections, based upon a multiplicity of criteria, but there is neither remainder nor overlap. Thus, for example:

Fon (5;6) constructs nine collections: the circles; the squares; the rectangles; the *n*'s; the *a*'s, *b*'s, and *x;* and the *p*'s, a *g,* and an *m,* and a *t* (Inhelder and Piaget, 1964, p. 53).

Here there is no homogeneity of classes at the same rank nor any attempt to arrange classes into different ranks. Nevertheless, all the objects are used and there is no overlap because no two identical objects are classified differently.

The next development described by Inhelder and Piaget consists of eliminating some of the fluctuations in the criteria. Thus, a classification might be made, for example, entirely on the basis of color. This means that a variety of shapes and materials may be put together into a single class, without any attempt to arrange an hierarchical classification. One criterion is used throughout to make the subdivision into classes.

Finally, the most highly developed type of classification consists of an hierarchical arrangement in which the various criteria are used to subdivide larger classes. For example:

Ker (6;4) starts with thirteen piles of which one is an enclosure made up of all the squares. After a number of tentative attempts, he ends with two boxes, one containing all the rectilinear forms (with the squares and the triangles both separated from the rest), and the other containing all the curvilinear forms, these being further divided into circles, sectors and so forth. There is one stray triangle among the sectors (Inhelder and Piaget, 1964, p. 54).

This example illustrates some of the problems of determining the level of functioning at which the child is operating. It looks as if Ker started out with a graphic collection in which he used the squares to make a box which would enclose some of the forms. This would clearly be a graphic collection. Then after a number of tentative attempts, he finally ends up with an arrangement of the objects which fits the criteria of an hierarchical classification. There is reason to doubt, however, whether he really sees this entire hierarchical classification as a system. Children's behavior in the stage of concrete operations shows much more clearly that the hierarchical system is governing the classification, rather than the classification's being a somewhat accidental intuitive result of the arrangement of the objects into physically distinct groups. Thus, for example:

Rob (8;2), given the materials, starts with four classes: (A) the circles, semi-circles, and sectors, (B) the triangles, (C) the squares, and (D) the rings. Then he puts together B and C, saying *"all the squares and triangles,"* but he keeps them separate in one box and then he puts together A and D, saying, *"all the rounds,"* which are also subdivided according to variety (Inhelder & Piaget, 1964, p. 55).

Here we get a much clearer feeling that the child is grouping the two classes together on the basis of a criterion rather than because they sort of feel better or look better. This overall plan for a classification system implies that in some sense all of the operations in the grouping of the hierarchical classification are simultaneously present in the child's thinking. Such a plan is an important criterion for the existence of a conceptual grouping. It is quite possible for the child to arrive through empirical trial at a clustering of objects that could also be arrived at through a conceptual scheme. One of the difficult tasks of the experiment in the Piaget tradition is to make the subtle distinction between behavior that is guided by cognitive organization and behavior that reaches the same objective result through some other psychological process.

Experiments on All and Some

One of the ways that the child's understanding of an hierarchical classification can be tested is to ask him some questions to see whether he understands the fact that subgroups are members of the higher ranking group. To bring out the nature of the terms *all* and *some* as these appear in logic and as they are necessary to the understanding of a classification system, Inhelder and Piaget devised the following experiment.

In the central experiment they laid out a row of counters that included red squares, blue squares, and blue circles but contained no red circles (see Figure 8-8). The child's understanding of this relationship could be investigated by giving him four boxes: red circles, blue circles, red squares, and blue squares and asking him which boxes he needed in order to reconstruct the arrangement. The child's understanding could also be tested by asking him questions. "Are all the squares red?" "Are all the circles blue?" etc. A typical error of the child of four or five years is to answer the question "Are all the circles

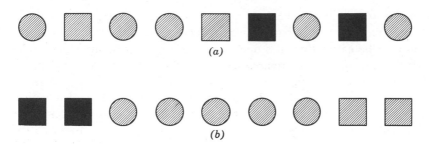

Figure 8-8. Materials for study of child's concepts of "all." In *b* elements are rearranged into graphic collections. Red is denoted by solid figures, blue is denoted by hatched-line figures.

blue?" in the negative and to justify his answer by saying, "because there is a blue square." It is as if the child did not clearly distinguish between the question "Are all the circles blue?" and "Are all the blue ones circles?" According to Inhelder and Piaget, the performance of the child who makes this error can result from his inability to form a logical class. He operates instead in terms of a graphic collection.

They point to the following data to support their interpretation. There are two logically equivalent questions to be asked about Figure 8-8. One is, "Are all the circles blue?" The other is, "Are all the red ones squares?" Despite the logical equivalence of the two, the first question is often answered more easily than the second.

To illustrate Inhelder and Piaget's interpretation, suppose we arranged the counters as illustrated in Figure 8-8b. The members of the three classes are arranged in graphic collections. The question "Are all the circles blue?" now could be paraphrased, "Is the collective object composed of circles all blue?" It is a little like asking if an actual object is "all blue." The child should find the question easier for Figure 8-8b than Figure 8-8a, though there is no empirical evidence for the assertion.

The child at the stage of nongraphic collections can behave the same way, even though all of the objects are not actually segregated. According to Inhelder and Piaget, he forms a collective object of the circles or of the reds, then tries to see whether the collective object composed of all the circles is entirely blue or the red collective object is all square. His success depends on how readily the perceptual characteristics of the objects lend themselves to the formation of a perceptual unit. Thus, if the red objects in some way stand out perceptually, the child can search this object to see whether it is entirely composed of squares.

On the other hand, if he fails to form such a collective object, he is likely to answer the question incorrectly. The question about blue circles may be easier than the one about red squares because the circles stand out or because there are only two red objects. At any rate, it is a perceptually clearer unit than the red.

Only when the child is able to understand the nature of a logical class and to search it to see whether every member has some particular characteristic is he able to answer both questions with equal facility. This does not really happen until the child is nine or ten years old. According to Piaget's data, even nine-year-old subjects do not answer the question, Are all the red ones square? with complete accuracy.

Another interpretation that Inhelder and Piaget offer for some of these findings is that the child, when asked if all the circles are blue, must really answer the question, "Are all the circles equivalent to some of the blues?" Inhelder and Piaget believe that the child does not understand the terms "all" and "some" accurately, so that he frequently answers the question, "Are all the blues, all the circles?" that is, do the blues and the circles completely correspond. Of course, for Figure 8-8*a* the answer to this question is "no." The experimenters present a variety of evidence for this interpretation. Some of the youngest children show a certain absolutism about what "all" and "some" mean. One child of age five, when shown three red squares, two blue squares, and two blue circles and asked if all the circles were blue, said "No, there are only two." Here it seems as if the word "all" should not be applied to such a small number of objects as two. There is evidence in other experiments that children tend to think of "all" as being a rather large number as though it meant "many" while "some" means about the same as "few."

Experiments on Class Inclusion

Still another way to investigate the child's understanding of an hierarchical classification is to determine whether he recognizes that there are more members in a class of higher rank than in one of its subdivisions. This is essentially the same experiment that was reported earlier (see p. 241) about the brown and white beads. This experiment has been repeated several times and in the volume by Inhelder and Piaget it is mentioned with respect to sets of flowers. The child is shown a number of flowers: primulas, violets, tulips, and others. As a preliminary check, the child is asked if all the primulas are flowers and also if there are other flowers that are not primulas. He usually has no trouble with these questions. He is then asked if there are more primulas or flowers. Here is one of the answers:

Per (8;3) has already constructed three classes: yellow primulas, primulas, and flowers. "Can one put a primula in the box of flowers (without changing the label)?"—*"Yes, a primula is also a flower."* "Can I put one of these flowers (a tulip) in the box of primulas?"—*"Yes, it's a flower like the primula."* When the experimenter does so, she changes her mind and puts it back with the other flowers: "Can one make a bigger bunch with all the flowers or with all the primulas?"—*"It's the same thing, primulas are flowers, aren't they?"*— "Suppose I pick all the primulas, will there be any flowers left?"—*"Oh, yes, there will still be violets, tulips, and other flowers."*—"Well, suppose I pick all the flowers, will there be any primulas left?" *"No, primulas are flowers, you're picking them too."*—"Are there more flowers or more primulas?"— *"The same number, primulas are flowers."*—"Count the primulas."—*"Four."* —"And the flowers?"—*"Seven."*—"Are they the same number?"—(astonished) *"The flowers are more."* (Inhelder and Piaget, 1964, p. 107).

This example shows another variety of error that the child may make before he understands the notion of hierarchical classification. It will be recalled in the experiment on brown and white beads that the commonest answer to the question, "Are there more wooden beads or brown ones?" is "Brown ones, because there are so few white ones." In other words, the child answers the question whether there are more brown than non-brown ones, rather than whether there are more brown than wooden ones. But children do not always answer this question the same way. Per answered the question upon the apparent assumption that if flowers are primulas, there must be the same number of flowers as primulas.

Even older children who are able to answer this question correctly may make the same kind of error in thinking about the complementary class. Take this quote from a child of eleven years and six months, who is making an hierarchical classification of a variety of animals:

Duv (11;6) "Are there more ducks or more birds?"—*But the ducks are birds as well."*—"Well, then?"—*"There are more birds."*—"And more birds or more animals?"—*"More animals, because birds are animals."*

"Now show me all the things on the table that are not ducks."—(he indicates those which are not birds)—"Is that all?"—"No." (which is correct)— "Show me all the things which are not birds."—*"The animals, those which don't fly."*—"Are those all living things?"—"Yes."—"Are there more living things which are not ducks, or more living things which are not birds?"— *"The same thing because the duck is the same thing as a bird."*—"Suppose that one hunter wants to kill all the ducks and another one wants to kill all the birds. Would there be more left after killing all the ducks or all the birds?" —*"More when I kill all the birds."*—"Why?"—*"If one kills all the ducks and all the birds, the ducks are birds as well."*—"Are there more living things which are not birds, or more which are not animals?"—"*The same thing, nothing.*"—"What do you mean?"—"*Birds are animals, so there is nothing left.*" (Inhelder and Piaget, 1964, p. 14).

The child is able to recognize that if *A* is included in *B*, there are more members of the class *B* than of the class *A*, but when asked about the complementary class he makes a similar error. (This involves the grouping of *vicariences,* Grouping II.) He recognizes that if you kill all the birds, you kill all the ducks as well since ducks are birds. He recognizes that the non-birds are included in the non-ducks, but when asked which is the larger class, "everything except ducks" or "everything except birds," he returns to the statement that ducks *are* birds and therefore there will be exactly the same number.

Inhelder and Piaget also report experiments showing the particular problems that children save with special kinds of classes. For example, it is much harder for a child to arrive at an hierarchical classification of a set of objects if there is one class that contains only a single object. If children do make various classifications, they tend to avoid those that leave a class with only one object in it. They find it even harder to consider a class that does not have any objects in it, the null class. In fact, if the child is shown a series of pictures of various kinds along with a number of blank cards, he has difficulty even up to the age of ten or eleven in recognizing that the blank cards form a class like any other. Long after childern reach the age at which they do not ordinarily leave a residual unclassified set of objects, they may leave the pile of blank cards alone as if somehow it were not even part of the universe of objects to be classified.

OTHER ASPECTS OF THE STAGE OF CONCRETE OPERATIONS

By this time we have discussed many of the features of the period of concrete operations either in terms of what is lacking in the preoperational period or in terms of the kinds of problems that can be solved with respect to classification. Piaget has made may more empirical studies of other aspects of the period of concrete operations, especially of the child's concepts of quantity, time, velocity, space, and geometry. We shall merely summarize the main finding.

The studies of quantity are fairly well summarized in the discussion of conservation of quantity (see p. 242). Conservation has been studied relative to a variety of characteristics: conservation of quantity of liquid, conservation of number, conservation of distance. Piaget has shown, for example, that the preoperational child does not assume that the number of objects in a row remains constant if the distance between objects is increased or decreased. The child seems to believe that a set of objects spread out over a long space contain more members than the same number of objects clustered closely together. The child also tends to believe, as was illustrated in an earlier example (see p. 242), that the length of a stick is not necessarily constant when the stick is moved forward or backward. Piaget has also shown that the child may believe that the distance between two objects is changed by intervening objects. Sometimes children seem to think that an intervening object extends the distance from A to B and they may justify this in terms of the length of the path required to get from A to B. Sometimes they seem to believe that an intervening object lessens the distance; the intervening object uses up some of the space between the two points (Piaget, Inhelder, & Szeminski, 1960).

Another program of experiments concerns the child's concept of space: his ability to follow a map, to recognize a map, to draw one; his ability to recognize the kinds of changes in shape that occur with projection; the child's ability to arrange objects in a straight line, when they do not happen to correspond to the straight lines of the background. Piaget also shows that the child thinks that a winding path between two points is the same length as a straight path between the two points if the beginning and end points of the two paths correspond. It is only when the child reaches the stage of concrete operations that he recognizes the difference between the distance separating end points of a path and the actual length of the path itself. In all these experiments, Piaget and his colleagues have taken various assumptions about the nature of space, time, logic, classes, or number and shown that the preoperational child seems not to operate on the same basic assumptions about the world as adults.

THE STAGE OF FORMAL OPERATIONS

At the stage of concrete operations the child learns all the various groupings and is able to apply them to objects he meets in the concrete world. But among the groupings there are relationships that are necessary for hypothetical thinking, which the child does not understand until he reaches the stage of formal operations. This stage begins at about the age of eleven and represents the adult stage of cognitive development. Many characteristics of formal operational thinking are not readily related to one another in a clear conceptual way, but are important in the development of problem solving ability.

The first of these has to do with the further development of the child's ability to understand logical relations among classes. In the period of concrete operations a child can understand the relationships presented to him, but in the period of formal operations he realizes the possible relationships so that he can design situations that will provide the information he needs. This is, of course, the experimental method of science. We might wait a long time and never come upon a case in which everything is so well controlled that we can establish the importance of a particular factor in the causation of an event. On the other hand, if we understand what kind of situation is required for the relationship to be established, we become able to design experiments to obtain confirmation or disconfirmation of the particular hypothesis. All of this requires the ability to think of all the possible kinds of relationships that can exist among events, rather than the simple ability to understand the actual relationships that occur.

Second, a part of the child's ability to conceive of all the possibilities is his facility in combinatorial thinking. In other words, he is able to review all the choices systematically so that he can go through them, sequentially if necessary, and know that he has exhausted them all. The various possible relationships among classes are described in the theory of formal logic and the child in the period of formal operations is able, in an intuitive way, to use the entire system of formal logic to obtain the kind of information he wants.

Third, and in a somewhat different vein, the child also acquires in this period some additional concrete constructs. For example, he is able to understand the problem of equilibrium in which there are two different inverses and which leads to the development of the 4-group. In addition, the period of formal operation has a number of other specific aspects. For example, the child does not acquire the concept of the conservation of volume until the period of formal operations, although he has already acquired the concepts of conservation of mass and of weight and of quantity. Volume, as we shall see, involves the equilibrium kind of balance between density and quantity.

With this preview, let us return to the discussion of the child's acquisition of formal logic. It will be necessary first to take a further excursion into formal logic itself in order to clarify what the child is able to do in the period of formal operations and see how it repersents an advance over the period of concrete operations.

Logical Operations

In the period of concrete operations children can multiply two characteristics together and obtain the matrix of possibilities. This matrix

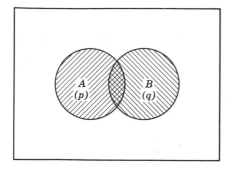

Figure 8-9. Diagram of relations of two classes. Two circles, one representing a class of objects *A* (cross-hatched in one direction) and another representing a class of objects *B* (cross-hatched in the other direction), which overlap.

of possibilities, when represented in logical terms, is the raw material from which all logical operations can be derived. Thus, in Figure 8-9 we see two circles, one representing a class of objects *A* (crosshatched in one direction) and another representing a class of objects *B* (cross-hatched in the other direction), which have some overlap. There are, therefore, four subdivisions of the space in the figure. One area is both *A* and *B*; a second is *A* but not *B*; a third is *B* but not *A*; and finally, a fourth is neither *A* nor *B*. These are the four cells in the two-by-two matrix that emerges when two classifications (*A* versus non-*A*) and (*B* versus non-*B*) are multiplied together.

Now instead of thinking of *A* and *B* as classes of objects, let us think of their elements as statements. For example, one statement, *p*, might be "a dog is bigger than a cat." This is true in some instances but not in others. So the class $\overline{P}$ represents instances where the statement *p* is true. Non-*P* or $\overline{P}$ represents instances where *p* is false. Similarly, *q* is another statement that also is true in some instances and false in others; for example, a dog has shorter hair than a cat. *Q* and $\overline{Q}$ represent instances of "*q* is true" and "*q* is false."

From this we can write a *truth table* for *p* and *q*, as in Figure 8-10. Here there are instances of all four possibilities, "*p* and *q* are true," "*p* is true, *q* is false," "*p* is false, *q* is true," and "*p* is false, *q* is false."

Suppose we now consider the various ways a truth table might look. It might be that *p* is always true while *q* is never true. The truth table

	p	$\overline{p}$
q	+	+
$\overline{q}$	+	+

Figure 8-10. Truth table for Figure 8-9.

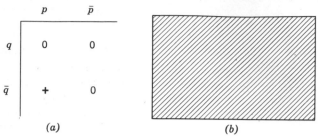

Figure 8-11. Truth table for p is always true and q is never true.

would then assume the form seen in Figure 8-11a. The plus in the $\bar{p}q$
cell indicates that there are instances of this combination. The zeros in
the other cells indicate that there are no instances of "p is true, q is
true," "p is false, q is true," or "p is false, q is false." In Figure 8-11b
the area representing P is crosshatched and includes the entire space.
There is no class Q at all. In other words, p is always true and q is
always false.

A second possibility is illustrated in Figure 8-12a: p is true sometimes and q is true sometimes, one or the other is always true, but both
of them are never true at the same time. For example, if p is the statement "a stick is longer than six inches" and q is the statement, "a stick
is equal to or less than six inches," one or the other is always true,
but both are never true. This state of affairs can be represented by the
diagram in Figure 8-12b. The entire space is taken up by P and Q, but
they have no overlap, so that there are no instances where both are
true and no examples where both are false. One or the other is always
true.

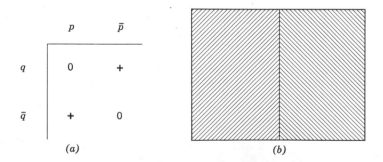

Figure 8-12. Truth table for p is true sometimes and q is true sometimes, but
never at the same time (a). p incompatible with q (b).

We have examined two of the possible arrangements of the truth table for p and q. Sixteen different possibilities are listed and illustrated in Figure 8-13. First there are the four tables in which just one cell of the four contains any instances. These are: (1) PQ, (2) $P\overline{Q}$, (3) $\overline{P}Q$, and (4) $\overline{PQ}$. Then there are six tables that can be obtained by combining each one of the single classes with every other one. For example, (5) $PQ + P\overline{Q}$ is equivalent to the class P itself and means that "p is always true." Table (6) $PQ + \overline{P}Q$, is equivalent to the statement "q is always true." (7) $PQ + \overline{PQ}$ describes a different sort of situation. It means that the two statements p and q are true or false in exactly the same instances. In other words, p and q are equivalent statements; for example, p says "a figure is square" and q says "a figure has four equal sides and four right angles." (8) $P\overline{Q} + \overline{P}Q$ states that p is incompatible with q; whenever p is true, q is false, and vice versa. (9) $P\overline{Q} + \overline{PQ}$ is equivalent to the statement "q is not true." (10) $\overline{P}Q + \overline{PQ}$ is equivalent to "p is false." Finally, there are four tables that can be made by combining any three of the original four. (11) $PQ + P\overline{Q} + \overline{P}Q$ is equivalent to the union of P and Q; either p or q is true or both are true. For example, "p, a number, is greater than 10; q, a number, is less than 100." (12) $PQ + \overline{P}Q + \overline{PQ}$ is an important statement; it says that p implies q. If p is true, q is true, but if p is false, there is no restriction on q's truth or falsity. (13) $P\overline{Q} + \overline{P}Q + \overline{PQ}$ states the converse of (12), that q implies p. (14) $P\overline{Q} + \overline{P}Q + \overline{PQ}$ states that either p or q is false or both are false. (15) represents the combination of all four of the original possibilities, $PQ + P\overline{Q} + \overline{P}Q + \overline{PQ}$, which states that p and q are not logically related, so that all four of the possibilities occur. The sixteenth class supplies logical completeness, representing the null class in which none of the possibilities occurs.

The importance of a working knowledge of these sixteen binary combinations is that through them we can test the validity of any logical relationship between two statements. Suppose one were testing the hypothesis that "when bananas are yellow, they are ripe." Here p states "bananas are yellow" and q states "bananas are ripe." The statement that "if bananas are yellow they are ripe" is a statement that "p implies q"; the yellowness of a banana implies that it is ripe. If the hypothesis is true, then truth table 12 should describe the situation: we should be able to find cases of bananas that are both ripe and yellow (PQ); we should find cases of bananas that are not yellow but ripe $(\overline{P}Q)$—this is true, since ripe bananas are sometimes black; and we should find cases where bananas are neither yellow nor ripe $(\overline{PQ})$. The

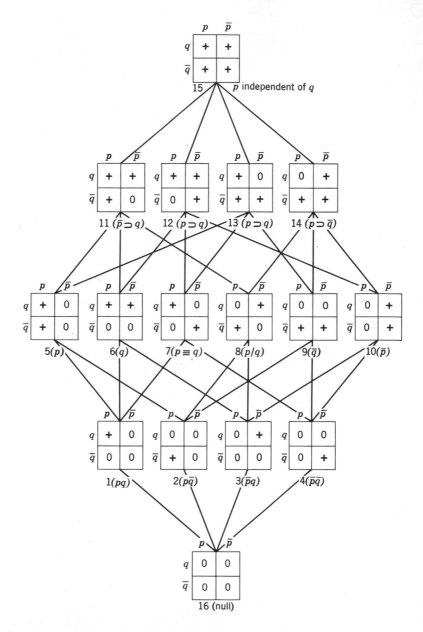

Figure 8-13. Truth table for sixteen binary operations.

critical case for testing the statement that p implies q is the failure to find any instance of $P\overline{Q}$, *that is, to find any instance of a yellow banana that is not ripe*. A person with a working knowledge of these logical relations would know immediately what crucial instances to search for in order to test the statement that p implies q.

Experiment on Separation of Variables

Inhelder and Piaget have tested the ability of school-age children to use these logical relations by posing problems in which a number of possible factors are interrelated and asking the children to formulate and test hypotheses about the particular relationship that pertains. One instructive experiment is reported in the volume, *The Growth of Logical Thinking from Childhood to Adolescence* (1958). The experimenters prepared a number of rods which had cross sections of different materials. As shown in Figure 8-14, each rod could be clamped to

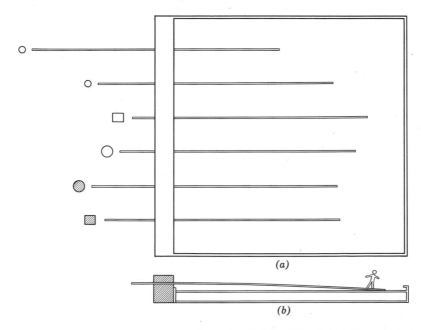

Figure 8-14. Experiment on separation of variables. The figure illustrates the variables used in the flexibility experiment. The rods can be shortened or lengthened by varying the point at which they are clamped. Cross section forms are shown at the left of each rod; shaded forms represent brass rods, unshaded forms represent non-brass rods. Dolls are used for the weight variable. These are placed at the end of the rod. Maximum flexibility is indicated when the end of the rod touches the water. (Inhelder & Piaget, *The Growth of Logical Thinking from Childhood to Adolescence.*)

the side of a shallow vessel of water, so that any desired length of rod extended out over the water. Dolls of various weights were then placed on the end of the rod. The crucial event was whether the rod would touch the water when the doll was placed on the end. Figure 8-14*a* shows the different sizes and cross sections of rods. Figure 8-14*b* is a side view illustrating the arrangement of the rod in the vessel and the doll so that the rod is bent sufficiently by the weight of the doll to touch the water.

The child was told that he could use any of the rods he wished and arrange them in any way he liked in order to find out when a rod would touch the water and when it would not. Several variables are involved in this problem and the important feature of the child's behavior is how well he isolates particular variables, holding other ones constant, in order to test a particular hypothesis. Children in Stage 1, even before the stage of concrete operations, like to put the doll on the rod and are very interested in whether it touches the water or not, but have neither an idea of the rationale behind it nor any ability to test systematically for the influence of any particular variable. Thus, for example:

Huc (5;5) after a number of trials put a hundred grams on a rod and waits as if it were going to descend in a moment. "Why don't all the sticks go down the same way?"—*"Because the weight has to go in the water."*—then he places 200 grams on a thick rod and 100 grams on a fine one.—"Which one bends the most?"—*"That one* (the fine rod)."—"Why?"—*"The weight is bigger here* (he points out 200 grams on the other) *it ought to go on the water."* We put 200 grams on the thin one which then touches the water and he laughs. "Why does it touch now?—*Because it has to."* (Inhelder and Piaget, 1958, p. 48).

Huc reports what he sees, but he is unable to recognize cause and effect relationships in this particular problem. He says that the small rod touches the water because the weight on the thick one is bigger. He also assumes that it is going to touch the water and waits for it to happen as if it would get around to it after a while.

In Stage 2, the period of concrete operations, the child is able to observe some of the relationships between variables as they appear to him, but the striking feature of his behavior is his inability to design the experiment so that particular variables are held constant. Thus, for example, the following protocol:

Mor (7;10) after having put the weight on a narrow rod which reaches the water says, *"It won't fall the same way with this one* (pointing to a thick rod) *because the other one is thinner."*—Then he changes the weight, *"This one isn't so heavy as the other one."*—He places a heavy weight on a short rod, and a light one on a long one predicting that the curve will be sharper *"because the the other weight is lighter than this one."* The experiment does not confirm this prediction, and then he lengthened the short rod.*"Oh! with the one* (thick one) *you have to do that."* The subject is asked to summarize what he has discovered up to that point by ordering the rods serially according to their flexibility.—"Which one bends the most?"—*"This one because it is the thinnest."*—"Next?"—*"That one."* (long and thin, metal)—"Next?"—*"That one* (short wood)"—"Next?"—*"This one* (which is thicker) *it goes with the weight* (heavy)."—"Next?"—*"That one* (heavy and metal) *it didn't go in the water because I had to do that* (lengthen it)." (*Growth of Logical Thinking,* p. 49)

Notice how Mor is able to arrange the rods in the order of flexibility through his own particular experience with them. By and large he arranged them in order of flexibility with the thinnest one first, but he didn't separate the concept of flexibility from either the amount of weight put on the rod or its length. He was also able to see intuitively a one-to-one relationship between the amount of weight it was necessary to put on a rod and its thickness. He said, "Oh! with the thick one you have to do that (put one more weight on)." He recognizes that the thickness of the rod and its length are compensating factors. What he is unable to do, however, is to arrange the experiment so that only one variable at a time is changed while the others are held constant. To illustrate the clear difference we quote the following protocol of a sixteen-year-old who is well into the stage of formal operations:

Dei (16;10) "Tell me first (after experimental trials) what factors are at work here."—Dei, *"Weight, material, the length of the rod, perhaps the form."*— "Can you prove your hypothesis?" (she compares the 200 gram and 300 gram weights on the steel rod) *"You see the role of weight is demonstrated. For the material I don't know."*—"Take these steel ones and these copper ones."—*"I think I have to take two rods with the same form. Then to demonstrate the role of metal I compare these two* (steel and brass, a square 50 cm. long and 16 mm. cross-section with 300 grams on each) *or these two here* (steel and brass with a round 50 and 22 centimeters by 16 mm. squared). *For length I shorten that one* (50 cm. brought down to 22 cm.). *To demonstrate the roll of form I can compare these two* (the round brass and the square brass 50 cm and 16 mm² for each)."—"Can the same thing be proved with these two?" (Brass round and square 50 cm. long and 16 and 7 mm². cross-section)—"No, *because that one* (7 mm ²) *is much narrower."*—"And the width?"—*"I can compare these two"* (round brass 50 cm. long with 16 and 7 mm² cross-section). (*Growth of Logical Thinking,* p. 60)

It is perfectly clear that Dei has the scientific method well in hand in this experiment. She wants to show that the shape of the rod affects its flexibility so she chooses a length and a weight that will make one of the two rods she is testing touch the water. Furthermore, she chooses the two rods so that they are the same length, the same weight is used on each of them, and the same material composes them.

According to Piaget, the child in separating these variables demonstrates an understanding of all of these various logical relationships which, though not necessarily verbalized, is in some sense explicit. It is this kind of understanding of the entire system of relationships among classes that marks the period of formal operations. If we contrast this knowledge of classes with those available in the period of concrete operations, we see that some of the class relationships were understood earlier but that the meaning of all of their combinations was not known.

Another way of expressing the same point is to say that Mor in the stage of concrete operations could extract information from a situation that was concretely presented to him. Perhaps—though the experiment was not run that way—he could even have extracted the correct solution to the problem had the experimenter run through a series of controlled experiments and let Mor observe what happened.

Dei's clear superiority was his ability to design a situation to provide the relevant information. In order to do this, the child must have some intuitive understanding of the sixteen binary situations as a set of hypothetical ones, and must then select the one that will provide the information he needs. It is the child's capacity to use the range of possible arrangements that marks the period of formal operations, whereas in the period of concrete operations, the child is more-or-less limited to extracting information from the concrete situations he observes.

Lattices and Semilattices

Piaget emphasizes that, mathematically speaking, this set of sixteen binary operations represents a complete lattice, whereas the groupings in the period of concrete operations are only semilattices. A lattice, a mathematically defined concept, is illustrated in Figure 8-15. Figure 8-15 shows a set of hierarchically organized classes of the kind we are familiar with from the period of concrete operations. Figure 8-13 shows the relationships among the 16 classes in the first set of binary operations. Figure 8-15 contains a largest class and there is a direct connection between that class and any other one. For any pair of classes in the whole set there is some other class that includes both of the pair. For example, D is the least upper bound of A and C'. This class which is common to both is called the least upper bound of the

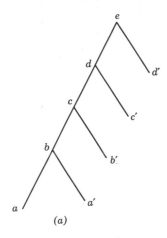

(a)

Figure 8-15. A semilattice.

two. The definition of a semilattice is that every two elements in a set have a least upper bound.

In Figure 8-13 there is a smallest set and also a largest set, even though there are a variety of branching pathways, all lead from the smallest to the largest through the various subclasses in the set. Thus, there is not only a least upper bound for every pair of classes but also a greatest lower bound. That is, for every pair of classes there is a class that includes both of them, and there is also a class that is included in both of them. This is the defining characteristic of a complete lattice as distinct from a semilattice. It will be seen that in Figure 8-15 there is no greatest lower bound for every pair of classes; the system fans out from a single smallest element. In Figure 8-13, however, it fans out from a single element but then converges back to another element so that it is closed on both sides.

Exactly how the child's thought processes reveal his ability to use this lattice is not clear, but Piaget feels that this ability is an important characteristic of the period of formal operations.

Combinatorial Thinking

It is not enough that the child must understand the relationship among the sixteen binary operations. The fact that these operations systematically cover all possible combinations of the four elementary classes in itself represents a kind of thought process which is acquired only during the period of formal operations. In order to list the sixteen binary operations we had to first take each of the four classes systematically one at a time, then describe every possible pair of classes, then every possible triplet of classes, and finally the combination of the quadruplet of classes. Before the child can use these binary operations he has to see that they really represent all of the possible combinations. The child's appreciation of the difference between all the combinations that actually occur and the entire range of possibilities is another acquisition of the period of formal operations.

To investigate this kind of combinatorial thinking, Piaget and Inhelder devised another experiment. The material is shown schematically in Figure 8-16. There are four bottles of colorless liquid labeled 1, 2, 3, and 4; and there is also a smaller vial containing colorless liquid from which a drop can be added to the liquid from the bottles in another container. The first bottle contains dilute sulfuric acid; the second, water; the third, oxygenated water; and the fourth, thiosulfate; the smaller flask labeled g contains potassium iodide (Figure 8-16).

To begin with, the two glasses are presented to the subject, one containing liquid from 1 and 3, and the other liquid from 2. While the subject watches, the experimenter adds several drops from g to each of

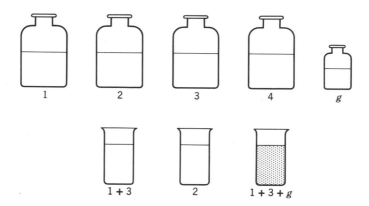

Figure 8-16. Materials for experiment on combinatory operation. This diagram illustrates an experiment in the problem of colored and colorless chemicals. Four similar flasks contain colorless, odorless liquids: (1) diluted sulphuric acid; (2) water; (3) oxygenated water; (4) thiosulphate. The smaller flask, labeled g, contains potassium iodide. Two glasses are presented to the subject; one contains 1 + 3, the other contains 2. While the subject watches, the experimenter adds several drops of g to each of these glasses. The liquid in the glass containing 1 + 3 turns yellow. The subject is then asked to reproduce the color, using all or any of the five flasks as he wishes. (Inhelder & Piaget, Growth of Logical Thinking from Childhood to Adolescence)

these glasses. The liquid in the glass containing 1 and 3 turns yellow, whereas the liquid in the other glass does not. The child is then asked to produce this color using any or all of the five flasks. Later he is asked to describe the function of the liquid in each of the bottles. In terms of function, 1 and 3 are necessary in order to produce the yellow color. Liquid 2 has no effect one way or the other; by itself it will not produce a yellow color but it may be added to a combination of 1 and 3 without effect. The fourth bleaches the mixture so that if it is added to a combination of 1 and 3 the yellow color will no longer be produced. This is the set of relationships the child must discover.

The important feature of this problem is that there is no way that the child can reason out ahead of time which combination of liquids will produce the color. It is something he must discover by trial and error. It is important, therefore, that he try all possible combinations of the different liquids in order to be sure of the effect of each. The child's ability to form all the possible combinations systematically is evidence that he is doing the combinatorial thinking of the period of formal operations. The following protocols are quotations representing the behavior at Stages 2 and 3. There are, in fact, some substages that can be delineated, but these are not essential. In Stage 2, or the period of concrete operations:

Ren (7;1) tries $4 \times g$ then $2 \times g$ then $1 \times g$, then $3 \times g$. *"I think I did everything; I tried them all."*—"What else could you have done?"—*"I don't know."* We give him the glasses again: he repeats $1 \times g$, and so forth. "You took each bottle separately; what else could you have done?"—*"Take two bottles at the same time."* (He tried $1 \times 4 \times g$, then $2 \times 3 \times g$, thus failing to cross over between the two sets of bottles, for example: 1×2, 1×3, 2×4, 3×4.) When we suggested he try others he put $1 \times g$ in the glass already containing 2 and 3, which results in the appearance of the color. "Try to make the color again."—*"Do I put in 2 or 3?"* (He tries 2×4, $2 \times 4 \times g$, then adds 3, then tries $1 \times 4 \times 2 \times g$.) *"No, I don't remember any more."* (*Growth of Logical Thinking*, p. 111)

Here it is quite clear that the child is able systematically to cover all of the single possibilities and that he tries g with each one. He is sure that he has covered all of the possibilities, but does not even consider the possibility of putting in more than one liquid with g. When this is suggested to him he tries various combinations but proceeds in no particular order and does not even remember what he has put together when, by chance, he does produce the color.

At a slightly later stage the child spontaneously recognizes the possibility of combining more than one bottle at a time with g, but is still unable to form all combinations systematically. On the other hand, when we come to the stage of formal operations we get a record as follows:

Sar (12;3) "Make me some more yellow."—*"Do you take the liquid from the yellow glass with all four?"*—"I won't tell you." (He tries first $4 \times 2 \times$ g, then $2 \times$ g $\times 4 \times$ g.) "Not yet." (He tries to smell the odor of the liquids, then tries $4 \times 1 \times$ g.)—*"No yellow yet, quite a big mystery!"* (He tries the four, then each one independently with g; then he spontaneously proceeds to various two by two combinations but has the feeling that he forgot some of them.) *"I better write it down to remind myself: 1 × 4 is done; 4 × 3 is done; and 2 × 3; several more that I haven't done."* (He finds all six, then adds the drops, then finds the yellow from 1 and 3 and g.) *"Ah, it's turning yellow. You need one and three and the drops."*—"Where is the yellow?" No answer. "In there." Pointing to g.—*"No, they go together."* "And two?" *"I don't think it has any effect, it's water."*—"And 4?"—*"It doesn't do anything either; it's water too. But I want to try again, you can't ever be too sure."* (He tries $2 \times 4 \times$ g.) *"Give me a glass of water."* (He takes it from the faucet and mixes $3 \times 1 \times$ water $\times$ g, that is, the combination which gave him the color, plus water from the faucet, knowing that $1 \times 2 \times 3 \times 4 \times$ g produces nothing.) *"No, it isn't water.—Maybe it's a substance that keeps it from coloring."* (He puts together $1 \times 3 \times 2 \times$ g, then $1 \times 3 \times 4 \times$ g.)—*"Ah, there it is, that one (4) keeps it from coloring."*—"And that?" (2)—*"It's water."* (*Growth of Logical Thinking*, p. 117)

This protocol shows how the child is struggling with the problem. To begin with, he does not understand the necessity for trying out every possible combination, yet spontaneously moves to pairs. He recognizes the difficulty in keeping track of them all, so he writes them down to be sure that he finds all six, and later collects a special sample of water so that he can determine whether 4 is the same as water. Since it is not he comes to the full solution of the problem. At a still later stage in the period of formal operations we find children recognizing the necessity for systematic coverage of all possibilities. Here they may start out to try every possible combination.

Equilibrium Problems—the 4-Group

A final development in the period of formal operations is the child's understanding of a variety of problems that are all abstractly similar and can be represented by the equilibrium of a simple balance. If a beam, as shown in Figure 8-17a, starts out in balance with equal weights at equal distances and is then thrown out of balance by adding weights to one side, it can be brought back into equilibrium in several ways. On the one hand, weights can be subtracted in the same

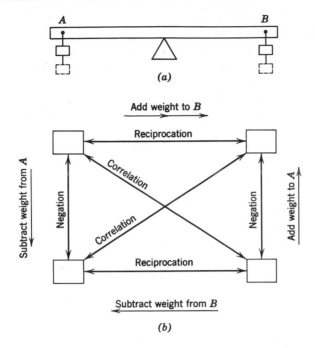

Figure 8-17. The 4-group illustrating equilibrium problems.

way they were added, thus restoring the situation to what it was. Another kind of equilibration can occur by moving the weights on the beam so that the heavier weight is brought closer to the fulcrum than the lighter one. This restores the balance but does not return the situation to its original state. The same kind of system can be seen in an even simpler case where the addition of weight to one side of a balance can be countered either by subtracting weight from that side or by adding weight to the other side.

The same double inverse occurs in a variety of fields. For example, the velocity of an object is equal to the distance it covers over a period of time. If the distance covered is increased while the time remains the same, the velocity increases. If one wished to bring the object back to its original velocity, one could either decrease the distance covered or increase the time it takes. Both of these restore the original velocity.

The relationship of the specific gravity, volume, and weight of a liquid is linked in the same way. The equilibrium problem arises whenever there is a simple law of proportions in which one variable equals the quotient of two other variables. The value of a fraction can be modified or restored to its original value by changing either the numerator or the denominator.

According to Piaget, these equilibrium problems involve two kinds of inverses, a negation of the original change or a reciprocation which changes some compensating factor. This system of negation and reciprocation produces a group structure that is not a grouping but an actual mathematical group. Figure 8-17*b* shows how the relationship among these operations form a group. There are four operations: negation, reciprocation, correlation, and identity. These are shown in Figure 8-17*b* where negation attains a balance by subtracting weight from one side and reciprocation achieves a balance by adding weight to the opposite side. The relationship between the opposite corners is one of correlation because this is a relationship that maintains the balance. The corners are the equivalent results of negation and reciprocation. Piaget has also shown how these operations form a mathematical group.

SUMMARY

In summary, we have seen the development of operational thinking in the periods of concrete operations and formal operations. In the period of concrete operations the child acquires an understanding of a variety of groupings; Piaget emphasizes that this understanding is oriented toward the actual observation of concrete events in the child's environment. He does not show in this stage the ability to relate these groupings to one another, or to see them all in terms of the universe of possibilities, and he has only an incomplete understanding of the variety of relations that may exist among various classes of elements. Later developments involve combinatorial thinking and an understanding of the full implication of propositional thinking, as well as the attainment of an understanding of equilibrium problems; all these are achievements of the period of formal operations.

NINE

Piaget's theory
of the developmental process

THE BULK OF Piaget's research has been concerned with understanding the child's thinking at particular periods of his life and with studying the differences among children of different ages. Perhaps because of Piaget's interest in the stages of childhood, many people assume that he believes these stages follow one another automatically and that his theory of development is a purely maturational one. It is not purely maturational; stages do not merely unfold in a predetermined pattern. However, Piaget's theory is not as clearly formulated nor as well studied empirically as his description of the characteristics of children at various periods in life, so the misunderstanding is not surprising.

Generally speaking, there are three main points of view about development. One is that development is an unfolding of the growth process, that it is maturational, and that therefore the characteristic of later stages can largely be predicted from a knowledge of the preceding stages. Probably nobody believes that all child behavior can be thus explained, but in different points of view we find a relatively greater or lesser emphasis on this aspect.

An alternate view is that the child's development is essentially the accumulation of the learning acquired from experiences in the environment. These bits of learning are relatively independent of one another and of the chronological age of the child. People holding such a view look for the cause of the development of any particular kind of behavior in the experiences where that behavior was learned. As with the purely maturational point of view, there is probably nobody whose theory is completely a learning theory, but, as we shall see, the S-R theorists have emphasized how behavior is learned in their research. Thus, we can see in their position a theory that is relatively close to environmentalism.

Piaget finds serious objection to both a maturational theory and a learning theory. He believes he has formulated a third view which is not merely a mixture of the two, but which depends on a third kind of developmental process, namely *equilibration*.

Piaget's arguments against a theory of cognitive development based purely on learning are stated at greater length than his arguments against a purely maturational position and should be described in more detail. Before reviewing these arguments, we should recognize that Piaget, in attacking a theory that the child learns the concept of class, or the object concept, or conservation of quantity, is not describing a position that anyone else has taken. In some of his writings he apparently believes that he is attacking the S-R theory that will be described later in this book (see p. 386 ff.) but he does not describe the S-R position accurately. Many of his arguments are relevant, however, for any learning theory and should be kept in mind in coming to any judgment about the relative value of various theories of development.

Piaget says that a learning theory is passive, that it describes the child being passively impressed by the environment and having habits imposed on him by the concatenation of experiences in its life. In contrast, he himself believes that the child is active, constantly acquiring new actions, and organizing them into operational groupings. All aspects of the child's behavior, even those that we have traditionally considered receptive, are active, as Piaget sees it.

For a learning theory of cognitive development we must discover how the child learns the object concept or the conservation of quantity concept or the reversibility of groupings. A theorist who believes that these basic assumptions are learned generally refers to two kinds of learning experience. One possibility is that the child's experience with the natural environment teaches him that there are permanent objects and that the quantity of liquid does not change when poured from one glass into another. It is, however, difficult to see just where the child does learn these beliefs in the course of his interaction with the environment. The object concept is so pervasive a basic assumption, involving so many aspects of the child's interaction with his environment, that it is hard to conceive of the specific experiences where such a belief would be formed. It is probably true that the child who has the object concept is able to satisfy more of his needs, attain his goals, and get along better in the world than the child who does not have this concept, so, in a sense, the object concept is rewarded. But still it appears in so many different behaviors that it is difficult to see how the belief would arise in the first place.

In the same way it is difficult to see how the child would acquire the belief that quantity is unchanged when liquid is poured from one vessel to another. As we saw in the earlier discussion (see p. 242) invariance of quantity is partly a matter of definition. Quantity is that aspect of the liquid that does remain invariant. Thus, invariance is partly a cultural norm as well as an empirical fact. What is culturally normative about invariance is the definition of quantity in such a way that it is independent of location, shape, and arrangement.

The introduction of cultural norms into these basic epistemological assumptions suggests a second major source of learning, namely social learning. Perhaps the child does not acquire the object concept directly from his interactions with the environment, but instead is taught these concepts by his parents. If he were taught such a concept, and if such a belief resulted in more frequently reinforced behavior in adapting to the physical environment, the combination of the social learning and its empirical effectiveness could account for the acquisition of the belief system.

The main trouble with this hypothesis is that there is no real evidence that adults do teach the child that objects are still there if they are out of sight. These beliefs are so tacit that they are seldom mentioned, although many of our verbal contacts with the child tacitly assume them. Furthermore, the child seems to acquire the most basic assumptions in infancy before he is able to respond to any explicit teaching.

In the same way it seems unlikely that we ever explicitly teach the child that the quantity of liquid remains unchanged when it is poured from one glass into another, or that the number of objects in a row remains the same if they are spread out more or clustered more together. Rather good evidence that we do not teach this belief lies in the fact that we adults are frequently surprised that children do not understand it. Adults do not view invariance of quantity as something that needs to be taught; it seems so obvious. And only infrequently does the child ever reveal his lack of understanding of invariance. He can attend nursery school for a year and never behave in any way that leads his teacher to suspect that in an experimental situation he will say that the number of roses in a row changes if they are clustered into a bunch. This is why nursery school teachers and other experienced people so frequently disbelieve the empirical results of Piaget's experiment. Despite their constant contact with children and their sensitivity to the child's thought processes, they have not realized that invariance is difficult for the child to grasp.

Another line of evidence that these cognitive organizations are not entirely the result of empirical learning is that they seem to involve a subjective feeling of necessity. When the child acquires the assumption of invariance of quantity, he also comes to believe it is unthinkable that the quantity would vary when the liquid was poured from a glass of one shape into a glass of another shape. This belief in the necessity of certain facts is in contrast to other beliefs that are more empirical in the sense that contrary evidence would merely change the belief.

Two experiments are relevant to this distinction between necessary and empirical relationships. One is an experiment by Morf (1959) in which he attempted to establish two concepts, one of which was purely empirical, while the other involved the logical necessity of concrete groupings. While the experiment did not demonstrate any clear result, its ingenious design clarifies the distinction between empirical and necessary relations. The particular organization Morf investigated concerned the reversal of spatial order when a sequence of objects is revolved in space. This experiment has been described briefly before (see p. 245). There are three beads in a tube in the order: red, yellow, blue. The tube is revolved 180° or 360° to see if the child knows what happens to the sequential arrangement of the beads. The 180° revolution, of course, reverses the order but leaves the middle bead still in the middle, whereas a 360° rotation leaves the original order unchanged.

In an attempt to find an analogous set of relationships that were purely empirical Morf devised the following experiment. There were two sizes of match boxes, large ones and small ones. On one end of the inside of each matchbox he glued a red bead, so that if the matchbox were opened slightly from that end, the red bead would be visible. On the other end of the inside of each matchbox he glued another bead. In the small matchboxes the other bead was also red, but in the large matchboxes the other bead was blue. The child's task was to look at the bead at one end of the matchbox and predict what color bead would be at the other end. He could tell, of course, if he had learned the relationship between the size of the matchbox and the similarity in the color of the beads at the two ends.

This problem is roughly analogous to the revolution of beads in the tube. If the tube is revolved 180° the bead in one end of the tube is changed in color, whereas if it is revolved 360° the bead at that end of the tube remains the same. Thus, the size of the matchbox has the same relationship as the number of revolutions of the tube to the similarity or dissimilarity in colors of beads. In each case the child knows what color the bead is at one point and has to predict its color under different circumstances. The difference between the two experiments is that the similarity of the color of the bead at two ends of a matchbox is quite arbitrary. An adult approaching the problem could discover this empirical fact. If he had learned the relationship and then was given matchboxes that violated his expectations he would merely conclude that the experimenter had changed the rule or that there were other matchboxes that violated the original expectation. He would not feel that any logical relationship had been violated. On the other hand, if one put a red, a yellow, and a blue bead into a tube, revolved the tube 180°, and found that the same color was at the same end as the start, one would feel that some kind of real legerdemain had to have occurred. A necessary relationship would have been violated and it would represent a much more disturbing disconfirmation of expectation.

Morf's experiment did not really answer the question whether children in the stage of concrete operations respond to the revolution of beads in the tubes as necessary relationships and the beads glued in the end of matchboxes as empirical relationships. He did find differences in the ability of children to learn the problem of the matchboxes depending on their age, but the empirical findings were quite complicated and not easily interpreted. The experiment is refered to primarily because it is a good illustration of what Piaget and his followers mean by a necessary relationship inherent in an organized grouping of relationships as opposed to a purely empirical regularity.

An experiment more relevant to the question of acquisition has been conducted by Smedslund (1961, a, b, c). He studied a child's concept of the invariance of weight when the shape of an object changed. The basic material consists of two identical balls of clay which the child agrees are alike and which are put on a balance to show they have the same weight. One of these balls of clay is then flattened into a pancake shape. The child was then tested to see whether he believed that the ball and the pancake of clay weighed the same.

This particular experiment is a useful one, because it permits an empirical check of equality through weighing. The child who believes that the pancake and ball of clay do not weigh the same can put them on the scale to discover that they do. It is possible, as Smedslund has shown, for children who have not yet reached the stage of concrete operations to learn through empirical trial that the two pieces of clay are the same weight even though one of them has been flattened into a pancake. Very young children cannot learn the invariance of weight, even empirically, but there is a group of children who are close enough to acquiring the concept of invariance that they apparently can profit from the empirical experience and learn that the two different-shaped bodies of clay are in fact the same weight.

Smedslund next introduces a variation. As he pounds one ball of clay into a pancake form he surreptitiously adds or subtracts a small amount of clay without the child's being aware of it. Now the two pieces of clay do not in fact weigh the same. If the child checked them on the scales they would not be balanced. How does the child respond to this violation of his expectation of invariance? Smedslund divides his subjects into two groups. One group has already acquired the concept of invariance by the beginning of the experiment and needs no empirical instruction that the two bodies of clay weigh the same even though of different shapes. A second group answers the question incorrectly to begin with, but through empirical checking on the balance acquires the notion of invariance. When the children in these two groups are then fooled by the surreptitious adding or subtracting of clay, Smedslund finds that half of those who had acquired the concept of invariance "naturally" refuse to accept the evidence that the ball of clay changed weight when it was flattened out. Such children say the scales had to be wrong, or the experimenter had done something, or that something was wrong. In other words, their belief in invariance is not strongly shaken by the contrary evidence, and they disbelieve the evidence rather than the hypothesis.

The other group of children who have acquired the concept of invariance through empirical checking on the scales respond quite differently when their expectations are violated. Every one of them unlearns the belief in invariance as readily as he learns it. They seem to say, "OK, then they aren't equal when you change the shape." Smedslund hypothesizes that since they acquired the belief empirically, it was subject to empirical disconfirmation. On the other hand, the children who have acquired a belief in invariance as kind of a logical necessity are quite resistant to any disconfirmation and refuse to give up their hypothesis merely because of contrary empirical evidence.

This experiment by no means conclusively demonstrates that children who acquire the concept of invariance in ordinary life do not do so empirically. We can have firm empirical beliefs that are resistant to change merely because they have been confirmed so often and not because we believe in their logical necessity. Perhaps the children who had already acquired the notion of invariance before the experiment had formed a much firmer belief in the notion of invariance than those who had acquired it more recently, merely because it had been confirmed over a longer period of time.

Nevertheless, there does seem to be a genuine problem here. Some beliefs are organized into systems, and by virtue of each single belief's being an inherent part of a total system of relationships, it shares in the strength of the whole. The disconfirmation of a belief in such a system throws the whole system into disarray and disequilibrium. In a logically related, coherent set of beliefs, the strength of any particular element is strengthened by its relation to all the other elements which are also empirically verifiable. In brief, when beliefs are organized into groupings, as Piaget describes them, the beliefs that make up this organized system acquire the quality of necessity because they are part of a whole coherent system and are sustained by the adaptive value of the system as a whole. However, when a belief is relatively independent of a system it does not have this property of necessity, and therefore will more readily be disconfirmed by contrary evidence.

When a single belief that is part of a large, coherent system is confronted by contrary evidence, the individual tends to explain away the evidence and save the belief. For example, if we saw an elephant appear out of thin air in the middle of a hallway we could not really accept this datum as contrary to our beliefs about the nature of the physical universe; we would attribute it to magic or a delusion. We would cope with it in some way, without modifying our basic beliefs. It is well known, of course, that people can develop this feeling of conviction about beliefs that are, in fact, untrue; these unjustified convictions are called prejudices.

This analysis of the relationship between empirical beliefs and logically necessary beliefs indicates the importance of explaining how a particular belief becomes a part of a large, coherent system. This is precisely what Piaget is trying to describe when he says that the cognitive functions of the child become organized into groupings that function as a whole and are activated as a whole whenever any part of the system is brought into action by contact with relevant empirical data.

Equilibration

Piaget's explanation for the process of cognitive development and particularly the development of organized belief systems is the process of equilibration. He does not assume that these systems develop without any previous experience. At the same time he insists that learning these beliefs one at a time, not merely coming into contact with the relevant empirical data, does not itself bring about operational thinking. Instead, Piaget assumes that the individual gradually acquires some of the elements of the operational system, perhaps through social learning or experience with the environment. At some point these unorganized ideas or beliefs produce a conflict, however. An unorganized system is not adaptive and leads to conflict and self-contradiction. The preoperational child, because his items of information are not all coherently organized, is constantly surprising his adult friends by being logical at one moment and apparently illogical the next. Piaget seems to argue that this same inconsistency also puts the child himself into conflict. Another possible source of conflict is that as the child confronts other children they all have different points of view, and this again presents the child with evidence that arouses a conflict.

Because these unorganized belief systems do contain inherent self-contradictions and conflict, force is set up to harmonize the child's ideas one with another. This is the process of equilibration. As a result of equilibration the child, independent of any further experience, tends to reorganize his beliefs into a coherent, harmonious, and equilibrated system.

Thus, the forces Piaget hypothesizes to explain the process of development are: first, certain maturational ones, although their exact role is not too clear; second, the results of experience with the environment itself; third, the result of explicit and implicit teaching of the child by other people in his environment; and fourth, the process of equilibration, which is set in motion whenever the child's belief system develops far enough to begin to contain self-contradictions.

There is not much empirical evidence to support the hypothetical process of equilibration; on the other hand, there is not much evidence to deny it or much to confirm any alternative hypothesis about the nature of cognitive development. There is evidence that before the period of concrete operations the child cannot merely be taught the right answers to questions about invariance and thus be brought to the period of concrete operations. It is true that the child close enough to the period of concrete operations may be brought into it by some specifically designed experiences which offer him empirical feedback for his beliefs, but this kind of experience is in the form of contradicting the child's expectations of noninvariance (see experiment by Smedslund, p. 293).

In summary therefore, although we do not have any clear evidence for equilibration in cognitive development, Piaget is pointing to a very important problem when he emphasizes the necessity of the child's beliefs becoming organized into some kind of a system. None of the other theories we discuss puts this same emphasis on the importance of the organization of knowledge and none raises with sufficient clarity the question of how organized information is acquired. Thus, even if Piaget's theory of equilibration turns out to be inadequate it is significant that he is pointing the attention of research workers to the problem of the acquisition of organized knowledge.

CRITIQUE

An evaluation of Piaget's theories and his research should be divided into two sections. First, Piaget has collected an enormous amount of empirical data on the development of various aspects of children's cognition. This empirical research ranges from earliest infancy to adulthood and has all been collected by Piaget, his colleagues, and his students at the J. J. Rousseau Institute. Second, Piaget has incessantly theorized about these data. Each of his empirical studies has a theoretical interpretation. There has been one marked change in the theory with the introduction in the early 1940's of the notion of grouping and the development of a system of logic. Some of his theories have been directly concerned with the understanding of children's thinking but large amounts of Piaget's theorizing have little direct relationship to developmental psychology. He has made contributions to the field of logic itself as well as to the field of epistemology and developmental psychology. We have, however, given no space to these theories and have instead looked upon Piaget's work as a developmental psychologist.

Piaget's empirical research has been marked by several characteristics. It has been badly controlled from the standpoint of experimental design and has been incompletely reported. Much of the empirical data has never been published; the reader is given only a sampling of verbatim excerpts and protocols to substantiate the empirical statements Piaget makes. Even when the data have been analyzed in a more orthodox fashion they have never been completely assesed or presented. The protocols that Piaget offers as evidence for his empirical generalizations are undoubtedly intended by him to be representative, but it seems likely that those chosen for publication have been selected to some extent. This does not mean that they have been biased to favor the hypothesis but they have very likely been selected to deal with it.

Thus, in the experiment dealing with the child's understanding of nested classes which uses the brown and white beads, the reader is led to believe that the typical answer of children, when asked whether there are more wooden beads than brown ones, is to say there are more brown ones because there are so few white ones. In a later study where essentially the same experiment was performed (1964), only with primulas and flowers instead of brown and wooden beads, it seems that the child frequently answers that there are the same number of flowers and primulas because all the primulas are flowers. This is a good illustration of the frustration that comes to the reader who would like to have an independent view of the raw data, not one filtered entirely through Piaget's interests and theories.

Thus, despite the enormous amount of empirical data and the general confirmation of the findings whenever these experiments are repeated by other people, one is still left with the fact that all of these experiments must be repeated and confirmed by someone else before we can be confident about the children's range of responses to the experimental situations, before we can know how many children are exceptions to the generalizations, and before we can come to an unbiased view of the empirical evidence.

These methodological criticisms notwithstanding—and they are serious—there is no question that Piaget's empirical research has contributed enormously to developmental psychology. In area after area he has broken new ground and performed new ingenious experiments; psychologists have been feeding upon his ingenuity since the 1950's and will undoubtedly continue to depend upon many of his innovations for years to come.

Piaget has also been courageous enough to try to look through the empirical findings themselves to an understanding of the thought process. In many ways his experimentation has been exploratory; he has been searching for an understanding of children's thinking, rather than testing a particular hypothesis about it. We are never clear when he is doing which; sometimes he reports data as if they confirmed an hypothesis, when in fact the data led him to form the hypothesis. If we look at his experimentation as exploratory and hypothesis-generating, many of the methodological criticisms lose their import. All research that generates new hypotheses must be independently confirmed and is no less valuable for that fact. Piaget's ingenuity and his insatiable curiosity for empirical investigation has made his work an enormous contribution to developmental psychology.

Turning now to the theory itself, we are of course in no position to estimate its final outcome accurately. In many ways it seems to have some of the same assets and liabilities as his empirical research. Piaget's theories constantly point to extremely important issues, and he theorizes about aspects of human thinking which many other psychologists have neglected. Piaget has put psychological insight ahead of operationalized theories, and it is important than there be people in the scientific world who make this choice. So, just as his experiments point to important questions but do not necessarily provide solid confirmation of hypotheses, Piaget's theories point to important issues and represent interesting hypotheses about them but do not yet represent a rigorous psychological theory of cognitive development.

Piaget's theorizing seems most provocative when he tries to describe the concrete factors in children's thinking. His analysis of the child's thinking in the invariance experiment includes the notion of reversibility, the mutual compensation of two dimensions, the assumption that if nothing is added and nothing taken away the quantity remains the same, and the difficulty the child encounters in using past experience for present judgment. This analysis seems extremely fruitful, even though much more experimentation needs to be done to determine to what extent and for which children these differing factors are important. Piaget has accomplished the creative task of theorizing. It only remains to test and refine his theory by designing experiments with all the appropriate controls. The results may disconfirm the theory but that does not reduce its value.

At this relatively concrete level of theorizing Piaget is very stimulating; however, he often shows no clear connection between the specific findings about children's thinking and the more abstract level of theorizing.

There is no clear logical connection between any of the groupings of concrete operations and the invariance of quantity. We have tried to point to as many connections as possible, but the effort is not very satisfactory. For example, the integration of past events with the present situation is an important cognitive characteristic, but it has little relation to groupings. Yet the concept of grouping, despite its lack of connection with the raw data of most of Piaget's experiments, seems a fruitful contribution because it attempts to describe the way thoughts are organized.

The notion of an organization is of course not new with Piaget, but even if the purely mathematical aspects of grouping are not fruitful, he does describe these organizations in a form that makes them more amenable to rigorous mathematical treatment. As we shall see later, this aspect of Piaget's theorizing has been developed by S-R theorists who do not find it difficult to coordinate the two theories at the level of language.

Whereas the general concept of grouping as an organization seems extremely productive, it is not apparent that the attempts to be mathematically rigorous about the concept of grouping and, in particular, to defend a particular set of eight groupings, are very rewarding. There is almost no evidence that children use all eight groupings or that the groupings are all acquired at the period of concrete operations. On the face of it, it seems likely that the later groupings, particularly the co-univocal multiplications, demand a much higher level of functioning than the simpler ones. There are more economical ways of describing these organizations, and the application of graph theory to the understanding of these organized systems of beliefs is as likely as Piaget's conceptualization to yield useful results. It also seems likely that there are more varieties of organizations than Piaget's eight groupings of concrete operations. The child's understanding of interpersonal relations can also be described in terms of organized systems of beliefs but it is difficult to see how such systems exemplify any of these groupings.

To sum up, Piaget has made an enormous contribution both empirically and theoretically and is probably the most productive developmental psychologist living at present. However, his attempts to develop mathematically rigorous theories have led him into realms of pure mathematics that may have little relationship to the cognitive development of children. This is no criticism of mathematics, but Piaget has felt compelled to assert that these mathematical constructs are closely and virtually related to the cognitive processes of children. In so doing he has gone beyond the empirical evidence and beyond his own intuitive knowledge of children's thinking which has generally stood him in excellent stead.

SIGMUND FREUD

Sigmund Freud and the Psychoanalytic Theory of Development

TEN

Freudian theory—
fundamental strategy and concepts

THE SCIENTIFIC THEORIES of behavior we have discussed thus far have stemmed from academic psychology. When we turn to psychoanalytic theory we come to a theory of different historical origin. It stems from the medical clinic rather than the university laboratory, from the attempt to help patients live more normal lives rather than the attempt to investigate theoretical questions on normal subjects. This difference in origin has far-reaching consequences for the theory.

Sigmund Freud was trained in medicine in Vienna in the nineteenth century. He began his career in neurology, but, after some experience with the hypnotic treatment of patients, gradually shifted his interest from the study of the physiological mechanisms of neural functioning to the psychological mechanisms of behavior. At first Freud used hypnosis in the treatment of his neurotic patients. While they were under hypnosis he could learn a good deal about their problems and difficulties, but what he learned did not seem to help the patients very much. Even if the therapist has a clear idea of the experiences that have made the patient neurotic and knows the psychological mechanism of the neurotic behavior, this knowledge does not help the patient to understand his problems.

Freud gradually devised the technique that became the standard procedure for psychoanalysis. The patient is instructed to report every thought and every idea that comes to mind. He is told that some of the ideas will be unpleasant and repugnant, others will seem too trivial to mention, and still others may be anxiety arousing, but that his job is to express them all, withholding nothing, and not try to make the stream of his ideas logical or coherent. These instructions are not easy to carry out; in fact, the realization that there are barriers of certain kinds to free expression of thought is an important part of the therapy.

In the course of his long lifetime, Freud listened to thousands of hours of these expressions of thoughts and feelings. They are the data from which the therapist and patient together discover the causes and mechanisms of the patient's disturbance. For Freud and other psychoanalytic investigators, these same expressions are the data for building a theory of personality development and functioning.

STRATEGY OF FREUDIAN THEORY

The strategy of Freudian investigations is to build a theory out of the verbal expressions of ideas and feelings and the self-descriptions voiced by unhappy, anxiety-ridden people who seek help from psychoanalysts. The raw data of Freudian theory are not limited to this source, but the theory is founded upon them.

In addition, psychoanalytic data come from the analyses of normal subjects, most commonly, but not exclusively, students planning to become practicing psychoanalysts. Psychoanalytic observations of children's play behavior are also available since free play substitutes for free association in child therapy. Moreover, in recent years, there have been many empirical investigations of psychoanalytic hypotheses carried out by both foes and proponents of the theory. However, psychoanalysts believe that these investigations are only ancillary and supportive. The basic data of the theory are the materials produced by individuals in psychoanalysis.

This strategy of investigation results in several consequences for the structure and content of the theory. The next few sections will review some of them.

The Study of Pathology

It is common practice in medicine to use pathological material for the investigation of normal functioning. The performance of many physiological systems has been revealed by the study of patients in whom that system does not function or functions improperly. Diabetes, for example, is a disease in which the pancreas does not work properly. As a result, the normal control over the level of sugar in the blood is lost. The study of diabetic patients has been of tremendous assistance in describing the normal functioning of the pancreas and in discovering that insulin is an important enzyme in the control of blood sugar. These findings have in turn led to the development of insulin treatment which has saved the lives of many thousand diabetic patients. This interaction among the study of disease, the investigation of normal functioning, and the development of effective treatment is common in medicine.

It is expected, therefore, that the careful study of the behavior of neurotic and psychotic patients would elucidate the normal processes of behavior, and that a medically trained investigator would capitalize on the opportunity to make such a study. Freud drew a parallel, however, between normal and pathological functioning. It is as if he assumed that every aspect of pathological functioning was also a part of normal personality, and that all pathology could be understood as the exaggerated, uncontrolled, or maladjusted activity of normal components of personality. The parallel with diabetes is still apt. Blood sugar is important in normal functioning; in diabetes, the mechanisms that control it are defective, so that blood sugar becomes a symptom of disease.

One kind of evidence which Freud frequently adduced to support an hypothesis about a personality component was that the same motivation appeared in a pathological form. Thus, it is hypothesized in Freudian theory that homosexual motivations are a part of everybody's personality. According to the theory, such motivation is one aspect of normal functioning. One support for this assertion is that there are overt homosexuals whose sexual feelings are directed toward others of the same sex. Similarly the existence of sadists, who obtain sexual satisfaction by the infliction of pain or injury upon their sexual partners, is taken to be evidence that normal sexuality contains elements of sadism and also evidence that "cruelty for the sake of cruelty" has sexual elements in it.

In general, then, psychoanalytic theory is supported by such evidence. Even the terminology used to describe the component of the normal personality is, like sadism, frequently the pathological name.

Concern with Thoughts and Feelings

A second consequence of the fact that psychoanalytic theory grew out of clinical practice is that the theory is more obviously concerned with an individual's thoughts and feelings than his behavior. The data available to Freud were restricted to what people said to him during their psychoanalytic treatment. In one sense this is a golden opportunity, and Freud used it that way, but it is also a serious restriction.

Freud never had much opportunity to observe his patient's social interaction and behavior in everyday life, but he did have access to frank statements of their thoughts and feelings which could hardly be obtained in any other way than from a patient in therapy.

Freud assumed, and psychoanalytically oriented psychologists agree, that a person's overt behavior can not be understood except by a knowledge of his motives, fears, feelings, and thought processes at the time. The same behavior can occur by way of different psychological mechanisms, but often the differences are revealed if the person tells how he perceives his own actions. These psychological differences are disclosed even more clearly if the individual can report all his thoughts and feelings. So psychoanalytic psychologists give these thoughts and feelings the same status as behavior, for they are part of the data the theory must explain. In fact, it seems as if many psychoanalytic explanations are more concerned with thoughts and feelings than with overt action. These thoughts which constitute raw data are not, of course, openly expressed. Many of them are inhibited or merely ignored when a person first attempts to follow the analyst's instructions to report everything in his mind. It is only after the long period of instruction and training which forms part of psychoanalytic therapy that many of these conscious and half-conscious thoughts are made accessible.

The data on which psychoanalytic theory is presumed to rest consist therefore of acts, conscious thoughts, and conscious feelings. Psychoanalysts believe that no theory that concentrates exclusively on acts and ignores thoughts and feelings can be complete or adequate. If thoughts and feelings are scientific data, then the expressions obtained from subjects trained, instructed, and motivated to report everything that comes to mind are essential data for theory building. Psychoanalysts have the belief that such data can be obtained only in the psychoanalytic setting, and thus psychoanalysts are the only people having access to the full range of raw data on which a theory must be built.

The pitfall in this line of reasoning is that only some of the patient's expressions can be accepted as accurately reflecting his conscious thoughts and feelings, and it is up to the analyst to decide which statements are truly expressive of the patient's thoughts and which are not. Psychoanalysts insist that it is possible to be unbiased in this judgment and thus obtain uncontaminated, theoretically neutral data.

In summary, the fundamental strategy for building psychoanalytic theory is to take as raw data not only overt actions but also thoughts and feelings as they flow through consciousness. Since many thoughts and feelings are not normally expressed, people must learn to express their conscious thoughts as fully as possible before the scientist can have an accurate record of raw data to analyze. Psychoanalysts are therefore in an advantageous position to obtain these raw data.

BASIC CONCEPTS OF PSYCHOANALYTIC THEORY

Instinctual Drives

One of the fundamental concepts of psychoanalytic theory is that of instinctual drive. The word was originally translated "instinct," but it now seems better to speak of these forces as drives, because they are not associated with specific behavioral patterns which mark many animal instincts. Instead, they are at the root of an almost infinite variety of behavior.

Freud described the conceptual properties of drives in an article entitled *Instincts and Their Vicissitudes* (1915). The most basic property of an instinctual drive is its *source*. Freud assumed that excitation arose in some region of the body and that the function of behavior was to reduce that excitation. These excitations may arise from different regions and require different sorts of activity to reduce them. The region from which the excitation arises is the source of the drive and the primary aim of every drive is the reduction of that excitation. This reduction of excitation is experienced as gratification.

The problem of the organism, so to speak, is to behave in such a way that gratification is obtained, but just what overt activity is satisfying varies from one age to another and depends upon learning and experience. The overt action that brings gratification is called the *external aim* of the instinctual drive. Thus, eating is the external aim of the hunger drive. Some of the aims of the sexual or libidinal drive may be sucking, looking at sexual objects, exhibiting one's body, embracing, or sexual intercourse. When Freud spoke of the vicissitudes of an instinctual drive he was describing some of the ways that the external aim of an instinctual drive might be changed and modified. The internal aim is persumably constant throughout.

In the attainment of satisfaction of instinctual drives, it is frequently necessary for some external person or object to participate. There must be an object (personal or impersonal) to be looked at, exhibited to, touched, and made love to. This object becomes an important part of the satisfaction of the instinctual drive and becomes emotionally significant to the individual. Thus, instinctual drives have objects that may also change from one period of life to another. The object may also under some conditions be the individual's own body or some part of it.

Three aspects of the instinctual drive are then its source (with its invariant internal aim), its external aim, and its object. Of these, the source defines the drive; the external aim and the object may change so that one cannot expect the overt behavior that is satisfying to a person to be a reliable indication of what instinctual drive is being satisfied. In addition, an instinctual drive has a strength or "impetus." This quantitative aspect of drive will be discussed in a later section.

The problem of deciding what drives exist is one that has never been satisfactorily solved in psychoanalytic theory—primarily because the proper label depends upon knowing the source and the internal aim of the drive, and these features of it are unobservable with present techniques. The overt behavior of people reveals innumerable kinds of activity that seem to be satisfying and there is not enough constancy in these external aims to suggest any clear classification of the underlying drives.

LIBIDO. Although there may be some doubt among psychoanalysts about the exact labeling of drives, there is no question that one of the characteristic features of Freudian theory is the importance assigned to sexuality as a basic drive and as a source of many significant personality adjustments. In fact, Freud gave the sexual excitation a special name: *libido;* the term is used quantitatively as an indicator of sexual energy. In psychoanalytic theory one may speak of the amount of libido discharged by some particular action.

The sexual flavor of many psychoanalytic explanations of behavior has made them seem far-fetched to many psychologists, and such interpretations as calling farming a symbolic rape of the mother have been difficult even for the sympathetic student of psychoanalytic theory to accept. It is the sexual nature of the theory that Freud pointed to when explaining the resistance the theory has encountered (see p. 379). Partially, the difficulty is a matter of terminology; Freud did use the term sexual in a wider sense than is customary. (We shall see how it is used shortly.) In part, the difficulty cannot be defined out of existence. Sexuality is believed by psychoanalytic theorists to account for many kinds of behavior that have no obvious overt sexual element. A child's anxiety over physical danger, for example, may be explained in psychoanalytic terms as a fear of castration. And the psychoanalyst genuinely means that the child has an unconscious fear his penis will be cut off. This fear is reflected in physical apprehensiveness. One need not agree with this interpretation, but it would be wrong to deny that it is a part of psychoanalytic theory. It is a part of the theory and there is psychoanalytic evidence for it. The fundamental importance of sexuality cannot be explained away or glossed over without doing real injustice to psychoanalytic theory.

However, Freud did use sexuality in a wider sense than is customary in nonpsychoanalytic language. The biological function of sexuality is procreation and preservation of the species. But in almost no case, human or otherwise, is the sexual act motivated by the desire to preserve the species. From the point of view of the participants in sexual intercourse, the motivation is the pleasurableness of the act itself. The biologically adaptive behavior is elicited and motivated by a mechanism that is not psychologically related to its biological function.

In the human species, furthermore, procreation is a complicated process. It involves conception, but conception does not always result from sexual intercourse. Furthermore, it involves a long pregnancy when the woman requires some degree of indulgence and protection. Finally, a child must be reared over a large number of years to survive and to maintain the human species. From the point of view of biological adaptation, therefore, much more than sexual intercourse is required for maintenance of the species, and Freud used the term sexual to cover them all.

Indeed, in the human species many sorts of feelings and pleasures, besides sexual pleasure, have become integrated into the pattern of mating and child rearing, and it is by no means easy to decide where the sexual element leaves off and some other element enters. In the behavior of heterosexual couples, for example, the sexuality involved in kissing, embracing, snuggling close together, and caressing can hardly be denied. Such mutual intimacy as smoking the same cigarette, drinking from the same wine glass, and the confidential exchange of intimate feelings certainly seems to have some sexual elements. The complex of pleasures that are all tied together in the heterosexual relationship of mates thus includes the pleasures of touching, looking, tasting, and exhibitionism, besides explicit genital sensations.

It was Freud's view that many of these activities were pleasurable in early childhood, but at that time they were not integrated into a complex of feelings which included genital sensations. They are all sources of pleasure, however—immediate, sensuous pleasure in the sensations themselves. Freud called this "organ pleasure"—pleasure in the use of the organ itself. Part of the process of maturation is the integration of these separate sensuous pleasures into a coherent set of sexual feelings which promotes the biological procreation of the species. He called these separate pleasures *partial instincts* because they are components of the sexual instinct in the mature adult. Since they are part of the sexual instinct in adults, Freud labeled them sexual; when they appeared in childhood, Freud spoke of them as pregenital to make clear their independence of genital activities.

As we shall see in the discussion of psychosexual development, psychosexual maturity involves not only the integration of these sensuous pleasures into a pattern of genital pleasure in sexual activity, but also includes the capacity for interpersonal love which can remain faithful under stress. Psychosexual maturity also includes parental love because it motivates the parents to provide the child with a warm secure environment that makes him into a genuine human being. All of these aspects of mature human behavior are biologically functional for procreation of the species, and in that sense they are all sexual. All of this makes sexuality a genuine cornerstone of psychoanalytic theory.

EGO-INSTINCTS. Although the libidinal drive is a more important drive from the point of view of personality organization, Freud recognized that a number of other drives like hunger, thirst, and escape from pain operated in the same way. He grouped these drives together under the rubric *ego-instincts,* and stated that they are all concerned with self-preservation, whereas the libidinal drive is concerned with species preservation.

Psychoanalytically speaking these ego-instincts are not very interesting. Theoretically they might have as complex ramifications as sexuality, but, they are so demanding of gratification and the possible ranges of external aims is so narrow, that they do not offer the opportunity for extensive repression and other defensive controls. A fetish for eating nothing but sawdust or complete celibacy about ingesting fluids are by the very nature of the drive not possible. The individual would die. Sexuality, on the other hand, is a strong drive but one that can be delayed for a long time and subjected to many sorts of control.

There is evidence that the manifestations of the ego-instincts can be repressed, and sometimes hunger will be used to illustrate defense mechanisms, but as a source of personality characteristics it is less significant than sexuality.

HOSTILITY AND AGGRESSION. Another important kind of human behavior is hostility and aggressiveness. In psychoanalytic therapy as much or more time is spent in unraveling the variety of ways that hostility can be expressed and in helping the patient accept it as a part of human nature as is spent in the exploration of the patient's sexual feelings. The existence and the importance of anger and hostility in human personality is not in question.

There is much less agreement on the instinctual roots of hostility. Since in sadism the inflicting of pain on the sexual partner is part of the pleasure of the sexual relationship, it might be possible to treat hostility as one of the components of the sexual instinct. Freud did discuss the relationship between sexuality and hostility in several papers and did view aggression as one normal and customary aspect of sexual feelings. Sexual intercourse is for many couples a violent affair, and quarrels are a normal part of many love affairs. An understanding of hostility must include some explanation of how it is interwoven with love and sexuality.

Hostility is also frequently a part of self-preservation and enters into competitive, self-interested activity. It is a response to frustration and might be viewed as a manifestation of the ego-instincts. During one period of his life, Freud inclined toward this conceptualization.

Later, however, Freud came to believe that hostility was part of a separate instinct, the death instinct, lying at the root of all destructive activities. The prevalence of gratuitous hostility throughout the world and its importance as a destructive force seemed to make it difficult for Freud to view hostility primarily as a tool of self-preservation. Hostility too frequently leads to self-destruction rather than self-preservation to make it sensible to call it self-preservation. When Freud advanced the notion of a death instinct he contrasted it to a life instinct that included both self-preservation (ego-instinct) and species preservation (sexuality). This formulation was not widely accepted, even among psychoanalysts who were otherwise quite orthodox in their adherence to Freud's beliefs.

THE DYNAMIC ASSUMPTION OF PSYCHOANALYTIC THEORY—CATHEXIS. What is the relevance of these instinctual drives for behavior? Psychoanalytic theory is perhaps as thoroughgoing a dynamic theory as is possible. According to the theory all behavior and all other psychological functioning are determined by the instinctual drives. Every perception, thought, feeling, and action discharges excitation that ultimately stems from the instinctual drives. All of the personality mechanisms are similarly propelled by a psychic energy and their operation disposes of that energy.

According to psychoanalytic theory the drive energy operates by *cathecting* various psychological structures in the personality. Freud viewed *cathexis* as somewhat like an electric charge that could energize an object or a region in an electric field. It describes the way that energy is distributed or deployed.

Cathexis functions in various ways. One of its services is to cathect ideas that are drive representatives and thus to bring about drive discharge. The drive itself has no direct behavioral expression. Although certain activities discharge the drive, there is no preformed or automatic mechanism by which the drive achieves the appropriate behavior. It is not connected to a specific action like a reflex or the instincts in animals.

The connection of the drive to its behavioral aim must be acquired by the individual after he is born, and the connecting link to behavior changes as the child grows up. In the adult, the performance of the gratifying behavior is carried out through conscious voluntary behavior, although the individual is generally not aware of what drive is being gratified by his activity.

The process by which the drive excitation produces behavior is complex and elaborate and will be described in detail in the next chapter. The intervening mechanism is *cathexis*. The drive cathects an idea or a drive representative which is then felt as an impulse to perform the gratifying behavior. The cathexis is the force that drives the idea into consciousness.

Other ideas besides those that are behaviorally acted out are also brought to consciousness through cathexis. A common usage of the term in psychoanalytic writing is to say that the objects of a drive (see p. 309) are cathected. The child's mother is, for example, a cathected object. In ordinary language this means that she is important to the child and valued by him. The psychological mechanism is that the idea of his mother and all ideas that involve her have a strong cathexis. He thinks of her often; what she asks the child to do tends to be carried out. In a sense she commands a great deal of cathexis in the child's psychological functioning. The child has "invested" cathexis in her.

Psychological structures in the personality can also be cathected. Barriers that prevent ideas from becoming conscious require cathexis for their operation. Thus, all defense mechanisms (see p. 328) represent the investment of some cathexis.

Even organs of the body can be cathected. The Freudian explanation of an hallucination, for example, is that the sensory system is so strongly cathected that it perceives some drive representative even if the corresponding object is not actually present in the external world. This widespread and general use of cathexis in different areas of psychological functioning reflects the basic psychoanalytic assumption that all types of behavior, thoughts, feelings, and other psychological processes, whether they are conscious or unconscious, are ultimately motivated by the instinctual drives. Cathexes are the carriers of this influence.

The details of the functioning of cathexis will be discussed later;

this discussion suffices to illustrate the way in which the basic assumption of drive. motivation and mental energy pervades all aspects of psychological functioning, according to psychoanalytic theory.

Unconscious Processes and the Psychoanalytic Theory of Consciousness

In the minds of many scientists, the most original of Freud's contributions to psychological theory was his assumption of unconscious mental processes. Long before Freud, of course, people knew that much activity of the nervous system took place without any conscious awareness of it. Breathing, and the frequency of the heart beat, as well as the automatized activities of standing, walking, etc., proceed under their own controls with only fleeting, if any, conscious awareness. Freud spoke, however, of phenomena of a different order; he spoke of unconscious mental activity like unconscious ideas, desires, feelings, and perceptions. In other words, he took the whole vocabulary of naïve psychology describing the contents of conscious awareness and proposed the hypothesis that such mental activity might occur unconsciously. Furthermore, he argued that these unconscious mental activities played an important role in psychological functioning, in mental health, and in the determination of behavior.

It is not so commonly realized that Freud attributed great significance to the process by which ideas became conscious because under normal conditions only conscious ideas are acted out. The connection between the drive that cathects the idea and the idea's becoming conscious is generally unconscious but the act itself is a conscious, voluntary one. Only in serious pathology are unconscious ideas acted out without becoming conscious; if so, the person performs the act like a sleepwalker. Normally, access to consciousness is a prerequisite for overt behavior.

What is significant for an understanding of Freud's conception of the unconscious is that a psychological process may not be conscious for several reasons. These different reasons are usually desribed by the terms *conscious, preconscious,* and *unconscious.* Consciousness contains those items of which we are actively aware here and now. Preconscious ideas are available to become conscious if they capture attention or if attention is turned to them. Unconscious ideas are those that are actively repressed and prevented from becoming preconscious. Sometimes the term *dynamic unconscious* is used to specify this repressed material. There are other psychological processes of which we are unaware, however, and Freud discussed some of them in his earlier writings. Drive and drive excitations cannot themselves become conscious any more than nerve impulses or physiological mechanisms. Outside the realm of psychoanalytic theory there are, of course, many other activities of the nervous system that are psychologically relevant but not conscious. Nonpsychoanalytic writers often use the term "unconscious" to include all processes of which we are not aware. The student must be cautious, therefore, in assuming that psychologists who use the term unconscious are all using it in the same way. The commonest error is to use the term to mean simply "unawareness" and to believe that that is what it means in psychoanalytic theory. In nearly all of psychoanalysis, the term *unconscious* means that the material is actively repressed, that is, *dynamically unconscious*.

Id, Ego, and Superego

The difference between a socialized adult and the unsocialized child is not a matter of different instincts or different amounts of instinctual drive, but a difference in the pattern of cathexis and other regulating mechanisms that determine how the instinctual drives are satisfied. This pattern of cathexis is largely described in terms of the three "structures" of the personality, the *id,* the *ego,* and the *superego*.

PRIMARY PROCESS. The young child is impulsive, easily aroused to overt expression of emotion, and finds it difficult to restrain or to delay the gratification of his desires. He cries easily and may go into an uncontrolled temper tantrum when he is frustrated or irritated. When he wants something, he wants it *now*. Experiments have shown that young children are more likely to choose some immediate pleasure, even though they could have more by merely waiting a short while (Mischel & Metzner, 1962). It is particularly difficult for the young child to give up some goal simply because it is unattainable. The five-year-old who wants a drink of lemonade or a piece of candy continues to fuss and demand it even when he is clearly told that there is not any to be had. He wants it and he can hardly stand the frustration of not getting it.

This general state of affairs is described in psychoanalytic terms by saying that the drive energy underlying these motives of the young child is *free energy* and that it is governed by the *primary process*. Primary-process functioning denotes not only the free expressiveness of feelings and the difficulty in accepting any delayed gratification but also various other characteristics of drive-oriented thinking. Primary-process thinking is most familiarly manifested in dreams where reality is distorted, where the same figure can be two people at once, where similarity in sound or appearance may be the basis for substituting one object for another, and where the sequence and organization of thoughts is governed by the instinctual drives. The primary process is described by Freud as being childlike, archaic, prelogical.

THE ID AND THE PLEASURE PRINCIPLE. Freud labeled one structure in the personality the *id* and described it as governed by these primitive primary processes. The infant's personality contains no other structure; the ego and superego develop later.

Psychoanalytic theory also describes the functioning of the id in another way, as being governed by the pleasure principle. The young child, like all the rest of us, does not like things that are painful, disturbing, or uncomfortable. He avoids them if possible, escapes them, or tries to shorten his exposure to pain. Under some circumstances escape from pain is sensible, but can be short-sighted, because an immediate escape from pain may in the long run lead to even more pain. The pain of a vaccination, for example, is not as great as the pain of the illness it prevents.

When some system of the personality functions to reduce the pain in an immediate sense, by repression for example, it is said to be operating on the pleasure principle. The id functions according to this principle but many of the defense mechanisms of the ego also function on the same basis. In fact, many of the maladjustments of the neurotic personality are due to the strong yet short-sighted motivation to avoid exposure to unpleasantness.

In contrast to the pleasure principle is the *reality* principle. This describes the functioning of the mature ego where painful events are recognized for what they are, even if the recognition is painful, and where short-term or immediate pain is undergone in the interests of a compensating reward in the future.

MODELS OF THE FUNCTIONING OF THE PRIMARY PROCESS. Rappaport (1959) has described three *primary models* of psychological functioning. One of these models is concerned with action, one with cognition, and one with affect. The models are called "primary" because, as they operate in the young child, they follow the primary process. They also describe the functioning of the id.

The primary model of action is described as follows:

Restlessness————————→Sucking on breast————————→Quiescence
(drive accumulation)   (drive satisfaction)   (drive absence)

The child, under the effect of drive excitation, becomes restless and fussy. He does not have any mechanism for obtaining or even searching for satisfaction. All he can do is yell more and more violently as the drive accumulates. If and when he is given the breast, he sucks. The drive-satisfying behavior is part of his repertoire, once the object of drive is present. After suckling long enough he subsides into quiescence. This is a primitive mechanism for satisfying a drive, and, of course, its effectiveness depends on the mother's interpreting the restlessness properly and providing the bottle or breast.

The primary model of cognition is summarized as follows:

Drive reaching———→Absence of drive object———→Hallucinatory idea
threshold intensity   of previous grati-
                                                                                fication

The primary model of action can describe the behavior of simple organisms where there is no guidance of behavior. However, the human infant has the potentiality for cognitive functioning, which is at the root of later development.

The primary model of cognition hypothesizes that one of the results of drive accumulation is an hallucinatory image of drive gratification. This hallucination does not occur automatically on the first occasion; instead, it depends upon the infant's memory of previous gratifications. In a simple sense, the infant has learned what it is he wants and thinks about it. Since he is very young, thinking and sensing are not different; so probably his thoughts are something like hallucinations. Here is an example of the psychoanalytic thesis that drives determine what becomes conscious, but that they are not the stuff of which conscious experience is made. The drive must have some memory as a vehicle for becoming conscious.

The hallucination of a previous gratification is energized by the drive, but it does not effectively discharge the drive. Cognitions are determined by drive, but since they do not discharge much energy they are not effective substitutes for the behavior that occurs when the drive object is present. When the aim of the drive is fulfilled, the energy is discharged more or less completely. Cognition, or conscious experiencing of the drive's representation, occurs when the aim of the drive is not achieved.

This kind of cognitive experience illustrates the primary process because the experience is determined solely by the drive and because the gratifying experience is hallucinated. In other words, the infant's experience is not influenced by what is actually present in the real world to be perceived, but rather by what he wants. The primary process is drive-oriented and not governed by considerations of reality. As the child matures, the gratifying experience is remembered and at the same time the present situation is accurately perceived, so that the child is in a position to bring about gratification in reality rather than merely in hallucination.

The third of the primary models described by Rappaport is the model of affect.

Drive————————→Absence of drive object————————→Affect discharge

Here again, the necessary condition is the frustration of the drive so that the energy is not discharged through actual gratification. The expression of the affect or emotion was viewed by Freud as a sort of emergency discharge of the drive cathexis. It discharges some of the drive energy, but not nearly as efficiently as does the gratifying or consummating behavior.

In summary, psychological functioning according to the primary process consists of being restless, of experiencing affect, and of experiencing an hallucinatory gratification of a drive as long as the drive is present but not discharged. When the aim of the drive is achieved, the organism goes into a state of quiescence in which there is no action, no affect, and no cognition. According to psychoanalytic theory, this is the way the id functions—or at least this is the way an organism would function if the id were the only system present.

EGO. The second system to develop within the child's personality is the *ego*. The ego is realistic; it is turned toward the outer world as well as toward the inner drives; it controls the drives by delaying, inhibiting, and restraining them in the interests of achieving their aims realistically. It represents the role of enlightened self-interest in the personality. Its functioning, if effective, results in attainment of the aims of the drives. In fact, it maximizes the eventual gratification that comes from drive discharge, but for this result to be achieved it may be necessary to inhibit drives for a period of time, to find detours to drive gratification, and to reconcile the incompatible impulses that may arise from the welter of instinctual drives.

One of the primary functions of the ego is to prevent drive discharge even when the drive object is present. In other words, the ego raises the threshold for drive discharge. This is equivalent to saying that the individual can tolerate the frustration of an ungratified drive. We shall see later that this tolerance for frustration may be used for a variety of purposes, both adaptive and neurotic, but the prevention of drive discharge or the control of impulse is an essential function of the ego.

A second function of the ego is to control the access of ideas to consciousness. Since a drive is acted out through a conscious impulse, the ego, by preventing the idea from becoming conscious, can prevent the behavior. As we shall see later, the various defensive mechanisms that are part of the ego may also distort consciousness in other ways.

A third function of the ego is to guide the behavior of the person toward those goals that are acceptable. Nearly all topics in the field of cognition are, in psychoanalytic theory, described as functions of the ego. Through ego functioning the individual selects an effective means to this goal, takes detours if necessary, and balances one value against another. In other words, these ego functions enable the individual to plan his behavior ahead of time.

A fourth function of the ego is logical thinking. As a result of the development of the ego, the individual is able to think about ideas in a logical sequence according to some systematic set of rules. This procedure is in contrast to the functioning of the primary process where the sequence of thoughts goes from one drive representative to another, regardless of logical rules or realistic factors.

A fifth function of the ego is to use the affect that accompanies drive frustration as a signal that helps the person to select what goal is important. If one is angry or sad or upset, the feeling is a sign that something is wrong, and this fact should be recognized. One's goals should be selected to relieve the feeling, even though relief from affect should not be the only goal. In primary-process functioning, the affect is an explosive discharge of emotional feeling. Such affective discharge does not facilitate effective functioning, but the feeling itself is indicative of what goals are important and what drives are unsatisfied. The ego, functioning according to the principles of secondary processes, uses this affect as a signal and integrates it with other considerations in deciding what to do.

In summary, the ego operates according to the principles of the secondary process, guided very much by reality considerations but in the service of the instinctual drives. Because of reality considerations, it is necessary to build up controls and defenses against certain forms of discharge of instinctual drive and to delay other forms of drive discharge. These controls are necessary in order that planning and other forms of goal-directed behavior may occur. At the same time the affect that accompanies the frustration of instinctual drives is controlled so that it becomes a signal that some sort of adaptive behavior is needed rather than an overpowering emotional impulse. All of these functions of the ego use ego cathexes that are ultimately derived from the instinctual drives.

In his theoretical writings Freud made a fairly sharp distinction between the id and the ego. To the id he attributed dynamically unconscious content, primary-process functioning, the pleasure principle, and drive cathexes. In contrast, the ego is partly conscious and partly not. It operates according to the secondary process, with neutralized cathexes. Actually, there cannot be such a sharp distinction, but rather a continuum from pure primary process to relatively pure secondary process. As Rappaport (1959) points out, the personality contains many layers of functions, with the higher ones controlling the operation of the lower. The controlling function is by no means always realistic; many of the controls prevent anxiety at the expense of realistic adaptive behavior. Throughout the continuum, however, the higher-level functioning is more realistic, more planful, and operates more with neutralized cathexes than the lower-level functioning.

SUPEREGO. Turning now to the superego, the third structural system of the personality, we face a whole new set of problems.

The ego-id distinction was developed by Freud to describe in theoretical terms the qualitative differences between the impulsive, emotionally labile, short-sighted behavior of the young child and the realistic behavior of the maturer individual. There is no disparity between the aims of the ego and those of id, merely differences in the means of attaining those aims. If the ego completely inhibits some expression of an instinctual drive it is because such an expression would not result in maximal drive satisfaction.

The difference between the superego and the id, on the other hand, is very much one of aims. There are many varieties of drive discharge that would be highly satisfying to the individual, but that would be very disruptive to the rest of the society in which the individual lives. One of the problems of human development in a society is the reconciliation of the conflict between egocentric satisfaction of the individual and maintenance of a social order. The conflict arises whether one views the social order as a mechanism for providing the maximum satisfaction for the maximum number of people, or sees it as a system of norms and standards and roles that may be imposed quite independently of individual happiness.

We want to discover how these societal rules become thoroughly incorporated into the individual personality so that the social system remains relatively constant over generations. For Freud the answer lies in the development of the superego, a part of the personality that may contain restrictions and controls over instinctual drives which absolutely prevent drive discharge.

In terms of the dynamic relation among the three systems, the id is the ultimate source of motivation for all of the systems and, in addition, represents the forces for direct immediate expression of instinctual drives. The superego represents the cultural restrictions on the expression of the instinctual drives that have been incorporated and accepted by the individual. The ego is the control center that must find behavioral patterns that provide the maximum of drive satisfaction within the restrictions of the superego and also within the constraints of the real world, including the social world.

It is important to recognize, however, that the superego is not necessarily an accurate representation of cultural norms. As we shall see in a later discussion of the development of the personality, the superego begins to be acquired in early childhood and represents the child's interpretation of parental prohibitions on sexuality, particularly the Oedipus complex. At that time the child's concept of punishment for sexuality is violent and unrestrained; he fears castration, for example. This violence of the superego is preserved because both the child's sexual desires for the mother and the castration fear are repressed; the castration fears are preserved, unmodified by later, more realistic conceptions of society's rules against overt direct expression of the instinctual drives. Thus, the restrictions and fears stemming from the superego may be unrealistically rigid, violent, and concrete. In many ways, therefore, the ego functions to find some compromise or reconciliation between primitive id impulses and equally primitive superego prohibitions and demands.

The mechanisms of ego-superego relations have not been described in as much detail as the mechanisms of ego-id relations. All the same processes of ego functioning are involved. In some manner impulses that are contrary to superego norms result in anxiety or guilt. Such impulses are then controlled to reduce the guilt they cause.

SUMMARY

This chapter has introduced the basic assumptions, strategies, and concepts of psychoanalytic theory. By now it is apparent how much psychoanalytic theory is focused on the explanation of the individual's thoughts and feelings at any moment. These are the data to be explained, and overt behavior is primarily the acting out of what one is thinking. The mechanism of this acting out is pretty much ignored, just as it is in naïve theory.

In the light of this fact, it is easy to see why psychoanalytic psychologists emphasize the importance of knowing a person's thoughts, and why they feel that a purely behavioral approach misses the boat. It is also clear why they do not trust simple answers to questionnaires and interviews; they want to know fully and completely what the person is thinking and feeling.

We have seen how the source of data in psychoanalysis could well have led to this viewpoint since in psychoanalysis, expressions of thought are more easily obtained than samples of behavior.

The basis concepts of psychoanalytic theory are:

1. The instinctual drives energize all human functioning.
2. The problem is to show how these instinctual drives energize the particular behavior that maximizes gratification.
3. There are two major influences that set limits on gratification of drives: reality, and the social rules as mediated by the superego.
4. The ego describes the machinery that achieves, more or less effectively, this maximal gratification. It gradually develops structures that channel the discharge of cathexis through cognitive activity, repression, and other defensive mechanisms.

ELEVEN

Freudian theory of psychodynamics

HAVING INTRODUCED the basic theoretical concepts of Freudian theory, we turn now to the internal psychological events that occur between the drive excitation and overt behavior. These are the vicissitudes that may prevent a drive from being realized quickly in an overt form but that may lead to eventual satisfaction of the drive. The term *psychodynamics* refers to the occurrence of these modifications of drives and the defenses against them under the pressures of various constraints.

Consciousness Controls Action

One of the basic principles of psychoanalytic theory is that access to consciousness is essential for the carrying out of an idea in action. Nearly all everyday behavior is voluntary and intentional. There are a few purely automatic responses and many automatized adjustments of the actions that execute our intentions, such as adjusting one's walk to the contours of the ground, but the bulk of the socially significant actions are conscious and deliberate. Freudian theory does not contain any detailed theory about the process by which conscious intent is carried out, but it is clear that if some concrete intention can be prevented from becoming conscious, the action will be blocked.

Thus, we see how important it is for Freudian theory to describe the conditions under which ideas may become conscious. Although consciousness is not sufficient to ensure the execution of an intention—we can consciously decide *not* to carry out some action—consciousness is certainly necessary.

The principle that behavior is controlled by access to consciousness may at first seem contradictory to the basic principle that many of the determinants of actions are unconscious. If we carefully examine one example of unconscious determination, a post-hypnotic suggestion, we shall see that it does not contradict the principle that action is controlled by access to consciousness. A post-hypnotic suggestion is carried out after the subject is no longer hypnotized. The hypnotist may inform the subject while under hypnosis that after he wakes up, he will hear a signal—three taps of a pencil on the desk. When he hears this signal he is to get up and open the window in the room. The hypnotist repeats these instructions a few times to be sure they are clear, then he awakens the subject with the instruction that he will remember nothing of what went on in the hypnotic trance. After the subject is awake the hypnotist questions him to check on whether there is any memory of the trance events or not. Then after fifteen or twenty minutes, the experimenter casually taps his pencil three times on the desk. He may do this in the middle of a conversation in an incidental way, or he may be quite obvious about it. The subject then gets up and opens the window, perhaps complaining that it is quite warm in the room. He may carry out the suggestion without ever remembering the suggestion given him during the hypnosis and without suspecting that his opening the window had any other reason than that he was feeling warm. In some cases, however, the suggested action is sufficiently inappropriate—to climb on the desk and crow, for example—that the subject does suspect that he may have been given a post-hypnotic suggestion and may try to resist it. What he reports is that the idea of performing the action keeps intruding on his thoughts, that it keeps nagging at him so that he may finally carry it out just to get rid of it. Or he may resist the impulse. The subject is not a completely docile slave of the post-hypnotic suggestion.

How is this obedience to a post-hypnotic suggestion consistent with the idea that access to consciousness controls action? What is important is to realize that in post-hypnotic suggestion the idea of opening the window is conscious; the subject does not move blindly and senselessly over to the window like a zombi. He gets the idea of opening the window as a conscious one; it is apparently a persistent idea which keeps intruding on consciousness. Its persistence in remaining conscious gives it its power. What is unconscious about the event is the relation of this conscious idea of opening the window to the hypnotist's earlier suggestion. From the standpoint of the subject, the idea pops into his head, without any clear antecedent thoughts leading up to it. It is the events leading to that thought that remain unconscious.

So it is with all unconscious determinants of behavior, according to Freudian theory. The concrete action itself and its particular goal is conscious; it must be conscious to be carried out as a voluntary movement. But many other aspects of that act may be unconscious. The act has many consequences in addition to the special goal of the behavior itself; these other consequences, or some of them, may be unrealized by the person executing the action, yet some of them may fit the unconscious drives that are satisfied by the action. Or, it may merely be that there are more determinants of the action than appear in consciousness.

From the point of view of Freudian theory, ideas are constantly coming and going in consciousness. Some of them are impulses to do something, some are perceptions or mental questions or merely idle thoughts. Some impulses are overtly acted out and others are not. For psychoanalytic theory, these ideas in consciousness are the raw data for psychological theory building. Thus, psychoanalysts believe that to restrict psychological theorizing to those ideas that are acted out overtly in motor behavior is to pass up the majority of the data.

The ideas in consciousness may come and go aimlessly or they may appear in lawful sequences determined by logic or mathematical rules. They may wander aimlessly or be directed to a single topic. The person's thoughts may stay away from unpleasant topics or they may be disciplined into focusing on harsh reality. According to psychoanalytic theory, all the essential features of psychological functioning are embodied in the content of the ideas that reach consciousness and in the sequence of ideas that flow through it.

In the young infant the ideas are hallucinatory pictorial images, although not necessarily visual. The contents are drive satisfactions and the sequence is by free association from one gratification to another. This is primary-process thinking.

Gradually as the child grows older, his ideation comes under control of the ego. The consciousness distinguishes between mental ideas and perceptions. The content may be a drive satisfaction or it may be neutral, and the ideas come in controlled sequences that lead to realistic solutions of his problems. This disciplining of ideation by the rules of reality and logic and the transforming of ideation from a kaleidoscope to a thinking instrument result in a tremendous improvement in the adaptive functioning of the child.

Not only the ideas themselves but also the associated affect, either pleasantness or unpleasantness, may be conscious. At first the child, under the control of the pleasure principle, rejects painful ideas and does not think about them. Another of the changes that come with the increased control of the ego in psychological functioning is that now the person can think about things that are painful and anxiety-producing. And often adaptive behavior can be achieved only by looking squarely at possible disaster in order to think how to avoid it.

The central importance of consciousness in Freudian theory is thus obvious. It is the idea in consciousness that may be acted out overtly; it is the sequence of ideas in consciousness that constitutes thinking and problem solving; it is the painfulness of some ideas in consciousness that result in defense mechanisms to keep consciousness anxiety free. Psychodynamics is basically concerned with the mechanisms that control the access of ideas to consciousness, the sequencing of ideas within consciousness, and the determination of what ideas are acted out in overt behavior.

Conditions Determining Access to Consciousness*

Two important conditions determine whether an idea has access to consciousness. The first of these is whether it has a certain quality of perceptuality and the second is whether it is sufficiently cathected.

QUALITY. The importance of quality in access to consciousness lies in Freud's conception of consciousness as a kind of sense organ, of a higher order than the eyes and ears. It is able to receive impressions from all the perceptual apparatus, but in addition can sense past remembered impressions and feelings—specifically pleasure and pain. But there are some sorts of mental or psychic events that are not in a form to be perceived by consciousness, just as there are many kinds of physical events that are not visible to the eye because they are not manifested as light. In order to have access to consciousness, mental events must be perceivable events like perceptions, memories, or feelings.

Drives or instincts do not have this quality of perceptibility and so they cannot become conscious in any direct manner. What can become conscious is the representation of a drive. So, for example, the visual image of the activity that is gratifying to a drive can become conscious; such an idea is then a drive representation. But such a visual image cannot convey any complete picture of the drive; it can include only one fairly specific instance of drive gratification. A much more complete and accurate representation of the drive can come through words. "The desire always to be better than anyone else in what one attempts" can describe in words the generality and intensity of com-

* The content of this section, although it stems from Freud, is largely taken from Gill (1963).

petitive motivation better than pictures can. While a person's awareness of his own competitive drive is not strictly an auditory or visual
image of a sentence, it is dependent upon the memories of words to
give it the quality of perceptibility. In fact, most, if not all, of the material of the preconscious is verbal in quality; when unconscious
material becomes so strongly cathected that it comes directly into consciousness or into a dream, it generally comes in the form of a sensory
image, not a verbal label.

To summarize, consciousness requires that the content have a quality of perceptibility. Most mental events do not have this quality but
can be represented in consciousness through the fact that they are attached to verbal or sensory memories that do have the necessary
quality. Verbal representations are generally speaking readily available to consciousness, and thus belong to the preconscious system.
Other material may have the appropriate quality but be unconscious
because it is repressed, while still other material may be unconscious
because it is not attached to verbal memories. Thus, Schachtel (1959)
suggests that the widespread lack of memory for events for early childhood is not that they are repressed, but merely that they are memories
of the preverbal period and thus have a nonverbal quality that makes
them less available to consciousness.

CATHEXIS. A second requirement for an idea's access to consciousness
is the attainment of a critical level of cathexis. Various factors contribute to the net cathexis of an idea. One is the drive cathexis attached to the idea, either from one of the basic instincts or from some
drive deriving from them. Ultimately, of course, the basic drives are
the determinants of all cathexis and all behavior.

This assumption that drive cathexis is one factor tending to bring
an idea into consciousness is found in other theoretical systems besides
Freud's. Stated in everyday language it is the assumption that we are
inclined to think about things we want and that are emotionally significant. Within limits the stronger the motivation, the more strongly
do the thoughts intrude themselves upon our minds. Very intense
motivations tend to be preoccupying and to exclude other thoughts
from consciousness.

Drive cathexis is not the sole determinant of access to consciousness,
however. One strong negative factor that may prevent a drive representation from becoming conscious it its repression. This is described
in Freudian language as the result of *countercathexis*. The countercathexis is opposed to the drive cathexis. It is as if the countercathexis
were subtracted from the drive cathexis to find the net cathexis which
gauges the intrusiveness of the idea.,

The countercathexis is basically determined by the pain or anxiety that the idea would bring or has brought with it to consciousness. We do not like to think about painful things; if they are painful enough it is almost impossible to keep our minds on them. This exclusion of thoughts on the basis of the pain produced is the basic reason for repression.

Drive representations may be painful for many reasons. To think about food when one is hungry and there is no prospect of eating is painful. Thus, there is a strong tendency to think about food when one is hungry and also a defensive tendency not to think about it because it only makes one aware of how hungry one is. One reason for repression can be to protect the person from the pain of conscious frustration when a drive is strong and its satisfaction is unavailable.

Another reason that a drive representation may be painful—anxiety-provoking is a better term—is that it threatens the individual's self-control. A person is afraid that he will act out the drive-cathected idea and wants not to think about it because that makes it less threatening. In pathological cases of obsessive ideas, for example, the main complaint is that the idea constantly intrudes upon consciousness and the person is afraid he will carry it out. For example, a young mother may be obsessed with the idea that she will kill her baby and is terribly anxious for fear that she will actually do it. According to psychoanalytic theory she unconsciously wishes the baby were dead. The wish is repressed, but the thought representing the wish intrudes itself upon consciousness and causes great anxiety.

In less pathological cases we can sometimes see young children in a tempting situation turn around and refuse to look at candy they have been forbidden to touch in an attempt to get rid of the temptation they fear they cannot resist. Or the alcoholic on the wagon may go around the block to avoid passing a familiar bar because he fears that he cannot resist the temptation to go in to get a drink. These are examples of defenses engaged in more or less consciously, but motivated by the anxiety aroused by the consciousness of one's own drives. When defenses like these are built into the personality—*structuralized* is the psychoanalytic term for it—the dangerous idea is prevented from becoming conscious at all. Since the reason for the defense is the painfulness of the idea if it were to become conscious, however, it might be more accurate to say that it is the painfulness of the idea when conscious that motivates the defense that prevents it from becoming conscious.

Still another reason that a drive representation may be painful is that it is so immoral, socially unacceptable, irrational, or outlandish that merely having such an idea seems to mean that one is a bad person, a crazy one, or in some way unacceptable to one's self-esteem. For a person who prides himself on his reasonableness or tolerance, the mere experiencing of anger and rage may be destructive to his sense of self-worth, even if he is not afraid that he will actually express his rage overtly. Or for a man who strongly feels that he is a faithful, loyal husband, the mere experiencing of sexual thoughts about other women may seem sinful or wrong.

Or ideas may be repugnant in and of themselves. Probably these are ideas that are defended against at a still deeper level, and perhaps built into the culture as horrible ideas. Thus, pictures of mutilations, deformities, horrible violence, or cannibalism, or even just perceiving someone being hurt can cause some people to hurt inside, to be nauseated, or to be terror-stricken. Probably most of us have one or another areas that are so sensitive that "just the idea is hardly bearable."

For a wide variety of reasons, therefore, ideas can be painful and thus provide motivation for excluding them from consciousness. The mechanism that brings about the exclusion is a countercathexis opposing the drive cathexis. The countercathexis reduces the probability that the idea will become conscious or perhaps it may fully prevent its access to consciousness.

Finally, there is a third type of cathexis that helps to determine whether an idea will become conscious. This is the *hypercathexis* attached to the idea. Hypercathexis is the concept Freud used to describe the fact that we can voluntarily pay attention to any object in our environment or can think about any idea that is preconscious.

No only can we attend to one thing at a time, we can also arrange our thoughts so that their sequence follows the rules of logic, or traces out a plan of action, or searches systematically for needed information. This systematic sequencing of thoughts and ideas according to some rule or plan is the essence of what Freud called the *secondary process*. This control over consciousness is the result of hypercathexis.

If drive cathexis were the only determinant of what entered consciousness, one's thoughts might be fixed upon some single drive satisfaction, although it is more likely that thoughts would roam from one variety of satisfaction to another. If, for example, a hungry person lets his thoughts roam freely, he may imagine different kinds of food, revive memories of Thanksgiving dinners, or picture in his imagination the experience of eating at a fine restaurant. Through the linkages of free association, his thoughts might include his mother, as well as other people and activities associated with eating. The thread connecting these thoughts is that they are all related to food. The sequence of free associations does not follow any rules of time and space; it may jump thousands of miles and twenty years from one thought to the next. The only organizing factor in purely primary-process thinking is the tie of the thought to the drive.

Repression and countercathexis eliminate some of the ideas that would occur if drive cathexis alone governed one's consciousness, but countercathexis cannot change the basic organization of the ideas or their sequence. As Freud pointed out, repression may shift the content of one's thoughts to remotely associated ideas that escape repression because they are not anxiety-producing. Nevertheless, ideas will still be brought into consciousness through drive cathexis, and their sequence and organization will still be determined by drives.

Through the development of hypercathexis, however, attention can control access to consciousness and change the organization. Ideas are partly under voluntary control when hypercathexis has developed, and their sequence can be governed by realistic plans and logical derivations.

Sometimes it is necessary to think about painful reality—a low bank account, or failure on an examination—in order to decide intelligently what to do. It may also be necessary to face one's own less desirable motivations and learn to deal with them. Facing reality can be greatly facilitated through the decision to pay attention to it, whether it is painful or not. Thus, hypercathexis sometimes can bring into consciousness ideas that would otherwise be ignored, although even the most assiduous attempt to think fully and completely about a topic cannot overcome strong repressions. But many items of information needed in everyday problem solving are not repressed; they are merely not obvious, not recently thought about, or merely unpleasant to dwell on. Attention and concentration can bring those ideas into consciousness and integrate them with other factors involved in problem solving.

Selective attention may also prevent some drive-cathected idea from becoming conscious by withdrawing hypercathexis from it or deploying it somewhere else. The free associations of a drive-cathected idea are not all relevant in planning a course of action, even when the motivation is to satisfy the drive. Attention should be directed instead toward means and instrumentalities that may not be drive-cathected at all. Thus, the individual can fix upon an objective, which is presumably drive-satisfying, and then focus attention upon means to that objective which are realistically important but not necessarily drive-cathected.

Why did Freud introduce the concept of hypercathexis instead of merely describing the phenomenon of attention? The concept of attention was obviously not originated by him nor is it unique to psycho-analytic theory. The answer to this question is threefold.

1. Defining attention as hypercathexis integrates the factors determining access to consciousness. *Drive cathexis* minus *countercathexis* plus *hypercathexis* must reach some critical value to bring an idea into consciousness.
2. The term *hypercathexis* emphasizes the common energy source behind all psychological functioning.
3. The term *hypercathexis,* being quantitative, embodies the economic point of view. The amount of cathexis available for attention is limited.

The first of these factors has been discussed but the second and third need some elaboration.

SOURCE OF ENERGY FOR HYPERCATHEXIS. Psychoanalytic theory assumes that hypercathexis, although ultimately based upon the drives, is conceptualized as neutral energy—neutral, that is, with respect to any particular drive. The conception of energy derived from drives but detached from them is not easy to understand; in some ways it seems self-contradictory. There are some things that can be said about it to make it more reasonable, however.

In the first place, all of this ego apparatus—attention, logic, realistic perception—is used in the service of the individual's motivations. People behave realistically and face painful facts not because the facts are real or painful, but because the person can obtain maximal satisfaction of the drives by facing reality and planning ways of circumventing difficulties rather than by ignoring them only to become frustrated by them.

We can also see how the ego apparatus is neutral, in the sense that it seems to satisfy diverse drives which are independent of, or even in conflict with, each other. Perhaps the derivation of the ego's cathexis from many different drives neutralize the ego to them all individually. Metaphorically speaking, the ego functions as an arbitrator whose salary is paid by both opposing parties.

Freud actually described two different properties of the cathexis available to the ego. It is *neutral* rather than drive-oriented, as we have described, and also *bound* as opposed to *free.* As the child matures his drives become less peremptory and less demanding of immediate gratification. This development is the result of a layering of defenses and controls. Controls over original drives result in derivative drives; they in turn require controls and defenses. As a result of this layering of one control structure on another, the basic drives are gradually tamed. The basic instinctual drives operate with free energy which is characterized by mandatory, immediate wish fulfillment. If the fulfillment is blocked by the unavailability of immediate gratification, hallucination of the drive-satisfying object and emotional expressiveness and affect discharge occur. This free energy permits no delay of gratification.

As the instinctual drives are gradually tamed by defenses and defenses against defenses, the energy involved in the various derivative drives gradually appears more inhibited or *bound*. These derivative drives do not result in such imperative, uncontrollable impulses for immediate gratification. Instead, they are amenable to delay, compromise, and reconciliation with other drives. Many of these derivative drives are not vital in the same sense as the basic ones. The quasi-needs studied by Lewin (see p. 111), such as wanting to mail a letter or the desire to continue in an interrupted task, can be conceptualized as derivative drives in psychoanalytic theory. Of course, they would be viewed by Freud as many, many steps removed from the basic instinctual drives but nevertheless energized by them. Such derivative drives as these are obviously amenable to delay and detour; they do not result in insistent unopposable impulses, riding roughshod over considerations of reality and common sense. Freud described the energy for such desires as *bound*. The similarity between neutral cathexis and bound cathexis is clear. There is little distinction between the ultimate level of derivative drives and the completely neutral planning of means to achieve a goal. The energy of the derivative drives is still motivational, but in a way that is as detached from the basic drives as is the neutral energy with which the ego apparatus functions.

The exact relation between bound energy and neutral energy is not stated precisely anywhere, but what is clear is the kind of behavior both concepts are intended to describe. Behavior is motivated in adulthood as well as in infancy and the drives of the adult are not weaker than those of the infant; the adult, however, shows a patience and self-control unseen in the infant. Freud felt that the cathexes of the adult were less demanding and more delayable, and he expressed this fact in terms of inhibited or bound energy. Also, there is a detachment about the adult's problem-solving efforts that led Freud to hypothesize that ego cathexes were neutralized (Gill, 1963).

ECONOMIC ASPECTS OF HYPERCATHEXIS. The fundamental assumption is that there is a limited amount of neutral and bound cathexis available for ego functioning. This scarcity puts a limit on the cathexis available for use as hypercathexis for attention. Thus, it is impossible to pay attention to everything at once. In fact, some psychologists have claimed that the focus of attention is very narrow and that mental activity involves rapid shifts of attention, scanning, alteration, etc. Many modern psychologists recognize the limited capacity of the organism to receive and process information (Hunter & Sigler, 1940; Broadbent, 1958). Freud conceptualized this limited capacity as a limited amount of cathexis.

Psychoanalytic theory also posits broader limits. Concentration, for example, the effortful paying of close attention to some topic, uses cathexis to exclude drive-cathected, anxiety-laden ideas. This concentration is achieved at the cost of cathexes available for effortless, flexible attention. If drive cathexes are so strong that large amounts of ego cathexis are required for repression and countercathexis, the cognitive functioning of the person may be handicapped.

Let us summarize the conditions determining access to consciousness. One is that ideas and drive representations must have a quality of perceptibility in order to be receivable by the sense-organ consciousness. This perceptibility may occur through sensory stimulation, sensory images, memories, particularly verbal memories, and through feelings of pleasure or unpleasantness. The second is that the idea must have a certain level of cathexis. This cathexis is contributed to by the *drive cathexis,* by *countercathexis,* and by *hypercathexis.* We have seen how the hypercathexis permits the attention to ideas and the sequencing of thoughts in obedience to reality considerations and logical rules.

Defense, Controls, and Cognitive Structures

The foregoing discussion conveys the impression that the countercathexis is somewhat like a dam. It raises the threshold of cathexis which an idea must possess before it can become conscious. The most strongly countercathected material is thus made virtually inaccessible to consciousness. This picture of countercathexis accurately describes only one defense mechanism: *repression.* There are, however, many other defenses and they function in many ways besides directly blocking access to consciousness. In addition, there are other sorts of control that do not block the expression of the drive but merely inhibit and tame it without forcing it into some altered expression.

DEFENSES VERSUS CONTROLS. Psychoanalytic theory distinguishes between defenses and controls (Rappaport, 1959). The essential difference is that defenses, by one means or another, distort consciousness and prevent the expression of the drive. Controls, on the other hand, inhibit the expression and modify it but do not really block the drive itself.

The modification of expression of hunger illustrates what is meant by control. Hunger is a basic drive, not perhaps the most significant for personality formation, but nevertheless basic. There is a difference between infant and adult expressions of hunger. The infant cries and is restless when he is hungry; adult hunger is geared to meal times and an adult, even if he is hungry, can put off eating and do something else until meal time. He can also take active steps to look for food rather than merely crying about it. Yet, it would not be accurate to say that hunger is repressed. Hunger is an acceptable motive in our society; it does not make a person ashamed or guilty to want food; very rarely does hunger energize behavior that has some other aim than eating. Although hunger is subject to *controls* by the ego and these controls operate through countercathexis, there are no significant *defenses* against hunger built into the personality. Hunger is tamed and controlled by the ego, but not altered into some derivative expression.

With sexual drives, the situation is quite different. There is, to be sure, a tamed, acceptable sexual drive in nearly all adults, which is openly expressed in the right places and toward the right people. This much is like hunger.

Psychoanalysis has stated, however, that sexuality is a drive that energizes many kinds of behavior which do not appear in consciousness to have any sexual connections or connotations. Much of the expression of sexuality is subject to elaborate defense mechanisms that repress some expressions and establish a variety of other derivative motives, such as sensual pleasures, warmth and sympathy, and such opposite motivations as prudishness and puritanism.

In other words, we can think of controls as taming the drive without bringing about any alteration of its basic nature, and defenses as preventing the expression of the drive. They bring about altered motivations whose connection with the repressed drive is unconscious.

Psychoanalytic Defense Mechanisms

Freud described a number of different sorts of defenses. The common feature of these defenses is that they distort the individual's consciousness in a way that prevents or alleviates the pain and anxiety that would be caused by a more realistic awareness of his environment or his own ideas and feelings.

Repression and displacement. Of these defenses, the cornerstone is *repression*. All other defenses are to some degree accompanied by repression. In all defenses consciousness is protected from the awareness of some psychic content, although consciousness may be modified in other ways, too. Repression is the simplest defense to conceptualize; it can be considered as a mere raising of the threshold of access to consciousness or as the mere subtraction of cathexis from a drive-cathected idea to prevent it from reaching the critical level of intensity necessary for conscious awareness.

A common accompaniment of repression is *displacement*. When some set of drive-representative ideas are repressed, the repression does not ordinarily include all the ideas that have any associative link with the central idea. One symptom that is not uncommon among patients is a handwashing compulsion. The patient must repeatedly wash and rewash his hands. The root of this symptom has been found in some cases to be guilt and anxiety about masturbation. The libidinal drive cathects the idea of masturbation, but such an idea is so laden with anxiety that it is repressed. Among the free associations to masturbation, the hand is a likely one. This idea along with other associations to the idea of masturbation is also cathected. Since masturbation is viewed as a dirty habit, washing is a sort of undoing of masturbation —undoing is another defense mechanism. At the same time the tender care of the hands expresses some of the cathexis of the genitals.

The important feature about the displacement is that hand washing does not arouse the anxiety that masturbation would. In fact, it relieves anxiety. Thus, the impulse to wash the hands can appear in consciousness and some of the libidinal drive energy is discharged in the acting out of the hand washing.

These ideas that are associatively linked with a repressed idea but are not themselves repressed are displacements. Because they are expressions of the drive that do not cause anxiety, they escape repression.

Freud's language sometimes suggests that there is something purposive and goal-directed about this displacement mechanism. When displacement is described as the appearance of repressed material in a disguised form, the language suggests the cloak and dagger: The forbidden idea chooses a disguise that will escape the watchful eye of the censor and manage somehow to get its message through to consciousness.

This picturesque language hides the essential simplicity of the displacement mechanism. A much better analogy would be water running through a small leak in a dam. The drive cathects all the ideas that are linked by a chain of association to the central drive representation, just as the water in a lake spreads out and wets the entire surface of the dam. If any of these associations are not painful they tend to become conscious, just as any water at the hole in the dam is pushed through. The mechanism is motivated by the drive energy but it is not a guided, planned circumvention of the repression. Nothing more complicated than the cathecting of a wide range of ideas associatively connected with the drive representation is required to account for displacement.

Freud described, however, how repression tends to spread. Once a displacement does become conscious, there is always the possibility that the associative link will consciously be traced backward. If its connection with the painful material is consciously recognized, it produces anxiety and will be repressed. Thus, repression spreads to exclude still more ideas. In a phobia, for example, it may be necessary for the person to avoid whole major classes of stimuli because they arouse anxiety through their associative links with unacceptable material. One patient's fear of going out into the street, for example, was traced back to her fear that she would become a prostitute and that was traced back to the desire for sexual experiences. The mere street environment aroused thoughts of "streetwalkers" and aroused such intense anxiety that the patient had to stay indoors to be comfortable.

REACTION FORMATION. In another defense mechanism, *reaction formation,* there is a distortion of consciousness in which the repressed motivation is replaced by its diametrically opposite motivation. Thus, hostility is overtly replaced by kindness, probably excessive kindness. Reaction formation is a protection against the acting out of the undesirable drive.

From a theoretical point of view, reaction formation consists of the establishment of a drive derived out of the countercathexis which prevents the appearance of the repressed material. Countercathexis describes the use of energy to prevent the consciousness of an idea; here that energy takes the form of a counterdrive. This counterdrive has all the characteristics of a drive. It provides its own drive cathexis for ideas that are its drive representatives and this cathexis tends to bring those ideas into consciousness; ideas can be organized by the primary process through association to this counterdrive. Such ideas can intrude upon consciousness and the impulses of the counterdrive can feel preemptory and imperative, and can be acted out in behavior. For this reason the counterdrive may itself be maladaptive and may, in turn, be inhibited or repressed by further controls and defenses. It differs from a primary instinctual drive in that (1) its energy is derived from the primary drives, (2) it was originally established as a reaction against a primary drive, and (3) it is a more tamed and inhibited and civilized drive than the primary drive.

Perhaps a hypothetical example—even though oversimplified and superficial—will illuminate the relation between the drive and the counterdrive or reaction formation. Suppose that kindness were established in a person as a reaction formation against a more basic hostility. A motivation to be kind expresses itself in various ways. When other people are in trouble, ideas for helping them out of their difficulties come into consciousness and impulses to express sympathy are elicited. Feelings of sadness become conscious when other people suffer tragedies.

The effectiveness of the counterdrive as a defense against hostility is seen in the fact that these kind, sympathetic ideas and impulses effectively prevent the appearance in consciousness of various expressions of hostility, such as a feeling of pleasure at other people's troubles and the impulse to take advantage of other people's vulnerability. This illustrates the defensive function of the counterdrive.

But the counterdrive has a life of its own and tends to organize ideas around it. It may well be maladaptive since its function is not primarily to help other people but to prevent the anxiety and guilt that would arise from awareness of the hostility. A person with such a counterdrive might find it hard to criticize another person, even if the criticism were constructive and helpful. The negative opinions expressed in the criticism would be too close to the repressed hostility for comfort. Or, the kindness itself could get out of hand and impel the individual to impulsively give away things he really needed himself, and then to regret their loss. The kindness might also take the neurotic form of giving and giving and giving, but becoming angry and hurt if the beneficiary were not sufficiently grateful. Here the repressed hostility finds an acceptable conscious expression along with the counterdrive.

As a result of these maladaptive consequences of kindness, some sort of defense and control might be established over the kindness. It might be a pessimistic, disillusioned belief that people are no good and do not deserve kindness; it might be a more modulated recognition that genuine kindness sometimes requires the acceptance of other people's distress or even at times the actual infliction of pain.

This is one example of the multiple layers of defenses and controls in which a defense requires a defense and then that defense must also be controlled. With these successive layers of controls, the resultant motivations become more and more civilized and acceptable, less demanding and peremptory, and more amenable to delay, detour, and planning. In psychoanalytic terms, the cathexis of these derivative motivations becomes more and more inhibited.

ISOLATION. A fourth defense is *isolation* and its close relative *intellectualization*. One common form of isolation is the repression of the feeling associated with the idea but not the content of the idea itself. Some people, for example, do not respond with anger and hostility when insulted or imposed upon. It appears at first that they are impervious, as if they did not understand what was happening. As it turns out, they are aware of the insult and of the intent, and they may even take action to respond more or less appropriately, but they do not feel angry—or perhaps it is better to say that they are not aware of their angry feelings. It is as if the conscious control over the expression of anger and hostility had become so habitual and structuralized that finally there were no angry feelings to control. Such people act all the time as if they were "playing it cool."

The relation to *intellectualization* comes from the fact that effective thinking and planning for the solution of emotionally significant problems always requires one to exert a certain control over one's feelings while at the same time clearly confronting the actual content of the problem. If an individual's boss is percieved to have been dictatorial, there is a real problem of how to behave. Perhaps one should protest, threaten to resign, or try to persuade him to act differently. The decision is more difficult if the person is overwhelmed by anger while making it. It is the affective side of the drive expression that gives it its preemptory and possibly uncontrollable quality.

Intellectualization consists in concentrating on the content of the problem and upon one's own goals, and in playing down the emotional elements. Separation of affect from content can thus be one mode of adaptive functioning. The danger in it lies in that the affective elements are also reflected in one's commitment to the goal. A purely cognitive understanding of a problem helps in selecting means to accomplish objectives, but does not help in staunchly adhering to the objective. Thus, intellectualizers may appear to be without basic values and goals. A completely intellectual approach thus turns out not to be any more adaptive than a completely emotional one. Affect may need control but it also needs to be felt.

Freud describes the mature ego as responding to the affect as a signal. The affect serves to indicate that what is happening is important and that the behavior must take this into account. With maturity, the affect is not uncontrollable; it does not explode in an emotional outburst. Instead, it functions as a signal that guides adaptive behavior and gives it a clear purpose. When operating according to the primary process, affect seeks emotional discharge; when operating according to the secondary process, it signals the significance of the problem to the person and helps to set the goal of adaptive behavior. Repression of affect prevents it from functioning as a signal.

Isolation of affect from content is the most commonly discussed example of isolation. More generally speaking, isolation consists of separating any mental events that naturally appear together. Thus, the man who cannot tenderly love any woman with whom he has sexual relations and who cannot feel sexual toward any woman he loves tenderly illustrates how tender love and sexual feelings may be defensively isolated from each other, each being expressed but at different times and with different people. How does the separation of sex and tender love prevent anxiety? There is no general answer. Perhaps in such a person sexuality might have strong aggressive overtones that are incompatible with tender love.

Isolation can also be illustrated by a strict separation of religion and science, which permits some scientists to study biological evolution and still believe in the biblical view of the creation. Another illustration is the psychological isolation of attitudes toward different races, so that one can demand freedom of the individual as a basic value and still feel that the Negro's striving for freedom is a dangerous rebellion against authority.

Generally speaking, therefore, isolation is a term describing the fact that two mental events that would normally impinge on each other are separated psychologically. By such separation, the individual is saved the difficulty of reconciling the two or dealing with them simultaneously. The various examples of isolation are not, however, all psychodynamically alike; repression of affect but not content is one kind of a psychodynamic process. The same general isolation mechanism might occur in a variety of specific psychodynamic mechanisms within the personality.

PROJECTION. There are other procedures of defense that operate on a different basic principle. A fifth important defense procedure is *projection*. Here the essential feature is the attribution of an undesirable characteristic or a dangerous drive motivation to another person. One of the classical illustrations is the prudish spinster's belief that other people are oversexed or sexually uncontrolled. Presumably, behind this belief is a libidinal drive. As a reaction formation, the individual is militantly nonsexual in her own behavior. Such a counterdrive would certainly decrease her chances of getting married.

The sexuality appears, however, in the preoccupation with other people's sexual behavior. Since the sexuality is attributed to someone else and since it is accompanied by disapproval, the thoughts of sexuality have access to consciousness. The disapproval also expresses feelings of hostility, and thus both sexuality and hostility find an outlet.

Another common phenomenon is hostility of a minority group member toward the minority group to which he belongs and his attribution to other minority group members the stereotype employed by the majority. Thus, a Jew who has turned away from his cultural group may become violently antisemitic and accuse Jews of being grasping, money-minded, and clannish.

These examples suggest that projection is frequently accompanied by hostility toward the person on whom the trait is projected. When the projected attributes are undesirable, projection can provide a defense that expresses both the motivation and hostility. People can, however, project feelings that they are embarrassed about or rather ashamed of, but that are not bad. Some people, for example, have great trouble in feeling proud of themselves or their family. They can sometimes express this difficulty by attributing these feelings to another person. The father who is proud of his children may be uncomfortable in expressing it himself but he may be able to project those feelings to his wife and gratefully accept them once they are projected onto another person.

In some ways projection is a subtler and more sophisticated distortion of consciousness than the previous defense mechanisms discussed. Projection is not so much a modification of the actual content of consciousness as a modification of the organization of consciousness. In projection, the thoughts and ideas themselves are conscious. As an expression of drive cathexis, the thought of someone else engaging in sexual actions is a reasonable direct expression of sexual drive. It would seem that only after the child has acquired a self-image and self-esteem would the attribution of a motive to another person be anxiety-relieving.

DENIAL. The last defense mechanism to be discussed by name is *denial*. It is perhaps one of the most primitive sorts of defenses, because it distorts cognition more severely than any of the others, and is therefore not present in the person who is not very young or seriously psychotic. Denial is perceiving the world in the way that one wants it to be rather than the way it is. Thus, it is directly related to the first hallucination of the drive-satisfying situation which Freud attributed to the young infant; at that time, however, the hallucination is not precisely a distortion of reality, since the reality-preceiving function of the ego has not developed. Still, it is clear that the infant does not distinguish between what he hallucinates and what he perceives.

Hence, as long as the ego is weak, the young child can deny unpleasant truths. Even the adult can deny facts if they are minor or unclear enough. The early signs of some impending disaster may thus be denied by those so inclined. In some people, a remark like, "I'm glad I haven't had a headache for so long" is soon followed by a headache. Freud hypothesized that the remark was an actual denial of the sensations that marked the beginnings of the headache.

As the child grows older, he is unable to deny clear reality, but he can still deny it in his play or in his daydreams. The adult can also daydream about things being the way he would like them to be, to escape burdensome reality for a while. In a gross sense, denial becomes impossible, however, once the ego is well developed. Defenses must then take some other form that does not twist and distort consciousness quite so violently.

This completes the list of defenses to be discussed at this point. Repression, displacement, reaction formation, projection, isolation, and denial are not the only methods by which the individual's cognition is organized and structured, or the only methods by which that structure may protect consciousness from pain and anxiety and the individual from his impulses. They are, however, some of the important defense mechanisms described by Freud.

We shall see later that modern psychoanalytic theorists have put these defenses into a much larger context than ego protection. They can be viewed as styles of perceiving and thinking which influence the individual's consciousness in many ways, as well as serve defensive ends. We shall come to this broader view of cognitive controls in the next section.

COGNITIVE CONTROLS AND COGNITIVE STYLES. Freud thought of defense mechanisms in relation to the prevention of anxiety aroused by drive motivation. Defenses represent one kind of cognitive functioning and reflect the individual's general cognitive style. Moreover, the general cognitive functioning of the individual may be influenced by the kinds of defenses he develops.

Since 1950, psychoanalytic psychologists have devoted much time to the study of cognitive styles and cognitive structures. The impact of this research has been to broaden the scope of the concept of defense so that a cognitive structure is thought of as a style or mode of perceiving that serves as a defense but also has effects upon all of the individual's functioning.

One cognitive style which has been investigated by George Klein and his colleagues (1954) is labeled *constricted control* as distinguished from *flexible control*. In one experiment on the distinction two groups of subjects were selected who differed markedly on the Stroop color-naming test. This test measures the subject's ability to ignore one aspect of a stimulus. The test material contains a long list of color words, red, green, blue, and yellow repeated over and over again in random order. These words are printed in colored ink, but the color of the ink is never the same as the color the word signifies. Thus the word *green* is printed in red ink, etc. The task of the subject is to name rapidly the colors in which the words are printed. His recital measures the extent to which the color name interferes with the performance. The performance requires a defense against the color name. One group of subjects in this experiment was selected because they showed a great deal of interference while the other group was much less bothered by the wrong color word.

This test seems at first to have little to do with psychodynamic defense mechanisms; as it turns out, though, the subjects showing high degree of interference manifested many other signs of a tendency to use isolation as a defense mechanism. One questionnaire, for example, asked the subjects about a number of aspects of everyday behavior. The subjects high on interference reported a variety of activities resembling compulsiveness: They emphasized precision and meticulousness, valued orderliness highly and were made uncomfortable by disorder; they tended to look at problems analytically, making many logical distinctions rather than using a more global intuitive approach. The contrast group was not so clearly described because its members were less like each other; in general, however, they seemed to allow intuitive and affective factors some influence in their cognition rather than trying to rule these factors out.

These two groups of subjects were also contrasted on a number of other experimental procedures designed to show the effects of need on perception and cognition. In one experiment the subjects were tested when they were quite thirsty and also when they were sated with water in order to show the ability of the subject to ignore drive-relevant stimuli. One of the tests was on the accuracy of estimating the size of a circular disk, which had a thirst-relevant picture or symbols on it. The high-interference subjects tended to underestimate the size, regardless of their degree of thirst and of whether the disk contained some need-relevant symbol, although the underestimation was greater when the subjects were thirsty. In contrast, the other group of subjects, showing less interference on the Stroop color-naming test, tended to overestimate the size of the objects and their overestimation was greater when they were thirsty.

Klein described the mechanism of constrictive control as a tendency to "package" stimuli into nonoverlapping units for the purpose of focusing on the main objects without visually exploring or responding to the periphery. This constriction of the cognitive field leads to a contraction of the perceived size of the object. The same procedure is even stronger when there is a compelling need present which threatens to impinge upon the perception. In fact, Klein believes that people showing constricted control are potentially very vulnerable to interfering needs. They have this procedure of cognitive constriction for coping with interfering stimuli when the stimuli are spatially separated under certain circumstances. Their vulnerability in the Stroop color-naming test arises from the impossibility of separating the conflicting stimuli since they physically overlap.

The high-interference group shows more direct evidence of a tendency to constrict its visual exploration. If there is a picture of an ice cream soda in the middle of a card surrounded by figures and letters randomly located in the periphery, the high-interference group tends to concentrate on the middle figure and to refrain from looking at the periphery of the card or from knowing what is out there.

The high-interference group shows constriction of freedom not only in visual eye movements, but also in free association. If a word like "dry" which is thirst-related, or "house" which is not is given to the subject as the beginning of a chain of free associations, the high-interference group shows many more associations that are close to the central meaning of the stimulus word; the range of free associations is constricted. However, if they are thirsty, the subjects showing constricted control are more vulnerable to direct intrusions of thirst words into the free associations to "house."

These findings are not completely clear and there is room for other interpretations of the data, but it does seem as if the use of isolation as a defense is part of a much broader pattern of cognitive style rather than being just a defense mechanism.

There have been other studies of cognitive style, all of which attempt to discover the general features of an individual's cognitive functioning as these appear in many different kinds of tasks. Although there is still much to be learned about such problems, the data suggest that the Freudian defense mechanisms may be part of a general style of perceiving and cognizing. If we think of defense mechanisms in this way, we can develop two hypotheses about the development of such a mechanism: One is that the mechanism developed as a defense and, as a result, the entire pattern of interaction with the environment is colored; the other is that such a stylistic variable develops out of the innate predispositions of the individual in interaction with his environment, and that it is used for defensive purposes. The research has not yet given adequate evidence to allow us to decide between these two possibilities; probably the truth includes both.

THE ESTABLISHMENT OF PERSONALITY STRUCTURES. When Freud introduced the id, ego, and superego, he called them structures; this aspect of Freudian theory is called the structural point of view. It is not easy to define what a structure consists of in psychoanalytic theory or how it is formed. The basic definition of any structure, of course, is that it is something that is stable, although not necessarily completely unchanging, and which persists from one situation to another embodying the various possible reactions to different situations. Because of its structure, an automobile will go rapidly when the accelerator is pushed down and slowly when the brakes are applied.

In earlier chapters we discussed the concept of a *dispositional variable*. This concept is closely related to that of structure. The structure of the automobile determines its dispositional properties, but the structure is not the same as a dispositional property. We can list or catalog the dispositional properties of an organism without having any idea about how they operate; when we describe a structure, we give some picture of how the organism functions, how its various properties occur, and how they are related to one another.

Let us illustrate this in Freudian theory. One of the dispositional properties of the mature person, but not of the infant, is that when a motivation is aroused, he will search out a course of action to satisfy it. Freud tried to explain how such behavior takes place by hypothesizing a structure of countercathexes, which delay the discharge of the drive, and a system of attention hypercathexes, which permit planful realistic thinking. He did not provide a complete or detailed description of the structure, but attempted a first approximation.

It is easy to have one misconception about a structure: that it is necessarily physical and located in some particular spot. However, Freud did not intend to say that the ego was a physical region or a part of the brain; his is not a spatial concept at all in the sense that it physically contains defense mechanisms, countercathexes, etc. Instead, it is called a structure because it consists of stable characteristics of the personality which determine how drive representations appear in consciousness and lead to drive discharge.

In discussing defense mechanisms, we have described some of the different kinds of structures that make up the ego, or, more accurately, the principles on which these individual structures work. There is not, however, a single repressive structure that performs all the repression in the personality; there are rather different structures concerned with different drives and motivations. An individual structure might, for example, be the tendency to turn away from an accident because the sight arouses pain and anxiety. Some of these operate respressively and others by other defense procedures; many illustrate several kinds of mechanisms. Although these structures must be interrelated into some sort of system of defensive mechanisms, we do not know how to count the structures, how to define each one, or how to describe their interrelationships.

In this section we will describe some of the psychoanalytic ideas about these structures and how they are formed; in view of the many problems listed in the foregoing paragraph, however, it should be clear to the reader that psychoanalytic theory is speculative and not yet clearly formulated on this point. The ideas presented in this section come largely from Rappaport (1959) and Gill (1963).

The basic hypothesis about the formation of a structure is that it is the result of a process that occurs again and again until it finally becomes habitual or structuralized. Gill uses the following example as illustration. Every dream is the result of an interplay of drive cathexes and defensive mechanisms which finally brings the dream into consciousness. The ordinary dream is, however, never repeated; it is a here-and-now psychic event whose formation is the result of an *ad hoc* process of adaptation or id and ego mechanisms. Some dreams become repetitive, however; instead of making up a new story each time, the dreamer falls into the habit of repeating the same dream over and over. It has then become structuralized, and represents the operation of a structure. This structure is dependent on the same drives and defenses that the first dream was, but is habitualized.

Structuralization of a dream illustrates the psychoanalytic view of how all structures are formed. Psychoanalytic theorists claim structures first appear as *ad hoc* problem solutions that resolve conflict or reduce anxiety. If the same conditions recur often enough, the adaptive process gradually becomes habitual and the solution is built into the personality as a structure.

In some cases, the first *ad hoc* process may be conscious or nearly so. These processes are often conscious analogs of the unconscious defensive processes that enable us to picture the origin of the defense mechanism. For example, one conscious defense is to look away from disturbing and unpleasant sights. Children may hide their eyes at the part of the movie that is too full of suspense to be bearable to them; adults may turn off the television set when it makes them so mad they cannot look any longer. This sort of overt behavior seems to resemble repression. Since consciousness is viewed as a sense organ in psychoanalytic theory, repression may be thought of as a sort of looking away that has become habitualized or structuralized. When we think of it as a mental act of looking away, we can conceptualize the formation of the structure as the learning of a habit to remove or prevent pain and anxiety.

Another example of conscious *ad hoc* adaptation to disappointment or anxiety is to busy oneself with other activities that are incompatible with the preoccupation. To embed oneself in a whirl of pleasant social activities helps prevent the painful consciousness of a loss; to indulge oneself with new clothes or fine .food in response to a disappointment occupies the mind with incompatible thoughts and also partially compensates the self with a benefit to balance the harm. These *ad hoc* conscious adaptive behaviors bear a certain resemblance to reaction formation, where a structured derivative motivation is established to counteract an unacceptable original motivation.

It is doubtful whether the defensive structures generally begin with such conscious *ad hoc* adaptive behaviors, however. It is more likely that these conscious adaptations are merely analogs that illustrate that the same kinds of defensive procedures operate at many different levels.

SUMMARY

This chapter has treated the psychodynamics of personality functioning, which describe the way the personality functions in concrete situations. The central postulate is that access to consciousness controls behavior, at least the voluntary behavior that makes up the large proportion of actions of people in everyday life.

For an idea to become conscious, it must stimulate the sense-organ consciousness; it must have a certain quality of perceptibility, such as perception, memories, and feelings have; and it must attain a critical level of cathexis. However, many of the mental events of which we are unaware do not have the quality of being perceptible by consciousness; one way that such material can become conscious is through being attached to verbal memories. In other words, much of consciousness is a verbal consciousness that can express otherwise inexpressible thoughts and drives.

The control of consciousness is also determined by the level of cathexis. Countercathexes may prevent ideas from becoming conscious, and hypercathexis under the control of attention permits voluntary control over one's thoughts. Because of this control thoughts can be organized logically and systematically.

There are many kinds of controls and defenses that distort consciousness to prevent anxiety, pain, and the acting out of unacceptable motivations. These have ordinarily been conceived as limited in scope, but recent research suggests that these defenses may be parts of a more ubiquitous cognitive style which colors the individual's whole contact with the environment, not merely his defense against unpleasant motivations.

TWELVE

Freudian theory—

development of personality

THE TWO PRECEDING CHAPTERS have described the theoretical frame-work of Freudian theory. This chapter will fill in the content of the theory as it describes the developmental process.

The Content of Freudian Theory

Freudian theory is far more differentiated and specific about the content of personality and the facts of development than any other theory discussed in this volume. It contains specific statements about the forms taken by the sexual instincts at various ages; it pinpoints the form of expression of hostility, dependence, and sexuality at different ages and under different caretaking regimes; and it details certain fantasies and fears that occur in all children. For example, Freudian theory describes the young infant's love for his mother by stating that he has fantasies of her total incorporation, as though the food and the person providing it were somehow inextricably confused with each other.

So specific a statement about the content of the infant's conscious-ness and the nature of his motivation is unusual in personality theory. It is perhaps bold or even foolhardy to stipulate such detail in a theory before it has been well documented, but such boldness in theoretical speculation makes Freudian theory the rich and impressive structure it is. Other psychologists, like everyone else who has had considerable contact with children, have tentative empirical hypotheses about the qualitative characteristics of children at different ages. Many people would agree about the physical activeness of three-year-olds, the management problems with fifth-grade boys, or the sensitivity and rebelliousness of the teenager, but these empirical hypotheses are not ordinarily incorporated into a single systematic theory.

One of the valuable features of Freudian theory is that it is specific, detailed, and rich in content. Its specificity makes it vulnerable but impressive. It is at present the only theory complex enough, detailed enough, and coherent enough to lead conceivably to specific predictions about individual cases. However, its specificity does not really make it testable. If any of its generalities does not hold for a specific child, there are innumerable explanations available within the context of its theory. In fact, it is not clear how psychoanalysts can use successes and failures to improve and modify the theory; to some extent, therefore, the richness of the theory is misleading. Nevertheless, the theory is quite specific, especially in two areas. First, it describes the course of personality development in considerable detail; second, it describes the nature of specific psychopathology in even more detail. In our discussion we shall describe only the developmental features of Freudian theory and shall not attempt to review the psychonalytic theories of the various psychopathologies.

THEORY OF DEVELOPMENT

The Basic Nature of Freudian Theory of Development

The Freudian theory of development can be summarized in general terms. There are two interlinked maturational processes. First, there is the maturation of the ego: as the child develops, his ego gradually differentiates out of the global personality of the neonate. In the course of this development, there is an increase in the reality principle and secondary processes, a development of neutralized cathexis, a gradual appearance of defense mechanisms, and generally a more differentiated understanding of interpersonal relations.

Paralleling this development of cognitive functioning, the child goes through the stages of psychosexual development as the primary source of libidinal gratification shifts from the mouth to the anus to the genitals. The child's instinctual aims gradually change, and thus the emotional impact of such socializing events as weaning, toilet-training, and the control over childhood sexual behavior also changes. Each of these events is frustrating as well as gratifying and is accompanied by typical patterns of anger and hostility love and satisfaction. Freud himself felt that psychosexual development was a predetermined maturational process, but some other psychoanalysts believe the psychosexual stages are the result of the sequence of socialization.

Whether psychosexual development is maturational or not, the behavior of the child's caretaker and the particular circumstances existing at the time of the major psychosexual stages strongly influence the course of personality development. Each stage can be thought of as confronting the child with a new problem, exposing him for the first time to a particular interpersonal relationship. Infancy, for example, puts the child in a passive-dependent relationship with other people, and thus serves as a prototype that influences the individual's adjustment to dependency in later life.

As a consequence of each stage, a certain amount of the individual's libidinal cathexes are fixated at that stage, and thus certain attitudes, fears, fantasies, defenses, and expectations are more or less permanently built into the personality. Major psychopathology results when excessive amounts of libido are fixated at an early developmental stage and the accompanying pattern of adjustment developed at that stage is maladapted to the demands of adult life. In the discussion that follows, the major periods of the child's life from birth to adolescence will be described in chronological order, together with the psychoanalytic hypotheses about the usual consequences of that stage in the child's life.

Birth—the Origin of Anxiety

The role of the birth experience in personality development is a good one to begin with, not only because it occurs early in life, but also because it highlights some of the problems of a psychoanalytic interpretation of personality development.

Psychoanalytic writers differ widely in their hypotheses about the specificity and profundity of the effects of the birth experience on personality. Freud's own interpretation is one of the most modest. He conceived of birth as exposing the child to anxiety for the first time in his life. This anxiety, as Freud envisaged it, is quite nonspecific. It is merely the experience of being flooded with stimulation and bombarded by excitation. The neonate, of course, has no protection against such stimulation. He has, until birth, lived in a sound-proofed, padded, darkened environment into which few stimuli penetrate. During birth, this situation changes abruptly and completely. The outside world is full of light, noise, tactual stimuli, and temperature changes which flood the organism beyond its adaptive capacity. The resulting psychophysiological emergency reaction is essentially the same as that which accompanies fear and anxiety reactions. This emergency reaction appears overtly as a high level of activity, gasping, crying, wiggling, a fast heart rate, etc. Since birth is the first occurrence of this reaction to a flood of stimulation, it can serve as a prototype for later anxiety reactions.

What is the exact significance of the statement that it is a "prototype?" First, it suggests that particular stimuli which would not by themselves elicit an anxiety reaction may become able to do so, because they accompany the disturbing stimuli of the infant's early postnatal life. Second, and more significant, the child may learn some adaptive mechanisms that protect him from this early flood of stimuli. These same adaptive devices may become habitual in later anxiety situations.

The adaptive devices of early infancy are necessarily quite primitive. One is merely the development of a higher threshold to stimuli. Freud describes this development as a protective shell. The higher threshold may be brought about in various ways. Sleep is one state in which the threshold to stimulation is higher than normal. Another mechanism for adapting to strong stimulation is to filter the stimulus out by not paying attention to it. The infant cannot control his own attention but whenever he is focused on some activity, like nursing, his threshold for irrelevant stimulation is raised. It is possible that the focused activity helps develop the ability to attend. Another psychological mechanism that raises thresholds is sensory adaptation. People become less sensitive to constant stimuli the longer the stimulus continues. Thus the neonate may "get used" to the stimuli of his environment so that they no longer arouse anxiety.

What are the consequences of these experiences for later personality development? The consequence may depend on the child's susceptibility. Children disclose individual differences in responsiveness and in the speed with which they adapt (Escalona, Leitch, et al., 1953). There are infants who continue to be abnormally sensitive to stimuli. They startle more readily than other infants and may be kept in a constant state of overstimulation. Escalona and Bergman (1949) have found that some seriously pathological children had an early history of hypersensitivity to stimuli. They speculate that some of the behavior patterns of childhood schizophrenia may represent pathological adaptations to this sensitivity. The failure of normal adaptation to occur may predispose the child to develop a more extreme protective mechanism which is momentarily adaptive but maladaptive in the long run.

In other cases, the experiences in early life may predispose the person to some particular kind of adaptive mechanism. There are people, for example, who are made sleepy by anxiety; it is a way of turning off the anxiety. Such an adaptive mechanism may have started early in infancy but need not be a result of only early infant experiences. As sleeping is a state relatively free from anxiety, the sleepy response to anxiety may be reinforced many, many times in the life of the individual. Comfortable as it may be, sleeping through anxiety does not solve the problem that causes the anxiety. Like almost every adaptive mechanism, sleep has its assets and its liabilities. What is important in the present discussion, however, is that the neonate's experiences in adapting to overstimulation can have some effect upon the adaptive mechanisms that function in later life.

Another effect of the birth process may be to endow certain experiences with the power to be comforting. For example, some children when they are scolded flee into a warm, dark closet and huddle against something soft and warm. Some psychoanalytic writers would identify this behavior as a "return to the womb." The child is recapturing some of the features of his prenatal life: darkness, being closed in, warmth, and contact with soft objects. Similarly, falling into the water in a dream is interpreted by some psychoanalytic writers as representing a return to the womb.

Whether such interpretations are farfetched or reasonable depends upon how differentiated is the neonate's experience of being born. Did it actually represent for him a transition from darkness and comfort to light and discomfort in a psychological sense? If it did, then darkness may indeed be a comforting absence of stimulation; if it did not, then the reversal of the transition cannot reasonably represent a return to the womb. It seems unlikely in terms of what we know of neonates, that they can experience birth as a coming out of the water, even though it is factually true that the fetus is enclosed in a liquid-filled sack and shifts to an environment of air when born. Thus, the interpretation of falling into the water as a return to the womb seems inherently unreasonable.

Psychoanalytic writers differ widely in the complexity of conscious experience they attribute to children of very young ages. Some attribute explicit and clear fantasies even to the young infant; others allow for the cognitive immaturity of the young child and argue that his fantasies, whether conscious or unconscious, must be compatible with his level of cognitive development at the time. All psychoanalytic writers feel, however, that these early experiences do predispose the child to certain patterns of reaction and adaptation which may become firmly established in the course of development.

The Oral Stage—the Development of Dependence

The first psychosexual stage following birth is called the *oral stage,* because the infant's primary source of pleasure and gratification comes from stimulation of the oral regions of the body. According to Freud's theory, this pleasure in oral activities develops through the connection between nursing and being fed. Eating gratifies the child; he is restless and crying when hungry but rapidly quiets when he gets the nipple into his mouth and begins sucking, and then goes off to sleep after he has nursed a while. This reduction of restlessness is the best evidence for the child's being gratified. Freud believed that through this association of oral stimulation and the gratification of feeding, the sensations of the mouth became pleasurable in their own right. As he stated it, the development of oral pleasure was *anaclitic* on eating.

Freud did not say explicitly that this mechanism by which oral sensations become satisfying was a general one. He did not hypothesize that any sensation that was consistently associated with a satisfying sensation acquired some pleasurable qualities of its own, but seemed to believe that there was also some genetic determination of the oral stage. It is difficult to determine the details of Freud's theory in this regard.

Regardless of how oral stimulation becomes pleasurable, Freud assumed that infants universally get libidinal satisfaction from stimulation of the oral region. The satisfaction is revealed overtly in the infant's tendency to mouth any object which he gets his hands on, to suck his thumb, and to engage in other sorts of spontaneous oral activity. The pleasure of the activity is also attested by the fact that even nonnutritive sucking quiets the restless infant. By the age of 4 or 5 months, the infant may quiet down as soon as he begins to suck his thumb.

In terms of the development of the libido, the infant's focus on oral pleasure is the key to this period; we cannot understand the effects of the oral stage, however, without knowing the status of the child's ego development at this period of life. For example, at this stage of development, the child has no concept of an external world with an independent existence of its own apart from his sensations of it. The sensations themselves are the reality for the infant (cf. p. 195). Furthermore, the sensations from the different modalities do not overlap; sights and sounds from the same objects do not have any intrinsic signs of a common origin. Only after each is perceived as a message from an external world can it be fully integrated. The child in early infancy does not distinguish, therefore, between sensations within the body and those from outside of it.

In another way, the child's immaturity is also evident. When he learns a new response because it has been rewarded, he does not understand the mechanism by which the behavior led to the reward; thus, he cannot discriminate between occasions when the act will lead to the reward and when it will not. The response is performed blindly, and it appears that the child assumes an almost magical power in the behavior to produce the reward (see Piaget's example, p. 200).

In psychoanalytic theory all these features of the infant's behavior are called *primary narcissism*. The term is intended to convey the lack of external objects in the child's psychological world and the exclusiveness with which pleasure is a matter of his sensations. The child is also described as having a sense of omnipotence, because he lacks an appreciation of the mediating chain of events which makes his actions effective.

In psychoanalytic writings, the "sense of omnipotence" is given another connotation. If an adult adopted the infant's attitude toward the world, apparently trusting implicitly that he will be provided for, and if he acted as if gratification were inevitably forthcoming, we might well call him egocentric, because for him the world centers on his own gratification. This is the actual state of affairs for the young infant; because of his real lack of power, he must be cared for. If that care is abundantly forthcoming, he acquires a trust that it will come. This can be seen as a sense of omnipotence, although it is doubtful if the infant actually feels all-powerful. Rather, he fails to appreciate how dependent he is.

One feature of the oral stage, especially the part before weaning, is normally a trustful passivity. If the infant is not cared for, and is consistently ungratified, whether because of parental neglect, the pain of illness, or the harshness of the environment, he is still necessarily passive. All he can do is to suffer; he cannot actively remedy his lot. Under these conditions, a sense of mistrust rather than of trust may develop. However, it is a passive mistrust, an expectation of no relief rather than an active fighting frustration or resenting of deprivation. Optimism or pessimism is thus seen as originating in the oral stage.

Another feature of this period stressed in Freudian theory is the particular nature of the child's relation to the objects of his drives—his love objects in a primitive sense. In the previous chapter, we described how the infant hallucinates the gratification of a drive when the drive is unsatisfied. The hallucination is maintained until the gratifying experience actually occurs, then disappears as the child quiets down and goes to sleep.

This fantasy of gratification is a "love object" of a sort for the child. It is partially independent of immediate sensations because it exists over a period of time despite changes in the circumstances. As an object it exists psychologically rather than in reality, although it must resemble the mother in some sense.

It is not easy to describe the fantasied object, but it is clear that the child's relation to it is peculiar. It is tied to oral sensations—for example, the fantasied experience is oral. Further, it disappears with gratification. Psychoanalytic theory describes this combination of orality and disappearance with gratification as a fantasy of "total incorporation." The love object disappears completely along with the consummatory behavior that is the gratification of the drive. Some valued objects like food are literally consumed by the course of the consummatory behavior; however, at the oral stage, the child has no other relation to a love object than this one.

This belief in total incorporation persists into the aggressive stage of the oral period when the child is approaching one year of age. By this time he does have some conception of external objects; he grasps them, eats them, and even performs some instrumental acts to obtain them. Thus, biting and eating an object are well within the understanding of a child at this level of maturity. The fantasy that he incorporates the objects of his libidinal attachment lives on, however. Perhaps it is because the child still does not clearly distinguish between the food he eats and the agent who feeds him.

What is probably more important than the fantasy itself is the fact that the love objects of the oral stage are not cherished after gratification. The bottle is rejected after the milk is gone. Whatever the nature of the infant's feeling of love for the cathected objects in his environment, the feeling loses strength after the infant is gratified. Infants thus show an egocentric possessiveness and a high-handed treatment of love objects that are reflected in the phrase "objects are loved only when they are consumed."

These features of the individual's relationship to love objects may last over into later life. Some men do discard women after they have made love to them. What such people experience as "love" disappears with the consummatory activity. Such an attitude toward a love object might be labeled oral because of its similarity to the relation of the infant to his love objects, and the psychoanalytic interpretation of such an attitude would retrace it to the experiences of the oral stage.

Any feature of an individual's behavior, especially his pleasure-seeking behavior, that resembles some feature of the oral stage is viewed in psychoanalytic theory as possibly stemming from the oral period. Oral features may take a variety of forms. Some are literally oral, kissing, smoking a pipe, nail biting. Some are metaphorically oral like "biting" sarcasm. Some, like "eating jags" replicate the fact that the oral stage is concerned largely with food. Some, like compulsive overfeeding of one's children, may be oral because they seem to equate food with love. Still others recreate the basic oral attitude toward love objects, the imperious demand for the love object when desire is high together with ignoring it the rest of the time. In still another version of orality the emphasis may be on the passivity of the oral stage. For example, a passive, unrealistic optimism that someone will appear to solve one's problems may be an oral trait.

According to psychoanalytic theory, the oral stage is divided into two substages. The earlier one is labeled *oral dependent*. The second phase occurs at the time of weaning and is called *oral aggressive*. It is aggressive partly because the child is typically frustrated—to some extent at any rate—by weaning and thus may be angry and uncomfortable. It is also oral aggressive because it corresponds to the growth of teeth. The oral activity of the aggressive period includes biting as well as sucking. The infant's biting on the breast may, in fact, be the precipitating factor in the mother's decision to wean the child from breast to bottle. Biting is, however, not solely aggressive; it is also a source of comfort for the infant suffering the discomfort of teething. We provide teething rings or their equivalent for infants at that stage. The oral traits of this aggressive period usually have an aggressive tone and are literally or metaphorically "biting."

Thus, psychoanalytic theory provides a theory of personality development which identifies the historical origin of certain personality traits as the oral period of the child's life. The general rationale for such a theory is not unreasonable, and the hypothesized mechanism for the later influences of the infant's behavior during the oral period is sensible enough. A theory of personality development should, however, not only identify the common root of a diverse set of consequences but should also predict under what circumstances one consequence rather than another will appear. How does psychoanalytic theory explain which consequences of the oral stage appear in what individual?

The appearance of oral traits in adult personality is viewed as a partial fixation of the libidinal cathexes on the drive objects of the oral stage. If this fixation involves large amounts of libido, there may be a serious reduction in the amount of libidinal energy available for maturer kinds of object relationships. There is much less clarity, however, about the particular circumstances that lead to fixation. Freud described such diverse causes of oral fixation as deprivation in the oral period, overindulgence in the oral period, a severe transition from the oral to the anal stage, and possibly constitutional factors. Not only does psychoanalytic theory contain no clear criteria for predicting that fixation will occur, but it also does not provide much basis for a prediction about the form the vestiges of the oral stage will take. Whether a person will bite his nails or indulge in biting sarcasm, whether he will overeat or be a gourmet, is hard to predict.

Psychoanalysis, because it is rooted in psychotherapeutics, is primarily concerned with the analysis of childhood experiences after the fact, rather than with prediction of the consequences ahead of time. The usual task of psychoanalysis is to construct a reasonable interpretation of the adult personality on the basis of information the patient reveals in his analysis. An interpretation after the fact is, however, always subject to doubt because it seems likely that any one of a number of different outcomes could have been explained with equal persuasiveness. It has happened too often that through some mix-up of records, a psychologist makes an impressive interpretation of the childhood factors explaining a particular individual's adult personality, only to find that by mistake he has used records from the wrong childhood.

Psychoanalytic theory is so rich in detail and allows for so many contingencies that it may not be testable on the basis of case histories. If a case history were constructed at random, using the first year's experiences of one child, the second year's experiences of another, a third year's experiences of still another, etc., would it obviously be an impossible case? Could the analyst say, on the basis of the theory, that the first year was incompatible with the second? This would constitute one possible test.

John Benjamin (1950) who has devoted much thought to the testing of psychoanalytic theory has suggested a similar device. We obviously cannot predict the adult personality from a knowledge of only the first year since the adult personality depends on later experiences as well as early ones. Perhaps the theory can, however, exclude certain kinds of outcomes on the basis of the first year's record. No matter what happens later, the theory may predict that this individual will *not* become schizophrenic.

These problems of prediction from childhood to adulthood are not specific to psychoanalytic theory; any theory describing the cumulative and interacting consequences of childhood experience has the same difficulties. It is because psychoanalytic theory is so detailed and rich in content that these prediction problems have become apparent.

The Anal Stage—Possessiveness

After the oral period there is a shift in the dominant source of the child's pleasure from the mouth to the anal region of the body. This shift marks the transition from the oral to the anal period of development. According to Freud, this shift of the dominance to the anal erotogenic zone is a part of the maturational process and occurs universally. Many other psychoanalytic writers, who otherwise follow Freudian theory quite closely, disagree with the assumption that the shift is inevitable or maturational. They are more inclined to attribute the shift to the fact that during the period of toilet-training, attention is focused upon anal functioning and the anal regions become the center of frustrating and rewarding experiences. Whether or not the anal stage is seen as a result of toilet-training, there is agreement among all psychoanalytic writers that the experiences of toilet-training influence the development of the personality.

The mechanisms by which the experiences of the anal period affect personality development are fundamentally similar to the mechanisms described for the oral period. Because of the interaction of the child's source of pleasure, his level of ego development, and the common experiences that occur during toilet-training, various types of dispositions are initiated at this stage which shape the future development of the personality. The central factors during the anal stage are, of course, quite different from those of the oral period; we will discuss some of these features of the anal period that may become prototypical for later development.

It is a primary assumption that the child obtains pleasure from anal stimulation. Such stimulation may remain the primary source of libidinal pleasure throughout life, as in various sexual perversions where the anal region replaces the genitals as the erotogenic zone. In males this replacement is most commonly found in some form of homosexual intercourse, but it is not characteristic of all homosexuality, nor is it limited to homosexuals.

Because of the close relationship between toilet behavior and anal stimulation, Freud assumed that both the distention accompanying bowel retention and the stimulation of bowel movements were sources of libidinal pleasure. These same activities are, of course, a focus of the toilet-training process. Parents reward and approve the child for a bowel movement at the proper time and place, but try to discourage the child from the same activity in the wrong circumstances. Constipation may be a source of worry to parents and lead them to focus attention even more sharply on anal functioning.

According to Freudian theory, various features of the anal period may become crucial for later development. For example, the child may view a bowel movement as a sort of a gift to the parent, and thus may identify feces with such gift objects as money, valuables, and jewels. In this manner the experiences of the anal period may condition the individual's whole attitude toward possessions and valuables. Miserliness is a pleasure in the accumulation and hoarding of possessions, which could have its historical origin in the pleasure of withholding feces. Stinginess is so common in certain kinds of people that it is one of a triad of traits constituting the *anal personality*.

Anal influences may be seen in other forms as well. The individual may, on the basis of early anal experiences, identify love with giving gifts or other material possessions. Just as the identification of love and food can be one consequence of the oral period of development, the identification of love and gifts may follow anal fixation.

To reverse the same identification of love and possessions, some people treat a loved person as if he or she were a valuable possession rather than an independent person. This concept of love as possession of the loved object is quite common in early childhood. Love for the infant in the oral stage was a complete incorporation of the loved object. In the anal stage there is some progress toward the mature concept of a mutual relationship between two equal and independent people in that possessions are somewhat more detached and independent than the food one eats, but during the anal stage love is still egocentric. The child owns his love objects and does not treat a human friend much differently from a favorite toy. This attitude toward love objects in adult life can obviously be the source of much friction and unhappiness because it leads to egocentric attempts to control one's loved ones.

Another bit of progress of the anal over the oral stage is that possessions are at least cherished, albeit selfishly. The loss of cathexis following consummatory behavior is not present during the anal stage. In fact, belongings may be cherished so much that the child refuses to consume them.

If the tacit assumption that loved ones are possessions stems from the anal period, it is quite obvious that there is a fair amount of anality among most members of our culture. It is the norm in our society to feel possessive and jealous about some sorts of love relationships. Marital love and sexual love in general is not expected to be shared. It is common to hear the expression that a wife or husband has been stolen by the third person in the triangle. Both the terms "shared" and "stolen" carry the implication that the loved one is a possession of the individual. This attitude has existed for a long time and mixed with it is the notion of masculine dominance. In many cultures, including our own, the wife is more a possession of the husband than vice-versa.

The prevalence of such anal features in culturally accepted behavior would not disturb a Freudian theorist. The complete transition from one developmental period to another without any remnants of the earlier period is never realized in real life. The assumption that the marital relation is an exclusive one and that each partner possesses the other is one factor leading to the maintenance of a monogamous relationship in our society.

A different feature of the anal period is the emphasis on cleanliness and neatness. It is obvious that one feature of toilet-training impressed upon children is to stay clean. Cleanliness can thus become a major issue for the individual, either in the form of obsessive cleanliness or defiant messiness, or in an alternation between the two. Just as possessions may be the anal period feature that becomes embedded in the personality, so cleanliness may become an important aspect of the personality, reflecting the influence of anal period development.

Often this cleanliness seems to be part of a more general fussiness and neatness, not only of physical possessions but also of thoughts. The anal personality is often pedantic. He tends to cling to tiny distinctions, to split hairs, and generally to be unable to tolerate any confusion or ambiguity. Since there is a fair amount of ambiguity in many issues of everyday life, an intolerance for this ambiguity leads to various sorts of maladjustment and to distortion of the individual's conception of the real world as he tries to make everything neat and tidy. Another related form of neatness is punctiliousness or clinging to the letter of the law. It is a form of literal obedience that may also stem from the experiences of toilet-training.

It is difficult to determine empirically whether or not the origin of these traits lies in the anal period, but there is evidence that the traits of the anal personality—parsimony, punctiliousness, and pedantry— do hang together. This coherence provides some empirical evidence for the Freudian theory of the origin of these three traits, because it is not easy to find other explanations for the correlations among them.

There are still other aspects of the period of toilet-training which may be psychologically significant for the child. By contrast with the oral stage, the child in the anal stage is more active. He is no longer merely a passive recipient of what happens; he acts on his own.

When the child reaches this stage, the problems of socialization change. He can now do some of the things that have previously been done for him but he does not do them spontaneously; he must be taught to do what he is expected to do. He can also now do things that are destructive and irritating; he must learn not to do them. In general terms, the child must learn to be autonomous, not completely dependent, but he must also accept limits to his autonomy and must learn to obey rules and commands.

Thus toilet-training, which teaches the child to go to the bathroom autonomously but not to wet or dirty his pants, epitomizes a much more general problem of socialization, autonomy and obedience. For the two-year-old, the problem is hard because he cannot solve it either by inhibiting his behavior or by actively behaving; he must sometimes act and sometimes inhibit, and he must do so appropriately in response to the right signal.

One of the less fortunate outcomes can be an overly inhibited child who has learned to do nothing spontaneously. He constantly doubts his own impulses and inhibits them. The anal personality needs clear signs as guides to what to do and what not to do. He doubts his own spontaneity and is looking for rules to which he can conform.

The opposite outcome is the compulsively autonomous child, who must express his defiance of restrictions. A certain amount of this defiance in the form of negativism is typical of the two- to three-year-old. Negativism is, of course, the refusal to obey any request just because it is requested. An extremely negative child may refuse to do something he likes to do only because it was requested of him.

Another psychological feature of this period is the appearance of shyness, an emotional reaction to being looked at, which is probably based on the closely related feeling of shame. One cause for shame can be a toilet accident; in some homes the child who wets his pants or bed is publicly ridiculed as "being just a baby."

Shame is a more general phenomenon, though. It is an emotion that seems to be aroused by the combination of two environmental factors: the public exposure of one's weakness, and some defect. Shame is thus distinguished from guilt which can be very private and which involves some moral sin or transgression. It is not obvious why the child's susceptibility to shame should appear during the anal stage but it is probably related to the importance put on "being a big boy" and possibly to the specific feelings aroused by toilet accidents.

Phallic Stage

The phallic stage, or early genital stage as it is sometimes called, has its name because at about the age of four the child's source of libidinal pleasure shifts to focus principally on the genital region. This shift, together with a gradually increasing ego maturity, creates a whole new set of problems and potentialities in interpersonal relations.

We shall start with the more obviously genital features of the preschool child's behavior. The child's pleasure, interest, and curiosity shifts from the anal to the genital regions of the body. During this period the child is curious about the anatomical differences between the sexes, the origin of babies, the role of the father in procreation, and the sexual activities of the parents. Every parent and preschool teacher has seen evidence of such interests in young children, and the existence of childhood sexuality is hardly debatable anymore. The empirical evidence of a shift from anal interests and bathroom talk to genital interests is not so clear. Masturbation occurs before the age of three—when the child is presumably in the anal stage. Anal jokes and bathroom talk certainly persist up into the elementary years. There may, however, be a real trend from anal to genital in preschool children's questions, curiosity, and interest, although empirical evidence for this is lacking.

Freud pointed not only to the pleasure in genital stimulation during the phallic stage, but also to the particularly high value put on the penis, both by boys and by girls. According to psychoanalytic theory, the penis is a valued possession by boys and the lack of a penis is often viewed by girls as a defect or mutilation. Because of the high value of the penis, the loss or the threat of loss of the penis has a major emotional impact. The child's discovery of anatomic sex differences enhances this concern over the loss of the penis.

Another feature of the period is the focus of love and affection on the mother, particularly by boys. It is only reasonable that the mother should be the chief focus of affection in young children. She is closer to the child, a nearly constant companion. She is the caretaker and source of security. Her interactions with the child are more intimate in a physical sense and many of the mother's caretaking activities and caresses are probably pleasurable in a sensuous way to the child.

With the child's interest turning to genital matters, this physical sensuousness may take on a frankly sexual flavor, especially if the child is a boy. He wants sexual relations with his mother. The four-year-old's ideas of sexual relations are often sketchy and inaccurate but they involve a number of specifically sexual features. They involve physical closeness, voyeurism, and exhibitionism, very likely mutual touching of genitals if the heterosexual sex play of preschool children is any guide. They may certainly include the notion of marriage and having children. The boy also recognizes that his sexual desires involve his replacing his father *vis à vis* his mother. This is one line leading to the Oedipus complex.

The mother is not unaware of the sexual flavor of the little boy's attention. Depending upon her own sex anxiety, her relation to her husband and various other factors, she may punish the child, or tolerantly avoid the problem. In any case, the child is not, however, permitted to satisfy his wishes.

A part of the child's interest in sexuality during this phallic period is his concern with the sexual relation between the parents, even if it is seen only as a special and exclusive intimate relationship between the mother and father. The child is mature enough now to recognize that the mother-father relationship resembles the love and tenderness of the mother-child relationship but is also different. The specificity of the child's speculations about the nature of their relationship varies widely from child to child. In some cases there is no question that children observe parental intercourse. Freud hypothesized that children commonly witnessed parental sexual relations; he referred to such witnessing as the "primal scene." Furthermore, he believed that even when there was no actual witnessing of parental intercourse, the child built a fantasy of it on the basis of such clues as sounds and parental remarks, conversations with other children, and other sources of information and misinformation. Freud also believed that intercourse was often interpreted as an aggressive attack by the father upon the mother.

The combination of circumstances outlined in the previous section —the boy's specific genital feeling for the mother, its rebuff by the mother, and its condemnation by both parents, simultaneous with acceptance of sexuality between the parents themselves—sets the stage for the psychological drama of the Oedipus complex. Since these events are different for boys and girls, the development must be described separately for each sex.

For a boy, the central features of the Oedipus complex are his feelings of hostility and rivalry toward his father and his fear of being hurt and castrated by the father. There is considerable evidence that the father-son relationship in most families is more strained and less comfortable than the mother-son relationship. There are many factors, however, that might account for this emotional ambivalence between father and son. The mother has had the nurturing role ever since the child was born. The father is more of a stranger, and, in many families, is referred to as the disciplinarian. Certainly the father often tries to inculcate the masculine ideal of aggressiveness, toughness, and independence into the child through a no-nonsense policy of nonindulgence.

There are thus many factors that might, to a degree, estrange father and son, but in Freud's view a crucial factor is rivalry between father and son for the mother. The young boy—usually unconsciously, of course—wants to enjoy the kind of relation with the mother that the father has and sees the father as a powerful and dangerous rival. He fears the father's retaliation in the form of castration.

This *castration anxiety* is a critical feature of the development in the phallic stage in boys. According to Freudian theory, the boy fears the loss of his penis and unconsciously fantasies that it will be cut off by his father. It is difficult to obtain solid evidence for this anxiety. There are some indications of it, and a consideration of the child's cognitive development may make it appear more reasonable. Children's dreams and fears are sometimes fears of mutilation and this is taken by some to be evidence of castration anxiety. It would be more convincing if the dreams were of castration, but even without that, physical mutilation seems a gratuitous fear. There is evidence that boys place a high value upon the penis and that its loss would be serious. For most men, in fact, the loss of "manhood" through an accident is viewed as more horrible and disastrous than the loss of a hand or foot. Men value sexual power highly and view sexual impotence as disgraceful. It is hard to justify this evaluation on strictly realistic grounds, so it seems possible that the high valuation on physical sexuality may stem from the fears of castration. The evidence is at best, however, not clear; by comparison with the evidence for hostility between father and son, the backing for a specific castration fear is very meager.

Even if the positive evidence is not convincing, the hypothesis is not ridiculous. The child is in a relatively immature stage of cognitive development and his fears can take unreasonable and unrealistic directions. Hostility toward the father, for whatever reason, is bound to be disturbing to the child. Thoughts of his father's death may enter his head and lead to speculations about how such an event would have its pleasant aspects. But such thoughts can also lead to fantasies of retaliation for such wishes.

At this stage, the child's imagination can run away with him. One dire, dreadful idea can lead to another, and even if the child does not actually expect such ideas to be lived out, they can be very frightening. Even adults can be made very frightened by intrusive fantasies of disaster, although they know perfectly well that their fears are exaggerated. The parent waiting for his teenager to come home in the car can picture all sorts of dreadful eventualities. In addition, childhood fears are not like adults' realistic apprehensions; rather, they have the quality of insistent thoughts that capture consciousness occasionally, cause anxiety, and are then repressed or disappear. This does not prove that the child does fear castration, but it may make the idea more reasonable.

The next step in the hypothesized development of the drama of the phallic stage is that the child gives up his sexual wishes because of the fear of castration. Rivalry with the father is too anxiety-provoking to be tolerated, so the boy identifies with the father. This mechanism of *identification with the aggressor* will be discussed in more detail in a subsequent chapter (see p. 460), but it will suffice to say that the evidence for such a mechanism is fairly good. One of the ways that people adjust to the continual presence of a feared and powerful person is to accept his values, become like him, and repress the hostility they feel toward him.

According to Freudian theory, this same process occurs normally in the boy's development. He identifies with the father and represses his hostility toward him, and also represses his sexual wishes for the mother. One of the consequences of the identification with the father is that it helps instill masculine interests and values in the boy.

FEMALE DEVELOPMENT. Freud was never as explicit about the course of development of the girl, except to hypothesize that the process was analogous. It involves sexual wishes toward the father, rivalry with the mother, and is ordinarily resolved by repression of the sexual desires, identification with the mother, and acceptance of femininity.

There is also a castration complex in girls, except that they presumably believe they have already lost a penis. Part of the problem is a devaluation of feminity since the all-important penis is lacking, and part of the eventual resolution is the acceptance of the female genitalia as valuable because women can have babies and men cannot.

The logic and dynamics of the psychoanalytic theory of the development of girls is, however, less clear than for boys. Since the girl, like the boy, is primarily attached to the mother pre-Oedipally, it is not clear how the sexual attachment to the father develops. Moreover, the dynamics of identification with aggressor do not seem as powerful if the girl thinks she is already castrated and so is her mother. The theory is not as satisfactory for girls as for boys. Freud realized this, but never resolved the problem clearly and elegantly.

SUPEREGO. Another consequence of the resolution of the Oedipus complex in both boys and girls is the development of the supergo. When the child identifies with his parent, he primarily identifies with the one of the same sex but to some degree he identifies with both. According to psychoanalytic theory, identification is a process of taking into one's own personality the personality of another person—as one perceives it, of course. The term for this is *introjection*. When the boy introjects his father, or the girl her mother, either child constantly then carries around a conscience, representing the parent's wishes, values, and standards. When the child transgresses, this inner voice reprimands him and makes him feel guilty; it is a part of the child's own wishes and values. There are many internal conflicts, as we all know from experience, between the person's motives and the dictates of his conscience or superego.

The superego develops, according to Freud, in the resolution of the Oedipus complex. The development occurs at this time partly because the child is mature enough to have a cognitive representation of another person: what he says, what he values, and what he approves and disapproves of. The ego must have a certain degree of maturity before it is capable of such activity. One of the potential problems of superego development is that the ego may not in fact be mature enough to know accurately what the parental values are. Often the child feels guilty about things his parents do not actually disapprove of. Much more frequently he is more rigid and condemnatory than his parents about certain of his faults. Thus, a parental value of neatness may be translated into a rigid hatred of, even anxiety about, the slightest bit of dirt. Freud said that the superego might be much harsher and more demanding than the parent.

At the same the child's superego may be more concrete than actual parental standards. It is difficult for the child at the first-grade level to have a clear conception of such values as justice, fairness, and tolerance in their abstract forms. Instead, he translates them into such concrete terms as dividing things evenly, taking turns, etc. In other words, his conscience may represent a rule of action rather than a principle of behavior. Gradually, as the child continues to mature, his superego becomes more realistic and principled, provided that the important values it represents remain conscious and accessible to change. It is when some dictate of the superego is repressed and remains primitive and immature that it causes unrealistic guilt feelings and hampers the normal behavior of the individual.

A second reason that the superego develops out of the Oedipus complex is that it relieves the child's castration anxiety and also his fear of loss of love.

The loss of the mother's love is a serious threat. The mother must have created a need for love and dependence through a long period of caretaking and indulgence before the threat of loss of love can be effective. In Freud's metaphor, the mother must have built up a large balance of love for her, through satisfying the child's wishes, before she can draw on that balance and use loss of love as a threat to enforce some of her demands and standards that are unpleasant for the child.

In ordinary circumstances, the loss of love is very threatening, however; that threat can also motivate an identification process. Once the child has introjected the parents, he carries around internal signals which both prevent him from transgressing and punish him if he does. The guilt feelings are themselves internal representations of the parents' punishment and disapproval.

In summary, the phallic period is complicated and exciting. It represents a period of strain and difficulty for the child which is often apparent in the behavior of four- and five-year-olds. Its normal resolution is important for normal development, and deviations in its resolutions lie behind almost all the neurotic difficulties of adults in our culture.

Latency Period

Following the many complexities of the phallic stage with its attendant castration fears, Oedipal feelings, and the development of the superego, the child goes into a period that is psychodynamically more placid. This corresponds to the elementary school years and is labeled the *latency period*. Freud, with his ever-present desire to root out the evolutionary origins of behavior patterns, speculated at one point that perhaps the human being had evolved from a species that reached adolescence at about age five or six. The phallic stage is then the vestige of that prehuman adolescence. The period between the two adolescences has some stability, while the periods before and after are full of rapid change, conflict, and psychological problems stemming from urgent libidinal demands. Whether this bio-anthropological speculation is sound or not, the view Freud presented of the latency period was one of relative stability.

This does not mean that changes do not occur during this period. In the psychoanalytic view, it is primarily a period of acquisition of culturally valued skills, values, and roles. The child learns many new facts during the school years; he acquires many skills in motor activity, in thinking, in reasoning; he learns many things about other people and is able to adapt to varied points of view of different people.

The superego is present throughout, but during this period it becomes more organized and more principled. Not only the parents but also other family members, teachers, club leaders, etc., contribute their portion to the child's value system. The child acquires a genuine value system if development goes well, and the conscious part of the superego becomes less concrete and uncompromising. Rubbing shoulders with people outside the family leads to more tolerance and also creates some problems of maintaining one's own value system in the face of divergent ones.

The peaceful connotation of the term latency period is, however, by no means an obvious, overt feature of this school-age period. It is a latency period in the sense that it does not bring new basic problems of close interpersonal relations, but there are many problems, nevertheless. The fourth, fifth, and sixth grades are commonly thought to be the most difficult to teach. Rebellion against authority and father-son conflict are common during this period. Boys in particular often show a messiness and carelessness about personal habits that is most distressing to the parent. This is also the time of sharp separation of boys and girls and rivalry between them. It is the time of gang formation, and it is the age when the beginnings of delinquency appear.

These characteristics of school-age children do not contradict the hypothesis of a period of sexual latency. Indeed, many of the features of latency are logical outgrowths of the Oedipal situation. Thus, the rapidly developing sex roles and the way they are sharply applied can be seen to result from the child's identification with the parent of his own sex and his emphasis on the proper sex tole. The rebelliousness, carelessness, and general intractability of boys can be seen as the magnification of the "he-man" traits, some of which are sufficiently antisocial to require further taming and control. There is evidence, however, that parents encourage these traits in boys and tolerate them at levels that they would not permit for girls. The fact that the traits may get out of hand and require firm control does not deny the fact that they are valued.

Whether there is any decrease in sexual activity during the latency period is hard to assess. Certainly, masturbation does not stop and under appropriate circumstances overt heterosexual activity may freely occur. Often this sexual activity is part of gang activities; it seems as if the sexual activity may be less intense and personal than during adolescence, and may only be one more display of a sex role rather than a falling in love. This is not inconsistent with the notion of a latency period. Nevertheless, one cannot escape the feeling that Freudian theory does not capture the flavor of this period nearly as well as it captures the intrafamilial turbulence of the preschool period or the problems of adolescence.

Adolescence

Freud himself believed that the basic structure of the personality was established by the end of the phallic stage. He viewed adolescence as a reactivation of the sexual drives which had been quiescent during the latency period. Adolescence is a reliving of the phallic stage but with several important differences.

One difference is that the adolescent has established relations outside the family. Whereas the four- or five-year-old could find no kind of a socially acceptable sexual relationship and therefore really had to renounce sexuality, the adolescent can find acceptable, socially approved heterosexual relationships outside the family. The love object has shifted from an incestuous to a nonincestuous one.

Freud did not, however, see the choice of a partner in adolescence as being independent of the previous stages. In many ways, the adolescent's attraction to a particular partner of the opposite sex is a repetition of the Oedipal choice. Sometimes the girl is explicitly chosen because she is like mother, as expressed in the song, "I want a girl just like the girl that married dear old dad." Often enough there are similarities between a girl's father and her boy friend. But in many cases the effect of the earlier stages is not so obvious. Depending upon how the Oedipal situation was resolved, the individual's conception of what the love relation is like may be colored strongly by familial patterns. A man may want his wife to be a caretaker and comforter to the partial exclusion of her role as sexual partner—he wants a mother and not a mistress in his love life. A woman may want to be dominated by her husband, yet fight domination. She can feel hostile toward the man she cannot dominate yet contemptuous of the man she can boss around. A boy may have so separated love and sex that he cannot have "dirty" sexual relations with the "pure" woman he wants to love.

A second important difference between the Oedipal and the adolescent love relationship is that the adult is less egocentric than the young child. The young child's love was first incorporative, then possessive, and then exploitative in the early stages of psychosexual development. All of these attitudes are essentially selfish and pleasure seeking. By adolescence, in contrast, love is more tender and altruistic. The shift from a love that is pleasurable to the self toward one that has as its goal the happiness of the love object is a highly important development. One of the adaptations to be learned during adolescence is the integration of tender feelings toward the love object with the obtaining of satisfaction for the self in a mutually rewarding relationship.

In some ways, therefore, the adolescent boy relives the Oedipal period during which his libidinal impulses were directed toward his mother. At the same time he must outgrow the type of strictly male identification which emerged during the latency period. As a result of the Oedipal situation, the boy identifies with his father and, as we saw, may have become exclusively male-oriented in his gang activities. With the emergence of adolescence, his libidinal drives may color his relationships with other boys in the direction of homosexuality. In fact, Freud believed that typically the adolesent went through a homosexual stage—the boy with a kind of hero worship of some male leader, the girl with a crush upon a teacher. These stages in adolescent development represent the beginning of acceptance of sexual feelings in the child who has repressed them during the latency period.

A relationship with a person of the same sex is, however, no better a solution than the relationship with the mother or father of the opposite sex during the Oedipal period. It is tolerated in our society as long as it does not take on any overt sexual flavor, but it cannot represent a satisfying solution for the great majority of adolescents. The next step is therefore the shift to a heterosexual relationship.

This shift seldom goes smoothly and swiftly into a permanent love relationship. Ordinarily, the adolescent has friendships of varying depths of intensity and sexuality with a number of counterparts. The deeper kind of relationship involving commitment of personal feelings, exchange of private opinions and thoughts, and the opening of the self-esteem to the possible pain of being rejected is threatening in many ways as well as being strongly attractive. Thus, the typical adolescent love affair involves many tentative advances, withdrawals, intense infatuations, and equally intense rejections. In the course of these courtship maneuvers and reactions, the child becomes able to commit himself emotionally to another person, to love that person in a tender as well as a pleasure-seeking way, to engage in overt sexual activities with pleasure and without guilt, and to understand the breadth of other activities that are part of a love relationship.

Adolescence, from the point of view of psychoanalytic theory, is not completely a matter of learning to be in love, although that is the central issue. At the same time, the adolescent is on the boundary between childhood and adulthood in other ways. He is faced with a choice of a whole way of life in terms of his job, his political activities, his ethics, etc. According to Erikson (1950), the most serious danger for the adolescent is the failure to establish a sense of identity and self-worth.

Although children obviously differ from one another in many ways, to a large extent they all occupy the same role in society; they live at home, they go to school, they go through a more-or-less standard curriculum. Their job, so to speak, is to acquire the knowledge, abilities, and values of our society. In adulthood, there is, however, a much larger diversity of roles. The activities of the college professor and the airline pilot differ much more than the activities of their children.

With this diversity of possible roles comes the threat of not having any roles at all. Everybody of a certain age is a child—it is what the sociologists call an *ascribed* role. But in our society the adult roles of occupation, spouse, community leader, or nonparticipant are *achieved* by the individual. It is essential for the person to have a place in his social environment in order to have a sense of his own identity.

To find this place in the face of these many alternating roles, the individual must decide what he wants to do and whether he is able to do it. He must take the responsibility for decisions that may shape the rest of his life. In order to take this independent step, the person needs a real sense of identity, of his own worth as an individual, and of his own self-esteem. He must stand up and be counted and take the responsibility for his actions.

Our culture does not make it easy for adolescents to do this. Educational needs greatly prolong the period when the adolescent is dependent upon his family for financial support. During this time both the child and his family recognize that the financial backing also legitimizes some control over the adolescent's decisions. Yet it is just the willingness to make these decisions and to live with the consequences of them that marks the assumption of a clear personal identity.

This identity and freedom from family control interact in various ways with the problems of dating, courtship, and marriage. First, there is the interpersonal relationship between the boy and girl. To fall in love in a deep sense is to give oneself to another person—it can seem to involve almost giving up one's own identity. Actually if the relationship is a healthy one both members of the pair are concerned about the various decisions to be made; there is an identity of "we" that prevents a real loss of personal identity, but it may not appear that way during courtship. In our culture this threat to one's identity is much greater for girls than for boys; girls are expected to subordinate their personal goals, particularly career goals, to the needs of their husband. When a baby arrives, it is customary for the wife to give up her own personal life to take care of the baby, at least for some time.

In the face of this threat of loss of control over one's life and one's independence, the individual must have a rather deep sense of his own personal identity and his own worth to be able to enter a marriage. If the adolescent is too dependent, marriage can result in a real loss of identity and in the failure to satisfy his own important needs because he does not exert his influence. If the adolescent is reacting against family control by being very independent, getting married with the entanglements that it brings may be like jumping from the frying pan into the fire.

CRITIQUE OF PSYCHOANALYTIC THEORY

ance are only examples of a general inclination for believers in psycho-analytic theory to come together in a kind of cult. Within the history of psychoanalysis, people have disagreed with Freud on various basic postulates and as a result have either broken off from the cult or been read out of the party as heretics. A second source of cultism in psycho-analysis is Freud's metaphorical phraseology. Although Freud's language often disguises the essential reasonableness of the mechanisms he described, one can find in other psychoanalytic writings a complete range from hard-headed responsible discussion to complete mysticism. The appeal of psychoanalysis to writers of fiction and drama and its general influence in all aspects of our lives is not because of the specific influence of psychoanalytic theory but rather because of the influence of a psychoanalytic way of thinking which takes many forms. Some children, for example, have been raised in a completely undisciplined fashion in the name of psychoanalysis. Many of these influences of psychoanalysis would surely be deplored by Freud.

The problem of psychoanalysis as a cult is not raised as a valid criticism of psychoanalytic theory, but as a recognition that there are differences between psychoanalytic theory and the total impact of psychoanalysis upon society. It is important in a discussion of theoretical positions to limit the discussion to the theory itself and not to criticize it because it is accompanied by other things we do not like.

The most important troublesome aspects of psychoanalytic theory have been discussed, but there are a number of specific features worth noting.

The Use of Pathology in Psychoanalytic Theory

Psychoanalytic theory makes sweeping assumptions about the general analogy between pathological and normal processes. The existence of a pathology is taken to be one line of evidence supporting the assumption that the same kind of process occurs in normal functioning; often the pathological label is given to that process in normal functioning. As we have seen, pathology is, in every aspect of medicine, an important source of knowledge about normal functioning; nevertheless, it is not a foregone conclusion that every pathological process is also a part of normal functioning. The fact that tubercular processes occur does not mean that there is a normal tubercular component of lung functioning.

The further fact that so much of the raw material upon which psychoanalytic theory is based is obtained from people suffering from anxiety who come to the analyst for help with their difficulties possibly represents a bias in the kinds of problems investigated by psychoanalytic theory. True enough, many nonneurotic, nonpsychotic people have been analyzed, but many of these are analysts in training who also do not represent a normal population. In fact, the ability of the individual to carry out the instructions of free association is itself a selective factor and makes it impossible for the raw data on which the theory is based to be really representative samples of the thoughts and feelings of the population as a whole. Although it is not clear whether this is a serious limitation or not, it nevertheless represents a possibility and emphasizes the importance of broadening the empirical base of psychoanalytic theory.

The Role of the Stimulus Situation in Psychoanalytic Theory

Perhaps because Freud collected his data from patients who were lying on the psychoanalytic couch rather than behaving in real life, and because the psychoanalytic situation remains reasonably constant during the psychoanalysis, the role of the stimulus in producing thoughts and feelings seems to be under-emphasized in psychoanalytic theory. Psychoanalytic theory emphasizes the role of instinctive motivation in the production of thoughts and feelings and contains an elaborate, sophisticated theory about the mechanism by which instinctual drives lead to thoughts and feelings and ultimately to behavior. The role of the stimulus situation has never been so clearly described. It has not been completely ignored, and all psychoanalysts would no doubt agree that the objects in the immediate environment of the individual are relevant for the activation of drives and for the production of thoughts and feelings. The role of the environment was in fact recognized by Freud in his discussion of dreams. He hypothesized that the contents of dreams were made up of the experiences of the day before, put together and woven into some kind of a theme under the influence of drive motivation.

The conceptualization of the roles of the stimulus and the drive in psychological functioning poses a puzzling problem. There is evidence to suggest that thoughts and feelings are to some extent determined by momentary stimuli. Given the appropriate stimuli a drive need not be strong for certain thoughts to become conscious and certain motives to be activated. An individual who sees a twenty-dollar bill lying on the ground stoops to pick it up, and it does not make much difference whether he needs money or not. Certainly he does not need to feel deprived to respond to this stimulus with motivated activity. On the other hand, it is also true that under conditions of deprivation, people's thoughts and feelings and behavior can be governed by internal drives, regardless of the suggestions presented by the immediate stimulus environment. People who are hungry do not need to see food in order to think about it nor do they need to be reminded by any kind of stimulus object to search for food. In fact, a high state of drive in animals can produce behavior *in vacuo:* a behavior pattern that is ordinarily instigated by stimuli is carried out in their absence. In some way, the motivational mechanism seems to involve the interaction of the stimulus environment and the strength of the drives; under some conditions each can govern behavior, regardless of the other. In investigating this interactive process, psychoanalytic theory has devoted is major emphasis to elucidating the role of the drives in behavior. The role of the stimulus needs considerably more attention if psychoanalytic theory is to have the generality to which it aspires.

The Process of Acting Out

Like other theories that emphasize the thoughts, feelings, and intentions of the individual, psychoanalytic theory has devoted relatively little attention to the actual process by which a conscious idea manifests itself in behavior. This criticism is appropriate to naïve theory; it has also been made of Lewinian theory, and it applies to psychoanalytic theory, too. It seems unlikely that people have a clearly conscious idea of every act they carry out even when the act is voluntary. Access to consciousness exerts strong control over the kind of behavior an individual will perform, but consciousness is certainly not the only factor that determines the details of voluntary behavior. The manner in which the behavior is carried out is adapted to the demands of the immediate environment, and this adaptation does not appear to be conscious. Thus, the typist types a word voluntarily but the actual sequence of acts of hitting the key in the proper order does not appear as a conscious, intentional one.

Not only is the understanding of this process generally important for the understanding of a theory of behavior, but it also has a special relevance for psychoanalytic theory. The style of behavior may express various unconscious factors without their necessarily cathecting a conscious idea. For example, the secretary who is angry may type a letter quite accurately, hit the keys in the right order, but pound the typewriter violently as she does it. Furthermore, anger may result in this kind of aggressive, violent style of typing, whether the secretary consciously feels anger or not. Many of these effects of feelings and drives are actually taken into account in psychoanalytic interpretations of concrete behavior, but it is not clear how they are treated in theoretical terms.

SUMMARY

In summary, the basic criticism to be made of psychoanalytic theory is that it focuses upon thoughts and feelings as the real data and these are relatively inaccessible. The implication is not that a theory based on this assumption must be discarded, but that it poses very real methodological problems. In the present form, psychoanalytic theory does not provide the kind of operational definitions of its terms that are necessary for a scientific theory; to a large degree, this failure in operational definitions depends on the fact that the focus of the theory is on thoughts and feelings rather than on overt behavior.

A second major criticism of psychoanalytic theory is that it is difficult to criticize because of its proponents' insistence that it can only be validated through the actual process of psychoanalysis. This limitation puts the control of the theory into the hands of a specially trained group of people who are not unbiased in their views about human behavior. Furthermore, the tendency of psychoanalysts to answer their opponents by attributing their criticism to resistance and repression is an unacceptable procedure in scientific discourse. Third, various areas of psychoanalytic theory have received considerably less emphasis than others and need to be expanded if the theory is to develop into a complete theory of human behavior. The role of the stimulus situation is one such area, and the actual process by which ideas and intentions are carried out in overt action is another.

Stimulus-Response Theories

JOHN B. WATSON

CLARK L. HULL

NEAL E. MILLER

B. F. SKINNER

JOHN DOLLARD

ROBERT R. SEARS

ALBERT BANDURA

RICHARD H. WALTERS

FOURTEEN

The basic elements
of the S-R strategy

ALL THE THEORIES discussed thus far have in one way or another accepted some major feature of naïve theory. Tacitly or explicitly they have tended to accept some aspect of mentalistic functioning. Lewin's concept of a life space is patterned after the naïve notion of a phenomenal world; Piaget's mental operations are based on the mental events in problem solving; Freud and the psychoanalytic theorists accept thoughts and feelings as primary given data.

Stimulus-response theories have traditionally taken a different position on the usefulness of such mentalistic concepts. The roots of S-R theory go far back into the history of philosophy, but the behavioristic movement in psychology began with the work of John B. Watson about 1910. The basic notion of association and the primary role of learning in the development of the child go back to the eighteenth and nineteenth centuries to the English empiricists: Locke, Hume, Mill, etc. In that tradition, the concept of association was basic, but it was the association of ideas and thoughts with one another; the concept of idea itself was not questioned. However, Watson, in addition to believing firmly that all behavior was learned by associationistic processes, also believed that only overt, observable behavioral concepts belonged in psychology. He discarded concepts such as consciousness, idea, thought, perception, goal, intention, will, and feeling as nonbehavioristic.

RESEARCH STRATEGY OF S-R THEORY

Although modern behavioristic S-R psychologists are no longer fixed upon outright rejection of all mentalistic concepts, their strategy is quite different from those investigating the theories previously described. The strategy of behaviorism consists in viewing the behavior of the person from the outside, ignoring the fact that the psychologist himself is a person. This view is sometimes called the "black box" approach. If we came upon a mysterious black box with various appendages that acted and behaved and responded to stimuli, we might watch it carefully, put it into different sorts of experimental situations, and finally develop a theory about the mechanism inside the box that would explain its reactions. Or, we might be content with writing down a set of empirical laws that related properties of the situation to the characteristics of the response. The advantage of the black box strategy is that we are not tempted to attribute to the box any of the subjective feelings and thoughts that we ourselves experience.

Experimental Approach

Besides being solidly behavioristic, S-R theorists also approach the problem of human behavior cautiously and experimentally. They are generally inclined to the point of view that psychological mechanisms and concepts should be developed in the laboratory where conditions can be controlled. Through years of such experimentation, a set of well-established facts has been accumulated and various explanatory concepts have been developed. The next step is to apply these concepts to the study of child development as it actually proceeds in real life.

The experimental approach is a natural one for S-R theorists, because they firmly believe that psychological mechanisms are widely applicable. Many of their principles of learning were worked out using animals as experimental subjects; they assume these principles are valid for humans also, although additional processes may be involved in human learning. Even when processes are studied in human subjects, the particular behavior is chosen because it can be manipulated experimentally. If the eyeblink response to an auditory stimulus can be acquired by pairing it with a puff of air, S-R theorists assume that the same principle will operate in the child's development if parental reproof is paired with physical punishment. Perhaps other factors may conceal the expected effect, but the basic principles are presumed to be valid for all stimuli.

This presumption might be wrong; the proof of it lies in its effectiveness as a strategy of research. Generally speaking, it has led to much valuable research on child development.

Parsimony

Stimulus-response theorists are also cautious in another way. They are parsimonious in theory building. Unlike the other theorists discussed, the major S-R theorists have been able to restrain their desires to sketch out rough global explanations for all human behavior and have generally applied their concepts first to apparently simple and uncomplicated problems where it seems that they are most likely to be adequate and sufficient. Although S-R theorists believe that S-R concepts can eventually account for all behavior, they are content to begin on a small scale and gradually expand the coverage. As a result of this strategy, these theorists are constantly subjected to the criticism that they oversimplify behavior. Their critics are always saying, in effect, that human behavior is far too complicated to be accounted for by the concepts so far developed.

Strictly speaking, of course, the critics are correct. Stimulus-response theorists do not say they have explained all the complicated types of human behavior; they do not promise that they will not need to introduce many new concepts. What they do argue is that new concepts should be introduced only as behavioral evidence requires them and should be limited to those that help to explain empirical findings. Furthermore, they have faith that such concepts will be adequate to explain all the complexities of human behavior. They are convinced they will never need to depend on subjective experience as evidence for a concept.

Openmindedness

Another consistent feature of the S-R approach has been a genuine openmindedness about theories—provided they meet the general criteria of the S-R point of view. In other words, the adoption of an S-R strategy has not resulted in a single S-R school. It is impossible to speak of S-R theory; there are too many of them. Stimulus-response theorists sometimes disagree over what assumptions should be adopted, but their disagreements are not divisive as those among different schools of pyschology have often been. Among S-R theorists one finds a general attitude that present theories are imperfect, and that if anybody wants to try out a different set of assumptions, that is fine. Let him discover how they work out.

There is also a genuine responsiveness to evidence. Most S-R theorists do not feel that it is a disgrace to modify one's theory or to add a new construct. In past controversies in psychology, a change in one's theory seemed to require an apology for having been wrong. Among S-R theorists there is a much deeper acceptance that theories are going to change and that science moves forward through modification of theory.

BASIC PRINCIPLES OF STIMULUS-RESPONSE THEORY

One of the basic tenets of S-R theory is that behavior is learned. The question to be asked about any kind of behavior is "How is it learned?" For example, conscience is conceived as a learned avoidance of anxiety, and anxiety is a learned internal response that acquires its effect through association with pain-producing stimuli. When S-R theorists study conscience they also ask how one learns such responses as confessing and apologizing. Or in a different field, perception is viewed by those S-R theorists who have engaged themselves in the problem as a learned perceiving response.

The emphasis upon learning in S-R theory does not stem from denial of the existence of innate behavior patterns nor an explicit conviction about the unimportance of genetic factors in behavior. The relative neglect of genetic factors is a result of a preoccupation with the problem of how behavior is learned. The theory is well equipped to deal with problems of learning; the learning question can be asked with respect to any new problem. Part of S-R strategy is to begin a research program with some problem that can be attacked on the basis of well-established concepts.

Stimulus-response theory not only emphasizes the view that behavior is learned, but also stresses that learned behavior is the result of many independent learning processes. The unit of behavior is the specific act, and each act is independently acquired. This belief carries a tacit assumption that through learning behavior is almost infinitely malleable and shapable. To take conscience again as an example, the more traditional views picture it as a system of behavior involving self-control to prevent transgressions, guilt feelings if one does transgress, and confession and making amends as devices for relieving guilt. The whole structure is viewed as unitary. Stimulus-response theory is more apt to view these different aspects of conscience as the results of separate learning processes, and to suggest that some people's conscience may help them to avoid transgressions and, vice versa, that guilt feelings can be learned without their having any effect upon self-control.

Furthermore, people can learn guilt feelings without learning any behavior for making amends.

To overstate the proposition for the sake of emphasis, S-R theory seems to assume that any combination and any sequence of behaviors —provided there is no physical incompatibility between them—can be learned, perhaps with equal facility. The theory contains no provision for inherent constraints upon the variety of behavior patterns that can be acquired. This viewpoint has frequently proved fruitful. For example, several varieties of conscience do exist. The unitary character of the usual conscience may well be a result of cultural norms rather than any inherent psychological structuring. On the other hand, the viewpoint has led S-R research away from questions about how responses are organized into larger units, unlike Lewin's life space and Piaget's groupings, which are attempts to describe how coherent sets of behavioral acts are organized and held together.

Still another presumption of S-R theory is that behavior is learned through external reinforcement. If asked how some behavior pattern was developed, an S-R theorist's first hypothesis is likely to be that the individual has been rewarded by somebody for doing it. The theory does provide for acts being self-rewarding, and in some situations it is possible that the events that reinforce behavior do not naïvely appear to be rewards. However, the basic approach is that behavior is learned through being reinforced.

The S-R approach to child development is that the child learns adult behavior patterns, adult values, and adult anxieties through the experiences of childhood. In the course of growing up, each of the child's actions is reinforced, punished, or ignored, and in the child's environment various stimuli are consistently associated with one another. Certain basic facts of learning are known. In order to understand child development, we need to show how the child's natural environment provides the experiences and rewards that teach the child to behave like an adult in his society.

The remainder of this chapter will review the basic facts of learning and the S-R conceptualization of them, with particular reference to those that are relevant for child rearing. The following chapter will present the specific hypotheses of social learning theory about child development.

Basic Facts of Conditioning

The basic concepts of many theories are often abstract and general. In contrast, the basic concepts of S-R theory are well-established empirical facts about the conditioning process. The study of a new field rests upon a base of these established facts and attempts to assimilate new phenomena and show how they are merely new examples of these basic facts.

There are two important kinds of conditioning. One is called *classical* conditioning because it was the type first investigated by Pavlov, the famous Russian physiologist who discovered the phenomenon of conditioning. The other type of conditioning is called *instrumental,* because the response of the organism is instrumental in obtaining reinforcement.

CLASSICAL CONDITIONING. In his original experiments, Pavlov conditioned the salivary response in the dog. The dog was operated on, so that the secretion of the salivary gland could be measured accurately, ordinarily in drops of saliva. The dog salivated whenever a food powder was introduced into his mouth. This salivary response to the food powder occurred on the first trial, so the salivation is called the *unconditioned response* and the food powder the *unconditioned stimulus.* The conditioning process consists of pairing some other stimulus with the unconditioned stimulus. In one of the famous Pavlovian experiments, a bell was rung slightly before the food stimulus was presented. After this combination of bell and food had been repeated a number of times, the dog began to salivate whenever the bell was rung, even if on that particular trial no food was given. So the bell is called the *conditioned stimulus* or *conditioning stimulus,* and the salivation to the bell the *conditioned response.*

The timing of the bell and food is important in this experiment. The conditioning is most rapid and effective if the ring comes just slightly before the food. If the bell rings a long time before the food appears, conditioning still occurs, but it takes longer to establish it. A delay in the unconditioned stimulus also has other effects on learning. If the bell, for example, sounds ten seconds before the food, then the salivary response to the bell occurs before the food itself is introduced. Early in the learning the salivation occurs immediately after the bell, but with more trials the response is gradually delayed longer and longer until finally the salivary response occurs almost ten seconds following the bell—just before the time the food is ordinarily given. In this experiment, the conditioning process results in a delayed response that quite accurately reproduces the delay between the conditioned and unconditioned stimuli. This is called *trace conditioning,* because the immediate stimulus to the salivation is not the sound of the bell itself but rather the memory trace of the bell.

It is important to note in this last experiment that the salivation

The rat is next put into the white compartment but not shut in completely, so that by jumping a hurdle he can get through a door into the black compartment. After a number of trials, the animal learns to jump the hurdle and does so immediately upon being put into the white compartment.

How are these findings to be explained? Going into the black compartment has never really allowed the rat to escape the shock; in reality, he has never actually avoided the shock by doing so, because the shock stimulus has been turned off during all the learning trials. In the earlier experiment the rat sometimes actually escaped shock by pressing the lever, but most of the time the shock was avoided so that the performance was rarely reinforced by escape from pain. The problem for a learning theory is to discover what reinforces the act of escaping from the white to the black compartment. The best hypothesis is that the reinforcement is the reduction in fear. Being put into the white box presents the rat with stimuli that elicit an internal fear response, which may be partly autonomic or partly muscular, or perhaps purely cortical. In any case, it is an internal response that is also a powerful stimulus. The reinforcement for the avoidance behavior is the lessening of the fear that occurs when the rat moves from the white to the black compartment.

Such a stimulus-elicited internal response that in turn serves as the stimulus for some overt behavior is called an *internal mediating response*. Behavior that occurs through the agency of such a mediating response is conceived as being a two-stage behavioral response: The first stage is the elicitation of the mediating response; the second is the response to the mediating stimuli.

There are numerous examples of such chains of responses where the action that constitutes each link in the chain is a response to the previous stimulus and also a stimulus to the next response in the chain. The sequence of acts in repeating a memorized list of words is one example. Once the sequence is initiated, it can run itself off, so to speak, without any further external stimulation. In skilled motor performances each act in the sequence is partially determined by the stimuli produced by the previous act but also partially determined by external feedback from the environment. The internal mediating response is conceived of as a link in such a chain of responses, but the middle link in the chain is not directly observable; instead, it is an hypothetical mediating response needed to explain observed behavior.

Avoidance behavior suggests another mechanism that might make behavior difficult to extinguish. The reinforcement—in the instance, fear reduction—is part of the response sequence itself and is independent of any external reinforcement. In principle the rat might never learn that the shock had been turned off, because he would keep on performing the act that would prevent the shock. Under ordinary circumstances the animal will occasionally fail to make the avoidance response quickly enough and receive the shock if it is still there; If the painful stimulus does not occur on these occasions, the response begins to extinguish and gradually disappears. In principle, however, the avoidance could be stabilized without further external reinforcement; Solomon, Kamin, and Wynne (1953), by using extremely painful stimuli, have produced avoidance learning that is apparently inextinguishable.

GENERALIZATION AND DISCRIMINATION. A final set of basic facts about conditioning describes the generality or the specificity of the response to the stimulus. The elementary fact is that if a response has been conditioned to a particular stimulus, the organism also responds to other stimuli besides the particular one employed in the original conditioning. If a dog is conditioned to a particular tone which is 256 cycles per second (middle C), for example, he also responds to neighboring tones; in fact, he will probably respond to all audible tones. The amount of response is strongest to the tone used for conditioning; the farther removed the stimulus is from the original, the smaller the response.

If the experimenter wishes to make the dog's response specific to one particular stimulus or to a narrow range of stimuli, he must teach the dog some *discrimination*. This is accomplished by presenting two stimuli successively and reinforcing one but not the other. Thus, the dog conditioned to a 256-cycle tone could be taught to discriminate a 256-cycle tone from a 300-cycle tone by reinforcing the 256-cycle tone and not reinforcing the 300-cycle tone. The same result could be accomplished through instrumental learning. The dog's response to the 256-cycle tone could be reinforced and his response to the 300-cycle tone extinguished. In this way organisms can be taught to make discriminations among stimuli up to the limits of individual capability. These phenomena are called *stimulus generalization* and *stimulus discrimination*.

Stimulus generalization is an important concept for explaining many features of the development of the child. The very young baby responds in much the same way to any person who picks him up and holds him: Any responses learned to one person generalize to other people. The baby gradually becomes more discriminating, however, and responds differently to his mother than he does to other people.

Indeed, it is common for infants to go through a period of "stranger anxiety," when they act shy and fearful of unfamiliar people, during the last part of the first year of life.

In one of his observations of a young infant, Piaget records how the little girl had learned to make the doll on her bassinet swing by jiggling her legs. Later she tried the same behavior when she wanted to make a jack-in-the-box pop out of its box. In S-R theory this behavior would be explained as a generalization of a learned response to a new stimulus. The common tendency of children just learning to talk to use the same word in a wide variety of situations beyond those that seem appropriate to an adult can also be thought of as stimulus generalization.

In learning the sounds of a language, both generalization and discrimination are essential. Any language has a variety of similar sounds that are all recognized as the same. For example, the /k/ sound is not the same in keel, kit, cat, and cool; in keel the tongue touches the roof of the mouth much farther forward than it does in cool. Yet, in ordinary speech one never hears the various sounds of /k/ as different. The difference in the tongue position which makes the difference between the /k/ sound and the /s/ sound is no bigger than the ones between the varieties of /k/, yet /k/ and /s/ must be discriminated in order to understand English. Each language has its own particular set of sounds which must be discriminated to understand the language; these are called phonemes. Every language also contains many different sounds which sound alike to the ordinary person; these are called the allophones of the phoneme. The same pair of sounds may be different phonemes in one language and merely variations on the same phoneme in another. The child gradually acquires these generalizations and discriminations in learning the language.

The examples of generalization introduced thus far represent primary stimulus generalization, because there is a natural similarity among the stimuli to which the response is generalized. However, there are other examples of generalization where the actual stimuli are not apparently similar at all. For example, if a response is learned to the word collie, it may generalize to the word poodle or hound. The words themselves are not similar; but their meanings are, and, of course, a person who did not know the language would not transfer a response from one of the words to the others. This type of generalization is called *mediated generalization,* because it depends upon a previously learned common response to all three words, namely, that they are all dogs. This common response reflecting the common meaning of the words is acquired in the course of learning a language. Mediated generalization describes the fact that if one has already learned a common response to two different stimuli, a new response learned to one of them will tend to generalize to the other stimulus. This common response may be overt, or, as in the case of the common meaning, it can be implicit and internal.

Concepts of Modern Behavior Theory

The previous section described a number of the elementary facts about learning and conditioning which are used as basic materials for the formation of various S-R theories. We now turn to the more abstract concepts in S-R theory to see how the facts of conditioning fit a broad theory of human behavior.

STIMULUS-RESPONSE. The basic concept of S-R theory is the response to a stimulus. All behaviors are viewed as overt responses elicited by stimuli. Skinner distinguishes between *respondents* and *operants* and assumes that the latter are emitted without elicitation by a stimulus. After an operant behavior has been reinforced a number of times, however, it is gradually brought under the control of a stimulus. Lever pressing occurs when the rat is put in a cage with a lever. The lawfulness of the behavior is described by specifying what response occurs in what stimulus situation. All lawful predictable behavior is, therefore, elicited by some stimulus or set of stimuli.

In Hullian theory, perhaps the best-known specific example of an S-R theory, this basic connection between stimulus and response is labeled excitatory potential, written symbolically as $_sE_r$, and defined as the strength of the tendency to make the response R, to the stimulus S.

HABIT. Several factors are necessary for a response to occur overtly. One of the basic factors is *habit*. In the concept of habit, S-R theory expresses the primacy of learning in the explanation of behavior. The habit is built up through learning, and its strength is a function of the number of times it has been reinforced. There are actually two kinds of habits, excitatory and inhibitory. In Hullian theory they are symbolized as $_sH_r$ and $_sI_r$. One describes the tendency to perform R when S is presented, the other, the tendency to inhibit R when S is presented. If the same response is involved the two counter each other.

Both habit concepts describe the effect of learning on behavior and constitute the sole factors relating a response to a stimulus. Whether a response actually occurs may depend on other factors, but the connection between a specific stimulus and a specific response is entirely a function of a learned habit linking the two. Furthermore, the habit is formed by reinforcement of the S-R connection.

DRIVE. If one tried to build a theory solely on the concept of the habit, he would have to assume that behavior in the presence of the same stimuli would always be the same. There would be nothing to reflect the state of the organism. The awareness of the organism's readiness to respond is contained in the notion of *drive*.

Drive, according to S-R theory, has several consequences for behavior. First, a drive serves to activate or sensitize all the organism's responses. In a state of high drive, the threshold for responses is lowered—therefore the organism tends to be more active and more responsive. This aspect of the drive concept is necessitated by the simple fact that an organism may have a strong habit but not display it. If a rat is well fed and sated with water he is sluggish. He may have been constantly exhibiting his learned response without error, but as he becomes satiated he no longer responds to the stimuli that previously elicited the habitual response. This is theoretically explained as a result of low drive. Animals are kept hungry during an experiment so that they will respond actively to the experimental procedures.

A second consequence of drive is that it sets the stage for reinforcement. Since any event that reduces the drive level reinforces instrumental learning, a state of high drive provides opportunities for reinforcement to occur. A bit of food is an effective reward for animal learning because the animal is in a state of hunger and the food slightly lowers the drive level. By lowering the drive level the food reinforces the response, so that the habit connecting the response and what preceded it is strengthened.

The activating effect of a drive does not produce a response which is particularly appropriate to the drive. A high drive level caused by thirst does not make the organism more responsive to thirst stimuli than to other kinds of stimulation. Neither is a hungry organism more sensitive to food stimuli because of the high drive. In S-R theory *drive* functions as a general activator. There is evidence for this hypothesis: If an animal is taught a maze when he is thirsty and is rewarded at the end of each run by a small drink of water, he will still actively run the maze if he is hungry. Habits formed under one drive function under various other drives, and behavior is not tied to the particular drive that was rewarded during the original learning. Actually, the animal will not run it as actively or as well, and we shall see why in a moment.

The nonselectivity of the drive concept does not mean that animals and humans cannot discriminate between drives and behave in a way that is appropriate for each one. A rat can be taught to take the route leading to food when he is hungry but to take a different route leading to water when he is thirsty. How is such behavior accounted for according to the theory?

The explanation is that each kind of drive state is assumed to be accompanied by distinctive drive stimuli—usually symbolized as S_D. Being kept without food for twenty-four hours raises the general drive level, but it also produces distinctive hunger stimuli, including stomach contractions. Being deprived of water raises the drive level and in this sense is not different from food deprivation; but, in addition, it produces its own stimulus, namely, dryness of the throat. These stimuli coming from inside the organism can become attached to learned responses like any other stimulus. Thus, the animal that discriminates between two paths, depending upon whether he is hungry or thirsty, does not do so because of differences in drive, but because of differences in the internal stimuli accompanying the physiological state that raises the drive level.

The theory in this form accounts for some of the curiously unadaptive behavior of young children. It is not uncommon for a preschool child to become fussy and whiny about five o'clock in the afternoon. The experienced mother is likely to give him a bite to eat or to get him his supper early; food calms things down and makes life pleasanter for all concerned. The child was hungry but did not do any of the things appropriate to hunger; he neither asked for food nor tried to get a piece of candy. He acted like an organism with a high drive level but did not discriminate the specific stimuli produced by hunger, or had never learned any appropriate response to that stimulus.

Although the concept of drive seems a sensible explanation for many of the experimental findings on animal learning, there are still unsolved problems. One controversy within the ranks of S-R theorists is whether or not all reinforcement can be viewed as drive reduction, and another is the nature of the drive state itself. In many ways Miller's position on drive reduction and reinforcement is the most elegant (1959).

Miller maintains that drives are strong stimuli and that every strong stimulus is a drive. That is, the drive activates responses and its reduction is reinforcing. Pain is the clearest example of how a stimulus may function as a drive. When a rat learns a response that removes him from a shock, it seems natural that the reduction in the shock stimulus reinforces the escape response. Many other drive states like hunger, thirst, and bladder tension produce stimuli that are reduced in strength when the drive is removed.

These stimuli do not only function as drives; they are also the stimuli to which responses are attached. Any stimulus has distinctive properties which distinguish it from other stimuli and permit it to become attached to a unique response. This is the *cue* function of the stimulus. At the same time all strong stimuli have a common *drive* property, namely, that a reduction in strength is reinforcing.

There would probably be no serious objection to the hypothesis that stimuli can function as drives, but Miller (1959) and some other reinforcement theorists assume that all learned responses are acquired by this sort of reinforcement, and that all reinforcement decreases the strength of a strong stimulus. When the hypothesis is broadened to this extent it arouses objection and disagreement from several quarters.

There are a variety of objections to the view that all learning is reinforcement learning, that all reinforcement is drive reduction, and that all drives are strong stimuli. These objections come from different people and are not all consistent with one another. Many people think that there are reinforcements that are not drive reducing. Some believe that the connotation of the drive reduction theory, especially the strong stimulus view, is that all reinforcement is an escape from or a reduction in an unpleasant state. Certainly in everyday life there are many positive reinforcements—smiles of approval, pleasant-tasting food, even challenging problems. This objection may be based on a misunderstanding of the drive reduction position.

There is, however, experimental evidence to support this objection. Water sweetened with saccharine, for example, can be used to rein force a learned response in hungry rats. Such a liquid has no food value so it cannot reduce the portion of the hunger stimuli that depends upon blood sugar level. It functions as a reinforcement even if it never reaches the stomach (Janowitz & Grassman, 1949). In this experiment the animals undergo an operation in which the esophagus is cut, so food in the mouth does not get to the stomach. It appears sensible to say that the sweetness of the liquid in the mouth is the basis for its reinforcing value, yet it seems difficult to identify what strong stimulus or what drive is reduced when sweet liquid is put into the mouth.

A different kind of objection comes from those who find many reinforcements that seem to be effective early in life and yet not related to any of the standard drives. Brackbill (1958) has shown, for example, that nodding, smiling, talking, etc., to the young infant may reinforce his behavior if the adult response is contingent upon the infant's.

Thus, for example, the frequency of smiling or the frequency of vocalization in the infant can be increased merely by responding to each smile or vocal sound with some social response like smiling or nodding. In other words, the behavior of children can be shaped by the common everyday sorts of responses of adults to infants, not necessarily by some act that relieves a basic biological drive.

Secondly, there is evidence to suggest that the child's response to these common social actions of adults resembles the properties of the basic biological drives. Gewirtz and Baer (1958) have shown that young children's behavior is readily reinforced by attention being paid to them. This finding is merely an example of the wide variety of social responses that function as reinforcers. But Gewirtz and Baer have also shown that the child can be deprived of attention or satiated with it for a period of time, and that this treatment affects his responsiveness to attention. The child who is kept alone with an unresponsive adult for twenty minutes before the experiment is quite responsive to adult attention, which is then a more effective reinforcer for him than for the child who has not been deprived of attention. On the other side, if the child receives a great deal of attention from an adult, he becomes less than normally responsive to attention in the experimental situation. Periods of warm affectionate interaction or periods of cold unaffectionate interaction have also been shown to change the child's responsiveness to adult approval and disapproval (Hartup, 1958). This sort of change in deprivation and satiation is, of course, reminiscent of the cyclic nature of drives. It also recalls some of the Lewinian experiments on complete and incomplete tasks.

The implication of these findings is either that drives need to be redefined and broadened or that reinforcement is broader than drive reduction.

In terms of theories of child development, it seems more sensible to accept both positive reinforcement and reinforcement that functions to reduce some active drive state. There is no clear reason why the two types of reinforcement should not be accepted. At one time in the development of S-R theory, positive rewards seemed to admit teleological explanations, which many psychological theorists would not accept. If the child acted in a goal-directed fashion, the causes of his behavior had to be present at the time of the action. It seemed teleological to ascribe the motive for the child's behavior to some positive reward that was not experienced until after the behavior was completed. Modern S-R theory has avoided that problem. The stimulus, not the reinforcement, is the cause of the behavior. Reinforcement functions after the act to increase the probability that such behavior will recur when the appropriate stimuli are again present. Therefore, there seems to be no reason why the reinforcement must modify a preexisting drive state; it can in principle be quite unrelated to the stimuli eliciting the behavior.

The reason for the insistence upon a drive reduction theory—by Miller, at any rate—seems to be that no better theory has been proposed. Miller admits that the purely drive reduction theory is probably oversimplified, but his convictions about the development of a science lead him to believe that a theory should not be discarded until a better one supplants it. Certainly people who believe in positive reinforcement do not have a better theory about how reinforcement operates; neither do they have a clear theory that will predict which experiences will be reinforcing and how strongly.

A different objection to reinforcement theory is that both classical and instrumental conditioning should be recognized as learning mechanisms. Reinforcement theorists have maintained that classical conditioning can be accounted for as instrumental learning.

The experiment on the acquisition of fear poses the problem clearly. Here the animal acquires the fear because it is associated with shock. Once the fear is acquired, the animal's learning of avoidance responses can be explained as a reduction of fear. But how about the acquisition of the fear response itself? If fear is a response, it must obey the laws of response acquisition—therefore, according to strict reinforcement theorists, it must have been reinforced. When the animal is put into a white box and shocked, just what stimulus reduction occurs to reinforce the psychophysiological response labeled fear? It seems as if acquisition of the fear response fits the picture of classical conditioning much more readily than the picture of instrumental learning, yet a strict reinforcement theorist must account for both sorts of conditioning in terms of reinforcement.

The question of whether the classical conditioning model should be given an independent status or viewed as a special case of reinforcement learning involves many of the same considerations as the drive reduction problem. Reinforcement theory is more parsimonious if it can account for all the data on conditioning. At the moment, however, it cannot account for the data of fear acquisition or even for the classical conditioning experiment of Pavlov where the bell acquires the ability to elicit salivation. On the other hand, there is clearly no superior alternative theory.

The central problem for an S-R theory of child development, however, is to discover how the child, using the mechanisms that have been established in rigorous experimental work, acquires various responses in the natural habitat in which he grows up. The Miller experiment and others on fear as a learnable drive are the source of a valuable principle applicable to child development, regardless of whether the fear is acquired through some reinforcement or solely through contiguity of the pain stimulus and some neutral one. Some of these theoretical issues can be bypassed, therefore, until the basic theory has been clarified or it becomes clear that research with children can throw some special light on the issues themselves.

INTERNAL MEDIATING RESPONSES. In explanation of avoidance behavior and its reinforcement, fear is described as an hypothetical internal response which is accompanied by stimuli whose reduction reinforces the avoidance response. The concept of a mediating response is also needed to explain mediated generalization; this concept states that the response is a verbal meaning common to words that superficially are not similar. This common meaning permits generalization of responses from one word to another. These hypothetical mediating responses have been employed widely in modern S-R theory to account for some behavioral phenomena in the field of cognition.

ANTICIPATORY GOAL RESPONSE. One of the earliest uses of the concept of a mediating response can be found in one of Hull's discussions of anticipation (1931). In the theoretical controversies of that period it seemed to many people that the S-R conceptualization of behavior was completely mechanical and did not allow for anticipation of the goal by the organism while it was making a series of responses aimed at it. Hull introduced the notion of an anticipatory goal response in an attempt to show that within the framework of S-R theory the organism could have some anticipation of the goal.

Experiment shows that learned responses tend to occur too early; they anticipate the situation in which the response is appropriate. In Pavlov's first experiments, the salivation of the dog frequently came before the introduction of the meat powder if there was a long interval between the conditioned and unconditioned stimuli. Moreover, in learning a sequence of responses, as in learning to run a maze, there is a tendency to make anticipatory errors. If, for example, the final turn of the maze is a right-hand one, there is a tendency for the organism to make a right-hand turn at the penultimate point of choice. Indeed if the points of choice in a maze are indistinguishable from one another, animals find it almost impossible to learn without error a pathway that contains a series of five or six left-hand turns followed by a right-hand one. They make the right-hand turn too early.

The concept of an anticipatory goal response is based on these findings. Some parts of the actual goal response occur early in the sequence of responses without in any way disturbing the actual performance. If the reward at the end of a maze is food, there is no reason why the animal cannot make anticipatory chewing movements even while navigating the maze to reach the goal box. Anticipatory errors actually disrupt the performance and gradually are eliminated, but such responses as chewing neither interfere with the performance nor delay the reinforcement. They can become a stable part of the behavior of the organism.

There is no actual evidence that animals consistently make chewing movements or other anticipatory responses before reaching the goal, but it seems reasonable that they do; Hull assumed that anticipatory goal responses did occur. In doing so, they represent a behavioral anticipation of the goal just as a person's mouth watering before dinner is an anticipation of food.

The next step in the reasoning is that anticipatory responses necessarily produce stimuli, which may in turm be attached to responses of the organism. In this way the anticipatory goal response can function as a mediating response to link some antecedent stimulus to some response.

VERBAL MEDIATING RESPONSES. The anticipatory goal response represents an early attempt to conceptualize some cognitive process in S-R terms; Hull conceived it as an overt response, not readily observable, but observable in principle. The concept of a hypothetical internal mediating response has gradually become acceptable to S-R theorists. Although some day we may learn how to observe these responses, they are at present hypothetical constructs whose justification depends upon their usefulness in accounting for otherwise inexplicable data.

One commonly postulated mediating response is the verbal mediating response. By reviewing the research that has used the verbal mediating response, we can see how such responses have contributed to developmental psychology.

The acquisition of language is a peculiarly human characteristic. Thus, when S-R theorists turned to the problem of describing the reasoning processes and other peculiarly human characteristics, they naturally looked to language to provide many of the explanations for these human behaviors. One series of investigations carried out by Spiker and his associates have studied the effect of applying verbal labels to stimuli (1963). These studies have shown, first of all, that subjects can learn to discriminate more quickly if readily distinguishable verbal labels are given to intrinsically similar stimuli. For example, if different names are given to two children who resemble each other, any future task requiring the discrimination of their pictures is facilitated. According to this theory, the verbal labels are responses attached to the two pictures and become parts of the stimulus pattern for later discrimination learning. Since the labels are distinct, the stimulus patterns including the labels are more distinctive than the same patterns without the labels. The research also showed that the more distinctive the names given the stimuli, the better the discrimination.

Learning distinctive verbal labels for similar stimuli requires, of course, that the two stimuli be discriminated. Because of their similarity, it takes a long time to learn to label the stimuli correctly. Once the distinguishing labels are learned, the discrimination can be readily transferred to new tasks involving those stimuli. In the Spiker experiment, for example, the child's final task was to learn to pick the picture that would "win" in a race. This task became relatively easy once the stimuli had distinctive names, even though during the learning of the labels there had never been any consistent reinforcement for choosing one rather than the other picture.

Spiker and his colleagues have also shown that giving the same name to different stimuli increases the tendency to generalize a child's response from one to another (Shepard, 1956). In an experiment on preschool children, the child was first taught to choose a red rather than blue light; then it was empirically determined how frequently he would respond positively to three lights similar, but not identical, to the red light: a reddish orange, an orange, and a yellow. This part of the experiment was merely to measure the amount of generalization to the intermediate lights. There was some generalization but also wide individual differences among children. Then the child was taught names for the lights, the same names being assigned to the red light and the three similar stimuli, while a distinctive label was given to the blue light. After this experience there was an increased tendency to respond positively to all three of the similar stimuli.

Still another experiment has shown the effect of a verbal label on a transposition experiment, one of the classic problems in learning theory (Spiker, Guerjoy, & Shepard, 1956). In a typical example of this experiment, the subject is first taught to respond to the middle-sized stimulus of three: That is, he is taught to respond to stimulus number 2, if the three stimuli 1, 2, and 3 are arranged in order. Suppose, then that the stimuli are changed to 2, 3, and 4, so that the originally reinforced stimulus, number 2, becomes smallest of the three. Will the subject continue to respond to stimulus 2 because it was the actual stimulus previously reinforced, or will he respond to the stimulus that is middle-sized in the new series? If the child transposes his response to the middle one, he is said to show a *relational* response; if he chooses the previously reinforced stimulus, his response is called *absolute*. Which response a child makes is a function of many factors.

The experiment by Spiker, Guerjoy, and Shepard shows that the readiness with which the relational response is acquired depends on the possession of a verbal response, "middle-sized." Thus, a large group of children were tested to see if they could label the middle stimulus in a test series when prompted as follows: "This is the big one (pointing to the large stimulus), this is the little one (pointing to the smallest) and this (pointing to the middle one) is_____." On the basis of this test, the children were divided into two groups: those who had the concept middle-sized and those who did not.

All the children were then given two learning tasks, one of which required the subject to select the middle-sized stimulus from a set of three when the absolute sizes were varied. The word "middle" was never employed during this experiment. In the other task, the subject had to choose the middle of three stimuli, but the sizes were kept constant so that he could also respond correctly on the basis of absolute size. It was found that the children with the concept did much better on the task demanding a relational choice, whereas the two groups were alike on the task that did not demand such a choice. Thus, it appears that the child may need to acquire a label for the relational concept before he can respond to that particular feature of the stimulus situation.

The effect of verbal mediating responses upon selection of the particular aspect of the stimulus to which to respond is further illustrated by several experiments on what is called the "reversal shift." First, we must explain what a reversal shift or (its opposite) a nonreversal shift is. Suppose there are four stimuli (as shown in Figure 14-1): a large white square, a small white square, a large black square, and a small black square. Suppose further that a subject is taught to select the

Figure 14-1. Stimuli for experiment on reversal shift.

black rather than the white square, regardless of whether it is the larger or smaller of the pair. This is done by presenting pairs of stimuli that differ both in size and brightness, but arranging the series so that half the time the black is smaller and half the time it is larger.

Once the subject, animal or human, has learned this discrimination, the problem changes or shifts. It is the shift that is labeled *reversal* or *nonreversal*. In a reversal shift, the correct response is changed from the black to the white; the same attribute, brightness, is relevant but the correct response is the reverse of what it had been. In a nonreversal shift, the correct response is either "smaller" or "larger"; either would be a nonreversal shift. Here the other attribute is made the relevant one.

Which shift should be the more difficult, the reversal or the nonreversal? From one point of view it should be the nonreversal. The subject has no tendency to respond to either larger or smaller and therefore should acquire such a response in about the same way as he learned the first problem. The shift from black to white requires the subject, however, to make a response that has been previously extinguished and does not occur at all. He must learn to make that response 100% of the time.

From another point of view the opposite prediction is made. If the organism is already responding to brightness, the shift from black to white merely requires changing the response, whereas the shift to larger or smaller requires the subject to learn to respond to a new aspect of the stimulus and also to learn which particular response "larger" or "smaller" is correct.

This problem has been studied for many years. Recently it has been investigated by Kendler and Kendler and their associates as an example of an internal verbal mediating response. Rats seem to find the nonreversal shift easier than the reversal shift, whereas college students find the reversal shift easier (1963). The hypothesis is that human adults have an internal verbal mediating response, brightness, involved in their response. As the Kendlers put it, the human adult response is a two-stage affair involving a mediating response while the rat's response is a one-stage response. This explains the difference between the two.

In studies of children, the Kendlers have shown that younger preschool age children behave like rats in this experiment; they prefer the nonreversal shift and find it easier. Children in first grade or above find the reversal shift easier (Kendler & Kendler, 1959). The shift seems to take place at just about kindergarten age and in a group of kindergartners, the advanced ones seemed to learn the problem in a two-stage process, while the slower ones learn it by a one-stage process.

Thus, evidence is beginning to accumulate that some of the differences between younger and older children with respect to cognitive processes can be explained in terms of the acquisition of language and the development of verbal mediating responses. The picture is far from complete and the role of verbal mediation is not clearly established, but this seems to be a promising line of research.

HABIT-FAMILY HIERARCHIES. Another concept introduced by Hull into modern S-R theory is that of a family of interrelated habits. These habits represent alternative pathways to the same reward. The basic phenomenon that demands such a concept is the remarkable ability animals and humans show to shift their behavior in order to reach a goal. It has been shown, for example, that rats who learn to run a maze are able to swim through the same maze with fair accuracy, even though the specific motor actions involved in running and swimming are different. If a rat who has learned a maze develops a cerebellar lesion which keeps turning him involuntarily to the right, he can still negotiate the maze, even though he must make a 270° right turn in order to make a 90° left turn in the maze. Cognitive theorists have argued that these findings require the concept of a spatial cognitive map of the maze. The particular acts used in traversing the maze are relatively unimportant; it is the spatial pattern and the location of the goal box that is learned. Once that is acquired the animal can vary the specific instrumental actions within a wide range.

Hull's answer to this argument was the concept of habit-family hierarchy. This hierarchy can be illustrated as in Figure 14-2. The several chains of habits are each represented by one of the S-R sequences in the figure. There is an hierarchy because all the branches end at the same point, a goal stimulus denoted S_g. In other words, at various times in the past each of these chains of responses has been reinforced so that each has been learned. Furthermore, the reinforcement has

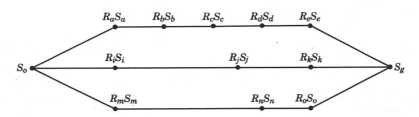

Figure 14-2. A habit-family hierarchy.

been the same for each sequence—that is, each has led to the same goal.

A second feature of the habit-family hierarchy is that the chains all begin at the same point (see Figure 14-2). In each of the chains the first response is attached to the same initial stimulus—in the maze this initial stimulus is the starting point. Furthermore the responses are also all responses to the same anticipatory goal response. As Hull thought of it, it consists of parts of the final response that were not antagonistic to running the maze and were carried forward to its beginning. The r_g in Figure 14-2 is the anticipation of the goal stated in S-R language.

Hence, the habit-family hierarchy represents a number of different sequences of actions, all of which have been learned to the same initial stimulus and involve the same anticipatory goal response. They represent alternative means of arriving at the goal (S_g). The individual members of the hierarchy do not ordinarily have the same strength, so one is more likely than another to be elicited. If the strengths are nearly equal because all have been reinforced equally often, equally promptly, and have involved equal effort, the organism may shift from one sequence to another on successive trials. But more important, if one of the chains of acts is prevented from occurring, the other alternatives are available.

Thus, the habit-family hierarchy describes in terms of sequences of acts the same range of possible behavior that is implied by the postulation of a cognitive map. The description of a map is a labeling of its points and a specification of the path from one point to another. The habit-family hierarchy also describes a set of points (stimuli) and the response that moves the person from one point to another. As far as a pure description of action is concerned, the two formulations are equivalent. This does not mean, of course, that the theories behind the two are the same.

S-R DESCRIPTION OF THINKING. The two concepts of habit-family hierarchy and internal mediating response are brought together in a recent volume by Berlyne (1965) which presents an S-R view of thinking. If one mediating response is admitted to the theory, it becomes reasonable to describe whole chains of mediating responses that intervene between the external stimulus and the overt response. If one introduces the idea of a habit-family hierarchy of symbolic mediating responses, the result is a complicated picture of the processes that lead from the stimulus to the response one that seems to incorporate for the first time in S-R theory the actual process of thinking.

One of the most recent attempts to systematize this view of thinking has been proposed by Berlyne. For him, as for other behavioristic theorists, the train of thought is represented by a chain of internal symbolic responses. Some of these responses symbolize external stimulus conditions. They are internal representations of external situations and are called *situational thoughts*. In the train of thought, the individual may think of a sequence of such situations—for example, when he anticipates a series of chess moves, he envisages the situation that would ensue after his first move or the result of the next move. Each of these situational thoughts is described theoretically as an implicit symbolic response.

In addition, Berlyne proposes that there are *transformational thoughts* which intervene between the situational thoughts and represent the action that must be carried out to change one situation into another. Thus, the train of thought consists of a situational thought followed by a transformational thought, then a situational thought, then a transformational thought, and so on until in the case of successfully directed thinking, the final situational thought represents the goal the person is trying to reach. The initial situational thought is, of course, the present situation. The train of thoughts maps a sequence of actions from the present situation to the goal. Although transformational thoughts may represent overt actions, like moving a pawn in chess, unlocking a door, or making a statement that will convince a customer, they may also represent other kinds of mental actions. For example, they may represent drawing an implication, deducing a consequence from a premise, or conceiving of a logical class, like the class of "all men."

Of course, not all sequences of thoughts are controlled, disciplined, or successful. Sometimes thoughts jump from situation to situation without intervening transformational thoughts—in fact, there may be no transformation in reality which connects the two situations. Thus, a person can think of his present situation and then of the goal even if there is no way to reach it. Berlyne's formulation of the thinking process seems to be potentially able to describe reverie and wishful thinking, as well as various kinds of realistic problem solving.

These transformational thoughts are similar in their properties to the "mental acts" and "operations" described by Piaget. They also describe the same disciplined sequence of thoughts for which Freud used the term "secondary process." They are no more observable and no more operational than are the "ideas" described in Freudian theory or the "thoughts" that are part of naïve theory. By tying such concepts to the body of S-R theory, however, Berlyne is assuming explicitly that such chains of thoughts are responses and thus must act like other responses in S-R theory. They are learned through reinforcement; they can be inhibited; they show stimulus and response generalization. In other words, these thoughts have all the properties of other responses. Berlyne has not achieved an explanation of thinking, but he has taken an important step in describing thinking in a theoretical language that contains principles of learning, inhibition, generalization, and displacement so that these other concepts can be brought to bear upon the thought process. What will happen when the specific predictions that follow from such principles are tested will determine whether the formulation is fruitful.

One extension of S-R theory into the study of thinking, then, is the great elaboration of the concept of implicit mediational responses to include long chains of such responses and their coordination to the naïve concept of "thought." A second extension of S-R theory is proposed by Berlyne in an attempt to describe the structure of knowledge by means of an elaboration of the habit-family hierarchy. It seems almost self-evident that in the course of thinking, our information becomes organized in some complex way, not just arranged in chains of thoughts. Numbers have many different kinds of relations; some are greater than others, some have the common property of being odd numbers, others are prime numbers. All sorts of rules and constraints have been described by mathematicians in their attempt to explicate the basic principles of the number system. In an attempt to represent this structure of knowledge, Malzmann (1955) and later Berlyne have built an S-R formulation of structure based on the habit-family hierarchy. All they have done is. to hypothesize that individual habit-family hierarchies may themselves be elements in a galaxy of habit-family hierarchies. In other words, they have described a many-leveled hierarchy of habit families. Such a compound habit-family hierarchy is pictured in Figure 14-3 (Berlyne, p. 191) and again in more complicated form in Figure 14-4 (Berlyne, p. 192).

This kind of structure seems particularly applicable to the types of problem solving in which a decision must be made at a number of levels. In planning a trip across the country, one may first decide whether to take a northern or southern route. These two main routes are elements in a habit-family. If the northern route is selected, there are decisions about which route to take from New York to Chicago, and so on, down until one is finally faced with the decision to turn right or left at the end of the driveway.

When computer programs are being designed to perform complex operations that simulate thinking, it has been found that efficient pro-

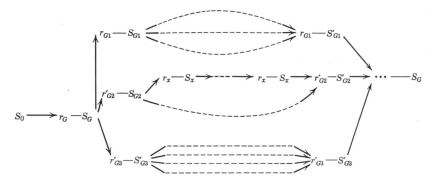

Figure 14-3. A compound habit-family hierarchy.

grams are arranged hierarchically so that a major decision is first made, and then, within the constraints of that alternative, various subdecisions are made and explored. If none of these succeeds, perhaps a different decision at the top level may be tried. An alternative approach puts every possible sequence of actions on a single undifferentiated list and routinely explores them one after another. This alternative is wasteful and time consuming, and does not simulate human thinking.

In Figure 14-3, we can see that each habit-family hierarchy is held together by a begining r_{g1} or r_{g2} and unified at the end by an S_{g1}, S_{g2},

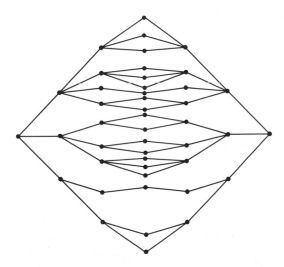

Figure 14-4. A more complicated compound habit-family hierarchy.

etc. These symbols represent subgoals in ordinary language, and the first major decision to be made is which major subgoal will become the goal of the planning. Then, in order to reach that subgoal, further choices must be made; perhaps one must select sub-subgoals that require more specific choices.

How does this view of the structure of thinking compare with that described by Piaget? He introduces the concept of grouping (see p. 185) to explain the structure of mental acts required to perform logical thinking. Berlyne believes that many of these same principles can be applied to the transformational thoughts involved in compound habit-family hierarchies.

For example, equivalent chains of transformations inhere in every habit-family hierarchy. This is the essential feature that marks the operations in a grouping: If the operations in a system form a grouping, there will be some operation that is equivalent to every combination of other operations, and the ways the operations are grouped in arriving at the final result are all equivalent.

At this point Berlyne is guided very much by Piaget's thinking. Berlyne asks what would be the result if the transformations in a compound habit-family hierarchy fitted the criteria of a group (see p. 179). Let us see what this means.

1. CLOSURE: The criterion of closure means that any two elements in a group may be combined and that an operation equivalent to the combination is also a member of the group. When we put this into a habit-family hierarchy, it seems that every sequence of transformations a-b can be replaced by a single transformation c, and that c is also a member of the hierarchy. Looking at Figure 14-5, we see that whenever the sequence a-b occurs, there must be another branch of the hierarchy that contains c instead of a-b. Furthermore, this must happen whenever the sequence a-b occurs in this particular compound hierarchy.

2. ASSOCIATION: The sequence a-b-c is equivalent to $(a$-$b)$-c and to a-$(b$-$c)$. If we trace this association in Figure 14-6, we will find that if the sequence a-b-c appears in a habit-family hierarchy, other branches of the hierarchy must contain d-c, where d is the resultant of a-b; a-e

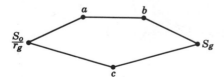

Figure 14-5. Closure in habit-family hierarchy.

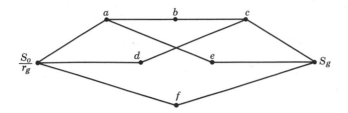

Figure 14-6. Associativity in habit-family hierarchies.

(where e is the resultant of b-c); and also, by closure f, a single transformation that is equivalent to all of the others.

3. IDENTITY: There must be a transformation O that can be introduced at any point in any chain of the habit-family hierarchy without modifying the structure. Thus, a-b must be equivalent to a-O-b. This means that there is potentially another branch of the hierarchy with the same beginning and end point (Figure 14-7). In terms of thinking this may mean that between a and b the thinking might stop momentarily without influencing the result, or that some sequence equivalent to O might intervene.

4. INVERSE: Every element must have an inverse. An inverse is depicted in Figure 14-8. In other words, introducing b and b^1 into the sequence is the same as introducing O into it.

We see in Figure 14-9 what this implies in terms of thinking. The sequence a-b leads to the result S_g. There may be a transformation c that leads off to some other end point, as illustrated in the top branch. But even if thinking takes the transformation c, it can be brought back to a sequence that leads to S_g by introducing c'. By closure, of course, there is a single transformation d that short circuits a-b.

So, if a habit-family hierarchy has a group structure, then:

(1) For *every* sequence of transformations there must be a single equivalent. (2) The associative law must hold for *every* set of three transformations. (3) *Every* transformation must have an identity. (4) There must be an inverse transformation for every transformation.

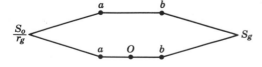

Figure 14-7. The identity in structure of habit.

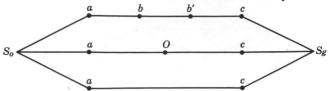

Figure 14-8. The inverse operation in a system of mediating responses.

These are rigorous criteria and there is no reason to assume that all or most habit-family hierarchies meet them. Thus, the formulation suggests that if Piaget is right, we can describe a habit-family hierarchy in a young child that would not have all the necessary properties for logical thinking, but might still contain many usable sequences of transformations that would achieve the logical result under some conditions.

Berlyne relates this group property of some habit-family hierarchies directly to the Piagetian problem of conservation of quantity.

A subject recognizing a quantitative invariant will possess a number of habit-family hierarchies of the following kind: All constituent chains will end with a common sequence of acts (for example, selecting a particular vessel as containing just enough liquid to quench one's thirst and then consuming its contents), but the earlier parts of the chain preceding this final sequence will consist of all possible successive combinations of transformation preserving the quantitative property, for example, all possible successive pourings of a mass of liquid from container to container.

The subject hierarchies will also show the following characteristic—(notation changed to fit text) where x represents any transformation that preserves the quantitative property, provided that the satisfaction of the motivation subserved by the hierarchy depends on this quantitative property. (Berlyne, p. 218)

In other words, between b and c there will be a hierarchy of transformations that form a group, since they all leave the amount of liquid invariant.

Thus, we are brought to the present state of S-R theory as it has

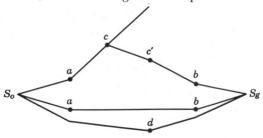

Figure 14-9. Role of inverse in directed thought.

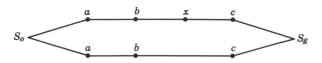

Figure 14-10.

been modified and extended in the attempt to encompass the problems of human thinking and, specifically, as Berlyne has attempted to integrate many of Piaget's concepts into an S-R language.

Whether it will be fruitful remains to be seen. But some of the assets of the S-R point of view are already apparent. By distilling the global process of thinking into individual implicit responses, Berlyne is able to represent many features of Piaget's formulations in S-R language. It would not be difficult to describe the sequence of ideas in consciousness or the structure of a cognitive map in the same language.

By putting this structure in S-R theory, Berlyne is able to draw upon a large body of experimental findings in addition to a large body of theory. He is also putting real constraints on the term "thought" by calling it a symbolic response. If, for example, thoughts are the result of reinforcement for thinking them, it may be that the theory can only predict thinking according to the pleasure principle, but not realistic thinking. Stimulus-response theory has never addressed itself to the particular problems of primary and secondary processes as Freud described them. And, to find a language bridge from one theory to another does not mean that the two theories can be translated into each other; if that were true they would be equivalent. The language bridge does, however, allow the theories to confront each other and it frequently raises interesting problems for both theories.

OBSERVATIONAL LEARNING. To round out the survey of the basic concepts of S-R theory, three more, different from those discussed, are needed. As S-R theory has gradually grown to include phenomena like thinking, anticipation, or fear, these have been encompassed in the general theory by the addition of new terms like implicit mediating response which do not modify the basic principles of habit formation.

As S-R theory has gradually been extended to include more and more complex behavior, some empirical facts have constituted building blocks without being completely coherent with the remainder of the theory. Observational learning, imitation, and the frustration-aggression hypothesis are all examples of empirical concepts used to explain the development of the child which are not yet themselves completely reconciled with the rest of S-R theory.

Observational learning describes the fact that people can learn behavior patterns merely by watching other people perform them, that their own acts can be reinforced or inhibited by observing reinforcements and punishments to other people, and that they can acquire conditioned emotional responses to stimuli which accompany a painful stimulus to another person.

IMITATION. Imitative behavior has been discussed by several psychologists in the S-R tradition in attempts to show how it might be rewarding, or how an imitative response might occur. Dollard and Miller in *Social Learning and Imitation* (1941) demonstrate that imitative behavior may be reinforced. The act of copying, although it involves many different specific actions, can function as a unitary response and be acquired by reinforcement principles. Dollard and Miller hypothesize that all imitation is the result of a person's being reinforced when his behavior matches the behavior of another person. Sometimes the reinforcement is extrinsic, as when a mother praises a younger child for copying some desirable behavior of his older brother. Sometimes the reinforcement occurs because copying the successful behavior of another person achieves the same reward as the other person obtained. In all cases, according to Dollard and Miller, the imitative response first occurs in a trial-and-error fashion like all other responses. They state that once it occurs it can be reinforced, but they do not hypothesize any mechanism by which a new response can first occur through imitation. In other words, Dollard and Miller say that imitation occurs, but that no new principle is involved.

A second hypothesis presented by Mowrer and others suggests that imitation can be self-reinforcing. It is a method by which the person can reinforce himself when the usual source of reinforcements is not available. For example, the child may say to himself the complimentary words or the supportive phrases which his mother uses to reward him. Or, he may admonish himself in the words of his parent before he does something wrong, and thus produce the stimuli that inhibit the behavior. Mowrer proposes that this mechanism underlies the imitative behavior of talking birds. The necessary precondition is that the bird be warmly cared for, so that it is content when its caretaker is around and distressed when he is absent. Then, if the caretaker repeatedly uses the same phrase, the bird gradually imitates these words and utters them as a replacement for the stimuli that were part of the caretaker's being present.

Mowrer (1960) also suggests that imitation may be facilitated or inhibited by observation of the reinforcements and punishments the model's behavior incur. Bandura, Ross and Ross (1963) have performed an experiment that shows the effect of reinforcement or punishment of a model on the amount of imitation. The model's behavior in this experiment was shown on film. In one film sequence, Rocky, the villain of the picture, meets Johnny, who is playing with an attractive set of toys. Rocky asks Johnny to let him play with some of them, but Johnny refuses. Then Rocky throws a ball at Johnny and shoots a dart gun at Johnny's toys. Johnny tries to spank Rocky, but is quickly overpowered. Poor Johnny is then beaten with a stick, and retires into a corner. The film ends with Rocky enjoying all the toys, while Johnny sits unhappily in the corner. Finally, Rocky packs all the toys into a sack and rides away with his loot. This, needless to say, is the film showing aggression rewarded.

In another film, where aggression is punished, Johnny thoroughly thrashes Rocky at the end of the film. Rocky flees to the corner, and Johnny packs up the toys and walks away. In the course of the film, Rocky displays the same aggressive acts that he did in the first film.

The subjects in this experiment were preschool children divided into four groups, those viewing aggression rewarded, those viewing aggression punished, and two control groups who did not see the aggressive behavior at all. One control group saw vigorous but nonaggressive behavior using the same props that were in the aggressive sequences, and the other was not exposed to a model at all.

After the experimental treatment the children played in an experimental room which contained a large collection of toys, among them the objects used by the models in the film. The play behavior of the children was carefully described. The children who had seen aggression rewarded displayed much more imitative aggressive behavior than children in the other three groups.

In a later experiment, Bandura showed that the children who were exposed to the punishment of aggressive behavior knew the model's actions. If given an incentive to display the aggressive acts they could do so readily, almost as readily as the children who saw aggression rewarded. Bandura argues that the punishment of the aggression did not hamper the acquisition of the aggressive behavior, it merely inhibited its display in the play situation following the movies (1962).

Bandura hypothesizes, therefore, that the mere exposure to the behavior of a model without any reward for imitation and without the model being rewarded for his behavior is sufficient for the learning of the responses displayed. The following experiment illustrates that fact and also shows the effect of previous experiences with the model in the child's readiness to imitate (Bandura & Huston, 1961). The experiment investigated direct instrumental imitation learned through reinforcement and incidental imitation of irrelevant features of behavior.

In the experiment two identical boxes were placed side by side about five feet apart. Both the model (a young lady) and the child were presumably subjects in the experiment. The experimenter, a third person, placed two little gummed stickers with pictures on them in one of the boxes, while the child and model were out of the room. Then the two returned and the model made the first choice. She selected the prearranged box and received a reward. Now the subject made his choice. If he chose the same box as the model, he too received a reward, and thus was reinforced for copying an actual choice. The experiment continued until the child had imitated the model four times in a row or until he had completed thirty trials without reaching a criterion.

The opportunity for incidental imitation arose from the fact that the model performed distinctive actions as she made her choice. At the starting point she said, "Here I go." As she walked toward the selected box, she chanted, "March, march, march." The boxes had little dolls sitting on the lid and the model aggressively knocked the doll onto the floor before opening the box. As she opened the box she said, "Open the box," she then removed one of the gummed stickers that served as a reward, pasted it on a picture hanging on the wall, and replaced the doll on the box. For a control group of subjects, the model performed quite different actions to be sure that the actions performed by the subjects would not occur except through imitation. (The researchers had to ignore the subjects' replacing the doll on the box because nearly all the control subjects performed that act spontaneously.)

This is the imitation situation itself, but actually it came last in the experiment. The experimental subjects were divided into two groups, based on the kind of interaction the subject and the model had had during two earlier play sessions. For half the group the previous interaction had been nonnurturant: the model brought the child to the experimental room, gave him toys to play with, and then busied herself with paper work in the far corner of the room. The other half of the subjects had two nurturant play sessions, in which the model sat close to the child, responded to his bids for help and attention, and was consistently warm.

There are several interesting findings in the experiment. One is that there was more spontaneous imitation of the irrelevant behavior than of the model's actual choice. Children seem to have a tendency to choose the opposite box from the model in a two-alternative choice, perhaps because they think that both boxes have rewards in them and the model already has the one from the box she selected. The most important result, however, is that there is a great deal of imitation of incidental actions and that nurturant subjects imitate the model much more than the nonnurturant group. In addition, one would expect that dependent subjects would be more imitative than independent ones; however, all the subjects had been rated on dependency in the nursery school, and this relationship did not emerge distinctly from the study.

This experiment is illustrative of several experiments on imitation. Another factor influencing imitation is the power of the model. A model who is introduced to the child as his new nursery school teacher is more imitated than one who is merely a person, despite the fact that the child and model have had no direct contact (Mischel & Grusec, 1965). There have been contradictory findings about whether a same-sex model or an opposite-sex model is imitated more. In the Bandura and Huston experiment the model was female for all subjects and there were no sex differences.

Exposure to a model may produce more than the display of specific imitative behavior; it may also encourage the display of other behavior patterns belonging to the same general class. For example, the aggressive behavior of children who have been exposed to an aggressive model includes not only the specific aggressive acts observed in the model, but also other sorts of aggressive responses which are already in the child's repertoire. In one experiment (Lovaas, 1961), the child could choose to activate either of two animated toys. One showed one doll hitting another whenever the starting button was pressed; the other showed a ball rising up to the top of a cage. Children exposed to aggressive models preferred the first toy to the second more than children shown a nonaggressive movie. Bandura speaks of this effect of exposure to a model as *disinhibition* of responses already in the child's repertoire of acts.

The experiment of Bandura and Huston shows that children who have had warm interactions with the model imitate her more than children whose interactions with the model have been neutral or cold. There have been several studies of the factors influencing a person's susceptibility to a model's behavior. In general, three sorts of factors seem relevant. First, a previous history of being rewarded for imitative behavior increases the probability of imitation. Second, a history of deprivation of rewards, low self-esteem, and general dependency produces more imitation than does a history of their opposites. Finally, a condition of emotional arousal seems to encourage imitative behavior, both when it is induced by situational factors (McNulty & Walters, 1962) and when it is the result of drugs (Schachter, 1962).

Bandura and Walters (1963) emphasize observational learning more than any other S-R theorists. They see it as an important mechanism for the acquisition of responses which are not reducible to reinforcement learning or to classical conditioning. For the two researchers, observational learning includes not only the copying of models and the responsiveness to the reinforcement a model receives, but also all forms of verbal instruction. Learning through verbal instruction is called symbolic imitation. Bandura and Walters contend that an actual model can be effectively represented in films and pictures, but .that even these stimuli are to some degree symbolic models. By a further extension, they argue that a verbal description of behavior is also a representation of the behavior itself, and so can be thought of as a model which the individual imitates when he carries out the verbally described behavior. Thus, the instructions to open a combination lock by making "two turns to the right to 47, one turn to the left to 14 then right to 26" are not essentially different as far as learning is concerned from a visual demonstration of opening the lock. Indeed, Berlyne states that such a sequence of acts can be represented by a series of symbolic mediating responses. It might be that both the imitation of a model and the following of verbal directions involve the representation of the actions by means of symbolic mediating responses, and that all stimulus situations that produce the same set of mediating responses are equivalent.

FRUSTRATION-AGGRESSION HYPOTHESIS. The third radical and innovative addition to the basic concepts underlying social learning is the acceptance of the hypothesis that frustration leads to aggression as a basic postulate, rather than trying to derive it from already existent principles of learning.

In 1939, in a thin book entitled *Frustration and Aggression* (1939), a group of S-R psychologists from Yale University proposed the hypothesis that frustration always resulted in aggression, although other sorts of behavior also followed. The hypothesis also stated that aggression implied frustration as an antecedent. It was stated very strongly: *frustration is a necessary and sufficient antecedent to aggression.* The aggressive behavior might be inhibited by other factors and thus not be overtly expressed, but it was always instigated by the frustration.

This hypothesis was taken explicitly from Freudian theory—actually from Freud's earlier theorizing about the sources of aggression before he introduced the death instinct. As stated in the book *Frustration and Aggression,* the relation is not derived from the principles of learning. It is possible to envisage how aggression toward a frustrating agent might be reinforced because of its success in removing the frustration; and, it is tempting if one is committed to learning theory, to try to account for aggression as a learned response to frustration. The authors of *Frustration and Aggression,* however, did not formulate their theory in that way. To them, the connection between frustration and aggression was a fact, regardless of what instinctive and/or learned mechanism explained the connection.

However, to simply state the connection between frustration and aggression does not provide any sort of satisfactory theory of aggressive behavior, so the authors presented a series of supplementary hypotheses to bring the theory of frustration and aggression into useful contact with actual behavioral data.

In the first place, both *frustration* and *aggression* must be operationally defined, although it is hard to do so in a strict S-R terminology. Aggression is defined as a *sequence of behavior whose goal-response is the injury of the person toward whom it is directed.* The term *goal-response* itself is an unusual one in S-R theory, but in this context it means the response in a learned behavior which ends the sequence and also reinforces the behavior that led up to it. In other words, aggression is defined as a learned habitual response that has in the past been reinforced by the fact that it injured another person.

It is difficult to say whether this definition covers all the various connotations of the term aggression, but it does pretty well. It includes physical injury, frustration of another person's behavior, social insults, and snubs. The destruction of inanimate objects by kicking them, etc., is considered as a displaced form of aggression. Feelings of anger, hostility, and irritation not reflected in overt behavior are viewed as inhibited aggression.

Frustration is defined as an interference or blocking of a behavioral sequence that prevents the goal response from occurring. In other words, we have learned a variety of behavioral patterns through the fact that in the past they have led to reinforcements. When such a learned pattern is interfered with so that it does not result in the reinforcement, it is frustrating. Such an event is also the beginning of the process of extinction of the learned behavior, but while the habit is still strong, the failure to receive the reinforcement is frustrating, and the frustration instigates aggressive behavior. An example of this is the behavior of the chimpanzees in Wolfe's experiment when the vending machine which gave food for tokens did not work (see p. 403).

With the two main terms in the hypothesis defined, the theory then states a number of other hypotheses concerned with the strength of the instigation to aggression, and with its various forms of expression. Different frustrations and different sequences of frustration may instigate aggression more or less strongly. The three hypotheses which account for this variation are:

1. The stronger the instigation to the frustrated response, the more the frustration is an instigation to aggression. In other words, interferring with well-learned and strongly reinforced habits is more frustrating and therefore more of an instigation to aggression than the blocking of weaker behavior patterns.
2. The greater the interference with a frustrated response, the stronger the instigation to aggression. A minor interference involving some readjustment and delay is less frustrating than the complete blocking of a response.
3. Frustration accumulates. A long series of frustrations may build, so that the final frustration instigates a tremendous amount of aggression just because it has been preceded by a long series of other frustrations, not because the particular frustration is so irritating.

All these hypotheses have a common-sense quality that makes them quite believable. At the same time they are couched in clear language and have basic terms which are operationally defined. It is worth pointing out, however, that the definitions are not completely operational. In particular the labeling of a response as "aggression" involves a great deal of tacit naïve theory. The response is defined in terms of its effect on the environment. It is not a simple response, but a class of responses which may include many different actions. Nevertheless, the class does not include the same response unambiguously. If a particular action hurt someone one time, and did not hurt anybody on another occasion, then it would be called aggression one time and not another. Naïve theory speaks of aggression in terms of intention as well as effect. Stimulus-response theory avoids the mentalistic word *intention,* but labeling all actions that hurt other people as aggressive responses regardless of intention does not really solve the problem, either.

The publication of *Frustration and Aggression* marks the beginning of a new trend in S-R theory in which operational purity has been sacrificed for the sake of making empirical studies of significant problems. Using this concept of aggression, many S-R theorists have made important contributions to the study of the development of aggression and of the environmental factors that foster its appearance. By treating aggression as if it were a response, they have applied many of the principles of reinforcement and conditioning to the problem and these have proved fruitful. As we shall see in the following chapter, many experiments performed under the general heading of *social-learning theory* have successfully applied the general strategy of S-R theory to behavior such as aggression, dependency, and conscience, which cannot be defined strictly in terms of the motor actions that constitute the response; common-sense definitions of the terms have been used and, as a result, important portions of naïve theory have been, so to speak, allowed into the theory through the back door.

This does not mean that the research has not been empirical or rigorous. When aggression is investigated, the researchers have been careful to see that different observers agree upon what behaviors are called aggressive. In an experiment it has often been possible to define aggression narrowly and operationally as hitting or as some other explicit act. Underlying the research, however, is the tacit assumption that aggressive responses do reflect some underlying unity in the personality even though they are manifested in quite different ways under different circumstances.

Summary

This chapter concludes the description of the basic concepts employed in S-R theory, especially as it relates to the development of the child. The next chapter will describe the way the development of the child in our society is actually conceptualized within this theoretical framework.

To recapitulate, the theory starts with the assumption that nearly all human behavior is learned and is done so piecemeal rather than in large chunks. There are two main principles of learning: One is that when two different stimuli repeatedly appear in close proximity to each other, the responses to one of them are gradually transferred to the other, the second is that if a response to a stimulus is followed by a reinforcement, the probability of that response to that stimulus is increased.

We have also seen how behavior may be learned under partial reinforcement, and that such schedules of reinforcement can produce responses that are resistant to extinction.

We have also examined the notion of a mediating response that may not be overtly manifested. Mediating responses are hypothesized to account for such phenomena as mediated generalization, learned drives, and the complex problem of directed thinking.

Stimulus-response theory also contains the frustration-aggression hypothesis that frustration is a necessary and sufficient condition for aggression. The aggression may be inhibited or displaced, or it may suffer the fate of any other response.

Finally, the concepts of S-R theory include observational learning. According to this principle, behavior may be acquired through the imitation of other people or through verbal instructions, and may be reinforced and inhibited by the observation of its consequences for another person.

FIFTEEN

Social-learning theory
of child development

ONE OF THE LEADERS in the development of S-R theory was Professor
Clark L. Hull of Yale University. Hull's own research was largely concerned with the behavior of rats in experimental situations, but he
formalized a view of behavior that was applicable to behavior in general. Among his students and colleagues, one group has been dedicated
to understanding the development of the child. These people include
O. H. Mowrer, Robert R. Sears, Neal Miller, John Dollard, and others
who have attempted to build a theory of child development on the
basis of both S-R theory and psychoanalytic theory. Couched in the
language of S-R, their theories depend on learning and reinforcement
as explanatory principles, but many of the hypotheses have been inspired by the writing of Freud. This view has been labeled *social-
learning theory*.

Sometimes it is said that social-learning theory is a translation of
Freudian theory into S-R terminology. Psychoanalytic writers clearly,
even violently, disagree, however. They point out that many fundamental assumptions of Freudian theory are not included, rephrased, or
even replaced in social-learning theory. The whole problem of consciousness and unconsciousness and the basic instinctual drives are ignored; the psycholanalytic formulation of psychosexual development is
also not treated.

These objections are quite justified. It is possible to rewrite one
theory into another on occasion in order to show that the essential

437

concepts are translated into a different language, and that the two theories are in agreement except for language. But this is not what the writers of social learning theory have done. They believe that many of the concepts of Freudian theory—including ones that psychoanalytic theorists consider essential—have no testable consequences and have therefore ignored them.

What social-learning theorists have done is to write a theory of social learning and socialization of the child that is inspired by certain Freudian hypotheses but that places the causal explanations and theoretical justification of these hypotheses within the S-R framework. Sears has put it clearly:

The reformulations of the theories—particularly that of anaclitic identification —were therefore less a translation of psychoanalytic language into behavior terms than conversion of a map of something seen into a set of operationally defined variables the interactions among which would account for the development of what was seen and for the differences among individuals in that rate of development. The research that followed must not be viewed as an attempted verification of psychoanalytic concepts, therefore, but as a testing of a behavioral theory that was suggested by psychoanalytic observations and was then constructed within the framework of an entirely different theoretical structure. (*Child Rearing and Identification*)

Thus, social-learning theory began as a psychoanalytically inspired S-R theory of the development of the child's social relations and personality. However, the findings of empirical research have led to revisions of the theory and have posed problems which are not rooted in psychoanalysis: in fact, recent social-learning theorists like Bandura and Walters seem to believe the psychoanalytic inspiration has generally produced misconceptions. Such research has also led to divergence among different social learning theorists as they have tried various hypotheses for explaining the empirical data of child development.

Cross-Cultural Studies of Child Rearing

Psychoanalytic theory is not the only root of social learning theory; a second is anthropology. Including anthropology may seem peculiar but is actually natural. Social-learning theory, like S-R theory in general, emphasizes the role of learning in the development of personality. Purely maturational concepts are not employed. Empirically, however, there is a great deal of similarity in the development of different children. They walk at about the same age, learn to go to the toilet at about the same time, boys generally tend to develop masculine behavior patterns while girls develop feminine ones. This similarity in the growth patterns of different children has often been made the central argument that some genetically controlled maturational process underlies child development.

If social-learning theory attributes most of these similarities among different children to learning processes, it must ascribe the common development of children to what is common in their environments. There must be some environmental factors that cause children to learn the same things at approximately the same age.

Two factors produce similarities in the environments of different children. One is that the physical environment operates according to the same laws for everybody: Falling rocks hurt anybody; fire burns; deep water presents a danger of drowning. These realities teach the child not to step off a cliff or to breathe when he falls into the water. Although children are not equally exposed to these realities, they will all learn the same things from the purely physical environment.

Another factor producing similarity in the learned acquisitions of different children is that within the same society customary patterns of child rearing ensure that different children will be exposed to the same influences at approximately the same age. They will be weaned, expected to walk and talk at about the same time, toilet-trained during approximately the same period, etc. And, not only the time but also the manner of training new skills is similar within a society. Weaning may be encouraged by putting pepper on the breast in one culture and by spoon feeding solid foods in another. This process by which a society trains its children to behave like adults is called *socialization*.

Societies may show marked differences in the age, sequence, and manner of socializing various kinds of behavior. These differences in child rearing provide the opportunity for a cross-cultural study of the consequences. If the custom in one group of societies is to wean children harshly early in life while in another group of societies it is to wean them gently at a later age, a comparison of the two groups of societies may reveal customs, beliefs, or personality traits that are consistently different. These variables that correlate with the age of weaning may contribute to our understanding of the consequences of weaning. Researchers have used cross-cultural studies on several occasions to explore some of the correlates of different child-rearing practices.

Despite the differences between societies, the problem of socialization in every society can be described in the same general terms. Socialization always involves changing the behavior patterns of a child from what they are early in his life to the accepted adult pattern. Whiting and Child (1953) label the early period the *period of in-*

dulgence. The infant is not required to eat with a spoon or to obey his parents immediately. For a period of time, he is permitted to behave naturally. Then, at some point in the child's life—a different point for different behavior systems—he is required to change his behavior toward the approved adult form. This interval is called the *period of socialization* for the particular behavior. Socialization may be gradual or abrupt, or harsh or gentle, and may involve punishment of the infantile pattern, reward of the adult pattern, or both.

As a result of this patterning of socialization, the child generally learns during the period of indulgence to find pleasure, satisfaction, and security in one kind of behavior. Then, during the socialization of that behavior he must relinquish his old mode of pleasure. On top of the previously learned behavior a layer of inhibitory learning may be imposed, probably accompanied by anxiety. At the same time, reinforcement of more adult behavior provides a new source of pleasure.

These points in a child's life when some particular behavior is under socialization pressure are the moments where various kinds of maladjustments may occur. The child may cling to the infantile mode of behavior, may develop hostility, or may adopt the more adultlike behavior but with considerable anxiety attached to it which prevents its functioning effectively. What happens at the beginning of the period of socialization depends upon how it is handled. Whiting and Child—borrowing from Freud—distinguish two sorts of reactions which might hamper smooth socialization. One, called *positive fixation,* represents the possibility that the infantile behavior was so rewarding that it is given up only with difficulty and retains a considerable amount of its pleasurable quality. The other, called *negative fixation,* represents the creation of so much anxiety over the change in behavior that the child has difficulty in making the transition. Thus, in weaning, nursing may be so rewarding that there is a positive fixation on it, or weaning itself may be so harsh and punitive that all eating becomes surrounded with a great deal of anxiety.

Whiting and Child made these distinctions in order to predict some of the consequences of the two in a cross-cultural study. They hypothesized that in those cultures where eating was positively fixated, eating would be associated with pleasant and anxiety-relieving connotations in the folklore of the culture. Specifically, they searched for beliefs that oral activity was therapeutic for illness of any kind. On the other hand, they hypothesized that in cultures where weaning was carried out quickly and harshly, eating was associated with anxiety and in those cultures it would be believed to be a factor in the causation of illness.

Generally speaking, the hypothesis of positive fixation did not receive much empirical support, but the hypothesis of negative fixation proved to be fruitful. In the Whiting and Child study, for example, the severity of socialization of a behavior system is significantly related to the presence of that system in explanations of illness. This hypothesis has proven valid, however, only for oral behavior, dependency, and aggression.

The particular symptoms Whiting and Child chose to study were rather exotic and not the most direct evidence obtainable of positive fixation or of anxiety over a behavior pattern. Cross-cultural studies are, however, dependent on the kind of information generally obtained by anthropologists in their field studies. Beliefs about illness happen to be information that is available for many societies, which is why it was chosen.

The theorizing behind the study of Whiting and Child will occur again and again as we review other investigations of the acquisition of dependency, aggression, etc.

The Development of Dependency

Early in the child's life he becomes psychologically dependent on the mother. Physically he is dependent on her from birth; his life depends upon her care. He does not show psychological dependency until he is a few months old, however. This dependence continues to some extent into normal adult life, but under ordinary conditions in our culture it is strongest during middle and later infancy, and then slowly declines throughout childhood as the individual becomes independent and self-reliant.

How is psychological dependence manifested? One sign is *attention-seeking behavior:* the child asks an adult to look at him or at what he has done; the child wants to be close to the adult, to sit in his lap, or to cling to him. If the child attracts attention, even if not overtly, it is taken as a sign of dependency; the child has learned responses that gain him attention and put him close to his mother or some other adult. Another sign of dependency is that the giving of attention or affection are reinforcers which can be used to teach the child other sorts of behavior. If the child's learning is strongly reinforced by adult attention, that child must need and want attention very much. Dependency can also be mainfested in a third way by the fear of being alone or the fear of a stranger.

According to social-learning theory, the development of dependency begins with the fact that the mother is the infant's caretaker and does many things that make him comfortable. The mother effectively relieves the child's hunger and pain on innumerable occasions during the child's early years. Thus, the mother's presense is frequently associated with being made more comfortable and her absence is often associated with being uncomfortable.

How does this produce signs of dependency? In the first place, the child's acts that call the mother, such as crying when uncomfortable, are often reinforced by her doing something that makes the child more comfortable. Thus, attention-getting is reinforced. Second, the continued association of the mother's presence and the baby's comfort makes the mere presence of the mother a source of comfort. The infant is often soothed and stops crying as soon as he sees his mother, before she actually does anything to relieve his physical distress. When he is frightened, just being near her may remove the fear. Third, the frequent association of the mother's absence and the child's discomfort can make her absence a stimulus to anxiety and fear. Separation anxiety occurs in practically all children, usually appearing during the last half of the first year of life.

There is ample evidence that social responses from adults, such as smiling, talking, or cuddling the infant, function as reinforcers for the child (Brackbill, 1958). In a more naturalistic setting, Rheingold (1956) has shown that social responsiveness by an adult can function to encourage social spontaneity in young children. She selected an experimental group of four six-month-old infants from the population of a children's institution. These children lived in one room, with their cribs side by side. The experimenter, to quote her report, "fed, bathed, diapered, soothed, held, talked to and played with these four babies for seven and one-half hours a day, five days a week, for eight weeks." In contrast, the children under the regular routine of the hospital received much less individual attention because of the large number of them assigned to a small staff. The children's physical needs were cared for and during these moments of social interaction the adults caring for them were generally friendly and playful; but, of necessity, the children were left alone much of the time. On a series of tests of social responsiveness, the experimental infants obtained higher scores than the control infants, not only in response to the experimenter, but also in response to an examiner who was present only once each week for the testing, and to a stranger who appeared for the first time at the end of the eight-week period.

These symptoms of dependency all generally develop by the time the baby is eight months old. From then on the situation becomes more complicated. For one thing, the cues that arouse anxiety and relieve it become subtler, and the intensity of the overt reaction is reduced. The child learns the distinction between maternal approval and disapproval. The mother's presence is not always associated with increased comfort for the child. Sometimes she is angry and speaks harshly without doing anything comforting, or she shows disapproval even while taking care of the child's needs. Gradually, according to the theory, the child learns to perform actions that bring approval; he is now content when she shows approval and anxious when she is disapproving. In other words, the nuances of the mother's expressive behavior become effective stimuli over and above her mere presence or absence.

The effectiveness of maternal approval and disapproval as reinforcers and anxiety arousers gives the mother a powerful tool for teaching the child the necessary rules of social life. The child is reinforced by approval for eating out of a spoon, for awakening dry in the morning, for going to the bathroom at the right time, and for innumerable other socially conforming actions. Gradually, nonconforming actions are either extinguished through nonreinforcement or actually inhibited by the anxiety aroused by maternal disapproval.

An experimental study showing the effectiveness of dependency in setting the stage for the acquisition of adult-approved behavior was performed by Hartup (1955). He first observed children in the nursery school in order to score each child's behavior on dependency. This score depended upon the frequency with which the child sought recognition and approval, sought necessary help, sought physical nearness and contact, and sought either positive or negative attention.

Using these measures, Hartup set up two groups of children matched on dependency and balanced with respect to sex. These two groups were eventually tested on the same set of learning tasks to measure the efficiency of learning, but before the test period the two groups were treated differently. In one group, the child interacted warmly and nuturantly with the experimenter for two five-minute periods. In the other group, the first five minutes were warm and nurturant, but then the experimenter said he could not play with the child any more, and instead read a book for the last five minutes. The theory underlying these two treatments is that during the first five minutes both groups establish some dependency on the experimenter because of the warm, rewarding relationship. Then, in the second five minutes, one group continues to enjoy this attention while the other group is deprived of it. In the second group, nurturance followed by its withdrawal is expected to create a state of high dependency as in the Gewirtz and Baer experiment (see p. 412). If this is true, the second group (labeled NW for nurturance-withdrawal) should learn more effectively when rewarded by the experimenter's approval. His approval should be more reinforcing for the NW group than for the other group (labeled C for consistent nurturance). Furthermore, this experimental manipulation should be more effective for highly dependent children than for less dependent ones.

As in many experiments on social interaction, there is a difference between boys and girls. For girls, nurturance withdrawal led to more effective learning than did consistent nurturance. Among the boys, only the highly dependent ones showed this result, whereas the boys low on dependency showed the reverse.

This simple experiment seems to indicate the power that can be exercised by the parent through withdrawal of nurturance once a dependent relation is well established. It also points to some complexities in the process which need further exploration.

It will be recalled that in one of the experiments on imitation (see Bandura & Huston, 1961, on p. 430), children who had experienced a series of two nurturant sessions with the model were more likely to imitate her in the experimental situation. Thus, the fostering of dependency in the child not only makes him responsive to direct reinforcements, but also makes him more susceptible to acquiring behavior patterns that the parent models for him.

Another feature in the development of dependency is the generalization of dependent behaviors to people other than the mother. This spread of dependency attachments results partly from the fact that the mother is not the child's sole caretaker; the father, the baby-sitter, and the nursery school teacher can all build their own attachments to the child. Another source of generalized dependency extends from the mother to other adults, particularly other women, who have a similar role. The power of an adult to dispense rewards and punishments may be an important basis for generalized dependency. The mother hastens this dependency when she tells the child to mind the baby-sitter while she is gone, or to pay attention to the nursery school teacher when he is at school.

Another complication in the development of dependency is that almost as soon as it is established, it must begin to be unlearned: The child must begin to be self-reliant. The parents may adopt a strategy of ignoring the child if he cries and fusses when nothing is wrong. As the child becomes older, he must learn gradually not to cling too closely or be too dependent. Parents achieve this in various ways, of course. One strategy is merely to ignore attention-getting behavior when it becomes too persistent and obnoxious. According to the principles of learning, such techniques should gradually teach the child to discriminate between legitimate and illegitimate bids for attention, and should ultimately extinguish illegitimate ones.

Whereas persistent nonreinforcement of dependency probably does eventually decrease it, there are other consequences to be expected during the process. The withholding of reinforcement, after a history of reinforcement, is frustrating. Thus, some emotional responses, perhaps aggression, might well be expected. In addition, we have seen from the experiment of Gewirtz (and also Hartup; see p. 443) that the withholding of attention after it has been freely given makes the child more responsive to attention, and more inclined to bid for it. Thus, the predicted course of events if some specific attention-getting behavior were suddenly to be nonreinforced would be a period of emotional upset, perhaps aggression, temporary increase in dependent behavior, and finally a decrease, as the discrimination between appropriate and inappropriate behavior were established. If, instead of complete nonreinforcement, the parent sometimes responded to the undesirable attention-getting, then the principles of partial reinforcement would apply. Much the same temporary emotionality and increase in dependency would be predicted, but instead of eventually disappearing, the child might show persistent and highly resistant attention-getting of the undesired form. Another possibility is that the parent, attempting to extinguish bids for attention, may ignore all the unwanted attention-getting bids except a few that are so violent and intense that they compel attention—temper tantrums, perhaps. Then the child may learn to be violent in his bids for attention.

Instead of merely ignoring undesirable attention-getting behavior, parents may actively punish it; this is the easy and impulsive way to respond if the parent becomes annoyed at the child's persistent bids for attention. Such punishment should, according to the theory, have two effects. First, it should teach the child to inhibit attention-getting behavior. Second, it should create an anxiety about dependency. Intense dependency anxiety may reduce the efficacy of the parent's use of affection, attention-giving, and approval in socializing other sorts of behavior. Bandura and Walters, who first formulated the concept of dependency anxiety, found that it was much commoner in excessively aggressive adolescents than in a control group. It displays itself in a defiant refusal to seek advice, to talk over problems with parents, or to behave affectionately toward them (Bandura & Walters, 1959).

One puzzling kind of child behavior has been hypothesized to result from the conflict of dependency and dependency anxiety. This is so-called *negative attention-getting*. The behavior itself is easily recognized. The child performs a whole series of irritating mischievous actions, each so clearly noticeable that there is no possibility that the child is accidentally misbehaving. Ordinarily, children who break a rule because they want very much to perform the forbidden action do so surreptitiously. Negative attention-getting is, however, an effort to attract attention not by asking for it, but indirectly by performing actions that are bound to bring adult attention although it will be disapproving. The explanation suggested from social-learning theory is that such behavior captures attention and thus satisfies dependency, but does so in a way that does not arouse dependency anxiety. It may very well arouse a fear of punishment, but perhaps for some children that is preferable to overt dependency.

It is good to recognize that not all social-learning theorists necessarily agree on all the details of the theory. As it happens, the evidence for the hypothesized effects of punishing dependency is not perfectly clear. There are data to show that punishment of dependency in the child does not always result in any decrease in overt dependency bids. In fact, the first and commonest response to the adult's rejection of dependency even by punishment is for the child to try even more vigorously to obtain attention.

Thus, although Bandura and Walters found that extremely aggressive adolescents showed inhibition of dependency and signs of dependency anxiety, Bandura (1960) in a similar study of preadolescent aggressive children found a more complicated situation. The parents of the aggressive children, like those of the aggressive adolescents, did tend to discourage and punish dependency. But there was now consistent correlation between parental punitiveness toward dependency and its frequency of appearance. In the case of aggressive boys, punishment of dependency by the mother was related to increased dependency on adults. In fact, the preadolescent aggressive boys showed a great deal of dependency behavior toward adults and also peers.

Perhaps it is this combination of dependency that is punished which produces the dependency anxiety and inhibition of dependency in the adolescent group. Whiting has hypothesized, however, that it is the combination of rewarding and punishing dependency that creates a dependency drive, and that the conflict between dependency and dependency anxiety adds to the strength of the drive. This is called the *conflict-drive hypothesis* and has been proposed as a general thesis for all sorts of conflicts, not merely dependency conflict.

Several different outcomes of both punishing and rewarding dependency seem theoretically possible and it is important to learn under what conditions each occurs. Every parent, for example, is inconsistent to some degree in his child rearing; for example, he may welcome bids for affection some days but not feel like it on other days.

It seems as if sometimes the result is merely that the child learns to discriminate the times when his attention-getting efforts are welcome and when they are not. The ability to respond to other people's moods is a valuable one. There are apparently other circumstances, however, when this inconsistent response does produce a conflict within the child over dependency. One might guess that such a result would occur if there were no cues permitting the child to develop the discrimination between one mood and another. In still other cases, the condition could be viewed as a partial reinforcement schedule and the result would be very persistent dependency attempts, difficult to extinguish. This discussion points to the fact that our understanding of dependency is far from complete.

SUCKING AND WEANING. Within the general study of dependent behavior, there is a separate stream of research in the study of nursing, sucking, and weaning. The investigations belong to the study of dependency, because nursing is one of the most satisfying kinds of mother-child interaction in early infancy and so it must contribute to the development of dependency. Weaning is also related to dependency because it is an early parental demand for independence. The relation of sucking and dependency is also suggested by the common belief that persistent thumb-sucking is an index of dependency in the child and that it provides a kind of do-it-yourself security for the child.

The theoretical issue that instigated the research on sucking is whether sucking is a primary drive or whether it develops in conjunction with nursing and acquires secondary reward properties. David M. Levy (1934, 1937) has advanced the hypothesis on the basis of his clinical experience that sucking is an infantile need that is independent of hunger. It is possible therefore that children can get their food so rapidly that their hunger for food is satisfied before their hunger for sucking. Levy's hypothesis is that thumb-sucking and other nonnutritional oral habits in infants are signs of insufficient sucking. He experimentally investigated this hypothesis by feeding pups with nipples that had different-sized holes in them. It required less sucking for the pup to get his fill from a nipple with a large-sized hole than a small one. He predicted and found that pups who did get milk very rapidly did show more accessory oral activity such as chewing on slippers and table legs.

An alternative hypothesis is that the sucking becomes pleasurable because it is associated with food satisfaction. According to this hypothesis, nonnutritive sucking is pleasurable only if it is preceded by a steady history of sucking in association with eating. Sears and Wise

(1950) investigated the two hypotheses in a study that took advantage of knowing that one group of pediatricians customarily recommended to their patients that the infant be spoon fed from birth; these pediatricians said that spoon feeding required the mother to hold the baby and personally administer the food, whereas bottle feeding could be done more impersonally, and they believed that the mother-child contact was very important.

If sucking deprivation leads to thumb-sucking, these babies should have shown a great deal of it. If the satisfaction of thumb-sucking depends on its association with feeding, these babies should have shown little of it—theoretically none. The results of the study are somewhat ambiguous, clearly supporting neither hypothesis. There was fairly clear evidence that the strength of the sucking response itself increased more in the infants who nursed and that infants who were weaned in the first week or so showed less disturbance over weaning than those weaned later in the first year. However, all showed about the same amount of thumb-sucking. This study as well as a later one (Sears, Maccoby, & Levin) also found that the child's disturbance at weaning was greater for children weaned at about a year than those weaned much later. Thus, both hypotheses received some support and some disconfirmation.

According to social-learning theory, thumb-sucking might well be interpreted as an action that reduces the anxiety of being separated from the parent. Because of its close association with the satisfying action of nursing and with the presence of the mother, the act of sucking can theoretically acquire reinforcement properties of its own. It might be a self-administered reinforcement. The fact that the child thumb-sucks would indicate a temporary separation anxiety; it might or might not suggest a long-lasting insecurity.

In summary, dependency develops from the association between the mother's caretaking behavior and the satisfaction of the child's drives in infancy. The pleasurableness of sucking develops the same way, according to social learning theory. The results are attention-getting behavior patterns and signs of distress at separation from the caretaker.

The later development of dependency reflects the conflict over it. Dependency is desirable, but so is independence. Thus, children may develop any of several patterns of dependency, avoidance of dependency, or strong dependency drives with inhibition of some of its manifestations. The pattern the child develops depends on the balance among reinforcements, withholding reinforcements, and punishments for dependency as well as on the surrounding circumstances.

Aggression

Aggression is perhaps the most difficult behavior system to explain, regardless of the theoretical approach taken. In the development of Freudian theory, we saw that Freud finally felt compelled to postulate a basic death instinct to account for aggression. He felt dissatisfied with the various alternatives that would tie aggression to the frustration of other instincts. In the book *Frustration and Aggression* (1939), however, all aggression is conceived to be rooted in frustration. Furthermore, aggression is taken as an inevitable consequence of frustration. It is not seen as an innate response, but as a learned one acquired through the rewards it brings.

The puzzling problem is to account for the appearance of aggression and hostility in situations where no specific frustration seems to instigate the aggressive action, and where by no stretch of the imagination can the aggression be seen as an attempt to remove the frustration. In everyday life we see examples of apparently pointless hostility, vandalism, and destruction, which seem to indicate that the individual behaving this way had an all-pervasive hatred of other people. Since such aggression seems to provide little reward, and frequently seems to bring the aggressor unhappiness, the ordinarily adaptive function of social learning as it appears in dependency, and the development of conscience and other systems, seems to be absent. One would think that aggression would be unlearned through hard experience, but obviously it is not; in fact, it often seems to be solidified rather than inhibited by harsh consequences. This is what makes aggression such a puzzle.

There is an innate behavior pattern that is a precursor of aggression. This is the crying and writhing and flailing of the infant when he is hurt and interferred with. This behavior pattern appears early in the child's life and is often called *anger*. The infant is not, however, angry *at* anything; he is just angry. His anger is an emotional state and the circumstances that arouse it, restraint of his body, interference with his activity, and intrusion on his comfort, are classified as frustrations.

Several things must occur before anger becomes genuine aggression. First, the behavior must be directed to hurting or damaging others; second, hurt to other people must become the reinforcement for the behavior.

An early step in this process is the stabilization of the anger response to certain stimulus situations through reinforcement. The response is sometimes reinforced by virtue of the fact that the writhing and flailing may remove the painful stimulus. In addition, as the child's motor control develops he pushes away intruding stimuli like the wash cloth that is scrubbing his ears or the intruding spoon when he is not hungry. The response is directed at the intruding stimulus, although crying and flailing are still prominent. Finally, anger is a signal that brings help from the mother, and this can serve to reinforce it. In other words, the precursors of hostile behavior and dependent behavior are partly alike. A pure distress signal may bring aid and relief from the mother; an angry yell and thrashing around may be annoying to the mother, but it still beings relief.

According to social-learning theory, the fact that angry behavior produces annoyance or pain in the mother is an important step in the acquisition of aggression. If the mother is annoyed while she cares for the baby, the signs of pain, irritation, or anger in another person become associated in the baby's mind with satisfaction of drives. Since such stimulus signs from other people are defined as the reward for aggression, and since the causing of pain is a part of the definition of aggression, the theory must account for the original association of pain, distress, and injury in other people with drive reduction.

It is easy to underestimate the actual efficacy of aggression. In particular circumstances in the home, aggression may be a more effective means of social control than dependency. A burst of real anger and annoyance may get through to the mother who is busy with other things in a way that a less forceful signal would not; anger can be a signal to the mother that the child is getting to the end of his rope. Although it seems to most parents that the child would be far better off to express his wants in a nonirritating way, his anger may indeed be more effective.

The usual response to aggression and anger in a young child is to cope with his problem, although this reinforcement is often accompanied by scolding and parental hostility. The behavior of the parent is not likely to extinguish the impulse to aggression; instead, it simultaneously tends to reinforce it and to create anxiety about it. Thus, aggressiveness in the child as an instrumental action for removing frustrations develops in a particularly conflicted way. It is reinforced, yet it is also punished. The child grows up more-or-less ready to respond angrily to frustration and also more-or-less inclined to inhibit the angry response because it arouses anxiety and fear of punishment.

Even if anger has been associated with removal of the frustration, it also seems to occur readily in conditions where it is ineffective. Some aggression, furthermore, seems to be self-rewarding and to occur even in the absence of any frustration. Every child on occasion displays unprovoked hostility in the form of teasing, ridiculing, pestering animals, or direct physical attacks. How does social-learning theory explain this gratuitous unprovoked and unadaptive aggression?

One explanation is the familiar process of secondary reinforcement. If anger and aggression are often enough associated with removal of frustration, then the stimulus feedback from injuring other people and causing them pain or embarrassment can become rewarding in its own right.

There is also another mechanism by which aggression can be self-rewarding, even in the absence of any instigation. This arises from the conflict-drive hypothesis (see p. 432). If one is angry but at the same time inhibits the expression of that anger, one is in conflict; this conflict itself adds frustration to the situations. Under these circumstances, the overt expression of anger, letting off steam, can result in a net drive reduction, even though one component of the situation, anxiety or fear of retaliation, may have increased in strength. At least the conflict is gone and the individual can feel a real relief in blowing his top and expressing his hostility.

DISPLACEMENT OF AGGRESSION. Aside from the problem of explaining how aggressive behavior is learned, there is also the puzzle of accounting for its object. If aggression were always directed toward the frustrating object or person, it would be easier to understand; however, one of the common features of aggression is that it is displaced and directed against something that is not directly frustrating. A dramatic example of displacement of aggression occurs when a group's hostility turns on some unfortunate scapegoat. Whenever a group is frustrated and has poor morale, one of its members may somehow attract the hostility of the group. Everyone turns on him, finds everything he does wrong, blames him for all its troubles, and finally makes his life so uncomfortable that he leaves the group (Lippitt & White, 1939).

Aggression is not the only kind of behavior that is displaced, but it is one of the most striking; therefore, we shall use it to illustrate the mechanism by which social-learning theory explains all displacement. This formulation of displacement was first developed by Miller (1948). The displacement mechanism is a special case of generalization, a phenomenon which has been known for many years and has been confirmed over and over again. If aggression is learned as a response to some stimulus objects, it would be expected to be generalized to other similar stimuli. However, this is not sufficient to account for displacement, because displaced aggression is not displayed toward the original object that aroused it, but toward some other object.

Miller's hypothesis is that displacement is the result of the counteracting forces of excitation and inhibition. In the home the child is spurred to aggression by the parent who provides the primary reinforcement for it. At the same time, however, the parent punishes expression of aggression and forces the child to inhibit the response. In most families the inhibition is strong enough so that the child is rarely, if ever, directly hostile to the parent. This is illustrated in Figure 15-1, where the relative strengths of the aggression and fixation are shown at the point marked *P,* for parent.

Both the tendency to respond aggressively and the inhibition of the response generalize to other stimuli that are similar to the parent. These might be other adults, dolls representing the parent, or other people like the school teacher who have authoritative roles. There are many possible dimensions of generalization.

The essential point of the explanation is that inhibitory tendencies have a narrower range of generalization than the responses they inhibit. This empirical finding has been confirmed in a variety of studies. Hence, in Figure 15-1, the generalization curve of inhibition is

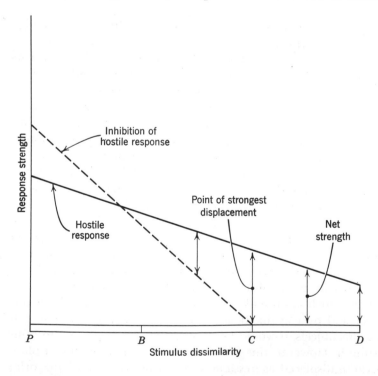

Figure 15-1. A model of displacement. (after Bandura & Walters, 1963)

steeper than the curve of excitation. The result of these different slopes is that at some point the curves cross. At points farther away from *P* than the crossover point, the aggressive response is higher than the inhibitory tendency, while in the region within the crossings, inhibition is stronger than excitation. Thus, in terms of overt behavior, we would expect that the aggressive response would not appear toward the parent nor other stimulus objects that were too similar, but toward some more dissimilar object.

It is easy to see the effect of different levels of inhibition and excitation on the amount of displacement. The higher the strength of the inhibition relative to excitation at the point of origin, the farther out will be the crossover point, and thus the remoter will be the objects that actually receive the displaced aggression. Notice also that the aggression is relatively weak at these distant points, regardless of its being greater than the inhibitory tendency. Thus, the aggressive response to the displaced object would be expected to be mild, delayed, and perhaps only symbolic (Figure 15-1).

There is some evidence that this kind of displacement does occur in children's doll play. Sears (1953) related the punitiveness of the mother to the frequency of aggressive action in nursery school and to the frequency of aggression in doll play. The curves are shown in Figure 15-2. The children of parents who are nonpunitive showed little aggression in either school or doll play, reflecting the existence of only little frustration to produce aggression. The children of moderately punitive mothers showed increased aggression both in school and in doll play. The children of highly punitive mothers showed a great deal of aggression in doll play but less than either other group in school. If maternal punitiveness resulted in marked inhibition of aggression in these children, the results could be explained by assuming that the adults in the nursery school were sufficiently similar to the mother so that inhibition toward them was greater than aggression. The dolls, however, were dissimilar, despite some similarities, so that they served to instigate uninhibited aggression.

THE ROLE OF IMITATION IN LEARNING AGGRESSION. Not all social-learning theorists agree that the learning of aggression is primarily a result of the child's experiences with frustration. Bandura and Walters (1963) believe that the evidence for the frustration-aggression hypothesis is not strong, and that most aggression can be accounted for by the fact that the child learns aggressive responses through imitation and that these responses are directly reinforced.

Bandura and Walters point to the fact that many actual responses

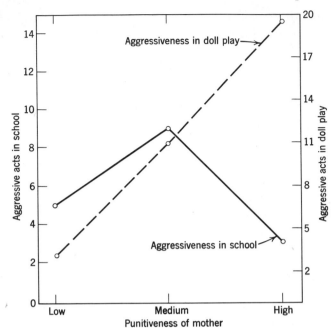

Figure 15-2. Relations of aggressiveness to punitiveness. (After R. R. Sears, *Amer. Psych.*, 6, 1953, 476–483.)

observed in aggressive episodes also occur in situations where there is no frustration and no intent to harm. Frequently, the responses are merely intense and violent forms that would not be considered agressive at all if they were performed more gently. For example, the touching, pulling, and tugging that frequently occur as part of attention-getting can appear in a more violent form of hitting, kicking, and yanking that seem to be acts of aggression rather than bids for attention.

These authors point to the fact that a father may spend time in playing active games with his child, perhaps kicking a football, punching a punchball, or tackling and roughhousing. He performs these acts himself and encourages the child to perform them too. He reinforces the child when he hits the punchball very hard or when he tackles effectively, or may actually compete with the child. Thus, the child acquires in a nonfrustrating situation many responses that can become aggressive in response to a frustration.

Several experiments (Patterson, Ludwig, & Sonoda, 1961; Cowan & Walters, 1963; Walters & Brown, 1963) all show that children who are reinforced for hitting an inflated doll or a specially devised "Bobo" clown that records the intensity of the punches, are more likely to respond in this way in a subsequent competitive physical-contact game or in free play. Furthermore, children on a partial reinforcement schedule showed more aggressive responses than those on a continuous reinforcement schedule.

Not only the specific responses, but also other forms of aggression can be made more frequent by reinforcement of aggression. Thus children who were reinforced for calling a doll "bad" or "dirty" were more likely in a later testing session to select an animated toy in which one doll hit another on the head than children who had been reinforced for calling a doll "clean" or "good." The reinforcement of verbal aggression resulted in an increase in nonverbal aggression.

Of course, children may also imitate responses they have seen a model perform. In some cases the model's behavior occurs in a nonfrustrative situation, while in other cases the model behaves in a way that would be called aggressive. These experiments were reported in the section of imitation (see p. 428). In all cases it is possible to show increases in aggression by the children exposed to the aggressive model.

There is evidence from several field studies that parents of children who are aggressive are themselves likely to behave aggressively and thus provide the child with models of aggression. Also, such parents are likely to actively encourage the child's aggression, especially toward people other than themselves.

A study by Bandura and Walters (1959) illustrates these points. The researchers compared 26 highly aggressive adolescent boys with 26 control boys. The aggressive boys were selected from adolescents who were under the supervision of probation services and who had a history of repetitive aggressive behavior. The control group was selected from boys designated by school counselors as neither markedly aggressive nor markedly withdrawn. The two groups were the same age, came from similar socioeconomic backgrounds, and were equal in intelligence. The mother and father of each of the 52 boys were interviewed; the boy himself was interviewed and each boy was also administered a test to assess his reactions to socially deviant behavior.

The aggressive boys showed much more direct aggression toward adults outside the home, particularly teachers. They also were more aggressive toward peers. They were not, generally speaking, more aggressive toward their parents, although the aggressive boys reported more feelings of hostility toward their fathers. Outside the home, the aggressive boys also showed more indirect aggression, but the sharpest differences between the aggressive and control groups were in direct aggression. For the aggressive boys the amount of direct physical aggression exceeded the amount of verbal and indirect aggression, whereas the reverse was true for the control group (see Figure 15-3).

The most striking source of these differences is that the parents of the aggressive boys encourage their children to be aggressive. They believe the boys should know how to fight and should stand up for their rights. The fathers in the aggressive group also tended to use physical punishment and deprivation of privileges as disciplinary techniques, while fathers in the control group tended to use reasoning more. Finally, the parents, especially the fathers, in the aggressive group, were less accepting of dependency from the boy than the fathers in the control group.

We see in this study many of the elements described earlier in the social learning theory of aggression: higher frustration, more punitiveness, more reinforcement from aggressive responses, and the use of physical punishment. There are also differences between the two groups in the development of conscience, but that discussion must wait until the section on conscience and self-control.

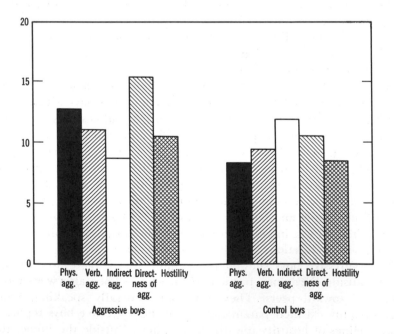

Figure 15-3. Comparison of aggressive and control boys on different types of aggression.

PHYSICAL PUNISHMENT. One reasonable consistent finding in studies of the effects of child-rearing practices is that in some way parental punitiveness toward aggression is associated with higher aggression in the child. This is especially true of physical punishment of the child (Glueck, 1950; Bandura, 1960; Sears, Maccoby, & Levin, 1957).

This is a finding that has not been easily explained; the social-learning explanation of it will be clearer after we have discussed the concept of identification in a later section. In general, however, it is concerned with the role of the parent as a model which the child copies. Thus, the parent who is overtly aggressive toward people in general, and toward the child in particular, provides a model of aggressive responsiveness and lack of inhibition, at the same time that he frustrates and angers the child. The child's overt aggression is counteracted by his punishment for it, but parents who sometimes punish aggression severely are not necessarily consistently punitive toward it. Two studies have investigated the variables of permissiveness toward the child's expression of aggression and punitiveness toward such expression. The two are negatively correlated, but the correlation is only $-.46$ in one study (Sears, Maccoby, & Levin) and $-.61$ for mothers and $-.26$ for fathers in another study (Bandura & Walters). The fact that the correlations are not nearer to -1.00 reflects the many ways of being nonpermissive of aggression in children without punishing them for it. and the ways of punishing aggression which do not use physical means closely resembling the child's own aggressive behavior.

SUMMARY. It is apparent that the social-learning theory of the development of aggression is not completely coherent; different people within the social-learning tradition emphasize different aspects of the problem. Nevertheless, the diverse emphases are not incompatible in many places.

First, it seems clear that many of the actions employed for aggressive purposes can be acquired in circumstances that do not involve frustration, anger, or aggression. Thus, a variety of intense and violent responses can be acquired by the child as part of his repertoire of behavior. Furthermore, according to social-learning theory, these responses move up on the hierarchy of potential responses by virtue of their being reinforced or displayed by a model who commands imitative behavior. To some extent they are actually acquired, but to some extent the learning experiences merely free them from inhibitory influences and makes them more available.

The problem of course, is how these responses acquired in one setting become instigated in frustration and conflict situations. This can be partly explained by the fact that they are observed not only in nonaggressive situations but also in aggressive ones. They may be acquired and reinforced in playful situations, then observed in the parent's behavior during genuinely aggressive episodes. Thus, they become available to the child when he is aggressive. When these responses are actually performed by the child they are reinforced or not reinforced, or more likely, are differentially reinforced and punished. For many highly aggressive children, it seems as if they are reinforced when directed toward other people than the parent and punished when directed toward the parent. Furthermore, they are much more likely to be reinforced in boys than girls.

Another problem is how the class of actions called aggressive becomes clustered so that aggressive behavior of one form generalizes to another form. Presumably this is the result of mediated generalization. In other words, the child learns the common label "aggressive" to a wide variety of actions when performed in the appropriate circumstances. The definition of aggression employed in *Frustration and Aggression* tacitly involves the notion of intent (see p. 432) for discussion), and nobody has been able to define aggression objectively yet realistically. Breaking into a cabin to escape from a blizzard is not aggressive, whereas the same action performed for revenge upon the owner is. Researchers in social learning have not been very interested in discovering the characteristics of an action which make people label it aggressive, but the problem is a reasonable one within the framework of S-R theory. People do show considerable, although not perfect, agreement in what they label aggression. As a part of social learning the child acquires the rules for labeling aggression as well as the acts that serve aggressive purposes.

Finally, the significance of infantile anger seems to be assumed in social-learning theory. Just how these early emotional responses fit into the theory of the development of aggression is not clear, but presumably they are relevant.

Thus, the child with his innate responses to interference gradually acquires responses that can serve aggressive purposes. He also learns the meaning of the label, so that he knows why he and other people are behaving in the way called aggressive in his culture. He is also taught to perform or to inhibit these responses in the appropriate circumstances by imitation and by direct reinforcement and punishment.

The Development of Conscience and Self-Control

THE ROLE OF IDENTIFICATION. Freud introduced the concept of identification into psychological literature. As we have explained, social-learning theorists have used Freudian theory as a source of hypotheses that can be couched in the language of S-R theory.

Identification begins with a preestablished dependency. As we have seen, dependency is marked by contentment when the child is with his mother and is being taken care of by her, and distress when he is separated from her or when she is present but not paying attention to him. Dependency is also characterized by the performance of a variety of behaviors that "ask" the mother to perform her customary caretaking activities which have become satisfying. The behavioral indices of dependency are attention-seeking—positive or negative—reassurance-seeking, touching, clinging, or staying near some particular person.

The facts that the theory of identification attempts to explain are that the child develops the ability to depend on himself, to control himself, and even to punish himself for transgressions. The various encouragements, instigations, and controls for behavior that are first carried by the parent become internalized so that the individual functions as his own caretaker. This aspect of identification is called *internalization* of social rules. More generally, identification involves imitation of another person's behavior, mannerisms, beliefs, and values.

One mechanism underlying this internalization and imitation is simple indeed according to social-learning theory. The child reinforces himself by saying to himself the approving words his parents use, controls himself by warning himself of the consequences of his acts, and punishes himself by reproving his own behavior.

This mechanism is even employed to account for parrots learning to talk, suggesting that when a bird becomes attached to its caretaker, it suffers a sort of separation anxiety when its owner leaves, and that repeating certain remarks that the caretaker had made is comforting.

With children, the stimuli emitted by the caretaker are reinforcing and satisfying even if they are produced by the child himself. This imitative behavior generalizes to an overall tendency to act like the caretaker. A generalized imitation of another person is called identification, and this particular type of identification corresponds to what Freud called *"anaclitic identification."* "Anaclitic" means dependent or "leaning upon."

Identification, then, primarily involves the imitation of another person. As we learned in the section on imitation, imitation is a prevalent phenomenon and need not involve a long history of dependency— although dependent children are more imitative than highly independent ones. Some social-learning theorists argue that identification is nothing but imitation (Bandura & Huston, 1961) but there are those who would give some special place to identification. If identification is different, its uniqueness is that it is a very generalized imitation of many characteristics of another special person. It involves not only the direct copying of selected performances but also the acquisition of another person's mannerisms, style, and other incidental features of his behavior. Finally, identification also involves the acceptance of the other person's values and beliefs.

Some social-learning theorists believe identification is the mechanism by which the child acquires certain important traits, which result in the child's behaving more like the adults around him. One result of identification is the development of conscience, involving the acquisition of the culture's moral standards, resistance to the temptation to break them, emotional upset and guilt over one's own transgressions, and disapproval of other people who violate these standards (prosocial aggression). A second consequence of identification is the acquisition of the roles and behavior patterns appropriate to one's own sex. The third is a more general kind of growing up—behaving like an adult, doing adult jobs, and achieving adult goals. Each of these identifications, of course, involves acquiring a large set of specific behavior patterns.

The boy's acquisition of a sex role involves special problems. If the boy is to become masculine through identification, it is necessary that he identify with his father or some other male figure. Since the mother is the primary caretaker of boys as well as girls, the mechanism of anaclitic identification would result in identification with the mother and actually retard masculinization of the boy. Freud described another mechanism of identification that applied particularly to boys, a defensive identification motivated by fear and anxiety (1923). Anna Freud gave this mechanism the label *identification with the aggressor*. Both kinds of identification are defensive, since they represent behavior mechanisms that reduce anxiety, but the defensive quality of the identification with the aggressor is especially clear. This type of identification occurs because the boy has ambivalent feelings toward his father: he feels some real love and affection and desire to be like him, but also feels rivalry with him as a competitor for the mother's affection and care. By identifying himself with the father, the boy reduces the anxiety engendered by his feelings of hostility. Identification with the aggressor is therefore particularly relevant for the acquisition of the masculine sex role. It also underlies the inhibition of aggressive impulses toward the father and turning them into self-aggressive guilt feelings.

IDENTIFICATION STUDY. A recent extensive study, *Identification and Child Rearing*, attempts to test all these consequences of identification. Sears, Rau, and Alpert (1965) sought to measure the variety of outcomes of a hypothetical identification process to see if they were correlated. Would children who showed one sign of identification also tend to show its other symptoms?

This study was carried out on a group of 40 children, 21 boys and 19 girls. These children were observed in a nursery school situation, and in a variety of experimental situations; their parents were interviewed about both the child's behavior at home and the parent's child-rearing practices. All of these observations were categorized and many different behavioral variables were scored for each child—several hundred, in fact.

Three main areas of behavior were measured for each child in the free play situation: dependency, aggression, and spontaneously adoption of such adult role behavior as helping with juice and cleaning up. To study the child's responses to particular instigations, the experimenters observed him in several experimental settings. One of these placed the mother and child together in several situations requiring interaction. One situation was designed to study the child's attention-getting behavior and other sorts of dependency toward his mother. The child was given toys to play with while the mother was given a task that would keep her busy; such a situation would incite attention-seeking behavior and also permit observations of the mother's responsiveness to it. Another situation involved playing a messy game to see how much the mother insisted on cleanliness and how much she tried to control the child's behavior. In a third situation, the child and his mother talked to each other over the telephone; the child was instructed to be himself and also to pretend he was various other people.

Still another experimental situation was designed to measure "rule quoting" by the child. He was left alone in a room with many nice toys that he was told he should not play with; then, while the experimenter was out, a younger child came into the room and began to play with the forbidden toys. Still another experimental situation measured the child's resistance to temptation. A final situation was designed to create guilt, in order to observe the child's responses to his own transgression. The child was told to watch a hamster carefully; then, as soon as the child failed to keep his eyes glued to the animal, it was dropped out of its cage through a trap door. From the child's point of view, he had lost the hamster. How would he respond?

These same variables were also assessed in doll-play fantasy scored by standardized doll-play technique.

By means of this large study, the experimenters measured a variety of behavioral variables which should be closely related. Including a number of independent measures of each of the major variables was an important advance over many earlier studies, because it permitted the discovery that the basic variables were not unitary factors, and that various symptoms of dependency or aggression or identification did not correlate. Basically, eight different measures of dependency emerged:

Observations in the free-play situation of the nursery school

1. Negative attention seeking—getting attention by disruption, aggressive activity with minimal provocation, defiance, or oppositional behavior.
2. Reassurance seeking—apologizing, asking unnecessary permission, or seeking protection, comfort, consolation, help, or guidance.
3. Positive attention seeking—seeking praise, seeking to join an in-group by inviting cooperative activity, or actually interrupting a group activity in progress.
4. Touching and holding—nonaggressive touching, holding, and clasping onto others.
5. Being near—following or standing near a particular child or a group of children or teacher.

Ratings based on mother-child interaction

6. Overall rating of the amount of dependency of all kinds during the two half-hour sessions.
7. Frequency of bids for attention while the mother was busy.
8. Frequency of bids for attention while mother was attentive to the child.

It would not be expected that all these measures should correlate positively with one another. For boys, however, none of these measures was significantly related to any of the others. For girls, there was a slight intercorrelation. There is some suggestion that *touching and holding* may be less mature forms of *positive attention-seeking,* but this is far from clear. In terms of the original intent of the study, the data reveal an embarrassing complexity that is not consistent with the way the original hypothesis was formulated. Dependency was hypothesized to be an antecedent for identification, but if none of the behavioral symptoms of dependency are related to each other, the hypothesis must be rephrased.

Similar problems emerge in other areas of the study.

The original hypothesis was that the five classes of behavior—*taking an adult role, prosocial aggression, appropriate sex-role behavior, resistance to temptation* and *emotional upset over transgression*—would be correlated, since they were all, by hypothesis, products of primary identification. Nevertheless, the results show that even within the classes of behavior, the separate measures are not highly correlated.

For girls, there are modest intercorrelations within the sets of measures of each of the four major variables, whereas for boys, only *aggression* and *resistance to temptation* appear to have any unity as variables. When the correlations between the major variables are examined, girls show a generally positive relation among all the measures except *resistance to temptation* and *emotional upset,* but boys show none at all.

Since it is clear that the various measures of dependency are not highly intercorrelated, the relation of dependency to identification must be studied variable by variable. If *seeking positive attention* is taken as a measure of dependency, then in girls it belongs to the same cluster of variables as *taking an adult role; prosocial aggression, femininity,* and *emotional upset following a transgression.* For boys, however, there is little relation between *positive attention-seeking* and any of the other hypothesized results of identification.

Furthermore, four parent variables were hypothesized to be related to the development of identification: *nurturance and warmth, love-oriented discipline* (as opposed to physical punishment and use of tangible rewards), a *high level of demand on the child for mature behavior,* and the parent's *holding up models of good behavior for the child to imitate.* These variables are themselves complex; parents differ from one situation to another in child-rearing practices and the two parents of any child do not necessarily agree. The original hypothesis can hardly be tested in any clear-cut fashion. In some cases, however, the data do clearly indicate a failure of confirmation or even suggest that the opposite hypothesis seems more supported.

The correlation between the child-rearing variables and the various measures of dependency shows that the expected relationship to nurturance is generally disconfirmed. High demands on the part of the parents for mature behavior in areas studied show some relationship to the dependent variables, but it is by no means unequivocal. Love-oriented discipline is negatively rather than positively correlated with dependency in girls, and shows little or no correlation for boys. The use of models in child-rearing does seem to have a number of positive relationships to various aspects of mature child behavior.

All in all, however, the theory does not come out too badly as far as girls are concerned. There is a certain unity, although not strong, among the various measures of identification. There is evidence that parents who make high demands on girls for mature behavior generally obtain it. For boys, however, the whole structure of variables seems to be different and seems not to fit with the hypothesis of primary identification.

One of the difficult problems in such research is that the multiple meanings and significance of the same behavior and of different behavior patterns are classified together. For example, in this research, the kinds of behavior that were intended to measure the child's taking adult roles in the nursery school turned out to be behavior generally typifying feminine adult roles. The adult-like activities available to children in a nursery school are behaviors such as cleaning up, passing out juice, and comforting younger children. These are adult types of behavior, but they are mostly maternal. Thus, for boys, the measure of taking adult roles also tended to measure femininity. It may be that most of the adult-like tasks at home are also tinged with femininity, and so taking adult roles may involve the boy in a conflict with his masculinity but not reflect at all his desire to grow up and become adult. Similarly, dependency may be an important source of reinforcement, but at the same time dependent behavior is more appropriate to the feminine than the masculine role. Hence, positive attention-seeking in girls appears in this study to be part of being feminine.

There is no conflict among the measures for girls and they can appear as part of a single syndrome.

The results of the study led the investigators beyond their original hypotheses to more complicated formulations, but it did not force them to reject the basic notion of identification. One way to analyze the data more searchingly is to investigate subgroups of subjects where these different variables are more independent of one another. For example, what are the antecedents of the girls who appear relatively masculine? It turns out that the variables marking this type of behavior, *negative attention-seeking, injury to objects,* and *masculinity,* are all related to the important role the father plays in their upbringing. Fathers of masculine girls tend to have taken care of their daughters during infancy more than the average father does; they were relatively permissive of sex play and aggression in their daughters, and tended to be warm, empathic, and emotionally demonstrative and to use praise rather than punishment. In this cluster, we find many of the characteristics predicted by identification theory, but displayed by the father rather than the mother. Since the father is a man, the girls acquire some masculine characteristics. For them, the identification hypothesis holds up very well. In the total group, they merely add to the confusion, since they deviate from the more common pattern of chacteristics among girls.

Similarly, if the antecedents of femininity in boys are examined, they are dependent on the mother; she rewards their dependency like fathers of masculine girls. She is also permissive, but not about sex and aggression; her permissiveness shows up in a leniency about household restrictions and standards of obedience.

Furthermore, in both the mother of feminized boys and the fathers of masculinized girls, there is often an estrangement from the spouse. It seems as if the parent in question takes over child-rearing responsibility from the other. Perhaps then the home is more simply structured and the identification mechanism is less complicated.

If we turn now to findings about girls, we find that the antecedents of femininity form a fairly coherent pattern. First, the mother rewards dependency, which is itself an aspect of femininity. The pattern of femininity is consistent with the sex and with the reward of dependency. The mother is trying to make her daughters feminine and she is feminine herself. The things she values, because of her own femininity, are consistent with the kinds of behavior she wants her daughters to show. Thus, for girls in general, dependency on the mother and her rewards for such dependency are positively correlated with femininity.

With boys, the problem is more complicated. The mother has a picture of the masculine personality and to some degree she wants her sons to be masculine. At the same time, she does not really value some of the masculine traits, especially overt sexuality and overt aggressiveness. Thus, if she had complete control over child rearing, she would find it hard not to discourage aggressiveness and sexuality in her sons. For this reason, sons from father-absent families tend to be feminized. In two-parent families, the father must counter the mother's influence to some degree and establish masculine traits in the boy. Femininity in boys comes about not because it is so much specifically rewarded by the mother as because the father fails to establish dependency and reward masculine traits.

As Sears, Rau, and Alpert summarize it:

The general principle may be stated that the *strength of the basic feminine personality pattern in girls varies with the amount of rewarded dependency by the mother, while the strength of its infusion into the boy's personality varies with the lack of such reward from the father.* We suppose that the girl is in less conflict, as to model, than the boy. The mother's rewarding for the girl has an influence proportional to the amount of it that occurs. The boy, on the other hand, has two models, one of which has held temporal primacy. The mother's rewarding of dependency strengthens his use of her as a model unless the father overcomes her influence by rewarding the boy's dependency himself. His influence is proportional to the extent that he does this. (*Identification and Child Rearing*, 1965, Chapter 7.)

The development of masculinity in boys, however, seems to depend upon additional factors which are not covered by the kind of reinforcement that comes with rewarding dependency or with primary identification. It is this additional problem in the development of boys, who must shift from a female to a male model, that led Freud to hypothesize the Oedipal period with its identification with the aggressor.

The study investigated the hypothesis of identification with the aggressor in several indirect ways. The most convincing finding would have been a high correlation between *resistance to temptation* as a measure of conscience and *masculinity,* but the correlation is negligible. Boys did appear to have a more tightly organized conscience than girls, that is, resistance to temptation and guilt over transgression were more highly correlated in boys than girls. These measures of conscience are negatively correlated with aggression and dependency. Furthermore, this pattern in boys is related to ambivalence in the father's feelings toward them. Fathers of boys with strong consciences were both affectionally demonstrative and hostile toward them.

All of this, while not clearly confirming the hypothesis that boys acquire their conscience and their sex role identification through the identification with an ambivalent father, is consistent with such a point of view.

A MORE ELEMENTARY VIEW OF THE DEVELOPMENT OF CONSCIENCE. Although the findings of the study of identification are interpretable, they do not provide impressive support for the basic theory. Among social-learning theorists, there are some who would argue that the concept of identification is unduly global. They believe that conscience and self-control develop because of direct reinforcement of the elements of the pattern and direct imitation. In fact, they believe the whole attempt to use psychoanalytic concepts as the basis for social-learning theory is unproductive.

The various elements of conscience can be acquired by direct reinforcement and punishment. Suppose the child is faced with the stimuli that would elicit some deviant prohibited behavior. If the child has been punished in the past for the act, he may have learned to inhibit the deviant response. The original stimuli to arouse the inhibition were the words of the parent or perhaps merely the sight of the parents. Gradually, however, the child learns to inhibit the response even if the parents are not present. The mechanism presumably underlying this behavior is the anxiety aroused by parental disapproval or punishment. At first, the stimulus for the inhibition is the parent's presence or the parental prohibition; gradually, however, the inhibitory tendency becomes elicited by the temptation itself, perhaps mediated by the child's stating the prohibition or rule to himself.

In order for this procedure of resistance to temptation to operate, it would seem that performance of the prohibited action or transgression should arouse anxiety. Hence, the guilt that normally occurs after transgression is the anxiety aroused; this anxiety was orginally aroused by parental reproof or punishment.

If anxiety is aroused by transgression, its relief serves as a powerful reinforcement for whatever behavior can achieve the relief. In normal home circumstances the parent has taught the child some way of making amends and has reinforced such behavior by restoration of approval or by positive praise. Making amends in our culture usually involves confessing and apologizing and undoing the transgression if possible. In addition, the child is often punished, and when the punishment is over the child is forgiven. Thus, even punishment may acquire anxiety-reducing properties.

The three components normally associated with the conscience are resistance to temptation, the feeling of guilt after transgression, and the existence of a variety of behavior patterns for making amends. These generally develop together, but are not necessarily dependent on one another and so in some homes might not exist together.

One factor that may be important in the differential development of the resistance to temptation and guilt feelings is the timing of the parental reproof. If the parent warns and reproves the child as he is about to transgress, the inhibition may become more directly attached to the temptation itself. If, however, the parent punishes the child after the crime is completed, the child learns directly to feel anxiety when he performs a deviant action, but the arousal of inhibitory anxiety may require longer to develop.

In experimental situations Aronfreed and Reber (1963) have shown the effect of the timing of punishment. The boys who were subjects in the experiment were taught to select the less attractive of two toys and not to touch the more attractive one. The punishment, which consisted merely of verbal reproof, was administered to one group as soon as the boys reached toward the attractive toy. For children in the other group, the reproof occurred after they actually had the attractive toy in their hands. Then in a test situation, the children were left alone with a new pair of toys and observed to see whether or not they touched the more attractive toy. In the group punished early, only 26% transgressed in the test situation. Transgressors were much more frequent in the group punished afterward (71%), almost as frequent (80%) as in the control group that was not punished at all. The same kind of difference has even been shown in pups. (Mowrer, 1960). Pups who were physically punished for approaching a forbidden food were more likely to resist temptation than pups who were punished while they consumed the food. On the other hand, the pups punished later were more likely to behave emotionally after the deviant behavior occurred.

The evidence does not all fall together neatly, however. Burton, Maccoby, and Allinsmith (1961) found quite different results in a study in which they tested each child's resistance to temptation and related his responses to child-rearing practices in the home obtained from a well-developed interview with the mother.

The experimental situation was a bean bag game in which the child tried to toss a bean bag over a partition so that it hit a wire on the other side. Presumably, this lit a light to show the score, although actually the lights were turned on secretly by the experimenter. There were various opportunities to cheat by not following the rules. After the child played a practice game, he was left alone and urged to see how many lights he could score to receive a prize. Each act of cheating was reinforced by lighting a light, and honesty was made difficult by giving the child only a single score for following the rules. The amount of cheating during this session was recorded. In a subsequent session all children played again while the experimenter watched; now all received four lights and all won a prize.

In the interview with the mother, the interviewer asked whether she stopped the child before he touched a forbidden object, or if she waited to see if he really played with it. The children who were stopped before touching were more likely to cheat in the experimental situation. The difference was significant and completely opposite to the hypothesis.

There have also been experiments investigating the conditions under which self-critical remarks and attempts to make amends occur. One study by Aronfreed (1963) is particularly illuminating. The experimental material consisted of a phalanx of toy soldiers in front of a larger doll representing a nurse, the whole array being at one end of a table so that the nurse stood on the very edge. The story was that the nurse was very kind and the soldiers were fond of her. Whenever there was danger, she had to hide. As the experimenter said this, he shoved her off the edge of the table into a padded box that was just below table top height.

The task of the subject was to shove the nurse off the table with a toy hoe or pusher without knocking down any more of the soldiers than was absolutely necessary. The child was given a pile of Tootsie Roll candies at the beginning of the session and was allowed to keep all that he had left at the end. On each trial, some of the candies were removed as punishment for knocking down soldiers. On trial number eleven, the test trial, the nurse doll was "discovered" by the experimenter to be broken. One of its arms came off. The experimenter then asked two sets of questions: one to elicit self-critical remarks, and the other to elicit suggestions for reparations. The first set merely consisted of "I wonder why it broke," and then if there was no answer, "Why do you think it broke?" The second set of questions were first, "Well, now that it is broken, I wonder what we should do?" and then, "What do you think we should do now?" The child's responses to these questions were coded for self-criticism and for reparative suggestions.

The experimental manipulations involved two factors. One was the cognitive structuring of the requirements, a labeling of the relevant aspect of the performance. For one set of subjects the experimenter's instructions emphasized being "careful and gentle," and the assessment of the damage that led to loss of Tootsie Rolls was worded in terms of "how careless and rough you have been." The other group of subjects was given the same objective rules, to push off the nurse while knocking down as few soldiers as possible, but without any labeling of the required behavior as being careful or gentle.

A second independent experimental variable was called control. In the high-control condition the subject decided for himself at the end of each trial how many Tootsie Rolls he should lose. In the low-control condition the experimenter made that decision, but the total loss of Tootsie Rolls was made to equal the number lost under the high-control conditions.

The results are shown in Figure 15-4. The total number of children in each cell of the table is 17, and all were boys.

Cognitive structures facilitate self-critical remarks. By providing the child with a label to describe his behavior, careful or careless, gentle or rough, during the trials where it is relevant to how many soldiers are knocked down, it is easier for the child to label his actions as careless or rough when the nurse doll is broken. On the other hand, the control dimension is related to reparative remarks. The child who evaluates his own performance and assigns his own punishment is more likely to suggest repairing the doll when it is broken.

These studies do not at all provide a complete theory of conscience development, but they do suggest that it is possible to separate out different aspects of moral development experimentally and to facilitate any one of them by appropriate training techniques.

OTHER ASPECTS OF SELF-CONTROL. Although conscience development, particularly resistance to temptation, has been the most com-

Frequency of self-critical and reparative responses
under four conditions of cognitive structure
and control of reinforcement at punishment
termination

Type of response	High cognitive structure		Low cognitive structure	
	High control	Low control	High control	Low control
Self-criticism				
Present	11	10	5	4
Absent	6	7	12	13
Reparation				
Present	14	4	10	6
Absent	3	13	7	11

Figure 15-4. Note—$N = 17$ in each of the experimental groups. Frequencies represent number of subjects who show any instance (one or more) of a given response and number of subjects who show no evidence of the response.

monly studied aspect of moral development, there are other types of self-control or social standards that the child must acquire. He learns, for example, to resist the temptation to settle for an immediate reward if a greater gain can be obtained by being patient. He learns to stick at a task even it it becomes boring or difficult or if attractive diversions are available. He learns to evaluate his own performance as successful or not, on contexts that are quite removed from crimes and transgressions.

There seems, in fact, to be some degree of generalization of behavior in the area of self-control, just as in aggression. Children who kept at an unattractive task in the face of temptation to stop were found to be less overtly aggressive in nursery school (Livson & Mussen, 1957). Children who chose a delayed larger reward rather than an immediate smaller one were less likely to cheat (Mischel & Gilligan, 1962, in Bandura & Walters).

One experiment by Bandura and Kupers (1963), shows how high standards can be established through imitation. The subjects in this experiment were shown a bowling game on which scores from 5 to 30 could be obtained. The player was allowed to help himself to a supply of candy whenever he wished, but the various models in the experiment used this candy as self-rewards. One model helped himself to candy and made satisfied comments whenever he obtained a score of 20, which, in this situation, was uncommon. In another experimental condition, the model rewarded himself for any score of 10 or more. A control condition contained no model at all. Another variable introduced was that the model might be an adult or another child about the age of the subject. Figures 15-5a and 15-5b show the results. The height of the bar graph represents the percentage of times the subjects reward themselves for scores of 5, 10 to 15, and 20 or above. Exposure to a model with high standards influenced the child to hold high standards for himself, a model with lower standards was also imitated, and children who had no model rewarded themselves freely for any kind of performance. The peer model was almost as effective as the adult model.

Although there is not a full literature available, it seems likely that any of the kinds of behavior discussed above can be influenced by a model. It seems even more likely that they can all be controlled to some degree by direct reinforcement, nonreinforcement, and punishment. In experimental situations the efficacy of these mechanisms are generally confirmed. It is when they are investigated in the home itself that we find so many contradictory findings. This is not surprising, since a real home contains many different factors operating in different, and probably not consistent, ways. Detailed information is also scanty about schedules of reinforcement, and this clearly is important. Thus, the unclearness of the results of field studies may be due to the complexity of the setting.

On the other hand, it may be that these experimental investigations do not really tap the important features of the acquisition of high standards, resistance to temptation, or guilt feelings. In the last experiment, for example, the child may have learned primarily from the model the social evaluation of different performances. It seems unlikely in such a short experiment so artificially arranged that the child actually acquired a willingness to hold up high standards for himself. This does not mean that the much longer exposure to models in the home would not build in standards of self-evaluation, but the findings of experimental studies must be confirmed by careful studies of child rearing in naturalistic environments.

Summary

In this chapter we have seen the development of social-learning theory. One of its features that is clear and different from other theories is that it is a theory in the making. Although every theory of child devel-

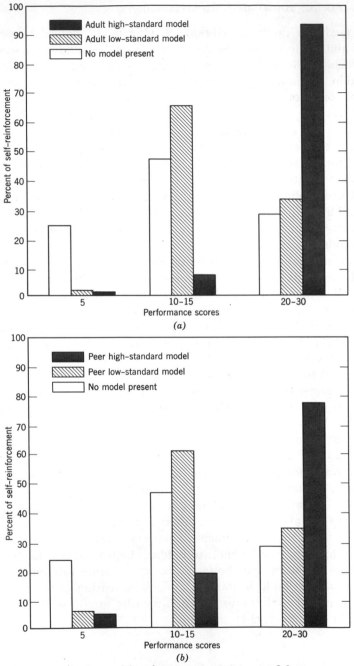

Figure 15-5. Standards resulting from exposure to a model.

opment was once a theory in the making, most of them are rarely modified once they are firmly stated. In this chapter, however, we have seen how social-learning theory is not firmly formulated; there are alternative ways for describing many of the phenomena, and, in addition, new studies bring up new data which pose new problems for the theory.

Thus, we have presented the basic elements of the theory, the role of dependency in infancy, and dependency anxiety. The combination of a broad habit system with the simultaneous existence of anxiety about the same behavior appears on several occasions in social-learning theory. The effect is hypothesized by some to result in a heightening of the drive as well as the appearance of the behavior patterns in a displaced form. Dependency is seen as the root of nearly all socialization, the gradual taming of aggression into a socially acceptable form, the appearance of various adult behavior patterns enforced through fear of punishment, and the appearance of identification and conscience.

In the identification study, one of the most recent major studies within social-learning theory, we see considerable evidence that the theory as ordinarily described is probably too simple. Its elements may be correct, but it looks as if more complexity will be required to account for the variety of phenomena in individual children.

We have seen, in addition, a whole set of studies within social-learning theory that have not been oriented toward psychoanalytic concepts, but rather have returned to the simpler concepts of conditioning. One major addition brought by these studies is the importance attributed to imitation and observational learning. The role of this kind of learning in S-R theory will be evaluated in the next chapter.

Thus, the theory is in the process of growth and modification. Certainly one strength of the theory is that it leads to empirical studies which modify without destroying it, and that its proponents can also be purely empirical in some parts of their investigations, and able and willing to absorb new facts that are relevant for a theoretical explanation.

At the same time, the very complexity of the empirical findings contains support for one of the basic tacit assumptions of the theory, that concepts like conscience, identification, dependency, and anxiety are not unitary, but are rather sets of partially independent specific behavior patterns whose organization can vary greatly from one person to another depending upon his particular child-rearing experience.

SIXTEEN

Critique of social-learning theory

THE DISTINCTIVE FEATURES of the S-R point of view are the following: (1) The objective viewpoint and the rejection of naïve concepts. (2) The use of an S-R language for describing behavior and concepts. (3) Parsimony in the introduction of new concepts. (4) The establishment of a concept through controlled experimentation and its use in the explanation of the development of behavior. The task of this chapter is to assess the development of the theory in each of these respects to determine how fruitful and facilitating it has been.

The objective viewpoint

One major premise of S-R theory has been that the human being should be studied objectively as if he were a strange black box to which one could not attribute any properties that were the result of the theorist's subjective knowledge of himself. All the properties of the organism must be hypothesized on the basis of his behavior.

As a consequence of this point of view the makers of S-R theory have clearly and self-consciously focused on the task of designing a comprehensive, coherent, testable scientific theory. The criterion of testability has been more important to them than to theorists of any other persuasion. Their writings and empirical reports have remarkable clarity. By and large, they are conscientious about stating the hypothesis, explicit in describing their methods for testing it, and clear in reporting the results. The standards of S-R theory require rigorous testing of an hypothesis against other alternatives. The high value put upon public repeatability of findings tends to make the description of experiments lucid.

A second result of these objectives is that research within the S-R framework has been more theoretically guided in its inception, planning, and development than psychological research in general. Despite its objective quality and close adherence to facts, S-R research is ordinarily not purely empirical. Since B. F. Skinner (1950) is militantly nontheoretical in his approach, the research in Skinner's tradition is perhaps an exception to the rule. Even Skinner's research, however, is guided and systematic. He has not investigated all problems unselectively or studied the influence of any and every factor in a completely unguided way. The S-R viewpoint, even when untheoretical, has for some reason encouraged systematic sequences of investigations leading to some edifice of fact and theory, rather than a spotty and random series of unrelated studies.

A third consequence of objectivity is that S-R theorists generally believe that a scientific theory is built primarily through the corrections required by disconfirmation of hypotheses rather than through the rigidity that comes from confirmation. This belief has led S-R theorists to report their findings fully, whether they are corroborative or not. The same attitude prompts S-R theorists to welcome alternatives and competing theories, provided that these accept the same scientific and methodological standards. In other words, S-R theory has been very responsive to the empirical findings of experiments.

It was the original intention of S-R theorists to keep their theory clear, rigorous, operationally defined, and objectively testable at every point of its development. The theory was expected to grow and to change through the attempts to correct bad predictions, but to be methodologically sound. It was also to develop modestly by tackling simple problems first and building the explanation for more complicated phenomena on the basis of the concepts established in simpler situations. Throughout its development, however, it was expected to stay clear, rigorous, and objective.

Two comments about this objective are in order. First, S-R theorists have tended to be severely critical of people who follow any other strategy for the development of a science. Second, S-R theory, particularly the social-learning theory of child development, has not lived up to this noble ambition.

THE STRATEGY OF THEORY BUILDING. Although natural scientists can have little objection to the long-term objectives of S-R strategy, these objectives may be achieved through other strategies. The particular choice of S-R theory to sacrifice comprehensiveness and plausibility in the early stages of development for rigor and objectivity is not the strategy that someone else might choose.

Stimulus-response theorists have tended, however, to assume that their strategy was as unassailable as their objectives. They have often attacked other theoretical positions with a moralistic, contemptuous tone which is lacking in disagreements among S-R theorists themselves about what particular assumptions should be made. Some S-R theorists automatically assume that any use of a term like goal, thought, or feeling is tantamount to mysticism; they dismiss any discussion of such terms as "ghosts."

The tone of such remarks has become increasingly mild in recent years, but even so, we find such a quotation as the following in Bandura and Walters (1963):

Whereas punishment occuring in a response sequence produces anxiety arousal that inhibits deviant behavior, self-punitive responses associated with the termination of punishment can have an anxiety-reducing function. In the former case, anxiety is reduced by the cessation of the deviant response; in the latter case it is reduced through the occurrence of the self-punitive response. *In neither case is there need to assume that some inner moral agent or faculty has played a role in regulating behavior.* [Italics not in original] (*Social Learning and Personality Development,* p. 185)

It certainly seems difficult to discriminate between an anxiety that is aroused by deviant responses and an inner moral agent. The authors have produced a plausible explanation about how an inner moral agent might operate, but their abhorrence of the label seems uncalled for.

There is a place for rigor and for tolerance in building a science. A formal theory must be rigorous and a statement of an empirical fact dependable. If a scientist reports an empirical result of his research, he must be able to verify it, and in this verification rigor and objectivity are essential. Stimulus-response theory has perhaps been too rigid, however, in assuming that all contributions to science must be factual. Theoretical speculation, even if it is not clean and rigorous, is not necessarily useless. Explanatory studies, observational reports, case studies, and other naturalistic investigations have a place in scientific literature, even though they are based on too few cases to be statistically significant, have no control group, or in some other way fail to meet the requirements for rigorous testing of the truth of an empirical statement. The mere fact that social-learning theory has fed itself on

Freud's observations and speculations for twenty-five years is evidence for the value of other strategies.

THE INTRODUCTION OF NAÏVE CONCEPTS INTO STIMULUS-RESPONSE THEORY. The history of S-R theory has been a gradual retreat from a purist position. The original intent was to build a theory that connected the stimulus to the response. The stimulus was defined as "proximal," that is, in the form that it actually impinged on the sense organs. Stimuli were not the objects in a situation, nor did the term stimulus include such events as insults or favors, because these were external and involved interpretation; they described the meaning of the stimuli rather than the stimuli themselves. The argument for a proximal definition of the stimulus is that the environment's meaning for the individual is transmitted through proximal stimuli. Instead of labeling a stimulus an insult, the S-R psychologist should describe the auditory stimuli that reach the individual's ear. Whatever is insulting about the stimulus must be contained in the pattern of proximal stimuli.

A similar restriction limits the definition of the response. A response was originally intended to include only the actual muscular movements, the secretions of glands, etc. The response was not to be defined in terms of its effect on the environment. The purists argued that people did not open doors, eat meals, or walk through the park. These are the effects of their behavior, but the responses themselves are muscular contractions in various combinations and sequences. Walking through the park is a matter of making the right muscle contractions in the presence of the right stimuli.

This argument is absolutely correct. Whatever impact the environment has on the organism is mediated by proximal stimuli; whatever effect the individual has on the environment is mediated by muscle contractions. Therefore, in principle, it was and still is possible to limit the psychological explanation to accounting for the motor responses to proximal stimuli. For the early S-R theorists the connection of stimuli to responses was largely the result of conditioning. Thus, for them the task of psychology was neatly and logically defined.

In the course of time, and for various reasons, this original purity was lost. Some features of the early S-R viewpoint were based on current but mistaken notions about the nervous system. When the brain was conceived as a sort of mammoth switchboard connecting incoming nervous impulses to outgoing channels of excitation in diverse and complicated ways, the concept of an S-R connection reflected current neurology. The same thought model made it easy to believe that each sensory end organ might be independently connected to a motor response. It was hoped that the stimulus situation might be fruitfully considered an aggregation of individual stimuli.

As evidence accumulated, both in neurophysiology and psychology, it became increasingly apparent that the connection between stimulus and response was exceedingly complicated. Stimuli interact with each other so that the effect of a combination of them is not predictable from a knowledge of their individual impacts. The brain is not a static mediator of nerve impulses, quiet except when stimulated. It is a living, spontaneously active organ with characteristic activity patterns even in the absence of external stimulation. It imposes its own organization on behavior, as well as mediating the effects of stimulus inputs. Furthermore, the effective stimuli may be configurational factors, such as the sharpness of a brightness gradient, or the peaking of a distribution of nervous excitation.

These facts about the nature of the nervous system do not invalidate the original principle that the environment's effect on the individual is channeled through the proximal stimuli, and that the individual's effect on the environment is mediated by his motor responses, but it makes the task of writing the laws connecting the two much more complicated. The nervous system's effect on research strategy is to slow down progress toward explaining such complicated problems as the relation of frustration to aggression. If one wants to investigate that relation but sticks to the strategy that every term must be objectively defined, one can spend a lifetime discovering what patterns of proximal stimuli signify frustration and what motor responses to what stimuli constitute aggression.

In response to these problems, some S-R psychologists have learned neurophysiology and have tackled the immensely important task of understanding the behavioral manifestations of various neurophysiological mechanisms. Others have concentrated on various important but restricted problems of learning, memory, and the like.

Social-learning theorists have tried to apply the S-R strategy to the problems of child development, but it has been necessary to modify the strategy of research. Phenomena such as frustration, insult, guilt, and dependency cannot be defined in the completely objective way theorists would like, but social-learning theorists do not propose to delay research on such problems until purely objective definitions become available. The problems are important; they can be studied profitably even if the definitions are sullied by a soupçon of subjectivity.

The main source of trouble with this modified strategy is that it apparently was not adopted consciously, or at least not announced publicly. The book *Frustration and Aggression* (Dollard et al., 1939), *Social Learning and Imitation* (Dollard & Miller, 1944), and *Personality and Psychotherapy* (Dollard & Miller, 1950), read as though the objective strategy were being followed, despite the fact that it was not. Whether social-learning theorists thought their definitions were objective is not clear, but it is evident that subjective concepts from naïve psychology had crept into the theory.

To take one example, the definition of aggression in all social-learning studies involves the intention of the aggressor. This is a term of naïve psychology. If the decision to introduce intention as a concept had been made explicitly, it seems likely that the research program would have been facilitated. For example, in *Frustration and Aggression,* there is a long discussion of the factors that influence the strength of the instigation to aggression. Nowhere is the intention of the other person mentioned, despite the common belief that an intentional injury instigates aggression more than an unintentional one. This is not to say that the hypotheses about instigation in the volume are not valid, but rather that the discussion seems curiously blind to one of the more obvious bits of naïve psychology.

Social-learning theory has produced much valuable research, but the research would have been facilitated had the subjective elements, like intention or expectation, been explicity recognized and labeled. The acceptance of them, *pro tem,* until their careful objective definitions could be achieved would not have involved any real sacrifice of principle. The reluctance to accept them openly has only muddied the waters. Sears, Maccoby, and Levin (1957) describe excellently how parents who are anxious about sex may resist calling the genital organs by their correct names. Instead, they say, "down there" or "don't touch that." The confusion that results is obvious. The reluctance of social-learning theory to label its subjective concepts by their subjective names has resulted in an analogous confusion.

EMPIRICISM IN STIMULUS-RESPONSE THEORY. Another feature of the strategy of S-R theorists has been to coordinate empirical research to theory and to let the theory guide the research. As S-R theory has been applied to more and more complicated problems, this objective has not been consistently maintained. Instead, purely empirical variables have been introduced into research, without being coherently tied to any fundamental theoretical point of view.

For example, *warmth* is an important variable in recent studies in social-learning theory (Sears, Maccoby, & Levin, 1957). Homes that differ in warmth tend to differ in many other variables. At the same time, warmth has never been defined theoretically in any precise way, either as a response in the behavior of the parent or as a stimulus to the child. It has been assumed in a common-sense way that children who are treated warmly by their parents probably receive more reinforcements for their behavior, that for them parental approval has been frequently associated with drive reduction, and that they have probably experienced fewer periods of high drive than children in a cold home. All of these are reasonable hypotheses about what a warm environment is like, but warmth itself has never been defined in S-R language, nor have these hypotheses about the accompaniments of warmth been empirically verified. Warmth is an important but essentially empirical variable without any clear theoretical underpinnings.

Another parental variable, *withdrawal of love,* is one disciplinary technique. It can be recognized with certainty only when the mother says to the child, "I don't love you anymore," or words to that effect, but it is often used to describe various sorts of verbal discipline where the parent describes to the child how his behavior hurts the parent, or even explains how it is bad. This disciplinary technique and all others are clearly defined, but none of them has any conceptual relation to the fundamental concepts of social-learning theory; they and the distinctions between them cannot be described in terms of reinforcement or punishment in the usual sense.

Empiricism is also reflected in the emphasis given to observational learning by Bandura and Walters (1963). The research on observational learning and imitation is very important, but Bandura and Walters do not integrate it into the main body of S-R theory. Just how does imitation occur? What events intervene between the stimulus (model) and the response (imitation)? Is there a tendency for any stimulus to be imitated? If not, what differentiates a model from a stimulus? The exploration of these problems is necessary for the development of a good social-learning theory. At the moment, the justification for the concept of imitation is merely that it occurs, not that it is related to the other concepts in the theory.

Thus, in general, social-learning theory had gradually become more empirical, in the sense that it is no longer considered necessary to define the variables in terms of their theoretical and conceptual relations.

Value of Stimulus-Response Language

Although many modifications in the theoretical structure of S-R theory have occurred, the language itself has not changed much.

Thoughts are called responses, perception is called a response, the meanings of situations are labeled stimuli.

This language has some specific theoretical significance which S-R theorists have not always tested before applying the label. Thus, if perception is properly called a response, it should be shown to be learnable through classical conditioning or reinforcement. Furthermore, implicit in the label is the concept that all perceptions have been so learned except for a few innate ones. These implications of the label have not been generally tested before the label is applied, however.

Instead, the labels *stimulus* and *response* have been applied quite freely to various aspects of psychological functioning; sometimes it seems that the only innovation has been the label. It is important, however, to recognize the value of S-R language itself and its real contribution to the fruitfulness of the S-R point of view. Every theory has definitions and terminology as well as contingent hypotheses couched in the terminology and given meaning by their definitions. Stimulus-response theory is no different; there is an S-R terminology which can be considered as independent of the assumptions, postulates, and hypotheses of the theory.

The value of the S-R language is that it contains so few tacit presumptions about the structure of the theory. It is close to a theoretically neutral terminology, whereas in many other theories the language itself puts constraints on the possible theoretical constructs which could be formulated in the language. Lewin's geometry, for example, contains many tacit constraints on the kinds of behavior which can be described (see p. 157).

There are two senses in which S-R language is theoretically neutral. First, the term S now includes all precipitating factors for an action and R describes any action whatsoever. S is given enough generality to include both internal and external stimuli; it puts no constraint on psychological events to say they are elicited by a stimulus. If the stimulus means the totality of input into the organism at a particular moment, then any kind of precipitating factor can be translated into S-R language. Similarly, if the response is defined as the totality of overt action elicited, it represents all of the behavioral evidence available at the moment. Thus, by definition, the observable elements in behavior as described in any theory can be translated into S-R language, because doing so does not require that any of the hypotheses of S-R theory must be adopted; the language is sufficiently neutral to describe any theory.

Second, S-R language is theoretically neutral because it does not state that certain constellations of stimuli and behavior necessarily go together. It is probably this atomistic feature of S-R language which has led S-R theorists to break down global clusters of behavior into their elementary components, as we have seen in the analysis of conscience. Any theorist who does assume that these constellations are unitary can state his belief as an hypothesis to be verified, rather than as a tacit assumption underlying the terminology. This is a useful course because it clarifies the assumptions of the theory.

Stimulus-response theory, despite the neutrality of S-R language, has made its own tacit assumptions and has sometimes not spelled them out clearly. Thus, in early S-R theorizing, the stimulus was assumed to be a mosaic of individual packets of stimulus energy which affected each of the sensory organs. The response was tacitly assumed to be a pattern of muscle contractions. Recently, though, the term *stimulus* has been used in a more common-sense way to represent a stimulus situation. Different situations having the same psychological meaning have often been given the same label, even though the actual elements of the stimulus situations are different. A black square, for example, is not the same stimulus at different distances or positions. Similarly, when response is defined in terms of its effect on its environment, a whole theoretical step is tacitly bypassed. It is perfectly acceptable to make such assumptions, but it is better to make them explicitly than to do so tacitly. Stimulus-response language, if used rigorously, can force theorists of all persuasions to be more explicit about their implicit assumptions.

Parsimony in theory construction

Stimulus-response theorists have adopted the criterion of parsimony as well as testability in theory construction, and have consistently tried to find the simplest theoretical explantation for the facts. In fact, they have given parsimony equal status with testability in the S-R strategy for theory building.

Parsimony is certainly a valuable asset to a scientific theory, but even as an ultimate objective it is more a matter of taste than of truth. Although in natural science we cannot accept an eventual theory that is untestable, we are not required to reject the more complicated of two theories that account for the same set of facts. Unnecessary complexity is to be avoided, but it is difficult to ascertain whether complexity is unnecessary or not. In some ways the adherence to parsimony has led S-R theory into more controversy than any other aspect of this strategy. Stimulus-response theorists frequently write about complicated issues and adopt the tone of "this is really not so complicated, it's nothing but ordinary learning." Although there is real value in searching for simple mechanisms to account for apparently complicated phenomena, it would seem well advised to be modest and tentative about the adequacy of the simple explanation until the complexities have been explored.

It is difficult to say whether the parsimony of S-R theory has retarded its development or kept it healthfully sound at the base. Certainly it is true that many of the concepts now incorporated in S-R theory are restatements of concepts that had been proposed much earlier and rejected by S-R theorists as unnecessary and unparsimonious. Much effort went into trying to discredit the empirical evidence for them or trying to explain them away as "nothing but" some familiar learning phenomenon. At one time, most S-R theorists took the position that cognition was unnecessary for a psychological theory; it seemed to them to interpose hypothetical constructs between the stimulus and the response, and to be guided by the common-sense nature of these constructs. When such mediating variables were first added to S-R theory, they were labeled in the language of motor behavior. They resembled the small chewing movement made by the rat as he traversed the maze and were called partial anticipatory goal responses. It eventually became clear that there was no real virtue in giving them the names of muscular activities. Gradually, therefore, they were attributed to cortical processes or were frankly recognized to be hypothetical constructs whose function was to account for behavior. At this time the concept of a mediating variable is commonplace in S-R theory and the distinction between one- and two-step processes as described by Kendler (1955, see p. 418) seems well accepted.

Curiously enough, the evidence for such a two-step process can still be attacked on exactly the same grounds that Lashley's (1942) explanation of the reversal shift was attacked years ago. It is not that data have forced new concepts, but merely that new concepts have become accepted.

Similarly, a purely drive-reduction theory of reinforcement can be maintained today as well as it was years ago. The argument against broadening the concept of reinforcement was that those who proposed to do so had not exhaustively eliminated every possibility of a drive-reduction theory. Until they had, parsimony should prevent its acceptance. Many S-R theorists now accept the idea that a variety of stimulus changes can be reinforcing, and that the purely drive-reduction theory should be abandoned.

The real danger of an argument based on parsimony is that it can easily prevent the introduction of fruitful new concepts, by requiring the innovator to prove that he can eliminate every possible explanation of the data in terms of the old concepts. Given a theory of any complexity, it is almost impossible ever to prove beyond a reasonable doubt that the traditional concepts are incomplete.

Despite the fact that the history of S-R theory reveals the gradual acceptance of many concepts that were at one time viewed as unnecessary, we still find the same philosophy operating. Bandura and Huston (1961), for example, argue that identification is "nothing but" incidental learning through imitation. The support for the argument is an experimental study showing that incidental learning through imitation can occur. But the sweeping claim that everything that has been attributed to identification is reducible to such incidental learning is more a statement of the parsimonious philosophy than a careful attempt to demonstrate the fruitlessness of the concept of identification.

Parsimony in S-R theory has also been an ambiguous principle in another respect. Parsimony with respect to the number of concepts in theory does not result in parsimony in the representation of the individual psychological mechanism. The difference between the two sorts of parsimony is well illustrated in one of Miller's discussions of mediating response (1959). If there are four stimuli and four responses such that each stimulus elicits every response, it is possible to picture sixteen separate connections, each of which is a simple $_sH_r$ (see Figure 16-1). Such a representation is parsimonious in that only one kind of

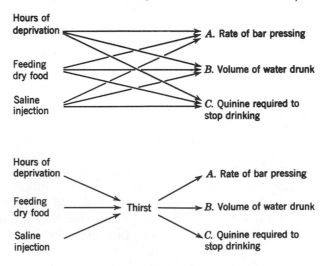

Figure 16-1. The role of a mediating response in a parsimonious explanation. (After Miller (1959).)

concept is involved, but is unparsimonious in the amount of wiring that is required to connect each stimulus with each response. The introduction of an internal mediating response can, however, simplify the wiring. Each stimulus can be connected to the mediating response, which in turn can be connected with each response. The model is less parsimonious in terms of concepts, but much more so in terms of the number of connections. If one is to make parsimony a basic tenet of a theoretical strategy, which sort of parsimony is to be cherished?

S-R theory is a theory of acquisition

Turning now to more specific problems of S-R theory, we see first of all that the theory was developed to explain the acquisition of behavior rather than the actual events that take place between stimulus and response. Every theory of human behavior must contain both a theory of action, which describes the process by which behavior at the moment is elicited and carried out, and a theory of acquisition, which describes the temporal sequence of events resulting in the formation of various kinds of dispositional variables.

The basic explanatory concept in S-R theory is habit. It is the only concept that relates the stimulus to the response. Other intervening concepts, like drive, change the probability that a particular response will occur, but they do not introduce any additional factors relating the response to particular stimuli. Habit, as its name suggests, is a concept from learning. The only operational definition of habit is a description of its acquisition.

The implications of this fact are extensive. If an experimenter wishes to study a particular kind of behavior from an S-R point of view, he tries to discover how it has been learned by devising an experiment in which that behavior can be systematically reinforced. If the behavior is acquired under these conditions, it is a learnable response. The experimenter knows what habit he is working with and can then study its characteristics. An important contribution of S-R theory to psychology is this experimental approach to behavior that stems from the experimenter's ability to produce any particular habit through a controlled learning process.

There is, however, no operational definition of habit in terms of behavior alone. We cannot identify an individual's habits by observing his behavior or by applying any set of experimental tests. If an experimenter is presented with a full-grown rat of unknown background, there are no clear procedures within S-R theory by which he can determine the rat's repertoire of habits.

This fact is obvious upon a little consideration. The experimenter could put the rat in a variety of stimulus situations and observe the rat's behavior. If he put him in a Skinner box and observed that he pressed the lever, he would know that some of the stimuli present in the box, or some particular combination of them, elicited the response. By an exhaustive analysis he might be able to specify what stimuli within this setting were necessary and sufficient for this response, but he would not know whether this response had been originally learned to these stimuli or whether it was a result of generalization and had been originally learned to different stimuli. He would have even more difficulty in discerning if the rat had once learned some other response to these stimuli but had also learned to inhibit it.

It may seem unimportant to know anything about the rat's behavior except how it responds to what stimuli. However, a knowledge of the rat's actual habit structure is necessary for predicting its behavior in any other situation than the particular one in which it is observed. If, in fact, the rat has a learned response to some stimulus in the situation and the response has been inhibited, then that response may appear in some other situation in which the inhibiting stimuli are removed. Similarly, if the response occurring in the present situation were a generalization from some different habit, then the response in some other situation might be much more intense than in the present one.

Thus, we see that a knowledge of the habit structure of the individual is important for prediction of his behavior, but that the diagnosis of this habit structure from observation or experimental test can only be done laboriously and can never be done completely. Speaking quite generally, one cannot determine the historical process by which a behavior pattern is acquired solely by observation or study of the end result. Different acquisition histories can lead to the same behavior. It was the consideration of this fact that led Lewin to distinguish sharply between systematic causation and historical causation (see p. 88). Stimulus-response theory has developed a purely historical theory of behavior.

The experimental approach of S-R theorists also has another implication over and above their concentration on the acquisition of behavior. If instead of setting up an experiment in which the experimenter determines what behavior is reinforced and what is not the experimenter is required to observe an organism in a natural habitat and determine what responses it is acquiring, the task is immensely more difficult. For one thing, the experimenter can decide upon the stimulus to which he will attach a response; in the natural habitat he must have some criterion for deciding what stimuli are present in the environment. Second, the experimenter can specify the response; how in the natural habitat is the changing kaleidoscope of activity to be divided into responses? Third, the experimenter can bring to bear a clear, obvious reinforcement, like food, and can use that reinforcement in one experiment after another. In the natural habitat he is faced with the immediate problem of deciding what events are reinforcers and what are not. These problems are not insoluble, but they are unsolved and are critical for the application of S-R theory to everyday life.

IMPLICATIONS OF AN HISTORICAL THEORY FOR CHILD DEVELOPMENT. The psychologist who wishes to study the causes of aggression in adolescents or of dope addiction in adults is put into a difficult situation by an experimental historical theory. He cannot diagnose the past history from the behavior; he cannot turn time backward to observe the learning history of the individual, and even if he could, he could not control the learning history to build in the habits he wanted.

This dilemma accounts for one of the typical strategies of social-learning theorists in explaining some feature of child development. They first devise a possible learning history that would result in the behavior to be explained, say dependence, guilt, or aggression. They then show in the laboratory that this hypothesized acquisition process can be reproduced and does indeed result in the behavior to be accounted for, and then assume that children who show the behavior have had the hypothesized learning history.

We find social-learning theory full of descriptions of hypothetical events in childhood that would, if they actually occurred, produce the behavior. For example, the learning of aggression is frequently made dependent upon the child's associating evidences of pain in another person with the reinforcement of having his own needs satisfied. There is no evidence that such a contingency ever occurs, or that it would function like secondary reinforcement if it did. Such events have not been systematically observed, instead they are hypothetical events, a sort of mythology of early childhood. As a matter of fact, this particular mechanism has never been reproduced in the laboratory to see if it would bring the predicted result.

Similarly, the presence of the mother associated with drive reduction is hypothesized to be the antecedent of dependence; and, inconsistency in parental reinforcements is hypothesized to constitute a partial reinforcement schedule that produces certain intractable responses. However, such conjectures cannot establish a theory of child development. Social-learning theorists have taken some of the experimentally established findings about learning and have attempted to imagine conceivable events in childhood that would produce the predicted behavior. This procedure is perfectly acceptable as a way of formulating hypotheses, but it is not a sound basis for establishing a theory.

There are two important fallacies in such procedure. One is the fallacy of judging that because A implies B, the occurrence of B proves the existence of A. There may be many possible mechanisms by which aggression is learned; direct reinforcement is only one. A second fallacy is that most of the mechanisms used to explain child development have been shown to produce certain behavior but not to produce the feelings or intentions that social-learning theorists have accepted as part of the definitions of aggression, dependence, or guilt. Thus, for example, none of the experiments on reinforcement of aggression acts or imitation of aggression behavior has established that such procedures lead to full aggression, involving anger and the intention to injure another person. Several writers (Sears, 1957; Bandura & Walters, 1959) recognize the anger of the baby as relevant for the development of aggression, but it is ignored in the experimental studies of acquisition.

In summary, the details of social-learning theory rest on shaky grounds. The behavioral mechanisms have been established and the theorists have been ingenious in suggesting how these mechanisms might occur in the child's natural habitat to produce the results, but the proof is left incomplete at that point.

LACK OF OBSERVATIONAL STUDIES OF CHILDHOOD. Given the state of affairs described, it would seem that S-R theorists would be eager to observe the actual events in the young child's home in order to discover what associations among stimuli actually occur with high frequency, to note the actual schedule of reinforcements, and to correlate these with the occurrence of dependence, aggression, etc. In fact, however, observational studies of the home have not generally stemmed from social-learning theory and have not been couched in the S-R language. Social-learning theorists have tried to obtain information about child rearing but only retrospectively through interview. Furthermore, they have described the home in terms of such variables as warmth or restrictiveness, not in terms of the frequency of association of reinforcement and signs of pain in another person, nor in terms of schedules of reinforcements. Thus, although the research has contributed to our knowledge of child rearing, it has not made the contribution to social-learning theory that might have been expected.

The methodological problems in such observational studies are serious. To attempt a genuine description of a child's environment in S-R terms requires a definition of the stimulus and the response, a criterion for marking the boundaries of particular stimuli and responses, a workable criterion for identifying reinforcements, and highly sophisticated recording procedures for keeping up with the fast-moving events of adult-child interaction. One of the reasons that the problems loom large, though, is that they have never been attacked. Stimulus-response theory has been based largely on experimentally produced responses which are applied without empirical check to the natural environment, and so, even the methods of making such a check are lacking.

Summary

Stimulus-response and social-learning theory have probably contributed more sound empirical data about the learning process in animals and humans than any other of the theories we have discussed. This type of approach is more objective and attempts to base its theories upon a sound empirical foundation.

In many respects, however, it has not lived up to these high standards. As the theory has developed, new concepts have been added, not ordinarily because they were demanded by data, but because they just happened. Various subjective elements have crept into the concepts without being explicitly recognized. Although the experimental work itself has been sound, the attempts to apply the concepts to the description of child rearing, or to any other aspect of real life, have frequently been highly speculative. The consequent variables have generally been carefully described, although not always without subjectivity. But the antecedent variables have been left unstudied and unobserved.

HEINZ WERNER

Heinz Werner—

The Organismic Developmental
Point of View

SEVENTEEN Heinz Werner's theory
of child development

AMONG THE MANY VALUABLE PEOPLE who left Germany and came to the United States at the time of Hitler's rise to power were a number of persons who became leading figures in American psychology. They brought to this country a point of view that was, and still is, atypical of general American psychology. One of these men was Kurt Lewin, whose theories were discussed in an earlier section. Another, Heinz Werner, is the subject of this chapter.

There is probably no psychologist whose work is more completely developmental than Werner's; his entire theoretical position revolves around the concept of development. His theories have not led to detailed descriptions of children's personalities as did Freudian theory, however, nor to the detailed description of the functioning of the child's mind as did Piaget's. He concentrated on the global problems of development and on discovering how different aspects of the individual's psychophysiological functioning interrelate. Although he and his colleagues and students conducted many empirical investigations, their research has done more to illustrate and confirm a general approach to psychological problems than to contribute knowledge of the actual development of children. Werner's influence is greater as the proponent of a general strategy of scientific investigation than as a source of significant facts about children.

In order to understand Werner's theories, it is important to consider his background and the psychological culture from which he emerged.

In psychology there has been a persistent conflict between the empirical view of human nature and opposing views which are less easy to characterize. Empiricism assumes that human behavior is learned through a process that was first called association and later, conditioning. The child, according to the view of empiricists, is a blank page at birth on which experience writes through the learning process. This tradition is represented in current theories of child development by social-learning theory.

The opposing psychological tradition is represented in this book by Lewin, Piaget, and now Werner. It is not so unified a point of view, nor so easily characterized, but it consistently contains some of the following elements.

First, it places much more emphasis than does empiricism upon inherent structures of the person which are rooted in biological processes. It has been called *nativistic* because some of the modes of individual functioning are assumed to be inherent rather than learned through experience. This inherent structure is sometimes viewed as being merely the operation of the dynamic laws of physical and biological processes; thus, for example, Lewin argued that behavior acted like an energy system with forces, resultants, and equilibria, and Piaget argues for a dynamic equilibration process which results in certain constellations of cognitive structure. Werner, however, drew more directly upon biological growth processes for the description of development.

These inherent or genetic factors put some constraints upon how the child can develop and what he can learn. For Werner, these constraints stemmed from the developmental process; for Lewin, they stemmed more from the dynamic laws of an energy system.

Second, this opposition to the associative, empirical tradition insists that the process of association or conditioning is *atomistic* and *mechanistic*. An association between two ideas, or the conditioning of a response to a stimulus, is a local event involving only those particular ideas or that particular stimulus and response. The developmental process, according to S-R theory, is the totality of all these specific events. The point of associationism is that it deemphasizes both the effect of the context in which an association occurs and the effects of a particular learning event upon the total functioning of the organism. In opposition to this atomistic point of view is a *holistic* or *organismic* view, according to which all changes in human behavior involve the total organism because the organism is an integrated whole. Research in the organism tradition has always emphasized the influence of the context upon the operation of any specific factor, and upon the interdependence of one aspect of human functioning on other aspects.

This holistic viewpoint has traditionally been strong in continental Europe, whereas empiricism and associationism flourished in Great Britain. Werner, like Lewin and Piaget, grew up in the traditions of continental Europe, was educated in Austria, and taught in Germany, where he was in close contact with a number of people who represented the holistic view.

Besides this general psychological tradition, there were more idiosyncratic factors in Werner's background that influenced his development. One was a persistent and early interest in aesthetics. A second was his knowledge of embryology and neurology; he taught courses in these fields and constantly used the developmental processes of biology as analogies for his conception of psychological development. Of course, he believed these parallels were more than analogies, since the human being is a developing biological organism. It was inconceivable to him that the developmental processes of the nervous system would not be reflected in behavioral development.

A third influence was his knowledge of both pathology and anthropology. It led him to conceive of development in a broader framework than the growing individual organism. As we shall see, he assumed that all developmental processes, social, cultural, and biological, had similar general principles, and that pathology represented either a developmental regression or arrest.

PRINCIPLES OF DEVELOPMENT

Generality of Development

One of Werner's basic assumptions about development was that it occurred in a wide variety of circumstances, not merely in the growth of an individual organism. He conceived of development as a process of change that could occur in the changes of a culture over time, in the development of a world view, in the development of cognition in the individual, or in the development of the embryo. He did not assume that every change was a developmental change. There were obviously some changes, even ones that represent growth, that could follow other principles. The growth of a bank account, for example, is not developmental. Neither would the growth of a coral reef be described as developmental. In other words, Werner said that only one variety of change could legitimately be called developmental. Whenever a developmental change occurred, it followed the so-called "orthogenetic" principles of development. As Werner pointed out, the orthogenetic principle is not empirically testable; it is a definition of a variety of growth which he believed occurred so widely that it would be well worth labeling, studying, and describing. Specifically, he postulated that the orthogenetic principles described the growth of the individual personality.

One of Werner's books, *Comparative Psychology of Human Development,* is devoted to a detailed description of the developmental process and its principles. In this book Werner documented his thesis that the changes from childhood thinking to adult thinking followed the same general principles as the change from the thinking in primitive societies to the thinking in technologically advanced societies.

The Parallel between Ontogeny and Cultural Growth

A similar hypothesis had been advanced earlier, that the ontogeny or individual growth of the child paralleled the cultural evolution of the human race. This hypothesis has fallen into disrepute for many reasons. In the first place, it seemed to imply that primitive societies were in some sense worse than advanced ones. Such a point of view has been held by people who have wanted to justify colonialism and who have had no respect for cultures other than the Western one with its high level of technological achievement. Second, the parallels drawn were often inaccurate and superficial. The impulsiveness and emotional expressiveness of the child at play may resemble in certain respects the dances and music of savages, but any careful description of a culture reveals complicated beliefs, patient planning, and often tremendous stoicism in the face of pain.

The modern tendency is to deny the validity of any concept of primitive cultures as distinguished from advanced ones. Werner believed there was valid meaning to the term primitive and tried to resolve some of the misconceptions about the concept of *primitivity* as he used it.

He pointed out first, that primitive thinking was not necessarily bad thinking nor that it was less effective in solving problems. There were circumstances where primitive thinking was more effective and more adaptive than the more differentiated thought processes of the adults in technologically advanced cultures. At the same time, he argued that there was a real difference between the kinds of thought processes found in various primitive societies and those that accompanied western technological advancement.

Whether or not the concept of primitivity is valid or useful, it is true that some of the reasons for denying it are emotional rather than empirical. With our modern emphasis on the equality of races and cultures, some people deny the existence of any significant difference between races and societies. There are established ethnic differences in the distribution of blood types and in the incidence of various diseases, yet people have denounced them as products of race prejudice. There may indeed be significant psychological differences among ethnic groups and among the several thousand cultures that currently exist, but these differences have nothing to do with racism as a political position. Werner wanted to emphasize the fact that what he called *primitive* was not lower or worse than what he called *differentiated.*

A second confusion Werner tried to dispel was that primitive patterns of organization were always chronologically prior to differentiated ones. Although it is empirically true that temporal change often goes from an undifferentiated to a differentiated organization, this is not always so. The important thing is that the orthogenetic principles do not logically imply that the more primitive precedes the more differentiated.

A third confusion arises from the fact that for Werner *primitive* was a sort of ideal construct which was logically possible, but which might not actually exist. Though at one end of a continuum, *primitive* might not be represented at all—just as nobody has an I.Q. of zero although the concept of I.Q. carries the logical necessity for an I.Q. of zero.

In other words, as used by Werner, development was a construct defined by the orthogenetic laws. If such a construct is useful, it should be empirically related to a number of other variables, which is a task for empirical research. In *Comparative Psychology of Mental Development,* Werner tried to show that the concept described some of the differences between young and older children, between primitive cultures and technologically advanced ones, and between the pathological thinking accompanying brain injury or schizophrenia and nonpathological thinking.

Some readers have thought that Werner believed that primitive adults, children, and schizophrenics were all alike. This is not Werner's view, however. There are some similarities among the three, but also many differences. Developmental status is only one aspect of personality; there can be many sorts of both primitive thinking and advanced thought processes. Werner was interested mainly in conceptualizing the similarities.

Werner's basic definition of development is best quoted directly from his own writings (1957).

It is an orthogenetic principle which states that whenever development occurs it proceeds from a state of relative globality and lack of differentiation to a state of increasing differentiation, articulation, and hierarchic integration. (*Concept of Development,* p. 126)

These are not easy concepts to understand. Perhaps it is best to examine one of the original usages of the concept of *differentiation* in embryology. The earliest stage of the embryo is the single cell, the fertilized egg. The first change that takes place is the division of this cell into 2, then 4, then 8, then 16. Instead of a single cell, there is now an organism divided into sixteen similar parts. Later, different types of cells begin to appear. An organism whose cells were previously alike now becomes an organism with different types of cells. The variety of types increases rapidly. By the time the baby is born his body contains a tremendous variety of different kinds of cells.

At first the cells are more or less independent of each other in terms of functioning; they all function the same way and are not coordinated. Gradually, however, their functioning becomes articulated. When, for example, a nerve cell transmits an impulse to the muscle cell which then contracts, the functions of the two cells are interdependent and articulated. Sequences of activity occur in which the order is determined by the relations among the cells. For a sequence of sounds to make a sentence, to cite an analogy, each sound must come at the right time and in the right order. Inarticulate speech may have the same sounds, but a chaotic ordering.

Along with this articulation, some of the cells develop control over others, so that if cells high in the hierarchy are destroyed, the whole articulation collapses, while if cells low in the hierarchy are destroyed, the disruption is less pronounced. One of the characteristics of all complex biological organizations is the dominance of some functions over others. In other words, there is an hierarchic organization and integration. Thus, we see how the orthogenetic principle is illustrated in the development of the biological organization.

There is a comparable development in behavioral embryology, that is, the development of behavior in the embryo. Coghill (1929) showed, for example, that in the development of the salamander, the earliest form of spontaneous behavior was a curl of the organism toward one side. Next appeared a curl to the other side, so that at one stage the embryo curls first one way then the other, repetitively. Each curl is produced by a contraction of the muscles in all the segments on one side of the body. The next, more differentiated, response is when the upper half of the body curls in one direction and the lower half in the other; this produces an S shape, which then becomes a reverse S, with the alternation resulting in a swimming movement. When the limb buds from which the legs develop first appear, their movement is part of the S-shaped motion. The right front and left rear legs move simultaneously, since both are in the middle of a region of contraction;

with the reverse S, the left front and right rear legs move. Thus, the coordination of the leg movements stems from the generalized un-differentiated contraction patterns. In other words, the legs do not first move independently and then gradually become coordinated; rather, their coordination is part of the less differentiated movements that exist even before the legs appear.

In these examples, it is not difficult to see what is meant by the terms *global, undifferentiated,* and *unarticulated.* When we come to the study of primitive thought processes or language it is not so easy to see what the terms mean, nor to accept the orthogenetic principle as an accurate description of development. Werner has, however, presented numerous examples of the orthogenetic principle in psychological development and lists five aspects of the developmental process.

Syncretic versus discrete. Syncresis means the fusion of qualities that at a later developmental level are discrete. Synaesthesia, or colored hearing, is one clear, though rare, example of syncretic fusion. For some people, sounds appear to have a color; trumpet music is golden. The sound elicits a visual experience of color along with the auditory experience of the sound. The color and the sound experiences are fused or syncretic rather than separate and discrete.

Animals and children treat objects as "things of action." The objects are apparently apprehended solely in terms of the responses to them. Thus, a child accustomed to chewing on the corner of a square rattle tried to chew on a round rattle, but kept moving it in her mouth searching for the comfortable corner to which she was accustomed (Shinn, 1909). Here the geometrical shape of the rattle was not discrete from its other properties and the perceptual properties apprehended by the child were more those of "chewableness" than anything else. Yet even chewableness does not accurately describe the child's syncretic perception.

Another example of syncretic functioning can be found in the research of Bridges (1932), who described the gradual differentiation of children's emotions. She detailed a primitive excitement which gradually differentiated into joy and distress; she reported that these two emotional states are not as discrete for the young child as for the adult. Distress then differentiated into fear and anger. These two emotions are also almost indistinguishable in the young infant, whereas in the adult they appear to be nearly opposite feelings.

An example of syncretism in normal adult functioning can be seen in the close relationship between taste and smell. The end organs and the neurology of the two senses are quite distinct, but we commonly attribute to the taste of food some characteristics that actually depend upon its odor.

This illustrates a point that Werner made quite explicit. The transition from syncretic to discrete is never complete, so that some syncretism is a part of adult experience. In addition, adults have available to them the option of experiencing in a more syncretic manner. Thus, we may see a landscape as gloomy and try to capture that feeling in a painting or a poem. Such an approach is syncretic—Werner called this particular example of syncretic perceptions *physiognomic*. Yet, the same person can also accurately describe the colors and forms and objects in the landscape in a way that is independent of the feeling factor. Furthermore, people with a good intuition use their syncretic perceptions and may develop them to a high order of skill. Syncresis is primitive, in the sense that it is characteristic of children and primitive man and of perception under conditions of impoverished input, but it is not, per se, maladaptive, disordered, or incompatible with the more discrete varieties of perception that characterize everyday adult life.

DIFFUSE VERSUS ARTICULATED. Articulation relates to the separateness yet coordination between the parts of an organization. Thus, articulated speech contains specific identifiable elements which appear in a specifiable sequence with relatively clear boundaries between neighboring sounds.

One characteristic of undifferentiated organizations is that the articulation is frequently diffuse and vague. Werner gives an example of diffuseness in the drawing shown in Figure 17-1b. Circularity and corneredness are both present, but each pervades the whole figure so that they are not represented in segregated parts of the drawing. Similarly, the drawing of a cylinder in Figure 17-1a shows both ends and the middle. This kind of a drawing is common among children. The parts are represented as segregated from one another, but are not properly articulated.

RIGID VERSUS FLEXIBLE AND LABILE VERSUS STABLE. The previous terms describe the structure of an organization; the present ones describe its functioning. The functioning of the primitive organization, or system, is both rigid and labile. One of the common characteristics of a child's behavior is rigidity. The child often tends to do the same thing over and over again in similar circumstances. Piaget described, for example, how the child would look under the pillow where he last found the watch even when he had watched it being placed under a different pillow (see p. 212). The child's enjoyment of the same story

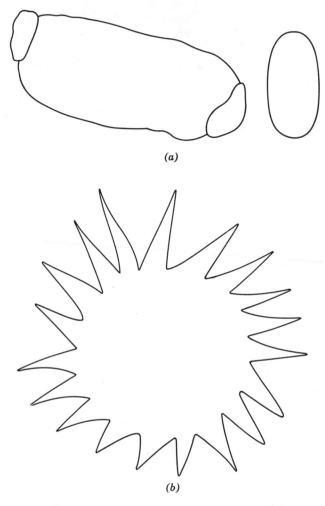

Figure 17-1. Diffuseness in a child's drawing. *a:* Childlike copies of a cylinder. Left—girl six years old (after Katz); Right—girl five years old (after Volkelt). *b:* Six-sided pyramid on a cylinder drawn by an eight-year-old girl (Hamburg Psychological Laboratory, Werner, *Comparative Psychology of Mental Development.*)

over and over again and his refusal to accept any variation in its telling is another example of rigidity.

In many lower species of animals the rigidity of adaptation may be striking. Gulls, for example, have a set of socially interactive behaviors that are released by the appropriate stimulus. The natural habitat of the gull does not contain too great a variety of circumstances, so this relatively automatized set of responses functions quite well. Rigidity can be seen clearly in experimental situations, however. A mother goose, for example, can be made to retrieve an egg that has rolled from the nest, and will continue the retrieval once it is begun, even if the egg is removed, so that she is apparently retrieving an imaginary egg (Lorenz & Tinbergen, 1938). The young nestling gull will peck at its mother's beak, which has a red ring around it, and thus obtain food, but it will prefer a pencil with three red rings to an accurate model of the mother's head (Tinbergen & Perdeck, 1950). The instinctive behavior of many species shows the rigidity and unmodifiability of a response to a stimulus.

The relative flexibility of the human species in comparison to lower species is marked. Differences between primitive and advanced cultures and between children and adults are similar. In the case of children, a randomness in behavior and a lack of conventionality can exist alongside greater rigidity. Thus, the child sometimes appears free and untrammeled by the rigid conventions that may hamper the creativity of the adult. If rigidity means, however, the ease of modification of an established pattern of response, children are generally less flexible than adults.

Rigidity of response is highly adaptive to a stable environment in which nothing new ever occurs, but it is generally maladaptive in an environment that changes radically. The flexibility of the responses of the human being compared to that of the lower animals, makes his behavior stabler and more adaptive in the sense of achieving his goals in diverse circumstances. In this sense, flexibility and stability go together, and both characterize the functioning of a differentiated, articulated organization.

In summary the orthogenetic principle states that a developmental process goes from the undifferentiated, syncretic, diffuse, rigid, unstable organization to the differentiated, articulated, flexible, and hierarchically organized system that is better adapted to the demands of a heterogeneous, variegated environment.

THE ANALYSIS OF MENTAL FUNCTIONING

Werner's description of the orthogenetic principle is easy to think of as a single line of progression. Actually, however, Werner viewed it more as a multiform process than a uniform one. The development does not unfold maturationally; instead, various different psychological processes appear at one time or another in the behavior of the child. There are many processes, but the maturer ones gradually take over and control the child's functioning, winning out, so to speak, over the less mature.

We saw something of this same conception in Piaget's view of development. The psychological functions that dominate during the sensorimotor stage are superseded by the processes of conceptual thinking; sensorimotor functions do not become conceptual or drop out of existence, however. Conceptual thinking has its own development beginning at the end of infancy. Gradually it takes over the control of adaptive behavior from the sensorimotor processes, but the processes of perception and automatized habitual functioning continue to develop. They become subordinate to conceptual thinking, but have their own development.

Werner emphasized this aspect of development more explicitly than does Piaget, and he also tended to analyze mental functioning into many more processes than Piaget. Werner's point of view contains the following assumptions:

1. Mental functioning may be analyzed into a number of different functions.
2. Some of these functions are at a lower developmental level than others, and the lower ones are subordinated to the higher.
3. The lower-level functions appear earlier than the higher. They reach a level where they dominate the functioning of the organism and then are superceded by higher functions. The influence of the lower-level functions on the functioning of the individual wanes except as they operate under the control of higher functions.
4. The same objective achievement may be brought about by different functions. Such different functions that result in the same achievement are called *analogous processes*.
5. Primordial functions may develop in some individuals to great heights and contribute substantially to effective functioning. For example, physiognomic perception is a more primitive level of functioning than detached geometrical perception, but physiognomic perception occurs in all people, and in the case of poets it may be highly developed and contribute significantly to the effectiveness of their poetry as an expression of human feeling.
6. Functioning at any level tends to stabilize and rigidify in such a way as to be adaptive to the environment. If some crisis or problem severely taxes the range of adaptation of the present system, a new level or kind of functioning is required. The reorganization of

functioning stimulated by such challenges begins with a regression or dedifferentiation to some lower level of functioning.

THE ACQUISITION OF WORD MEANING. These principles of mental functioning are illustrated in a study carried out by Werner and Kaplan, *The Acquisition of Word Meaning* (1952). This study describes various psychological functions, showing how those at each level dominate behavior for a while and are gradually superseded. It also shows that some of the transitions or reorganizations may take place rapidly. The developmental process may thus be divided meaningfully into stages when it is qualitatively analyzed in terms of how the child functions as judged by objective ..chievement.

The task presented to the subjects in this experiment was to discover the meaning of a nonsense word from its usage in a series of sentences. Twelve different series of sentences were used. The child was informed at the beginning of the experiment that he would be presented with twelve words that he had never heard before, and that these words were used in a little town out West and were not spoken anywhere else. It was made clear to the child that in each series of six sentences, the word had only one meaning. The experimenter concluded with, "I want you to try to find out what these words mean. I will show you one sentence at a time. After you read the sentence tell me what you think the word may mean. Tell me everything you are thinking."

After the child responds to the first sentence he is asked in what way the meaning he gave fits in the sentence. He is then given the second sentence with the first still in view. After his interpretation of the word in the second sentence he is asked how it fits that sentence and then how it fits the preceding sentence. One of the nonsense words in the experiment is LIDBER. Here are the sentences that use the word LIDBER:

1. ALL THE CHILDREN WILL *lidber* AT MARY'S PARTY.
2. THE POLICE DID NOT ALLOW THE PEOPLE TO *lidber* ON THE STREET.
3. THE PEOPLE *lidbered* ABOUT THE SPEAKER WHEN HE FINISHED HIS TALK.
4. PEOPLE *lidber* QUICKLY WHEN THERE IS AN ACCIDENT.
5. THE MORE FLOWERS YOU *lidber* THE MORE YOU WILL HAVE.
6. JIMMY *lidbered* STAMPS FOR ALL COUNTRIES.

These sentences and eleven other similar sets were given to five groups of children, 25 in each group. The groups differed in average age from nine years (8 years 6 months to 9 years 5 months) to thirteen years, by yearly intervals.

Before a child can perform satisfactorily on this test, there are a number of different concepts and modes of functioning that he must have acquired, and others that must be discarded. Some of these cognitive achievements are concerned with the nature of language, some with the meanings of words, and some with the tacit conventions that govern the test situation.

1. RIGIDITY OF MEANING. The child must think of solutions to each of the sentences but keep them tentative and be willing to revise them until he arrives at a single solution that fits all of the sentences. For example, one child interpreted the word *soldeve* as "bumpy" in the sentence, WHEN WE WERE DRIVING IN THE EVENING WE DID NOT FEEL SAFE BECAUSE THINGS ON THE ROAD SEEMED TO *soldeve*. In another sentence, PUTTING THE DRESS ON THE SUNNY LAWN MADE THE COLOR OF THE CLOTH *soldeve,* the child said the word meant "different color". The child declared that "different color" didn't fit the first sentence because it was about "bumpy". In other words, he took his first solution as fixed and could not keep it tentative until he had seen all the sentences. This sort of rigidity and other variations of it are found somewhere in every child's performance, but its frequency declines with age. Figure 17-2 shows the frequency of such rigidity at the various ages.

2. CONCRETE SYMBOLISM. The child must recognize that the nonsense word is a symbol for an unknown and that it may mean anything. Some children picked meanings for the nonsense word because of similarity of sound. One child (8-8), for example, said LIDBER was leave. The child said, "It doesn't fit any sentence—but 'lidber' sounds like 'leave' so that must be it." Another child (9-3) said HUDRAY was "hurry." This assumption of the concrete similarity between the symbol and meaning is a problem primarily for the youngest children.

Another kind of concrete symbolism is somewhat different. Werner called it *sentence realism* because it seemed to involve the tacit assumption that the sentence was imparting actual concrete information about a single object rather than the variety of objects that might be symbolized by a single word. One sentence, for example, said, A CORPLUM MAY BE LONG OR SHORT, THICK OR THIN, STRONG OR WEAK. In this series, CORPLUM means a stick or piece of wood. One child said it was "door" because a door was "thick and long." Another child said, "You are going to put all of them in one sentence, long, short, thick, thin, strong, weak? So it doesn't make sense—so it's wrong." Because he assumed that CORPLUM was a single concrete object that had to be long and short, thick and thin, strong and weak, he was sure that was impossible.

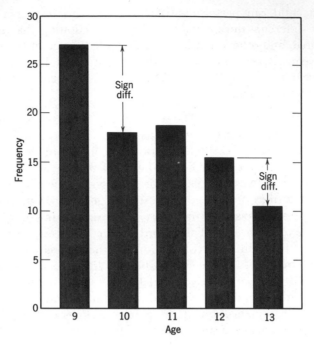

Figures 17-2. Frequency of rigidity of response among children of each age level. The differences marked "Significant Difference" are statistically significant.

Another child found the right solution to CORPLUM. He fit it into the sentence, THE PAINTER USED A CORPLUM (stick) TO MIX HIS PAINTS, and also into the sentence, YOU CAN MAKE A CORPLUM SMOOTH WITH SANDPAPER. But then he said that maybe some painters did not like smooth sticks. He was assuming that the same stick used to mix the paints was the one that could be made smooth with sandpaper, instead of conceiving of a stick as a label for a class of objects.

Figure 17-3 shows the frequency of these various kinds of concrete symbolism with age. This kind of psychological functioning appears early and practically disappears by the age of twelve.

3. WORD SENTENCE FUSION AND HOLOPHRASIS. A third problem reveals itself in a variety of ways, and is more difficult to describe. The child must recognize that the word is a distinct portion of the sentence which is transferable into other sentences, and that it has a distinct meaning which is not shared with the rest of the sentence. He must

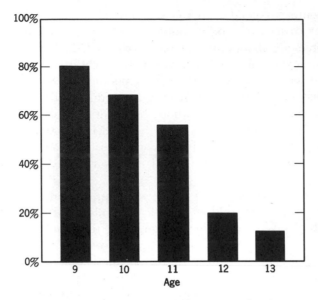

Figure 17-3. Percentages of children at different ages showing concrete realism.

also recognize that its meaning can also be transferred to other sentences. This represents the differentiation of a word from the sentence in which it appears.

Another kind of differentiation is also required. The word *stick* refers to only one part of the total situation described in the sentence, "The painter used a stick to mix his paints." If the word, CORPLUM, is used to refer to the entire situation of a painter stirring his paint with a stick, it is called *holophrasis*. In primitive languages some words have holophrastic meanings. In one language, for example, *zembela* means "to hop across earth seared by great heat." As a language grows and advances, the meaning of a word becomes limited to an element of a situation, because such limitation is more efficient and adaptive. If we had a different word for every concrete situation the vocabulary would be impossibly large. Words continue to have connotations, however, that express more than their denotative meanings; the connotation is holophrastic. For example, the words *determined* and *stubborn* have similar denotative meanings but quite different connotation.

Both kinds of differentiation, the word from the sentence, and its meaning from the situation, are reflected in this experiment. In the younger children the meaning of the word is at times confused with the entire sentence of which it is a part. For example, one child, age 9

years 5 months, responded to the sentence PEOPLE TALK ABOUT THE
BORDICKS OF OTHERS AND DON'T LIKE TO TALK ABOUT THEIR OWN, as follows. "People talk about other people and don't talk about themselves,
that's what BORDICK means." Then, when the child came to sentence
four in that series, PEOPLE WITH BORDICKS ARE OFTEN UNHAPPY, he said,
"People that talk about other people are unhappy because say this
lady hears someone is talking about her and then she'll get mad."
Sometimes the meaning attributed to the word is almost a restatement
of the sentence; at other times it is a condensation or an evaluation of
the whole sentence. Werner called all these variations "sentence core
concepts."

A sentence core concept may occur when an individual sentence is
interpreted, but many children handle the individual sentences in a
differentiated way, that is, they assign some reasonable meaning to
the word. The regression to a sentence core concept comes when the
child tries to find a single meaning for all the sentences. For example,
in finding a meaning for LIDBER one child said, "play," for the first sentence. Then, in sentence 5 he said, "The more flowers you *pick off* the
more you will have next year." When he tried to fit the two meanings
together he used them both: "If I '*pick*' a lot of flowers I can '*play*'
flower store."

In other cases the meaning of the word is taken to be a whole concrete situation, even though it is not part of the sentence. One example of this type of holophrastic use of a word comes from the record of
a child aged 10. In the series of sentences using LIDBER, he assigned the
meaning "collect" to LIDBER. In sentence 6, JIMMY "collected" STAMPS
FROM ALL COUNTRIES. One might think now he had the whole problem
solved because "collect" does fit all the sentences, but when this child
went back to fit the meaning into the previous sentences, the meaning
he transferred was not just "collect" but "collect stamps," so that his
translation of sentence number 2 became, THE POLICE DID NOT ALLOW
THE PEOPLE TO "collect stamps" ON THE STREET, and then went on to
explain "because it would be untidy to collect stamps on the street on
a windy day; they would be flying all around."

Sometimes the holophrastic use of the word is developed and then
the actual circumscribed word is dropped out, so that the child is left
with the neighboring parts of the sentence as the concept. One child
offered "do" as the meaning of PROTEMA in the sentence, PHILIP ASKED
JOHN TO HELP HIM PROTEMA HIS HOMEWORK. This child really thought
of PROTEMA holophrastically as "do his homework," but in other sentences only the homework part of the concept was transferred, and the
original meaning, *do,* was dropped completely.

Usually the accessory attributes of the holophrastic concept come from the sentence in which the concept appears, but sometimes a broader meaning comes from some outside situation. Thus, one child offered "plant" as the meaning of CONTAVISH in the following series:

1.   YOU CAN'T FILL ANYTHING WITH A *contavish*
2.   THE MORE YOU TAKE OUT OF A *contavish* THE LARGER IT GETS
3.   BEFORE THE HOUSE IS FINISHED THE WALLS MUST HAVE *contavishes.*
4.   YOU CAN'T FEEL OR TOUCH A *contavish.*
5.   A BOTTLE HAS ONLY ONE *contavish.*
6.   JOHN FELL IN A *contavish* IN THE ROAD

As he tried to fit this word into various sentences, it became clear that what the child had in mind was not just a "plant," but an entire flower pot containing dirt plus the things growing out of it. He sometimes used one part of this aggregate, sometimes another, to fit the demands of the various sentences. For example in sentence 2, he said, "The more dirt you take out of the inside of the plant the larger the "plant" gets (more room in the pot).

All of these examples can be considered problems of differentiation. In one way or another the child fails to differentiate the total sentence or the global situation and takes a word that refers to some part of it as referring to the whole. He may then use some other part of the totality in another sentence, without quite realizing that he no longer is using the same word with which he started.

4.   INTEGRATION OF MEANINGS OF A WORD. Still another process arises in the solution of the problems. The child may fit a set of individual meanings to the word in the various sentences and now have to find some way of integrating them into a single word. For example, one child gave the solution "lie to" for PRIGNATUS in the sentence, BOYS SOMETIMES PRIGNATUS THEIR PARENTS. Then he used the word "cheat" in the sentence, MARY DID NOT KNOW THAT JANE USED TO PRIGNATUS. Since "lie to" and "cheat" are both concrete instances of a more general term "deceive," one can integrate the two concrete meanings into a more general one that fits both sentences and that also fits a third sentence, YOU MAY PRIGNATUS SOMEONE BUT YOU WILL NOT GET AWAY WITH IT OFTEN. This illustrates integration by generalization.

Werner pointed out that children used a variety of other genetically inferior processes to integrate separate meanings of the nonsense word. He distinguished three of them: *aggregation, pluralization,* and *transposition.*

The simplest form of aggregation is merely to put the individual meanings together. One child gave the meaning "gay" for a word in one sentence, and "get" for it in another. His overall solution was "gay and get." At other times the aggregate solution is made somewhat more coherent by the invention of a relationship among the various meanings. For example, one child gave the meaning "paint" for CONTAVISH in the sentence, BEFORE THE HOUSE IS FINISHED THE WALLS MUST HAVE CONTAVISHES. In another sentence, he gave "air" as the solution for CONTAVISH in YOU CAN'T FEEL OR TOUCH A CONTAVISH. When he aggregated the two, he reinterpreted the first sentence as follows: "The walls must have 'air' before the house is finished so the 'paint' will dry."

A second, much less primitive, process for combining the meanings of a word from different sentences is pluralization. If aggregation is the mere putting together of different meanings and the advanced process is generalization, the searching for what is common to the various meanings, pluralization falls in between. It represents finding a vague general concept that encompasses all the meanings. Thus, for example, one child offered "dripple glass" as the solution for YOU CAN'T FILL ANYTHING WITH A CONTAVISH, and "jack-in-the-box" for THE MORE YOU TAKE OUT OF A CONTAVISH THE LARGER IT GETS. She explained her words in each sentence. "You can't fill up a dripple glass because the water will leak out and everything" and "When you take the jack-in-the-box out of the box it gets bigger—it stretches." When the child tried to find a single meaning she used "plaything," a too-general word which does not fit either sentence as well as the original word did.

Other children combine individual meanings in a much vaguer way, asserting only that the individual meanings are "kinda like" each other. Werner called this transposition. For example, one child offered "dirty" as the meaning of SOLDEVE, in the sentence, THE DINNER WAS GOOD BUT THE FRUIT WE ATE WAS SOLDEVE. Then he offered "burnt" in the sentence, PUTTING THE DRESS ON THE SUNNY LAWN MADE THE COLOR OF THE CLOTH SOLDEVE. He explained, "The sun burnt a little hole in it; burnt is dirty-like."

5. LABILITY OF USAGE OF WORDS. Still another problem is the child's failure sometimes to distinguish between the different functions a word may have in a situation. Thus, for example, some children will find a solution that is transitive in some sentences and intransitive in others. One child, struggling with the meaning of PRIGNATUS, used "ignore" in the sentence BOYS SOMETIMES PRIGNATUS THEIR PARENTS. Then in the next sentence, A GOOD MAN WHO TELLS THE TRUTH WILL NEVER PRIGNATUS, the child used "be ignored." "people will always listen to him."

Thus, we see how Werner identified a variety of processes that represented ways of dealing with the problems presented by this experiment. Some of them are inferior to others, but each is a way of coping with the task. In addition, each of these processes has its own developmental curve. The use of the entire sentence as the meaning of the word declines rapidly and almost disappears by age eleven. The processes of *pluralization* and *aggregation of different solutions* are more advanced. Both processes actually increase in frequency between ages 9 and 10, and then decline as the process of generalization supersedes them.

In his analysis of these data, Werner combined all of the processes representing the most primitive types of thinking, such as word-sentence fusion, calling them *A*-processes. Then he combined the more advanced processes, like pluralization, that are still not adequate for this task and called them *B*-processes. Figure 17-4 shows the frequency of these processes at different age levels.

One reason Werner arranged the table in this fashion was to illustrate his hypothesis that the developmental process was not a single-line development, but that it was best described as the replacement of primitive processes by more advanced ones, which were, in turn, re-

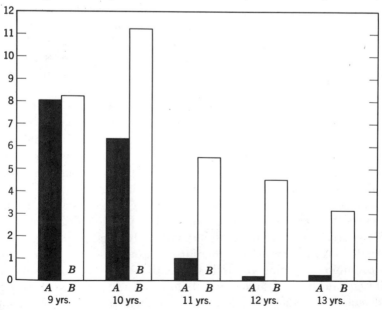

Figure 17-4. Age changes in different kinds of cognitive processes. Frequency of *A* and *B* processes.

placed by still more advanced ones. Notice that A-processes decline steadily with age, but B-processes peak at age 10 and then decline.

Another point illustrated by the table is that some of these processes drop out rapidly at a particular age. Between 10 and 11, for example, the A-processes practically disappear. In examining the developmental curves for some of the individual processes, it is often apparent that there are much larger changes at some years than at others. This irregularity in the age curves led Werner to hypothesize that many of the developmental changes in individual processes were abrupt rather than gradual. The apparent gradualness of development may be the result of using some measure of achievement that depends on a wide variety of functions, so that it averages out the abrupt changes in individual functions.

Not only is there an abrupt loss of some functions, but also other functions, though relatively primitive, continue to appear even among the oldest children in the sample, and would probably appear in an adult sample, too. These primitive functions may assist in solving the problem, provided that the individual can go beyond them. Referring to the example (p. 512) of pluralization, we can see how an adult, in working out his solution, might well develop the hypothesis that PRIGNATUS had "something to do with not respecting one's elders." This much constraint upon the search for a word that actually fits the sentences could be very useful. When the child does not have the more advanced processes, however, he may leave the solution at this stage and feel that he has solved it. As a final answer such a solution would be classified as pluralization.

Finally, we can find in this experiment examples of what Werner called analogous functioning, where the same answer can be obtained by genetically different level processes. Thus, many of the older children in this study could find quite satisfactory solutions for an individual sentence. Thus, the boy who interpreted LIDBER as "collect stamps" arrived at this solution by a translation of JIMMY LIDBERED STAMPS FROM ALL COUNTRIES into "Jimmy collected stamps from all countries." From this sentence alone, his psychological functioning leads to precisely the same result as a more advanced one.

Analogous functioning of different processes poses a serious problem for psychologists doing research with children. So often we find that children can solve a problem in a behavioral way, yet reveal basic misunderstandings when we inquire about their solution. For example, one might ask whether a child knew the meaning of right and left. He could hold up his right hand correctly. If one shows him two objects, a red and a blue pencil, he can say accurately that the blue pencil is to the right of the red one. In one sense he demonstrates his knowledge of right and left. However, if there are three objects, say red, blue, and green pencils, he may deny that the blue pencil is to the right of the red one. For him only the green pencil is to the right. Right and left are not relative words pointing to the relation between two objects, but absolute terms identified with his own right and left hand. The challenge to research psychologists is to design experimental situations where the subject's behavioral response is an accurate reflection of the underlying psychological processes.

In summary, Werner conceived of development as a shift from processes that were undifferentiated to those involving differentiation and hierarchical organization. All of these processes may be available to the mature organism and usable in his adaptive behavior, but the younger or more primitive organism will be limited to the kind of functioning that corresponds to the more primitive of these processes. Werner's interpretation of the results from the study of the acquisition of word meanings illustrates how these hypotheses can be applied to the interpretation of children's behavior in an experimental situation.

MICROGENESIS

Werner, as we pointed out early in this chapter, was a thorough-going developmentalist. Nowhere is this more evident than in his studies of microgenesis. He attempted to extend the developmental concept from the relatively slow changes that occurred in the growth of the individual, or the even slower one in cultural change, to the actual process by which a thought or a perception or a judgment is elicited. In other words, he hypothesized that in the fraction of a second required to perceive an object, that perception developed from an early undifferentiated perception through a sequence of developmental stages to a differentiated articulated and organized one. The primitive perceptions of the young child or the schizophrenic patient reflect the halting of this developmental process at some point before the differentiated perception appears.

The experiments on which this hypothesis is based often halt the microgenetic development at some point, by presenting the stimulus for so brief an exposure that there is not time enough for a fully articulated perception to form. As the time of presentation is gradually lengthened, the development of the perception can be studied in detail.

One early experiment in microgenesis supports the hypothesis that in some subjects at least, the development of recognition of a word goes through a stage where the word's general sphere of meaning is apprehended even though the word itself is unrecognizable (Werner, 1930). Since this experiment was conducted before Werner left Germany, the stimulus words are in German. The subject was shown each stimulus word for 1/50 second and asked to report all he could about it. Then he was allowed another 1/50 second look and required to make another report. The quick looks were repeated until the subject finally recognized the word or phrase clearly.

One protocol follows. The stimulus was the phrase "sanfter Wind," which is translated as "gentle wind." Here are the subject's responses following each tachistoscopic presentation.

1. "———? Wind   What stood before 'wind' feels like an adjective specifying nature of the wind; feels like 'warm' or something similar. Definitely not a word defining direction."
2. "—ter Wind   Know now that the 'heavier' than 'warm'—somehow more abstract."
3. "—cher Wind   Now it looks more like an adjective of direction."
4. "—ter Wind   Now again somewhat more concrete, it faces me and looks somewhat like 'weicher Wind' (soft wind) but 'ter' is in my way."
5. "Now very clearly 'sanfter Wind.' Not at all surprised. I had this actually before in the characteristic feel of the word and the looks of it."

Werner pointed not only to the emergence of a sphere of meaning prior to recognition of the word, but also to the fact that there was some organismic involvement in the process. The subject says that it "feels" like warm, not that it looks like warm. It is as if the first presentation still lacked differentiation of the separate sensory modalities in the process.

Before leaving this experiment, we should point out that there are alternative interpretations of these findings. What is the stimulus to which the early spheric responses correspond? Did Werner imply that the word was actually recognized at some level, but that only its general sphere of meaning was available for a report? This seems a difficult interpretation to justify. One possibility suggested by other investigators is that the early response is an interpretation based upon the parts of the stimulus not necessarily whole letters, that were actually recognized. Because of the characteristics of the language, the recognizable parts do provide a clue to the general meaning of the word, even though they do not give its exact spelling. If this is true, the process is quite different from that proposed by Werner. The general spheric meaning would not represent an early stage of perception, but rather a relatively sophisticated interpretation based upon partial information about the word.

More recently, Werner and his colleagues investigated microgenesis in the development of an interpretation of Rorschach cards. The Rorschach test is widely used in clinical studies of personality and personality disorders. It consists of ten ink blots, some in black and white, some in color. The subject is asked to look at each card and tell, "What it looks like, what it might be." These responses are then scored in a variety of ways, but a group of Werner's colleagues (Hemmendinger, Freed, & Phillips), have constructed a genetic scoring of the Rorschach test, based upon developmental theory.

One of the usual scores used in interpreting the Rorschach test is whether the response of the subject is a whole response, a detail response, or a rare-details response. If the subject reports that the whole blot looks like something, that is a whole response. But there are different sorts of whole responses. Some are vague and general, like "clouds," "an anatomical drawing," or "smoke and flames," without any specification of details and any serious effort to fit the contours of the blot to the actual shape of some object. Clouds can be any shape, so that it is easy to say that a blot is shaped like a cloud.

Other whole responses are much more specific and differentiated. If the subject says that some blot looks like two ballet dancers whirling, and that they are wearing ballet skirts and tall head dresses, it is a much more differentiated whole response, provided, of course, that there is some reasonable correspondence between the parts of the blot and the various figures reported in it.

In between these two kinds of whole responses, there are responses to the shape of some detail in the blot. A detail requires some differentiation of the blot into parts, but not the organization of these parts into an articulated whole. The same can be said for the responses to the rare and tiny details of the blot. These responses require differentiation of the whole into parts, but not necessarily an integration.

From these examples we can see how developmental criteria can be used. Once this scoring system is developed, it becomes possible to use it to study developmental phenomena. Figures 17-5, 17-6, 17-7, and 17-8 show the way these different kinds of responses are distributed under a variety of conditions. Figure 17-5 shows the percentages of each developmental type of response as the exposure time is gradually increased. After a 0.01-second exposure, most responses tend to be global,

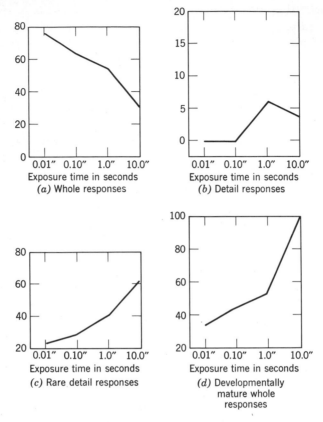

Figure 17-5. Effect of exposure time on frequency of different kinds of Rorschach responses. (After Werner (1957), pp. 142–3.)

diffuse, whole responses. As the exposure time is gradually lengthened, responses to details gradually become dominant and the percentage of developmentally mature, whole responses also increases.

To support the hypothesis that this microgenetic development reflects the same process occurring with age, Werner compared the age curves for these same responses with the curves for exposure time (see Figure 17-6). There is a striking parallel between the curves in Figures 17-5 and 17-6. Werner's hypothesis is, that in young children the development of the perception of the ink blots halts at some early point just as it can be halted by a short exposure time.

Figure 17-7 also shows the differences between two groups of schizophrenic patients and a normal sample on the same developmental

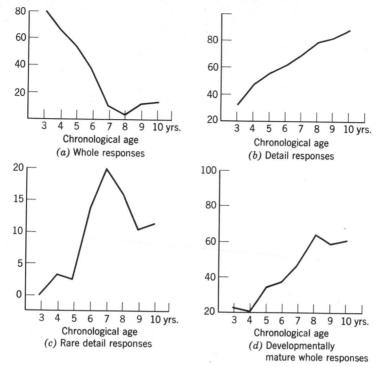

Figure 17-6. Rorschach responses at different chronological ages. (After Werner (1957), pp. 142–3.)

variables. The hebephrenic and catatonic types of schizophrenic are judged to be more pathological and more regressed than the paranoid schizophrenic.

Again, Werner's hypothesis is that in the pathological subjects, the normal developmental process resulting in an articulated response is halted in midstream. To give still more support for this particular interpretation, Werner also compared the curves for schizophrenics and normals to different degrees of exposure time (see Figure 17-8). At the .01-second level of exposure, the schizophrenic and normal sample are not very different. The striking feature is that the schizophrenics' responses do not improve with longer exposure times, whereas the responses of the normal sample do. Thus, Werner argued that in the microgenetic development of the response, the schizophrenics in this sample were functioning only at a primitive level that could occur with only a fraction of a second exposure time.

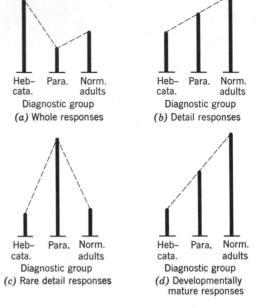

Figure 17-7. Rorschach responses in different diagnostic groups. (After Werner (1957), pp. 142–3.)

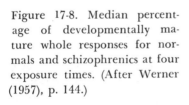

Figure 17-8. Median percentage of developmentally mature whole responses for normals and schizophrenics at four exposure times. (After Werner (1957), p. 144.)

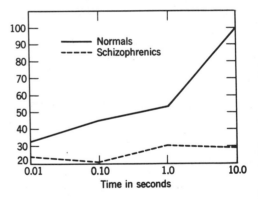

SENSORITONIC THEORY OF PERCEPTION

Werner's major emphasis was his concept of development, but one line of his research stemmed from another aspect of his general theoretical point of view. Werner called himself an organismic psychologist. The organismic point of view is related to gestalt psychology, represented in this book by Kurt Lewin.

Gestalt psychology developed in protest against the atomism of a psychology based on association. It insists that psychological functioning depends on the operation of interdependent psychological systems rather than on sets of independent elementary acts. One of the favorite findings of gestalt psychology is that the psychological functioning and properties of a stimulus depend on its context as well as on its characteristics as a stimulus. Wertheimer, the founder of the gestalt tradition, studied apparent movement extensively as an example of the effect of a context. A flashing light by itself is perceived to flash off and on, but it is in no way remarkable. If another flashing light is placed a short distance away, and its flashes are timed to alternate with those of the first light, the observer sees one steady light moving quickly back and forth between the two positions. The total stimulus situation has psychological properties not possessed by either isolated stimulus.

Organismic psychology is based on the belief that all behavior and all responses are reactions of the total organism to the total stimulus situation. It has always remained a protest position. Organismic psychologists are often content with the mere demonstration that everything in the psychological situation influences everything else in it; they seldom go beyond this point to a specific theory to predict just what the influence will be.

Werner was an organismic psychologist, but in his sensoritonic theory of perception he tried to advance beyond the mere fact of organismic functioning to an actual theory about the mechanism. Seymour Wapner has been an important colleague of Werner in developing this theory. The basic postulate of the sensoritonic theory of perception is that "a perceptual property is an experience which corresponds to a particular relation between organismic state and stimuli from an object" (Werner & Wapner, 1956, p. 316). Let us fill in some background for this hypothesis.

In the naïve view of perception described in Chapter 1, we assume that perception is a function of the stimulus object; in other words, the perception is a function of the stimulus object, except in cases where there is some visual defect which spoils the transmission. This naïve view is clearly oversimplified; nevertheless, many students of perception argue that it is generally a reasonably accurate representation of the stimulus object.

There is an opposite tradition in the study of perception, however. Some researchers have primarily investigated the effects of a person's motives, beliefs, and attitudes on his perception. These investigators believe perception involves a process of projection in which perceptual experience reflects various organismic factors such as motivation, attitude, and set. The Rorschach test, for example, is based upon the assumption that if the subject is given an ambiguous stimulus like an ink blot, his perception of it can be used as a measure of such personality variables as impulse and impulse control, sensuousness, negativism, and introversion-extraversion.

It has been a persistent problem in psychology, therefore, to devise a theory that is able to account for both the accuracy of the perception of the external stimulus and the projective aspects of perception which reflect organismic factors. The sensoritonic theory represents one such attempt, and its basic postulate, as stated, is that perception is a function of the relation between the organismic state and the appropriate stimuli. Research on this theory has tended to concentrate upon the perception of verticality, perception of the mid-line, the "straight-ahead point," or the perception of the horizon ("eye-level point"). One of the basic experiments arising from this research is the *rod and frame* experiment.

In the rod and frame experiment, the subject is placed in a dark room and shown a luminous rod that appears as a bright line in his visual field. He has controls for adjusting the tilt of this line, and his task is to move it until it looks vertical. Under the control condition he is seated in an upright chair and his head held rigidly upright. Under these conditions, most subjects are quite accurate in their judgments about the verticality of the rod. This standard control condition may be varied in several ways. In one type of experiment, the subject's body is tilted in one direction or the other by movement of the chair in which he is seated. He is asked to adjust the rod until it looks vertical. By vertical is meant a true vertical, parallel to the walls of the room, not to the longitudinal axis of the subject's body. In other experiments, the line is surrounded by a luminous square frame. This frame may be tilted in one direction or the other and the subject must adjust the rod until it appears vertical. Or both he and the frame may be tilted in the same or opposite directions, and again he tries to judge when the line is vertical.

We shall use the experiment in which there is no frame but the body is tilted, to explain the way the sensoritonic theory operates. The term *sensoritonic* refers to the assumption that the tonus of the organism, the level of muscle tension, and all the rest, are functions of the pattern of sensory inputs. Sometimes this organism tonus is balanced. If so, it is in equilibrium and stable. When the pattern of sensory inputs is unbalanced or asymmetrical, however, there is a tendency for the organism to return it to balance. The balance can sometimes be restored by a movement of the body, and at others by a change in the perceptual experience.

Returning to the problem of verticality, Werner assumed that when the body was upright, the organism was in balance in relation to the sensory input. There are several sense organs involved, particularly those in the middle ear. When the body is upright, the input to these sense organs on the two sides of the body is balanced. The visual sensory input can also be balanced or unbalanced. A balanced visual input is one that is symmetrical about the vertical axis. If the sensory input from the gravity system and the input from the visual system are both balanced, the perceiver judges the rod to be vertical, and his own body to be upright. The entire system is in balance, and there is a stable relationship between the organismic state and the stimulus input.

Werner symbolized this relation as $o_X Rs_X$. The R refers to the relationship, o represents the organismic state, and s the sensory input. The state of balance is indicated by the fact that both o and s have the same subscript. If the relationship were unstable, the o and the s would have different subscripts: $o_X Rs_Y$ or $o_Y Rs_X$. The hypothesis of sensoritonic theory is that in such an unstable relation, the organismic state tends to change until the balance and stability of the relationship is restored. Given $o_X Rs_Y$ there is a tendency for o_X to change to o_Y, so that the relation becomes $o_Y Rs_Y$, which is balanced.

It is important not to fall into a misunderstanding at this point. The example suggests that s in the formula refers to sensory input from the outside, and the o to the somatic and visceral sensations that come from the organism. This is not generally true. The basic sensoritonic assumption is that all stimuli, either from the inside or outside, affect the tonus of the organism. The contributions to o may stem from somatic or external stimuli.

How, then, are the s and the o different? Werner assumed that the state of s was determined by stimuli from the object being judged or attended to. Thus, in the experiments on the verticality of the line, the balance or imbalance of s is determined by the stimuli from the line. The o factor is determined by all the extraneous stimulation; it might come from gravity, or from the visual frame if the frame were present. If the subject were asked to judge whether his body was upright or not, then the gravity stimuli would contribute to s in the formula.

How does all this work out in the perception of the vertical? Figure 17-9, taken from one of Werner and Wapner's articles, illustrates the theory. The two researchers defined a hypothetical equilibrial axis of the body that was vertical (represented o_0) whenever the extraneous forces on the right and left balanced. When the body tilted to the left,

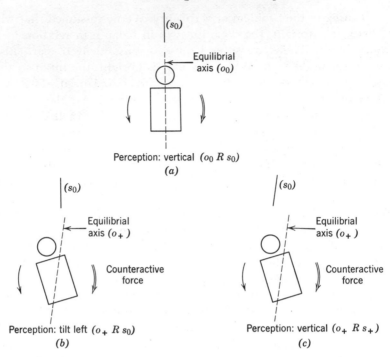

Figure 17-9. Sensoritonic balance and perception of verticality. Hypothetical mechanism of the effect of body tilt on the perception of verticality (shown for left body tilt only). (a) Body erect (0_o), rod at plumb line (S_o); (b) body left, rod at plumb line; (c) body left, rod adjusted to apparent vertical. (After Werner and Wapner (1956), p. 321.)

the hypothesis was that compensatory muscle tension on the right side of the body was evoked, so that the equilibrial axis tilted to the right (o_+). If, in this condition, the rod was actually vertical (s_0), the relation was imbalanced o_+Rs_0, and this imbalance resulted in the perceptual experience of the red appearing tilted to the left. If the subject were asked to adjust the rod until it appeared vertical, he would rotate it toward the right until a balanced relationship o_+Rs_+ was restored. This same effect on the equilibratory axis could be obtained by other kinds of extraneous stimulation besides actual tilting of the body. Direct electrical stimulation of the left neck muscle, auditory stimulation of the left ear, or counterclockwise rotation of the body about the vertical axis, all shifted the equilibrial axis to the right.

Sensoritonic theory can also predict another sort of phenomenon: the adaptation of the organism to a stimulus. For example, if one continually looks at a slightly tilted line, he will over a period of time, see the line gradually seem to lose its apparent tilt. In terms of sensoritonic theory this is explained as follows: A left-tilted line initially represents the relation o_0Rs_-. This results in a perception of left tilt, but it also is an imbalanced condition which tends to become equilibrated. According to the theory, the equilibrial axis of the body gradually moves toward the left. The relation gradually balances by becoming o_-Rs_-, and this balanced relationship also corresponds to the perception of a vertical line.

A more suprising finding which stems from sensoritonic theory is the effect of completely extraneous stimuli upon the perception of the vertical or the median plane (straight-ahead position). If, for example, a subject fixates the right-hand edge of a rectangle, the apparent median plane moves to the left. The figure is then seen placed more symmetrically than it is. Figures that are physically located so that their midline is straight ahead, but which have some unidirectional dynamic quality, like a hand pointing, or a bird flying, also shift the apparent median plane. A picture of a bird in flight pulls the apparent median plane in the direction of the flight; if such a figure is adjusted until it appears straight ahead, it will be adjusted to the left of the objective median plane.

Finally, Werner attempted to integrate his concepts of development of sensoritonic theory to account for some of the age differences in the effect of body tilt on the apparent vertical and also for differences between schizophrenics in their response to the body tilt experiment. The empirical findings themselves are unexpected. The adult, it will be recalled, tends to adjust the apparent vertical to the right if his body is tilted to the left. The left body-tilt arouses compensatory muscle tension that produces an actual sensoritonic imbalance in the opposite direction. With young children and with schizophrenics, this does not happen. Up to the age of ten at least, children adjust the rod so that it tilts in the same direction as the body tilt.

To state it somewhat differently then Werner, it is as if the adult recognizes that his body is tilted and out of line with the objective upright, and so, in trying to allow for the known tilt of his body, he exaggerates his tilt and overcompensates. His action may be seen as a tendency to counteract a recognized discrepancy between the body and the external world.

Now, if we assume that for the young child there is less differentiation between the body and the external world, then the external world is egocentrically bound to the position of the body. We might predict that, for very young children, the apparent vertical would coincide with the actual body axis. This would be true for everybody if the body were tilted in a fashion that made it impossible to know it was tilted, say in a weightless condition in space. The apparent upright would be the same as the longitudinal axis of the body. The overcompensation, then, is the result of the adult's recognition of his body's being tilted, and is an attempt to discriminate his longitudinal axis from the true vertical. The partial failure of that discrimination accounts for the opposite direction of the distortion in young children.

DIFFERENTIATION AND FIELD-INDEPENDENCE

From this point on, the story of Werner's contributions to developmental psychology shifts from his hands to those of the people whom he has influenced. One of these in particular, Herman Witkin, was never a student of Werner's. Although he developed many of his ideas quite independently, Witkin was influenced by Werner and his research fits so neatly into the Werner tradition of developmental studies that it seems appropriate to include an account of his work in a chapter on Werner's theories.

Witkin's research is reported in *Psychological Differentiation* (1962). He employed the concept of differentiation to interpret the findings on a diverse battery of measures used on children. The central set of measures assessed each child on a variable called field-independence; these tests will be described in a moment, but they included the rod and frame experiment as well as others. The personalities of the children were then studied in a variety of ways: They were tested on intelligence, their responses to the Rorschach and the Thematic Apperception Test were obtained, and each child was interviewed; the mothers of the children were interviewed to ascertain the early life experiences of each child; and, certain subsamples were followed longitudinally over a period of years.

The central thesis of the work is that psychological differentiation is an imporant personality variable with manifestation in many areas of behavior. It increases with age, but there are individual differences among children of the same age. Psychological differentiation may be fostered or retarded by early life experiences and by the parent-child relation.

The concept of *field-dependence* originally came from studies by Witkin on the perception of the upright. The experiments were more elaborate than the Werner experiments, including not only a tilting rod, a tilting frame, and a tilting chair, but also a whole tilting room.

The tilt of all of these objects could be independently controlled. Sometimes the subject had to adjust the rod to the vertical, sometimes to the room, and sometimes to his own body. In many ways, however, the rod and frame test and the body adjustment test seem closely related. Both measure the ability of the subject to pay attention to, or analyze, one set of sensory cues without being influenced by a variety of extraneous and conflicting ones. In order to show that these abilities were not primarily related to the subject's sensitivity to the particular cues of gravity and the visual upright, Witkin and his coworkers adopted a third, completely different test of the same variable. It is called the embedded figure test and requires the subject to identify a simple figure that is embedded in a larger one in such a way that the contours of the embedded and surrounding figures coincide at many points. Figure 17-10 shows one example. In this experiment, the ability of the subject to abstract or analyze one stimulus out of a confusing setting of extraneous stimuli is clearly tested. This test correlates with the rod and frame test and the body adjustment test, and is also related to a variety of perceptual tasks. All in all, there is evidence that the tests of field-dependence do have a common factor, and that the ability to perform in tests of field-dependence is relevant to other perceptual abilities. Witkin wants to show that it is related to a still broader field of behavioral characteristics, and that it is one indication of the degree of the child's developmental differentiation.

In order to show the breadth of the concept field-dependence versus field-independence, the investigators explored its correlations with various indices of intellectual functioning. The three tests that best measure field-independence, the body adjustment test, the rod and frame test, and the embedded figure test, were included in a factor analysis along with the various subtests of the Wechsler Intelligence Scale for Children (WISC). One of the three factors which emerged is called the analytical field approach. It includes all of the measures of field-independence and, in addition, some tests on picture completion

 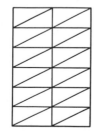

Figure 17-10. An embedded figure.

and block design, as well as other tests of intellectual functioning which require the isolation of an object or an idea out of an embedding context. This feature is the basis for the label *analytical field approach*. It implies the ability to decompose a field into its independent parts. Some other tests of intellectual functioning that also correlate with this analytical factor pose certain insight problems. In these problems, the subject must construct some object or accomplish some objective using materials that are not obviously useful. For example, a pair of pliers may need to be tied to the end of a piece of rope as a weight so that it can be tossed from one side of a gap to another. The kind of problem correlated with field-dependence is one in which this same object must be used both conventionally and unconventionally; one such problem requires the subject to use a pair of pliers in a conventional way to remove a nail from a board, and also to use the same object as a support for a shelf. The ability to use an object in an unconventional way seems to require the ability to see its inherent characteristics, regardless of its more conventional uses.

If this analytical field approach were reflected in both perceptual and intellectual functioning, Witkin and his colleagues felt that it would be detectable in a variety of other performances. For example, it should be reflected in the subject's responses to the Rorschach ink blots. They devised a rating scheme for judging whether a Rorschach response required a low or a high level of organization. In some ways this rating scheme is more refined than the scoring of the Rorschach according to developmental level and less concerned with the ability of the subject to integrate the parts of the blot into a single hierarchically organized interpretation. In general, however, it is quite similar to the scoring developed by Werner's group. This scoring of the Rorschach performance correlated positively, although not highly, with the scores on the perceptual tests, and also with the index of analytical approach in intellectual functioning. If the perceptual and intellectual tests are fused into one measure, a *cognitive index,* the correlation with the Rorschach scoring is .37.

The investigators also attempted to measure the articulateness of the subject's experience in everyday life. For this purpose they devised a scheme for scoring the interview with the subject. The interview itself was quite general. It dealt with school work, free-time activities, the child's plan for a vocation, his knowledge of current events, his health, and his family relations. In scoring the interview protocol for cognitive clarity, the rater paid little attention to the actual content of the child's answers to the interview questions. Instead, he was primarily interested in evidence that the child's cognitive picture of the world was clear, detailed, and articulated. For example, the following are the responses of two subjects to similar questions. The first is rated high on cognitive clarity, the second, low.

Example of response suggestive of cognitive clarity:

Examiner (*E*) How do you become a doctor? *S:* It's a very long feature, you have to first go to college and then to a special university.

E: And after you finish the special university? *S:* Then you get an office and the equipment you need for your work—but you start working in hospitals so you'll get patients to know you.

Example of response suggestive of lack of clarity:

E: How do you become an accountant? (Which the subject now plans to be) *S:* Well, that I don't know— I'll have to ask my father.

E: How do you become a doctor? *S:* You go to a doctor school and learn to be a doctor.

E: How long does it take? *S:* I dunno, maybe 14 or 15 years—but I figure it could take me one year. (Can give no explanation of this.)

These examples exemplify the general difference between high and low cognitive clarity in children 10 to 12 years of age. We cannot be sure, of course, that their everyday experience is organized in the same way as their answers; the difference between them might be partly their skill in verbal expression. The answers certainly suggest that the second child lives in a diffuse and confused world with little clear structure. The score for cognitive clarity in the interviews is correlated .77 with the perceptual scores of field-independence and .53 with the tests of analytical ability in intellectual functioning.

These are not the only differences found related to the measures of field-independence. Differences also appear in the child's sense of identity, in his controls and defenses, and in the consistency of his behavior over time. Furthermore, there is some evidence that people who differ widely from the norm on measures of cognitive functioning and clarity tend to develop distinctive patterns of psychopathology if they become mentally ill.

The investigators believe there may well be a genetic factor in the origin of these differences. There is evidence, for example, that identi-

cal twins perform more nearly alike on the rod and frame test than do
fraternal twins. In addition, the interviews with the mothers of the
children in the study suggest that mothers of psychologically less-
differentiated children are themselves less differentiated. They seem to
lack assurance and confidence in their own roles; they are less satisfied
about having realized their own potentialities than mothers of highly
differentiated children. They complain more, act more fatigued, and
generally seem less satisfied with their role, their friends, and themselves.

The similarity between mother and child is attributed by Witkin to
the mothers' child-rearing attitudes and proclivities. The investigators
listed six indicators suggesting that the mother has inhibited the
child's psychological differentiation.

1. She regards the child as delicate, in need of special attention or
    protection, or she regards him as irresponsible.
2. She does not accept a masculine role for the child (all subjects
    were boys).
3. Because of fears, anxieties, or emotional ties, the mother markedly
    limits the child's activities and his expeditions out into the com-
    munity.
4. She provides physical care for the child that would be more appro-
    priate for a younger child.
5. Her maternal control is not designed to help the child achieve
    mature goals or become responsible. In some cases, it is consis-
    tently directed against the child's asserting himself.
6. The mother limits curiosity and stresses conformity. Her punish-
    ments are emotional and irrational, and her discipline is severe.

When the mother interviews were rated according to these criteria,
the overall score was significantly related to the perceptual and cognitive indices of the children. Witkin, in this study, has shown the generality of the trait he calls *psychological differentiation*. By looking
carefully at many different areas of behavior, he can discern the variable's operation.

There are, of course, other aspects of the child's behavior that are
not described by this variable. Witkin's care in defining the variable in
each area of behavior is one of the noteworthy features of the research.
Psychological differentiation does not even encompass all the developmental aspects of behavior. It is unrelated to some aspects of intellectual development and related to others. From Werner's point of view,

Witkin's variable would be one of the psychological processes involved in development. Werner might have felt that the term psychological differentiation was broader than the specific variable as it is behaviorally defined. In any case, Witkin has provided definitions and measuring instruments for an aspect of Werner's concept of development.

CRITIQUE

Werner's theoretical position is a coherent organismic and developmental theory, but by comparison with Freud, Piaget, or the social-learning theory, it is limited in scope and shows little concern for explaining common everyday behavior of children. Neither does the theory, despite its emphasis on the developmental point of view, lead to any prediction about what kind of childhood experiences are antecedents of what kind of adult characteristics.

The most important contribution Werner's theory could make to the field of developmental psychology would be the introduction of a clear theory of the maturational and developmental process. There can hardly be any doubt that part of the growth of the child is maturational. We know this is true with respect to physical growth; it seems almost inconceivable that there is not a genuine maturational process in psychological development as well. Werner emphasized the nature of the developmental process throughout his career and tried to describe development in general theoretical terms.

One threat to the fruitfulness of his conception is the possibility that what Werner called development is only the result of adaptation and learning processes. If his view of development is merely the description of the symptoms of adaptation, then it provides no explanation of development because the causal factors lie in the learning and adaptive process.

Many of the features of mature or advanced behavior as Werner described them are adaptive. It is not difficult to see that an organism must show some degree of differentiated, articulated, and hierarchically organized behavior if it is to adapt to the demands of a complex environment. Stimulus-response theory has described processes of discrimination and chaining of responses into sequences that can result in differentiated, articulated behavior patterns. If we pursue the S-R hypothesis a little further, we can find in social-learning theory the development of individual responses and their waning in importance as a more adaptive response becomes predominant. We can add to these considerations the fact that all organisms look undifferentiated and disorganized during the early trials of a learning process, before effective responses have been acquired. However, the mere fact that developmental processes do progress from diffuseness and undifferentiation to articulation and discrimination does not mean that a principle of differentiation is required to explain this evolution.

Nevertheless, none of these arguments militates strongly against Werner's theories. The many examples of syncretic thinking, concrete symbolism, or word-sentence fusion he described have not been explained by any theory of learning. Certainly the analogy he drew between the principles of embryological development and psychological development suggests that differentiation is not always learned. There is a good chance that Werner actually captured some of the important principles of the maturational process underlying the growth of children. Two of the theories already discussed contain a principle of differentiation in development. Werner's contribution was to explicate this developmental principle in much more detail than anyone else, and to suggest it in new contexts, like microgenesis.

If we accept for the moment the general validity of the orthogenetic principle, we find that it is still not very clear or detailed. Despite Werner's explication, the principles of development are still not stated in a detailed enough way to lead to rigorous predictions. The terms global, diffuse, and syncretic can be convincingly exemplified, but cannot be explicitly defined. For this reason they are difficult to apply to new areas. For example, how would syncretism be identified in a young child's errors on his arithmetic paper? Probably syncretism is responsible for some of the errors, and it might be useful to recognize the role of syncretic thinking in teaching arithmetic. Clear criteria of these features of immature functioning would be most helpful.

The same difficulty applies to the sensoritonic theory of perception. If all perceptual experience is hypothesized to be a relationship between S and O, it must be possible to recognize the relationship in general perception. The terminology of the theory applies to the particular situations where it was developed, but how does it relate to size constancy, for example? In many perceptual experiments it is not clear what goes with S, and what with O.

The same criticism can be applied to most of the concepts Werner developed to explain his findings. Vagueness is, however, characteristic of most concepts at this stage of the science, and we have certainly found many examples of diffuse concepts in our survey of theories. The more important question is whether Werner's concepts can lead to fruitful research and eventually be incorporated in truly adequate theories. Werner certainly applied these concepts widely to diverse fields in his own lifetime. He was able to translate them into empirical research, and they led him to some interesting empirical findings that no other point of view has suggested. This is why Werner's concepts are potentially valuable for development psychology.

TALCOTT PARSONS (left) and R. FREED BALES (right).

Talcott Parsons

and Robert F. Bales—

The Sociological Viewpoint

EIGHTEEN   The family as a social system

THE FINAL THEORETICAL VIEW of child development to be discussed in this volume is unusual, because it is the work of sociologists looking at child development as one aspect of the functioning of a social system rather than as the growth of an individual person. Although the view of Parsons and Bales draws heavily on Freudian theory, its unique feature is its picture of the changing role of the child in the family and its concern with the dynamics of family interaction which bring about the socialization of the child.

The sociological view of the family as an interdependent system of individuals operating within the norms of the society requires some readjustments in the psychologists' customary view of parent-child relationships.

THE PSYCHOLOGICAL AND SOCIOLOGICAL VIEWS OF CHILD DEVELOPMENT

It has become traditional in developmental psychology to consider that the personality of the child is the result of his upbringing. For example, positive correlation between physical punishment as a child-rearing practice and the child's aggressiveness is often interpreted as a causal relation. The physical punishment is assumed to somehow produce aggressiveness. This is one possible interpretation of the correlation, but there are other ways of viewing the relationship. Another possibility is to think of the child-rearing practice as the result of the child's behavior. If asked to explain their use of physical punishment, parents may very well say that the child is so disobedient, does so many things they cannot permit him to do, and is so recalcitrant to milder forms of discipline that they finally turn to physical punishment as a last resort; in short, the aggressiveness and antisocial behavior of the child cause the parent to punish him severely.

Many of the other established correlations between child rearing and the child's personality can also be reinterpreted as adaptations of the parent to the behavior of the child, rather than as a casual relation between child rearing and its effects on personality development. Richard Bell (1965) has tried to see how adequate a theory of the established correlations between parent behavior and child behavior he could devise if he viewed every correlation as an effect of the child upon the parent rather than of the parent upon the child.

Psychologists, of course, are primarily interested in the mechanisms by which behavior occurs. One of the causes of behavior at any moment is the stimulus situation; therefore, any theory of behavior must specify the chain of events which lead from the stimulus to the response. Another causal factor in behavior is the personality of the individual: his abilities, needs, and attitudes. The individual personality changes over time, partly as a result of growth or maturation and partly as a result of environmental events. There is, therefore, a causal connection between the environment of the individual and changes in his personality. Child-rearing practices do influence the development of the child, and there is nothing misdirected about searching for this causal connection between the practices and the child's development.

The difficulty in the traditional causal interpretation of the correlation between child-rearing practice and child personality arises from the fact that these correlations are obtained in naturalistic situations, not in the laboratory. In experimental studies of social-learning theory, the experimental treatment, such as nurturance is applied to one group of subjects but not to another. Which child is treated nurturantly and which is not is determined by chance; the child's own personality has no bearing on whether he is in the nurturant or nonnurturant group. In these circumstances, the behavioral differences between the two groups can be considered the results of the experimental treatment.

In a naturalistic situation like the home, the circumstances are different. Each person in a situation stimulates the others around him who, in turn, stimulate him. In such an interacting system, there gradually emerges a stable pattern of behavior on the part of all members of the system. Each person habitually behaves toward others and responds to their behavior in ways which will obtain satisfaction and avoid punishment from them.

This mutually adaptive adjustment operates through the behavioral mechanisms of the individuals concerned. However, the behavior patterns of each person cannot be explained adequately without accounting for his effects upon the behavior patterns of the others in his environment, as well as for their influence on him.

From the standpoint of child development, it is clear that the infant and his mother form a mutually responding pair, and that the properties of each affect the other. An irritable and sensitive child creates an environment for the mother and produces maternal behavior patterns unlike those that would have occurred for a passive and lethargic child. Social-learning theory has to some degree used this point of view of the mother-child pair, or "dyad." Sears introduced the notion of the dyad into developmental psychology (1953). However, research on social-learning theory has not emphasized the reciprocal reinforcements and punishments within the mother-child pair, but has concentrated more upon the mother as a provider of reinforcement and the child as the recipient. This tendency is also found in all the other psychological theories we have examined.

The basic idea of a social system is that its different components mutually fit and adapt to one another. Operating a society would be a tremendously complicated task if anybody had to do it. It requires the feeding, clothing, and housing of all its members. A successful society wards off its enemies. A successful society also contains both controls on emotional responses, so that they will not upset the apple cart, and releases for them. It provides a socially useful job for everybody and a haven away from the job. Finally, it contains children who must be raised to be responsible members of the society, with the appropriate values, beliefs, and training to fill its diverse jobs. Every society spontaneously achieves this mammoth job of coordination. It is the job for sociologists to find out how.

From this vantage point, the problems of individual psychology and child development look different than they do to the individual psychologist, whose concern is with the internal mechanisms by which the individual person adapts to his environment. Talcott Parsons is a sociologist who has investigated such child development problems. In a long series of papers and books, he has attempted to develop a general theory of human action that can account for individual behavior but can also cope with the problems of social system. His theory of child development is only a tiny piece of this huge canvas. We shall be primarily concerned with that piece, but we cannot study it without getting some perspective upon his general theory of action.

GENERAL THEORY OF ACTION

Despite his primary concern with the organization of social systems, the point of reference for Parsons' analytical scheme is the individual actor. In other words, he recognizes that all social organization and disorganization is ultimately mediated by the behavior of the individual. He uses the actor more as a point of reference and an executive agent than as a living organism, however. The *actor* is the part or functioning aspect of the individual that makes the decisions. Although actors are embodied in physical organisms, Parsons describes the needs, drives, and emotions of the individual as a part of the situation with which the actor must cope. Furthermore, the situation that confronts the actor in Parsonian theory is not unlike the psychological environment described by Lewin (see pp. 87 ff.). It is the situation as it affects the actor, not the totality of physical sensations impinging upon him. It is organized and contains certain objects that are in the physical environment, but it also includes objects in the social, cultural, and symbolic environment. It does not include objects that are ignored or filtered out and have no influence upon the actor's decision. Again, like Lewin, Parsons ignores the problems of perception by which the physical world is represented psychologically. This does not mean that Parsons considers that the psychological situation is free from reality considerations; there are obviously many factors that constrain the psychological situation and make it realistic, but Parsons is not interested in the process of perception.

The problem of the actor is to choose among the various goals available to him and to allocate his efforts, time, and other resources among them. Allocation does not mean choosing one and giving up another. Since actual behavior has many different and interrelated consequences, careful planning may enable the actor to achieve many of his goals, so that he will not need to give priority to some at the expense of others.

This conceptualization of the actor facing the problem of satisfying a diverse set of needs in a situation containing various constraints could be the beginning of a psychological analysis of behavior. Parsons does not proceed in that direction, however. He does not ask about the actual mechanism of choice; instead, he uses the choice paradigm to describe some general features of behavior called *pattern variables*. These will be discussed in a later section (see p. 547).

For Parsons, the individual actor always brings to a situation an organized personality, a style of life, and many habitual patterns of perception, evaluation, and action. This complex interdependent system can itself be analogously described, says Parsons, as a kind of social system.

One of the basic assumptions of Parsonian theory is that every complex, dynamic, interdependent system for allocating resources follows the same laws, faces the same problems, and selects from the same set of basic alternatives as every other dynamic social system, irrespective of level. This view that all systems are dynamically analogous, or isomorphic, stems, perhaps, from Parsons' contact with physiology. He was particularly influenced by L. J. Henderson (1913), who drew analogies and parallels among homeostatic physiological systems, the adjustments of the individual personality, and the structural equilibria of major social systems.

We have already in this volume met this general view of personality organization as a dynamic equilibrated system: once in Lewin's theory and more strikingly in Piaget's. There are, however, many variants on this same general view. One, in particular, emphasizes the parallelism among all systems, cells, physiological systems, ecological systems, personalities, and cultures. Theorists taking this view emphasize the universality of the problems faced by all systems. Persons adopts this point of view; he repeatedly emphasizes the essential similarity between systems at all levels, and he views his theory as a general theory of systems, not merely a specific theory of social systems.

Although he views every system as basically isomorphic with every other one, Parsons obviously devotes most of his attention to the analysis of social systems. Since the development of the child is viewed as a part of the family social system, the next section will describe the terminology of social systems.

THE DESCRIPTION OF A SOCIAL SYSTEM—SOCIAL ROLES

The simplest form of a social system is a two-person system or dyad. Since the first social system in which the child participates is such a dyad, it is appropriate for our analysis. Let us begin, however, with the formation of a dyad between two adults.

As soon as two people begin to interact, each of them is seeking to obtain certain rewards and satisfactions from the other and to attain certain goals through the other. Each person tries, therefore, to behave in a fashion that will elicit from the other the kind of behavior that he finds rewarding or goal achieving. In Parsons' language, a dyad consists of *ego* and *alter*. There would be no basis for interaction if alter were not a significant person in ego's situation, and if there were not a reciprocal significance of ego for alter. Ego must predict how alter will respond, in order to elicit the desired responses from him. Alter is faced with the same problem. If the two are strangers, they may make many mistakes and may each elicit responses that they do not want. If the dyadic relation persists, however, ego and alter will begin to know each other and to develop some mutual expectations. Each will possess some individualized knowledge of what actions upset the other, and gradually develop specific habits of responding to the other. In a harmonious relationship, each person's behavior provides rewards for the other and fulfills the other's expectations.

Mutual interdependence of ego and alter may take a variety of forms. It may result in a division of labor with respect to tasks facing the dyad. It may also result in comfortable, established patterns of communication and mutual responsiveness. Gradually, if the relationship is stable and viable, these interactions fall into customary patterns. In a particular situation one person is expected to take a particular responsibility and to behave in a particular way.

This expectation defines a *social role*. For example, in most American families it is the husband's role to cut the grass, to repair lamps, to earn the family income, and to make out the income tax. The mother's role in most families includes child care, particularly for infants, cooking, housework, and participating in community activities. In particular families these roles may be different; the husband may get breakfast and the wife dinner; or, the husband may dress the older child, the wife the younger child. In other families, the wife also works and brings in income, and the housework is done by a hired maid. In every family, however, some set of expectations has been established for each person. If the person does not live up to the demands of the role, it is upsetting to the smooth functioning of the family and is likely to bring some sanctions.

In social systems which are more complex than the dyad, there are many diverse social roles necessary for the functioning of the system. In fact, the *social role* is the primary unit for the analysis and description of a social system. To describe the system of roles in a complex system, it is necessary to distinguish between two terms: *status* and *role*. In an individual dyad or even in a specific small group, the roles of the different members are worked out to fit the abilities and tastes of the members of the group. In larger society, however, many roles are predefined. These are positions in the social order that must be filled, and they are filled by many different people at different times. By contrast, the way a man and wife privately arrange their division of duties might be left completely to the individuals; in that case, different couples might adopt dissimilar arrangements that were mutually satisfactory to the couple.

In fact, however, there are cultural norms about the role of husband and the role of wife, so that the husband's role in one family is generally similar to the husband's role in another family. The husband's role includes earning income for the family. At an earlier time, the wife's role practically forbade her to earn income; at present it is possible, but not expected, that the wife will work outside the home. The wife's role includes the major responsibility for child rearing. These features of the two roles are not absolutely demanded, but they are so generally expected that any couple trying to reverse the roles would find itself subjected to a variety of pressures, jokes, and outright disapproval. This culturally defined job that is filled by a large number of different people is an example of a *position* or a *status* in the social system. The actual behavior the man does in filling this position is called the *role*.

If we listed all of the *positions* in a social system, together with the duties, rights, and prohibitions of each, we would describe the machinery by which that social system survived. Some of these positions must be concerned with the providing of food, clothing, and shelter to the members of society. Some must be concerned with child rearing, both to protect the child and socialize him. These are obviously necessary positions, but in any complex society there are many other essential roles like middlemen, executives, and religious personages. There are even socially deviant roles, like prostitutes, disapproved of by members of the society, but apparently functional in the viability of the social system.

This conception of society is called by sociologists the *structural-functional* point of view. It sees society as an interdependent set of positions all somehow adapted to the demands on the society and the needs of its individuals, while at the same time being suited to easing the strain that social living entails and facilitating the welfare of the system's members. The sociologists who adopt this view must examine the various positions and roles in the society and, by careful analysis, show how each is functional and how it relates to the functions attached to other positions. This analytical activity is called *structural-functional* analysis.

In a functional analysis of a social institution or a behavior pattern, there are both *manifest* and *latent* functions (Merton, 1949). The manifest function is the overt purpose of which everyone is aware. The latent function is often an unrealized consequence of a custom or role that helps maintain the social system. For example, buying material things is obviously a way of trading the work one does for the things one needs through the medium of money, and one tries to get as much value as possible for one's money. Another, but more latent function of buying goods is to display one's wealth and to achieve status through conspicuous consumption. For this purpose the high price on an article makes it more valuable, regardless of its inherent value.

A structural-functional analysis of a custom, role, or institution tries to draw out all the ways that the role or institution meets some problem of the social system and seeks to discover the probable consequences if the custom did not exist. Parsons is one of the pioneers in formulating this structural-functional point of view, and he and his students are its leading proponents in American sociology. From his analysis of various kinds of roles and positions in a society and a study of their interrelation, Parsons has gradually developed a general theory about the way such systems function. He believes that there are certain universal problems in social systems and limited ways of meeting the problems if the system is to be orderly, stable, and in equilibrium.

For Parsons, the maintenance of orderly integration and equilibrium in a social system poses a significant problem for the general theorist. In any close examination of a society, it is easy to find all kinds of strains that threaten the system's stability. A social equilibrium is, in this respect, unlike the various biological systems which remain stable under varying environments. All mechanisms by which the body's temperature is kept at 98.6° harmonize smoothly with each other. The problems with which the system must cope are external ones, such as the wide variety of temperatures and humidities to which the body is exposed. The social system, however, has certain inherent functional problems that inevitably bring about strain. For example, the roles of the individuals could all be meshed together to meet the demands of diverse habitats and solve various problems of environments in a machinelike fashion, if the individuals were robots. But since they are not, a difficulty arises from the fact that individual people with their own motivations, impulses, and temperaments must fit into these roles.

Not only do individuals not necessarily fit neatly and perfectly into society, but also the subsystems that have vital social functions to perform acquire certain characteristics that may put them out of gear with the larger system in which they are embedded. An army, for example, by virtue of the demands of its function in society, puts a high value on unquestioning obedience by everybody to anybody higher in the hierarchy. Such a rule clearly has a functional value in combat. However, the same value is inconsistent with the values of a freely competitive business economy or a democratic political system.

Thus, a society inevitably has a certain patchwork quality. The strains of the workaday world are soothed by retreat into individualistic family life. The competitive morality of the weekdays, which, if carried to its logical conclusion, would lead to internal schism, is partially overcome by an ethical morality preached on Sunday. Whole institutionalized systems of sub rosa behavior, like gambling or prostitution, are needed to provide some adjustment to the individualistic appetites of people and to the maladjustments which other strains in the society produce.

The Pattern Variables

One of the most provocative of Parsons' theoretical contributions to the structural-functional analysis of the social system is his description of five dichotomies, or pattern variables, that represent the predisposition of any particular social system toward certain fundamental choices. These pattern variables distinguish one social system from another, and in a large society many different dichotomies are represented within the totality. A family is a social system, but it is not like a business; neither is a family or a business like a hospital, and none of them is like the army or the theater or the Senate. According to Parsons, the differences between social systems can be described by differences in the pattern variables. Furthermore, he maintains that the pattern variables are sufficient to describe all differences among social systems, insofar as their patterns of social functioning are concerned.

The pattern variables are described as the resolution of certain basic dilemmas or choices in the mode of orientation. This is not to suggest that they are matters of personal choice, but simply that they are the alternatives that exist.

AFFECTIVITY VERSUS AFFECTIVE NEUTRALITY. Some social relationships in our society are emotional and involve affect as a part and parcel of the relation. The relation between spouses is expected to be affective in our society. A husband-wife relation that is not affective is considered an unlikely marriage. In contrast, the relation between a doctor and his patient is more neutral; if it does become strongly affective, it is likely to endanger the doctor's good judgment. Thus, there is a general principle that doctors should not treat members of their own family for serious illnesses, and that psychiatrists should not accept their personal friends as patients.

The expectation of affectivity in the marital relationship does not mean that there are not some families where affective neutrality prevails. Similarly, the norm of neutrality for the doctor-patient relationship does not preclude some doctors becoming strongly emotionally involved with their patients. The norm of our society is for the family members to be affectively related, but individuals may deviate from the norm. There are, however, consequences of this deviance; other aspects of the relationship will also be deviant, and the deviance may entail social sanctions.

Incidentally, the marriage relationship is not characterized by affectivity in every culture. In some societies it is much more businesslike than in our own. In such societies, marriage has a different function, and often some of the functions played by marriage in our society are found in a different relationship in those societies—lover-mistress, perhaps.

SPECIFICITY-DIFFUSENESS. This pair of alternatives describes a different dimension of social relationships. In a *diffuse* relationship, all aspects of the personalities of the participants are involved, whereas, in a *specific* one, the relationship is focused on selected elements. The role of professor is defined in terms of teaching, research, and academic affairs. As long as the professor is doing a good job, his colleagues would defend his right to be politically active or passive, to join an offbeat religious movement, or to get to work at eleven o'clock in the morning. He can even have an affair as long as it is not with his student. This last would violate the presumed affective neutrality of a professor and his student and would endanger the maintenance of uniform standards of evaluation.

On the other hand, the relation between child and father is diffuse; there is no aspect of the son's life and personality that the father considers irrelevant and none of his business; nor is there any aspect of a father's behavior that is not relevant to his children. A psychiatrist's relation to his client is also diffuse, in that no aspect of the client's behavior is irrelevant, but the situation is quite different in the other direction. The executive's role with his secretary is generally specific; if it becomes diffuse, the label "office wife" is used to describe the fact.

UNIVERSALISM-PARTICULARISM. Whereas the two previous variables describe relationships between people, the third variable describes alternative ways of classifying another person or a social object. The question is whether the other person should be judged in terms of some universal objective frame of reference or in terms of his personal relation to ego. Aspirants for the Olympic team are judged and selected for their skill in their chosen sport; all candidates are marked according to the same universal and objective criteria; whoever is highest with respect to the criteria is selected. Spouses, on the other hand, are chosen particularistically. It is the quality of the relationship between the two people, rather than a general criterion like "good cook," which governs marital choice. In a different way, kings are also chosen on particularistic grounds. The oldest son of a king becomes a king on his father's death; within wide limits, it makes no difference what his other characteristics are.

QUALITY-PERFORMANCE. This pair of alternatives describes whether another person is judged in terms of some *quality,* perhaps described by, "who he is," or in terms of his *behavior,* "what he does." The qualities used to judge a person may be of all sorts: age, sex, beauty, membership in a family or race, but they have nothing to do with his behavior. In these days of civil rights, qualitative criteria for jobs, offices, and political privileges are condemned. There are other roles, however, that are selected on such a basis. The legal right to sign a contract, membership in the 150-lb. crew, membership in the League of Women Voters are all determined by qualitative considerations. On the other hand, many positions are achieved by performance, and the roles of professor, janitor, and congressman are so defined.

SELF-ORIENTATION VERSUS COLLECTIVITY ORIENTATION. The final pair of variables describes the attitude that prevails in a relationship. When two horse traders bargain, each is expected to be self-interested; it is the other fellow's job to look out for himself. A doctor, on the other hand, is not supposed to be self-interested in his relation with the patient—until it comes time to collect the bills. It is unethical for him to prescribe drugs because he receives a kickback, to recommend an expensive operation because he would make more money from it, or to tell a patient he is healthy because the doctor wants to get home to dinner quickly.

Parsons uses these pattern variables primarily to analyze various social systems and to trace out the way that particular combinations of pattern variables are functionally useful for the maintenance of that particular sort of social relationship. This type of analysis is among the most exciting in Parsons' work.

From the standpoint of child development, it is clear that a tremendous body of rules and principles underlies interpersonal relations within a social system. It is obvious how large a task is involved in socialization. As we shall see, Parsons' theory of socialization shows how the child has opportunities to learn about all these combinations of pattern variables, and thus to become prepared for the complex task of living an adult life in a social system.

THE PLACE OF CHILD-REARING AND SOCIALIZATION IN THE SOCIAL SYSTEM

From the standpoint of society, socialization is essential in maintaining its viability. This does not mean that parents consciously raise children to promote the future welfare of the society; it merely means that if the child-rearing practices of a society do not produce adults who fit its role system, the society will either disintegrate or change into a different one. The maintenance of a social system over a number of generations signifies *de facto* that the children are brought up to function in the system in much the same way as their parents did. Thus, socialization is viewed as one of the requisite tasks for a persevering social system.

Let us look for a moment at some of the behaviors that are a part of the socialization process. In psychology we are so accustomed to thinking of socialization in the limited sense of acquiring parental values that we sometimes forget about the breadth of its requirements. First, socialization requires the production of people with the appropriate abilities in approximately the right numbers for the roles to be filled in the social system. A social system needs soldiers, priests, hunters, farmers, distributors, mothers, chefs, and diplomats. Some of these roles are incompatible with others; they cannot be filled from a homogeneous population. At the same time some abilities, like learning the language, are required of practically everybody. Child-rearing practices, each one the result of the individualistic treatment of one child by his family, must, *in toto,* produce approximately the proper numbers of people with these abilities.

A second aspect of socialization is the transmission of information from the older generation to the younger. Some of this information is tied closely to each role; thus, a fisherman must know what kind of bait is eaten by what kinds of fish. Some information is distributed widely, such as knowledge about social rules, geography, and religious belief systems. As a result of child-rearing and socialization, this culturally accumulated information is passed on, but again is passed on differentially. Some people learn some information, other people learn some other, nobody learns it all, everybody learns some in common; and, in sum, the entire body of information that is essential for the functioning of the system is transmitted.

A third aspect of socialization is the development of motives and values that tie the social system together cohesively. A society in which people obtain satisfaction and enjoyment out of performing their roles is much stabler than one in which role performance is burdensome or distasteful, yet, it is obvious that not every role is to everyone's taste. People committed to particular roles in a society can learn through socialization to enjoy and feel valuable in their roles, but the socialization of motives and values goes beyond this. The ethics, values, and loyalties of a society are means by which the individualistic motivations of people are prevented from producing social schism. For example, it may be the case that honesty is *not* the best policy. Viewed from an individualistic, utilitarian point of view, the requirement to tell the truth may more frequently prevent than facilitate an individual's gaining the maximum rewards. However, it does seem clear that a culture could hardly endure if nobody's statement could be trusted. Even the individual who gains from dishonesty must often depend on other people's honesty to reap his ill-gotten gains. Honesty is probably the best policy for the social system and thus indirectly for the individual, but not directly for the individual achieving his own goals. This divergence between the individual's self-interest and the social value of honesty is resolved by making honesty an ethical matter. Children are socialized to feel anxious to guilty when they are dishonest, and are thus taught to become better members of the social system. As Freud said, the superego is an essential feature of civilization, despite the fact that it may be disadvantageous or even destructive for some individuals.

In summary, socialization involves all aspects of personality: abilities, knowledge, motivation, conscience, and feelings. In each area of socialization, there are some items that are common to all members of a culture; these distinguish one culture from another. But within a culture there are also equally important differences in abilities, knowledge, and values. These differences must be distributed in approximately the same way from one generation to another if the social system is to remain stable.

Once we look at this formidable list of requirements for the socialization process, we might wonder how it ever happens successfully. It sounds as if a full-blown computer would be required to solve the logistical problem of supplying the social system in the next generation with the proper supplies in the proper quantities. Yet it does happen over and over again, without any real planning at all. By and large, people raise their children in their own fashion, with never a worry about whether there will be too big a supply of diplomats and not enough engineers.

INTERACTIONS IN SMALL GROUPS

The work of Parsons on the socialization process stems from the consideration of the family as a social system, but also it depends heavily on the work of Robert F. Bales, who extensively studies the interactions that occur within small groups (1950). The primary reference for the application of Parsonian theory to the family is a book by Parsons and Bales, *Family, Socialization and Interaction Process* (1955).

Before describing the theory of socialization as presented in that book, it is beneficial to briefly review the work that Bales had done in the study of small groups and to see how it blends with the work of Parsons. Bales' studies of small groups are concerned with the process of group interaction and the way these interactions change over the group's history. The groups studied were not stable subsystems of a continuing society, but arbitrary collections of adults, usually undergraduates, brought together for an experiment. Each group was given some problem or series of problems to solve in succeeding sessions. As the members of the group gradually became familiar with each other, they settled into certain roles, and their interactions in solving a problem tended to follow a predictable sequence.

These experiments are reported in several places; the primary reference is Bales, *Interaction Process Analysis* (1950), where the method of describing interactions within the group is outlined. An interaction is any remark or action made by one person and directed toward another person or toward the group. The set of categories used by Bales for describing an interaction consisted of twelve categories as follows:

A. Positive Reactions

1. Shows solidarity, raises other's status, jokes, gives help, rewards.
2. Shows tension release, shows satisfaction.
3. Agrees, shows passive acceptance, understands, concurs, complies.

B. Problem-Solving Attempts

4. Gives suggestions, direction, implying autonomy for others.
5. Gives opinion, evaluation, analysis, expressed feelings, wish.
6. Gives orientation, information, repeats, clarifies, confirms.

C. Questions

7. Asks for orientation, information, repetition, confirmation.
8. Asks for opinion, evaluation, analysis, expression of feeling.
9. Asks for suggestion, direction, possible ways of action.

D. Negative Reactions

10. Disagrees, shows possible rejection, formality, withholds help.
11. Shows tension increase, asks for help, withdraws "out of field."
12. Shows antagonism, deflates other's status, defends or asserts self.

In this classification of interactions among the members of a problem-solving group, we find goal-directed actions, questions, and problem-solving attempts; we also find socially disruptive interactions and positive integrative ones. According to Parsons and Bales, these interactions do not primarily occur as expressions of individual personality and temperament, but rather as predictable offshoots of problem-solving activities in a group. Problem solving or any other group task inevitably creates tension. Some people do not like the assigned task and resent participating. Others feel they are not competent to contribute to the group activity and feel ashamed or embarrassed. A person with a good idea may have to point out weaknesses in someone else's proposal and thus arouse antagonism. Hence, it is only natural that task-oriented behavior creates emotional tension.

A social system, even a temporarily collected small group, makes provision for solving these tensions and conflicts and keeping them from splintering the group. Actually, socioemotional relationships are maintained in two different ways. First, there is a tendency for two sorts of leaders to arise in any group, a task leader and a socioemotional leader. The task leader is identified in Bales' experiments by a questionnaire to the members of the group after the problem is solved. One person is generally judged to have contributed most of the ideas for problem solving, and to have led the group in its efforts to cope with the assigned problem. He is the task leader. The socioemotional leader is the best-liked member of the group. Both of these people contribute a great deal to the discussion and they are not sharply differentiated from each other in terms of their behavior, but the "idea man" tends to have more interactions classified as "problem-solving attempts," while the best-liked man puts out more actions in the "positive reactions" area, like giving encouragement, laughing, and expressing group solidarity.

The repair of interpersonal relations can also be seen in the sequence of phases of group activity. There is a balancing of accounts over the session as a whole. Early in the session there is an over-balance of problem-solving attempts, but the balance tends to be restored at the end by a period of joking and friendly interactions largely in the area of social solidarity.

These findings and other considerations have led Parsons and Bales to describe the interactions of a task-directed group in a four-phase cycle of activities. The first phase is *adaptive,* labeled *A,* and includes the struggle to attain the goal, the period of preparation of facilities, and planning. The second phase brings the task-directed activity to an end with *goal attainment,* labeled *G*; at that point the social system shifts to the problems of interpersonal relations which have been disturbed by the focus on task-oriented activity. The third phase of task performance is a period of *integrative* or *I* activity, represented by the period of joking and congratulations at the end of the problem-solving session. The fourth phase is called the period of *latency, L.* More difficult to understand than the others, this phase occurs after the group separates and seems to provide a period of relaxation where the individual members take care of their own business and rest up for the next battle with an external problem.

This cycle of *adaptation–goal attainment–integration–latency (A-G-I-L)* describes the sequence in task performance, that is, in a situation where the problem is external. There is also a sequence of phases of activity where the problem facing the group is one of social control. Such a problem arises whenever a group member deviates from group norms. This process, which Parsons first described in his analysis of the psychotherapeutic process, consists of the same phases, but they occur in the opposite order. The first phase is a stage of *permissiveness* (or latency) in which the main objective of the therapist is to accept the patient's remarks and behavior for what they are. The second phase is *supportive* (or *integrative*) during which a strong positive relation is built up between the patient and therapist. Parsons labels the third phase *denial of reciprocity* and says it corresponds to the *goal gratification* phase of task performance. In this phase, the therapist, while being friendly, refuses to become emotionally involved in the patient's problems; he establishes that the inter-personal attachment previously formed goes in only one direction. He does not concur in the patient's deviant values, nor is he emotionally identified with the patient. Instead, the therapist begins to exert pressure to bring the patient back into adjustment to the realities of social life. He points out the realistic consequences of deviant behavior, thus making clear to the patient the rewards and punishments entailed by his deviancy. Because of the solidarity previously built up, the patient can accept this pressure, and in the ideal case discovers a socially conforming kind of behavior that is also compatible with his personal values. This corresponds to the *adaptive* phase. Thus, the sequence of social control is *latency (permissiveness)–integrative (supportive)–goal gratification (denial of reciprocity) –adaptive (manipulation of rewards)*.

THE PHASES OF SOCIALIZATION

All of this has been a long but necessary digression from the presentation of the Parsonian theory of socialization. The essential process of socialization is to be found in the social-control model. The child is born a deviant, in the sense that many aspects of his behavior must be changed if he is to become a socially conforming adult. His upbringing can be seen as an endless repetition of the social-control cycle, as one after another of his childish infantile behavior patterns are changed into the adult form. Socialization of any behavior takes place in a sequence of phases consisting of (1) *permissiveness*, (2) *establishing a strong basis of love through support by the warmth of the socialization agent*, (3) *the introduction and presentation of adult norms*, and (4) *finally, rewards and punishments to bring the child into conformity with adult norms*.

Parsons and Bales add something more to the process. They believe the whole period of childhood can be divided into four large stages of personality development which correspond to the stages of psychosexual development as described in Freudian theory. However, to the sociologists these four stages (oral, anal, latent, and genital) also represent a sort of supercycle of the phases of social control (latency, integration, goal attainment, and adaptation).

The argument can best be followed with the aid of Figure 18-1, taken from *Family, Socialization, and Interaction*.

According to Parsons, the neonate is a bundle of separate and uncoordinated segmental needs such as hunger, thirst, and pain avoidance. Each need clamors for satisfaction independently of the others and in a way that is uncoordinated with other aspects of the baby's activity.

Oral Dependency

The first crisis in personality development—corresponding to the oral crisis in psychoanalytic theory—occurs when the mother denies

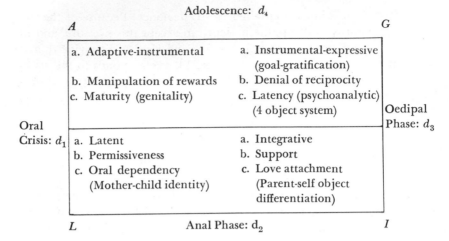

Figure 18-1. Phases of Socialization; a. task-performance phases (*AGIL*), b. learning-social control phases (*LIGA*), c. phases of psychosexual development, d. crises of transition

the child's demands for gratification of every separate need on demand, but instead rewards a more diffuse dependency upon the mother. This is the stage of *oral dependency*. The term *diffuse* is used advisedly because diffuseness is one of the pattern variables; it describes a state in which all of the mother's activities directed toward the child are important to him: her smiles, her closeness, her withdrawal. Before this stage, the mother-child relation was more specific; the only activities of the mother that really impinged upon the child were those that directly catered to his need of the moment. As a result of the child establishing this more diffuse dependency relation with the mother, the segmental needs of the child can, on occasion, be subordinated to the "collectivity" (the total personality). Thus, the personality achieves its first integration into a system. At the same time, the child becomes a member of his first social system, a system consisting of *mother and child*.

In this system, the mother's role can be described in terms of the pattern variables. Her relation to the child is marked by *affectivity* rather than *affective neutrality;* it is *diffuse* rather than *specific;* it is *particularistic,* since it depends upon this being her child and is not elicited by all babies; it is based upon *quality* rather then *performance,* since it is the fact of being a baby that is important, not the specific acts that the baby performs; finally it is *collectively oriented*—the mother continually sacrifices her own personal comfort for the welfare of the child. This little social system is not completely described by these pattern variables, however, because in it the mother bears the entire responsibility for both task performance and socioemotional integration. The foregoing pattern of variables emphasizes the socioemotional aspect of her relation to the child.

We can also see the task-oriented, instrumental role. The mother feeds the child, for example, and here her behavior is less diffuse and more specific. She feeds him when he is hungry and when he performs certain acts indicating hunger—although in some mother-child systems feeding may be more an expression of fondness than a specific response to hunger.

In this mother-child system there is little room for differentiation of roles; the mother plays all those roles associated with power—task leadership and socioemotional integration. The child is the recipient of all of them. According to Parsons, differentiation of the social system into two people is nonexistent for the child who does not, in any sense, see himself as part of a social system.

The Love-Dependent Personality

The first psychological differentiation of the mother and the child's roles—from the standpoint of the child—comes in the next stage, as a result of the anal crisis. This period, according to psychoanalytic theory, occurs about the time the child is two to three years old. His primary relationship is to his mother, and this is the time when the child's problem is learning the proper balance of autonomy and obedience or conformity. The problem of autonomy vs. conformity is epitomized in toilet-training.

Parsons would not deny any of these characteristics of the anal period, but he describes the period in his own terminology and emphasizes aspects of the mother-child relationship which are not treated in the usual psychoanalytic discussion of the period (see Figure 18-2).

First, Parsons emphasizes that in this period the child psychologically enters into a social system, by differentiating himself from his mother and becoming psychologically a part of a dyadic relation. In this dyadic social system—as seen by the child—the mother is marked by superior power and the *instrumental* role, while the child is in a weaker position and more *expressive*. The term *instrumental* describes the role that is concerned with solving external problems. The task leader in a group has an instrumental role. The term *expressive* refers to being more concerned with expression of feelings; the socioemotional role is expressive. In the present discussion the term describes

Superior power: Instrumental	Objects cathected: self; objects internalized: parent. Need-disposition: dependency Performance type: alter-oriented, asking for and giving care; narcissistic, self-indulgence. Sanction type: alter-oriented, accepting care; narcissistic, self-gratification.
Inferior power: Expressive	Objects cathected: parent; objects internalized: self. Need-disposition: autonomy Performance type: alter-oriented, loving alter; narcissistic, self-love. Sanction type: alter-oriented, receiving alter's love; narcissistic, self-love.

Figure 18-2. The Love-dependent personality

the fact that the two-year-old depends on the mother for instrumental actions to achieve his goals.

Second, the child begins during this period to acquire the patterns of behavior and the needs that go along with both roles of the social system. An important hypothesis in Parsons' theory is that the child does not merely learn his own role in the family, but that he gradually gains knowledge of the entire social system with all its roles. He begins to learn in an elementary way how social systems function and thus is prepared eventually to take any role in a system. At the same time, he acquires the dispositions for needs that go along with these roles.

This two-person system contains two important features, one associated with the mother's roles, the other with the child's. According to Parsons, during this phase the mother gradually shifts from being an object of dependency to being a loving mother in a maturer sense. She gives the child love and support but she denies him an overly dependent relationship. She requires some autonomy of the child and rewards him, making him more independent. She also denies the child too much autonomy which she punishes by withdrawal of love. In Parsons' language, the child shifts from a dependency personality to a love-dependency personality.

Third, in the dyadic interaction that constantly occurs within this social system, the child often asks for help or care and his request is generally accepted and filled. He is also frequently given care and help that he does not ask for and thus learns to accept help from a more powerful person. He is also frequently urged to be autonomous, and his autonomous independent performances are appreciated and approved. In this way love becomes differentiated from caretaking: love comes from being independent.

On other occasions the child is required to do things he does not want to do; he is required to be autonomous in one sense, but is not allowed to do what he wants. Obedience requires acting independently rather than accepting care, but also renouncing another sort of autonomy. Too much autonomy, particularly disobedient autonomy, leads to maternal disapproval and "withdrawal of love." Thus, within this social system, the child is exposed to examples of giving and accepting care, and asking for care and responding to such bids for dependency. He knows what it is to be autonomous and sees what it is to require autonomy. He learns what it is to love, to receive love, and to withdraw love. Although the child has been on only one side of many of the reciprocal relations, he has learned both his role and his mother's.

Furthermore, Parsons argues that the child learns to perform many of these actions toward himself, or narcissistically. The narcissistic form of giving care is to be self-indulgent; the narcissistic form of accepting care is self-gratification; the narcissistic form of loving and receiving love is self-love.

These, then, are the dimensions of relations that become psychologically meaningful in the contest of the mother-child dyad. In addition to learning what these various needs mean, the child also learns something about the appropriate circumstances for each of them—everybody shows all of these needs in some relations and on some occasions. Thus, the child begins to learn the mutual balance and interdependence among these actions and acquires expectations of appropriate responses to his acts.

Finally, there is plenty of room within this system for different children to acquire different personalities. No child fails to acquire the idea that asking for help is one way of getting it, but some children develop a personality in which asking for help plays a much more dominant role than in other children. Or, a child may learn about asking for help but also learn to be anxious about it and inhibit such tendencies.

Thus, although Parsons calls this the "love-dependent" personality, it is not a personality type, nor do all children have the same personalities in this period. What is common to them all is a set of interpersonal relations; loving, punishing, dependency, or nurturance is not an unknown quantity for any child. Yet the balance of such actions which becomes the individual's customary stance in actual behavior varies from one family to another and develops in such a way that the particular mother-child pattern of interactions tends toward stability.

To note another aspect of Parsons' thinking, we should return to Figure 18-1. We can observe that this whole anal phase of development is seen as *integrative* following a "latent" phase described as the period of oral dependency. Despite the fact that the phase is integrative, its achievement involves a complete subcycle of phases, marking the transition from oral dependency into the love-dependent stage of personality. This subcycle has its own *L-I-G-A* phases and is described in Figure 18-3. Parsons' view of development always consists of a subcycle within a larger cycle within a still larger one. Later we shall see a detailed example of a still smaller subcycle within one of these subcycles. The Parsonian theory of development always contains wheels within wheels within wheels (Figure 18-3).

Postoedipal Phase of Personality Structure

The next phase of personality development stems from the Oedipal crisis (see Figure 18-1). Recalling psychoanalytic theory, we remember that the Oedipal crisis for boys is the period when the boy develops sexual desires for his mother and hostile feelings toward his father because of the latter's preferred position. He also fears his father, specifically fearing some genital injury or castration. As an outcome of this conflict, he identifies with the father, and through this identification moves into the latency period. During latency, sexual desires are reduced as the boy acquires appropriate sex roles and concentrates upon the acquisition of skills in noninterpersonal areas. A further consequence of the Oedipal crisis is the acquisition of a conscience representing the voice of the father, through which the values of the culture are transmitted.

Parsons generally accepts the psychoanalytic theory of this crisis, but just as in the love-dependency period, he reformulates it, emphasizing somewhat different aspects of the period than did Freud; Parsons par-

A   G

Establishment of solidarity system of mother-child reciprocal love and care Internalization of self and mother as objects Autonomous love need-disposition.	Rewarding of accep-table performances Denial of a) overdependency b) overdemanding autonomy c) anal aggression.
Oral dependency and mother-child iden-tity Imposition of auton-omy demands.	Establishment of love dependency-expecta-tion of reward for autonomous perform-ance.

L   I

Figure 18-3. Phases in the development of love-dependency personality. Process moves counterclockwise starting in L.

ticularly tries to put it into the broader framework of the family as a functioning social system. From the Parsonian standpoint, the major transition for the child during the Oedipal period is from his integrated membership in a two-person system, consisting of mother and child, to a four-member social system consisting of mother, father, child, and opposite-sexed sibling. The personality of the child simultaneously divides into a four-unit personality structure with the acquisition of need dispositions that are appropriate to all four roles. These four roles describe the nuclear family and are diagrammed in Figure 18-4.

According to Parsons, the essentials of the nuclear family can be encompassed in this four-member system. Not all families actually have all four members, and there may be further discrimination in the roles

	Instrumental priority	Expressive priority
Superior power	Father (Instrumental superior)	Mother (Expressive superior)
Inferior power	Son (Instrumental inferior)	Daughter (Expressive inferior)

Figure 18-4. The structure of the four-person family.

in families with multiple siblings of the same sex, but the basic elements of the nuclear family consist of these roles.

There is cross-cultural evidence that in most societies where there is a nuclear family the father is the task, or instrumental leader and the mother is the expressive leader or socioemotional integrator of the family. When 75 cultures were examined by Zelditch (1955) on the basis of ethnographers' reports, he took statements such as the following to represent instrumental leadership: Boss-manager of the farm, leader of the hunt, the final court of appeals, final judge and executor of punishment, discipline and control over the children. The expressive leader is characterized by such descriptions as mediator, or conciliator of the family—soothes over disputes, resolves hostility in the family—affectionate, solicitous, warm, emotional to the children of the family,—the comforter, the consoler, relatively indulgent, and relatively unpunishing.

The attitudes of family members toward the instrumental leader are respectful, constrained, reserved, and on occasion, hostile. On the other hand, family members are generally at ease in the presence of the expressive leader, and are emotionally attached in a warm and close relation.

The rating of the typical family in a culture is not easy, but in general 44 out of 56 societies seemed to confirm the hypotheses that the two leadership roles were differentiated, and that the instrumental role was allocated to the father while the expressive role was allocated to the mother. Actually, the cross-cultural regularity of this pattern is not essential for the Parsonian theory of personality development in the American family. There is certainly a great deal of evidence that the American family is generally organized in this differentiated way, although the pattern was probably much clearer one hundred years ago than it is today.

With this digression into cross-cultural research, we will return to the main line of Parsons' argument.

For him, the outstanding feature of the child's personality development during the Oedipal period is his acculturation into the basic social system of the nuclear family. The same general principles employed in explaining the introduction of the younger child into a dyadic social system also apply to this more complicated period. These common principles are first, that the transitional crisis is itself organized into the sequence of phases typical of all social-control mechanisms, and second, that the child adopts the pattern of the entire organized social system of the family thereby learning appropriate behaviors for all the roles within it, even though he does not himself fill all those roles. This conception is reminiscent of Piaget's insistence that the child acquires the entire logical system of class inclusion, or class multiplication, and not just the particular individual elements that he may have been taught. The social system is a rather logically coherent system of interpersonal relations which come from living on a nuclear family.

The personality structure that Parsons hypothesizes for the post-Oedipal period is summarized in Figure 18-5. It is important to recognize that the father is a new figure introduced into a previously exclusive relationship between the mother and child. A further significant fact is that, because of his instrumental role in the family, the father generally initiates new demands upon the child. At an earlier period the mother was both instrumental and expressive. In this new period, she retains her expressive role of integrator and conciliator, while the father takes on the more instrumental role of disciplinarian. From the point of view of the child, the father is the fly in the ointment; he is the intruder, the one who is demanding and denying. The mother becomes, if anything, more completely the family conciliator. This view suggests a basis for the hostility of the son toward the father which is somewhat different from the sexual pattern described by Freud, although Parsons accepts the importance of the sexual undertones.

It is important, of course, that the parents act in concert and not play their instrumental and expressive roles too exclusively. The child is helped to accept the father's demands because the mother, with whom he has already established stable relationships, supports the father's demands on the child. Vis-à-vis the parents, the child is in the inferior power position and the parents use their power to demand maturer behavior from the child. Of course, the child tries to play one parent against the other and may succeed on occasion, but generally the parents do not oppose each other. The mother does not actually

	Superego Instrumental	Id Expressive
Superior power:	Objects cathected: self (masculine); objects internalized: father. Need-disposition: conformity. External orientation: performance: control of alter; sanction: esteem. Internal orientation: P: self-control; S: self-esteem.	Objects cathected: self (feminine); objects internalized: mother. Need-disposition: nurturance External orientation: P: giving pleasure; S: response. Internal orientation: P: self-indulgence; S: self-gratification.
Inferior power:	Objects cathected: father; objects internalized: self (masc.). Need-disposition: adequacy. External orientation: P: instrumental performance; S: approval. Internal orientation: P: "reality testing"; S: self-approval.	Objects cathected: mother; objects internalized: self (fem.). Need-disposition: security. External orientation: P: giving love; S: acceptance. Internal orientation: P: harmonization; S: self-love.
	Adaptive Functions Ego	Integrative Functions

Figure 18-5. The post-Oedipal personality structure

soften the father's demands for maturity, but makes them more palatable by conciliation and provides the loving reward for conformity that the father finds more difficult to provide in his disciplinary instrumental role.

Turning to the need dispositions that emerge through this period (see Figure 18-5), we find many more complications than in the earlier period. What was called *dependency* in the earlier stage has now differentiated into *conformity* and *nurturance*. The giving and accepting of care now consists of giving and accepting control on the one hand, and giving and accepting nurturance on the other. In the earlier dependency both aspects were merged and undifferentiated.

Just as in the previous stage, these attitudes may describe interpersonal relations or self-directed actions. Thus, the child in this period becomes capable of self-control and self-esteem. Psychoanalytic theory describes this aspect of the personality as the superego.

On the expressive side, the important difference between nurturance at this stage and the earlier caretaking is that nurturance consists of giving pleasure freed from cultural normative requirements. Nurturance is the gratification of another person's needs and is reinforced by the fact that the other person responds to it. As the child adopts these maternal roles in the nuclear family, he becomes able to be nurturant freely and openly, without strings. This noncontingent desire to benefit another is an important part of a warm, loving personality.

Love in the dyadic phase of development had two roles, reward for autonomy and provision of security. In the post-Oedipal phase these two aspects of love are differentiated; it is as if love and respect had differentiated out of a previous amalgam. The respect is for adequacy in instrumental functioning and, like other attitudes, can be directed toward the self in a sort of pride or self-approval. Love, like nurturance, is at this point also noncontingent; it requires nothing of the other person but loving in return.

The fact that love and respect are differentiated does not mean that most love relationships do not contain both elements. It merely reflects the fact that the two can be independent. One can and does respect people's competence and approve of them, without feeling that particularistic attachment called love. Thus, as seen in Figure 18-5, the need disposition for one of these aspects of love is "adequacy," the other is "security." The difference between the two is that one is contingent upon performance—"achievement-oriented" in Parsons' terminology —while the other is a kind of insured sense of safety and well-being that does not need to be earned or lived up to. Parsons describes this noncontingent love of the mother which gives alter a sense of security, on the right side of the bottom half of Figure 18-5. When this same sort of noncontingent approval of one's own person is developed, it is a sort of self-love and self-esteem which leads to a personal sense of security.

Parsons conceives of the child's relation with the father as achievement-oriented. The father demands achievement and gives or withholds approval in terms of whether it is deserved. This is a less warm and less comfortable relation than the noncontingent love of the mother for the child. In terms of socialization, the object of the father's demand is to bring about mature behavior from the child, while the mother's noncontingent love maintains the solidarity of the family.

This approach presents stereotyped relations between each of the parents and the child. In an actual family, the father and mother play both roles on occasion; the differences between mother and father are average differences, not absolute ones. It is true, however, that as the father enters into the socialization process, he tends to take on the instrumental role more frequently than the mother.

How does this shift involve the Oedipal complex in the Freudian sense? The Parsonian explanation for the Oedipal complex stems from two factors. One is that the mother-child relation exists before the four-person social system, so that the social system must be modified from the earlier two-person system into the four-person system. There is resistance to any change, and if change is required the system tends to move along the line of least resistance. Thus, with the increasing maturity of the child and increasing maturity demands upon him, the natural development of the mother-child social system is for the child gradually to take on an instrumental role in relation to the mother, and in that sense occupy the role that is already occupied by the father. There is also a tendency for the child, since he has already incorporated the mother's role and learned nurturance, to adopt this role in relation to the father.

A second factor is the existence of eroticism in the mother-child relationship in the pre-Oedipal period. Parsons used the term erotic in the same sense as Freud, to mean a pleasure in bodily contact. The mother's contact with the child in child care is erotically satisfying to the child and to a lesser degree to the mother. This eroticism belongs to the expressive side of the personality rather than to the instrumental; it is diffuse, particularistic, and based on quality rather than achievement.

Thus, Parsons says the tendency for the child to move into the father's role in the social system, when accompanied by a maintenance of the eroticism of the pre-Oedipal relation, creates a sexual rivalry in which the eroticism of the child must be repressed. This is a restatement of Freudian theory.

The identification of the child in the four-person family is, however, more complicated than Freud described it. Parsons does not even mean quite the same as Freud by "identification"; he means the establishment of a collectivity, or a "we" to which the child is attached. Because Parsons emphasizes the importance of the entire nuclear family as a social system, he separates out several collectivities that exist and argues that each represents an identification. One collectivity is the entire family "we" against the rest of the world. A second is the collectivity of the mother and father, the parents. On the other side there is the "we" of the children. On occasion the latter two collectivities are opponents. Another collectivity is father and son, the men in the family. In various ways the males of the family may feel thay are a group which does not include the mother and sisters. The counterpart is the collectivity of the females in the family.

Thus, in moving from the two-person to the four-person system, the boy begins with an identification with his mother, which expands to include the whole family; in addition, he acquires a sex role identification with the father, and a "child" identification with his siblings. For the girl, the process is somewhat simpler, since her sex role identification coincides with the pre-Oedipal identification.

Further Differentiation of the Personality

With the completion of the Oedipal period, the child is incorporated into the full complexity of the nuclear family and the variety of roles and attitudes it encompasses. The next development results from the child's explorations and emotional involvements outside the home. In one sense, the child of six has developed a male or female sex role, but it is a particularistic sex role because it is described by the activities of the boy and father, or at most, the men in the immediate family, or the women in the family. In this respect, all the roles and attitudes of the six-year-old are particular to the family and depend on the relations among the people in the family. In the next stage, these roles are generalized through the child's relations with other adults outside the home and through his relations with other boys and girls.

As Parsons views the process, these outside contacts bring about a further differentiation of the four need dispositions of the Oedipal child: nurturance, conformity, security, and adequacy. To grasp the total concept, let us examine what Parsons calls the genealogy of need dispositions, from the first stage on (Figure 18-6). Here the development is described in terms of the pattern variables along which each differentiation is made. There are five pattern variables. The first is the mere establishment of a collectivity of the personal need dispositions rather than segmental drives. Each of the other four represents a splitting along a new dimension. The result of the set of sixteen need dispositions is shown in the right-hand column. The first split into the two-person system, mother and child, is based on a power difference and splits *specificity* from *diffuseness*. Dependency is more specific; autonomy is more diffuse. Each of these, then, splits on the *affectivity*

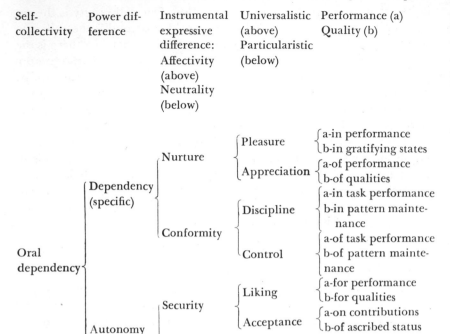

Self-collectivity	Power difference	Instrumental expressive difference: Affectivity (above) Neutrality (below)	Universalistic (above) Particularistic (below)	Performance (a) Quality (b)

Figure 18-6. Geneology of Need-Dispositions.

versus affective neutrality dimension, as described in the shift from a two-person to a four-person social system. Nurturance is more affective, conformity more neutral; security is more affective, adequacy more neutral.

In the post-Oedipal development, two further differentiations occur. One is along the lines of universalism and particularism. The other is between performance and quality; the results of this split are outlined in Figure 18-6. The labels attached to these later differentiations are, unfortunately, far from obvious. For example, the need disposition for nurturance in the four-person system differentiates along the universalistic-particularistic dimension into pleasure and appreciation. Of the two, Parsons calls pleasure more universalistic and appreciation more particularistic. Someone else might feel the reverse is true. The trouble here is that the English language is not prepared to cope with the precise distinctions Parsons wishes to make. Parsons' labels are shown in Figure 18-6, and the reader is welcome to agree or disagree with them.

The important point for Parsons is that nurturance and every other need disposition become more discriminating. Nurturance can be expressed on the basis of universalistic criteria, or for particularistic reasons—and the need is slightly different for the two. Pleasure can be felt in performance or it can be merely a gratifying state enjoyed for its inherent quality. Every other need goes through these same differentiations.

THE DYNAMICS OF THE SOCIALIZATION PROCESS

Having reviewed the course of development, we can now return to the more detailed analysis of the actual dynamics of socialization. One of Parsons' important contributions is an emphasis upon the fact that the socialization process is an activity of an entire social system and that there are dynamic reasons why the family socializes the child. The goal of the family is almost never to prepare the child for membership in the society, although, on some occasions, parents are clear about the fact that their aim is to educate the child to behave as a proper four-year-old, or as a proper ten-year-old. Mostly, the socialization of the child takes place through interactions in which the motivation is directed toward some immediate goal, or where the actual socializing behavior is based on a feeling aroused by the child. The mother's motivation for toilet-training may be composed of a dislike for changing diapers, a wish to reduce her load of laundry, and pride in having a child who is dry earlier than her neighbor's, supported, of course, by a knowledge that toilet-training is one of the tasks of motherhood and by a belief that she is doing the child no harm. The father, who perhaps participates in this process by getting the child up to go to the toilet in the late evening, may be motivated by the desire to assist the mother in whatever she wants to do, or to let her go to sleep early. Siblings may contribute to the process by making fun of the little brother who wets his pants; for them, the motivation may be a mixture of hostility and a feeling of superiority. Yet, all of these diverse motivations result in a coordinated pressure on the child to become more mature.

This is a good example of a *latent function* of the behavior of all of these people. The function of toilet-training, from the standpoint of the society, is socialization, but that is not the reason the people involved do it. It is a latent function of their activities. In contrast, the function of the elementary school, to teach the child the information needed for adult life, is quite explicit or *manifest*.

One of the problems for a sociologist is to analyze the behavior patterns that have latent functions to see how they happen to occur, what motivates them, and how they are timed and coordinated so that the latent function is, in fact, fulfilled without anybody knowing it. The particular contribution of Parsons to this problem is his attempt to describe the functioning of the social system in socialization. Since all such activities put strains on the social system and require adaptations from every member, it is important to analyze how the family social system functions in each step of the socialization process. Parsons presents a detailed, although hypothetical, example in *Family Socialization and Interaction Process* (1955, p. 202 ff). Each step of the socialization process is described as a cycle from *latency* to *integration* to *goal attainment* to *adaptation*. For the child, socialization is a sequence in which he is a deviant to begin with, and through the socialization process comes into harmony with the social system. Each step in the sequence is a tiny bit of psychotherapy which follows the general pattern of the therapeutic process Parsons outlines. Unlike psychotherapy, where there is a single therapist, socialization is a job for the family as a whole. For the family, socialization is a task. The family, therefore, goes through the sequence of phases in the reverse order to the child; namely, *adaptation, goal attainment, integration,* and *latency*. Let us see how it works out in one specific example.

TIME 1. This stage represents a stable state that exists just before the particular socialization sequence begins. In this example, this stable state is assumed to occur in a family in which there are two parents, the child who is being socialized (labeled *ego* in this discussion) and one sibling of the opposite sex, older than ego. This is the standard family that Parsons describes in the Oedipal development of the child.

At Time 1, the family accepts ego as a "little child" primarily associated with his mother in a two-person system. The rest of the family treats him more as a possession than as a participating member of the group. The mother thus has several roles. In the family she is wife of her husband and mother of the older sibling, but she is also the mother of ego in a two-person system. In the family, her role as ego's mother leads her to maintain the proper limits of the ego-mother system. She protects the child from too many demands and gives the care and love he needs. On the other hand, she does not let the ego-mother relationship take too much of her time and energy from the family.

At Time 1, ego is well integrated in the pre-Oedipal period, able to be dependent enough, yet autonomous enough to accept care, and to love in return.

TIME 2. Now we come to Time 2, when this stable system is disturbed. The disturbance arises partly from the fact that ego is maturing and is capable of performing at a higher level than previously. His family, recognizing this maturity, begins to have higher expectations for him. "He is getting too big" to continue some of his childish habits. The family, at this point, moves into the *adaptive* phase of the cycle by preparing to make new achievement demands of ego. Its demands are primarily mediated by the mother, but instigated and supported by the family. She is herself a member of the family, so she is not merely conforming to external pressure. Rather, she takes the responsibility for changing the child's behavior as a result of her membership in the broader family. This pressure on ego in the mother-ego system occurs through her withholding part of the care that she has formerly given and asking the child to take it on for himself. This demand disturbs a previously stable mother-child relationship. The disturbance is felt more by ego, but it is also felt by the mother. Partly, she may have enjoyed the role that she previously had; partly, she does not like to make the child unhappy. At this point, she may receive support and encouragement from the family to help her meet the disturbance.

From the point of view of the child, this is the permissive phase of socialization. The mother withholds some care, but does not demand that the child perform his new responsibilities perfectly. She recognizes his dilemma, and is lenient at first about lapses, and does not punish by withdrawal of love. She is also permissive about ego's aggression. As the pressure is applied, ego is deprived of something he had come to expect, and is understandably frustrated and angered by it. As a consequence, he may show other forms of undesirable behavior; perhaps he regresses in some other area of maturity or becomes irritable and obnoxious. Part of the permissiveness of this phase is the acceptance of these reactions, although they may well be the most difficult for the mother to accept. At this point she again receives support from the family. The other family members may also need some patience and tolerance toward ego.

TIME 3. In the G phase, *goal attainment* for the family, the child begins to accept his new responsibilities and the family is succeeding in its socialization task. This success entails several consequences however. The child begins to be a member of the family, not merely of the two-person system, and so the family must reciprocate and treat him like a family member. New achievements deserve new status. At the same time, the family and the mother must be selectively rewarding, so that the child continues to develop and mature. This phase also marks the liquidation of part of the old mother-child relation. The mother may find ego's new, eager self-reliance difficult to accept, and again she needs support from the family. Gradually, she herself shifts from a supportive person to a selectively rewarding one. There are also new responsibilities for the father and the sibling in this new four-member family. The mother must relinquish some of her former role to the father, and this may be difficult.

Thus, we see that if the social system is to negotiate the socialization process successfully, each member of the family must respond to the demands of the situation at each phase, not only with respect to ego himself, but also with respect to one another.

TIME 4. In the next or integrative phase, the process of incorporating the child into the family is the most prominent feature. The child, in being accepted by the family, must himself accept a different kind of gratification than he was formerly accustomed to. He must come to value the kind of support and family membership that is provided by being a member of the family. Thus, for the child, it is a period of *adaptation* to a new status, in which certain of his previous desires are repressed, others are modified to fit new circumstances, and still others are acquired.

With the final resolution of these problems, the child and the family return to a period of latency until a new problem comes along.

Regardless of whether all the details of this process are confirmed, it is clear that Parsons makes an important contribution to the understanding of socialization by recognizing how the entire family is involved. There must be motivation to socialize; socialization is a result as well as the cause of changes in family structure. At each step there are problems in family relationships, as well as personal problems for each member. These problems are partly resolved because the social system has ways of meeting crises and the members are led to support each other at critical junctures. Unless there were such mechanisms, it is likely that the family would fail to accomplish its function.

CRITIQUE OF PARSONS

The primary evaluation to be made of Parsons and Bales is the acknowledgment of the important positive contribution made by their recognition of the role of the family in child development; not merely that the family affects the child, but that the child affects the family. Child development is not a process that occurs only in the child.

If it is true that the natural unit for the description of child development is the family rather than the child, the implications are important. It means that the theoretical description of child development as it actually occurs will be couched in terms of family variables. It is important to distinguish between the roles of individual and family variables in this process.

The family functions by way of individual psychological processes: the instigation of aggression, defense mechanisms, learned behavior, etc. We need research on these processes to determine what children of various ages learn, how they think, and how their defense mechanisms operate, etc. Many of the processes need to be studied in laboratory situations, so that the results can provide developmental psychology with an armamentarium of mechanisms with which to understand the process of development in real life.

The developmental processes themselves can be studied individualistically, provided that an environment is supplied which does not respond to the behavior of the child himself, or which responds to it only in specified ways. Certainly animal environments can be so arranged, and we can learn much from animal experimentation. There are some naturally existing institutional environments thay may be sufficiently constant and unresponsive to the child's actions to be used for developmental studies.

It is probably impossible, however, to isolate the development of the child from other family variables in studies of human families over time. Such families should be studied, but they must be investigated as units; the investigations must not assume that the changes in the child are developmental processes in the child alone, nor solely causal factors influencing the parent. We must look at families as systems; we must observe the interactions that go on in families and identify them as reinforcements, punishments, and instigations to emotional responses. Knowing the elements of such interactions, we can tackle the problem of describing family development and formulating theories about how the family, including the child himself, develops in a complex society.

This is the major contribution of Parsons and other sociologists to the understanding of child development. Parsons, in particular, because he has struggled so long to include all the facets of a social system—its organization, its dynamics, its strains and methods of coping with them, and its treatment of deviance and the socialization process—certainly has made an important contribution to this fuller understanding.

We may question whether both the specific concepts developed by Parsons for describing personality and personality development and his detailed view of the child's socialization in the family structure will be fruitful in facilitating empirical research. Parsons himself almost never engages in empirical research beyond the careful analysis of social systems on the basis of his own knowledge and guided by his intuition. Many of the features of Parsons' theories are not readily translated into empirical research, although they may stimulate research efforts.

As far as Parsons' own specific description of the developing personality of the child is concerned, there are many points that can be legitimately questioned. One can hardly help thinking that Parsons strains for an orderliness in development that emphasizes the parallelism and isomorphism between the personality as a miniature social system of need dispositions and the broader social system. This assumption of parallelism is not necessary, even though there are certain analogies between maintenance of the integrity of the personality and the social system. The attempt to find a single need-disposition for each role the child acquires in his socialization seems gratuitous. One may accept completely the importance of viewing the child-mother as a two-person social system. There seems no solid reason why the corresponding personality of the child must also be a two-unit one. This does not deny the cogency of what Parsons says, as much as it questions the ultimate completeness and exhaustiveness of his concepts. The pattern variables are very interesting and helpful in making sense out of many aspects of interpersonal relations, but the assumption that each of these global terms is unitary and that together they exhaust the possibilities seems groundless.

Similarly, the assumptions that phases of socialization match the phases of psychotherapy and that these are neatly related to the phases of problem solving by groups, is largely unsubstantiated—although not disproved. Whenever Parsons analyzes concrete processes, one cannot help but be impressed by his grasp and understanding of the process and the fruitfulness of his view. However, as soon as one tries to make it fit the general theory, there is so much ambiguity and even discrepancy that the general theory seems forced. The necessity for forcing it seems to stem from Parsons' need to establish an isomorphism between child rearing and every other process of handling deviance. The parallels are stimulating, but the assumption of complete parallelism seems too confining.

In summary, Parsons does a tremendous service in pointing out the necessity for taking the social system as the unit for analysis, but the details of the theory must await further justification. At this point, they do not seem the most promising set of variables to employ, but if they succeed only in stimulating research, they will have accomplished their scientific mission.

Conclusion

NINETEEN

Toward an integrated theory

of child development

THIS VOLUME BEGAN its examination of theories of child development with an analysis of the common-sense notions of behavior and development as a foundation on which other theories are built. Then we surveyed, in turn, six scientific theories of child development: Lewin's, Piaget's, Freud's, S-R theories, Werner's, and Parsons and Bales'. In this final chapter we compare and contrast these six theories. Out of this comparative analysis comes a list of psychological mechanisms and hypotheses that are found in several different theories. This list is a rough outline for an integrated theory, and it seems possible to use the six theories as source material for devising a single one.

The resources for theory building are not limited, however, to the content of the six theories described. There are other theories, particularly older ones, which contain useful hypotheses: Koffka (1924), Stern (1926), Buhler (1930), and Gesell (1946). In addition, there are special theories concerned with a single aspect of development. For example, several people have concerned themselves with the particular problems of acquiring language (Lewis, 1951, 1957; Church, 1961). Then there are the theories stemming from the Soviet Union. Those of Vitgotsky (1962), Luria (1963), and Zaparozhets (1960) are interesting, although none of them seems a major general theory in the same sense as the six discussed here. Further, there are hundreds of empirical studies of child behavior and development. Not tied closely to any theory, these studies are obviously valuable materials for any aspiring theory builder.

In no sense, therefore, does this chapter present a general integrated theory of child behavior and development. It will attempt, however, to survey the lessons to be learned from these theories and to suggest some concepts that are widely enough employed to be candidates for inclusion in an integrated theory.

COMPARATIVE ANALYSIS OF SIX THEORIES OF CHILD DEVELOPMENT

The six theories discussed in this book will be compared in two ways. First, it seems only fair to let each theorist have his say about the other theories in the group. In some cases these comments are available for inspection. When they are, we will of course refer to them. In addition, it seems possible to intuit what some of the theorists might be expected to say about the other theories in terms of the theorist's own values and central beliefs.

A second comparison will be the author's own. From the vantage point of a detached onlooker, it is possible to point to similarities, incompatibilities, and differences in emphases among the various theories.

One Theory Speaks about Another

STIMULUS-RESPONSE THEORY. The central comment that most S-R theorists would have about all of the other theories is based upon the importance they attribute to rigor, parsimony, and operational testability. None of the other theories approaches S-R theory in its maintenance of a strictly rigorous development, in its emphasis on operational definitions, and in a serious attempt to make theory lean and parsimonious. In recent years, S-R theory has become more relaxed in the hands of social-learning theorists and people like Berlyne who are attempting to couch cognitive processes in S-R language, but S-R theorists are always among the rigorous, hardheaded psychologists. Consequently, S-R theorists would generally agree that all of the other theories presented in this volume are global and loose.

Some S-R theorists would certainly criticize Freud and Piaget as being mentalistic, speculative, and perhaps completely far-fetched. On the other hand, the S-R theorists have used Freudian theory as a source of theoretical ideas more than theorists of any other persuasion. One S-R theorist after another has attempted to reformulate an S-R theory of psychoanalytic hypotheses, and there have been some corresponding attempts on the part of psychoanalysts to integrate psychoanalytic theory and S-R theory (French, 1933). Similarly, Berlyne has frankly drawn upon Piaget's concepts in attempting to reformulate them in S-R language. Thus, although there is a general criticism of the softness of the other theories, there is also a respect for the insights they contain.

PIAGET. Piaget's views of the other theories are more difficult to intuit because he has not spent much time in theoretical controversy. His comments on associationism suggest that he views S-R theory as too passive and mechanistic. S-R theory pictures the child as the recipient of environmental contingencies and reinforcements, rather than as an active participant in the developmental process.

Piaget also has implicitly commented on psychoanalytic theory in his discussion of symbolic schemas (see p. 231). It is fair to say that he believes it is a source of fruitful hypotheses. He has developed his own notions of symbolic schemas to deal with the same kind of data that led to Freud's theories of primary-process thinking and dreams. In most respects, Piaget is interested, however, in specific problems of conceptual thinking, whereas Freud and psychoanalytic theorists have devoted little energy to the description of conceptual thinking. They have tended to be more concerned with the way primary processes interfere with or hamper cognitive functioning than with the nature of the secondary process itself.

FREUDIAN THEORY. Psychoanalytic theorists have a single major criticism of practically every other psychological theory. It was first expressed by Freud and has been echoed widely since. Psychoanalysts believe other psychological theories are superficial and oversimplified, failing to deal with the deep and genuinely important problems of personality functioning; this criticism is more frequently directed toward the S-R theory than toward any of the others. A somewhat related criticism is that none of the other theories sufficiently emphasizes drives as causes of behavior.

Rappaport, one of the major psychoanalytic theorists after Freud, found many parallels between psychoanalytic theory and the theories of Lewin and Piaget. He thought Lewin's concept of tension and tension reduction was quite similar to the psychoanalytic theory of drive, whereas the S-R theory of drive reduction was a different kind of theoretical concept. Rappaport and the other ego psychologists among psychoanalytic theorists do emphasize more than Freud himself did the importance of describing secondary processes. For this reason many studies of cognitive functioning are used by Rappaport as the source of ideas for psychoanalytic theory.

LEWIN. Lewin's criticisms of S-R theory were made public in the early forties and are limited to those he raised in his theoretical controversy with Hull. He certainly felt that S-R theory was too atomistic and molecular. Lewin emphasized the organization of cognitive structure and felt that S-R theory was in error in trying to describe complex behavior as the combination of many elementary behavioral acts.

Lewin criticized Freud for his historical point of view (1937); he believed that Freud's theory allowed for past events to influence present behavior without any currently operating intervening mechanism. Lewin's own emphasis was much more upon the contemporaneous, systematic causes of events. Psychoanalysts cheerfully rebutted this argument, and staunchly defended the essential importance of past experience as a cause of present behavior. The controversy between the two, viewed from the present, seems to be largely one of terminology. Lewin was not happy labeling the historical root of a personality characteristic a cause. On the other hand, he did admit that there were such historical roots. Psychoanalytic theory does not assume that childhood events influence adult behavior except through the fixations of cathexes that continue from the time of the childhood event up to adult life. This fixation is the contemporaneous cause that produces the manifestations. In addition to the existence of fixation, precipitating events are required to trigger overt neurotic disturbance.

Despite this controversy, Lewin, like so many of the other theorists, had great respect for the insights of Freud, and felt that they should be put into a more scientific language; he himself made no serious attempt to do so, however.

WERNER. Like Lewin, Werner came from the tradition of Gestalt and organismic psychology, and like Lewin, he had been an opponent of associationism and of S-R theory practically from the cradle. He, too, felt that S-R theory was mechanistic, that it failed to describe the organization of behavior. He certainly believed that differentiation could not be described in S-R terminology. Furthermore, he argued that S-R theory was not developmental in his sense of the term; it was not concerned with the genetic process, but with molecular acquisitions of new behaviors which are added to the child's already existing repertoire. In view of the importance that he gave to the description of development, he would certainly have criticized psychoanalytic theory in terms of the specific concept of development. Although not seeing eye to eye, he and Lewin both included the concept of differentiation in their theories; however, Lewin defined it in a much simpler fashion, as the number of regions in the life space. Werner surely felt that this formulation of differentiation missed nearly everything that was important about it.

PARSONS. Parsons has been so busy writing in the fields of sociology and economics that he has never really actively engaged in controversy with other theories of child development. He is obviously sympathetic to psychoanalytic theory, and incorporates it fully into his own theory of socialization. He must certainly feel that his role is to emphasize the child's participation in the family as a social system and to insist on analyzing the entire social system as a part of the socialization process. He would point to this gap in all of the other theories described in this book.

The Patchwork Quilt of Theories of Child Development

This survey of the theories of child development clearly shows how little they overlap. There are few issues on which any two theories actually confront each other and produce different predictions in the same situation. The theories generally talk past each other; each is concentrated on some particular area of child behavior and development to the exclusion of many of the questions which other theorists regard as fundamental. At certain points the theories deal with the same subject matter in different terminologies, but these points of contact are less common than the place where they are nonoverlapping.

THE QUALITY OF CHILDLIKE BEHAVIOR. Lewinian theory, for example, has always appealed to teachers of young children. It manages somehow to capture and make clear the situational causes of child behavior. The best example of this is Lewin's analysis of detour behavior (see p. 106). The child is pulled toward the goal by a force and has difficulty in turning against that force to go away from the goal. Although this hypothesis needs supplementary assumptions to become a genuinely testable hypothesis of detour behavior, it does capture an important quality of the young child's behavior. As a matter of fact, in many ways it captures the young child's behavior better than the adult's. The Lewinian view of the adult who is able to take a detour is not nearly as colorful or as convincing as his view of the child who is unable to take the detour. The Lewinian conceptualization of the differences between children and adults is one of the few such descriptions that occur in the literature of child psychology. He couched this description in his own theoretical language, but he was facing an important issue which almost no other theorist has done. Werner's discussions of child behavior have a similar quality, but as we shall see, they are more concerned with the child's symbolic conceptual functioning than with his overt behavior.

The one thing Lewin did not put into his discussion of his contrast between children and adults is the children's impulsiveness and the preemptory quality of their motivation. Freudian theory is almost the only one that faces the fact that young children are impulsive, that they do have a hard time waiting, and that they demand immediate gratification. Piaget's language does not contain the vocabulary to describe impulsive behavior, and there is no way in S-R theory to describe the difference between reflective and impulsive behavior. As far as overt behavior is concerned, Lewin and Freud each dealt with one aspect of it.

In discussing infancy, Piaget gives valuable detailed descriptions of the behavior of the infant at different ages, although even his description is far from exhaustive. Piaget has, however, in no place presented a comparable discussion of the quality of behavior of the preschool child. As soon as the child is old enough to engage in conceptual or quasi-conceptual thinking, Piaget's interest is focused almost entirely on the child's thinking rather than on the quality of his behavior.

SYMBOLIC FUNCTIONING IN CHILDREN. Another aspect of the psychological function of children is their conceptual thinking, or symbolic functioning. It seems clear that the symbolic processes in children and their overt, everyday behavior have somewhat different characteristics and qualities. One of the surprising things about Piaget's findings is that so many sensitive observers of children had never discovered them before Piaget conducted his experiments. Nursery school teachers with years of experience find it almost impossible to believe that the child thinks the number of objects changes as one spreads them out or clusters them together. For some reason, in an experimental situation where he must deal with the problem in terms of language and engage in conceptual thinking about it, the child reveals weaknesses and defects that are seldom, if ever, manifested in his overt behavior. It seems, therefore, that the area of symbolic functioning in children is, in some sense, a different area from their everyday behavior.

Piaget and Werner are the two theorists in our group who make major contributions to the understanding of symbolic functioning. Yet, even though both of them deal with the same set of problems, it is hard to translate Werner's concepts into Piaget's, or vice versa. On the other hand, they are not in disagreement with each other. Werner described the lack of articulation and the lack of differentiation of the child's concepts, and gave many illustrations to exemplify these characteristics. Piaget talks about egocentrism and the lack of psychological groupings, and has solid empirical data to support his interpretations. Even so, the two theorists rarely seem to be talking about the same thing. The fact that Piaget's and Werner's descriptions of the cognitive functioning of preschool children have so little to do with each other may be due to the difference in focus: Werner focused on describing the conceptual thinking of the preschool child, whereas Piaget wishes to discover how the thinking of the preschool child lacks certain essentials for mature functioning; in other words, Werner searched for the causal factors in preoperational thinking, whereas Piaget focuses upon operational thinking and, except for egocentrism, presents few explanatory principles to account for the way the preoperational child thinks. Whatever the reason, Piaget and Werner seem neither to agree nor disagree with each other, but rather, in some sense, to be irrelevant to each other.

The two of them are almost alone in their study of the symbolic functioning of children. Psychoanalytic theory contains some recognition of the lack of logic and the archaic rules of primary-process thinking, but Freud never really explicated this in the thinking process of children. Instead, he concentrated upon the peculiar logic of dreams and neuroses. Despite certain superficial similarities, these are not much like the conceptual thinking of young children.

THE DEVELOPMENTAL PROCESS. If the behavior of children is one important subject matter for a theory, the development of children is another, and among the theories that have been reviewed, several are primarily concerned with development.

The study of development can take several forms, and Werner chose to investigate almost entirely the conceptual nature of the developmental process. He described it as differentiation, the establishment of an hierarchical organization and of articulation. Of the other theorists, only Lewin gave even passing attention to the nature of the developmental process, and he also adopted differentiation as a primary developmental concept. Lewin's use of differentiation was, however, so different from Werner's that the two words hardly meant the same thing as used by the two men.

ANTECEDENT-CONSEQUENT RELATION. Despite Werner's interest in development, his research contains nothing on the actual childhood antecedents of various kinds of personality characteristics. On the other hand, S-R theory is exclusively devoted to the elucidation of the effects of early experience on later behavior variables. There are practically no discussions in any of the S-R literature of the general differences between children and adults. Stimulus-response theory does not deal in theoretical terms with the impulsive, alogical behavior and thinking of the young child, but is instead concerned completely with discovering the way behavior is learned and the learning conditions that lead to the acquisition of behavior patterns.

Curiously enough, none of the other theories gives any space at all to the problem of how children learn. It is certainly an important area, and one that needs exploration and investigation, but it has been left almost entirely to S-R theory to exploit it.

Freudian theory does, of course, contain hypotheses about the historical roots of adult behavior. It does so in a way, however, that hardly seems to touch S-R theory. To read Freud, one might believe that the child never learned any behavior because he had been consistently rewarded for it. For Freud the historical roots of adult behavior were the fixations of infantile cathexes that would otherwise have been outgrown. The variables of childhood experiences that receive attention from psychoanalytic theory are, therefore, those concerned with weaning and toilet-training, and the Oedipal complex. The separation of psychoanalytic theory and social-learning theory is highlighted by the fact that the important psychoanalytic variables, weaning, toilet-training, and the Oedipus complex, have never been theoretically integrated, despite their inclusion in many studies by social-learning theorists.

The particular emphasis of Parsons' theory is quite understandably the child's development in a social system. It is not to be expected that the sociologist would investigate children's logic, or the specific antecedents of adult behavior. For Parsons, child development is a fringe topic representing one aspect of the functioning of one kind of social system. His efforts have been primarily directed to elaborating the functioning of social systems in many other contexts.

The conception of child development obtained from these six scientific theories is like a patchwork quilt. Each theory has its own focus and emphasis, and is, in the main, concerned with questions the other theories ignore. There are some points at which the theories do touch a common ground because they are dealing with the same problem. There are also differences in the basic psychological stance of the different theories which lead them to adopt different kinds of concepts, but these clear differences of opinion are often tangential to the main impact of each theory.

This patchwork quality in theories of child development is disturbing, because it would seem that a group of people purporting to write theories of child development would find themselves more frequently writing about the same thing. On the other hand, it is perfectly natural that research programs and theoretical investigations follow the bent of the investigator. It is also significant that none of the topics emphasized by any of the six theories is unimportant.

The fact that these theories do not overlap also implies that they do not conflict. It may be possible, therefore, to write an eclectic yet integrated theory of the development of the child that capitalizes on the wisdom in each of the six theories. This hope is supported by the fact that the theories do contain certain common hypotheses despite their general isolation from one another. In the next section we discuss a number of general hypotheses of child behavior and development which do seem to find some support in the various theories.

RECOMMENDATIONS FOR AN INTEGRATED THEORY

A Neutral Molecular Language

A review of the theories reveals how the different languages in which they are stated becloud both the similarities and the differences between the concepts posed by the psychological theorists. For example, both Piaget and S-R theorists obviously believe that the words "schema" and "habit" are different, but it is extremely difficult to state the difference in any precise way. One essential step for either the reconciliation of theories or the discovery that they are unreconcilable, therefore, is the adoption of a neutral language in which the concepts of all the theories can be described without distortion.

The properties of a good language and a good theory are quite different. A theory should be testable, that is, falsifiable. A theory explains some behavior, but it declares that other behavior will not occur. A theory that can account for any conceivable behavior is untestable. A good language, on the other hand, should be able to express any content, whether it is true or not. It should be able to describe both possible and impossible situations. For example, nobody necessarily believes ghosts exist because he uses the word "ghost." The language needs, however, to contain the word as long as people have comments to make about ghosts, even if the comments only express skepticism about their existence.

A good language should also be unambiguous. It should make clear what the speaker means but still permit him to express any idea he wishes.

A neutral language for psychological theories should contain several sorts of terms. In the first place, it should be able to describe the terms suggested as replacements for *stimulus* and *response* in order to avoid some of the tacit, as well as explicit, assumptions of these two terms when they are patterned on the model of S-R language. Stimulus-response language is a relatively neutral descriptive one, and part of S-R theory's value has been its ability to describe so many different concepts in this language. The terms *situation* and *event* would be too constraining, unless the situation were described in terms of both the external environmental and internal situational factors. The psychoanalytic concept of drive can be described as an internal stimulus situation, but could not be so described if the situation were restricted to *external* elements.

Similarly, the term *event* cannot be limited to overt behavioral acts if it is to describe the concepts contained in theories. It must also include internal psychological events like thoughts and feelings to permit theorists of various persuasions to state accurately what their theory means, and to require them to be relatively unambiguous.

A common language does not need to be restricted to concepts that have operational definitions, because many of the concepts central to theories do not have them. It is more important for the language to be able to describe each theory accurately than to meet the criteria of operationalization. Since psychoanalytic theory is concerned with the contents of consciousness, these contents have to be described, and they can be described as the occurrence of certain psychological events that correspond roughly to the naïve concept of thought or idea. Some theorists may wish explicitly to exclude all such concepts from his theory. That, of course, is his prerogative. The function of a *language,* however, is not to exclude any concepts.

If situations and events can be described in sufficient detail to permit the discrimination of each situation from every other and each psychological event from every other, it is also possible in this neutral language to describe the dispositional variables that are an important part of the theory. A dispositional variable is defined in terms of "if–then" statements (see p. 11) and can be completely described by a constellation of such statements in which *if* describes a situation and *then* describes an event. If the language contains words for events such as anger, love, beliefs, and ideas, the scope of possible dispositional variables is broad. The value of such a neutral language can be illustrated by attempting to distinguish *need* from *attitude.* The terms are related, but it is extremely difficult to know the precise relationship between the two concepts. The attitudinal term *likes* might be defined in terms of such situation-event statements as the following: *A* likes *B* means that if *B* is hurt, *A* will feel sad; if *B* is benefited, *A* will feel happy; if *B* is injured by somebody, *A* will feel angry toward that person. Writing out the meaning of the term in this way has something in common with making the concept operational, but is not restricted to terms that are themselves behaviorably definable at the present time. A need like nurturance can, in contrast, be defined as follows: *A is nurturant* means that if *anybody* is injured, *A* feels sad. The difference between the need and the attitude is thus made clear. As defined here, the attitude involves the same kinds of situations and feelings as need, but the two terms represent different constellations. In the case of attitude, all the situations involve another particular person; in need, the same psychological events are oriented around the quality of the situation rather than around the person.

A neutral theoretical language must also describe developmental processes. Development represents a change in dispositional variables over time. Thus, the developmental concept can be reduced to a situation-event language by describing the change in the disposition, and, in turn, describing the disposition in terms of the situation and event.

Event Concepts

Child and developmental psychology must include a theory of behavior that describes and explains how a child responds to his environment at a particular time. In child psychology we are particularly interested in the age of the child and in the behavioral characteristics that distinguish him from children of other ages. Child psychology can thus be considered a branch of comparative psychology.

Comparative psychology engages in comparisons of different species, of normal and pathological behavior, of different personalities and of children of different ages, to discover their common features of behavior and their individual differences. Its intent is to formulate a general theory with the common elements incorporated into the basic structure. The differences among people are then described in terms of differences in the values of the parameters in general theory. The general theory itself depicts the sequence of psychological events that occur between the stimulus and the response.

In this section we discuss some of the kinds of psychological events which should be included in this general theory of child behavior.

BEHAVIORAL EVENTS. It is accepted, as a matter of course, that overt behavioral events are obviously to be included. However, accepting behavioral events can introduce a number of knotty problems about how to describe them. Should they be described in molecular terms as muscle movements, or in more global terms which detail the effects of the behavior on the environment? The theories surveyed generally describe behavioral events in terms of their effects on the environment. No one has yet been able to define satisfactorily such words as *harming, benefiting, sympathizing,* and *persuading* in a completely molecular way. Although we can argue that a thoroughly satisfactory theory should be able to define these words in a molecular fashion, there seems to be tacit agreement to bypass the problem for the present.

One of the theses of this attempt at integration is that any theory of child behavior and development that can now be devised is a prototheory; it will not be entirely satisfactory as a scientific theory, because we are not at the stage to write one. What is intended is the development of some ground rules which can guide the formulation of a better and more general prototheory than is currently available. In this spirit, we can accept a definition of overt behavior based on its goal or environmental effect rather than its actual execution.

In the same spirit, it would seem advisable to accept both thoughts and feelings as hypothetical events in an integrated theory. Thoughts and feelings are either explicitly admitted, or some euphemism for them is employed, in every one of the six theories examined. In psychoanalytic theory, they are stated explicitly, but *mental acts,* as used by Piaget, *cognitive structure,* as described by Lewin, and the *internal mediating response* in S-R theory all reflect the gradual awareness that at the present stage of science we need to accept these mental events as constructs. Mental events are not data; they are hypothetical constructs. At the present time, we know only in principle how they might be given operational definitions. There is no single behavioral act that corresponds to each thought and idea we may infer. What can be operationally defined are various structures of thoughts and feelings. Thus, for example, we believe that logical behavior depends on the operation of an organized set of thoughts. Once the theory is clearer, logically coherent behavior can be used as operational definition for such sets of thoughts. But we must admit that at the present time our knowledge is not sufficient and our theories are not ingenious enough to bridge the acknowledged gap.

It is also conceivable that advances in neuropsychology may discover some physiological indicators which will provide solid operational definitions of thoughts or feelings. Certainly it seems that modern neurological advances are coming closer and closer to bringing mental events under experimental control. These neuropsychological advances contribute to the general feeling that, at some future point, thoughts and feelings will be elements of a scientific theory that is solidly grounded in empirical data.

In addition to accepting mental events, it also seems wise to admit inhibitory acts or events as hypothetical constructs. Inhibitory responses have been part of S-R theory for a long time because it has been possible experimentally to produce inhibition through conditioning procedures. It is extremely difficult, however, to diagnose the presence of inhibitory acts in the overt behavior itself—harder, in fact, than to identify thoughts and feelings. Since inhibitory acts are important elements of S-R theory and play an important role in psychoanalytic theory, however, it seems likely that they will continue to be useful as explanatory concepts in a theory of behavior.

Multilevel Functioning

The survey of the theories in this book attests to the complexity of human functioning. Nearly every theory admits that the same overt act can be mediated by different causal mechanisms. Werner labeled this hypothesis *analogous functioning* and perhaps gave it more explicit attention than anyone else. Piaget, in describing the analogy between sensorimotor functioning and conceptual thinking, also indicates different ways in which the same behavior can occur, although he does not emphasize this particular aspect as much as Werner did. The attempt to encompass cognitive functioning in S-R theory has also led to the distinction between a one-step and a two-step process for learning the same discrimination. The two mechanisms are distinguishable through the transfer of this discrimination to a later problem. Alternative bases for the same action are implicitly recognized throughout psychoanalytic theory.

Furthermore, most of the available theories contain, in one way or another, the hypothesis that there are two main types of behavior mechanism. One kind of behavior is called at various times *cognitively mediated, conceptual, symbolic,* or *secondary-process.* Opposed to it is the other, more direct mechanism of behavior, called *sensorimotor* and *primary-process.* The definitions of the two kinds of processes in different theories do not jibe completely, but neither do they seem to contain any genuinely incompatible elements.

All these theories seem to accept the principle that the cognitively mediated or conceptual process is in some sense higher than and dominant over the other. In adult functioning, voluntary behavior seems to be governed by conceptual processes, whereas the direct sensorimotor processes occur either as automatized habits or as a less reflective, more impulsive kind of behavior. Ordinarily, the higher functioning controls the lower.

Finally, another aspect of this general hypothesis is that the direct sensorimotor primary process develops early in life, and that it controls the behavior of the child more than the behavior of the adult. Cognitively mediated or conceptual functioning is seen as developing later in the child's life, and gradually comes to take control over important behavioral events.

Thus, it appears that a relatively detailed general hypothesis lies latent in many of the current theories. Each theory, in one way or another, features one aspect of this hypothesis. The hypothesis is also consistent with many neurological findings about the control of higher centers over lower ones. The details of the functioning of this mechanism in child development need more explanations; there may, for example, be more than two levels of this functioning. Nevertheless, there seems to be a fair consensus among theories that there is a primitive, noncognitive functioning which is gradually superseded and controlled by a more advanced cognitively mediated logical process.

Motivation and Affect

When we compare the six theories on the problems of motivation, it is striking to note that they partially agree, but that there is a considerable area of nonoverlap between theories and relatively little actual disagreement. The concepts of motivation and affect are designed to account for a variety of phenomena associated with motivated behavior. Some of the characteristics of motivation are made explicit in one theory, some in another, but nearly every one of them is explicated in more than one theory.

SENSITIVITY TO STIMULI. One aspect of motivation, explicitly conceptualized as *drive* in S-R theory, is that a highly motivated organism is more responsive to stimulation than a less-motivated organism. In Hullian theory, the strength of the habit is multiplied by the strength of the drive to determine the strength of the response tendency.

REINFORCEMENT AND PLEASURE. A second aspect of motivation is that certain kinds of acts are rewarding, reinforcing or pleasurable, depending on the organism's motivation. There are really two parts to this hypothesis. One part is that the consummatory behavior itself is accompanied by an affective state, which we call pleasantness in everyday language. The other is that this consummatory activity has rewards for the behavior that preceded it and increases the probability that such behavior will recur. In some theories, particularly naïve theory, it is tacitly assumed that these two consequences of consummatory behavior are the same; that the activity must be rewarding in the sense of being pleasant, before it can be rewarding in the sense of reinforcing the behavior that led up to it. There is good evidence that these two aspects of motivation are not necessarily identical, and that some kinds of behaviors reinforce learning without being pleasant, and possibly vice versa.

GUIDANCE OF BEHAVIOR—THE TARGET. Another aspect of motivation, which is particularly emphasized in Lewinian theory, is that motivated behavior has a goal or target toward which it is guided. The cues that guide the behavior come as feedback from the environment and result in a type of guided behavior which is roughly analogous to the behavior of guided missiles. The target has been viewed by Lewin and others as an essential feature of motivated behavior, and it certainly is one aspect of motivation that any theory must account for.

DRIVE STIMULI. A fourth aspect of motivation which enters into a variety of theories is that the motivation itself can function as a stimulus: one motive can be distinguished from another. The hypothesis that motive states are stimuli is also based on the fact that under conditions of high motivation no external stimulus is required to elicit behavior. The state of motivation functions as a part of the situation that elicits behavioral events. All of this is explicitly stated in Hullian theory under the concept of a drive stimulus (Sd). For Hull, drive stimuli were limited to such things as hunger and thirst; perhaps other kinds of drive stimuli will be required in the future. At any rate, one aspect of motivation is its function as an instigator of behavior and as a cue for discrimination.

TENSION, DEPRIVATION, AND SATIATION. A fifth aspect of motivation which continually recurs in these theories is the view of motivation as a tension which rises and falls. In psychoanalytic theory the tension aspect of motivation is identical to its stimulus function. The level of tension is taken to be a stimulus to restless behavior, and the reduction in excitation constitutes the gratification. A property of tension, and perhaps the basic reason for conceptualizing it, is that it can be raised and lowered by conditions of deprivation and satiation. Deprivation and satiation are explicit in Lewinian theory, and have led to many studies of satiation. Deprivation is also explicit in psychoanalytic theory. In S-R theory, food deprivation has long been an established mechanism for the control of motivation. The work of Gewirtz has, however, raised the hypothesis that all kinds of reinforcers can be made more or less effective by periods of deprivation or satiation.

FRUSTRATION, AND ITS AFFECTIVE CONCOMITANTS. A final aspect of motivation is the existence of frustration. It is conceptualized as the

Conclusion

prevention of goal attainment, by the establishment of certain kinds of barriers to reaching the target. In S-R theory, frustration is assumed to instigate aggression. In other theories, aggression or anger is assumed to be a common, although not universal, consequence of frustration. We can assume that there are affective reactions to the frustration, just as there are to the consummation, of a motive. We can also assume that various sorts of interpersonal behavior are instigated by frustration.

There are, then, eight aspects of motivation: (1) sensitization to stimuli; (2) the pleasant affect accompanying consummatory behavior; (3) the consequences of consummatory behavior as a reinforcement in the learning process; (4) the existence of a target for motivated behavior; (5) the existence of drive stimuli which may elicit behavior and provide cues for discrimination of motives; (6) a tension aspect which is raised and lowered by deprivation and satiation; (7) the existence of frustration and its associated affect, and (8) frustration as an instigator of interpersonal behavior not directly related to goal attainment. In different theories, different constellations of these eight effects are packaged together in a single concept. In S-R theory, for example, drive, which sensitizes the organism to stimuli, is also the element that is reduced to produce reinforcement. In psychoanalytic theory, the excitation that serves to instigate behavior is also the one discharged by reinforcement. We might take a lession from S-R theory in other areas and attempt to break down motivation into elementary parts in order to study each of them separately. It seems entirely possible that under some conditions motivations may have only one of the eight effects. It seems likely that guided target-directed behavior is acquired as the child grows and very possibly involves conceptual or cognitive mediation. Not every barrier to goal attainment produces frustration. The separation of motivation into these different elements is suggested by their appearance in different combinations in the various theories.

Research in child psychology can make an important contribution to general behavior theory in the area of motivation, because these different aspects of motivation seem to appear at different ages. Young infants can be angry, but not aggressive. Deprivation can lead to restlessness, but not to goal-directed behavior. How these different aspects of motivation are related at different ages and which ones are learned and which mature are questions asked in child psychology; their answers will help determine the structure of general theory.

One hypothesis about motivation, explicated in both Lewinian and in psychoanalytic theory, is that it elicits thoughts about the target and consummation of the motive. Freud viewed this as the basic mechanism for the development of all cognitive functioning. Lewin did not go so far in this direction, but nevertheless, explicitly recognized the hypothesis. It is also a tacitly accepted hypothesis in some other psychological theories.

Still another hypothesis in the motivational area proposed by several theories is that young children are impulsive and their motives preemptory. Not only do their motives capture behavior, but their emotions are also easily expressed and difficult to control. In everyday psychology it appears that the control over expression of emotion is not not very different from the control over motivations. Both are preemptory in early childhood and gradually become more and more controlled as the child grows older. Psychoanalytic theory treats this problem much more fully than any of the others. Although the theoretical explanation may be inadequate, the empirical hypothesis seems sensible. Motivations become tamed as they become more refined and concrete, and their taming is part and parcel of the functioning of the secondary process. Furthermore, the emotional expressions of the young infant are purely expressive; they gradually become integrated into the motivational system so that they become guides to the instigation of motives. Thus, the young infant's anger gradually matures into directed hostility or hatred as it appears in the older child.

Maturation

One of the other concepts that seem to have some necessary role in an interrated theory of child development is maturation. As it happens, none of the theories surveyed in this volume has placed primary emphasis on the role of maturation. Gesell's work (1946), which has not been reviewed, is probably the best example of an almost purely maturational theory. Lewin spoke of maturation but put no particular emphasis on its predetermination. Freud pointed to a maturational process in both ego and psychosexual development; but the maturational process in psychosexual development has been deemphasized by many otherwise orthodox psychoanalytic theorists. Piaget denies that his developmental theory is maturational, but it is not clear whether he denies all maturational factors or merely denies that maturation is a sufficient explanation of development.

The essence of the maturational concept is that one factor in the child's developmental sequence runs off on a time schedule rather than being tied to environmental events. It is not necessary that the maturational sequences grow at the same rate in all children, because maturation cannot be tied to chronological age. Nevertheless, the most important evidence for the maturational process is the appearance of clear chronological age differences. At the same time, however, chronological age differences can stem from a variety of causes. In the light of the survey of these theories, it does seem as if a concept of maturation is a valuable one in a general integrated theory of child development, and that considerable empirical research is needed before the exact nature of this concept can be adequately described.

Principles of Conditioning

In an integrated theory of child development, it seems wise to capitalize on the large body of empirical data stemming from S-R theory and explicated in the principles of conditioning. By and large, these principles have been poorly used by other theoretical positions, although many of the same phenomena are described in other theoretical languages. S-R theory has been empirical; it has been rigorous in its experimentation, and the empirical facts of conditioning are, by now, well established, although there can be disagreement about the interpretation of them.

Whether the facts of conditioning represent a sufficient repertoire of learning principles to account for all aspects of child development is certainly open to question, but it seems almost impossible that the principles of conditioning do not apply to children growing up in the home. Children do learn some aspects of their adult behavior because they have been consistently rewarded for it.

Acquisition of New Behavior

Although there is a large body of material on conditioning theory incorporated into S-R theory, these principles only describe the way behavior becomes stable, predictable, and controllable once it occurs. There is nothing in S-R theory to explain the occurrence of a behavior pattern for the first time except a tacit assumption that it is accidental. Skinner, for example, can teach animals and children complicated forms of behavior, but solely by beginning with the type of behavior that is likely to occur. Bandura and Walters suggest imitation, but they do not account for it theoretically. A large part of the criticism of S-R theory has been directed to its neglect of other processes of performing a new form of behavior.

In the survey of the empirical data on which the theories in this volume are based, at least four kinds of mechanisms have been suggested for the acquisition of new behavior. One of these is imitation, extensively investigated by Piaget at the infancy level and experimentally studied in considerable detail by social-learning theorists. In some versions of social learning, imitation is now accepted as a primary mode of acquisition of behavior.

In his description of stage 5 in infancy, Piaget describes a second source of new behavior: the child spontaneously varying his behavior about the established schema. These variations are accidental in a sense, but, assuming that the child plays spontaneous variations on a familiar theme, suggest some lawful limits to what can be expected in the way of new behavior; for this reason, it surely deserves a place in a general integrated theory of child development. Piaget is the only theorist who specifically emphasizes the deliberate variation of behavior for the sake of change.

The third way that people perform acts they have never done before is through verbal instruction. It is not clear how verbal instruction leads to the behavior, but in some cases it seems that such instruction programs a sequence of already available elementary acts. In his description of stage 4 in infancy, Piaget discusses the beginnings of this kind of programming and the conditions that permit it, where two schemas are put together as a means toward an end.

Finally, new acts also occur through that traditional mechanism labeled insight. which may not be very different from control through verbal instruction. The only hypothesis about this process is that a cognitive representation of the act occurs as a solution to a problem. Then the representation programs the actual behavior to produce the act itself. These mechanisms—in addition to the genuinely accidental occurrence of new behaviors—suggest a number of hypotheses about the ways that particular kinds of new behavior are developed at different ages in the child.

CONCLUSION

We come finally to the end of the trail. Common-sense theories of development have been compared to six scientific theories. The six do not include all there is to be known about child behavior and development, but together they represent a large body of research work in the field. Each of these theories has been examined in some detail and criticized. In this final chapter, the six theories have been compared with each other and found to have a patchwork quality. The six are concerned with different aspects of child development more than they are focused on different explanations of the same behavior. This fact suggests eclectic integration of the theories, provided that they can be reconciled in language.

There do seem to be areas of agreement among the theories, and several hypotheses are independently suggested by one or more of the theories. These have led to a list of general hypotheses about child development that present some specifications for a general integrated theory.

First, there is a need for a neutral, molecular, nontheoretical language.

Second, child development is partially a theory of behavior and action, and partly a theory of change in behavior.

Third, in a theory of behavior, a number of different kinds of behavioral events are admitted as theoretical concepts. These include not only overt behavior, but also such hypothetical events as thoughts, feelings, and inhibitory acts.

Fourth, all of the theories seem to accept in some form an idea of multilevel functioning. This hypothesis states that one primary and primitive mechanism of behavior occurs early in the child's life, and another, described variously as secondary, conceptual, symbolic, or cognitively mediated, develops as the child grows. In the course of development, the second level of functioning gradually assumes control over the first, although the first continues to function in an important subsidiary role.

Fifth, various aspects of the concepts of motivation have been discussed by the theorists: these include sensitization to stimuli, the affective concomitant of frustration and gratification, the reinforcing effect of consummation on previous behavior, the guiding of behavior toward some target, the operation of a stimulus component to drive which enables it to elicit responses in itself, and finally, a tension aspect to drive, which is contributed to by deprivation and satiation. It may be that different aspects of this motivational complex function in different people under different circumstances. The study of the motivation of children of different ages offers an important avenue for the refinement of this conceptualization.

Sixth, there is a general acceptance of the projective hypothesis, namely, that motivation tends to produce relevant thoughts.

Seventh, many of the theories generally accept the idea that through the process of development, motives and affects are somehow tamed, and that the early preemptory demands of motivation and emotion on the child are gradually refined and civilized into a much more controlled adult expression.

Eighth, the concept of maturation seems to be an essential one someplace in the theory of child development, although its exact role in a theory of behavior is by no means clear.

Ninth, the empirical principle of conditioning, which have developed through years of experimentation led by S-R theorists, are well substantiated and other theories contain aspects of them. It would thus seem wise to accept them and to assume that many aspects of the child's behavior are learned through reinforcement and conditioning.

Tenth, there are ways by which new acts are performed in addition to the accidental production of behavior on which S-R theory has traditionally focused. Some of these have already been investigated within the theories themselves. These modes of performing new actions include the imitation of other people, the spontaneous and deliberate variation of one's own behavior for the sake of something new, the production of new behavior through verbal instruction, and the discovery of new forms of behavior in the course of cognitive problem solving.

In retrospect, the theories do not turn out badly. In many ways they support each other, and, in total, suggest a kind of prototheory of child development which, although obviously incomplete, badly defined, and surely wrong in some respects, is a feasible and workable basis for further research and for more refined theory building.

Bibliography and Author Index

Adler, D. L. Types of similarity and the substitute value of activities at different age levels. Unpublished doctoral dissertation, State University of Iowa, 1939. **114.**

Ames, A., Jr. Visual perception and the rotating trapezoidal window. *Psychol. Monogr.*, 1951, *65*, No. 7 (Whole No. 324). **222.**

Aronfreed, J. The effects of experimental socialization paradigms upon two moral responses to transgression. *J. abnorm. soc. Psychol.*, 1963, *66*, 437–448. **468.**

Aronfreed, J., and Reber, A. The internalization of social control through punishment. Unpublished manuscript, University of Pennsylvania, 1963. **467.**

Baldwin, C. P., and Baldwin, A. L. The development of children's concepts of kindness. In preparation, 1966. **13.**

Bales, R. F. *Interaction process analysis, a method for the study of small groups.* Cambridge, Massachusetts: Addison-Wesley Press, 1950. **552, 553.**

Bandura, A. Relationship of family patterns to child behavior disorders. Progress report, United States Public Health Research Grant, M1734. Stanford University, 1960. (Cited in Bandura and Walters, 1963.) **446, 457.**

Bandura, A. The influence of rewarding and punishing consequences to the model on the acquisition and performance of imitative responses. Unpublished manuscript, Stanford University, 1962. (Described in Bandura and Walters, 1963.) **429.**

Bandura, A., and Huston, Aletha C. Identification as a process of incidental learning. *J. abnorm. soc. Psychol.*, 1961, *63*, 311–318. **429, 444, 459, 484.**

Bandura, A., and Kupers, Carol J. The transmission of patterns of self-reinforcement through modeling. *J. abnorm. soc. Psychol.*, 1964, *69*, 1–19. **470.**

Bandura, A., Ross, D., and Ross, S. S. Imitation of film-mediated aggressive models. *J. abnorm. soc. Psychol.*, 1963, *66*, 3–11. **429.**

Bandura, A., and Walters, R. H. *Adolescent aggression,* New York: Ronald, 1959. **445, 455, 457, 488.**

Bandura, A., and Walters, R. H. *Social learning and personality development.* New

York: Holt, Rinehart and Winston, 1963. **431, 452, 453, 457, 470, 476, 480.** (Quoted with permission of the publishers.)

Barker, R. G. An experimental study of the resolution of conflict by children. In Q. McNemar and M. A. Merill (Eds.), *Studies in personality.* New York and London: McGraw-Hill, 1942. Pp. 13–34. **104.**

Barker, R. G., Dembo, T., and Lewin, K. Studies in topological and vector psychology, II: Frustration and regression: An experiment with young children. *Univer. Iowa Stud. Child Welf.,* 1941, *18* (1). **94, 116, 133.**

Barker, R. G., and Wright, H. F. 1951. *One boy's day.* New York: Harper, 1951. **131.**

Barker, R. G., and Wright, H. F. *Midwest and its children; the psychological ecology of an American town.* Evanston, Illinois: Row-Peterson, 1955. **131.**

Bavelas, A. Communication patterns in task oriented groups. *J. acoust. Soc. Amer.,* 1950, *22,* 725–730. **125 ff.**

Bell, R. Unpublished manuscript, National Institute of Mental Health, 1965. **540.**

Benjamin, J. Methodological considerations in the validation and elaboration of psychoanalytical personality theory. *Amer. J. Orthopsychiat.* 1950, *20,* 139–156. **358.**

Berlyne, D. E. *Structure and direction in thinking.* New York: Wiley, 1965. **420 ff.**

Brackbill, Yvonne. Extinction of the smiling response in infants as a function of reinforcement schedules. *Child Develpm.,* 1958, *29,* 115–124. **411, 442.**

Braithwaite, R. B. *Scientific explanation.* Cambridge: Cambridge University Press, 1955. **52.**

Bridges, K. M. B. Emotional development in early infancy. *Child Develpm.,* 1932, *3,* 324–341. **501.**

Broadbent, D. E. *Perception and communication.* New York: Pergamon Press, 1958. **334.**

Bruner, J. S. The course of cognitive growth. *Amer. Psychologist,* 1964, *19,* 1–15. **243.**

Buhler, K. *The mental development of the child.* New York: Harcourt, Brace, 1930. **579.**

Burton, R. V., Maccoby, Eleanor E., and Allinsmith, W. Antecedents of resistance to temptation in four-year-old children. *Child Develpm.,* 1961, *32,* 689–710. **468.**

Cartwright, D., and Festinger, L. A quantitative theory of decision. *Psychol. Rev.,* 1943, *50,* 595–621. **152.**

Cartwright, D., and Harary, F. 1956. Structural balance: A generalization of Heider's theory. *Psychol. Rev.,* 1956, *63,* 277–293. **127.**

Church, J. *Language and the discovery of reality.* New York: Random House, 1961. **579.**

Coghill, G. E. *Anatomy and the problem of behavior.* New York: Macmillan, 1929. **115, 500.**

Conant, J. B. *On understanding science.* New Haven: Yale University Press, 1948. **6.**

Cowan, P. A., and Walters, R. H. Studies of reinforcement of aggression, I. Effects of scheduling. *Child Develpm.,* 1963, *34,* 543–552. **454.**

Dollard, J., Doob, L. W., Miller, N. E., Mowrer, O. H., and Sears, R. R. *Frustration and Aggression.* New Haven: Yale University Press, 1939. **432 ff., 449, 458, 479.**

Dollard, J., and Miller, N. E. *Personality and psychotherapy.* New York: McGraw-Hill, 1950. **479.**

Erikson, E. H. *Childhood and society.* New York: Norton, 1950. **371 ff.**

Escalona, S., Leitch, M., and others. Early phases of personality development: A non-normative study of infant behavior. *Monogr. Soc. Res. Child Develpm.,* 1953, *17,* No. 1 (Whole No. 54). **352.**

Escalona, S., and Bergman, P. Unusual sensitivities in very small children. In Vol. III. *The Psychoanalytic Study of the Child.* New York: International Universities Press, 1949. **352.**

Estes, W. K. Toward a statistical theory of learning. *Psychol. Rev.,* 1950, *57,* 94–107. **77.**

Farber, M. L. Studies in topological and vector psychology III: Imprisonment as a psychological situation. *Univer. Iowa Stud. Child Welf.,* 1945, *20.* **26.**

French, T. M. Interrelations between psychoanalysis and the experimental work of Pavlov. *Amer. J. Psychiat.,* 1933, *12,* 1165–1203. **581.**

Freud, S. (1915) *Instincts and their vicissitudes.* London: Hogarth Press, 1958. **309.**

Freud, S. (1916) *A general introduction to psychoanalysis.* New York: Liveright Publishing Corp., 1935. **379–80.** (Quoted with permission of the publishers.)

Freud, S. (1923) *The ego and the id.* London: Hogarth Press, 1947. **460.**

Gesell, A. *Infancy and human growth.* New York: Macmillan, 1928. **119.**

Gesell, A. The ontogenesis of infant behavior. In L. Carmichael (Ed.), *Manual of child psychology.* New York: Wiley, 1946. Pp. 335–373. **595.**

Gewirtz, J. L., and Baer, D. M. Deprivation and satiation of social reinforcers as drive conditions. *J. abnorm. soc. Psychol.,* 1958, *57,* 165–172. **412.**

Gill, M. M. Topography and systems in psychoanalytic theory. *Psychol. Issues,* 1963, *3,* (2), Monograph 10. **327, 333, 346.**

Glueck, S., and Glueck, Eleanor. *Unraveling juvenile delinquency.* Cambridge: Harvard University Press, 1950. **457.**

Harary, F., and Norman, R. Z. *Graph theory as a mathematical model in social science.* Ann Arbor: Institute for Social Research, 1953. **127.**

Hartup, W. W. Nurturance and nurturance withdrawal in relation to the dependency behavior of preschool children. *Child Develpm.,* 1958, *29,* 191–201. **412, 443.**

Heider, F. *The psychology of interpersonal relations.* New York: Wiley, 1958. **9, 127 ff.**

Hemmendinger, L. A genetic study of the structural aspects of perception as reflected in Rorschach responses. (Cited in Werner, 1957.) **517.**

Henderson, L. J. *The fitness of the environment.* New York: Macmillan, 1913. **543.**

Hoppe, F. Erfolg und Misserfolg. *Psychologische Forsch.,* 1930, *14,* 1–62. **110.**

Horney, Karen. *New ways in psychoanalysis.* New York: Norton, 1939. **380.**

Hull, C. L. Goal attraction and directing ideas conceived as habit phenomena. *Psychol. Rev.,* 1931, *38,* 489–506. **414.**

Hull, C. L., Hovlund, C. I., Ross, R. T., Hall, M., Perkins, D. T., and Fitch, F. B. *Mathematico—deductive theory of rote learning.* New Haven: Yale University Press, 1940. **77.**

Humphreys, L. G. The effect of random alternation of reinforcement on the acquisition and extinction of conditioned eyelid reactions. *J. Exp. Psychol.,* 1939, *25,* 141–158. **401.**

Hunter, W. S., and Sigler, M. The span of visual discrimination as a function of time and intensity of stimulation. *J. exp. Psychol.,* 1940, *26,* 160–179. **334.**

Inhelder, B., and Piaget, J. *The growth of logical thinking from childhood to adolescence.* New York: Basic Books, 1958. **279, 280–281, 284, 285, 286.** (Quoted with permission of the publishers.)

Inhelder, B., and Piaget, J. *Early growth of logic in the child: Classification and seriation.* New York and Evanston, Illinois: Harper and Row, 1964. **238, 241, 262, 263–64, 265, 266, 267, 268, 271–72, 298.** (The quotations on these pages are taken from pp. 53, 54, 55, 107, and 144 *The Early Growth of Logic in the Child* by Barbel Inhelder and Jean Piaget. Copyright English translation © Routledge and Kegan Paul Ltd., 1964. Reprinted by permission of Harper and Row, Publishers.)

Janowitz, H. D., and Grossman, M. I. Some factors affecting the food intake of normal dogs and dogs with esophagastomy and gastric fistula. *Amer. J. Physiol.,* 1949, *159,* 143–148. **411.**

Jucknat, M. Performance, level of aspiration and self-consciousness. *Psychologische Forsch.,* 1937, *22,* 89–179. **110.**

Kaila, E. Die Reaktionen de Sauglings auf das menschliche Gesicht. *Ann. Universitatis Aboencis,* 1932, *17,* 1–114. **206.**

Karsten, A. Psychische Saltigung. *Psychologische Forsch.,* 1928, *10,* 142–254. **113.**

Kendler, T. S. Development of mediating responses in children. In J. C. Wright and J. Kagan (Eds.), Basic cognitive processes in children. *Monogr. Soc. Res. Child Develpm.,* 1963, *28,* No. 2 (Whole No. 86). **418.**

Kendler, T. S., and Kendler, H. H. Reversal and nonreversal shifts in kindergarten children. *J. exp. Psycholo.,* 1959, *58,* 56–60. **418.**

Klein, G. Need and regulation. In M. R. Jones (Ed.), *Nebraska symposium on motivation.* Lincoln, Nebraska: University of Nebraska Press, 1954. Pp. 224–280. **343.**

Koffka, K. *The growth of the mind.* New York: Harcourt, Brace, 1924. **579.**

Kohler, W. *The mentality of apes.* New York: Harcourt, Brace, 1925. **107.**

Kounin, J. S. Experimental studies of rigidity: The measurement of rigidity in normal and feeble-minded persons. *Charact. & Pers.,* 1941, *9,* 251–272. **114, 116, 117.**

Lashley, K. S. An examination of the "continuity theory" as applied to discriminative learning. *J. gen. Psychol.,* 1942, *26,* 241–265. **483.**

Levy, D. M. Experiments on the sucking reflex and social behavior of dogs. *Amer. J. Orthopsychiat.,* 1934, *4,* 203–224. **447.**

Levy, D. M. Primary affect hunger. *Amer. J. Psychiat.,* 1937, *94,* 643–652. **447.**

Lewin, K. *Dynamic theory of personality.* New York: McGraw Hill, 1935. **87.**

Lewin, K. *Principles of topological psychology.* New York: McGraw-Hill, 1936. **87.**

Lewin, K. The conceptual representation and measurement of forces. *Contr. Psychol. Theor.,* 1938, *1* (4). **100.**

Lewin, K. Studies in topological and vector psychology III: Constructs in psychology and psychological ecology. *Univer. Iowa Stud. Child Develpm.,* 1945, *20* (1). **132.**

Lewin, K. *Resolving social conflicts.* New York: Harper and Row, 1948. **87.**

Lewin, K. *Field theory in social science.* New York: Harper and Row, 1951. **87, 144, 150.**

Lewin, K., Dembo, T., Festinger, L., and Sears, P. Level of aspiration. In J. M. Hunt (Ed.), Vol. 1. *Handbook of personality and behavior disorders.* New York: Ronald, 1944. Pp. 333–378. **110.**

Lewis, M. M. *Infant speech: A study of the beginnings of language.* (2nd ed.) New York: Humanities Press, 1951. **579.**

Lewis, M. M. *How children learn to speak.* New York: Basic Books, 1959. **579.**

Lippitt, R., and White, R. K. The social climate of children's groups. In R. G. Barker, J. Kounin, and H. F. Wright (Eds.), *Child Behavior and Development.* New York: McGraw-Hill, 1943. Pp. 485–508. **133, 151.**

Lissner, K. Die Entspannung von Bedurfnissen durch Ersatzhandlung. *Psychologische Forsch.,* 1933, *18,* 218–250. **114.**

Livson, N., and Mussen, P. H. The relation of ego control to overt aggression and dependency. *J. abnorm. soc. Psychol.,* 1957, *55,* 66–71. **470.**

Lorenz, K., and Tinbergen, N. Taxis and instinctive action in the egg retrieving behavior of the Greylag goose. In C. Schiller (Ed.), *Instinctive Behavior.* New York: International Universities Press, 1957. Pp. 176–208. **504.**

Lovaas, O. I. Effect of exposure to symbolic aggression on aggressive behavior. *Child Develpm.* 1961, *32,* 37–44. **431.**

Luria, A. R. *Higher cortical functions in man.* New York: Basic Books, 1966. **579.**

MacCorquodale, K., and Meehl, P. E. On a distinction between hypothetical constructs and intervening variables. *Psychol. Rev.,* 1948, *55,* 95–107. **147.**

Malzmann, I. Thinking: From a-behavioristic point of view. *Psychol. Rev.,* 1955, *62,* 275–286. **422.**

McNulty, J. A., and Walters, R. H. Emotional arousal, conflict, and susceptibility to social influence. *Canad. J. Psychol.,* 1962, *16,* 211–220. **431.**

Merton, R. K. *Social theory and social structure.* Glencoe, Illinois: Free Press, 1949. **545.**

Miller, N. E. Studies of fear as an acquirable drive: I Fear as motivation and fear-reduction as reinforcement in the learning of new responses. *J. exp. Psychol.,* 1948, *38,* 89–101. **404, 451.**

Miller, N. E. Liberalization of basic S-R concepts: Extension to conflict behavior, motivation and social learning. In S. Koch (Ed.), Vol. 2. *Psychology: A study of a science.* New York: McGraw-Hill, 1959. Pp. 196–292. **410, 411, 484.**

Miller, N. E., and Dollard, J. *Social learning and imitation.* New Haven: Yale University Press, 1941. **428, 479.**

Mischel, W., and Gilligan, Carol. Delay of gratification and resistance to temptation. Unpublished manuscript, Stanford University, 1962. (Cited in Bandura and Walters, 1963.) **470.**

Mischel, W., and Grusec, J. Determinants of rehearsal and transmission of neutral and aversive behavior. *J. Pers. soc. Psychol.,* 1966, *3,* 197–205. **431.**

Mischel, W., and Metzner, R. Preference for delayed reward as a function of age, intelligence and length of delay interval. *J. abnorm. soc. Psychol.,* 1962, *64,* 425–431. **316.**

Morf, A. Apprentissage d'une structure logique concrete: effets et limites. In A. Morf, J. Smedslund, Vinh-Bang, and J. F. Wohlwill, L'apprentissage des structures logiques. *Etudes d'epistemologie genetique,* Vol. 9. Paris: Presses Universitaire de France, 1959. Pp. 15–83. **292.**

Mowrer, O. H. *Learning theory and behavior.* New York: Wiley, 1960. **428, 467.**

Murray, H. A. *Explorations in personality.* New York: Oxford, 1938. **27.**

Osgood, C. E., Suci, G. J., and Tannenbaum, P. H. *The Measurement of Meaning.* Urbana, Illinois: University of Illinois Press, 1957. **29.**

Ovsiankina, M. Die Wiederaufnahme von unterbrochener Handlungen. *Psychologische Forsch.*, 1928, *11*, 302–382. **113, 155.**

Padilla, S. G. Further studies on the delayed pecking of chicks. *J. comp. Psychol.*, 1935, *20*, 413–443. **197.**

Parsons, T., and Bales, R. F. *Family, socialization and interaction process.* Glencoe, Illinois: Free Press, 1955. **552 ff.**

Patterson, G. R., Ludwig, M., and Sonoda, Beverly. Reinforcement of aggression in children. Unpublished manuscript, University of Oregon, 1961. (Cited in Bandura and Walters, 1963.) **454.**

Phillips, L., and Frano, J. Developmental theory applied to normal and psychopathological perception. *J. Pers.*, 1954, *22*, 464–474. **517.**

Piaget, J. Une forme verbale de la comparaison chez l'enfant. *Arch. Psychol., Genève*, 1921, *18*, 141–172. **171.**

Piaget, J. *Psychology of intelligence.* New York: Harcourt, Brace, 1950. **174, 179, 223, 250.**

Piaget, J. *Play, dreams and imitation in childhood.* New York: Norton, 1951. **190, 194, 230 ff.** (Quoted with permission of the publishers.)

Piaget, J. *The origins of intelligence in children.* New York: International Universities Press, 1952. **176, 190 ff., 241.** (Quoted with permission of the publishers.)

Piaget, J. *The construction of reality in the child.* New York: Basic Books, 1954. **190 ff.** (Quoted with permission of the publishers.)

Piaget, J., Inhelder, B., and Szeminska, A. *The child's conception of geometry.* New York: Basic Books, 1960. **244, 273.**

Piaget, J., and Lambercier, M. Recherches sur le developpement des perceptions. III Le problème de la comparaison visuelle en profondeur (constance de la grandeur) et l'erreur systematique de l'étalon. *Arch. Psychol., Genève*, 1942–43, *29*, 255–308. **225.**

Piaget, J., and Taponier, S. Recherches sur le developpement des perceptions. XXXII L'estimation des longeurs de deux droites horizontales et parallèles à extrémités decalées. *Arch. Psychol., Genève*, 1955–56, *35*, 369–400. **224.**

Rappaport, D. The structure of psychoanalytic theory. *Psychol. Issues*, 1960, *2*, No. 2 (Monograph 6). **317, 334, 346.**

Rheingold, Harriet L. The modification of social responsiveness in institutional babies. *Monogr. Soc. Res. Child Develpm.*, 1956, *21*, No. 2 (Whole No. 63). **442.**

Riesen, A. Arrested vision. *Sci.*, 1950, *183*, 16–19. **197.**

Rogers, C. *On becoming a person: A therapist's view of psychotherapy.* Boston: Houghton-Mifflin, 1961. **86.**

Schachtel, E. G. *Metamorphosis: On the development of affect, perception, attention and memory.* New York: Basic Books, 1959. **328.**

Schachter, S., and Singer, J. E. Cognitive, social and physiological determinants of emotional state. *Psychol. Rev.*, 1962, *69*, 379–399. **431.**

Sears, R. R. A theoretical framework for personality and social behavior. *Amer. Psychologist*, 1951, *6*, 476–483. **453 ff., 541.**

Sears, R. R., Maccoby, Eleanor E., and Levin, H. *Patterns of child rearing.* New York: Harper, 1957. **448 ff.**

Sears, R. R., Rau, Lucy, and Alpert, R. *Identification and child rearing.* Stanford,

California: Stanford University Press, 1965. **438 ff.** (Quoted with permission of the publishers.)

Sears, R. R., and Wise, G. W. Relation of cup feeding in infancy to thumb-sucking and the oral drive. *Amer. J. Orthopsychiat.*, 1950, *20*, 123–128. **447, 448.**

Senden, M. (von). *Space and sight.* New York: Free Press, 1960. **31.**

Shepard, W. O. Effects of verbal training on initial generalization tendencies. *Child Develpm.*, 1956, *27*, 311–316. **416.**

Shinn, Millicent W. Vol. 1. *Notes on the development of a child.* Berkeley, Calif.: The University Press, 1909. **501.**

Skinner, B. F. Are theories of learning necessary? *Psychol. Rev.*, 1950, *57*, 193–216. **475.**

Sliosberg, S. A contribution to the dynamics of substitution in serious and play situations. *Psychologische Forsch.*, 1934, *19*, 122–181. **121.**

Smedslund, J. (a). The acquisition of conservation of substance and weight in children, I. Introduction. *Scandinavian J. Psychol.*, 1961, *2*, 11–20. **293, 296.**

Smedslund, J. (b). The acquisition of conservation of substance and weight in children, II. External reinforcement of conservation of substance and weight, and of the operations of addition and subtraction. *Scandinavian J. Psychology*, 1961, *2*, 71–84. **293, 296.**

Smedslund, J. (c). The acquisition of conservation of substance and weight in children, III. Extinction of conservation of weight acquired "normally" and by means of empirical controls on a balance scale. *Scandinavian J. Psychol.*, 1961, *2*, 85–87. **293, 296.**

Smyth, P. *Life and work at the Great Pyramid during the months of January, February, March and April, A.D., 1865, with a discussion of the facts ascertained.* Edinburgh: Edmonston and Douglas, 1867. **46.**

Solomon, R. L., Kamin, L. J., and Wynne, L. C. Traumatic avoidance learning: The outcomes of several extinction procedures with dogs. *J. abnorm. soc. Psychol.*, 1953, *48*, 291–302. **406.**

Spiker, C. C. Verbal factors in the discrimination learning of children. In J. C. Wright and J. Kagan (Eds.), Basic cognitive processes in children. *Monogr. Soc. Res. Child Develpm.*, 1963, *28*, No. 2 (Whole No. 86). **415.**

Spiker, C. C., Guerjoy, I. R., and Shepard, W. O. (1956) Children's concept of middle sizedness and performance on intermediate size problem. *J. comp. physiol. Psychol.*, 1960, *53*, 89–94. **416.**

Spitz, R. A., and Wolf, K. M. The smiling response: A contribution to the ontogenesis of social relations. *Genet. Psychol. Monogr.*, 1946, *34*, 57–125. **206.**

Stagner, R., and Karwoski, T. F. *Psychol.* New York: McGraw-Hill, 1952. **222.**

Stern, W. *Psychology of early childhood: Up to the sixth year of age.* New York: Holt, 1924. **579.**

Thurstone, L. L., and Thurstone, T. G. Tests of primary mental abilities for ages five and six. *Sci. Res. Associates*, 1946. **148.**

Tinbergen, N., and Perdeck, A. C. On the stimulus situation releasing the begging response in the newly hatched Herring gull chick. *Behav.*, 1950, *3*, 1–38. **504.**

Tolman, E. C. *Purposive behavior in animals and men.* New York: Century, 1932. **84, 86.**

Vigotsky, L. S. *Thought and language.* Cambridge, Mass.: Massachusetts Institute of Technology, 1962. **579.**

Walters, R. H., and Brown, N. V. Studies of reinforcement of aggression III. Transfer of responses to an interpersonal situation. *Child Develpm.*, 1963, *34,* 563–572. **454.**

Werner, H. Die Rolle der sprochempfindung im prozess der gestaltung ausdruckmassig erlebter worter. *Z. Psychol.*, 1930, *10,* 149–156. **516.**

Werner, H. *Comparative psychology of mental development.* (rev. ed.) Chicago: Follet, 1948. **503.**

Werner, H. The concept of development from a comparative and organismic point of view. In D. Harris, *The concept of development: An issue in the study of human behavior.* Minneapolis: University of Minnesota Press, 1957. **499, 518** ff.

Werner, H., and Kaplan, E. The acquisition of word meanings: A developmental study. *Monogr. Soc. Res. Child Develpm.*, 1952, *15,* No. 1 (Whole No. 51). **506.**

Werner, H., and Wapner, S. Sensoritonic field theory of perception: Basic concepts and experiments. *Rev. psicologia,* 1956, *50,* 315–337. **521** ff.

White, R. K., and Lippitt, R. *Autocracy and democracy: An experimental inquiry.* New York: Harper, 1960. **132.**

Whiting, J. W., and Child, I. L. *Child training and personality.* New Haven: Yale University Press, 1953. **36, 439.**

Witkin, H. A., Dyk, R. B., Faterson, H. F., Goodenough, D. R., and Karp, S. A. *Psychological differentiation: Studies of development.* New York: Wiley, 1962. **526.**

Woodcock, Louise P. *Life and ways of the two-year-old.* New York: Dutton, 1941. **106.**

Zaparozhets, A. L. The development of perception in the pre-school child. In P. H. Mussen (Ed.), European research in cognitive development. *Monogr. Soc. Res. Child Develpm.*, 1965, *30,* No. 2 (Whole No. 100). **579.**

Zeigarnik, B. S. Ueber das behalten von erledigten und unenledigten handlungen. *Psychologische Forsch.*, 1927, *9,* 1–85. **112.**

Zelditch, M., Jr. Role differentiation in the nuclear family: A comparative study. In T. Parsons and R. F. Bales, *Family, socialization and interaction process.* Glencoe, Ill.: Free Press, 1955. Pp. 307–352. **562.**

Subject Index

Abilities, in naïve psychology, 11
  primary mental, 148
Accommodation, in Piaget's theory, 176 ff.
Acquisition of new behaviors, 596–97
  of word meaning, 506 ff.
Adaptation, in Piaget's theory, 172–73, 176
  in social systems, 541
  perceptual, in sensoritonic theory, 524
Adaptive phase in small group interaction, 554
Addition, of asymmetrical relation, 257
  of classes, 185, 239, 252 ff., 263
  of path segments, 122, 183
  of symmetrical relations, 260
Adolescence, in Freudian theory, 369 ff.
Adult role, learning of, 462
Affect, in Freudian theory, 319 ff., 326
Affectivity, pattern variable, 547
Aggregation, in development of word meaning, 511
Aggression, in Freudian theory, 312
  in S-R theory, definition, 433
    development of, 449 ff.
    frustration and, 432 ff.
    role of imitation, 428–29
"All," experiments on child's concept of, 268
Anaclitic identification, 459
Anal personality, Freudian theory, 360–61
Anal stage, Freudian theory, 359 ff.

Antecedent-consequent relations, in theories of child development, 585
Anticipatory goal response, 414
Anxiety, origin of at birth, 351 ff.
  role in psychodynamics, 329–30
Aristotelian explanations, 89, 154
Articulated vs. diffuse, Werner's theory, 502
Assimilation, 176 ff., 198 ff.
  generalizing, 199
  recognitory, 200
  reproductive, 198
  role in adaptation, 176–77
Association, criteria of mathematical group, 183, 424
  principle of in learning, 397
Assumptions, role of in scientific theory, 40–41, 52
Attention, hypercathexis, 330
Attention-seeking behavior, 441
Autonomy, characteristic of anal stage, 362
Avoidance learning, 404

Balance principle, 20, 28, 127 ff.
Behavior, definition in field theory, 92
  role of learning in S-R theory, 394
Behaviorism, cognitive, 62, 69, 71
  S-R, 61, 68, 71
Behavior setting, in field theory, 136

Bi-univocal multiplication, of relations, 260
of classes, 255
Bound cathexis, 332–33

"Can," in naïve psychology, 10
Case histories, problem of prediction, 42, 358
Castration anxiety, 310, 363 ff.
Cathexis, 313 ff., 328 ff., 330, 332, 337
Causal explanations, in field theory, 144, 151
in natural science, 46
lack of in naïve psychology, 64 ff.
vs. teleology, 67
Centrality of regions, 122
Child development, comparison of theories, 580 ff., 583 ff.
integrated theory, 587 ff.
Children, characteristics of, in field theory, 116 ff.
in naïve psychology, 30
Circular reaction, 197, 205, 214
Class, *see* Logical class
Classical conditioning, 396
Classification, 239 ff.
see also Addition of classes
Closure, criterion of mathematical group, 182, 424
Cognition, in field theory, 91–92, 97
in Freudian theory, 318, 326, 342
in naïve psychology, 12 ff., 64
in Parsonian theory, 542
in Piaget's theory, 221 ff.
in S-R theory, 405, 414 ff., 420 ff.
in Werner's theory, 501 ff.
Cognitive behaviorism, 62, 69, 71
Cognitive controls, 342
Combinatorial thinking, 283 ff.
Command, in naïve psychology, 23
Conceptual thinking, 223 ff., 226 ff., 229 ff., 235
Concrete operations, stage of, 192, 249 ff.
Conditioning, description, 396
relation to reinforcement, 413
Conflict, in field theory, 87, 103
Conflict-drive hypothesis, 446
Conscience, in Freudian theory, *see* Superego
in naïve psychology, 24

Conscience, in social learning theory, 458 ff.
Consciousness, in Freudian theory, 315 ff., 324 ff.
in naïve psychology, 12, 14
Conservation, length, 225
quantity, 242
role of reversibility, 243
Contiguity principle, 397
Control, cognitive, 342
difference from defenses, 334
role of consciousness, 324
Co-univocal multiplication, of classes, 256
of relations, 262
Countercathexis, 328, 337
Critiques, of field theory, 138 ff.
of Freudian theory, 374 ff.
of naïve psychology, 56 ff.
of other theories by each theorist, 581–82
of Parsons and Bales' theory, 572 ff.
of Piaget's theory, 297 ff.
of S-R theory, 474 ff.
of Werner's theory, 531 ff.
Cross-cultural research, 439
Cultism in psychoanalysis, 380

Death instinct, 313
Decentering, 247
Defense mechanisms, 334 ff.
Denial, 341
of reciprocity phase in small group interaction, 554
Dependence, development of in social learning theory, 441 ff.
Deprivation, field theory, 111
Freudian theory, 358
integrated theory, 593
naïve theory, 35
S-R theory, 409 ff.
sucking, 448
Desire, naïve theory, 16
Detour behavior, 106
Diameter of a system, 123
Differentiation, field theory, 115
of schemas, 202
Werner's theory, 500, 530
Diffuse vs. articulated, Werner's theory, 502
Direction, definition of, 100

Discrimination learning, 406, 416
Dislike, 17, 18, 21
Displacement, 335, 451
Dispositional variable, definition, 11
Drive, Freudian theory, 309 ff.
  integrated theory, 593
  S-R theory, 409 ff.
Drive cathexis, 328
Drive reduction, 410
Drive representation, 327

Effort, naïve psychology, 15
Ego, 316 ff.
Egocentrism, 244
Ego instincts, 312
Embedded figure test, 527
Emotion, see Affect
Empirical definitions, 49
  statements in a theory, 52
Enjoyment, naïve theory, 16
Epistemology, 178
Equalities, grouping of, 251
Equilibration, 290, 295 ff.
Equilibrium, child's understanding of,
  286
Expiation, in naïve theory, 26
  in S-R theory, 462 ff., 467 ff.
Expressive role in social groups, 557, 562
Extinction of a learned response, 399

Falsifiability of a theory, 49
Father, effect on identification, 464
  instrumental role, 562
Field-dependence and independence,
  526 ff.
Field theory, advantages of geometrical
    representation, 158 ff.
  Aristotelian thinking, 154
  balance principle, 127
  behavior setting, 136
  centrality of regions, 122
  cognitive structure, 97
  concrete causal explanation, 144 ff.
  conflict, 87, 103
  criticism of other theories, 582
  definitions, behavior, 92
    direction, 100
    neighboring region, 97
  detour behavior, 106
  developmental changes, 116 ff.

Field theory, diameter of a system, 123
  differentiation, 115 ff.
  geometrization, 94, 157 ff.
  graph theoretical representation, 125
  group atmosphere, 132
  lack of dispositional variables, 142
  lack of operational definition, 91 ff.,
    138
  lawfulness of individual behavior, 151
  level of aspiration, 110
  life space, 87
  naïve concepts in, 85, 140
  needs, 112 ff.
  organizational dependence, 119
  psychological ecology, 130
  psychological forces, 98
  quality of childlike behavior, 583
  realism, 120
  simple dependence, 119
  substitute valence, 114
  substitute value, 114
  systematic vs. historical causation, 153
  topology, 95
  valence, 101
  Zeigarnik effect, 112
Fixation, in Freudian theory, 351
  in S-R theory, 440
Flexible vs. rigid, Werner's theory, 502
Formal operations, stage of, 193, 273 ff.
Four-group, 286
Four-unit personality structure, 561
Free will, 70 ff.
Freud, Sigmund, biography, 304
Freudian theory, adolescence, 369 ff.
  affect, 320
  aggression, 312
  anal personality, 360–61
  anal stage, 359 ff.
  anxiety, 329 ff., 351 ff.
  attention hypercathexis, 330
  castration anxiety, 310, 363 ff.
  cathexis, 313 ff., 328, 330, 332, 337
  cognition, 326 ff.
  cognitive controls, 342
  consciousness, 315 ff., 324 ff.
  constricted control, 343 ff.
  controls, 334 ff.
  countercathexis, 328, 337
  criticism of other theories, 581
  critique of, 374 ff.

Freudian theory, cultism, 380
  death instinct, 313
  defense mechanisms, 334 ff.
  denial, 341
  dependence, 354 ff.
  displacement, 335
  drive representations, 327
  ego, 316 ff.
  ego instincts, 312
  fear of loss of love, 367
  fixation, 351
  hypercathexis, 330 ff.
  id, 316 ff.
  identification with aggressor, 366
  instinctual drives, 309 ff.
  intellectualization, 339
  interpretation of criticism as resistance,
      378
  isolation, 339
  latency period, 368 ff.
  libido, 310 ff.
  Oedipus complex, boys, 363 ff.
    girls, 366
  oral stage, 354 ff.
  partial instincts, 311
  pathology, role of, 306, 381
  perceivability and access to conscious-
      ness, 327
  personality structures, 345
  phallic stage, 362 ff.
  pleasure principle, 317
  possessiveness, 359 ff.
  preconscious, 315
  primal scene, 364
  primary narcissism, 355
  primary process, 316 ff., 320
  projection, 340
  psychosexual development, 349 ff.
  quality, access to consciousness, 327
  reaction formation, 337
  repression, 329, 335
  secondary process, 320, 326
  structuralization, 346
  superego, 316 ff., 321, 366 ff.
  unconscious, 315 ff.
  validation of theory, 377
Frustration, aspect of motivation, 593
  in field theory, 105
  in S-R theory, 432
Frustration-aggression hypothesis, 432

Generalization, mediated, 416
  of a learned response, 406
Generalizing assimilation, 199
General Theory of Action, 542
Genetic epistemology, 179
Geometrization in field theory, 94, 157 ff.
Goal attainment phase in small group
      interaction, 554
Graphic collections, 265
Graph theoretical representation, 125 ff.,
      158 ff.
Great pyramid theory, 46
Group, mathematical, definition of,
      180 ff.
  habit family hierarchy and, 424
  permutation, 180
  relation to adaptive behavior, 184 ff.
  relation to concept of space, 195
Group atmosphere, 132
Grouping, addition of asymmetrical rela-
      tions, 257
  addition of symmetrical relations, 260
  additive composition of classes, 252 ff.
  bi-univocal multiplication, of classes,
      255
    of relations, 262
  co-univocal multiplication, of classes,
      256
    of relations, 262
  difference from group, 185
  equalities, 251
  logical vs. infralogical, 250
Guidance of behavior—aspect of motiva-
      tion, 593
Guilt, 26, 462 ff., 467 ff.

Habit, naïve psychology, 33
  S-R theory, 408
Habit family hierarchy, 419 ff.
Habituation, 34–35
Historical causation, 88
Holophrasis, 508
Hypercathexis, 330 ff.
Hypothetical constructs, 147 ff.

Id, 316 ff.
Identification, 366, 458 ff.
Imitation, in acquisition of new behav-
      iors, 596
  in Piaget's theory, 212 ff.
  in S-R theory, 427 ff., 470

Impersonal action, 9
Imposition, 27
Indeterminism, 71
Inhibition of a learned response, 400
Insight, in acquisition of new behavior, 597
Instinctual drive, 309 ff.
Instrumental conditioning, 397
Instrumental role, 557, 562
Integrated theory, mechanisms for acquiring new behavior, 596 ff.
  mental events, 590
  motivation, 592
  multilevel functioning, 591
  neutral molecular language, 587
  principles of conditioning, 596
  situation and events, 588
Integrative phase in small group interaction, 554
Intellectualization, 339
Intention, naïve theory, 15, 16, 57 ff.
  Piaget's theory, 203
Interaction process analysis, 552
Internalization of social rules, Freudian theory, 316 ff., 366 ff.
  Parsons and Bales' theory, 559
  social learning theory, 459
Internal mediating response, 405, 414 ff., 418 ff.
Intuition, 245 ff.
Invariance in scientific theories, 186
Inverse, mathematical group, 183, 425
Isolation, 339
Isomorphism of personality and social system, 574

Lability vs. stability, Werner's theory, 502
Language, role of, Piaget's theory, 237
  S-R theory, 480
Latency period, 368 ff.
Latency phase in small group interaction, 554
Latent functions, 545
Lattice, mathematical, 282
Law of effect, naïve psychology, 32
  S-R theory, 398 ff.
Learning, theory of vs. theory of behavior, 485
Level of aspiration, 110

Lewin, Kurt, biography, 86
Lewinian theory, see Field theory
Libido, 310 ff.
Life space, 87 ff.
Like, naïve psychology, 17–18
Logical class, concept of, 238
  inclusion, 270
Logical operation, 274
Logical thinking, Freudian theory, 320
Logical vs. infralogical groups, 250
Love-dependent personality, 557
Love object, nature of, 356, 360

Manifest functions, 545
Masculinity, development of, 366, 464
Maturation, Freudian theory, 350
  integrated theory, 596
  naïve theory, 36
Means-end behavior, infancy, 211
Mediated generalization, 407
Mental image, Piaget's theory, 219, 230
Methodology, principles of natural science, 40 ff.
Microgenesis, 515
Mother, expressive leader in family, 562
Motivation, field theory, 98 ff., 112 ff.
  Freudian theory, 309 ff.
  integrated theory, 592 ff.
  naïve theory, 12 ff.
  Parsons and Bales' theory, 542
  Piaget's theory, 177, 197 ff.
  S-R theory, 409 ff.
Multilevel functioning, 591
Mutual assimilation of schemas, 201

Naïve psychology, 8 ff.
  ability, 11
  balance principle, 28, 127
  "can" and "try," 10
  characteristics of children, 30
  cognition, 12, 14
  cognitive learning, 32
  command, 23
  conscience, 24
  consciousness, 12, 14
  critique, 56 ff.
  cultural convention, 7
  definition, 8
  dislike, 17, 18, 21
  dispositional variables, 17

Naïve psychology, effort, 15
    expiation, 26
    fortune, 28
    free will, 70 ff.
    guilt, 26
    habit, 33
    habituation, 34–35
    impositions, 27
    intention, 15
    law of effect, 32
    like, 17, 18
    obligation, 24
    ought forces, 24
    perception, 12, 13
    personality, 28
    personal vs. impersonal action, 9
    punishment, 32
    repetition, 33
    responsibility, 24
    sentiments, 19
        development of, 35
    single factor explanation, 73
    teleology, 65
    values, 25
    want, 16
Natural science, methodology, 40
    nature of prediction, 44 ff.
    of human behavior, 41
    teleology, 67
Need-dispositions, genealogy of, 568
Needs, co-satiation, 114
    effect on memory, 112
    in field theory, 111 ff.
    resumption of interrupted tasks, 113
    satiation, 113
    spread of tension, 114
Negative attention-getting, 445, 464
Negative fixation, 440
Neonate, reflexes of, 204
Neutral molecular language, 587
Nonbehaviorism, 63
Nongraphic collections, 265
Nonreversal shifts, 418
Nurturance, effects of, 431, 443, 459

Object concept, 195, 206, 209, 213, 216
Objectivity of S-R theory, 475
Obligation, 24
Observational learning, 427
Oedipus complex, 363 ff.

Operant learning, 398
Operational definition, importance in
        S-R theory, 475
    lack of in field theory, 138
    role in scientific theory, 49, 57
Oral dependency, in Parsons and Bales'
        theory, 555
Oral stage, 354 ff., 356
Organismic psychology, 496
Organizational dependence, 119
Ought forces, 24 ff.

Parsimony, in anal personality, 361
    in S-R theory, 393 ff., 482 ff.
Parsons and Bales' theory, 534 ff.
    adaptation in social systems, 541
    adaptive phase in small group interac-
        tion, 554
    affectivity vs. affective neutrality, 547
    critique of, 572
    denial of reciprocity in small group
        interaction, 554
    expressive role, 557, 562
    four unit personality structure, 561
    genealogy of need dispositions, 568
    general theory of action, 542
    goal attainment phase in small group
        interaction, 554
    instrumental role, 557–62
    integrative phase in small group inter-
        action, 554
    interaction process analysis, 552
    isomorphism of personality and social
        system, 543, 574
    latency phase in small group interac-
        tion, 554
    love-dependent personality, 557
    manifest and latent functions, 545
    oral dependency, 555
    pattern variables, 547
    permissive phase in social groups, 554
    post-Oedipal phase in development,
        560
    quality vs. performance, 549
    self-orientation vs. collectivity orienta-
        tion, 549
    socialization, dynamics of, 569
        phases of, 555
    social roles, 543
    social system, role of socialization, 550

Parsons and Bales' theory, specificity vs. diffuseness, 548
  status distinguished from role, 544
  structural-functional point of view, 545
  supportive phase in small group interaction, 554
  universalism vs. particularism, 548
Partial instincts, 311
Partial reinforcement, 401
Pattern variables, 547
Pedantry in anal personality, 361
Perceivability, role in access to consciousness, 327
Perception, naïve psychology, 12, 31
  Piaget's theory, 221 ff.
  Werner's theory, 520 ff.
Perceptual constancy, 226
Period of indulgence in socialization, 439
Permissive phase in small group interaction, 554
Permutation group, 180
Personal action, 9
Personality structures in Freudian theory, 345
Phallic stage, 362 ff.
Piaget, Jean, biography, 171
Piaget's theory, accommodation, 176
  adaptation, 173–76
  addition of asymmetrical relations—grouping V, 257
  addition of symmetrical relations—grouping VI, 260
  additive classification system, criteria, 263
  additive composition of classes—grouping I, 252
  "all," concept of, 268
  assimilation, 176, 198 ff.
  bi-univocal multiplication, of classes—grouping III, 255
  of relations—grouping VII, 260
  cause, concept of in sensorimotor stage, 196
  circular reaction, 197 ff.
  classification, 239
  closure of a mathematical group, 182
  combinatorial thinking, 283–84
  conceptual judgment, 223 ff., 235, 244
  conservation, 225, 242 ff.

Piaget's theory, co-univocal multiplication, of classes—grouping IV, 256
  of relations—grouping VIII, 262
  critique of, 297 ff.
  decentering, 247
  differentiation of schemas, 202
  egocentrism, 244
  equalities, grouping of, 251
  equilibration, 290, 295 ff.
  equilibrium problems, 286
  formal operations, stage of, 193, 273 ff.
  four group, 286
  genetic epistemology, 178 ff.
  graphic collections, 265
  group, mathematical, 179 ff., 195
  grouping, distinction from group, 185
  of concrete operations, 252 ff.
  logical vs. infralogical, 250
  imitation, development of, 212 ff.
  intention, criteria, 203
  intuition, 245
  language, development of, 237 ff.
  lattices, mathematical, 282
  logical operations, 274 ff.
  means-end behavior in infancy, 211
  mental representations, 219, 230
  mobility of schemas, 194
  mutual assimilation of schemas, 201
  nongraphic collections, 265
  object concept, development of, 195, 206, 209, 213, 216
  perception, 221 ff.
  play, stages in development, 233 ff.
  prehension, development of, 206
  preoperational period, 191, 221 ff.
  primary circular response, 205
  reality, concept of in sensorimotor stage, 195
  reflexes, 204
  reversibility, 243
  schema, 194 ff.
  secondary circular responses, 205
  sensorimotor period, 190, 193 ff.
    stage I, 204
    stage II, 204 ff.
    stage III, 206 ff.
    stage IV, 211 ff.
    stage V, 214 ff.
    stage VI, 217 ff.

Piaget's theory, seriation of quantity, 258
"some," concept of, 268
space, concept of, 195, 213, 219
symbolic schemas, 230 ff.
tertiary circular response, 214
thumb-sucking, 205
verbal schemas, 235
Play, development of, 233
Pleasure principle, 317
Pluralization in acquisition of word meaning, 511
Positive fixation, 440
Post hypnotic suggestion, 325
Preconscious, 315
Prehension, development of, 206
Preoperational period, 191, 221 ff.
Primal scene, 364
Primary circular response, 205
Primary mental abilities, 148
Primary narcissim, 355
Primary process, 316 ff., 326
Primitivity as defined by Werner, 498
Projection, 340
Projective hypothesis, 112, 328, 595
Presocial aggression, 462
Psychoanalytic theory, *see* Freudian theory
Psychological ecology, 130
Psychology as a natural science, 42
Psychosexual development, 350 ff.
Punishment, effect of, 400, 457
naïve psychology, 26, 32

Quantity, conservation of, 241 ff.
seriation of, 258

Reaction formation, 337
Realism, field theory, 120
Recognitory assimilation, 200
Reflexes, role in development, 204
Reinforcement, 397 ff., 409 ff., 592
Repression, 329, 335
Reproductive assimilation, 198
Requests in naïve psychology, 22
Resistance to psychoanalytic interpretations, 378
Resistance to temptation, 458 ff.
Responsibility for actions in naïve psychology, 24
Reversal shift, 418

Reversibility, Piaget's theory, 184, 243
Rigid vs. flexible in Werner's theory, 502
Rod and frame experiment, 522, 526
Rorschach test, genetic scoring, 517

S-R theory, *see* Stimulus-response theory
Satiation, 113, 593
Schema, 173 ff., 194
Scientific theory, 43 ff.
assumptions, 52
criteria of, 44 ff.
definitions, 52
effect of confirmation, 53
effect of nonconfirmation, 54
empirical definitions, 49
falsifiability of, 49
operational definitions, 49, 57
predictions, 44 ff.
public verifiability, 47, 50
Secondary addition of classes—grouping II, 253
Secondary circular response, 205
Secondary conditioning, 402
Secondary process, 320, 326
Self-orientation vs. collectivity orientation, 549
Semantic differential, 29
Semi-lattice, 282
Sensorimotor period of development, 190, 193 ff.
Sensoritonic theory, 520 ff.
Sentiments in naïve psychology, 19 ff., 35
Seriation of quantity, 258
Sexuality, meaning of in Freudian theory, 310
Signed graphs, 127
Simple dependence in field theory, 119
Socialization, 439, 550
phases of in Parsons and Bales' theory, 555
dynamics of, 569
Social learning theory, *see* Stimulus-response theory
Social roles, 543
Social system, isomorphism with personality, 574
role of socialization, 550
"Some," concept of, 268
Space, concept of, 195, 213, 219

Specificity vs. diffuseness, Parsons and Bales' theory, 548
Spontaneous recovery of a learned response, 400
Spontaneous variations in behavior, 214, 597
Stable vs. labile, Werner's theory, 502
Status, distinguished from role, 544
Stimulus-response behaviorism, 61, 68, 71
Stimulus-response theory (S-R theory), aggression, 433, 449 ff.
 anaclitic identification, 459
 anticipatory goal response, 414
 attention-seeking behavior, 441
 avoidance learning, 404
 classical conditioning, 396, 413
 conflict-drive hypothesis, 446
 conscience, development of, 458
 contamination by naïve concepts, 477
 contiguity principle, 397
 criticism of other theories, 580
 critique of, 474 ff.
 cross-cultural studies, 439
 dependency, 441 ff.
 discrimination, 406, 416
 displacement of aggression, 451
 drive, 409 ff.
 experimental approach, 392
 extinction of a learned response, 399
 frustration-aggression hypothesis, 432 ff.
 generalization of a learned response, 406
 habit, 408
 habit-family hierarchy, 424 ff.
 history of, 391
 identification, 458 ff.
 imitation, 428 ff.
 inhibition, 400
 instrumental conditioning, 397
 internalization of social rules, 459
 internal mediating response, 405, 414 ff.
 lack of observational studies, 488
 learnable fears, 404
 mediated generalization, 407
 negative attention-getting, 445
 negative fixation, 440
 nurturance withdrawal, effect of, 443
 objectivity, 474
 observational learning, 427 ff.
 operant learning, 398

Stimulus-response theory, parsimony, 393
 partial reinforcement, 401
 positive fixation, 440
 punitiveness, effect of, 457
 reinforcement, 395 ff., 409 ff.
 secondary conditioning, 402
 self control, 470
 socialization, 438 ff.
 spontaneous recovery of a learned response, 400
 sucking and weaning, 447 ff.
 thinking, 419 ff.
 trace conditioning, 396
 verbal mediating response, 415, 416
Structural-functional point of view, 545
Structuralization of personality, 346
Subjectivity of scientific theory, 56 ff.
Substitute valence and value, 114
Sucking and weaning, 447
Superego, 316 ff., 321, 366 ff.
Supportive phase in small group interaction, 554
Symbolic schemas, 230 ff.
Syncretism, 501
Systematic causation, 153

Teleology, 67 ff.
Tertiary circular response, 214 ff.
Theory building, role of common sense, 6 ff., 61 ff.
 strategies of, 77
Thinking, S-R theory of, 420 ff.
Thumb-sucking, 205, 448
Topology, 95
Trace conditioning, 296
"Try," in naïve psychology, 10

Unconscious, 315, 321 ff.
Universalism vs. particularism, 548

Valence, 101
Values, in naïve psychology, 25
Verbal mediating responses, 415, 416
Verbal memories, role in access to consciousness, 328
Verbal schemas, 235

Want, in naïve psychology, 16
Weaning, 357, 447
Werner, Heinz, biography, 492

Werner's theory, 491 ff.
    acquisition of word meaning, 506 ff.
    aggregation in discovery of word mean-
        ing, 511
    analysis of mental functioning, 504 ff.
    articulated vs. diffuse, 502
    concrete symbolism, 507
    criticism of other theories, 582
    developmental principles, 497 ff.
    differentiation, 500
    embedded figure test, 527
    field dependence and independence,
        526 ff.

    holophrasis, 508
    microgenesis, 515
    pluralization, 511
    primitivity, 498
    rigidity of meaning in interpretation
        of words, 507
    rigid vs. flexible, 502
    rod and frame experiment, 522, 526
    sensoritonic theory, 520
    syncretism, 501

Zeigarnik effect, 112

THE ROMAN SATIRISTS
AND THEIR MASKS

Stephen Fry as the satirist Juvenal in the BBC2 programme (August 1995) 'Laughter and Loathing'.